GROWTH AND DEVELOPMENT OF TREES

PHYSIOLOGICAL ECOLOGY

A Series of Monographs, Texts, and Treatises

EDITED BY

T. T. KOZLOWSKI

University of Wisconsin
Madison, Wisconsin

T. T. KOZLOWSKI. Growth and Development of Trees, Volume I — 1971; Volume II — 1971

DANIEL HILLEL. Soil and Water: Physical Principles and Processes, 1971

In Preparation
J. LEVITT. Responses of Plants to Environmental Stresses

Growth and Development of Trees

T. T. KOZLOWSKI

DEPARTMENT OF FORESTRY
UNIVERSITY OF WISCONSIN
MADISON, WISCONSIN

Volume II

Cambial Growth, Root Growth, and Reproductive Growth

ACADEMIC PRESS *New York and London* *1971*

ACADEMIC PRESS, INC.
111 Fifth Avenue, New York, New York 10003

United Kingdom Edition published by
ACADEMIC PRESS, INC. (LONDON) LTD.
Berkeley Square House, London W1X 6BA

LIBRARY OF CONGRESS CATALOG CARD NUMBER: 70-127688

PRINTED IN THE UNITED STATES OF AMERICA

TO MAUDE

CONTENTS

4. Measurement of Cambial Growth

5. Root Growth

6. Specialized and Modified Roots

7. Flowering

8. Fruit, Cone, and Seed Development

9. Control of Reproductive Growth

Bibliography   440

PREFACE

This two-volume treatise characterizes important features of growth and development of trees and other woody plants during their life cycles. The need for this work was indicated by greatly accelerated research and a rapidly expanding body of information on the nature and control of growth of woody plants. These volumes were planned as text or reference material for upper level undergraduate students, graduate students, investigators, and growers. The content is sufficiently interdisciplinary to make it useful to academics as well as those involved in the practice of growing trees and other woody plants for fruit crops or wood as well as for esthetic reasons. The subject matter will be of interest to arborists, foresters, horticulturists, plant ecologists, plant physiologists, plant anatomists, tree breeders and geneticists, plant pathologists, entomologists, soil scientists, meteorologists, and landscape architects.

The viewpoint in these books is largely developmental, with strong ecological and physiological overtones throughout. In organizing the chapters, an attempt was made to adhere to the following central objectives: (1) To present a comprehensive treatment of the current state of knowledge of the important events in growth of the perennial woody plant. (2) To highlight the significant changes which take place in vegetative and reproductive growth as woody plants progress from juvenility to adulthood and, finally, to a senescent state. Such an emphasis seemed especially important because ontogenetic changes often have not been treated in depth or have been overlooked in the literature on tree growth. (3) To interpret the effects of external and internal controls of vegetative and reproductive growth. Considerable attention is given to important spatial and temporal variations in growth. Among the reasons for this emphasis was my realization that cambial growth generally has been described in terms of an "annual ring" at a single stem height. As cambial growth varies markedly with stem height the need was evident for dealing with the developmental architecture of a tree axis in three dimensions. To this end particular stress has been placed on variations in production and maturation of cambial derivatives at different stem heights and along branches. (4) To present significant reference material selected from the world literature so as to make the work authoritative and well documented.

Despite the explosive accumulation during recent years of research data, both controversies and deficiencies exist in information on several aspects of growth of woody plants. When possible an attempt was made to present conclusions that seemed most reasonable in the light of available data. Nevertheless, certain interpretations must be considered tentative, and some of the conclusions presented may be reinforced and others revised as new information becomes available.

I wish to express a debt of gratitude to a number of friends and colleagues who contributed in various ways. Particularly, I acknowledge the help of J. Johanna Clausen who read the first draft of most chapters and made many valuable suggestions. Individual chapters were also reviewed by R. F. Evert, W. E. Hillis, B. F. Kukachka, P. R. Larson, A. C. Leopold, G. C. Marks, J. D. Matthews, Daphne J. Osborne, Diana M. Smith, G. R. Stairs, R. G. Stanley, E. L. Stone, H. B. Tepper, T. A. Villiers, Y. Waisel, P. F. Wareing, H. E. Wilcox, and S. A. Wilde. To all I express my sincere appreciation for their generosity and kindly counsel.

T. T. KOZLOWSKI

CONTENTS OF VOLUME I

ERRATUM TO VOLUME I

The third line on page 40 of Volume I should read: xylem in containing cytoplasm and in lacking *rigid* cell walls. The efficiency of

GROWTH AND DEVELOPMENT OF TREES

Chapter 1
CAMBIAL GROWTH

Increase in girth of trees occurs primarily from meristematic activity in the vascular cambium (hereafter called cambium), a sheathing and cylindrical meristem located between the xylem and phloem of the stem, branches, and major roots. A relatively small amount of increase in girth is traceable to meristematic activity of the phellogen (also called cork cambium). Two types of cell division occur in the cambium, additive and multiplicative. Additive division involves periclinal (tangential) division of cambial cells and recent derivatives to produce secondary xylem and phloem. Multiplicative division consists of anticlinal (radial) divisions of cambial cells which provide for circumferential expansion of the cambium.

Mature Xylem and Phloem Increments

Following winter dormancy the cambium of Temperate Zone trees is re-activated as periclinal cell divisions are initiated to produce xylem centripetally and phloem centrifugally. New annual increments of xylem and phloem are thus inserted between old layers of these tissues causing the stem, branches, and major roots to increase in thickness.

XYLEM INCREMENTS

The annual rings of wood stand out prominently in stem or branch cross-sections because of rather consistent variations in cell size and density of wood formed at various times during the growing season. As mentioned in Volume I, Chapter 1 the xylem formed early in the season is composed of larger cells than that formed later. Wood formed early also is less dense than that formed late in the growing season. Because of the uniformity of composition of gymnosperm xylem, changes in cell wall thickness are closely correlated with changes in density. In angiosperms, however, the density of xylem depends not only on wall thickness but also on the proportion of various cell types present. This proportion is relatively constant within a species and even within many genera, although it does vary within a season. In species of different angiosperm genera, however, the arrangement of cells and proportions of different cell types vary greatly.

Because of the consistent periclinal divisions of the cambium, the young undifferentiated xylem and phloem cells are regularly aligned in radial rows. In gymnosperms such a regular radial arrangement is generally maintained throughout differentiation of tracheids. In contrast, in angiosperms, the early alignment of cambial derivatives in the xylem is obscured as some cells, such as vessel members, enlarge greatly, and distort the position of rays and adjacent cells. Hence, it is not uncommon for a uniseriate ray to approach a large vessel and then bend around it (Figs. 1.1 and 1.17). In *Quercus rubra* uniseriate rays were displaced tangentially more than 100 μ by expanding vessel elements. Multiseriate rays, however, were not affected by the enlarging vessel elements (Zasada and Zahner, 1969).

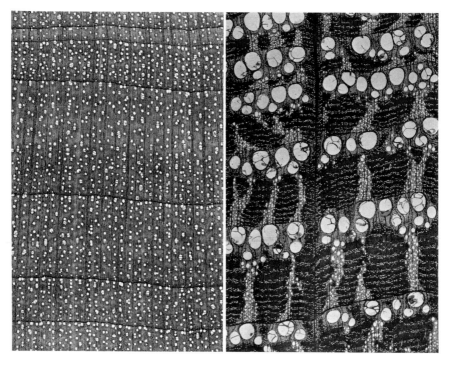

Fig. 1.1. Stem transections showing variation in vessel diameters and distribution within annual growth increments of a diffuse porous species, *Acer saccharinum* (left) and a ring porous species, *Quercus alba.* ($\times$ 12.) U.S. Forest Service, Forest Products Laboratory photo.

As may be seen in Fig. 1.1 angiosperms are classified as ring porous or diffuse porous. In ring porous trees, such as *Quercus, Fraxinus,* and *Ulmus,* the diameters of xylem vessels formed early in the growing season are much larger than those formed later. In diffuse porous trees, such as *Populus, Acer,* and *Betula,* the vessels generally are of small diameter, and those formed early in the growing season are of approximately the same diameter as those formed late.

Contact Zones

Considerable variation exists in the outer contact zones of annual xylem growth increments. In areas of high rainfall and cold winters the contact zones, as seen in transections of stems or branches, between annual xylem increments are well defined in comparison to those in species growing in extreme environments. In the juvenile core of the stem of a normal tree, the transition is gradual in rings nearest the pith and becomes increasingly abrupt in the older wood. In old trees the demarcation between xylem increments generally is very sharp. Some extreme examples of cambial growth in certain species growing in the very arid region of West Texas were cited by Glock, Studhalter, and Agerter (1960). In that region, cambial activity varied among twigs from complete cessation to continuous but decreasing activity, followed by an increasing rate. Because of such variations, contacts between xylem increments were sharp, definite, indefinite, or diffuse. A single branch cross-section sometimes showed all four types of contacts. Wide variations in sharpness of contact also occurred in the longitudinal direction. Outer contact zones of annual growth increments sometimes were not as sharp as borders between intraannual rings. As borders of annual rings were sharp or diffuse, they often could not be distinguished by cell structure from the outer borders of annual increments (Glock and Agerter, 1962).

In tropical and subtropical trees annual rings often are indistinct or absent, especially in diffuse porous woods. In India, where diffuse porous species account for over 90% of all dicotyledonous woods, some species have distinct growth rings and others do not (Chapter 2). The specific anatomical features which delineate growth rings in tropical woods may vary greatly among species. In *Acacia catechu,* for example, growth rings are outlined by narrow bands of marginal parenchyma and sometimes by thick-walled fibers in the outer latewood. In *Bombax malabaricum* the growth rings are identified by radially compressed fibers and parenchyma cells in the outer latewood. The xylem increments of *Shorea robusta* have many irregularly shaped parenchyma bands which sometimes are mistaken for annual rings. These do not always encircle the tree and do not always form only once a year. When they do form annually they are not produced during the same month each year (Chowdhury, 1939).

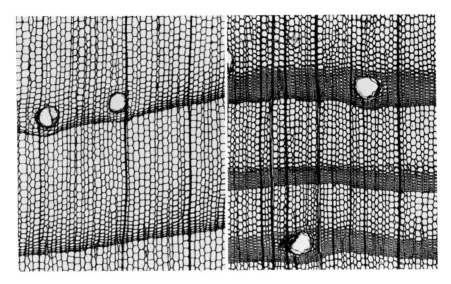

FIG. 1.2. Variations in transition from earlywood to latewood in gymnosperms. Gradual transition in *Pinus lambertiana* (left) and abrupt transition in *Pinus palustris.* (× 27.5.) U.S. Forest Service, Forest Products Laboratory photo.

Earlywood and Latewood. The wood of low density usually (but not always) produced early in the season will be called "earlywood." The part of the annual xylem increment which usually is produced late in the growing season and is of higher density than wood produced early in the season, will be called "latewood" (Fig. 1.2).

Earlywood and latewood have been used in the literature as synonyms for "springwood" and "summerwood," but the latter terms are really misnomers because either type of wood may be produced in more than one season in the same year. Chalk (1937) suggested that the terms springwood and summerwood be abandoned but their wide usage has persisted despite their manifest shortcomings. Glock, Studhalter, and Agerter (1960) also objected to the terms earlywood and latewood because the latewood sometimes was found at the beginning of a growth layer as fragments within an annual increment, intermittent circles, and complete circles preceding the latest earlywood of an increment. They preferred to use the terms "lightwood" and "densewood," which placed emphasis on actual structure of the tissues and were not identified with the time when tissues formed or with their relative position within a growth layer or increment.

The boundary between earlywood and latewood in the same ring can be very sharp or gradual (Fig. 1.2). The boundary is sharp in hard pines, *Pseudotsuga, Larix,* and *Juniperus.* Ladefoged (1952) found an abrupt earlywood–latewood transition in ring porous angiosperms and a gradual one in diffuse porous species. Various arbitrary methods of clearly characterizing both earlywood and latewood have been advanced. One of the most popular standards is that of Mork (1928) who considered a latewood tracheid to be one in which the width of the common wall between the two neighboring tracheids multiplied by 2 was equal to, or greater than, the width of the lumen. When the value was less than the width of the lumen the xylem was considered to be earlywood. All measurements were made in the radial direction. Mork's definition originally was applied to spruce xylem but has been adopted widely for use with wood of gymnosperms. It is not useful for angiosperm woods.

PHLOEM INCREMENTS

The annual sheaths of mature secondary phloem are much thinner than the increments of secondary xylem. This is because less phloem than xylem is produced annually, old phloem tissues often are crushed, and eventually the external, nonfunctional phloem tissues are shed.

In many woody plants the phloem is divided by various features into distinguishable growth increments. However, these are not nearly as clear and distinctive as are annual increments of the xylem. Often the structural differences of early phloem are rendered indistinguishable by collapse of sieve tubes and growth of parenchyma cells.

In branches of *Juglans regia* the annual phloem rings were not crushed except for early-season phloem which was somewhat compressed. The phloem annual ring was made up of distinct tangential bands, making it possible to identify seasonal growth increments (Fig. 1.3). Each phloem increment was divisible into early- and late-season tissue. Early-season phloem, composed primarily of large sieve tubes, was separated from late-season phloem by a band of fibers. Late-season phloem was composed of a mixture of narrow sieve tubes, parenchyma cells, and sometimes an incomplete tangential band of fibers (Schaad and Wilson, 1970).

In some species the annual increments of phloem can be delineated because early phloem cells expand more than those of the late phloem (Artschwager, 1950). In *Pyrus malus* tangential bands of fiber sclereids and crystal-containing cells are characteristic boundaries of annual growth of phloem (Evert, 1963b). Early- and late-phloem increments sometimes are also identifiable by features of phloem parenchyma. For example, phloem parenchyma cells produced early have little tannin and they collapse when the phloem eventually becomes nonfunctional. In contrast, the tannin-laden, late-phloem parenchyma cells become turgid. Hence, their appearance is useful in identifying limits of annual increments. In some species the annual increments of

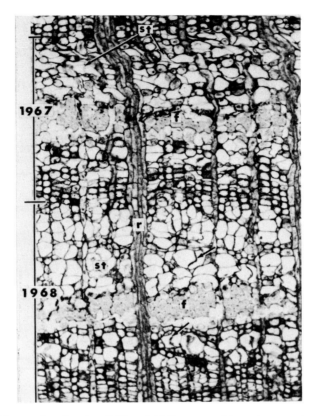

Fig. 1.3. Transection showing 1967 and 1968 season phloem increments of branch of *Juglans regia*. The degenerated sieve tubes (st) in the 1967 phloem are collapsed more than those of the 1968 phloem. f, fibers; r, ray. [From Schaad and Wilson (1970).]

phloem can be identified by the number of distinct zones of various cell types produced.

In angiosperms the seasonal timing of production and differentiation of various elements of the phloem varies considerably. In *Robinia pseudoacacia* periclinal divisions and sieve element differentiation began early (late March or early April) in Madison, Wisconsin. The first new sieve elements arose from undifferentiated, overwintering cells in the outer part of the cambial zone. Concurrently other cells divided periclinally without first expanding radially. By comparison, phloem fiber primordia usually were first produced in mid-May, by which time about half the seasonal phloem increment had already been laid down. At maturity the phloem fibers were associated with strands of crystal-containing cells. Secondary wall formation in phloem fibers and crystal-containing cells occurred slowly. Hence, mature sieve elements were located adjacent to fibers with only partially thickened walls (Tucker and Evert, 1969).

In gymnosperms the annual increments of secondary phloem are especially difficult to outline histologically. Although differences occur in diameters of early- and late-sieve cells these often are obscured by pressures from expansion of parenchyma cells. In *Chamaecyparis* and *Thuja* the early formed fibers of an annual increment have thicker walls than do fibers formed later. According to Huber (1939) and Holdheide (1951) the early phloem of *Pinaceae* is made up almost wholly of sieve elements. As sieve elements collapse they form a dark band which outlines the boundary of the annual increment. Using such criteria, Srivastava (1963) attempted to identify annual growth increments in phloem of a variety of gymnosperms. The results were variable. Some species, including *Pinus jeffreyi, Picea pungens, P. excelsa* and *Larix decidua* had distinct growth increments. In a number of other species the boundaries of growth increments were not readily discernible either because phloem parenchyma cells were scattered or because no clear line of crushed sieve cells could be identified between successive bands of phloem parenchyma, as in *Pinus murrayana* and *Abies concolor.*

Conducting and Nonconducting Phloem

The layer of phloem which has conducting sieve tubes is exceedingly narrow. For example, the layer of conducting phloem was reported as 0.2 mm wide in *Fraxinus americana*, 0.2–0.3 mm in *Quercus, Fagus, Acer,* and *Betula,* 0.4–0.7 mm in *Juglans* and *Ulmus,* and 0.8–1.0 mm in *Salix* and *Populus* (Holdheide, 1951; Zimmermann, 1961). Because of distortions of tissues in the nonconducting phloem it is only in the narrow conducting zone that important characteristics of phloem tissues can be recognized. These include shapes of various phloem elements, presence of nacreous walls, structure of sieve plates, and variations among parenchyma cells. After sieve elements cease functioning, several important changes occur in the phloem including intensive sclerification, depositions of crystals, collapse of sieve elements, and dilatation of phloem tissues resulting from enlargement and division of axial and ray parenchyma cells. The extent to which each of these changes occurs varies with species.

Production of Xylem and Phloem

More than 90% of the cambium is comprised of elongated, spindle-shaped cells called fusiform initials. The remainder of the cambium is made up of short ray initials. Cambia may be classified as storied (or stratified) and nonstoried (or nonstratified). In storied cambia (e.g., *Diospyros, Robinia,* and *Tamarix*) the fusiform initials and cambial derivatives appear in horizontal tiers in tangential view. In contrast, nonstoried cambia (e.g., *Acer*, *Pinus*, and *Populus*) have fusiform initials and derivatives with overlapping ends (Figs. 1.4, 1.5).

There has not been general agreement on a standard definition for the cambium. Whereas some investigators regard the term cambium to refer exclusively to a uniseriate layer of cambial initials, others consider the cambium to be a zone which includes both cambial initials and their recent meristematic derivatives, the xylem mother cells and phloem mother cells. The latter choice is supported by difficulty in recognizing a uniform uniseriate layer of initials and their great instability. In this chapter the entire zone of dividing cells, including the xylary and phloic initials as well as the

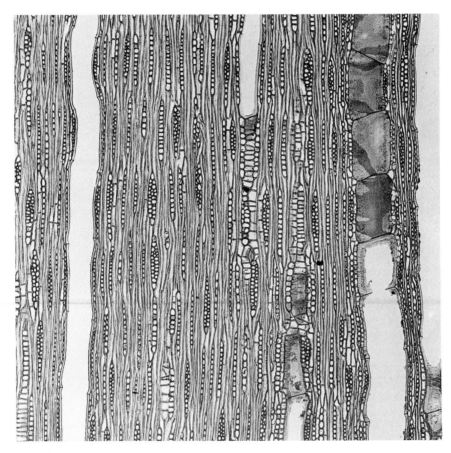

FIG. 1.4. Tangential section of xylem of *Diospyros virginiana* showing storied elements. U.S. Forest Service photo.

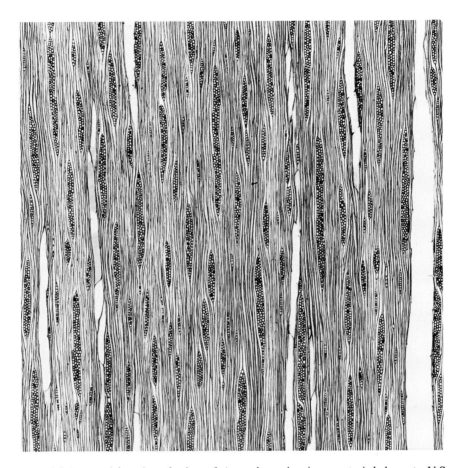

Fig. 1.5. Tangential section of xylem of *Acer rubrum* showing nonstoried elements. U.S. Forest Service photo.

uniseriate layer, will be called the cambial zone or cambium. As thus defined, the cambium in dormant trees often varies from 1 to as many as 10 cells wide (Figs. 1.6, 1.7). The width of the cambium in growing trees is extremely variable. Bannan (1962) reported the cambium to be 12–40 cells wide in fast growing trees and 6–8 cells wide in slow growing ones; in transection the cells of the cambium are arranged in radial series.

Most investigators agree that cambial reactivation in temperate zone trees actually involves two stages. The first of these, called "preliminary change" by Ladefoged (1952), is considered to be a prelude to resumption of the second phase which involves mitotic activity to produce cambial derivatives. There does not seem to be general agreement, however, on the processes

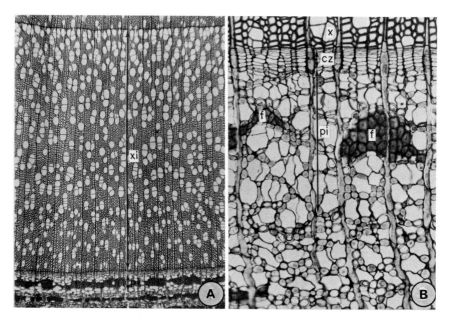

FIG. 1.6. Mature xylem and phloem increments of *Populus tremuloides*. (A) Xylem (xi) and phloem increments (pi) of trees samples in late November, 1962. (B) Outer part of 1962 xylem increment (x), the cambial zone (cz), and mostly nonconducting phloem. The phloem included all of the 1962 increment (pi) and part of 1961 increment. f, fibers. [From Evert and Kozlowski (1967).]

involved in the first or preparatory stage of cambial activity. Some observers have reported that during the first stage the cambial cells lose their dark appearance and become transparent. Although some investigators reported a general swelling of the cambial zone at the time of reactivation (Ladefoged, 1952; Wareing, 1958a), others have been unable to confirm this. For example, Alfieri and Evert (1968) found no initial general expansion of the cambial zone in *Pinus resinosa*, *P. strobus*, or *P. banksiana*. However, individual cambial cells expanded before undergoing division. An absence of a swollen cambial zone in several angiosperms has also been reported (Evert, 1960, 1963b; Derr and Evert, 1967). During reactivation of *Tilia americana* cambium, the cell walls became translucent with disappearance of lipid materials, but there was no noticeable increase in their dimensions (Deshpande, 1967). Some investigators have indicated that the preliminary change began at bud bases and moved basipetally (Ladefoged, 1952) but most data indicate that this phase begins at about the same time throughout the tree axis.

CAMBIAL GROWTH AND SHOOT ACTIVITY

Internal control of cambial growth will be considered in detail in Chapter 3 of this volume. However, as a prelude to describing cambial growth characteristics it is important to emphasize that, to a large extent, cambial growth is regulated by physiological activity of the crown and specifically by translocated products produced by shoots.

As the second or mitotic phase of cambial growth begins, the first few cell divisions may be scattered and discontinuous at different stem levels in large trees having buds on many lateral branches. Nevertheless there is considerable evidence that, once seasonal cambial growth is initiated, its control is propagated in a basipetal direction (Wareing, 1958a; Larson, 1963b). The downward progression of a xylem growth wave from the bases of buds toward the stem base has been well documented (Kramer and Kozlowski, 1960; Wilcox, 1962a). In one-year-old *Fraxinus americana* seedlings, in which the terminal bud was the only bud to elongate, the first appearance of mitotic activity was in leaf primordia. The reactivating mitotic figures could then be observed in the procambial cells and in the cambium at the base of the bud and subsequently lower down in the stem (Tepper and Hollis, 1967).

Evidence for basipetal propagation of seasonal xylem production comes from various sources. For example, many investigators have observed that

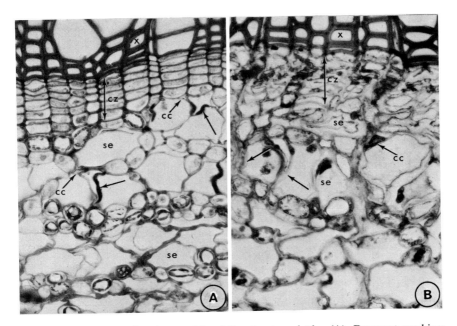

FIG. 1.7. Dormant and active cambia of *Populus tremuloides*. (A). Dormant cambium. The xylem, cambial zone, and some nonconducting phloem are present. Definitive callose is still present on some sieve elements. Sampled March 10, 1965. (B). Active cambium. Outer xylem, cambial zone, and newly formed sieve elements with nacreous walls may be seen. Sampled May 7, 1964. Details: unlabeled arrows point to definitive callose in (A) and to nacreous thickenings in (B); cc, companion cell; cz, cambial zone; se, sieve element; x, xylem. [From Evert and Kozlowski (1967).]

the cambium in the part of a pruned branch above the uppermost bud remains inactive whereas xylem and phloem are produced below the same bud. Disbudding shoots during the dormant season also greatly impedes cambial growth in the same shoots, further emphasizing the importance of control of cambial growth by shoots. As will be pointed out later, however, phloem formation in some species is not as well correlated with visible shoot activity as is xylem production.

Cambial activity to produce xylem and phloem is thought to be stimulated by growth hormones which are formed in buds and leaves and translocated downward in the branches and stem (Volume I, Chapter 8). However, appreciable xylem production does not always start simultaneously around the branch circumference. Studhalter, Glock, and Agerter (1963), for example, cited several investigators who found that diameter growth sometimes began first on one side of a branch at the bud base and spread downward in a wedge. In gymnosperms cambial activity has been reported to occur earlier on the lower side of leaning stems and branches than on the upper side. According to Bernstein and Fahn (1960), late-summer pruning of grapevines in Israel stimulated a second period of cambial activity which began in mid-

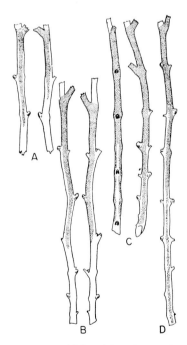

FIG. 1.8. Pattern of late-summer cambial activity of pruned grapevines. (A) 12 days after bud opening, (B) 16 days after bud opening, (C) 20 days after bud opening, (D) 24 days after bud opening. Stippling represents area of active cambium. [From Bernstein and Fahn (1960).]

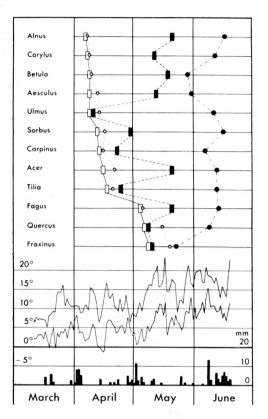

FIG. 1.9. Average time of beginning of appreciable cambial growth at different tree heights in angiosperms.
☐ Base of bud; ■ stem height of 1.3 meters; ● roots at depth of 10 cm and 1.5 meters from the stem base; ○ time of bud opening. Rainfall and maximum and minimum temperatures are given below. [From Ladefoged (1952).]

September and lasted until the middle of November. During the first few days xylem production was restricted to small patches below the opening buds. Ten days later cambial activity had extended downward and sideward from the patches so they continued in two lobes (Fig. 1.8). By that time the cambial activity near the uppermost opening bud had expanded completely around the cane. The cambial strips on the sides of the cane occupied by dormant buds were reactivated last. When cambial activity began in *Acacia raddiana* seedlings, xylem was at first formed in small isolated patches. Later cambial activity spread throughout the entire branch circumference (Fahn, Waisel, and Binyamini, 1968). Following bud break in *Tilia americana* cambial growth was suddenly accelerated at the bases of axillary buds in one-year-old stems, with activity greatest in the regions of bud traces. In a given internode, cambial activity was greatest in the regions of bud traces and least in the leaf traces of the node above. Toward the base of each internode cambial activity tended to become uniform around the circumference (Deshpande, 1967). Tepper and Hollis (1967) observed that portions of the cambium below the bud scales remained dormant longer than the rest of the cambium just below the terminal bud of *Fraxinus americana* seedlings. This suggested that, together with limited mitotic division in scales, there was insufficient production of growth hormones in bud scales to stimulate early cambial reactivation just below the scales.

Xylem production at the bases of buds may begin before, after, or simultaneously with bud opening. In *Fraxinus americana* seedlings cambial reactivation to produce xylem was correlated with bud opening (Tepper and Hollis, 1967). Both Ladefoged (1952) and Zasada and Zahner (1969) found xylem production in ring porous-trees to occur well before bud opening, indicating that biochemical activity and downward transport of cambium-stimulating growth regulators often precede actual bud opening. In mature *Quercus rubra* stems, the first vessel elements of the season were initiated simultaneously throughout the stem and branches about 2 weeks before visible bud enlargement. However, the first-formed vessel elements may have been initiated in overwintering derivatives as no mitotic activity was found in buds until several weeks after initial differentiation of vessel elements.

Ladefoged (1952) showed differences among species in time of seasonal initiation of xylem production. In some mature ring porous angiosperms the production of xylem began at the bases of buds one to nine days before buds opened. In some diffuse porous species cell division below the bud began as much as a week before bud opening and in other species about two days before buds opened. In general, cell division at the bud base began 5 to 15 days in gymnosperms before buds opened. *Larix decidua* was an exception, however. In this species there was little shoot elongation in connection with bud opening of dwarf shoots, and cell division did not occur until shortly before or simultaneously with growth of long shoots. These relationships are shown in Figs. 1.9 and 1.10.

The rate at which the xylem growth wave moves downward in a tree varies with environmental conditions and with species. In a number of ring porous angiosperms, the hormonal stimulus moves downward very rapidly, with xylem production detectable throughout the branches and main stem shortly after its initiation below the buds. In contrast, in some diffuse-porous angiosperms, xylem production extends gradually downward into the large branches and main stem.

According to Ladefoged (1952), cell division to produce xylem in the lower stem of ring porous species (*Ulmus, Fraxinus,* and *Quercus*) began a few days before or up to the time of bud opening. In diffuse porous species (*Alnus, Betula,* and *Acer*) xylem was not produced in the lower stem until after the trees had partly or completely leafed out (Fig. 1.9). Cockerham (1930) reported a period of 9–10 weeks between initiation of xylem differentiation in twigs of *Acer pseudoplatanus* in late April and in roots in July. Activity of the cambium ceased in the twigs in late July and in the roots in late September. Hence, cessation of xylem production throughout the tree covered a period of 8–9 weeks. Phipps (1961) found that initiation of diameter growth in the lower stem of ring porous species in Ohio was related to the time of bud swelling, but in the diffuse porous species studied it was correlated with leaf unfolding. Ladefoged's (1952) data showed that the rate of downward movement of xylem production in gymnosperms was intermediate between the rate of movement in ring porous and diffuse porous angiosperms (Figs. 1.9, 1.10). In *Pinus taeda* diameter growth at the stem base was observed only a few days after it began in the top (Young and Kramer, 1952).

Several investigators have emphasized that the rate of downward progression of a xylem growth wave in stems is considerably modified by site and environmental conditions. Apparently the growth wave moves downward

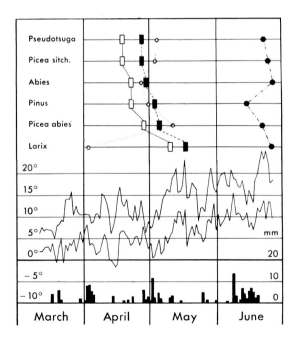

Fig. 1.10. Average time of beginning of appreciable cambial growth at different tree heights in gymnosperms.

☐ Base of bud; ■ stem height of 1.3 meters; ● roots at depth of 10 cm and 1.5 meters from the stem base; ○ time of bud opening. Rainfall and maximum and minimum temperatures are given below. [From Ladefoged (1952).]

in the twigs and main stem more slowly in suppressed than in dominant trees. Bannan (1955) and Kozlowski and Peterson (1962) noted that in suppressed trees diameter increase near the stem base began later and ended sooner than in dominant trees. In *Thuja occidentalis* suppressed trees ceased growing in late July whereas dominant trees grew until the end of August or early September (Bannan, 1955). Ladefoged (1952) also observed early cessation of xylem production in suppressed trees.

Kozlowski and Peterson (1962) studied seasonal growth characteristics of 34-year-old red pine (*Pinus resinosa*) trees in dominant, intermediate, and suppressed crown classes. In each of 2 successive years dominant trees started diameter growth earlier, grew faster, and increased in diameter for a longer time than intermediate trees. Suppressed trees grew negligibly. In both dominant and intermediate crown classes, the rate of diameter growth was greater in the upper stem than in the lower stem. Diameter growth often started, then stopped, and later in the season it resumed.

TIME OF INITIATION OF XYLEM AND PHLOEM

Reports in the literature on the order of seasonal initiation of xylem and phloem production in trees of the temperate zone are varied. Many early researchers reported that annual xylem production preceded phloem formation (Cockerham, 1930; Fraser, 1952; Bannan, 1955; Artschwager, 1945) whereas others stated that formation of xylem and phloem began and ended at about the same time (Knudson, 1916; Lodewick, 1928; Artschwager, 1950).

In many of these early studies little information was available on ontogeny of sieve elements, and differentiating sieve elements often were not properly identified. Furthermore, as Evert emphasized (1963b), early researchers paradoxically applied dissimilar criteria of cell development on opposite sides of the cambium. For example, differentiation of phloemward cells which had overwintered in the cambial zone usually was interpreted as maturation of phloem mother cells left over from the previous season. New phloem production was not considered to begin until new phloem mother cells were derived from cambial initials. In contrast, differentiation of overwintering xylem mother cells was accepted as representing cambial activity and xylem production. Hence, the criteria on which the widely held view that xylem formation preceded phloem formation was founded are open to serious question.

In several ring porous angiosperms phloem differentiation throughout much of the plant axis began slightly earlier or about the same time as xylem differentiation. For example, in *Robinia pseudoacacia* phloem differentiation began about a week before xylem differentiation (Derr and Evert, 1967). In a wide variety of diffuse porous angiosperms and in gymnosperms, phloem differentiation occurred first and sometimes preceded xylem differentiation by several weeks (Figs. 1.7, 1.11). For example, in *Pyrus communis* phloem differentiation preceded xylem differentiation by 8 weeks (Evert, 1960) and in *Populus tremuloides, Pyrus malus, Pinus banksiana, P. resinosa,* and *P. strobus* by as much as 6 weeks (Davis and Evert, 1965; Evert, 1963b; Alfieri and Evert, 1968).

Evert (1960) found that in the diffuse porous species, *Pyrus communis,* in California, one or two rows of elements in the middle of the cambial zone expanded during the first half of March and quickly differentiated into sieve elements and companion cells. At approximately the same time cambial activity began with production of phloem initials. By late March or early April one or two rows of new sieve elements were formed. At the end of April or early May up to 6 rows of functional sieve elements were found. As may be seen in Fig. 1.11 phloem differentiation in *Pyrus communis* preceded xylem differentiation by 8 weeks, sieve element differentiation was

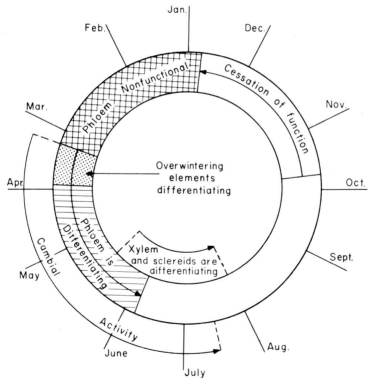

Fig. 1.11. Seasonal changes in cambial activity of *Pyrus communis.* [From Evert (1960a). Originally published by the Univ. of California Press; reprinted by permission of The Regents of the Univ. of California.]

completed 6 weeks before xylem differentiation ceased, and differentiation of sclereids and xylem occurred almost simultaneously.

In *Pyrus malus* new sieve elements began differentiating slightly before or at the beginning of cambial activity in early April. Practically all cambial cells divided periclinally at least once before undergoing differentiation. From early April until mid-May, cell division was slow. By May 21, 4 to 6 rows of new sieve elements were present, but the first 1 to 2 rows of new vessel elements were only initiating enlargement. Cambial activity reached a maximum in late June to early July and it ceased in most branches by the end of July (Evert, 1963b).

Periclinal division of ray initials in *Pyrus malus* occurred in a short time and began later than in fusiform initials. Ray initials first divided when xylem production began in mid-May, about 6 weeks after divisions had started in fusiform cells. Prior to that time ray cells in the cambial zone elongated radially to keep pace with the phloemward increase by early July. Thereafter the new ray cells elongated radially.

It is reemphasized that for the first month and a half of cambial activity in *Pyrus malus* most of the new cells were produced on the phloem side. By mid-May, 4 to 6 rows of mature or partially differentiated sieve elements had formed. This amounted to about two-thirds of the total produced for the year. Phloem production then continued for an additional 10 weeks but only 2 to 3 additional rows of new sieve elements were produced during that time. Phloem production was completed by late July or early August (Evert, 1963a).

AMOUNTS OF XYLEM AND PHLOEM PRODUCED ANNUALLY

The order of precedence of formation of cambial derivatives appears to have no direct relation to the amount of tissue produced annually on opposite sides of the cambium. By the end of the growing season the number of xylem cells cut off by the cambium greatly exceeds the number of phloem cells produced. This is true even in those species in which initiation of phloem precedes initiation of xylem. As seen in stem cross sections as many as 100 rows of tracheids were produced in a radial file each season by *Pseudotsuga menziesii* trees as against only 10 or 12 rows of phloem elements (Grillos and Smith, 1959). In *Abies concolor* xylem and phloem cells were produced in a ratio of 14 to 1 (Wilson, 1963).

In some species at least, the annual xylem increment is influenced more by environmental stress than is the phloem increment. As conditions for growth become unfavorable, the xylem–phloem ratio often declines. In *Thuja occidentalis* the xylem–phloem ratio varied from 15 : 1 to 2 : 1, depending on tree vigor (Bannan, 1955). In *Carya pecan* seasonal increment of small, 2-year-old, fruit-bearing branches had a xylem–phloem ratio of less than 3, but in rapidly growing branches the ratio often exceeded 5 (Artschwager, 1950). Tucker and Evert (1969) found wide variations among individual *Acer negundo* trees in width of their phloem increments. In most trees the phloem increments were smaller than the xylem increments. In trees with small xylem increments, however, the phloem and xylem increments were almost equal in size. These relations apparently do not hold for certain subtropical species which lack recognizable annual growth rings in the phloem. In *Eucalyptus camaldulensis*, for example, the ratio of xylem to phloem changed only in a narrow range under different environmental conditions. A similar xylem–phloem ratio, about 4 : 1, was found for fast-growing and for slow-growing trees. The ratio also was rather independent of the width of the cambial zone (Waisel, Noah, and Fahn, 1966b).

CAMBIAL GROWTH IN RELATION TO LEAF GAPS

Leaf gaps are gradually closed by extension of a cambium which develops from leaf gap parenchyma (Fig. 1.12). This cambium produces xylem toward

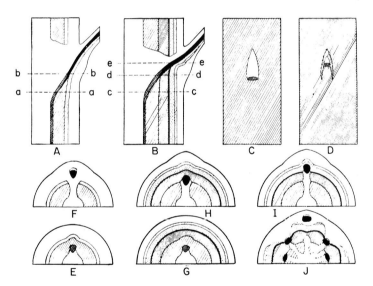

FIG. 1.12. Burial of leaf traces by secondary growth. (A) Before the beginning of secondary growth. (B) After appreciable secondary growth. Note (1) that the gap is partially closed, (2) the phloem is pushed away from the base of the trace, and (3) the xylem is buried. (C, D) Face views of surface of vascular cylinder. (C) corresponds to stage shown in (A); (D) to stage shown in (B). (E, F) Transection at *a-a* and *b-b* in (A); (G, H, I) transections at *c-c*, *d-d*, and *e-e*, in (B); (J) transection below a node, showing departures of five traces, with bases buried to different degrees. [From "An Introduction to Plant Anatomy" A. J. Eames and L. H. MacDaniels (1947). Used with permission of McGraw-Hill Book Company.] Primary xylem, lightly cross-hatched; secondary xylem, heavily cross-hatched; primary phloem, finely stippled; secondary phloem, coarsely stippled.

the inside and phloem to the outside. The gap narrows with successive xylem production until finally it is closed. The length of time required for closure is variable. In most angiosperms leaf gaps are closed in the first season, but 2 or 3 years sometimes are required for closure of wide gaps.

Sometime after leaf fall occurs in deciduous angiosperms, the leaf trace is ruptured by the lateral pressure of cambial-produced tissues. In the lower part of the leaf trace the primary xylem is buried by secondary tissues and the phloem is slowly moved outward. In the upper part of the trace, however, the continuous production of secondary tissues exerts a pressure on the trace near the region where the trace crosses the plane of the cambium, until finally the trace is broken. The length of time required for rupturing the trace varies with the size of the trace, the rate of cambial growth, and the angle of the trace across the cambial plane (Eames and MacDaniels, 1947). A trace which passes through the cortex at an acute angle is broken quickly because much of its length is exposed to the outwardly directed pressure of secondary tissues. By comparison, the more horizontally oriented traces are broken slowly. After rupture, the parenchyma tissue which fills the break is converted to cambium. Eventually cambium formed in the gap is connected with cambium of the lower part of the trace. Subsequently the end of the leaf trace below the point of rupture is imbedded by secondary xylem produced by the new cambium (Fig. 1.13).

As in angiosperms, the leaf traces of gymnosperms are broken under the

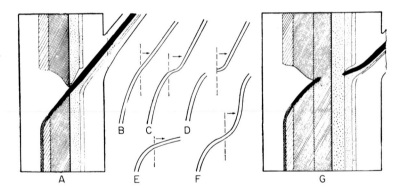

Fig. 1.13. Rupture of leaf trace in deciduous angiosperms. (A) At end of first growing season the gap is closed and the base of the trace buried in secondary xylem. (B, C, D) The trace during the following season (dotted lines represent the cambium); (B) trace unchanged; (C) trace stretched and bent; (D) trace broken with outer part carried outward; (E) trace which ruptures slowly; (F) form which ruptures quickly; (G) section of node at end of second growing season. Trace ends are separated by secondary xylem and phloem. [From "An Introduction to Plant Anatomy" A. J. Eames and L. H. MacDaniels (1947). Used with permission of McGraw-Hill Book Company.]

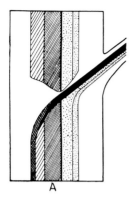 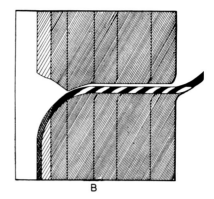

Fig. 1.14. Extension of trace in gymnosperm leaves: (A) at end of first growing season; (B) at end of fifth season, with tissues outside the cambium omitted. The primary parts of the trace (black) are separated by a secondary part (black and white). Like the primary part, the secondary part breaks, but rupturing is continuous and the trace is rebuilt. [From "An Introduction to Plant Anatomy" A. J. Eames and L. H. MacDaniels (1947). Used with permission of McGraw-Hill Book Company.]

action of diameter growth. However, unlike the situation in angiosperms, new vascular elements are formed in gymnosperms and these are successively broken and replaced by elements which form toward the stem periphery (Fig. 1.14). Hence connections are maintained between leaf traces and the most recently formed xylem ring. Such connection tissue often is produced for a few years after leaf fall. In *Picea excelsa*, connection tissue was formed for 5–6 years after leaf abscission occurred. After formation of connection tissue ceases, the last elements produced usually are broken by diameter growth and the leaf gap is filled by parenchyma tissue and a cambium grows across the gap (Tison, 1903).

In some deciduous gymnosperms the sequence of events in the vicinity of leaf traces is similar to that in deciduous angiosperms. In *Ginkgo*, the leaf trace is broken 1 or 2 years after leaf fall. This also was true for most leaf traces of *Larix europaea* although Tison (1903) observed some leaf traces with connection tissue which traversed up to 3 annual rings.

Differentiation

After xylem and phloem daughter cells are cut off by the cambium, they differentiate in sequential and overlapping phases. Wilson, Wodzicki, and Zahner (1966) consider differentiation of cambial derivatives to occur in three phases: (1) the immediate derivatives of the cambial initial may retain capacity for continued division. Such cells are the xylem and phloem mother cells; (2) cells which have stopped dividing usually enlarge in a radial direction (vessels also undergo tangential enlargement); (3) after radial enlargement ceases such processes as secondary wall formation and lignification either continue or are initiated. Some cells such as phloem parenchyma cells and sieve elements do not become lignified.

During differentiation, most cambial derivatives are altered morphologically and chemically into specialized elements of various tissue systems (Figs. 1.15–1.17). Derivatives produced on the centripetal side of the cambium may differentiate mostly into one of four types of elements: vessel members, fibers, tracheids, or parenchyma cells. Derivatives on the centrifugal side eventually become sieve elements, parenchyma cells of various types (including companion cells and albuminous cells), and sclerenchyma cells (fibers and sclereids). Derivatives of ray initials undergo relatively little change during differentiation. However, ray tracheids of gymnosperms are greatly altered as they develop secondary walls and lose their protoplasts.

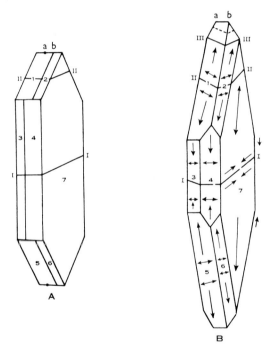

Fig. 1.15. Changes in form of a gymnosperm tracheid during differentiation. (A) cambial initial, (B) mature tracheid. As the tracheid increases in volume it elongates and the ends become more acute. The radial walls widen and tangential walls narrow. Corresponding parts are shown by Arabic and Roman numbers and by a and b. The length of the cell is reduced approximately 50 times. [From Wardrop (1954).]

Early season   Mid-season   Late season

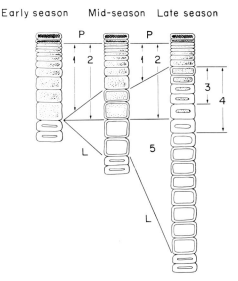

FIG. 1.16. Variations in radial files of tracheids of *Pinus resinosa* trees at different times during the growing season. 1, Primary wall zone; 2, cytoplasm zone; 3, flattened latewood cells; 4, Mork latewood cells; 5, mature earlywood; P, phloem; L, latewood of the preceding year. [From Whitmore and Zahner (1966).]

DIFFERENTIATION OF SECONDARY XYLEM

The ontogenetic changes in derivatives which are cut off on the inner side of the cambium vary with cell type. Whereas vessel members, tracheids, fiber tracheids, and libriform fibers develop secondary walls and end walls of vessels become perforated, the derivatives of ray initials change little during differentiation. However, the ray tracheids of gymnosperms are greatly altered as they develop secondary walls and lose their protoplasts. Changes in cell size also vary appreciably among different types of xylem derivatives.

Timing of Phases of Differentiation

There often is considerable overlap in the various phases of differentiation of cambial derivatives. For example, laying down of secondary walls in xylem cells frequently is initiated before growth of the primary wall ends. Expansion of xylem cells often ceases by the time lignification is initiated.

In *Pinus strobus* most cell divisions to produce xylem occurred in May and June in Madison, Wisconsin. Differentiation of xylem began in early May and continued into September. Seasonal development of secondary xylem in *Pinus strobus* was gradual. Xylem mother cells were at first small cells with thin walls. They then enlarged radially but still retained thin walls.

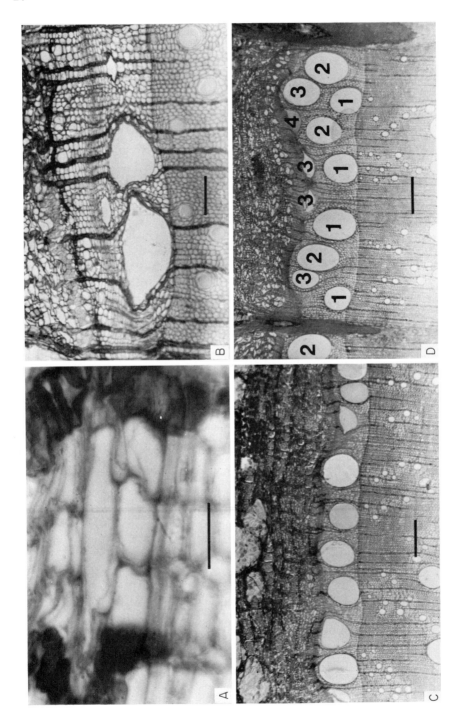

When these cells achieved radial diameters characteristic of mature tracheids, deposition of secondary walls began and continued until the walls became thick and rigid (Murmanis and Sachs, 1969).

Differentiation of tracheids lagged considerably behind cell division in rapidly growing *Pseudotsuga menziesii* trees. Mitoses began in March and progressed rapidly in April, but the first formed tracheids usually did not develop secondary walls until late April or early May. Thereafter, differentiation of secondary walls occurred rapidly. In a 15-year-old tree with wide growth rings there were about 40 mature tracheids in each tier by May 24; 20–25 tracheids with protoplasts and partly thickened walls; and 20–25 tracheids with no evidence of secondary walls (Grillos and Smith, 1959).

Full differentiation of individual cambial derivatives usually occurs in a few to several weeks from the time of their production. The duration of differentiation varies with species, cell type, and for a given type of element, it varies with the time during the growing season when the element was produced. Skene (1969) studied the duration of various aspects of differentiation of tracheids in 14-year-old *Pinus radiata* trees in Australia. The time required for radial expansion of tracheids was longer early in the season than later in the season. Whereas about 3 weeks were required for radial expansion of earlywood tracheids, latewood tracheids completed expansion in approximately 1.5 weeks. The reduced time for cell expansion late in the season was associated with a decrease in the number of expanding tracheids and restricted amount of their expansion. In contrast to duration of cell expansion of earlywood and latewood tracheids, the time required for deposition of the secondary cell wall increased greatly as the season progressed. Whereas only 3–4 weeks were required for wall thickening in the spring, 8–10 weeks were required in the autumn. Inasmuch as the volume of cell wall material per tracheid was similar in earlywood and latewood cells, the progressive seasonal increase in the time necessary for wall thickening indicated a reduced rate of cell wall deposition for latewood cells.

There is considerable variation in expansion of xylem cells which are produced at different times in the growing season. This is well known in gymnosperms, with diameters of tracheids produced early in the season greater than those cut off later. Angiosperms also show variations in size

---

FIG. 1.17. Stem transections showing early season xylem production in 60-year-old *Quercus rubra* trees. Latewood of the previous year is shown at the bottom of each photograph. (A) Tangentially expanding element on April 10, differentiating in the second cell removed from the previous year's latewood. Scale line is 25 μ. (B) Expanding vessel elements and earlywood appearance of April 27. Scale line is 100 μ. (C) Earlywood on April 15 as leaves first emerged. Scale line is 300 μ. (D) Earlywood on May 31, when foliage was fully expanded. Numbers indicate successive tangential rows of vessels. Scale line is 300 μ. [From Zasada and Zahner (1969).]

among cambial derivatives produced at different times of the growing season. For example, the vessels of greatest diameter in *Castanea crenata* were produced in March and April, with slightly smaller ones produced thereafter until July. Diameters of vessels produced in August and September were very small. Fibers of maximum diameter were not produced until late summer. Fiber diameters increased gradually beginning in March but fibers of maximum diameter were not recorded until July. Thereafter only fibers of small diameter were produced (Ito, 1957).

The rate of differentiation of various types of cambial derivatives is quite variable. For example, in ring porous angiosperms, secondary wall formation of vessels commonly precedes that of other contiguous elements. In *Quercus rubra*, for example, expansion and lignification occurred faster in vessel elements than in imperforate xylem elements tangential to maturing vessel elements (Zasada and Zahner, 1969). Girdling experiments with *Populus tremuloides* (Evert and Kozlowski, 1967) also illustrated variations among various elements in timing of their differentiation. Below phloem girdles applied to stems early in the growing season, parenchyma cell walls at the end of the season were primary in nature and unlignified whereas vessel member walls were thickened and lignified. Apparently, with isolation of the cambium in the lower stem from hormonal shoot products, vessel member differentiation took priority over that of other cell types in the xylem.

Increase in Cell Size

During differentiation the cambial derivatives enlarge in patterns which vary with species. As water is taken into the vacuole, turgor pressure increases and cells expand.

When differentiation of a cambial derivative begins, the protoplast is enclosed in a thin and elastic primary wall. Diameter increase of such cells precedes elongation. Most diameter increase in the xylem occurs in earlywood elements with those of latewood undergoing only negligible increase.

The vessel elements of *Quercus rubra* expanded in two stages: first a rapid enlargement to nearly full tangential dimension, followed by slow radial expansion to full size (Fig. 1.17). The maximum tangential dimension was attained within a week after expansion began. The appreciable turgor pressure of vessel elements permitted their expansion into the less turgid, soft tissues located tangentially to enlarging vessel elements. At this early stage, expansion of vessel elements in the radial direction appeared to be blocked on the inside by mature latewood of the previous annual increment and on the outside by the turgid cambial meristem backed up by lignified bark tissues. Thus, radial expansion was delayed until space was provided for it by outward displacement of the cambium (Zasada and Zahner, 1969).

Cambial derivatives in the xylem increase in size in variable patterns. Cells which develop into vessel members expand radially and tangentially but do not elongate appreciably. Tracheids and fibers undergo some radial expansion and they elongate in amounts which vary among different plant groups. In angiosperms the tracheids and fibers elongate greatly. Size increase of gymnosperm tracheids is traceable largely to radial expansion and only in a minor way to cell elongation. Bailey (1920) noted that tracheid length in some gymnosperms exceeded cambial initials by as much as 20%, whereas in the angiosperms studied cambial derivatives increased in length up to 500%. According to Wilson (1963), radial enlargement predominated for both tracheids and sieve cells of *Abies concolor*. However, tracheids elongated but did not enlarge tangentially. Tracheids elongated to a maximum of 13%. The amount of new wall produced by growth in length was not significant when compared to that traceable to a 400% increase in radial diameter which took place in only 6–10 days. It should be remembered that cambial initials in gymnosperms are much longer than those of angiosperms. Hence, even though there is proportionally little increase in length of cambial derivatives in gymnosperms, they nevertheless are considerably longer when fully developed than are the cambial derivatives of angiosperms. Variations in tracheid length of immature and mature tracheids of two species of gymnosperms are given in Table 1.1.

Considerable evidence is available which shows that growth in length of differentiating tracheids is restricted to cell tips or at least to the apical zone. The growing cell tips penetrate between neighboring cells where the intercellular layer is still not lignified (Wardrop and Dadswell, 1953). The occurrence of forked, flattened, or otherwise altered tips of cambial derivatives, when these are not characteristic of cambial initials, favors a theory of tip growth. Schoch-Bodmer and Huber (1952) stated that branching of fibers of *Sparmannia africana* was caused by splitting of the growing tips. In later

TABLE 1.1

VARIATION IN TRACHEID LENGTH OF TWO SPECIES OF GYMNOSPERMS IN SUCCESSIVE ZONES FROM THE CAMBIUM[a]

Species	Average length of tracheids (mm)			
	Zone 1[b]	Zone 2	Zone 3	Zone 4
Pinus radiata	1.41	1.45	1.51	1.55
Pseudotsuga menziesii	2.43	2.53	2.63	2.59

[a] The zones were 40 μ thick. In zone 1 only primary walls were present, and in zone 4 tracheids were mature. [From Wardrop and Dadswell (1953).]

[b] Cambium.

stages of growth, forking of fibers could be caused by growth inhibition comparable to that of hyphae, root hairs, or other cells showing local apical extension. These views were supported by Bannan's (1956) observations of forked tips of enlarging tracheids of *Thuja occidentalis*. Bannan (1956) noted that puckers occasionally developed along flanks of tracheid tips. These apparently resulted from unequal growth or local areas of accelerated growth of the wall along the flanks of the cell tip. Sometimes growth in length continued after outlines of bordered pits were discernible in walls remote from the tips. The tips apparently followed a path of least resistance and intruded between the nascent tips of bordering cells. Further evidence of restriction of growth to cell apices lies in the observation that areas of pits in xylem cells correspond to the length of cambial initials (Wardrop, 1964b).

The walls of most mature xylem cells consist of a thin primary wall (P) and a thick secondary wall (S) (Fig. 1.18). The cementing substance between cells is termed the middle lamella (ML). The primary wall forms at cell division in the cambium and encloses the protoplast during the time that surface growth of the cell continues. The lamellated secondary wall forms after surface growth is completed.

Cell wall constituents include (1) matrix substances (e.g., noncellulosic

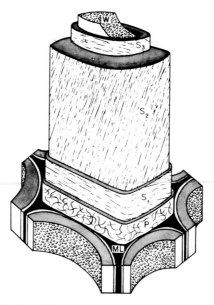

FIG. 1.18. Diagram of cell wall organization of a mature tracheid. ML, middle lamella; P, primary wall; S_1, S_2, and S_3, secondary walls; W, warty layer. [From Coté (1967), "Wood Ultrastructure" Washington Univ. Press, Seattle, Washington.]

polysaccharides), (2) framework substances, and (3) encrusting substances (primarily lignin). Both matrix and framework substances form during wall formation whereas encrusting substances form only after some wall thickening has occurred (Fig. 1.19).

The structure and formation of the cell wall of xylem cells have been described by Wardrop (1964b). Various layers of the wall differ in arrangement and orientation of cellulosic microfibrils or micelles (Fig. 1.20). Primary walls are not lamellated and tend to have loosely packed microfibrils. On the inner surface these usually are orientated transversely to the longitudinal axis, but their orientation may be different on the outer surface. At cell corners of mature cells, heavily lignified longitudinal ribs of microfibrils often are present. In secondary walls of fibers and tracheids, the outer layer (S$_1$) contains lamellae of alternating left and right handed (S and Z) helical organization. The middle layer (S$_2$) has many lamellae in which the microfibrils are oriented at a small angle to the longitudinal axis. The inner layer (S$_3$) sometimes is thin or absent. When present, its lamellae have microfibrils orientated at a large angle to the longitudinal cell axis. The thin secondary walls of parenchyma cells have an organization resembling that of fibers. In vessels the secondary walls generally have a 3-layered structure similar

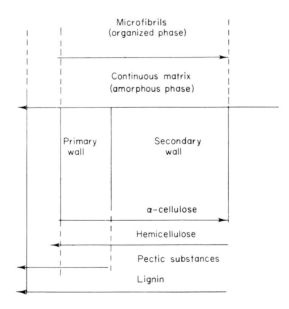

FIG. 1.19. Distribution of chemical components in the mature cell wall. The arrows indicate directions of increasing relative concentration of various components. [From Northcote (1963).]

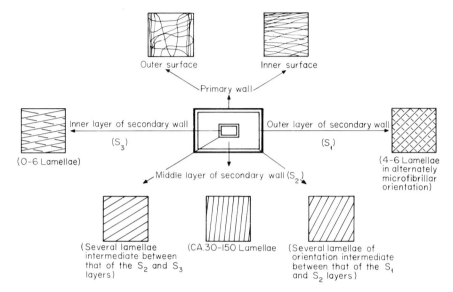

FIG. 1.20. Diagrammatic representation of cell wall organization of mature fiber or tracheid showing texture of various cell wall layers. [From Wardrop and Harada (1965).]

to that of fibers. However, in the more specialized vessels the layering is less obvious.

Wardrop (1964b,c) presented evidence that both vesicular secretion and lamellar apposition were involved in cell wall formation in differentiating xylem. Vesicular secretion appeared to be involved in the incorporation of matrix and encrusting constituents into the wall while apposition elaborated the cellulose framework.

Cellulose is quantitatively the dominant component of cell walls and is formed at all stages of cell development. Cellulose synthesis begins before surface growth is actually completed and formation of the secondary wall is initiated. Deposition of material of the S_1 layer begins near the center of the cell and proceeds toward the apices, as indicated by various lines of evidence. For example, gymnosperm tracheids in which secondary wall formation was incomplete had only primary walls at the tips (Wardrop and Dadswell, 1953). Decreased birefringence was noted from the middle of tracheids to the tips (Wardrop and Harada, 1965). When plants were grown in labeled CO_2 and autoradiographs of partially differentiated cells examined, the radioactivity was distributed evenly in cells having only primary walls. In contrast, in cells undergoing secondary wall formation, maximum radioactivity was recorded in the center of the cells with a gradual decrease toward the tips (Wardrop, 1964b). In compression wood the S_2 layer of the secondary wall has a system of helical fissures parallel to the direction of microfibril orientation. In partially differentiated tracheids of compression wood the fissures are clearly evident near the middle of the cells but can be hardly seen toward the tips (Wardrop and Dadswell, 1952). Finally, cross-sections of differentiating fibers taken near the tips usually show that less secondary wall formed there than in a cross-section taken near the middle of the cell, or that no secondary wall has yet formed near the tip. These several observations suggest that in a developing cambial derivative the lamellae of the secondary wall are deposited as shown in Fig. 1.21, with more lamellae near the center of the cell than at its extremities.

Lignification

Lignin, the material that makes plants "woody," is a very large polymer molecule with both aliphatic and aromatic components. It is basically derived from phenylpropane, a 6-carbon benzene ring attached to a straight side chain of 3 carbon atoms. These units are variously interconnected by carbon–carbon or carbon–oxygen–carbon (ether) bonds, giving lignin a complex three-dimensional structure (Harkin, 1969). The degree of lignification varies among plant groups and species, cells, and different parts of the same cells. Whereas tracheids of gymnosperms and vessels of angiosperms are heavily lignified the fiber tracheids and libriform fibers of angiosperm woods usually show only slight lignin deposition.

Deposition of lignin, which is considered a filling or cementing process, occurs within the existing framework of the cell wall. However, lignification and cell wall construction are not mutually exclusive processes and addition of lignin to the cellulose of the cell wall begins early in cell wall development.

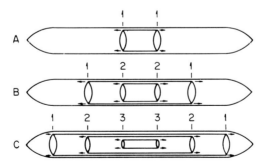

Fig. 1.21. Stages in formation of three successive lamellae (1,2,3) of the secondary wall of a differentiating fiber. The primary wall is not undergoing growth simultaneously. [From Wardrop (1964b).]

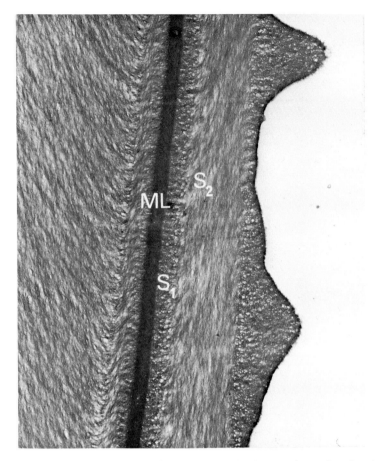

Fɪɢ. 1.22. Lignin skeleton of *Pseudotsuga menziesii* xylem as shown in a longitudinal section through a portion of a double cell wall (S_1 and S_2). Celluloses and hemicelluloses were removed and the intact lignin residue remained. Note the rather uniform distribution of lignin across the secondary wall except at the lumen lining. At the middle lamella (ML) the lignin has a different character than at some distance from it. [From Coté (1967).]

In *Pinus resinosa*, for example, lignification of tracheids was underway by the time their radial expansion ceased and secondary wall formation began.

Lignin is deposited in the microcapillaries which are between and parallel to the microfibrils of cellulose. Hence, the mature secondary wall of lignified cells is comprised of interpenetrating systems of cellulose and lignin (Fig. 1.22). Kremers (1957) showed that large amounts of energy and metabolic reserves were used in lignification. He estimated that about 20 g of material were present in the mature cell wall for every gram that was present in the primary stage. About 11 g of the 20 were represented by cellulose and 5 by lignin.

Lignin deposition begins first in the region of the intercellular layer and then extends to the secondary walls. Deposition of lignin can first be seen in differentiating fibers when surface growth stops and secondary thickening begins. According to Wardrop (1957), lignin is first found in primary walls next to the corner thickenings of the intercellular layer. It is then deposited on the primary wall and is noted on tangential walls first and then on radial walls. As lignin is deposited cell by cell only during a growth period, the amount of lignification may vary considerably in tangentially adjacent cells. At the beginning of a growth period, lignin first appears in cell corners of new cells and is not continuous with the lignin of cells which formed during a previous growth period (Wardrop and Bland, 1958). In the mature cell the final concentration of lignin is greatest at the outside regions of the wall (Northcote, 1963).

Wardrop (1957) showed that lignification of *Pinus radiata* tracheids lagged behind synthesis of cellulose and other cell wall constituents. In a *Pinus radiata* differentiating zone of xylem some 40 cells wide, the secondary walls of the tenth or eleventh cell from the cambium were completely formed, but lignification was only in incipient stages and confined to the corners of cells.

TABLE 1.2

SEASONAL COURSE OF GROWTH AND LIGNIFICATION OF THE ANNUAL RING OF *Picea abies*[a]

Date	Width of annual ring (mm)		Percentage of lignified part in relation to	
	Produced	Lignified	Ring width produced	Total annual ring width
May 26	0.525	0	0	0
June 2	0.885	0.145	16.4	2.8
June 9	1.730	0.462	26.7	9.1
June 17	1.910	0.710	37.5	12.7
June 23	2.260	0.885	39.4	16.1
July 1	3.160	2.220	70.0	43.5
July 7	4.160	3.150	75.4	61.5
July 14	4.800	4.010	83.5	78.8
July 22	4.880	4.350	89.0	85.5
July 28	4.950	4.500	91.0	88.5
Aug 4	4.990	4.750	95.0	93.5
Aug 11	4.990	4.990	100.0	100.0

[a] Stem height 1.3 meters. [From Mork (1960).]

In the thirty-first cell from the cambium, however, lignification was virtually complete in both the primary wall and intercellular layer, and it was occurring in the secondary wall. Some idea of the seasonal lag in lignification behind cell wall production in *Picea abies* may be gained from Table 1.2.

In fully differentiated xylem cells, Sachs, Clark, and Pew (1963) found the greatest density of lignin in the middle lamella, the primary walls, and the S_3 layer. In *Pinus taeda* xylem, the lignin in the middle lamella was dense and without structure, and it was laterally oriented on either side of the middle lamella. Lignin in the S_3 layer was almost as dense as in the middle lamella. In angiosperms, lignin also was dispersed throughout the cellular structure, but more of it was concentrated in the middle lamella, and the secondary wall was less dense than in gymnosperms.

Although the middle lamella and primary walls (ML + P) of xylem of angiosperms and gymnosperms are rich in lignin, it appears that in gymnosperms these layers contain something less than 40% of the total lignin. Berlyn and Mark (1965) calculated that the ML + P layers occupied only about 10–12% of the volume of gymnosperm wood and were about 80–90% as dense as the secondary wall. As wood contains about 25–30% lignin, the ML + P layers combined had to contain less than half of the total lignin.

Ringing experiments have shown that some lignification can occur below a bark girdle. This indicates that lignin precursors exist in the cambial region or are synthesized there independently from material translocated from the shoots. Nevertheless, the utilization of auxin precursors in lignification is under strong apical control. Evidence for this view comes from observations below bark girdles of marked reduction in lignification and changes in differentiation involving production of unlignified parenchyma rather than lignified tracheids (Wardrop and Bland, 1958).

DIFFERENTIATION OF SECONDARY PHLOEM

Both similarities and differences in differentiation of phloem and xylem cells have been shown. Cell expansion, wall thickening, and lignification occur in derivatives cut off on both sides of the cambium, but in different amounts. Ordinarily the derivatives on the phloem side divide before differentiation is initiated. This may involve divisions which produce more derivatives or groups of sieve elements and associated companion cells and parenchyma cells.

Increase in Cell Size

The amount of cell expansion during differentiation varies among phloem components. Sieve tube members usually show the greatest increases in diameter whereas fibers expand little. Ray cells expand somewhat but otherwise do not show marked changes during differentiation.

Cell Wall Thickening

Unlike the bulk of xylem cells which develop rigid, persisting walls a large proportion of the phloem cells remain soft-walled and eventually collapse or become greatly distorted. Some phloem elements develop secondary walls and others do not. The walls of mature sieve elements vary considerably in thickness. When nacreous wall thickenings are absent, the sieve elements of angiosperms have only primary walls. Nacreous thickenings sometimes disappear, suggesting they should not be classified as secondary walls. In one group of gymnosperms, the Abietineae, secondary wall formation occurs in sieve elements. However, evidence for lignification of sieve elements is lacking. Infrequent sclerification of companion cells after sieve elements become nonfunctional has been reported for *Tilia americana* (Evert, 1963c).

Phloem fibers develop secondary walls, with the timing of wall thickening varying among species. In *Tilia*, secondary wall formation of fibers occurs in the conducting phloem. In *Prunus*, however, fibers in the functional phloem have only primary walls and secondary wall formation occurs only after sieve elements cease functioning. The walls of phloem parenchyma and ray cells in the active phloem are primary and lignified. Following phloem inactivation, the ray and axial parenchyma cells either are not altered or they develop secondary walls and differentiate into sclereids. Parenchyma cells in the old phloem may become sclerified without assuming characteristics of sclereids (Esau, 1964, 1965b).

Ontogeny of Sieve Elements

Inasmuch as sieve elements are the principal cells concerned with translocation of food, much interest has been shown in their development and structure.

Sieve elements are living cells which are joined to other sieve elements by groups of pores in cell walls. During differentiation of sieve elements, metabolic activity declines as indicated by disorganization of the nucleus and reduction in mitochondria and ribosomes. The tonoplast also breaks down. Despite these changes sieve elements function as living cells for some time.

Evert and Alfieri (1965) described ontogeny of sieve cells in several species of gymnosperms. Cambial derivatives or phloem initials which gave rise to sieve cells had a thin parietal layer of cytoplasm enclosing a large vacuole. The cytoplasm contained oil globules, mitochondria, plastids, and a nucleus with several nucleoli. As differentiating sieve cells expanded, the plastids became arranged at primary pit fields of future sieve areas. Shortly thereafter slime bodies, which had appeared in the cytoplasm, elongated giving rise to strands. The nucleus began to lose chromaticity and nucleoli disappeared.

During early sieve cell ontogeny, secondary wall thickening occurred in some gymnosperms (*Larix, Picea, Pinus*) but not others (*Juniperus*). Sieve area pores were traversed by continuous slime strands. Finally the tonoplast disappeared. The necrotic nucleus was present near the lateral wall. As sieve cells were becoming inactive, large amounts of definitive callose were deposited at sieve areas. The strands broke down and sieve cell contents disappeared. Later callose also disappeared.

Important aspects of sieve element ontogeny in *Ulmus americana* were reported by Evert *et al.* (1969). Following the last division of the sieve mother cell, the young sieve element expanded radially and tangentially and underwent additional vacuolation. The fully expanded sieve element had a large central vacuole surrounded by a thin layer of parietal cytoplasm. During expansion of the sieve element, slime bodies appeared in the cytoplasm. Initial evidence of sieve plate development consisted of callose deposits on both sides of the developing sieve plate at sites of the future pores. Eventually the pore sites became perforated, with those near the margins of sieve plates undergoing perforation before those in the centers of the plate. At maturity the sieve elements had a parietal network of fine strands of slime which was continuous from one sieve element to the next through the sieve plate pores.

Small amounts of callose are present in sieve areas of mature conducting sieve elements. As a sieve element begins to senesce, however, the amount of callose increases. When sieve elements finally become inactive, their sieve areas either have very large amounts of definitive callose or none as callose is lost from old, inactive sieve elements.

In *Robinia pseudoacacia* in Wisconsin cessation of function began with narrow spring sieve elements. Large amounts of definitive callose were found on sieve plates and sieve areas by June. Most of these cells collapsed by the middle of July but some remained turgid up to August. In early September callose accumulation increased on the first formed, wide sieve elements. Subsequently these sieve elements collapsed together with associated companion cells and related parenchyma cells. Definitive callose was not removed until the following spring. Then most of it gradually disappeared leaving only small amounts on old sieve plates by midsummer. By late November, only the late formed sieve elements were turgid. By late December they collapsed also and no functional sieve elements were present from late December until early April (Derr and Evert, 1967).

In most species the sieve elements function for a single season, but in a few genera including *Vitis, Tilia, Liriodendron, Rubus,* and possibly *Rosa* they remain functional beyond one year. For example, in *Vitis* and *Liriodendron* sieve tubes remained functional during the second year (Esau, 1948; Cheadle and Esau, 1964). Sieve tubes of *Tilia americana* were reported to remain alive for up to 5 years and those of *T. cordata* for 10 years (Holdheide, 1951; Evert, 1963c). In *Quercus alba* most sieve elements became functionless during the same season they were produced by the cambium. However, the last formed sieve elements of each annual growth increment remained functional through the second season (Anderson and Evert, 1965). In various evergreen dicotyledons and gymnosperms, the phloem probably remains active in carbohydrate conduction for two seasons (Grillos and Smith, 1959; Esau, 1965b).

The sieve tubes of *Vitis* function for at least two seasons, with periods of activity interrupted by winter dormancy. The dormant phloem has heavy masses of callose on the sieve plates and sieve areas. When the phloem is reactivated in the spring the callose dissolves gradually. Phloem reactivation is initiated near the cambium and then progresses to other phloem areas. Reactivating phloem is distinguishable from dormant phloem by the thin callose masses and conspicuous slime in the former (Esau, 1965b).

In most angiosperm species examined, the sieve tubes are functional only during the season in which they are formed. This is true for *Pyrus communis*, *P. malus*, *Robinia pseudoacacia*, and *Populus tremuloides*. However, a few species of angiosperms have some functional sieve tubes throughout the year. For example, in *Acer negundo* the first functional sieve elements were those that reached maturity before the cambium was reactivated in the spring. These overwintering sieve elements did not become inactive until after newly formed, functional sieve elements were present (Tucker and Evert, 1969).

Functional sieve tubes also were present throughout the year in *Pinus banksiana*, *P. resinosa*, and *P. strobus*. In a given year's growth increment, however, all but the last formed sieve cells stopped functioning during the same season they were produced. The last formed sieve elements overwintered and remained functional until new sieve cells differentiated in the spring (Alfieri and Evert, 1968).

When sieve elements of gymnosperms become inactive they collapse. In angiosperms, however, the characteristics of inactive phloem vary considerably among species. In *Juglans*, *Liriodendron*, *Populus*, and *Tilia* the shape of inactive sieve elements is not very different from that of active ones. In contrast, in *Acer negundo*, *Aristolochia*, and *Robinia* the inactive sieve elements and their associated cells collapse. Tucker and Evert (1969) noted that as sieve elements of *Acer negundo* became inactive they lost turgor and underwent partial collapse. During the winter the radial walls of the partially collapsed sieve elements had a wavy appearance. As cambial growth resumed in the spring these sieve elements were further compressed and distorted (Tucker and Evert, 1969).

It is generally agreed that mature sieve elements lack nuclei and lack a boundary layer between cytoplasmic and vacuolar contents. However, agreement is lacking on the time of disappearance of the nucleus and tonoplast during sieve element differentiation. Some investigators reported perforation

of sieve plates and lateral sieve areas to occur after disappearance of the
nucleus and tonoplast (Esau, 1965c). Others reported that perforation preceded disappearance of the nucleus (Evert *et al.*, 1966). Nuclei have also been
reported in mature sieve elements of several woody angiosperms. For
example, in *Ulmus americana* the nucleus and tonoplast did not disappear
until after sieve plates were perforated, if they disappeared at all (Evert
et al., 1969). Nuclei in sieve elements of gymnosperms have also been reported to remain in a necrotic state in the mature cell (Evert and Alfieri,
1965).

Dilatation of Phloem Tissues

As trees grow in diameter, tangential stresses always occur in the bark.
These may be accommodated in varying degrees in several ways. To a
limited extent the cells of bark tissues can stretch and become distorted.
Thereafter, adjustments to tangential stresses are made by (1) circumferential
increase of the cambium by anticlinal divisions, (2) a limited amount of
simultaneous growth of all the phloem cells near the cambium, (3) proliferation of parenchyma cells to form expansion or dilatation tissues, and (4)
longitudinal cracking or fissuring of the dead outer bark (Whitmore, 1962a,
1962b).

As mentioned, tangential stresses which develop in the bark of growing
trees may be accommodated to a considerable extent by enlargement and
division of axial and ray parenchyma cells to form tissues which are inserted
among existing tissues. Such expansion tissues may take various forms.
The dilatation of phloem rays, a form of noncambial secondary growth,
is a common feature of many species of *Citrus* and *Tilia* (Schneider, 1952,
1954, 1955; Esau, 1965b). Esau (1965b) applied the term intercalary, secondary growth to dilatation of stems and roots outside the vascular cambium
in order to contrast such growth with cambial secondary growth.

The degree of ray dilatation is highly variable among species. Within a
tree some rays dilate while others do not; or cell divisions may be localized
to a part of a ray (Schneider, 1955). In *Citrus sinensis* phloem ray cells are
stretched tangentially and divided by radial walls to form masses of parenchyma tissue (Schneider, 1952).

Expansion tissues in Dipterocarpaceae formed in fingers by widening of
phloem rays; in wedges by proliferation of a number of adjacent rays and
intervening phloem blocks, or as a pseudocortex (Whitmore, 1962a). In
Eucalyptus the formation of wedges of parenchymatous tissues usually ac-
commodates the outer phloem to increased stem girth (Chattaway, 1953).
Commonly associated with tangential expansion of parenchyma tissues of
the phloem is a distortion of ray direction. Lack of dilatation of uniseriate
and biseriate rays, as in *Pyrus malus*, appears to be characteristic of many
woody dicotyledons.

CHEMICAL CHANGES DURING DIFFERENTIATION

The chemical composition of cambial derivatives changes markedly during their differentiation (Table 1.3). According to Stewart (1966), the weight

TABLE 1.3

VARIATIONS IN CHEMICAL COMPOSITION OF WOOD CELLS OF *Populus tremuloides* DURING DIFFERENTIATION[a]

Component	Percent at stage				
	1 Wood scrapings	2 Softwood	3 Stringy wood	4 New wood	5 Year-old wood
Lignin	1.4	2.8	8.2	16.0	19.1
Cellulose	19.8	34.8	42.8	45.8	46.4
Mannan	1.1	1.3	1.7	2.1	2.4
Xylan	7.2	12.3	18.0	16.0	16.2
Uronic anyhydride	15.6	12.9	7.7	5.8	4.8
Protein	20.0	16.2	6.2	1.9	0.6
Ash	10.4	7.0	3.3	1.1	0.4
Arabinan	4.2	3.3	1.4	0.7	0.5
Galactan	6.2	4.3	1.6	1.2	0.6
H_2O (fresh wt. basis)	—	86	—	48	39

[a] From Kremers (1964).

increment of a fiber cell wall during deposition of the secondary wall and addition of lignin, as well as extraneous substances, may be as much as 1000%. The weight increment of differentiating phloem cells usually is less than that of xylary cells because of a thinner wall in a differentiated cell of the former.

Whereas cambial cells are highly hydrated, those of fully differentiated cambial derivatives are much less hydrated. Thus the progressive increase in cellulose, lignin, and hemicellulose in developing cambial derivatives as they mature is accompanied by dehydration. According to Kremers (1964), three types of dehydration are involved in differentiation:

1. Chemical dehydration, resulting from conversion of small molecules into large ones, as illustrated by the following tabulation.

Starting material	End product	Reaction
Glucose	Cellulose	$n(C_6H_{11}O_5) OH \rightarrow (C_6H_{10}O_5)_n OH + (n-1) H_2O$
Xylose	Xylan	$n(C_5H_9O_4) OH \rightarrow (C_5H_8O_4)_n OH + (n-1) H_2O$
Coniferyl alcohol	Lignin	$n(C_{10}H_{12}O_3) T_nO \rightarrow (C_{10}H_{10}O_3)_n + n H_2O$

2. Mechanical dehydration, resulting from deposition of cell wall materials and displacement of water by air

3. Physical dehydration, involving equilibration with the environment after a derivative has matured

Several investigators have studied the chemical composition of cambial zone cells and of cambial derivatives in various stages of differentiation. A few examples will be given.

During differentiation of xylem cells of both gymnosperms and angiosperms, there is a decrease in the percentage composition of ash, nitrogen, pectic acid, galactan, and arabinan. In contrast, percentage composition of cellulose, lignin, and xylans increases during xylem differentiation (Table 1.3, Fig. 1.23). Such chemical changes are consistent with morphology of wood formation (Kremers, 1963, 1964).

The composition of samples taken in the cambial zone indicates that the primary wall is high in noncellulosic polysaccharides and contains less than 20–30% cellulose and little or no lignin. The cambial zone contains considerable inorganic ash, protein, and 80% ethanol-soluble material (Stewart, 1969). The cytoplasm of cambial cells is relatively rich in nitrogenous compounds such as enzymes, peptides, amino acids, nucleic acids, lipoprotein

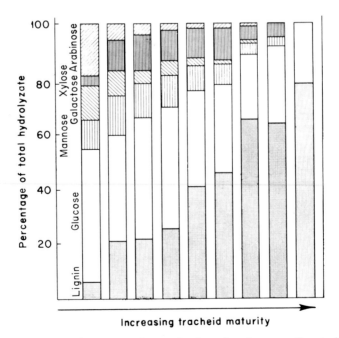

FIG. 1.23. Model showing progressive production of various constituents in walls of *Pinus resinosa* tracheids during their development. [From Larson (1969a).]

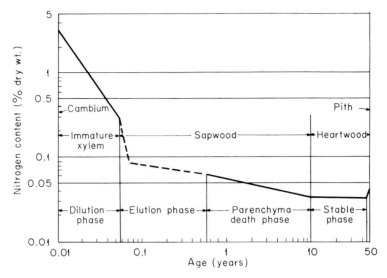

FIG. 1.24. Changes in nitrogen during various stages in maturation of xylary tissues. [From Cowling and Merrill (1966).]

membranes, and other compounds. After cambial cells undergo secondary wall thickening and lignification, the percentage of nitrogen in the cytoplasm and primary walls of these cells is diluted by addition of cellulose and lignin. Hence, percent nitrogen by weight decreases. Following lignification, the xylary cambial derivatives in most species die rapidly and abruptly lose much of their nitrogen (Fig. 1.24). There are exceptions, however. For example, *Tamarix aphylla* fibers may remain alive for 20 years (Fahn and Arnon, 1963). In contrast to vascular elements of most species, the long-lived axial parenchyma and ray parenchyma cells of the sapwood maintain their nitrogen contents at comparatively high levels.

Larson (1969a) studied differentiation of tracheids of 5-year-old *Pinus resinosa* trees. Following radial expansion the first file of tracheids already had a secondary wall indicating rapid deposition of the S_1 layer. The outer S_2 layers also were deposited in a short time. His data showed that the synthesis of each wall constituent represented a continuum, with each component either increasing or decreasing in a definite relationship as the tracheid matured (Fig. 1.23). Within the secondary wall, the cellulose–hemicellulose ratio of 60:40 stayed rather constant, but the proportion of different hemicellulose sugars varied with tracheid maturity. Lignin increased from approximately 20% in the outer wall to almost 70% near the lumen.

Thornber and Northcote (1961a) determined changes in chemical composition of cambial derivatives during differentiation in *Acer pseudoplatanus*,

Betula platyphylla, *Fraxinus elatior*, and *Pinus ponderosa*. Secondary thickening of xylem cells walls occurred by formation of α-cellulose, 47%; hemicellulose, 20%; and lignin, 33%.

During transition of a sapwood cell to a heartwood cell in the angiosperms, there was an increase in cell weight, largely due to greater deposition of α-cellulose than of lignin and hemicellulose. In *Pinus ponderosa*, the mean weight of a heartwood cell was less than that of a sapwood cell and this reflected a loss in the weight of each main component, primarily α-cellulose.

In another study Thornber and Northcote (1961b) determined the carbohydrate composition of the α-cellulose, hemicellulose, and pectic substances in cell walls of phloem, cambium, and sapwood and heartwood cells of *Fraxinus elatior*, *Betula platyphylla*, *Acer pseudoplatanus*, and *Pinus ponderosa*. The carbohydrate composition of cambial cell walls was similar for each species. In the angiosperms secondary wall thickening was accompanied by formation of glucans (56–67%), xylans (20–33%), uronic anhydride (8–11%), and mannans (2–6%). Thus the hemicellulose and α-cellulose of the secondary walls are composed of polymers made up from D-glucose, D-xylose, D-glucuronic acid, and D-mannose. There was little change in the amount of arabans per cell and the amount of galactans decreased. In *Pinus ponderosa*, cell wall thickening involved formation of larger amounts of mannans (22%), arabans (1%), and galactans (0.3%) and lower percentages of the other constituents. The xylans produced during secondary wall formation appeared to contain more uronic anhydride than was deposited in the primary cell wall. Transformation of a sapwood cell into a heartwood cell involved additional formation of glucans and mannans in the angiosperms and xylans in *Pinus ponderosa*. In the angiosperms, pectic substances (galactan, araban, and polygalacturonic acid) were lost during heartwood formation.

The individual polymers which are common to both primary and secondary walls of cambial derivatives show some differences in chemical composition. Thornber and Northcote (1961b) found that in both *Acer pseudoplatanus* and *Betula platyphylla* the percentage of 4-*O*-methylglucuronic acid in the hemicellulose component of cambial cell walls was less than that in the hemicellulose that was synthesized during secondary wall thickening. The xylans contain all the 4-*O*-methylglucuronic acid residues present in the cell walls of higher plants. Therefore, Thornber and Northcote (1962) isolated these polysaccharides from cambial, phloem, and xylem cells of *Acer pseudoplatanus* and *Pinus sylvestris* and compared their structures. The percentage of 4-*O*-methylglucuronic acid in the xylan fraction from primary cell walls of the cambial region was lower than that in xylem fractions obtained from differentiated tissues. The xylan in *Acer pseudoplatanus* phloem contained twice the number of 4-*O*-methylglucuronic acid residues for a given number of xylose units than the xylan of the xylem. However, in *Pinus sylvestris* the phloem contained only half as many uronic acid residues as that of the xylem. Therefore, during differentiation of a phloem cell from a cambial initial in *Pinus sylvestris* fewer 4-*O*-methylglucuronic acid residues were added to the xylans than during development of a xylem cell. This situation was reversed in *Acer pseudoplatanus*. The glucomannans laid down during secondary wall thickening in pine were similar in composition to those deposited in the primary cell wall. However, the glucomannan fractions deposited during formation of phloem cells were richer in mannose.

Expansion of the Cambium

As a tree stem increases in length and girth the cambial sheath increases in area primarily by adding cells rather than by appreciably increasing the average size of existing ones. Increase in number of cambial cells involves: (1) increase in length of the cambial sheath by the addition of new cells primarily from the procambium behind root and stem tips; and (2) increase in girth of the cambial sheath by anticlinal division of existing fusiform cambial cells throughout it, either by simple radiolongitudinal multiplicative division or by pseudotransverse division followed by apical intrusive growth. Whereas radiolongitudinal division is restricted to those species of angiosperms with storied cambia, pseudotransverse division occurs in other species of angiosperms and in gymnosperms.

Pseudotransverse Division

In pseudotransverse division the somewhat sigmoidal wall laid down near the center of the dividing fusiform initial may vary from short and almost transverse to elongate and inclined (Fig. 1.25). Usually the partition averages about 15% of the length of the dividing cell but sometimes it may be a third to as much as a half of the length of the original cell (Bannan, 1964). The direction of inclination of the new walls usually is similar in neighboring cells (Hejnowicz, 1961). After pseudotransverse division occurs, each of the two new daughter initials is slightly longer than half the length of the former initial. The cells then elongate during several periclinal divisions until the original length is attained, and then another pseudotransverse division may occur (Fig. 1.26). A marked feature of cambial response is a tendency for anticlinal divisions to be restricted to a narrow band or layer of cells which may be called initials. Although frequent periclinal divisions occur in xylem mother cells, anticlinal divisions in them are rare.

Characteristic of pseudotransverse division of fusiform initials is overproduction and accompanying loss of cells, resulting in only small net gain in cell number, together with effective renewal of the cambium. Major factors

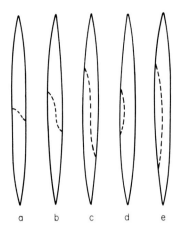

a   b   c   d   e

FIG. 1.25. Tangential view of fusiform initials showing various types of anticlinal division involved in multiplication of cambial cells. Pseudotransverse division (a–c); lateral division (d, e). [From Bannan (1967).]

in survival of fusiform initials during intracambial competition appear to be cell size and degree of contact with vascular rays. In both slow and fast growing trees, the longer sister initial of a pseudotransverse division is more likely to survive than the shorter initial (Bannan, 1957c; Evert, 1961). The surviving long initials have most ray contacts. The newly formed initials which are short and have few ray contacts either lose their capacity for periclinal division and mature or they undergo reduction in size and become converted to ray initials.

The rate of anticlinal division is somewhat higher in fusiform initials which contact fusiform rays than in initials which touch only uniseriate rays. In pines, for example, the differences in rate of division between the two classes of fusiform initials averaged 17% for 9 species (Table 1.4). In *Pseudotsuga menziesii* and two species of *Picea*, the differences in rate of anticlinal division in cambial cells with and without contact with fusiform rays were only 6 and 7%, respectively (Bannan, 1965b). The higher rate of division in cells touching fusiform rays apparently was due to the greater area of ray contact. The increase in the recorded rate of anticlinal division was not due primarily to a stimulation of division but rather to survival of more daughter initials resulting from anticlinal division. The importance of ray contacts to survival of fusiform initials suggests rather intense internal competition for assimilates (Bannan, 1956; Bannan and Bayly, 1956).

In addition to changing with environmental conditions, the frequency of anticlinal division of cambial initials varies with growth rate and species,

Whereas most fusiform cambial cells which divide anticlinally do so by pseudotransverse division, a small percentage divide anticlinally to produce segments off the sides of the initials (Fig. 1.25). Bannan (1957b) found such division to occur in only about 2% of the cases studied. These divisions to produce segments illustrate the relation between size of cells and their ultimate fate. If the segments are short they usually fail. If they are of intermediate length they generally undergo reduction to ray initials. The longest segments continue to function as fusiform initials.

In *Pyrus communis* about 50% of the new initials were lost from the cambium and 15% were transformed to ray initials. Hence, only 35% of the new initials survived and repeated the cycle of division (Evert, 1961). Failing initials at the time of their origin were 34% shorter and had 37% less ray contact on the average than surviving initials (Evert, 1961). Bannan (1956) found in a study of 1900 cases that the surviving initials contacted 53% more ray cells than initials which eventually failed. Cambial initials sometimes decreased in length before they disappeared. Bannan (1953) suggested this was because failing initials may not have been able to retain enough water for normal expansion.

TABLE 1.5

VARIATIONS AMONG SPECIES IN RATES OF ANTICLINAL DIVISION OF CAMBIAL CELLS AND CELL LENGTH AT DIVISION[a]

Species	Rate of anticlinal division (per cm xylem)	Cell length (mm)
Pinus banksiana	1.6 ± 0.2	3.15 ± 0.10
Pinus contorta	1.1 ± .2	2.71 ± .10
Pinus resinosa	1.9 ± .2	3.27 ± .07
Pinus lambertiana	1.3 ± .2	3.85 ± .10
Pinus strobus	2.4 ± .2	3.58 ± .06
Picea glauca	1.0 ± .1	3.60 ± .05
Pseudotsuga menziesii		
Coastal	1.4 ± .1	4.02 ± .12
Interior	1.7 ± .2	3.39 ± .08
Larix laricina	2.2 ± .2	3.28 ± .10
Tsuga canadensis	1.7 ± .2	3.76 ± .04
Abies balsamea	1.4 ± .1	3.47 ± .10
Sequoia sempervirens	2.6 ± .4	4.59 ± .13
Thuja occidentalis	2.2 ± .1	2.59 ± .03
Cupressus pygmaea	2.3 ± .3	3.03 ± .17
Cupressus sargentii	3.4 ± .3	2.85 ± .08
Juniperus virginiana	4.0 ± .5	2.04 ± .10

[a] From Bannan (1967).

TIMING OF PSEUDOTRANSVERSE DIVISION

Detailed investigations of timing of pseudotransverse division of cambial cells have been performed for relatively few species. Such studies show that most pseudotransverse divisions of multiplying fusiform cambial cells occur toward the end of the growing season, often just before the last latewood elements are formed. The late summer divisions are followed by tip elongation of the newly formed cambial cells. In the following year, the cambial cells elongate only slightly during development of approximately the first quarter of the annual ring. Thereafter, the rate of elongation of cambial cells increases and reaches a maximum in the last quarter. There also is a similar seasonal trend in loss of fusiform initials. In several species of *Chamaecyparis* and *Thuja*, losses of cambial initials tended to increase toward the end of the growing season, with more than 40% of the losses occurring during the last quarter (Bannan, 1951b). In *Pyrus communis* most anticlinal divisions which accounted for circumferential growth of the cambial cylinder also occurred toward the end of the surge of radial growth in late June and early July (Evert, 1961).

Fusiform cambium initials divide pseudotransversely at intervals which are not very closely related to the rate of circumferential increase. For example, Bannan (1960b) noted that pseudotransverse divisions occurred at a high rate in old stems where circumferential expansion was minimal. In *Thuja occidentalis* the rate of anticlinal divisions of initials remained about the same despite difference in width of rings or increases in girth. An increase in frequency of divisions did not occur except when ring width was below 0.3 mm. In *Pinus strobus* the frequency of division was more readily changed by reduction in ring width, with a marked increase occurring when xylem width was less than 1.3 mm (Bannan, 1962).

ELONGATION OF CAMBIAL CELLS

Tip growth of fusiform cambial cells involves an intrusion of some cells among others. However, as Bannan pointed out (1956), there must be some slippage between the expanding wall of a neighboring cell. When appreciable elongation of tip sides occurs, intrusive and interpositional growth (Schoch-Bodmer and Huber, 1952) as well as sliding growth might occur to some degree, and clear distinctions among these are difficult to make.

Fusiform initials elongate by apical growth. In some species much greater elongation of initials occurs consistently at one end but in other species this relation does not hold. For example, in *Pinaceae* the direction of growth of fusiform initials following pseudotransverse division is most often upward (Bannan, 1968). This contrasts with a prevalence of downward elongation of fusiform cambial cells in *Thuja occidentalis* (Bannan, 1960a). In *Pyrus communis*, however, no polarity in direction of elongation was found (Evert, 1961). Rapid elongation which accompanies loss of an initial above or below a cell suggests the importance of internal hydrostatic pressure in growth of initials.

Close correlation exists between survival of fusiform cambial cells, after pseudotransverse division, and the direction of major cell elongation. In the Pinaceae the upper of the two sister fusiform initials that are formed in pseudotransverse division is more likely to be the forerunner of a continuing cell series than is the lower sister initial. In species in which downward elongation of fusiform initials predominates (e.g., *Thuja occidentnlis*), the lower sister initials show higher frequency of survival than do the upper sister initials (Table 1.6). The correlation between direction of survival and major cell elongation suggests unequal distribution of growth controlling factors throughout fusiform initials.

MULTIPLICATION AND DEVELOPMENT OF VASCULAR RAYS

On the basis of their origin the vascular rays of trees are classified as primary or secondary. Primary rays, which arise at the outer margins of the primary xylem, originate from cells of the primary body which are called

TABLE 1.6

RELATIVE FREQUENCIES OF FAILURE AND SURVIVAL OF SISTER FUSIFORM INITIALS FOLLOWING PSEUDOTRANSVERSE DIVISION[a]

Species	Percentage of pseudotransverse divisions			
	Failure of both derived sister series	Continuation of lower sister series	Continuation of upper sister series	Continuation of both sister series
Pinus ponderosa	15	24	31	30
Pinus resinosa	18	24	30	28
Pinus lambertiana	13	18	32	37
Pinus strobus	17	24	30	29
Pseudotsuga menziesii	18	22	28	32
Picea glauca	15	24	27	34
Tsuga canadensis	20	18	26	36
Sequoia sempervirens	18	21	27	34
Juniperus virginiana	18	21	27	34
Cupressus sargentii	14	27	19	40
Libocedrus decurrens	15	25	20	40
Thuja occidentalis	20	25	20	35

[a] From Bannan (1968).

primordial ray initials (Barghoorn, 1940b). Secondary rays originate in the cambium from fusiform ray initials which are derived from fusiform initials during secondary growth.

Although primary rays tend to become widely separated as tree stems and branches increase in circumference, a rather constant balance is maintained between the number of rays and fusiform initials (Bannan, 1955). While new fusiform initials are added as previously described, additional secondary rays also are produced from ray initials which arise from fusiform initials in one of the following ways (Barghoorn, 1940a).

1. Formation of a single ray initial at the end of a fusiform initial. The segment cut off at the tip of a fusiform initial may be reduced to one or several ray initials (Barghoorn, 1940a, b; Bannan, 1950, 1951a; Evert, 1961).

2. Formation of a single ray initial at the side of a fusiform initial. The cell division occurs at or near the central region of the fusiform initial (Whalley, 1950). The cell which is cut off may become shortened before it is converted to one or two ray initials (Evert, 1961).

3. Segmentation of entire fusiform initials to produce a vertical series of individual ray initials.

4. Derivation of ray initials from radial plates (radially arranged sheets of parenchymatous tissue characteristic of Pinaceae). This specialized type of ray origin is relatively unimportant.

There has been some controversy about the relative importance of the first three methods of ray origin mentioned above. Some investigators (e.g., Barghoorn, 1940a; Braun, 1955) stated that most secondary rays of gymnosperms originate by division of the ends or sides of fusiform initials. According to Bannan (1950, 1953) and Whalley (1950), however, most secondary rays of *Chamaecyparis* and *Thuja* are derived by segmentation of fusiform initials and only few from divisions off the ends or sides. In angiosperms all three types of ray origin occur commonly. In *Pyrus communis* 48% of the new ray initials originated through reduction in length of fusiform initials followed by conversion to ray initials; 39% arose from a segment cut off the end of a fusiform initial, and 13% arose from a segment cut off the side of a fusiform initial (Evert, 1961).

Rays usually originate as single cells or uniseriate strands in both gymnosperms and angiosperms. Sometimes, however, multiseriate rays of angiosperms may originate by division and reduction of a group of tangentially and vertically contiguous fusiform initials (Philipson and Ward, 1965).

Ray Development in Gymnosperms

As the new secondary rays of gymnosperms undergo developmental changes they tend to develop a constant height and cell number. Thus, low rays tend to increase in height and high rays to decrease in height in processes which occur independently. Increase in ray height is brought about variously by (1) increase in size of initials, (2) transverse anticlinical division and subsequent increase in size, or (3) fusion of rays. The very high rays of roots and stems of gymnosperms originate by ray fusion. Rays which are separated by tracheids often come together as intervening fusiform initials are eliminated (Barghoorn, 1940a). As high rays tend to decrease in height by loss of initials from margins or central portions, they represent a temporary phase of ray development. Hence, continued loss of fusiform initials is required for formation of high rays.

Rays decrease in height either by loss of ray initials from the cambium or by splitting of a high ray into two parts. The former method occurs only rarely. Decrease in height of rays by splitting depends on intrusion of the apex of a fusiform initial between the ray initials until separation into two rays occurs. According to Barghoorn (1940a), decrease in ray height by splitting occurs more often in high rays than in low ones and thus tends to stabilize ray height within a species.

Ray Development in Angiosperms

Because of the presence of both multiseriate and uniseriate rays in angiosperms, ray development is somewhat more complex in angiosperms than in gymnosperms. Ray development in angiosperms is characterized by an overall rhythmic pattern of ray origin, increase in size, and splitting. Secondary rays usually originate in the cambium as uniseriate rays. These also develop into multiseriate rays which subsequently divide into smaller rays. By production of new rays and division of old ones, ray tissues are dispersed throughout the xylem and remain in balance with multiplying fusiform initials.

Uniseriate rays develop into multiseriate rays by increasing in width and height. This may involve increase in size of ray initials, division of ray initials followed by growth of daughter cells, addition of fusiform initials to cells, or ray fusion.

Decrease in size of rays is brought about by loss of ray initials from the cambium (Barghoorn, 1940b, 1941a; Evert, 1961), splitting of rays as a result of elongation and transformation of ray initials into fusiform initials (Chattaway, 1933, 1938; Bannan, 1941, 1950), and splitting of rays by intrusion of fusiform initials between ray initials (Esau, 1960; Evert, 1961). Ray initials are lost more often in angiosperms than in gymnosperms.

In some species the absence of rays constitutes a highly specialized condition associated with reduction in cambial growth and often with anomalous secondary thickening. Reduction of rays sometimes occurs in plants which have undergone modification in relation to a xerophytic or otherwise unfavorable environment. Phylogenetically the elimination of rays is brought about by transformation of ray initials to fusiform initials (Barghoorn, 1941b).

Phellogen or Cork Cambium

Although most increase in girth of stems, major roots, and branches is the result of production of xylem and phloem tissues by the vascular cambium, a small amount can be traced to meristematic activity of a lateral meristem called the phellogen or cork cambium. By periclinal division the phellogen, which consists of only one type of initial, produces phellem (cork) cells to the outside and phelloderm cells to the inside. The three layers (phellem, phellogen, and phelloderm) together constitute a periderm, a protective secondary tissue which in most species replaces the epidermis early in the life of a seedling.

The activity of the phellogen is relatively slow under normal conditions. Some idea of the much greater cell production by the vascular cambium than by the phellogen can be gained from data of Waisel, Liphschitz, and Arzee (1967). During the month of April the vascular cambium of *Robinia pseudoacacia* produced 20–25 xylem cells. By comparison, a month of phellogen activity produced only one or a few layers of phellem cells.

The seasonal activity of the vascular cambium and the phellogen, in some species at least, appears to occur independently. For example, in *Robinia pseudoacacia* the phellogen exhibited two short annual periods of activity, whereas the vascular cambium was active for one continuous period. In old branches the cambium was active from March to the end of August. The duration of activity of both the phellogen and vascular cambium was greater in young than in old branches.

The suberized phellem cells are dead, arranged in radial rows, and they lack intercellular spaces. Two common types of phellem occur, and both may be present in the same tree. In one type the cells are hollow, thin-walled, and wide in a radial direction. In the other type of phellem the cells are thick-walled and flattened radially. In *Abies, Pseudotsuga, Celtis, Populus, Salix,* and *Ulmus* the phellem is composed predominantly of thin-walled cells. In *Betula, Fagus,* and *Liquidambar,* however, the majority of phellem cells are thick-walled (Srivastava, 1964). In *Robinia pseudoacacia* the two cell types are produced seasonally. The early phellem consists of thin-walled cells and the late phellem of thick-walled cells (Waisel, Liphschitz, and Arzee, 1967). In some species of *Betula* the presence of both thin- and thick-walled phellem results in peeling of bark in thin sheets as separation occurs between the two layers. Unlike phellem cells, those of the phelloderm, which resemble cortical parenchyma cells, remain alive and their walls are unsuberized. Sometimes they contain chloroplasts and sclereids and other specialized cells. In some species (e.g., *Populus tremuloides*) they may carry on appreciable photosynthesis (Strain and Johnson, 1963).

Phellogens of different species vary in the number of layers of phellem and phelloderm they produce (Table 1.7). Usually at least two layers of phelloderm are produced but a few species form several layers and some may not produce any phelloderm at all. More phellem than phelloderm layers are usually formed.

In cork oak (*Quercus suber*), the initial phellogen which develops in the epidermis consists of an abundance of phellem (cork) cells and relatively few phelloderm cells. When the first layer of cork is harvested the phellogen dies, but a new phellogen forms deeper in the cortex and produces cork faster than the original phellogen. After the second and subsequent harvest

TABLE 1.7

VARIATIONS AMONG GYMNOSPERM AND ANGIOSPERM SPECIES IN NUMBERS OF PHELLEM AND PHELLODERM LAYERS IN THE PERIDEM[a]

Species	Layers of	
	Phellem	Phelloderm
Gymnosperms		
Abies grandis	Up to 40	2–6
Chamaecyparis thyoides	5	1–2
Cupressus macrocarpa	3–10	2–6
Juniperus virginiana	2–5	2–5
Larix laricina	5 or more	2–5
Libocedrus decurrens	5	2–5
Picea glauca	Variable, often more than 20	2–3
Pinus monticola	10 or more	2–8
Taxodium distichum	2–5	About 2
Thuja occidentalis	2–5	2–5
Tsuga heterophylla	Usually more than 10; variable in different rhytidomes	2–3
Angiosperms		
Acer saccharum	3–5	2–4
Alnus rubra	Continuously developed	2–3
Liquidambar styraciflura	Several	2–4
Platanus occidentalis	10 or more	3–5
Quercus alba	2–5	1–2
Salix nigra	Several	2–3
Ulmus americana	Several	2–4

[a] From Chang (1954a,b).

of cork, other phellogens form to continue the process of cork formation throughout the life of the tree (Eames and MacDaniels, 1947).

PERIDERM FORMATION

The epidermis of the stem ruptures and is sloughed off as trees begin to increase in diameter by cambial growth during the first year. Before the epidermis is lost, however, most trees form a cylindrical periderm at some depth outside the vascular cambium which is relatively constant for a species. In stems of most genera of trees (e.g., *Populus*, *Juglans*, and *Ulmus*) the first periderm arises in the cortex just within the epidermis. There are exceptions, however, and in *Pyrus* and *Quercus* stems the first phellogen is formed in the epidermis. In *Robinia pseudoacacia*, *Gleditsia triacanthos*, and species of *Pinus* and *Larix* the first phellogen forms in the second or third cortical layer of the stem. Particularly deep initiation of first periderms is characteristic of *Thuja*, *Berberis*, and *Vitis* stems. In these genera the first phellogen is initiated near the phloem or in phloem parenchyma.

In some trees (e.g., species of *Betula*, *Abies*, *Carpinus*, and *Fagus*), the first periderm persists and remains active for many years. In the majority of tree species, however, the first periderm is replaced within a few years, or even in the first year, by periderms which form successively deeper in the cortex. In those species in which the first periderm characteristically is initiated in very deep tissues, as in *Vitis*, the subsequently formed periderms are complete cylinders like the first periderm. By comparison, in species in which the first periderm is a superficial encircling layer, the second and subsequent periderms arise as arcs or lunes which curve toward the outside of the tree axis. The successive periderms are active for varying lengths of time. In some species they function for several years, in others for a few years, and in still others (e.g., *Vitis*) they may originate annually or seasonally as in *Robinia*. Some trees, such as *Fagus*, may retain a superficial periderm for life, and others, such as *Abies*, *Betula*, and *Prunus*, may do so for many years (Srivastava, 1964).

Cambial Growth in Wound Healing and Grafting

Healing of deep stem wounds in trees involves sequential production of callus tissue and formation of a new vascular cambium by conversion of callus cells to cambial cells. A phellogen is also regenerated during the wound healing process. Abundant callus formation usually is associated with healing of longitudinal frost cracks in tree stems. Such wounds may recurrently open and reheal in response to sudden temperature decreases and increases. During the rehealing phase, vertically oriented protrusions of abundant callus tissue, the so-called "frost ribs," often develop along the edges of the wound.

Although the origin of callus may vary considerably among species, in most woody plants the vascular rays usually make the major and sometimes the only contribution to callus formation. Sometimes other components of the cambial zone contribute variously to production of callus tissue. Thus, wound callus may be produced by parenchyma of xylem rays and phloem rays, undifferentiated xylem cells, and cortical tissues (Sass, 1932; Sharples and Gunnery, 1933; Barker, 1954; Noel, 1968).

The amount of callus formed during healing of stem wounds may vary with the size of the wound. Callus formation in shallow wounds sometimes is restricted or absent. The amount and rate of callus production following wounding may also differ among species of plants. For example, callus was produced earlier and much more abundantly by injured *Populus* and *Acer* stems than by those of *Pyrus* (Soe, 1959). Formation of a new vascular cambium was independent of the amount or rate of callus production. Formation of a phellogen preceded regeneration of the vascular cambium. The new phellogen became active as soon as the callus pad was well developed.

Initiation of new cambium in wounded trees often has been associated with the original cambium at the edges of a wound as in *Hibiscus* (Sharples and Gunnery, 1933) and *Populus* (Soe, 1959). In some species, however, regeneration of a new cambium does not depend on the position or presence of an existing cambium at the sides of the wound. For example, in wounded *Trema orientalis* stems, a new vascular cambium was differentiated in the middle of the callus (Noel, 1968).

The early activity of a newly regenerated cambium may be normal or abnormal. In *Hibiscus* the new cambium produced normally distributed tissues (Sharples and Gunnery, 1933). This contrasts with very abnormal distribution of vascular tissue which formed during healing of stem wounds in *Trema orientalis* (Noel, 1968), *Populus, Acer, Malus,* or *Pyrus* (Soe, 1959). In *Populus*, new xylem and phloem elements were cut off soon after the vascular cambium formed (about 9 days after wounding) but the first formed derivatives were abnormal and distorted. Normal production of xylem and phloem was first observed at approximately 20 days after wounding.

Grafting

In grafting, the cambium of an excised branch (scion) is placed in contact with the cambium of a rooted plant (stock) in order to bring about a cambial union between the two. Before differentiation of connecting vascular tissues occurs, wound callus tissues, which are formed by both the stock and scion, form and fill the voids between them. The stock and scion may produce about the same amounts of callus tissue, or one member of the union may produce considerably more than the other. In pine grafts, for example, the

stock produced most of the wound callus tissue (Mergen, 1955). In *Pseudo-tsuga menziesii* grafts the production of callus by the scion exceeded that by the stock for the first 7 days. Within 10 days, however, most callus was being contributed by the stock (Copes, 1969). Such a reversal in the order of callus contribution by the scion and stock also was reported in grafts of *Picea abies* and *Pinus sylvestris* (Dormling, 1963).

As the cells damaged in the grafting operation turn brown and die, the callus cells produced by the stock and scion are separated by a brown boundary line of dead cells, called the isolation layer, between them. In some genera (e.g., *Citrus* and *Prunus*) wound gum may develop along the isolation layer. Early in the grafting process, hypertrophy, or cell enlarge-ment of uninjured cells, occurs on both sides of the isolation layer. The enlarged cells subsequently divide profusely to produce callus tissue in a process called hyperplasia. Within a few weeks, isolated tracheary elements may begin to differentiate in the callus and across the isolation layer. Shortly thereafter the isolation layer breaks down and is resorbed. Eventually vas-cular cambium is formed through the intermingled callus of the stock and scion. The new cambium usually forms first where existing cambia of the stock and scion are in contact with callus tissue. Subsequently, cell division occurs in the callus to form a cambium and extend it until it meets other newly formed, converging cambial cells. When derivatives are produced by the new cambium, vascular continuity is established between the stock and scion of compatible combinations. In bud grafts the converging cambium differentiates in the callus mass, usually beginning at the edge of the bark flap, following the line of the original wound surfaces until it finally joins with the cambium of the bud. Shortly thereafter, rapid growth occurs in the cambium of the bud shield and the bud is gradually lifted out of the bark slit. As normal vascular tissues are formed from the joined cambium in compatible combinations, the graft union increases in strength (Mosse, 1962).

Incompatibility in Graft Unions

Successful grafting depends not only on contact between cambia or other meristematic tissues, but also on compatibility between members of the graft union. Incompatibility in graft unions occurs commonly (Fig. 1.27). Incompatibility may refer to failure of grafted partners to unite in a me-chanically strong union, poor health, or premature death where failure is

---

FIG. 1.27. Incompatibility of graft unions. (A) Six-year-old trees of Oullins Gage on Common Mussel broken smoothly at the union; (B) apricot (var. Croughton) on plum root stock (Brampton); (C) planed surface of a trunk section of Williams Bon Chretien (pear) on Quince A, showing different rates of oxidation in pear and quince, and a strongly oxidized parenchyma layer between them. Courtesy of East Malling Research Station.

caused by differences between the stock and scion. The severity of symptoms of incompatibility may range from rapid and complete failure of stock and scion to graft or sudden collapse in the first year to vigorous growth in the first year and a subsequent slow decline. Sometimes symptoms of incompatibility are delayed for many years. For example, when varieties of pear are grafted to quince, incompatibility may be greatly delayed (Garner, 1967).

Causes of incompatibility in graft union have been studied much more extensively in orchard trees than in forest trees. Different types of graft incompatibility have been variously classified. Herrero (1956) placed graft incompatibilities into four categories.

1. Graft combinations where the bud failed to grow out

2. Graft combinations where incompatibility was due to virus infection

3. Graft combinations with mechanically weak unions, in which the cause of death of trees usually was breakage, and poor health, if demonstrated, was due to mechanical obstruction at the union

4. Graft combinations where poor health was not directly due to abnormal union but was associated with abnormal starch distribution

Mosse (1962) placed graft incompatibilities of fruit trees into two broad groups, translocated and localized incompatibility. Translocated incompatibility was associated with (1) accumulation of starch above the union and absence below it, (2) phloem degeneration, (3) different behavior of reciprocal grafts, (4) normal vascular continuity at the union, although there might be marked overgrowth of the scion, and (5) early effects on growth. Localized incompatibility was associated with (1) breaks in cambial vascular continuity, (2) similar behavior of reciprocal combinations, and (3) gradual starvation of the root system with slow development of external symptoms.

Copes (1967) studied graft incompatibility in *Pseudotsuga menziesii* trees. Two major internal symptoms of incompatibility were found during the first 2 years after grafting: (1) initiation and penetration of suberin zones in bark areas of the unions and (2) initiation and development of xylem wound areas. Suberin symptoms were first seen in the cortex at 84 days after grafting and the xylem wound areas at 15 months. The suberin symptoms intensified with age. Incompatible clones differed from compatible ones in depth of suberin penetration. During the first year, necrosis of phloem and cambial cells was noted near suberized tissues. Regrafting occurred in those incompatible grafts which did not die early in the second growing season. Growth rate, grafting techniques, and spring phenology did not appear to be causes of incompatibility, but viral infections and biochemical antagonisms were not ruled out as causes. Much more research is needed on the nature and causes of incompatibility in graft unions.

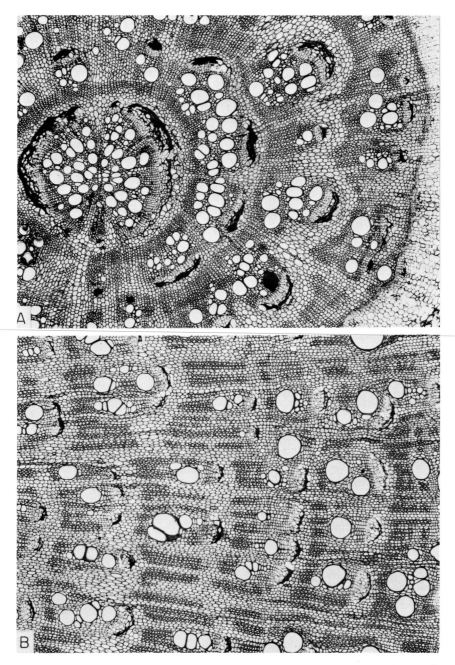

Fig. 1.28. Anomalous cambial growth in *Bougainvillea*. (A) Transection of root with one normal and three anomalous secondary growth increments. (B) Transection of old stem showing several anomalous secondary growth increments. Darkly stained materials, crushed phloem cells. [From Esau and Cheadle (1969).]

Anomalous Cambial Growth

Most information on cambial growth characteristics has been obtained from studies of temperate zone trees. Secondary growth of such species is considered to be normal. In a number of tropical species of trees and lianas, cambial growth deviates commonly from the normal pattern. For example, Obatan (1960) reported anomalous cambial growth in 108 species of woody lianas in 21 families of plants in Western Africa. Anomalous or atypical cambial growth may be found in some plants in which the cambium is in normal position. In other plants the cambium is atypically located. Often anomalous cambial growth is the result of unequal activity of various cambial segments, changes in amounts and position of xylem and phloem, or production and activity of successive cambia.

In some families of angiosperms (e.g., Amaranthaceae, Chenopodiaceae, Menispermaceae and Nyctaginaceae) and certain gymnosperms (lianas of the genus *Gnetum*, and in *Welwitschia* and members of the Cycadales) a series of successive functional cambia form. Usually the normal cambium functions for a while and then dies. New cambia then form sequentially toward the outer stem surface. Each successive cambium functions in a normal manner but only for a limited time. Thus the wood is comprised of alternating bands of xylem and phloem. An example of a species forming successive external cambia is *Avicennia resinifera*. In this species, the first of the supernumerary cambia arises by division of the inner cells of the cortex and subsequent cambia arise within derivatives of the preceding cambium. In transection, the mature stem of *Avicennia* consists of a series of units, each of which is produced by a single cambium. Each unit consists from the inside out, of sequential bands of parenchyma, secondary xylem, secondary phloem, and sclereids (Studholme and Philipson, 1966).

Bougainvillea also forms successive cambia, each of which originates among derivatives of the preceding cambium (Figs. 1.28, 1.29). Each cambium is bidirectional and produces xylem inwardly and phloem outwardly. Vascular tissues are produced in the following order: (1) conjunctive tissues and xylem fibers, (2) phloem, (3) more xylem with vessels and more phloem. The phloem and xylem differentiate from radially seriated derivatives. However, radial seriation may be obscured by divisions among phloem initials and growth adjustments in differentiating xylem.

In some woody plants strands of secondary phloem are found within the secondary xylem. The origin of such "included phloem" varies. In *Combretum*, for example, a portion of the cambium may cut off derivatives inwardly which differentiate as phloem (Pfeiffer, 1926). In *Strychnos* strips of the cambium stop growing. As the cambium at the sides moves outward, the gap gradually heals over leaving a strand of included phloem in the

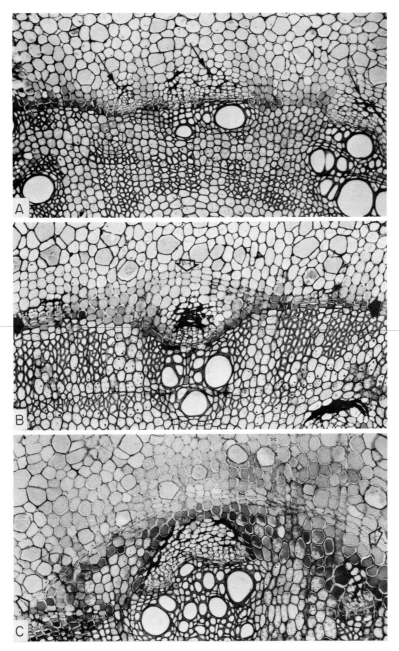

FIG. 1.29. (A) Anomalous cambial growth of *Bougainvillea* as seen in transections of roots. (B) The cambium forms a continuous layer outside the xylem. Phloem at arrows. (C) A new cambium (open arrow) has originated outside the phloem of the oldest bundle and is continuous with the old cambium (solid arrows). The new cambium (open arrows) is in a slightly later stage of development than in (B). [From Esau and Cheadle (1969).]

xylem (Cockrell, 1941). In some species certain portions of the cambial cylinder produce more xylem than phloem and other portions cut off more phloem than xylem. In some desert shrubs, such as *Peganum harmala*, *Zygophyllum dumosum*, and *Zilla spinosa*, marked discontinuities in cambial activity around the axis result in formation of ridged stems which often split (Ginzburg, 1963).

As emphasized by Esau (1965b), the various forms of anomalous secondary thickening are difficult to classify into distinct groups because of their diversity and intergrading with normal forms of cambial growth. Some idea of the complexity of anomalous cambial growth may be gained from observations of secondary thickening in lianas of the tropical and subtropical family, Bignoniaceae. In members of this family several types of anomalous secondary thickening occur. These include development of wedge-shaped masses of phloem in the xylem, occurrence of secondary rings of xylem and phloem in the secondary cortex or pericycle, fissured xylem, and inversely orientated bundles abutting on the pith. Sometimes more than one such anomaly is found in the stem, but generally the phloem wedges develop first and the other anomalies develop later (Metcalfe and Chalk, 1950).

Suggested Collateral Reading

Bannan, M. W. (1962). The vascular cambium and tree ring development. *In* "Tree Growth," (T. T. Kozlowski, ed.) Chapter 1. Ronald Press, New York.

Esau, K. (1965). "Plant Anatomy." Chapters 6, 11, 12, 15. Wiley, New York.

Fahn, A. (1967). "Plant Anatomy." Chapters 14–18. Pergamon Press. Oxford.

Larson, P. R. (1969). Wood formation and the concept of wood quality. *Yale Univ. School Forest. Bull.* 74.

Northcote, D. H. 1963 Changes in the cell walls of plants during differentiation. *Symp. Soc. Exp. Biol.* **17**, 157–174.

Philipson, W. R., and Ward, J. M. (1965). The ontogeny of the vascular cambium in the stem of seed plants. *Biol. Rev.* **40**, 534–579.

Srivastava, L. M. (1964). Anatomy, chemistry, and physiology of bark. *Int. Rev. Forest. Res.*, 1, 204–274.

Stewart, C. M. (1966). The chemistry of secondary growth in trees. *Div. Forest Prod. Tech. Paper* 43. CSIRO, Melbourne, Australia.

Stewart, C. M. (1969). The formation and chemical composition of hardwoods. *Appita* **22**, 32–60.

Thornber, J. P., and Northcote, D. H. (1961). Changes in the chemical composition of a cambial cell during its differentiation into xylem and phloem tissues in trees. I. Main components. *Biochem. J.* **81**, 449–455.

Wardrop, A. B. (1964). The structure and formation of the cell wall in xylem. *In* "The Formation of Wood in Forest Trees," (M. H. Zimmermann, ed.), pp. 87–134. Academic Press, New York.

Wardrop, A. B., and Dadswell, H. E. (1953). The development of the conifer tracheid. *Holzforschung* **7**, 33–39.

Wilcox, H. (1962). Cambial growth characteristics. *In* "Tree Growth," (T. T. Kozlowski, ed.), Chapter 3. Ronald Press, New York.

Wilson, B. F., Wodzicki, T., and Zahner, R. (1966). Differentiation of cambial derivatives: proposed terminology. *Forest Sci.* **12**, 438–440.

Chapter 2

VARIATIONS IN CAMBIAL GROWTH

It sometimes is assumed that seasonal cambial growth of trees is uniform in time and space and involves annual laying down of a xylem sheath of uniform thickness surrounding the entire stem and branches. Such erroneous assumptions often result from observations taken at a single height on a cross section of a branch or stem showing annual xylem increments of approximately equal thickness around the circumference. Actually, cambial activity is basically variable and intermittent. It may be general over a tree at times, and during other periods, as during drought, it may be localized. Trees generally produce a sheath of xylem which varies in thickness and structure at different stem or branch heights and, at a given stem height, it often varies on different sides of the tree.

Variations in growth rings

Diversity among xylem increments is shown by missing xylem rings, false or multiple rings, discontinuous rings, and frost rings in transections of stems and branches of Temperate Zone trees. These will be discussed separately.

MISSING RINGS

Under certain conditions all or portions of the cambial sheath fail to show any growth at all. Young *Pinus palustris* trees, for example, remain in a dormant "grass stage" for periods up to 15 years or even longer, during which they do not grow in height nor form annual rings. As these trees form annual rings only after height growth finally begins, ring counts at the stem base represent years elapsed since height growth began, rather than actual tree age (Pessin, 1934).

Within a species the incidence of missing xylem rings increases as environmental stresses intensify. Fritts *et al.* (1965) studied tree ring characteristics along a transect from the forest interior to a semi-desert forest border. As moisture deficits became greater toward the semi-arid forest border, the percentage of absent xylem rings increased sharply. Many trees which form complete xylem increments in the upper stem often do not form any annual xylem rings in the lower stem. This is especially true as trees become suppressed or old. Bormann (1965) showed an increasing tendency of suppressed *Pinus strobus* trees to cease cambial growth at the stem base (Fig. 2.1). Harris (1952) reported that *Pinus radiata* stems showed no xylem production in the lower stem for 11 consecutive years. As branches undergo successive suppression during their development, those in the lower stem often fail to produce annual rings at the point of juncture with the main stem (Reukema, 1959; Labyak and Schumacher, 1954).

FALSE OR MULTIPLE RINGS

The cambium often does not become either active or inactive as a unit. Cambial function is extremely responsive to environmental fluctuations, especially water deficits. False, multiple, or intraannual rings often form when cambial activity occurs in several growth flushes within the same year. Under these conditions rhythmical alternations of earlywood–latewood

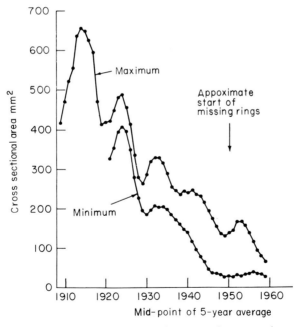

FIG. 2.1. Effects of aging on cambial growth of suppressed *Pinus strobus* trees. Data given as 5-year means of annual maximum and minimum cross sectional area of secondary xylem [From Bormann (1965).]

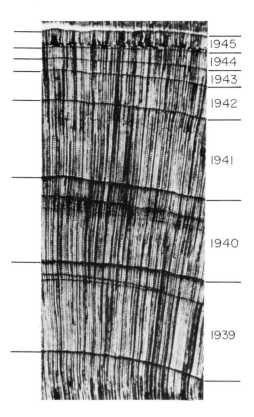

Fig. 2.2. Multiple rings formed during 1939 and 1940 in branch of *Cupressus arizonica*. [From Glock, Studhalter, and Agerter (1960).]

production are repeated within a growing season. Much of the literature shows that when multiple rings form in the same year the usual number is two, but quite often more are formed. Citrus commonly forms two or three (Bartholomew and Reed, 1943), and many examples of annual growth increments containing as many as 10 or more distinct rings have been cited (Glock, Studhalter, and Agerter, 1960). Some examples of false rings are shown in Figs. 2.2 and 2.3.

Experienced observers can generally identify false xylem rings of gymnosperms by a narrow latewood band near a wider latewood band and by a rather indistinct earlywood–latewood transition. In normal rings the boundary between the latewood of one year and the earlywood of the next year is rather abrupt. In false rings, however, the earlywood–latewood boundary is somewhat more gradual (Larson, 1956). Exceptions to these conditions often are encountered and many false rings are as clearly defined to the naked eye as are true annual rings. Thus, the presence of multiple rings often leads to serious overestimations of tree age by inexperienced observers. Sometimes false rings of angiosperms can be identified by distribution and size of elements within them. For example, the vessels in false rings of *Acer monospessulanum*, *A. campestre*, and *A. tataricum* were not as uniformly distributed as were vessels in normal rings. False rings had more groups of vessels and more radial rows of vessels per unit area then did normal rings. Furthermore, the diameters of vessels in false rings were narrower than in vessels of normal rings (Vasiljevic, 1955). The abundance of multiple growth rings varies among species, individual trees in the same species, and various parts of the same tree. Multiple growth rings are commonly found in multinodal pines of the southern United States (e.g., *Pinus taeda, P. echinata, P. palustris,* and *P. elliottii*). The formation of multiple rings is promoted by abrupt environmental changes as well as various injuries by insects, fungi, or fire. Multiple rings also tend to form during years of heavy fruiting (Tingley, 1936).

Production of lammas shoots usually is accompanied by formation of multiple (intraannual) rings, at least near the tip of the shoot. However, exceptions occur as shown by Guard and Postlethwait (1958). They suggested that the absence of false rings in *Quercus palustris* branches which formed lammas shoots may have been due to the relatively short time between end of growth in the first flush and beginning of the next growth flush. The shoots of the second flush were formed in midsummer. False or multiple rings are common in arid regions. Glock and Agerter (1962) showed, for example, that the abundance of multiple rings varied from 0 to 15% and averaged 6% in trees growing at or near the lower forest border in West Texas.

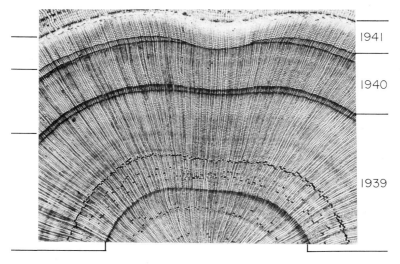

1941

1940

1939

FIG. 2.3. Multiple rings formed in 1939 and 1940, followed by single rings in 1941 in branch of *Cupressus arizonica*. [From Glock, Studhalter, and Agerter (1960).]

FIG. 2.4. Complexity of cambial growth in *Cupressus arizonica* in Texas, showing discontinuous rings, frost rings, and distinct as well as diffuse boundaries between xylem increments. Photo courtesy W. S. Glock.

Kawana and Kawaguchi (1957) described "colored growth bands" within annual rings of heavily fertilized *Cryptomeria japonica* trees. Although these bands macroscopically resembled false rings, they were caused by concentric circles of resin cells, in transverse section, within abnormally wide xylem increments which formed in response to added fertilizers.

DISCONTINUOUS RINGS

When cambial dormancy or death occurs on one side of a tree, varying numbers of xylem layers are formed on different radii of stem or branch cross-sections (Fig. 2.4). According to Studhalter, Glock, and Agerter (1963), some 40 different terms have been used in the literature as synonyms for partial or discontinuous xylem rings which do not complete the stem or branch circumference but run into an older ring. Discontinuous rings occur commonly in trees of arid zones. Elsewhere they are prevalent in overmature trees, heavily defoliated trees, suppressed trees of the understory, senescing branches, and stems of trees with one-sided crowns. In the latter group, the ring discontinuities characteristically occur on the narrow stem radius below the underdeveloped crown. Partial rings are more likely to be found in the roots and in the lower stem than in the upper stem of a tree. Usually discontinuous rings are composed of both earlywood and latewood, but sometimes growth layers form with earlywood that fails to complete the stem or branch circumference and is bounded by latewood that does. One-sided cambial dormancy usually results from deficient production and restricted downward translocation of hormonal growth regulators from the unbalanced or physiologically inefficient crowns.

Many investigators have documented the existence of discontinuous rings and only a few examples will be given. Larson (1956) found an increasing frequency of discontinuous rings from the stem top to the base of suppressed *Pinus elliottii* trees in Florida. All of the discontinuous rings were identified as a fused latewood type characterized by a basipetal fading out of earlywood and fusion of latewood bands of xylem. O'Neil (1963) observed both discontinuous and missing rings in stem cross sections of *Pinus banksiana* trees that had been severely damaged by the Swaine jack pine sawfly (*Neodiprion swainei*) in Quebec. Severe defoliation by this insect occurred in the late 1940's and 1950's, and the stands subsequently deteriorated. The partial or missing rings occurred more commonly among intermediate and suppressed trees than among dominant or codominant ones. Glock (1937) noted that in the High Sierra of California, branches of western junipers had cambial growth restricted to the underside. Usually about one-third or less of the circumference of a branch of these trees had active cambium. One specimen showed functional cambium for only 15% of its circumference. Because of such restriction

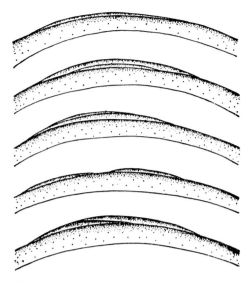

Fig. 2.5. Types of Lenses. From top to bottom: simple; compound with outer one longer than inner one; compound with inner one longer; concurrent; overlapping. [From Glock, Studhalter, and Agerter (1960).]

of growth to the undersurface, the branches were so eccentric in cross-section that vertical diameters exceeded horizontal diameters by 3–5 times.

Discontinuous rings of a very complex nature are especially common in the extreme environments of semi-arid regions and forest boundary areas. For example, in several species of trees in the forest border of Texas, Glock, Studhalter, and Agerter (1960) observed that very few annual xylem increments had only a single layer throughout their entire extent over the roots, stems, and branches. In the very arid parts of southwestern United States the complicated annual growth layers which form have been described as lenses, half-lenses, or arcs. Lenses were considered to be closed partial growth layers resulting from localized cambial activity. These were further classified as simple, compound, concurrent, or overlapping lenses as shown in Fig. 2.5. Lenses open at one end were termed half-lenses (Fig. 2.6), whereas arcs were open at both ends. Structurally a half-lens was considered to be part of the main growth layer, whereas a lens represented a patch of xylem added to the main growth increment (Glock, Studhalter, and Agerter, 1960).

FROST RINGS

Severe frosts after annual growth starts sometimes injure the cambium causing formation of abnormal "frost rings." Frost rings consist of an inner part made up of cells killed by the frost and an outer part of abnormal xylem cells produced after the frost. Frost rings of gymnosperms can be identified by underlignified, abnormal tracheids, collapsed cells, and traumatic paren- chyma cells (Fig. 2.7). The rays generally are laterally displaced and ex- panded at the frost rings. The structure of individual frost rings varies con- siderably among species. In a given species it varies with the degree of frost and activity of the cambium at the time of frost. The location of a frost ring often dates the frost, with early spring frosts causing the abnormal ring to be located at the beginning of the annual ring. Frost rings are most likely to occur on thin-barked stems. Hence, within the same tree, frost injury to the cambium tends to be more severe near shoot apices than lower down in the shoot. Small twigs are injured more than large branches, and the latter are injured more than the main stem (Peace, 1962).

Glerum and Farrar (1966) noted that frost rings of gymnosperms began where normal tracheids graded into incompletely lignified ones (Fig. 2.8). These graded into deformed tracheids which were unlignified or nearly so and had thinner walls than normal tracheids. To the outside of these was a dark amorphous layer consisting of collapsed cells. This layer was followed by traumatic parenchyma cells with thin unlignified walls and cell contents. Finally there were irregularly shaped tracheids which were not arranged in regular files but had lignified walls and bordered pits. These tracheids, which were much shorter than normal ones, graded into normal tracheids as the frost ring ended. Frost damage of increasing severity was reflected in frost

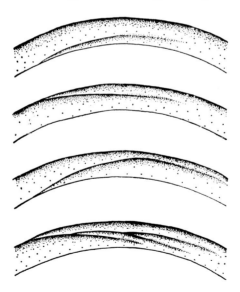

FIG. 2.6. Types of half-lenses. From top to bottom: interior; exterior; thick interior; compound exterior. [From Glock, Studhalter, and Agerter (1960).]

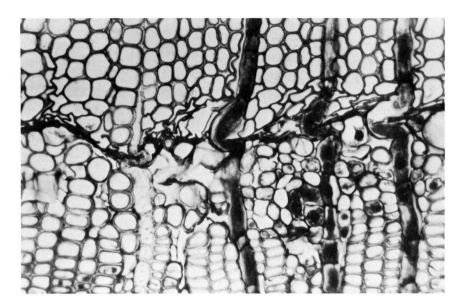

FIG. 2.7. Frost ring. The cambium is near the bottom of the figure. The effects of frost are indicated by collapsed tracheids, displacement of rays, and excessive production of parenchyma tissue. U.S. Forest Service photo.

rings with progressive increase in traumatic parenchyma cells and abnormal tracheids, slow return to production of normal tracheids, and decrease in cambial growth subsequent to the injury. The dead cells in the inner part of the frost ring were former cambial zone cells, mostly xylem mother cells and immature tracheids, which had been in various stages of differentiation at the time of the frost. Differentiating tracheids appeared to be more susceptible than xylem mother cells to frost. Some cambial cells were killed and this

FIG. 2.8. Formation of frost rings in gymnosperms. (A) Light frost damage in xylem of *Picea glauca* stem. The dark line represents a layer of crushed cells, below which are deformed and incompletely lignified tracheids. Above this layer are some parenchyma cells and abnormal tracheids. (B) Moderate frost damage from another part of the same tree as in (A). (C) Severe frost damage in *Picea glauca* stem. Note greater abundance of parenchyma cells than in (B) and marked reduction of cambial growth following the frost injury. (D) Frost ring in *Larix laricina*. In most places normal tracheids, rather than abnormal ones, developed next to the band of crushed cells. (E) Frost ring in *Picea mariana* frozen late in the growing season. Abnormal tracheids are adjacent to the cambial zone. Note lateral expansion of ray and phloem distortion. (F) Transection of normal *Picea glauca* stem at the end of the growing season, showing regularity of radial files of cambial derivatives on both sides of the cambium. [From Glerum and Farrar (1966).]

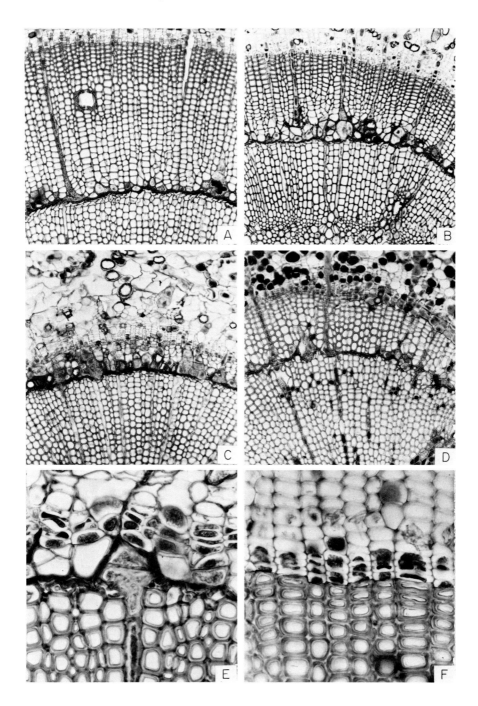

apparently was responsible for disrupting the normal radial continuity of xylem cells. The phloem was much less susceptible to frost damage than were immature xylem and cambial cells.

Variations in Duration of Cambial Growth

It is exceedingly difficult to quantify accurately for any species the number of days of cambial activity during the year. Usually, however, in a given region seasonal cambial growth of evergreens as a group continues for a longer time than it does in deciduous trees (Winget and Kozlowski, 1965). Duration of cambial growth also varies in different parts of the stem and branches within the same tree. The cambium of a suppressed tree may produce xylem for only a fraction of the time during which the cambium of an adjacent dominant tree remains active (Kozlowski and Peterson, 1962). The influence of crown class and competition on cambial activity will be considered in more detail in Chapter 3, this volume.

Wide variations among species in duration of the grand period of growth were recorded by Jackson (1952). Cambial growth of some species lasted only about 80 days and for others up to 200 days. Several of the species which initiated growth early had long grand periods of growth, while some of the late starting species exhibited short ones. Eggler (1955) also emphasized wide variations in lengths of growing season of different species. He reported that in Louisiana diameter increase of all the measured *Taxodium distichum* and *Celtis laevigata* trees stopped by the end of July at the latest, whereas in some *Platanus occidentalis* and *Nyssa aquatica* trees it lasted until November.

Ladefoged (1952) divided tree species of Denmark into the following three groups on the basis of rapidity with which the annual ring was laid down: (1) *Fraxinus excelsior*, characterized by very rapid formation of the annual ring. About half the ring was formed in May and June and after July very little wood was laid down; (2) *Picea abies* and *Larix decidua*, characterized by rather rapid formation of the annual ring. About half the ring was formed in May and June, and after July wood formation was not very active; (3) *Betula pendula, Fagus sylvatica, Alnus glutinosa, Acer pseudoplatanus,* and *Quercus robur* characterized by late formation of most of the annual ring. In this group only a third to a half of the annual ring was laid down in May and June. Cambial activity was unusually active in late summer, with one-third to one-fourth of the annual ring formed in August and early September.

Cambial growth of many tropical and subtropical trees may continue for all or most of the year, resulting in indistinct growth rings or absence of rings. (Figs. 2.9–2.10). In southern Florida, *Pinus elliottii* var. *densa.* a subtropical pine, grew appreciably in diameter for 10 months and made small amounts of

Fig. 2.9. Cambial growth in tropical trees. Indistinct growth rings of *Boswellia serrata*. Photo courtesy of Forest Research Institute, Dehra Dun, India.

growth during the other 2 months. Two major peaks of cambial growth were noted, one in the spring and another in the autumn. The main period of cambial growth was initiated in early February and reached a peak during the first half of March. Almost 40% of the year's growth occurred from February

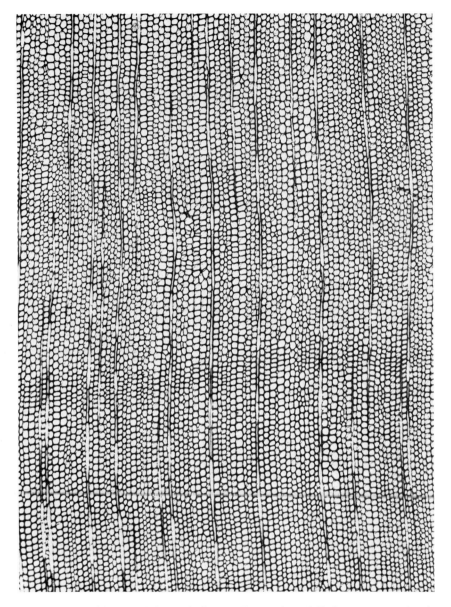

Fig. 2.10. Cambial growth in tropical trees. Transection of *Podocarpus* stem showing absence of growth rings. Photo courtesy of Forest Products Research Laboratory, Princes Risborough, England.

through April (Langdon, 1963). However, the total amount of growth and its seasonal distribution varied among years in response to climatic variations.

Vertical Distribution of Cambial Growth

The rate of cambial growth, the distribution of earlywood and latewood, and the anatomy of cambial derivatives often vary greatly at different stem heights. The annual xylem sheath laid down by the cambium varies in thickness at different stem heights in a consistent way (Onaka, 1950; Duff and Nolan, 1953; Larson, 1963b). The annual ring is quite narrow in the upper-most internode of the bole (Fig. 2.11). Ring width then increases for a few internodes and becomes thickest at the stem height where there is maximum leaf volume. Below the crown the variation in ring thickness with stem height depends on crown development. In dominant trees the ring narrows below the crown and thickens again near the stem base. In suppressed trees the whole ring is thinner than in dominant trees, the point of maximum ring thickness is at a greater relative stem height, and below the point of maximum thickness the annual ring narrows rapidly and does not show thickening near the base of the tree. Often severely suppressed trees have missing or discontinuous rings at the base of the stem. This was substantiated by Chalk (1930) who found that in dominant *Pseudotsuga* trees approximately equal amounts of xylem were laid down at all levels in the stem below the crown. In suppressed

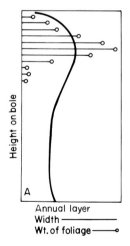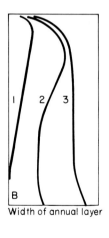

FIG. 2.11. (A) Variations in thickness of the annual ring at various stem heights. (B) Variations in thickness of the annual ring at various stems heights in suppressed (1), dominant (2), and open-grown (3) trees. [From Farrar (1961).]

trees, however, xylem production stopped toward the stem base. Harris (1952) noted that suppressed *Pinus radiata* trees had fewer than the expected number of annual rings at the base of the stem. In one 24-year-old tree the cambium at the stem base remained dormant for 11 years. In contrast, open grown trees may show increases in ring thickness from the height of maximum foliage all the way down to the base.

Farrar (1961) discussed changes in vertical distribution of the xylem sheath of plantation-grown conifers as they aged. When the trees were very young the thickness of the annual ring decreased from the tree apex to the base (Fig. 2.12). As trees aged, however, their crowns began to close and competition among trees increased. At that time a point of greatest ring thickness became apparent at the stem height where there was the maximum amount of foliage. Below this point the annual xylem thickness decreased progressively to the stem base. These observations were in accord with those of Reukema (1961) who found that growth rings were widest near the stem base in young *Pseudotsuga* trees. As the trees became older, the position of maximum ring width moved continuously upward.

Seasonal latewood production begins near the base of the stem and then moves upward. Thus the width of the latewood band tapers from the base of the stem upward and almost disappears near the tip. This developmental

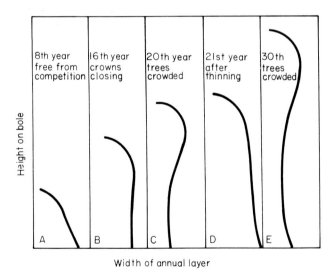

FIG. 2.12. Variations in thickness of the annual ring at various stem heights in plantation-grown conifers of varying age. (A) At 8-years, when crowns extend to the base of the tree; (B) crowns closing; (C) lower branches are dead; (D) shortly after thinning when crowns have been exposed to full light; (E) competition is again severe and crowns have closed. The horizontal scale is greatly exaggerated. [From Farrar (1961).]

pattern is regulated by age and distance from the crown (Larson, 1969b). Control of latewood formation is discussed further in Chapter 3, this volume.

The structure of xylem in roots often varies greatly from that of stems. Root xylem usually is lighter in weight (although it may be heavier in gymnosperms), often does not retain the ring porous characteristics found in the stem, or the earlywood vessels do not vary much in diameter from latewood vessels (Fig. 2.13). Except for earlywood vessels of ring porous species, the vessel members, tracheids and fibers in roots often have larger diameters than those in the stem (Table 2.1).

Vertical Alignment of Cambial Derivatives

Xylem elements often deviate markedly from strictly vertical alignment and thereby produce " spiral grain." The presence of spiral grain can often be seen in debarked trees (Fig. 2.14), telephone poles, power line poles, and piling. In living trees spiral grain can often be detected by following the direction of bark cracks.

Perhaps the most significant characteristic of spiral grain is its nearly universal occurrence. It has been reported in over 200 species of woody angiosperms and gymnosperms and appears to be a normal rather than

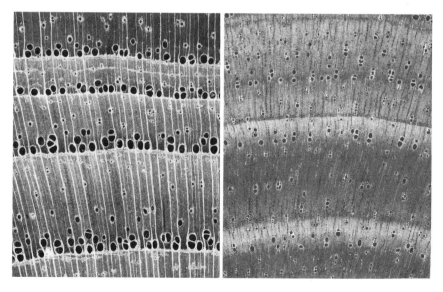

FIG. 2.13. Transections of stem (left) and tap root (right) of *Fraxinus excelsior* showing variations in xylem structure. [From Patel (1965).]

TABLE 2.1

VARIATIONS IN VESSEL DIAMETERS IN THE STEM AND TAP ROOTS OF DIFFUSE POROUS SPECIES[a]

	Year	Radial diameter (mm)		Tangential diameter (mm)	
		Stem	Tap root	Stem	Tap root
Aesculus hippocastanum	1958	0.059	0.066	0.041	0.050
	1959	0.056	0.062	0.039	0.048
	1960	0.057	0.069	0.042	0.051
	1961	0.060	0.062	0.042	0.051
	1962	0.063	0.064	0.042	0.049
Populus canadensis	1958	0.095	0.132	0.073	0.102
	1959	0.095	0.149	0.071	0.107
	1960	0.093	0.141	0.071	0.104
	1961	0.098	0.159	0.075	0.115
	1962	0.100	0.169	0.078	0.125

[a] From Patel (1965).

abnormal feature of tree growth. For example, in one study of 594 mature trees of several species, Northcott (1957) found that 99.6% had spiral grain. Koehler (1931) reported that 99% of the *Abies lasiocarpa* trees he examined had spiral grain, and Herrick (1932) noted that 77% of 1527 trees examined exhibited marked spiralling of xylem elements.

Wide interspecific and intraspecific variability occurs in the direction and degree of inclination from the vertical of wood elements. In some species the inclination of elements in the mature tree is predominantly to the left and in others to the right. Within species marked differences often are found in spiral grain characteristics between trees in the same locality as well as between localities. In addition differences in vertical alignment of wood elements occur within a given tree at different stem heights, in successive xylem rings at a given stem height, (Fig. 2.15), in different radii, and in branches as compared with the stem (Bannan, 1966). Spiral grain generally amounts to deflections of a few degrees from the vertical. Sometimes, however, extreme spirality, beyond that normally found in a species develops at certain sites. Noskowiak (1963) cited an extreme case of spiralling of tracheids in *Pinus balfouriana* trees which had grain angles of up to 40°. A few investigators have reported that in extreme cases the grain may be nearly horizontal, especially toward the base of the stem (Liese and Ammer, 1962; Bannan, 1966).

Several investigators have reported a consistent pattern of development of spiral grain during the life of gymnosperm trees with the direction of spiraling in young trees becoming reversed in older ones (Northcott, 1957). For example, wood of young *Pseudotsuga menziesii* trees twisted to the left, but as

Fig. 2.14. Adjacent *Pinus ponderosa* trees, showing extreme spiral grain (left) and straight grain (right). U.S. Forest Service photo.

the trees aged the direction was reversed to the right (Vité and Hendrickson, 1959). Noskowiak (1963) found that in the first ring from the pith of *Pinus resinosa* the grain angle was usually zero or at a small left angle, then increased rapidly to a peak left angle and eventually reached zero again. Finally the grain angle increased in magnitude to the right in older trees (Fig. 2.16). Although the general tendency for changes with tree age in direction of spirality of elements prevails in many gymnosperms, differences occur among them in direction of initial declination, intensity of spiral, and time spent in each phase. Nicholls (1967) found similar basic patterns of pith-to-bark variations of grain deviation for four provenances of *Pinus pinaster*. However, provenances differed in the age at which maximum grain angle was attained.

CAUSES OF SPIRAL GRAIN

There has been much speculation about the basic cause of formation of spiral grain. As emphasized by Noskowiak (1963), it often is difficult to distinguish specific causes of spiral grain from variables associated with it. Among the major factors with which the degree of spiralling of xylem elements has been correlated are species, heredity, growth rate, stem height, and age of trees (Noskowiak, 1963).

Several investigators have shown that the direction of spirality of xylem elements is correlated with the direction of pseudotransverse divisions in

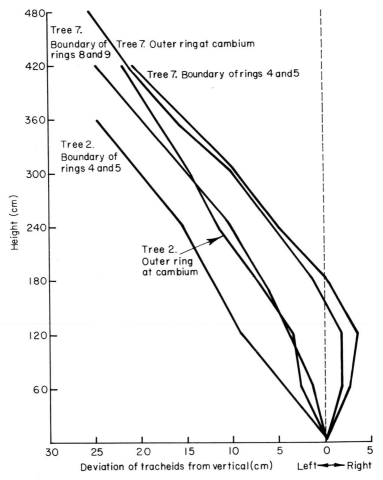

FIG. 2.15. Variations in spiral grain in different annual rings of two *Larix decidua* trees. [From Kozlowski, Hughes, and Leyton (1967).]

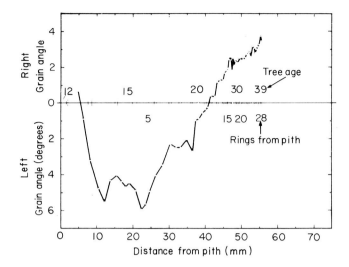

FIG. 2.16. Variations in spiral grain in different rings of a 39-year-old *Pinus resinosa* tree, with grain angle reversing from left in young trees to right in old trees. [From Noskowiak (1963).]

cambial cells. Most fusiform initials in a sector of the cambium have newly formed partitions inclined in the same direction, with usually less than 10% of the divisions occurring in the other direction. Bannan (1966) noted that in gymnosperm species which had grain in the outer wood slanted to the right, a rightward tilt of division of cambial cells persisted for a longer time than did a leftward tilt. In species with grain slanted to the left, a leftward tilt of pseudotransverse division prevailed. Hejnowicz (1968) also found that the orientation of pseudotransverse divisions in the cambium of *Pinus sylvestris* and *Picea excelsa* was correlated with the direction of spiralling. When reversals occurred in tilt of pseudotransverse division, associated changes also occurred in slope of the grain.

Bannan (1966) concluded that spiral grain is not traceable to a simple cause. A positive correlation between orientation of anticlinal divisions in cambial cells and direction of cell elongation over most of the cambium would tend to induce spiral grain. Deflection of elements from the vertical presumably would be in the direction of orientation of partition in pseudotransverse division. The periodic reversals which occur in orientation of anticlinal division appear to act against excessive development of spiral grain. A complicating feature is that sometimes agreement is lacking between change in orientation of pseudotransverse division and alteration in spirality of cambial derivatives (Bannan, 1966). Much more research is needed on causes of spiral grain.

EFFECTS OF SPIRAL GRAIN

There has been much interest in spiral grain because it has a number of important economic as well as biological implications. A few of these will be mentioned briefly.

Spiral grain, which often is considered to be one of the worst defects of wood has detrimental effects on strength, seasoning, and machining properties of wood. Spiral-grained wood dries out rapidly and warps excessively. It often is responsible for twisting of boards during seasoning and for twisting of plywood. Spiral-grained telephone poles in service often twist as moisture content of the air changes. This sometimes induces tension stress in transmission lines which are attached to cross arms. Twisting usually is in the same direction as spirality and the amount of twisting depends on the severity of the spiral grain (Wellner and Lowery, 1967).

The vertical alignment of xylem elements in the sapwood influences the upward path of water transport and the distribution of water throughout the crown. Water tends to move upward in xylem elements in patterns that follow the slope of the grain (Vité, 1959; Kozlowski and Winget, 1963; Kozlowski, Hughes, and Leyton, 1966). Rudinsky and Vité (1959), for example, described five major water conduction patterns that were associated with tracheid alignment in gymnosperm stems. These included:

1. Spiral ascent, turning right. Water ascended in a spiral band that ran from the outermost xylem ring clockwise toward the center of the stem.
2. Spiral ascent, turning left. Water ascended in a spiral band which ran counterclockwise from the outer ring toward the center of the stem.
3. Interlocked ascent. Water ascended so as to produce a zigzag pattern in stem transections.
4. Sectorial, winding ascent. Water ascended in a sector which tended to wind around the tree.
5. Sectorial straight ascent. Water ascended in a vertical sector.

When water ascended vertically its distribution in the crown was very restricted. In contrast, the distribution of water in the crown was very complete when spiral ascent occurred. These observations were confirmed for several species of angiosperms and gymnosperms by Kozlowski and Winget (1963) and Kozlowski, Hughes, and Leyton (1966, 1967). In angiosperms having spiral grain, water ascended in a spiral pattern. In those having interlocked grain the water path was delineated in stem cross-sections as a zigzag pattern. In gymnosperms, all of which had spiral grain, a pronounced spiral pattern of water ascent was shown for both seedlings and pole-sized trees.

Variations in paths of water movement in tree stems, have important practical applications. For example, many systemic chemicals, which are used in control of insects and diseases, ascend in the transpiration stream when injected into stems. For this reason the distribution of injected chemicals in the crown is influenced by specific patterns of water movement which, in turn, are related to vertical alignment of xylem elements in the sapwood (Kozlowski, 1964b).

Paths of water conduction also influence host–parasite relations of vascular wilt diseases. For example, patterns of water conduction differ between the red and white oak groups Members of the red oak group that are inoculated with the oak wilt fungus (*Ceratocystis fagacearum*) usually transport spores efficiently in the xylem and develop rapid and widespread wilting of much of the crown. By comparison, members of the white oak group distribute spores less efficiently and develop wilting symptoms on more restricted parts of the crown (Parmeter, Kuntz, and Riker, 1956; Kozlowski, Kuntz, and Winget, 1962).

The extent of spiral grain may affect tapping practices with rubber trees. In *Hevea brasiliensis* both the latex vessels and peripheral wood fibers were arranged in a spiral inclined from left to right. The angle of inclination was a clonal characteristic and was much more variable within some clones than others. The alignment of latex vessels had some bearing on latex yield. When the inclination of latex vessels was to the right upward as usual, a tapping cut sloping in the opposite direction (e.g., to the left upward) resulted in cutting more vessels for a given proportion of the tree circumference (Gomez and Thai, 1967). In the case of *Hevea* buddings, steepening the slope of a correctly orientated tapping cut from the recommended 30°–45° (for trees with vessel inclination of 3°–4°) would increase the length of cut to be tapped by 22% and yield by 2–3%. In the case of seedlings with vessel inclination of 4–5% steepening the tapping cut from the recommended 25°–45° might increase yield by 4–5%. However, because of greater taper and more rapid decline with height in number of latex vessels in seedlings than in buddings, steepening the tapping cut probably would not cut as many more latex vessels as a theoretical model indicated.

Variations in Size of Cambial Derivatives

Probably because of the importance of tracheid dimensions as indices of wood quality an unusually rich literature has accumulated on variation in size of cambial derivatives. Interest has centered on variations within trees, among species, and among different geographic regions. These will be discussed separately.

WITHIN TREE VARIATIONS

In a given tree the size of cambial derivatives varies markedly with tree height, from the pith outward at a given stem height and across the annual ring (Spurr and Hyvärinen, 1954; Dinwoodie, 1961).

Variations with Tree Height

Within a growth ring the length of cambial derivatives of both gymnosperms and angiosperms usually increases for some distance up the stem and then decreases progressively to the apex of the annual increment. The xylem elements at the top of a ring usually are shorter than those at the base. The point of maximum tracheid length occurs at successively higher levels in each successive ring from the pith (Dinwoodie, 1961).

The shortest xylem elements in a tree often occur in the inner wood of branches and young stems. Tracheids in branches often are only half as long as those of the same age in the stem (Jackson, 1959). Wood structure of gymnosperm roots is exceedingly variable, and root tracheids may be much longer or shorter than those in stems (Riedl, 1937; Dinwoodie, 1961; Bannan, 1965a). In angiosperms the relations of fiber length in root, stem, and branch wood are much more consistent than in gymnosperms. According to Fegel (1941), fibers of angiosperm stems are longest, those of roots about 10% shorter, and those of branches about 25% shorter than in the stem.

Variations from the Pith Outward

At a given stem height the length of cambial derivatives in the ring near the pith is very short. Cell length increases rapidly in the next few rings, and then more slowly until a maximum length is reached. Thereafter, cell length may remain constant or nearly so, may decline slightly, or may fluctuate. The distance from the pith at which cambial derivatives reach maximum length varies with species, growth rate, and age. (Dinwoodie, 1961, 1963).

According to Sanio (1872), *Pinus sylvestris* tracheids reached a maximum length between the 25th to 60th rings from the pith, and were of essentially constant length thereafter. Similar patterns have been reported for other species including *Pinus taeda* (Bethel, 1941), *Picea abies* (Bisset and Dadswell, 1949), and *Pinus radiata* (Dadswell, 1958). In contrast, some decrease in fiber length near the stem periphery has been reported for *Sequoia sempervirens* (Bailey and Faull, 1934), *Pinus sylvestris* and *Picea abies* (Helander, 1933), and *Fraxinus excelsior* (Bosshard, 1951). Dinwoodie (1963) found a fluctuation in tracheid length of *Picea sitchensis*, toward the stem periphery, after a maximum length was reached. Elliott (1960) concluded that tracheid length was largely a function of age in the early years, but in the mature tree ring width exerted a greater effect than age. In *Picea sitchensis* trees up to 360 years old, Dinwoodie (1963) noted that the effect of age on tracheid length was more important than distance from pith in the first 15 rings from the pith. In rings 50 and beyond, however, distance from the pith accounted for more variation than age.

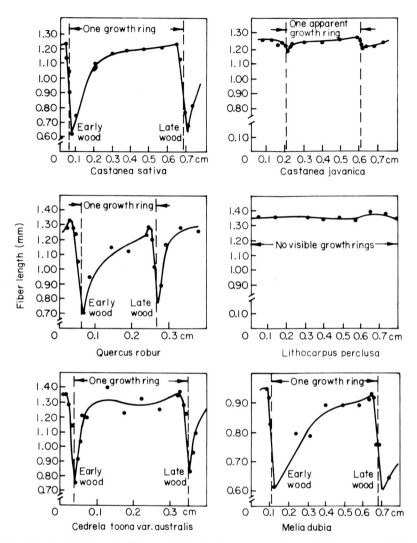

Fig. 2.17. Variations in fiber length in different parts of annual increments of forest trees. [From Bisset and Dadswell (1950).]

Variations across an Annual Ring

Many investigators observed that the length of cambial derivatives often increased from the first formed earlywood to the last formed latewood and then decreased sharply across the boundary of the annual ring (Figs. 2.17–2.18). Some variations of this general pattern may be expected, and these

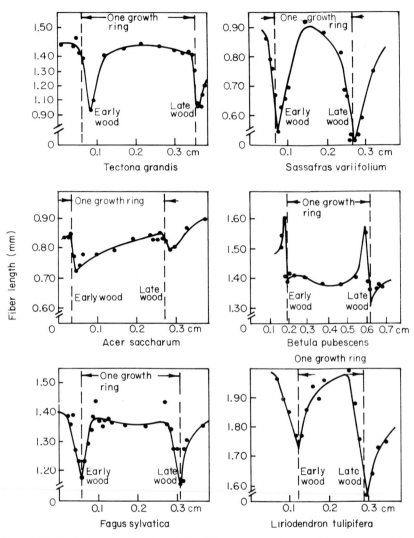

FIG. 2.18. Variations in fiber length in different parts of annual increments of forest trees. [From Bisset and Dadswell (1950).]

also appear to be coordinated with the timing of pseudotransverse divisions. In *Pinus taeda*, *P. echinata*, and *P. elliottii* fiber length increased through the earlywood to maxima that occurred at distances of from 47 to 72% of the ring width, and then it decreased to the end of the latewood (Jackson and Morse, 1965). Sometimes pseudotransverse division in the cambial zone may not occur until after cessation of all seasonal periclinal division. When this happens the shortened cells appear in the first formed wood of the next

TABLE 2.2

AVERAGE LENGTHS OF FIRST AND LAST FORMED PHLOEM ELEMENTS (SIEVE TUBE
MEMBERS AND PARENCHYMA STANDS) IN 7 SUCCESSIVE GROWTH INCREMENTS
OF *Pyrus communis*[a]

Growth increment	Average length (microns)	
	First formed elements	Last formed elements
1	299	461
2	409	462
3	367	479
4	420	476
5	369	475
6	362	467
7	384	462

[a] From Evert (1961).

growth increment. Dinwoodie (1963), for example, noted a decrease in cell
length at the first formed earlywood of *Picea sitchensis*. Sometimes, as in fast
growing trees, the first anticlinal divisions occur relatively early and a maximum length of cambial derivatives is correspondingly localized in an early
formed portion of the ring. When a false ring forms, the premature development of latewood often is correlated with an increase in tracheid length. In
species lacking distinct growth rings the length of cambial derivatives may
change only slightly over distances covering growth of several years. Hence,
Castanea javanica, which lacked distinct rings, showed little variation in
fiber length over considerable distance in a radial direction. However, cambial
derivatives of *Castanea sativa*, with distinct rings, showed the usual marked
variations (Fig. 2.17).

The pattern of variation across the annual phloem increment is similar to
that across the xylem increment (Evert, 1961). For example, the average
length of sieve tubes and parenchyma strands of *Pyrus communis* increased
from the first to the last formed elements of each growth increment (Table
2.2). The rapid decreases in length of cambial derivatives near the end of an
annual increment appear to be related to the timing of the pseudotransverse
divisions which account for increase in cambial circumference. Following such
anticlinal divisions the radial files of cambial derivatives are short.

SPECIES VARIATIONS

Various investigators have shown differences in length of cambial derivatives among genera and species. Such comparisons sometimes are difficult
to make because of variability in cell sizes among trees, within species, and
in different parts of the same trees. Nevertheless, in gymnosperms, studies of

TABLE 2.3

Variations in Tracheid Size in Earlywood of Various Species[a]

Species	Ring width (mm)	Tracheid length (mm)	Tracheid diameter (μ)	Length/width ratio
Juniperus osteosperma	0.1–0.5	1.59 ± 0.07	23.5 ± 0.6	68:1
Cupressus arizonica	1–2	1.70 ± 0.05	23.2 ± 0.3	73:1
Juniperus virginiana	1–2	1.98 ± 0.09	25.1 ± 0.5	79:1
Pinus contorta	1–2	2.90 ± 0.09	35.4 ± 0.4	82:1
Cupressus sargentii	1–2	2.91 ± 0.08	31.8 ± 1.0	91:1
Pseudotsuga menziesii				
Interior Br. Columbia	1–2	3.14 ± 0.07	38.1 ± 0.4	82:1
Coastal Br. Columbia	1–2	3.62 ± 0.09	41.5 ± 0.6	87:1
Pinus resinosa	0.1–0.5	3.21 ± 0.10	36.7 ± 0.4	88:1
Picea glauca	1–2	3.34 ± 0.09	36.8 ± 0.9	91:1
Abies balsamea	1–2	3.36 ± 0.08	35.4 ± 0.6	95:1
Pinus resinosa	1–2	3.36 ± 0.08	37.4 ± 0.4	90:1
Pinus ponderosa	0.1–0.5	3.37 ± 0.08	35.6 ± 0.8	95:1
Tsuga canadensis	1–2	3.63 ± 0.11	38.8 ± 0.4	94:1
Pinus strobus	1–2	3.73 ± 0.09	41.8 ± 0.6	89:1
Pinus lambertiana	1–2	3.98 ± 0.07	44.5 ± 0.7	90:1
Sequoia sempervirens	1–2	4.12 ± 0.12	43.7 ± 1.0	95:1

[a] Samples were taken at breast height from stems 10–20 inches in diameter. [From Bannan (1965a).]

material selected to minimize the more obvious sources of variability confirmed the existence of differences in cell size among species. For example, Bannan (1965a) found great interspecific variation in tracheid length of samples taken at breast height in earlywood or peripheral rings of gymnosperm stems of similar size and growth rate (Table 2.3). High correlation was noted between potential growth capacity and size of cambial derivatives, with gymnosperm trees which normally achieve large size, such as *Sequoia sempervirens*, *Pinus lambertiana*, and *P. strobus* having the longest tracheids. The shortest tracheids generally occurred in gymnosperms with low growth potential and those growing on poor sites. These included *Juniperus osteosperma*, *Cupressus arizonica*, and *Juniperus virginiana*. Tracheids were smaller in Cupressaceae than in Pinaceae. Differences in ratios of tracheid length to width followed a pattern similar to that in different parts of trees, with the ratio tending to be high when tracheids were large. The correlation between size of cambial derivatives and growth capacity which Bannan found in gymnosperms does not hold for many angiosperms. For example, *Acer saccharum* has very short fibers but attains a large size. In the genus *Eucalyptus*, a wide array occurs in both length of cambial derivatives and tree size.

FIG. 2.19. Compression wood in stem of *Pinus taeda*. U.S. Forest Service, Forest Products Laboratory photo.

In addition to species variations some regional differences in tracheid size within species have been reported. Such variability often is related to climatic differences, and it usually is small in comparison to individual tree variation. Much of the variability in tracheid size is heritable as shown by provenance studies and growing progenies in similar environments (Dinwoodie, 1963).

Reaction Wood

Rates of cambial growth differ considerably on upper and lower sides of leaning stems. Such growth eccentricities in inclined stems are associated with local formation of reaction tissues which differ physically, chemically, and anatomically from normal tissues. In gymnosperms reaction wood forms on the lower side of leaning stems and is called compression wood. In angiosperms reaction wood usually, although not invariably, forms on the upper side of leaning stems and is called tension wood. The reaction anatomy of gymnosperm and angiosperm xylem will be discussed separately.

Compression Wood

In gymnosperms abnormal wood called compression wood (also called Rotholz, Druckholz, bois rouge, and redwood) forms preferentially on the lower side of inclined stems and branches and may occasionally form in various amounts on opposite sides of stems (Figs. 2.19–2.23). According to Westing (1965a), compression wood functions in the righting of inclined stems and branches, apparently by expanding during and after cell differentiation. As soon as vertical orientation is attained, compression wood stops forming.

The formation of compression wood is a geotropic phenomenon involving growth promotion on the lower side and growth inhibition on the upper side. The production of compression wood occurs normally in leaning trees, and it may be readily produced by artificial inclination. Westing and Schulz (1965) found that leaning *Pinus strobus* and *Tsuga canadensis* stems had produced compression wood continuously for 30–72 years. Shrubby gymnosperms which lack a central axis, such as *Juniperus horizontalis*, *Pinus mugo*, and *Taxus cuspidata* commonly produce considerable compression wood. Westing (1965b) found strong correlation between bending of terminal

Fɪɢ. 2.20. Bands of compression wood in stem of *Sequoia*. U.S. Forest Service, Forest Products Laboratory photo.

Fɪɢ. 2.21. Transection of *Picea* stem showing compression wood forming in bands around the entire stem. U.S. Forest Service, Forest Products Laboratory photo.

shoots and the amount of reaction wood produced. Compression wood formation was blocked by artificially supporting terminal shoots in a vertical position. Westing (1961) observed that bending of terminal leaders of *Pinus strobus* caused compression wood to form. Cambial growth of the upper surface was depressed 2.4 % per week of displacement, whereas growth of the lower surface was increased 4.9 %. After a lag of one week, the formation of compression wood was proportional to the degree of displacement from the vertical. Each added week of stem inclination caused 7.2 % more compression

Fig. 2.22. Transection of stem of *Pinus taeda* showing compression wood after growth increase. U.S. Forest Service, Forest Products Laboratory photo.

wood to form. Ewart and Mason-Jones (1906) were among the early workers who induced formation of compression wood by twisting seedlings of several species of gymnosperms into vertical loops.

Westing and Schulz (1965) described a case of an inclined *Tsuga canadensis* tree which developed enough righting strain to cause mechanical failure in the form of tearing in the stem. Providing a branch with artificial support at its existing angle causes cessation of compression wood development, indicating that compression wood normally counteracts the downward pull of the branch weight (Westing, 1965). Although compression wood may be found in roots, it occurs there less commonly than in stems and branches (Patel, 1963; Westing, 1965a).

The structure of compression wood differs greatly from that of normal wood, with compression wood having tracheids which are more nearly round in cross-section (Fig. 2.24). For this reason large intercellular spaces occur in compression wood. All compression wood tracheids are very thick-walled, so that no ready distinction can be made between early- and latewood. The inner layer (S_3) of the secondary wall of compression wood tracheids usually does not form or it develops poorly. The inner layer (the middle S_2 layer of normal wood) of compression wood is very thick throughout the ring. Because of more anticlinal divisions in compression wood, the tracheids generally are much shorter than in normal wood.

Compression wood has several commercially undesirable characteristics which adversely affect its utilization. It is harder, denser, weaker, and more brittle than normal wood. It twists and warps excessively because its longitudinal shrinkage may be up to 10 times as great as that of normal wood. Compression wood tracheids have about 20% less cellulose and 28% more lignin than normal wood. Furthermore, the cellulose of compression wood is less crystalline than that of normal wood. Noncellulosic polysaccharides are

FIG. 2.23. Eccentric cambial growth and compression wood in *Pinus ponderosa*. U.S. Forest Service, Forest Products Laboratory photo.

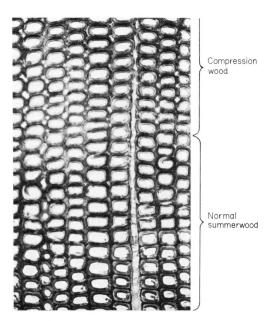

FIG. 2.24. Compression wood and normal wood of *Pinus palustris*. U.S. Forest Service, Forest Products Laboratory photo.

similar in both types, except for galactan which is about twice as high in compression wood as in normal wood (Westing, 1965a).

TENSION WOOD

Inclined angiosperm trees exhibit both eccentric cambial growth and reaction anatomy. Tension wood forms characteristically on the upper side of leaning angiosperm stems and apparently occurs more commonly in some species than others. Whereas *Fraxinus* and *Tilia* showed no marked anatomical modifications in response to inclination, *Fagus* and *Eucalyptus* showed pronounced changes (Wardrop, 1964a). Families with unusual tendency to produce tension wood include Anacardiaceae, Annonaceae, Burseraceae, Combretaceae, Euphorbiaceae, Lauraceae, Leguminosae, Moraceae, and Ulmaceae (Wardrop, 1964a).

The development of tension wood is often, but not always, associated with eccentric growth. Some leaning trees of *Paulownia* and *Catalpa* have been reported to show no growth eccentricity (Hughes, 1965). When both excessive growth and tension wood occur, their locations usually coincide, but sometimes they occur on opposite sides of branches or leaning stems. For example, in naturally leaning *Quercus rubra* trees, greatest radial increment usually occurred below the zone of maximum crown development which was on the underside of the lean, but tension wood developed on the other side. In contrast, trees that were tipped by high winds had greatest crown development on the upper side of the stem. In such trees both maximum cambial growth and tension wood formation were on the upper side of the stem (Sorenson and Wilson, 1964). In S-shaped or recurved stems the eccentric growth may occur on different sides at different heights. The production of reaction tissue in branches is complicated and appears to be more directly related to morphogenetic pattern than to upper and lower sides (Berlyn, 1961). In deciduous angiosperms tension wood is best developed in earlywood, and it does not extend through all the latewood. However, in some evergreen angiosperms such as species of *Eucalyptus*, tension wood often extends throughout the earlywood and latewood (Wardrop and Dadswell, 1955).

Gelatinous fibers, which can be identified microscopically by the gelatinous appearance of secondary walls, are a characteristic feature of tension wood (Fig. 2.25). Although they occur most abundantly on the widest portions of eccentric annual rings, they also are found on the shortest radii of stems and in concentric stems. Gelatinous fibers may occur singly, in small groups as in *Populus deltoides* (Berlyn, 1961) or in broad bands. The distribution of gelatinous fibers in sporadic groups appears to be characteristic of several

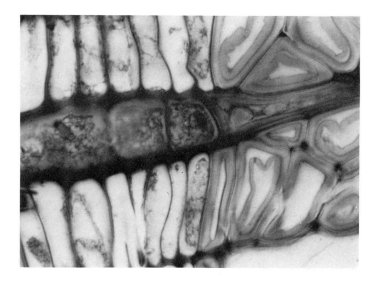

Fig. 2.25. Transverse section of the cambium showing subjacent gelatinous fibers of *Populus deltoides*. [From Berlyn (1961).]

families including Anacardiaceae, Combretaceae, Lauraceae, Moraceae, and Salicaceae. In *Populus deltoides* an increase in the amount of gelatinous fibers was correlated with a decrease in diameter and wall thickness of nongelatinous fibers. Hence, the environmental conditions which regulated expansion and differentiation of gelatinous fibers also controlled development of associated xylem elements (Kaeiser and Boyce, 1965).

Tension wood is not as easily discernible to the naked eye as compression wood. Tension wood has fewer and smaller vessels than normal wood and has proportionally more thick-walled fibers. Ray and longitudinal parenchyma cells are unaltered. Vessels of tension wood usually are well lignified, but sometimes they show reduced lignification. Fibers, in contrast, invariably show marked reduction in lignification. Reduced lignification of the G layer is a common feature, and Dadswell and Wardrop (1956) believe that the sparse lignification is a more important feature of tension wood than are associated anatomical changes.

The cell wall layer designated as S_2 or S_3 in normal wood is replaced in tension wood by an unlignified, often convuluted layer, designated as the G layer. When the S_2 layer is thus replaced, the new designation is $S_2(G)$. Sometimes the G layer is produced in addition to the S_1, S_2, and S_3 layers of normal xylem (Fig. 2.26). As the G layer consists almost entirely of cellulose it has a highly ordered parallel molecular orientation. The thickness and form of the G layer vary conspicuously among species as well as trees within species. In some genera such as *Acacia* the G layer is convoluted, and in *Eucalyptus gigantea* it may almost fill the cell lumen (Wardrop, 1961). Scurfield and Wardrop (1962) found the degree of convolution sometimes to be so great that the perimeter of the convoluted layer was greater than

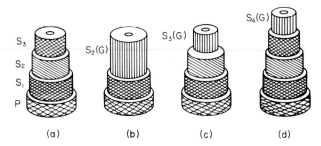

FIG. 2.26. Organization of cell walls in normal wood fibers and reaction wood fibers. (a) normal wood fiber of structure $P + S_1 + S_2 + S_3$; (b) reaction wood fiber of structure $P + S_1 + S_2 (G)$; (c) reaction wood fiber of structure $P + S_1 + S_2 + S_3 (G)$; (d) reaction wood fiber of structure $P + S_1 + S_2 + S_3 + S_4 (G)$. P, primary wall; S_1, outer layer of secondary wall; S_2, middle layer of secondary wall; S_3, inner layer of secondary wall: S_4, gelatinous layer. [From Wardrop (1964a).]

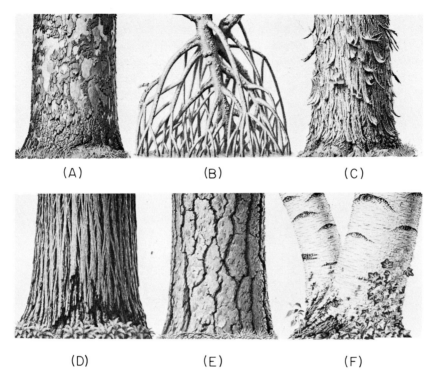

Fig. 2.27. Variations in bark patterns. (A) *Platanus*, (B) *Rhizophora*, (C) *Carya ovata*, (D) *Sequoia*, (E) *Pinus ponderosa*, (F) *Betula papyrifera*. Photo courtesy St. Regis Paper Co.

that of adjacent, nonconvoluted regions of the wall. X-ray diffraction studies showed that the molecular orientation in the G layer tended to parallel the fiber axis (Wardrop and Dadswell, 1955).

The initiation of tension wood occurs at the time of cambial division. Evidence for its induction early in cellular ontogeny comes from observations showing that gelatinous fibers developed in inclined seedlings within 6–10 days after bending (Casperson, 1960). According to Berlyn (1961), the gelatinous layer may be observed immediately subjacent to the cambium (Fig. 2.25).

Reaction phloem tissues also occur. Scurfield and Wardrop (1962) found considerable variation among angiosperm species in tendency for asymmetric phloem development. In *Lagunaria pattersonii* and *Pittosporum undulatum* eccentric phloem development was pronounced; in *Eucalyptus* it was definite but less marked; and it was uncertain in other species. When reaction phloem formed, it appeared to be anatomically similar to normal phloem, but the numbers of various types of phloem cells were greater. In *Eucalyptus*, for example, the sequence of sieve tubes, companion cells, parenchyma, and fibers was repeated more often on the upper side of the stem. However, in species which formed phloem or pericyclic fibers there was a tendency for these to develop unusually thick walls on the upper side of the stem.

The formation of reaction tissue is a geotropic phenomenon as shown by several lines of evidence. For example, compression wood forms toward the focus of gravitational attraction under conditions of a reversed gravitational field. When trees were grown upside down, compression wood formed on the morphologically upper sides of branches, which physically were the lower sides (Wershing and Bailey, 1942). If trees are grown on a revolving table the compression wood forms on the outer side of the stem (Jaccard, 1939). The internal control of formation of reaction wood appears to be regulated by growth hormones as discussed in Chapter 3, this volume.

Variations in Bark Patterns

The appearance and structure of bark are very distinctive for a species and often an excellent diagnostic feature for it (Fig. 2.27). Bark patterns vary among species from smooth to scaly to deeply fissured. Such differences result from variations in growth rates of bark tissues, in formation of periderms, and in rates of shedding of outer bark.

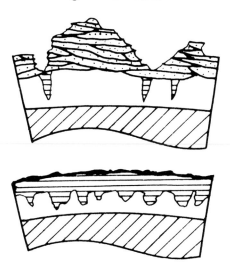

FIG. 2.28. Variation among species in expansion tissue. *Quercus* (above) has relatively little expansion tissue (shown by horizontal hatching) and a thick outer bark divided into layers by periderms. *Fagus* (below) has considerable expansion tissue and practically no outer bark. [From Whitmore (1963).]

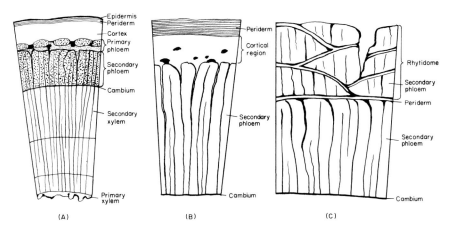

FIG. 2.29. Variation in periderm formation. (A) Young stem. (B) Mature bark of species which does not form rhytidome. (C) Mature bark of species which forms abundant rhytidome. U.S. Forest Service, Forest Products Laboratory photo.

As a tree increases in girth, the bark tends to expand at first by stretching. Later parenchyma cells in the inner bark divide to form expansion tissues which accommodate the strains of circumferential expansion. However, the specific pattern of production of expansion tissues differs considerably among species. For example, expansion tissue in *Fagus* is continuous at the inner bark surface whereas in some species of *Quercus* it occurs in narrow wedges (Fig. 2.28). *Quercus* bark also grows much faster and produces more periderms than does *Fagus* bark. The dead tissues of the outer bark of *Quercus* cannot form expansion tissues as the tree increases in girth so the outer bark becomes fissured. In contrast, *Fagus* bark with almost no dead outer tissues remain smooth (Whitmore, 1963).

Some species of trees form only superficial periderms and have no rhytidome (Fig. 2.29). Others with deep periderms form rhytidome which may have abundant parenchyma and soft phellem, as in *Ulmus*, or abundant fibers, as in *Carya* and *Robinia*. In *Fraxinus americana*, the fiber-containing bark splits to form a diamond shaped pattern. The scalebark patterns of pines are related to their periderms forming as overlapping scale-like units. By comparison, ring bark patterns form when the phellogen consists of a cylindrical sheath. In *Vitis*, for example, cylinders of tissue separate from the stem.

Bark patterns are appreciably influenced by the manner of separation of dead tissues from the stem. In some trees, such as *Platanus*, the dead tissues separate as scales through outer, thin phellem layers. In many trees (e.g., *Quercus* and *Robinia*) the several layers of rhytidome adhere to one another.

In old *Sequoia* and *Pseudotsuga* trees, for example, the thick, deeply-fissured bark may represent several hundred years of accumulated old phloem which was cut off by arcs of persistent periderms. Although the number of periderms formed varies among species, it alone is not always correlated with bark thickness. This was emphasized by Panshin, De Zeeuw, and Brown (1964) who showed that the four periderm layers of *Tilia americana* collectively were thinner than the one periderm layer of *Picea rubens*.

Some species of *Eucalyptus*, such as the "stringybarks," form very loose and fibrous barks (Chattaway, 1953, 1955). Their texture results from great expansion of parenchyma tissue outside the innermost periderm. This expansion occurs after the periderm forms and just before the cells die and are converted into rhytidome. The expanded phloem parenchyma and ray cells separate the patches of phloem fibers which characterize these barks and thereby produce a loose and spongy tissue.

Suggested Collateral Reading

Bannan, M. W. (1966). Spiral grain and anticlinal divisions in the cambium of conifers *Can. J. Bot.* **44**, 1515–1538.

Bisset, I. J. W., and Dadswell, H. E. (1950). The variation in cell length within one growth ring of certain angiosperms and gymnosperms. *Aust. Forestr.* **14**, 15–29.

Dinwoodie, J. M. (1961). Tracheid and fiber length in timber. A review of literature. *Forestry* **34**, 125–144.

Duff, G. H., and Nolan, N. J. (1953). Growth and morphogenesis in the Canadian forest species. I. The controls of cambial and apical activity in *Pinus resinosa* Ait. *Can. J. Bot.* **31**, 471–513.

Farrar, J. L. (1961). Longitudinal variations in the thickness of the annual ring. *Forestr. Chron.* **37**, 323–331.

Glerum, C., and Farrar, J. L. (1966). Frost ring formation in the stems of some coniferous species. *Can. J. Bot.* **44**, 879–886.

Glock, W. S., and Agerter, S. R. (1963). Anomalous patterns in tree rings. *Endeavour* **22**, 9–13.

Hughes, J. F. (1965). Tension wood: a review of literature. *Forestr. Abstr.* **26**, i–xvi.

Ladefoged, K. (1952). The periodicity of wood formation. *Dansk. Biol. Skr.* **7**, 1–98.

Larson, P. R. (1963). Stem form development in forest trees. *Forest Sci. Monogr.* **5**.

Larson, P. R. (1963). Stem form and silviculture. *Proc. Soc. Amer. Forest.* 103–107.

Larson, P. R. (1969). Wood formation and the concept of wood quality. *Yale School of Forestr. Bull.* **74.**

Low, A. J. (1964). Compression wood in conifers. A review of literature. *Forestr. Abstr.* **25**, xlv–li.

Noskowiak, A. S. (1963). Spiral grain in trees. A review. *Forest Prod. J.* **13**, 266–275.

Patel, R. N. (1965). A comparison of the anatomy of the secondary xylem in roots and stems. *Holzforschung.* **19**, 72–79.

Wardrop, A. B. (1964). The reaction anatomy of arborescent gymnosperms. *In* "The Formation of Wood in Forest Trees," (M. H. Zimmermann, ed.), pp. 405–456. Academic Press, N.Y.

Wardrop, A. B. (1965). The formation and function of reaction wood. *In* "Cellular Ultra-structure of Woody Plants," (W. A. Coté Jr., ed.), pp. 371–390. Syracuse University Press, Syracuse, N.Y.

Westing, A. H. (1965). Formation and function of compression wood in gymnosperms. *Bot. Rev.* **31**, 381–480.

Chapter 3

CONTROL OF CAMBIAL GROWTH

Introduction

The number, size, and distribution of cambial derivatives are determined by controls of several sequential phases of cambial growth such as maturation of overwintering xylem and phloem cells, division in the meristematic cambial sheath to produce new xylem and phloem cells, increase in size of cambial derivatives, increase in cell wall thickness, transition from production of earlywood to latewood, and division and subsequent growth of fusiform cambial cells to provide for increase in the circumference of the cambial cylinder. The various aspects of cambial activity are very efficiently coordinated and are responsive to many fluctuating environmental factors whose influences are mediated through internal physiological processes, especially food, hormone, water, and mineral relations. Because the influences of environmental factors are interdependent and interacting it often is difficult to evaluate the specific role of individual environmental components in cambial growth (Kozlowski, 1949). This chapter will discuss external and internal control of cambial growth.

Control of Cambial Growth by Tree Crowns

It cannot be emphasized too strongly at the outset that cambial growth is largely regulated by the basipetal flow of products synthesized in the crown, especially carbohydrates and hormonal growth regulators. Both the amount and type of annual xylem increment as well as its distribution along the stem and branches are influenced by physiological activity of the crown in a predictable way. The amount of leaf surface, the distribution of the crown along the stem, and the metabolic activity of leaves, all of which affect cambial growth, are influenced by environmental fluctuations, plant competition, site, management practices, and catastrophic events such as premature defoliation. Because of the very important regulatory role of products produced in shoots on cambial growth, any external influence on the formation of leaf primordia, on subsequent expansion of these primordia, or on the capacity of shoots to synthesize carbohydrates and hormonal growth regulators may be expected to play some contributory role in control of cambial growth.

The dependence of cambial growth on a continuous supply of substances provided by the shoot system is dramatically illustrated by stimulated cambial growth above stem girdles and inhibited cambial growth below them. Such girdles prevent downward transport in the phloem, causing a greater than normal accumulation of carbohydrates and hormonal growth regulators above the girdles and a deficiency of these substances below them. Wilson (1968) found an increase, above phloem severing stem girdles of *Pinus strobus* trees, in number of xylem and phloem cells cut off by the cambium, apparently because of a higher than normal mitotic index (percent of cambial zone cells in mitosis) and longer duration of mitotic activity. Percentage increase in phloem production above stem girdles generally was greater than the increase in xylem production. Below the girdle, cell division and cell enlargement stopped within a few weeks after trees were girdled and cell wall thickening continued at a very low rate.

Leaf Development and Cambial Growth

The seasonal development of leaf area in trees, which influences cambial growth markedly, varies greatly among species (Chapter 1, Volume I). Such variations are traceable largely to differences in the rate of production of leaf primordia by apical meristems, the area attained by individual leaves, and the number of apical meristems as determined by branching habit (Wareing, 1964). High correlations often exist between cambial growth of trees and seasonal increase in leaf production. For example, leaf growth continues for much of the summer in high yielding heterophyllous species of *Populus* and *Eucalyptus*. The extremely rapid growth of some tropical species such as *Trema guineensis* and *Musanga cecropioides* is due more to their capacity for continuous leaf production than to very efficient dry weight production or energy conversion (Coombe, 1960; Coombe and Hatfield, 1962). Similarly, recurrently flushing pines such as *Pinus caribaea*, *P. radiata*, *P. taeda*, *P. echinata*, and *P. palustris*, which continue to increase their leaf surface throughout the growing season, generally have high yearly increments in diameter.

Voluminous data are available which show that cambial growth is greatly influenced by leaf development and only a few examples will be given. In Japan, for example, wood production in stems of *Zelkowa serrata* and *Chamaecyparis obtusa* increased with increasing amount of foliage per tree (Satoo and Senda, 1958; Satoo, Negisi, and Senda, 1959). The greater the number of leaves the greater was wood production in *Populus davidiana* trees (Satoo, Kunagi, and Kumekawa, 1956). However, stem increment per unit amount of foliage decreased with increasing amount of leaves per tree. In contrast, the amount of branch wood produced by a unit amount of foliage increased with an increasing amount of foliage per tree. Although stem wood production was not linearly related to the amount of leaves per tree, when branchwood and leaf production were added to it and hence dry weight increment considered, growth and amount of foliage approached a straight line relationship. This suggested that the lower efficiency of foliage of dominant trees in producing stem wood was caused by differences in distribution of dry matter in various parts of the tree and by respiratory losses by nongreen tissues.

Duration of leaf retention is an important factor in overall tree development. For example, the evergreen habit of most gymnosperms provides them with a mechanism for rapid accumulation of photosynthetic products and growth regulators early in the frost-free season and late into the autumn. Pisek and Winkler (1958) showed that once the new needles matured, photosynthesis of *Picea excelsa* and *Pinus cembra* remained more or less constant until late autumn.

Winter photosynthesis, especially during mild winters, has been amply demonstrated, and there has been much debate over its importance. For example, *Picea* trees near Innsbruck gained considerable dry matter in the fall until prolonged frosts occurred, and again in the spring as soon as temperatures increased (Pisek and Tranquillini, 1954). In Japan the photosynthetic activity of *Chamaecyparis pisifera* in winter amounted to about one-third of the summer rate (Nomoto, Kasanaga, and Monsi, 1959). The evergreen *Cinnamomum* carried on photosynthesis all winter in Japan (Saeki and Nomoto, 1958). In the southeastern United States *Pinus echinata* trees had minimal carbohydrate reserves in the autumn but they increased very appreciably during the winter (Hepting, 1945).

Pollard and Wareing (1968) demonstrated that *Pinus sylvestris* and *P. radiata* seedlings at Aberystwyth, Wales showed appreciable increases in dry weight during the winter. Generally, the dry weight increment was concentrated in roots and stems, although a substantial increase in foliage weight occurred in *P. radiata*. This was the result of production of new needles in addition to growth of other needles.

In the coastal area of Norway, Hagem (1962) investigated dry weight increase in young *Picea* and *Pinus* trees in the mild winter months from 1934 to 1945. During most winters the young plants increased in dry weight, with the lowest increment occurring during weeks of low light intensity in December and January. Occasionally small decreases in dry weight were recorded for parts of a season but for entire seasons there was a net increase in dry weight because of excess photosynthesis over respiration. Hagem concluded that in coastal areas, with high winter temperatures and low frost, short periods of dormancy alternated with periods of high metabolic activity and dry weight increment.

Vertical Distribution of Cambial Growth

As mentioned, the architecture of a woody stem reflects the capacity of the crown for producing carbohydrates and growth regulators. Hence, the relation of crown size to length of the stem which is devoid of branches markedly influences annual xylem increment along the bole. Both tree age and environmental conditions which influence metabolic activity of crowns exert a strong effect on the distribution of xylem increment at various stem heights. In young trees, with physiologically active branches along most of the main stem, the height of maximum ring thickness is relatively low in the stem. As trees age and lower branches become physiologically inefficient, the relative height of maximum ring thickness gradually moves upward. During years of high rainfall or conditions otherwise favorable for growth the point of maximum xylem increment occurs at a relatively lower level in the main stem than under conditions unfavorable for vigorous crown activity (Smith and Wilsie, 1961). Also during years which are favorable to rapid growth the added metabolites are translocated to the lower stem and markedly affect growth there. Hence, xylem increment of the lower stem exhibits a greater sensitivity, than does xylem production within the crown, to environmental fluctuations from year to year (Larson, 1963b).

Effects of Suppression

The influence of suppression is to decrease total xylem increment and to alter its distribution along the tree stem and branches. These changes may result from late initiation of cambial growth, early growth cessation, and decrease in growth rate under intense competition (Kozlowski and Peterson, 1962; Winget and Kozlowski, 1965). As suppression of aging *Pinus strobus* trees increased, xylem production was gradually reduced throughout the stem, but with proportionally more xylem deposited at upper stem levels. Eventually the cambium near the stem base produced only discontinuous rings or none at all. Finally, xylem production was restricted to upper parts of the tree only. Hence, discontinuous and missing rings were found at increasingly higher stem levels in older trees. This overall trend was modified by climatic changes from year to year so the site of xylem production fluctuated somewhat either upward or downward in the tree. Nevertheless, the net effect over a period of years was one of concentrating the reduced amount of xylem in the upper stem (Bormann, 1965),

Seasonal duration of cambial growth often is shorter in suppressed trees than in dominant trees of the temperate zone. Kozlowski and Peterson (1962) showed a progressive delay in initiation of cambial growth in the lower stem with increasing suppression of *Pinus resinosa* trees. Early cessation of cambial growth in increasingly suppressed trees was reported by Winget and Kozlowski (1965). Unit growth rates of dominant, codominant, and intermediate *Tsuga canadensis* trees were similar until mid-June. The growth of the more suppressed crown classes then slowed down, with that of the most suppressed trees decelerating fastest. Hence, the greater the degree of suppression, the less likely a tree was to maintain physiological activity for a long time and consequently its competitive ability declined rapidly in the latter part of the growing season.

Bassett (1966) determined the amounts and duration of diameter growth of various crown classes of 30-year-old *Pinus taeda* trees in southern Arkansas. Measurements were taken at breast height during each of five successive growing seasons. Dominant trees not only grew faster but continued growing for a longer time than did the suppressed trees (Table 3.1). Whereas dominant and codominant trees continued growth into October and a few into November, diameters stopped increasing by late July in suppressed trees. On the

TABLE 3.1

Variations in Duration of Circumferential Increase of Different Crown Classes of 30-Year-Old *Pinus taeda* Trees at Various Times within the Growing Season.[a]

Crown class	% of growth period during which trees increased in circumference					
	March 1–May 31	June 1–Aug. 16	Aug. 16–Oct. 31	March 1–Oct. 31	During wet year (1961)	During dry year (1963)
Dominant	96	79	66	80	96	58
Codominant	90	66	53	70	92	46
Intermediate	77	43	38	53	79	28
Suppressed	51	15	17	28	49	8

[a] Data are averages for 5 growing seasons (1960–1964) and for a wet year (1961) and a dry year (1963). [From Bassett (1966).]

average, dominant and codominant trees expanded during 80 and 70%, respectively, of each of the five seasons. Diameter increase of large-crowned trees occurred continuously from early March through June, and then recurrently during two-thirds of the rest of the growing season. Intermediate and suppressed trees increased in diameter during 53 and 28%, respectively, of the five growing seasons.

Diameter growth is more sensitive than height growth to suppression. Bormann (1965) noted earlier and markedly more severe reduction in cambial growth over height growth of suppressed *Pinus strobus* trees. During the latter 30 years of life suppressed trees made half their total height growth but less than 20% of their total diameter growth.

EFFECTS OF THINNING

When a stand of trees is thinned the amount of growing space for both the roots and crowns of residual trees is increased. The released trees respond to the more favorable environmental conditions by slowing down upward crown recession, increasing crown width and leaf growth, increasing branch size, and producing more branch wood than they did before the thinning. These changes inevitably lead to an increase in physiological activity of the crown which in turn is followed by increase in cambial growth and redistribution of xylem increment along the stem.

The release of a tree by thinning not only increases total xylem increment but also has the effect of producing a more tapered tree by greater stimulation of xylem production toward the stem base than at upper stem levels or by redistributing xylem increment to favor the lower stem. Hence, change in taper can occur following thinning by redistributing growth along the stem and without immediately increasing growth in volume.

After thinning, trees of good form show a shift of xylem production in a downward direction while radial growth in the crown in inhibited (Fig. 3.1). Sometime later, when the crowns and roots of released trees expand, volume growth is increased as more xylem is deposited throughout the entire stem. The most important change, however, is an increase in xylem increment in the lower stems of released trees. Several years later, when the intensity of competition increases again, the vertical form of the xylem sheath subsequently laid down changes again and maximum ring width occurs near the stem height which supports most foliage. The stem then tapers below this point until near the stem base where there is an increase in ring width. As Farrar (1961) noted, the large increases in diameter at breast height following thinning often given an erroneous impression of increase in volume of the bole unless the suddenly greater stem taper is taken into account.

The degree of total growth response to release by thinning varies with

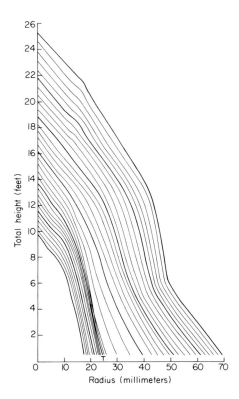

FIG. 3.1. Effect of thinning closely grown *Pinus ponderosa* trees on cambial growth at different stem heights. Before thinning the annual increment was widest in the lower stem. After thinning the annual increment was greater in the upper stem. [From Myers (1963).]

crown development of individual trees. Dominant trees with large and physiologically efficient crowns often show minimal response to thinning. In contrast, trees of intermediate and suppressed crown classes show proportionally greater response (Larson, 1963a,b).

Because the annual accretion of xylem at upper or lower levels of the stem is a function of the capacity of the foliage to synthesize carbohydrates and growth hormones the size of the crown strongly determines the degree of stem taper. Stems of open-grown trees with long crowns tend to be more tapered than stems of trees with small crowns in closed stands. These differences are related to variations in both rate of xylem increment along the entire bole and in its vertical distribution along the stems. As height growth is independent of stand density and the rate of radial growth is greater along the bole of large-crowned trees than in those with small crowns, this alone causes increased taper in the former. In addition, open-grown trees with large crowns tend to distribute significant amounts of metabolites to the lower stem, resulting in appreciable xylem increment there, further increasing stem taper. As crown length is decreased in closed stands and competition among trees is intensified, xylem increment along the entire stem is decreased and also concentrated in the upper part of the tree resulting in a stem which approaches cylindricity. Hence, strongly suppressed trees tend to have very nearly cylindrical stems (Larson, 1963b). For these reasons trees must be planted relatively close together in plantations to achieve acceptable stem form. After this has been accomplished, thinning can be imposed to concentrate wood production on selected trees. Original wide spacing may produce trees with too much taper to be usable.

EFFECTS OF PRUNING

The influences of removal of branches on xylem increment and stem form are the reverse of those of thinning. As pruning tends to inhibit cambial growth at the stem base, the accretion of xylem following branch removal becomes concentrated in the upper stem. Pruning, therefore, tends to reduce stem taper but whether it does so appreciably depends on its severity and timing as well as on crown characteristics of the tree prior to pruning.

Pruning of branches influences cambial growth of open-grown trees more than in stand-grown trees as the latter already have cylindrical stems and high crowns. The amount and distribution of xylem increment of open-grown or large-crowned trees depends greatly on the intensity of pruning. As pruning severity is increased and more branches are removed, the greater is the decrease in xylem production and upward displacement of growth leading to a decrease in taper (Larson, 1963a). The correction of stem form by branch pruning in strongly tapered trees is also modified by age of trees, with stems of old trees less susceptible than young ones to such modification. The failure of many pruning experiments to alter stem form often has been traceable to removal of too few branches or too great a delay before pruning. As emphasized by Larson (1963a, 1963b), tree stems become more cylindrical with increasing age and stand density. Thus, either a delay in pruning or removal of only a few branches from trees in closed stands may not be followed by noticeable changes in stem form.

The effect of pruning severity on xylem deposition along the bole of 14-year-old *Pinus taeda* trees was demonstrated by Young and Kramer (1952). Their experimental trees were pruned so the amount of crown left was 50, 35, or 20% of total tree height. Crown size of pruned trees had a marked effect on the amount of diameter growth below the crown but a relatively minor effect on growth within the crown. Trees with 50% crowns grew most in diameter and those with 20% crowns grew least, except in the upper stem where rates of diameter growth were similar. Diameter growth decreased with increase in distance below the crown in all pruned trees but the amount of reduction increased as crown size was decreased by pruning. In trees with 50% crowns, diameter increase at the stem base was about half as great as it was at the top. However, in trees with only 20% crowns, diameter increase was only a sixth as great as it was in the upper stem. In addition to altering the amount of xylem production, pruning also tends to alter wood quality. In heavily pruned trees the crowns are smaller than in unpruned trees, leading to a more abrupt latewood transition down the stem, and an increase in the percentage of latewood in the lower stem (Larson, 1969b).

Defoliation and Cambial Growth

The importance of products supplied by leaves on cambial growth is dramatized by the inhibitory influences of defoliation by insects, fungi, fire, adverse weather, and pruning on xylem deposition. The amount of xylem increment and its distribution along the stem in response to defoliation differ with species, the defoliating agent, the severity and timing of defoliation, and physiological predisposition of the host tree. Although it often is stated that reduction of cambial growth is proportional to the amount of defoliation (Church, 1949), this generalization should be viewed cautiously. Defoliation by some insects inhibits cambial growth more than does pruning of an equivalent amount of foliage. This is so because some insects remove foliage which is most active in synthesizing foods and growth regulators whereas pruning of forest trees, which ordinarily is confined to lower branches, removes the more shaded leaves which have relatively low physiological efficiency. Furthermore, some insects preferentially defoliate suppressed trees whose restricted food reserves would be unlikely to sustain tree growth through severe defoliation. Rose (1958) compared the effects of defoliation by adverse weather and by the forest tent caterpillar (*Malacasoma disstria*) on cambial growth of *Populus tremuloides*. As adverse weather defoliated trees severely early in the season, the beginning of cambial growth was delayed until a new crop of leaves had emerged from undamaged shoot tips, bud rudiments, or dormant buds. In contrast, effects of defoliation by *Malacasoma* on cambial growth were not appreciable until several weeks after insect feeding began. The amount of foliage consumed by young *Malacasoma* larvae was small. The production of foliage until the time of the last instar larvae occurred faster than foliage destruction by the insect and cambial growth early in the season was not greatly suppressed. Regardless of the severity of defoliation by *Malacasoma*, xylem cells were produced by the cambium for 3–4 weeks before the last larval stage was reached and heavy

FIG. 3.2. Effect of defoliation by spruce budworm during 1867–1877 on cambial growth of *Picea glauca*. Photo courtesy Canada Department of Forestry and Rural Development.

defoliation occurred. Subsequent inhibition of xylem production in the lower stem depended on the severity of final defoliation. If trees were completely stripped of leaves, xylem production ceased by the time defoliation was complete, and even if trees refoliated, no additional xylem cells were produced for the remainder of the season. If defoliation was less than complete, the amount of xylem produced was proportionally reduced and cessation of cambial growth occurred early.

Reports of responses of cambial growth to defoliation by fire have varied all the way from no significant reduction in xylem production to marked decrease in xylem increment followed by death of trees. Unfortunately some of the reports of negligible reduction of diameter growth following rather severe defoliation are difficult to evaluate because of the confounding effect of increased growth in residual trees as a result of reduced competition. Furthermore, the effects of fire on cambial growth generally have been based on examination of xylem increment at a single stem height shortly after defoliation. Hence, additional studies are needed on effects of defoliation on cambial growth throughout the stem axis during the year of the defoliating fire as well as in subsequent growing seasons.

DEFOLIATION BY INSECTS

The impact of insect defoliation on the amount of cambial growth and its distribution along the stem is extremely variable. Single severe defoliations often kill gymnosperms. Angiosperms and deciduous gymnosperms, such as *Larix*, usually survive single defoliations, probably because their destroyed foliage is rapidly replaced. Nevertheless, two severe defoliations in the same year may kill angiosperms also. There also is considerable variability in response to defoliation among various gymnosperms in the same genus. For example, the recurrently flushing southern pines of the United States, such as *Pinus taeda* and *P. palustris*, withstand a severe defoliation better than do northern pines, such as *P. resinosa*.

Some insects rapidly remove a large part of the total leaf surface whereas others do so gradually. In addition some insects remove only current-year foliage of gymnosperms, others remove only old foliage, and still others remove both old and new foliage. Defoliators such as spruce budworm (*Choristoneura fumiferana*) may destroy all current-year foliage without greatly affecting xylem increment at the base of the tree during the first year of defoliation. However, xylem increment in the upper stem usually is very much reduced. After the first year of such defoliation, xylem production at the stem base, as well as at the top, is greatly reduced (Figs. 3.2–3.3).

Although inhibition of cambial growth following defoliation has often been attributed to a decrease in carbohydrate supply, such a response

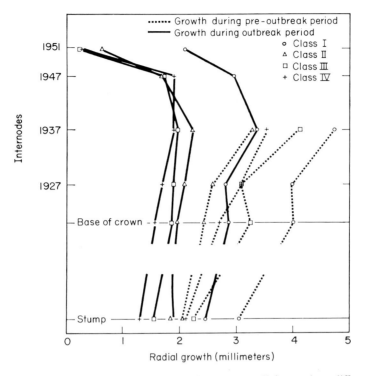

FIG. 3.3. Effect of defoliation by spruce budworm on radial growth at different stem heights of *Abies grandis*. Radial growth is compared for an outbreak (1946–1956) with the pre-outbreak period (1935–1945). Data are given for four classes of defoliation, with class I representing lowest amount of defoliation and class IV the most severe defoliation (see Table 3.2). [From Williams (1967).]

undoubtedly involves a more complicated control mechanism than one involving only carbohydrate deficiency (Kozlowski, 1969). Although photosynthesis and translocation of carbohydrates to the lower stem are reduced by defoliation, it should be remembered that the supply of hormonal growth regulators also is reduced. Isolation of the lower stem of trees by phloem blocks during the dormant season virtually prevented xylem production during the entire growing season (Evert and Kozlowski, 1967). When phloem blocks were imposed after cambial growth was already initiated, a rapid inhibition of cambial growth was noted. Cambial growth did not appear to be affected directly by availability of food because axial and ray parenchyma cells contained considerable starch before and after resumption of seasonal cambial activity and throughout the period of phloem and xylem differentiation. Hence, the importance of hormonal growth regulators supplied by the leaves should not be overlooked in evaluating the physiological impact of defoliation on cambial growth.

Responses to insect defoliation often are apparent early in the upper stem and much later in the lower stem. Stark and Cook (1957) found a lag of about 2 years in reduction of xylem increment in the lower stem as a result of defoliation of *Pinus contorta* trees by the lodgepole needle miner (*Recurvaria starki*). C. B. Williams, Jr. (1967) studied the effect of defoliation by spruce budworm (*Choristoneura occidentalis*) on cambial growth of *Abies grandis, Pseudotsuga menziesii,* and *Picea engelmannii.* Radial growth during an infestation was compared with growth before the attack. This was done for six different stem heights and for four different classes of severity of attack. Cambial growth was impeded by spruce budworm attack but the degree of response varied with the extent of damage, species, and stem height (Table 3.2). Cambial growth of *Abies grandis* was suppressed most and that of *Pseudotsuga menziesii* least. In all species radial growth was reduced to a greater extent within the crown than near the ground. Average radial increment for the outbreak period was much less in the upper crown than elsewhere along the stem (Fig. 3.3).

The time of year when defoliation occurs greatly affects the seasonal curve of diameter growth and, especially, survival of trees. Severe defoliation of gymnosperms early in the summer, before shoot expansion has ceased and buds for the subsequent year have formed, often kills trees whereas late summer defoliation, after buds have formed, is more likely to insure survival as primordia for the ensuing leaf crop are already present.

Benjamin (1955) described cambial growth response of *Pinus echinata* to early and late season defoliation by the red-headed pine sawfly (*Neodiprion lecontei*). Early season defoliation by the first generation of the insect was followed by reduction in xylem increment during the same season, with recovery occurring during the subsequent growing season. However, late season defoliation by the second generation of insects did not inhibit cambial growth appreciably during the same year but did so in the following year. This delayed effect of defoliation by the second generation of insects resulted because most of the annual xylem increment was already laid down before defoliation was initiated. By comparison, defoliation by the first generation of sawfly began before annual radial growth was well advanced.

Environmental Control of Cambial Growth

The environment can be considered to consist of various climatic, edaphic, and biotic components (Kramer and Kozlowski, 1960). Among the most important environmental factors which play a contributory role in control

TABLE 3.2

EFFECT OF FOUR DEGREES OF DEFOLIATION BY SPRUCE BUDWORM ON AVERAGE CAMBIAL GROWTH OF *Abies grandis* AND *Picea engelmannii*[a]

Damage class[b]	*Abies grandis*			*Picea engelmannii*		
	Pre-outbreak radial increment (1935–1945) (mm)	Outbreak[c] radial increment (1946–1956) (mm)	%[d] reduction	Pre-outbreak radial increment (1935–1945) (mm)	Outbreak[c] radial increment (1946–1956) (mm)	%[d] reduction
I	3.96	2.55	35.6	1.52	1.53	0
II	2.56	2.12	17.2	1.47	1.35	8.2
III	2.89	1.77	38.7	1.29	1.06	17.8
IV	2.85	1.74	39.0	—	—	—

[a] From Williams (1967).

[b] Class I   Little or no defoliation; less than 30% of tips dead; no top killing.
Class II   About 50% of tips dead; crown recovering from defoliation.
Class III   More than 50% of tips dead; few branches present in an otherwise live crown; crown not recovered from defoliation; tree may or may not survive.
Class IV   More than 50% of branches dead; top usually dead; crown producing little foliage; recovery slight—tree apparently dying.

[c] Adjusted values. Average damage growth minus deviation from the experimental average × error regression coefficient.

[d] Adjusted averages for *Abies grandis* were significantly different at the 5% level; adjusted averages for *Picea engelmannii* were not significantly different at the 5% level.

of cambial growth are light, water, temperature, mineral supply, composition of the atmosphere above and below ground, soil physical and chemical properties, insects, other plants, and various animals. Cambial growth is also greatly modified by cultural practices, reproductive growth (Chapter 8), and shoot growth.

As previously mentioned, fluctuations in environmental stresses ultimately affect cambial growth to a large extent by altering the flow of leaf products down the branches and stem. Hence, environmental factors eventually influence cambial growth both by affecting formation of leaf primordia and their expansion as well as by influencing physiological activity of fully expanded leaves. Thus, cambial growth responses to environmental factors can be rapid (as in the case of a sudden freeze which kills young leaves) or they can be long delayed (e.g., the influence of environment on number of leaf primordia formed). In addition to influencing cambial growth indirectly through crown activity, some environmental factors (e.g., internal water deficits) may affect cambial growth directly (Kramer, 1964; Whitmore and Zahner, 1967).

Many problems exist in evaluating the effects of environmental components on cambial growth of the woody perennial plant. An abrupt change in environment does not alter cambial growth similarly in all trees in a stand. This may be the result of differences among trees in exposure, crown size, depth of rooting, inherent growth characteristics, physiological preconditioning of trees, and other causes. Furthermore, the influence of a drastic environmental change often affects cambial growth markedly in some parts of a tree and not others. Another problem in evaluating environmental control of tree growth is that a given degree of environmental stress early in the growing season generally affects cambial growth differently than does a stress of similar magnitude exerted late in the season.

Still another problem in assessing environmental control of growth is that different internal control systems probably are involved in various phases of cambial growth. For example, there is evidence that tracheid enlargement and tracheid wall thickness are controlled by different mechanisms. For example, an increase in temperature reduced tracheid wall thickness in *Pinus* without affecting tracheid diameter (van Buijtenen, 1958). Richardson and Dinwoodie (1960) presented evidence that tracheid wall thickness was a function of net assimilation rate whereas tracheid diameter was determined by other factors.

Caution should be exercised in ascribing cause and effect relations to correlation analysis of growth and individual environmental factors. As emphasized by Fritts (1960), changes in a particular environmental component may be correlated with other factors which may exert a direct influence on growth. Correlations may cause it to appear that the factors analyzed influence cambial growth. This is especially true if the causal factors with which it is related are not included in the analysis. Another difficulty in evaluating climatic control of cambial growth is that different species in the same general area actually grow under different physiographic conditions and their growth is correlated differently with climatic variables.

Voluminous literature is available describing attempts to relate cambial growth of trees to changes in weather. As Zahner and Stage cautioned (1966), many such attempts have not accounted for most of the observed growth variance when all weather measurements were treated as absolute values. It should be remembered that a given amount of precipitation early in the growing season when soil moisture may be at field capacity will have little effect on cambial growth, whereas half that amount later in the season when soil is dry will affect cambial growth markedly.

There often is a shifting in importance of various environmental factors in control of cambial growth. Temperature was shown by Fritts (1956) to control cambial growth of *Fagus sylvatica* early in the growing season. However, later in the season as soil moisture approached the wilting percentage, water deficits exerted a major controlling influence on growth (Fritts, 1959a, b). Data of Kozlowski, Winget, and Torrie (1962) also showed that the importance of temperature to cambial growth of *Quercus ellipsoidalis* on sandy soil in Wisconsin varied at different times of the growing season. Correlation of cambial growth and temperature declined in late summer as soil moisture supplies were depleted and growth was very responsive to water deficits.

Lag Effects of Environmental Factors

Inasmuch as cambial growth depends on food and hormonal growth regulators synthesized in leaves, it is not too surprising that the climate of a given season can exert a carryover effect on cambial growth during the following year. Important in this lag effect is the role of climate in influencing the number of leaf primordia which will overwinter in the bud and expand during the subsequent season. Hence, total leaf areas of trees and associated carbohydrate and hormone supplies during a given year often are affected by weather of the previous year. Several investigators have found that cambial growth of trees was correlated with weather of both the current and previous year. A few examples will be given.

Fritts (1962) found that environmental conditions of the previous year were equally or even more effective than those of the current year on ring width variation of *Fagus grandifolia*. Ring width was inversely related to the severity of drought during August of the previous year and somewhat directly related to May–July temperature of the previous years. The lag effect of temperature on cambial growth in Finland is most pronounced near timber line where cambial increment often is low in the year following a climatically unfavorable one (Mikola, 1962).

Using regression analysis Zahner and Stage (1966) studied the influence of water deficits and temperature during the period from May to October of both the current and previous year on basal area growth of *Pinus monticola* in northern Idaho. Figure 3.4 shows the trend of partial regression coefficients for predicting basal area increment from water deficits and temperature. The upper curves show effects of water deficit independent of temperatures. Water deficits during June of both the current and previous year were inhibitory to growth. Small positive effects in August were interpreted as showing that growth was relatively insensitive to moisture stress at that time. Temperature reversed its effect from the previous to the current year. Higher than average temperatures in the previous year favored cambial growth in the subsequent year, but higher than normal temperatures in the current year impeded growth early in the season and had little effect later in the season.

Site Factors

As mentioned, the productivity of a given site depends on many impinging factors. Of these light, water, temperature, and fertility are widely recognized as among the most important. Their influence on cambial growth will be discussed briefly.

LIGHT

Effects of light intensity on cambial growth are complicated and are mediated through physiological activity of leaves and export from leaves of carbohydrates and hormonal growth regulators. Light conditions during one year will influence the formation of leaf primordia and the number of leaves produced during the subsequent year. Thus, a lag effect of light conditions on cambial growth may be expected. In addition light conditions greatly alter the expansion and structure of leaves (Chapter 6, Volume I) and thereby control the potential production of assimilates and hormonal growth regulators. Finally, any effect of light intensity, light quality, or length of day which influences shoot growth or synthetic capacity of fully expanded leaves may be expected to subsequently affect cambial growth.

Light Intensity

To a considerable extent the importance of light in controlling cambial growth can be shown by variations in patterns of growth of dominant and

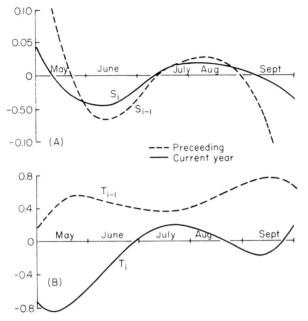

Fig. 3.4. Trends of partial regression coefficients of water deficit (A) and temperature (B), showing the importance of these variables in cambial growth of *Pinus monticola* at various times during the growing season in Idaho. [From Zahner and Stage (1966).]

suppressed trees. The former have higher rates of cambial growth and usually a longer seasonal duration of cambial growth. The increased cambial growth of residual trees following thinning of a stand also is partly a response to improved light conditions.

Duff and Nolan (1953) compared trees of different growth rates and found that xylem increment along the bole was distributed in the same consistent pattern. They combined inferior site conditions conducive to narrow xylem rings, and superior sites conducive to wide rings, with conditions of open growth and closed or shaded growth. They also studied cambial growth of trees which in their youth passed from one environmental condition to another. The influence of light in modifying the increase and decrease of xylem increment appeared whether trees were grown on fair or good sites and whether the succession was from open to shaded conditions or the reverse. The growth pattern of increased xylem increment for several internodes downward from the apex followed by decreasing xylem increment was repeated. This pattern could be modified in degree but not in kind over a variety of environmental conditions.

The increased cambial growth in dominant over suppressed trees, and in

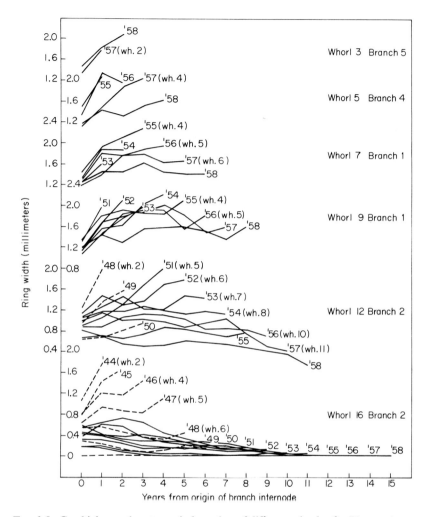

FIG. 3.5. Cambial growth patterns in branches of different whorls of a *Pinus resinosa* tree that was released from suppression at the end of the 1950 growing season. Solid lines show rings produced after release; broken lines before release. In parentheses following the year of ring formation is the number of the whorl in which the ring was produced. [From Forward and Nolan (1961).]

residual trees following thinning of a stand, is an integrated response to an overall improved environmental regime with greater availability of water and minerals as well as light. Perhaps, therefore, cambial growth in variously shaded branches of a tree is a more direct indicator, than is growth in the main stem of the importance of light to cambial growth.

Cambial Growth Patterns in Branches

During their development the branches of many trees, especially gymnosperms, undergo successive suppression. Many pines, for example, produce annually a whorl of branches at the base of the terminal leader. Each whorl from the apex downward has older branches and, as branches are overlaid by more whorls, they are progressively more shaded. Hence, their growth characteristics change with age as their environment is altered.

Forward and Nolan (1961) studied the pattern of xylem increment at nodes of branches of varying age in 25- to 30-year-old *Pinus resinosa* trees. In a wide range of environments there was an increase in xylem width followed by a decrease from the branch apex through the upper internodes. This pattern, which could be modified quantitatively, was a constant feature of all upper branches. In trees that had been grown in the open, suppressed, or suppressed and later released, the upper branches and parts of lower ones that were formed while near the tree apex, showed a pattern of cambial growth similar to that of the main stem. As a branch was progressively suppressed during aging there was a redistribution of its cambial increment and, in the lowermost whorls, growth of the xylem sheath was restricted at

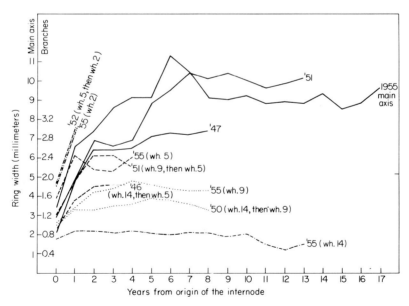

FIG. 3.6. Cambial growth patterns in the main axis and branches of different whorls of an open-grown *Pinus resinosa* tree. The solid lines represent the main axis and the other lines the branches. After each line appears the year of formation of the axis or branch and in parentheses the number of the whorl in which the branch finally occurred followed by the whorl in which it occurred when the ring was formed. [From Forward and Nolan (1961).]

showed a typical pattern of increasing width of the annual ring for several internodes down the branch from its apex. In whorl 9, however, the ring produced in 1958 was somewhat modified, indicating this whorl was undergoing suppression by whorls above it. Whorl 12 contains annual rings that were produced before as well as after the tree was released. Ring width decreases in rings formed in 1948–1950. In 1951 the tree showed the greatest effect of release and produced a ring that increased greatly in width down to the fifth internode. Hence, it showed a pattern of xylem increment similar to that in open-grown trees. This branch was then in the fifth whorl from the apex. In 1959, when it was in the ninth whorl, it showed suppression and lack of growth pattern. In the sixteenth whorl, only the branches that had been in the uppermost 5 whorls at the time the ring was formed showed pattern. The pattern was suppressed in the 1948 ring which then was in whorl 6. After release, the branch was already in the ninth whorl and, unlike higher branches, it continued in its condition of suppression.

Figure 3.6 shows the ring widths produced in different years in four branches of an open-grown *Pinus resinosa* tree. The branches were in whorl all internodes. Hence, even in open-grown trees the lower branches were suppressed.

Some idea of the distribution of cambial growth in branches of a *Pinus resinosa* tree that had been released from suppression at the end of the 1950 growing season may be gained from Fig. 3.5. Branches in whorls 3, 5, and 7 14 initiated in 1942, whorl 9 initiated in 1947, whorl 5 initiated in 1951, and whorl 2 initiated in 1954. The upper 9 whorls show a typical pattern of xylem increment, but in the 14th whorl the pattern is absent probably because of shading by upper branches.

The ring sequences of a suppressed tree with 9 leaf-bearing whorls are

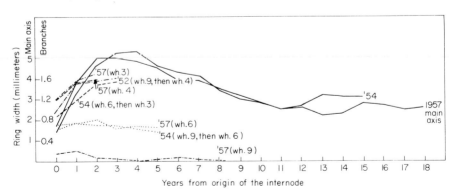

FIG. 3.7. Cambial growth patterns in the main axis and branches of different whorls of a suppressed *Pinus resinosa* tree. For further explanation see legend of Fig. 3.5. [From Forward and Nolan (1961.)]

shown in Fig. 3.7. Maximum ring width was attained in the main stem within 3 years from the origin of the internode. Xylem rings that were produced when a whorl was third or fourth from the top showed definite pattern, but in lower whorls the typical pattern was missing. The branches of lower whorls in this tree were shaded more than were branches at the same level on open-grown trees. Hence, only upper branches of suppressed trees showed no inhibition of cambial growth.

Lower, suppressed branches of many trees may fail to form annual rings for several years before the branches die. For example, in 35- to 77-year-old *Pseudotsuga menziesii* trees Reukema (1959) noted lack of agreement between numbers of rings in bases of live branches and in tree stems near the point of intersection. Often there were 9–10 fewer rings in the base of the branch than in the stem. In *Pinus ponderosa* the number of missing annual rings in branches increased from the top of the tree downward, reflecting greater suppression of the lower branches (Andrews and Gill, 1939). In *Pinus sylvestris* and *Picea abies* a number of outer annual rings of the stem bent outward toward a knot and then narrowed and finally disappeared in the base of the branch (Rommell, 1937, 1940, 1941). Such observations indicate that suppressed lower branches often are unable to supply foods and growth regulators for growth of the main stem (Kramer and Kozlowski, 1960). Labyak and Schumacher (1954) observed that a branch of *Pinus taeda* in the lower half of the crown with fewer than three branchlets, or one in the lower fourth of the crown with fewer than five branchlets, did not contribute to development of the main stem. Obviously the pruning of lower "negative" branches will not detract from diameter increment of the main stem.

Photoperiod

Both the amount and nature of the cambial growth increment are responsive to daylength. In many species of trees the continuation of cambial growth has been linked to continuous shoot expansion. When shoot elongation stopped in these species cambial growth ceased shortly thereafter (Priestley, 1935). This relationship appears to be the result of stimulation of cell division in the cambium by hormones produced by actively growing shoots. Hence, in some species any effect of photoperiod on shoot growth will secondarily influence duration of cambial growth. There are many species, however, which have a very short period of shoot expansion and a much longer duration of cambial growth. Daylength also influences cambial activity in the latter group. For example, the duration of cambial activity in *Pinus sylvestris* seedlings, which has a short period of shoot elongation, was greater under 15-hour than under 10-hour photoperiods. Cambial growth in the species could be prolonged in the autumn by supplementing natural photoperiod with artificial light (Wareing, 1951). Wareing and Roberts

(1956) showed that photoperiod also had an important effect in controlling cambial growth of *Robinia pseudoacacia* seedlings. Experimental plants were first exposed to short day conditions to cause shoot extension to cease. If such seedlings were further exposed to short days for several weeks, cambial growth ceased. If, however, seedlings were exposed to long days after shoot extension stopped, cambial activity usually was resumed. Girdling experiments demonstrated that the cambial stimulus, which originated in the leaves when they were exposed to long days, moved only downward in the stem.

The effects of photoperiod on cambial growth appear to largely involve control of internal hormonal balances. As discussed in Chapter 8 of Volume I the onset of bud dormancy under short days appears to be controlled by an accumulation of inhibitors. That photoperiodic effects of meristematic activity involve a hormonal control mechanism rather than one operating by influencing food supply is shown by experiments in which growth is increased when natural daylength is prolonged by supplementary light of such low intensity that it has little effect on food supply. Bamberg, Schwarz, and Tranquillini (1967), for example, found that the photosynthetic capacity of *Pinus cembra* was about the same when it was exposed to natural daylength and to 12- and 8-hour photoperiods.

In addition to controlling duration of cambial growth, photoperiod greatly influences the specific gravity of wood by controlling the proportion of large to small diameter cells in the annual xylem ring. Larson (1962a) noted that daylength exerted a strong influence on tracheid diameter of young *Pinus resinosa* plants. Long days promoted needle elongation and production of large diameter tracheids. Short days caused cessation of needle elongation and a transition to narrow diameter tracheids. Exposure of plants to long days caused an increase in cell diameter even when the intensity of the added light was below the level necessary for appreciable photosynthetic activity. Larson concluded that the influence of photoperiod on tracheid diameter was largely indirect and was associated with auxin production and distribution of terminal meristems. Waisel and Fahn (1965a) found that photoperiod affected cambial growth of *Robinia pseudoacacia*, with the types of derivatives formed influenced more than the width of the xylem increment. The effect of photoperiod on cambial growth is discussed further in the section on earlywood–latewood relations in this chapter.

SOIL MOISTURE

Throughout the entire life span of a tree cambial growth is exceedingly sensitive to available water. In forests soil water deficits often are of long duration and they usually become especially critical during the time of year when other environmental factors, including light and temperature, are at

optimal levels (Kozlowski, 1955, 1957, 1958, 1968c, d, e, f, 1969). In central
Ohio, for example, soil moisture during the summer may remain below wilting
percentage for periods in excess of a month (Fritts, 1956). In the southern
United States severe droughts lasting from 2–6 weeks occur quite frequently
(Moyle and Zahner, 1954).

Several aspects of cambial growth, including the number of xylem cells
produced, seasonal duration of cambial growth, proportion of xylem to
phloem increment, time of latewood initiation, duration of latewood production, and distinctness of the earlywood–latewood transition are responsive

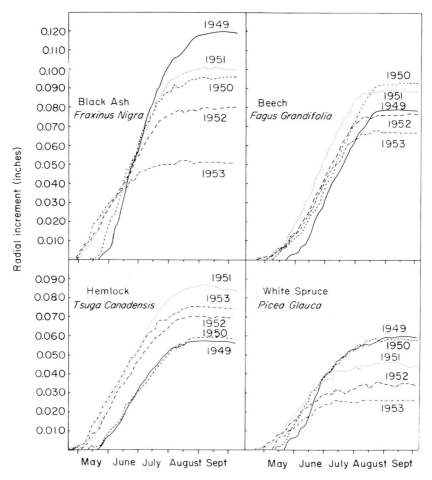

FIG. 3.8. Variations in time of cambial growth initiation, rate of growth, and duration of
growth of four species of forest trees during 5 successive growing seasons in Ontario,
Canada. [From Fraser (1956).]

to the amount of rainfall and its seasonal distribution. During a dry year, cambial growth continues for an abnormally short part of the growing season and only a thin sheath of xylem is produced. Some species may make twice as much diameter growth during a year of abundant rainfall as during a dry one (Fig. 3.8). The correlation between xylem increment and rainfall usually is higher in arid regions than in those of abundant rainfall (Kozlowski, 1964; Fritts, 1967).

Cambial growth often slows or stops during midsummer droughts and resumes or accelerates when the soil is recharged by rain. For example, Zahner (1958) found that during a dry summer diameter growth of *Pinus taeda* in Arkansas essentially ceased by August. However, it resumed during September, which was unusually rainy, and continued through October. One-third of the total annual xylem increment was laid down during September and October.

Annual radial growth of 2 species of angiosperms and 2 species of gymnosperms for 5 consecutive years in Ontario, Canada is shown in Fig. 3.8. The large differences for each species in time of cambial growth initiation, time of growth cessation, and rate of growth reflect wide differences in environment among years. In three out of four species, least growth occurred in 1953, a year of intense midsummer drought. *Tsuga canadensis* did not grow least in 1953, presumably because of much earlier growth initiation in that year than in 1949 or 1950 (Fraser, 1956).

In Arkansas Smith and Wilsie (1961) found high correlations between width of the xylem ring of *Pinus taeda* and June to October soil moisture deficits of the current season. Their observations were confirmed by those of Bassett (1966) who studied the effect of drought on the amount and seasonal duration of diameter increment of various crown classes of 30-year-old *Pinus taeda* trees in southern Arkansas. Diameter at breast height of dominant trees increased during 96% of the growing season in a wet year but during only 58% of the season in a dry year. Suppressed trees increased in diameter during 49% of the season during a wet year and only 8% of the season during a dry year (Table 3.1).

Regional anomalies in growth rings often are related to the amount and distribution of seasonal rainfall. This was shown by Glock and Agerter (1962) who characterized three distinct growth types as related to rainfall regime. These included the California, west Texas, and northern Arizona growth patterns. The California pattern developed in a region of winter rain and dry summer. Radial growth was initiated at the beginning of the growing season when practically all the soil moisture available for the year was already present in the soil. Under these conditions the growth rings were uniform in thickness and had sharp margins. Only rarely did partial growth layers develop. In contrast, the west Texas regime was characterized by summer rainfall only. When growth began in the spring only some of the water that would be available during the year was present in the soil. In fact, most of the water that eventually would be used during a year did not become available until after the first flush of growth. During the summer season wet periods were interspersed with short or long dry periods. Under this regime multiple rings formed commonly in one year. The growth layers often showed diffuse margins and variable thickness. Partial growth layers or lenses occurred commonly. The northern Arizona regime involved a rainy period in summer and another one in winter. Variability ranged widely and was low for several rings and then high for a series of succeeding ones. Ring borders varied from diffuse to distinct. Partial growth layers and discontinuous rings occurred. The northern Arizona pattern appeared to have alternating series of growth layers. Some of these had characteristics of the California type while others resembled the growth patterns of the west Texas type.

Bassett (1964b) estimated available soil moisture in the surface foot of soil in an Arkansas pine forest for 21 growing seasons. Soil moisture estimates were then combined with estimates of potential evapotranspiration to calculate indices of potential growth. Linear regressions of measured

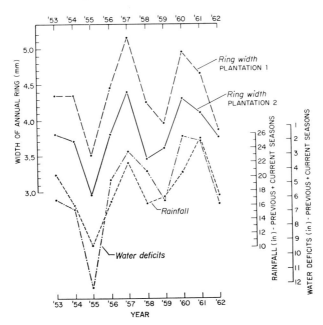

FIG. 3.9. Relations of xylem increment (ring width) in two 21-year-old *Pinus resinosa* plantations in Michigan and rainfall and water deficits for a 10-year period. [From Zahner and Donnelly (1967).]

potential growth on calculated potential growth accounted for 95–97% of the variation about the regression lines.

Several investigators have emphasized that variation in growth distribution throughout the stem in young trees depends on the age and size of the tree when successive xylem increments form. In order to assess most accurately the effects of environment on cambial growth of young trees, it is important to stratify annual xylem rings vertically in relation to the position of the crown at the time the xylem sheath was produced (Duff and Nolan, 1953). Measurements of xylem increment made from samples taken at a fixed height from the ground are independent of crown position only for rings which formed after crown height stabilized in mature trees. With these considerations in mind, Zahner and Donnelly (1967) studied effects of water deficits from 1952 to 1962 on ring widths for successive internodes of 21-year-old *Pinus resinosa* trees, at constant ring numbers from the pith. Xylem width was correlated with both rainfall and daily values of water deficit calculated for April through October 5 during each year according to the method of Zahner and Stage (1966). Water deficits of both the current and previous year affected xylem increment greatly, with 68% of the growth variation associated with current-season (May–September) moisture conditions, and 14% with moisture conditions of the previous season (July–September) (Fig. 3.9).

It should be emphasized that cambial growth is inhibited by soil moisture deficits because generally these also are associated with internal water deficits in trees. However, internal water deficits in trees are not controlled by soil

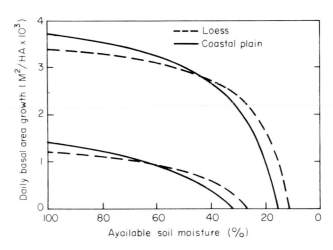

FIG. 3.10. Relation of cambial growth (basal area increment) of *Pinus taeda* to soil moisture availability at two rates of soil moisture depletion. [From Moehring and Ralston (1967).]

moisture alone. Rather they are controlled by relative rates of absorption of water through roots and loss of water by transpiration. As Kramer (1962) emphasized, internal water deficits in trees can result from excessive transpiration, slow absorption from dry, cold, or poorly aerated soils, or combinations of these. Thus, internal water deficits in trees may develop and inhibit cambial growth when soil moisture availability is relatively high but air humidity is low causing high transpiration. Conversely, internal water deficits in trees may be low when the soil is partially dry but air humidity is high and transpiration is consequently low.

Moehring and Ralston (1967) showed that the rate of depletion of soil moisture accounted for more of the variation of cambial growth in *Pinus taeda* than did the actual soil moisture content. Regardless of the amount of water available during the summer, cambial growth was inhibited when soil moisture loss was rapid. As may be seen in Fig. 3.10, when available moisture was above 40–60%, cambial growth was only slightly affected by soil moisture content but appreciably influenced by the rate of moisture loss. Such data indicate that the rate of depletion of soil moisture often is a better indicator of transpiration and internal water balance of trees than is soil moisture content.

In well-watered soils, recurrent temporary water deficits in leaves because of excessive transpiration during the day are not serious because leaves tend to rehydrate at night. However, afternoon wilting of leaves of trees growing in progressively drier soils becomes serious because leaves are less likely to recover turgidity at night and become ineffective in synthesizing carbohydrates and hormones required for growth of tissues.

TEMPERATURE

It is well known that cambial growth varies with temperature regimes. Rapid early cambial growth in the spring depends largely on warming of the air to a critically high temperature. Thereafter, the rate of cambial growth usually increases as the temperature is raised to some critical threshold value. At very high temperatures, cambial growth declines. At extremely high or low temperatures cambial growth often is influenced by injury to the shoots or directly to the cambium.

Cambial growth responses over the noninjurious range of temperatures involve complicated effects of temperature on coordination of such processes as cell division and elongation, photosynthesis, respiration, hormone synthesis, enzymic activity, synthesis of chlorophyll, and transpiration. Temperature also influences cambial growth by affecting leaf growth. For example, a pronounced increase in growth of *Pseudotsuga menziesii* seedlings was the result of a temperature influence on production of leaf area rather than the effect of photosynthesis per unit of leaf (Brix, 1967).

Temperature influences photosynthesis directly and indirectly by regulating respiration and transpiration (Kozlowski and Keller, 1966). As Kramer observed (1962), with temperature increase above a critical value, photosynthesis is checked because of an increase in respiration. Temperature increase also accelerates transpiration and produces internal water deficits which cause stomatal closure, bringing about a decrease in photosynthesis. These observations are in accord with those of Pisek and Winkler (1959) who observed that apparent photosynthesis of *Pinus cembra* seedlings increased up to temperatures of 10–15°C and then decreased. At 35° respiration exceeded photosynthesis and CO_2 was given off by the needles. Decker (1944) observed that increasing the temperature from 30° to 40° decreased CO_2 uptake by *Pinus taeda* and *P. resinosa* seedlings.

Seasonal Cambial Growth and Temperature

The profound effects of temperature on cambial growth of trees have been well documented. Temperature often influences the thickness of the annual ring through its effects on time of initiation of cambial growth, and on the rate and seasonal duration of cambial growth. As mentioned earlier, a critically high temperature is necessary to initiate shoot activity and in turn to stimulate the basipetal flow of an initial xylem growth wave. Fraser (1956) found that average radial growth of trees in Canada was greatest in years with high vernal temperatures and attributed the increased growth to a lengthened growing season due to the earlier initiation of cambial activity. As shown by Daubenmire and Deters (1947), an unseasonal drop in temperature in the middle of a growing season causes greatly decreased growth rates, further emphasizing the critical role of temperature in controlling cambial growth.

The effects on cambial activity of latitude and altitude, which are mediated to a large degree through temperature, are well known and only a few examples will be given. In the Temperate Zone the cambium of a wide range of species is active for a longer period as the length of the frost-free season is increased. At timberline cambial growth may last for only a few weeks. In the forest–tundra ecotone of Canada on the east coast of Hudson Bay the cambium of *Picea glauca* was active for less than 2 months (Marr, 1948), whereas further south at Chalk River, Ontario, cambial growth of *Picea glauca* continued for about a month longer (Fraser, 1962). Dramatic examples of control of cambial growth by temperature may be seen on mountainsides where annual ring width of trees often decreases progressively up to timberline.

Hustich (1948) concluded that radial growth of trees in northern European countries was controlled by temperature during the growing season. According to Brier (1948), nearly half the variation in annual tree growth in northern

Finland was accounted for by the regression on local summer temperature and mean atmospheric pressure. Mikola (1950) considered temperature to be the decisive environmental component controlling tree growth in northern Finland. The influence of drought on cambial growth was obvious only in unusually dry summers on the driest sites. The deleterious effect of excess moisture showed up only on wet peatlands in rainy summers. In northern Finland cambial growth was depressed from 1902 to 1911 and then increased continually for a number of years. The decreased growth in the early 1900's and the increasing trend thereafter were closely correlated with mean July temperature (Mikola, 1962). Higher correlation between cambial growth and July temperature in northern than in southern Finland was attributed to other important factors in the south which modified the temperature effect as well as to the longer growing season in the south.

Siren (1963) emphasized that summer temperatures were correlated with thickness and structure of annual rings at the subarctic and subalpine tree line. Xylem rings of gymnosperms were particularly good indicators of temperature changes. One study showed that at least three-fourths of the effect of climate on xylem increment in a subarctic area was related to air temperature of both the current and previous summer. There also was a lag effect of temperature during the preceding 10 years on cambial growth. Variations in precipitation had relatively negligible effect on cambial growth.

Haugen (1967) compared major trends in tree ring indices representative of the northern timberline, including Alaska, the northern Urals, Scandinavia, and Labrador for 50-year intervals beginning with the year 1650. The observed similarities in oscillation of tree ring indices among these areas were regarded as reflecting trends of June or July temperatures. Other evidence of the depressing effect of low temperature on cambial growth is found in Bray's (1966) correlation of glacial minima in British Columbia during 1655–1723, 1799–1833, and 1873–1913, with glacial maxima in northwestern North America.

Several studies have shown a rather rapid response of cambial growth to temperature change. Kozlowski, Winget, and Torrie (1962) found that daily radial growth of *Quercus ellipsoidalis* in central Wisconsin was correlated with daily maximum and minimum temperatures. The correlations varied during the growing season, with a general tendency to decline in the latter part when growth appeared to be influenced more by water deficits than by temperature. There also was an indication of a 1-day lag effect of temperature on cambial growth. In fact, in some instances radial growth was better correlated with temperature of the previous day than of the day of growth measurement. These observations were in accord with those of Fritts (1960) who found that maximum temperature of the day preceding growth may influence radial increment in some species. There apparently are variations among species in lag responses to temperature, for Fritts (1959a) reported that the average temperature of the day prior to the measurement day was directly related to diameter growth of *Quercus alba* and *Acer saccharum* but not to that of *Quercus rubra*. Fritts (1960) also found *Quercus alba* to be somewhat more affected than were *Quercus rubra* or *Acer saccharum* by high temperature of the day previous to growth measurement.

The time involved in transport of carbohydrates and growth regulators may partly account for a lag in cambial growth of the lower stem in response to environmental factors. As the rates of basipetal translocation of carbohydrates in tall trees may vary from 1 to 3 meters per hour, considerable time may elapse before photosynthate from the leaves reaches the stem base (Kramer and Kozlowski, 1960). Furthermore, hormones also move with photosynthetic products in the phloem. Hence, a significant time lag between synthesis of carbohydrates and of hormones, as well as their basipetal translocation and ultimate utilization in cambial growth in the lower stem may be expected.

Larson (1967) showed that cambial growth of *Pinus resinosa* seedlings was favored by intermediate temperatures (Table 3.3). He also noted that day temperature was more critical than night temperature and postulated that xylem production was reduced to some extent by inhibition of photosynthesis at low day temperatures and by increasing respiration at high day temperatures. Latewood development was much more sensitive than earlywood development to temperature. This relationship was ascribed to the greater dependency of latewood over earlywood on current assimilates.

Temperature Extremes and Cambial Growth

As mentioned, cambial growth is responsive to temperature over a considerable range because of its influence on rates of, and coordination among, physiological processes regulating various aspects of cambial growth. In addition, extreme temperatures above and below such a range often have profound effects on cambial growth. For example, extremely low temperatures often inhibit cambial growth either indirectly by injuring the shoot or root system or directly by injuring cambial tissues, e.g., by winter sunscald or by producing frost rings (Kramer and Kozlowski, 1960).

Waisel and Fahn (1965a) compared effects of high and low temperatures as well as long and short days on cambial growth of *Robinia pseudoacacia*. Temperature affected activity of the cambium while photoperiod determined the types of derivatives which matured. At high temperature (28°C day temperature, 20° night temperature) the cambium was active, while at low temperature (18° day temperature, 12° night temperature) it was not.

As emphasized throughout this chapter, a physiologically active shoot system exerts an important controlling influence on cambial increment by

TABLE 3.3

EFFECTS OF FOUR COMBINATIONS OF DAY AND NIGHT TEMPERATURES ON VARIOUS ASPECTS OF CAMBIAL GROWTH IN *Pinus resinosa* SEEDLINGS[a]

Temperature (°C)		Basal area increment (mm²)	Ring width (mm)	Earlywood width (mm)	Latewood width (mm)	Latewood (%)	Specific gravity	Cell wall thickness (μ)
Day	Night							
23.8	12.8	4.75	0.754	0.374	0.378	50.4	0.402	6.51
18.3	12.8	3.60	0.565	0.329	0.236	41.7	0.382	6.24
29.2	18.3	3.54	0.683	0.345	0.338	49.3	0.343	5.13
23.8	18.3	4.49	0.729	0.340	0.389	53.5	0.402	6.62

[a] From Larson (1967).

synthesizing carbohydrates and hormonal growth regulators (Evert and Kozlowski, 1967). Hence, winter desiccation injury to gymnosperm foliage, or direct thermal injury to buds or leaves, may be expected to decrease cambial growth during the subsequent growing season. Frost kill of young leaves in the spring occurs commonly and may be expected to have an overall depressing effect on cambial growth during the same year. It may also influence cambial growth the following year by influencing formation of leaf primordia in late summer.

Cambial growth often is affected by winter sunscald of stems which appears to be caused by rapid freezing of tissues after they are unseasonably warmed by the sun. Godman (1959) described winter sunscald injury to young *Betula alleghaniensis* trees in Michigan. The injured stems showed callus tissue above the line of snow depth on the south and southwest sides of the tree. The injury apparently occurred during the 1947–1948 winter. The xylem ring produced in 1948 was narrow and merged with the previous year's ring back of the callus tissue formation. Sunscald injury to *Liriodendron tulipifera* trees also occurred in Michigan during the 1947–1948 winter (Shipman and Rudolph, 1954).

SOIL FERTILITY

Mineral cycles in forests involve annual litter fall, and its subsequent breakdown, liberation of minerals, and their reabsorption. However, repeated harvesting of timber crops reduces mineral supplies and such depletion may result in critically low levels for tree growth, especially in soils low in native fertility (Kramer and Kozlowski, 1960). For these reasons there is much concern with the need for applying fertilizers to forests in order to increase wood production (Holmes and Cousins, 1960; Mustanja and Leaf, 1965; Swan, 1966). Many sandy nursery soils also are low in fertility and growth of nursery stock often requires regular fertilizer applications. The importance of minerals to cambial growth (Fig. 3.11) is shown in the voluminous literature showing stimulating effects of fertilizers on growth of trees. A few examples will be given.

Swan (1965) demonstrated that growth of *Pinus banksiana* seedlings in an infertile forest soil could be increased to different degrees by addition of various combinations of minerals (Table 3.4). Adding nitrogen alone increased seedling weight fivefold. Adding nitrogen and phosphorus together increased growth four times over adding nitrogen only. When nitrogen and phosphorus deficiencies were corrected, the limiting factor was potassium, the addition of which increased growth 2.5 times as much as did nitrogen and phosphorus combined. However, the addition of all essential elements in appropriate balance caused by far the greatest growth stimulation. The

0   1   2   3

Inches

FIG. 3.11. Effect of mineral supply on cambial growth of *Pinus radiata* in New Zealand. Narrow rings were formed for the first 14 years after planting in 1927. One ton per acre of superphosphate applied in 1952 caused formation of wide rings beginning 3 years after fertilizer application. Photo courtesy of G. M. Will.

TABLE 3.4

GROWTH RESPONSES AFTER 223 DAYS OF *Pinus banksiana* SEEDLINGS IN A NUTRIENT-DEFICIENT FOREST SOIL TO WHICH VARIOUS NUTRIENT SOLUTIONS WERE APPLIED[a]

Nutrient solution treatments	Fresh weight per plant (g)
Control (water)	0.22
Nitrogen only	1.13
Phosphorus only	0.49
Potassium only	0.26
PK	0.54
NK	0.90
NP	4.69
NPK	11.73
Complete solution[b]	16.12

[a] From Swan (1965).
[b] Solution containing nitrogen, phosphorus, potassium, magnesium, calcium, sulfur, boron, copper, zinc, manganese, molybdenum, and chlorine.

latter practice increased growth by about 73 times as compared to adding water alone, emphasizing the importance of mineral deficiency in growth control.

In Florida, Hoekstra and Asher (1962) applied commercial fertilizers around 21-year-old *Pinus elliottii* var. *elliottii* trees. Twenty pounds of 7-7-7 or 3-18-6 fertilizers were applied per tree in April and an additional 20 pounds were applied to some trees 6 weeks later. Radial increment was determined five years after treatment (Table 3.5). The trees responded to fertilizer applications for 3 years after treatment, with a peak during the second year. By the fourth year radial growth of fertilized trees was similar to that of control trees. Cambial growth was related to the amount of nitrogen applied in the presence of phosphorus and potassium.

Finn and White (1966) applied fertilizers to a 20-year-old, slow growing plantation of *Liriodendron tulipifera* trees in southwestern Michigan. Adding 336 pounds of nitrogen, 73 pounds of phosphorus, and 139 pounds of potassium per acre increased diameter growth by 85%. The increase was associated with accelerated physiological activity in the crown as leaf weight increased, leaf color changed from yellow-green to green, and leaf abscission was delayed. The beneficial effects of fertilizers persisted for at least 5 years.

The importance of minerals in controlling cambial growth of shade trees

TABLE 3.5

RADIAL GROWTH OF *Pinus elliottii* VAR. *elliottii* 5 YEARS AFTER FERTILIZERS
WERE APPLIED TO 21-YEAR-OLD TREES[a]

Treatment		Nitrogen per tree (lbs)	Radial growth (mm)	% of control
Fertilizer	Amount (lbs)			
Control	0	0	15.7	100
3-18-6	20	0.6	17.8	113
3-18-6	40	1.2	19.0	121
7-7-7	20	1.4	19.8	126
7-7-7	40	2.8	20.1	128

[a] From Hoekstra and Asher (1962).

was shown by Himelick, Neely, and Crowley (1965). They applied fertilizers around *Quercus palustris*, *Fraxinus americana*, and *Gleditsia triacanthos* trees. Fertilizer was applied at the rate of 6 lbs of N, P_2O_5, or K_2O per 1000 sq. ft of area, a rate commonly recommended for shade trees. Ring width of trees receiving nitrogen in the fertilizer was significantly increased over that in control trees. Application of phosphorus and potassium did not increase cambial growth, nor did a combination of phosphorus, potassium, and nitrogen increase cambial growth more than did nitrogen alone. Addition of minor elements to NPK produced no added growth response. The addition of nitrogen to the soil resulted in increasing stem circumference by 52% in *Quercus palustris*, 39% in *Fraxinus americana*, and 73% in *Gleditsia triacanthos* var. *inermis*.

Although many such instances of increases in cambial growth and wood production following addition of fertilizers to forest trees and shade trees can be cited, many other examples of lack of growth response to fertilizers also exist. The absence of response to added fertilizers often results from adding mineral elements which are not deficient or adding deficient minerals in inadequate amounts. Hence, correct diagnosis of specific deficiencies is important. Visual symptoms, soil analysis, foliar analysis and soil bioassays are variously helpful in diagnosing mineral deficiencies (Kramer and Kozlowski, 1960; Swan, 1965).

Internal Control of Cambial Growth

The important internal requirements for cambial growth are similar to those for shoot growth and include carbohydrates, hormonal growth regulators, water, mineral elements, and other regulatory substances. Deficiencies of any of these may inhibit cambial activity, with the speed of cambial response varying greatly under a given deficiency. For example, internal water deficits will develop faster than mineral deficiency as mentioned earlier. Environmental stresses ultimately cause a critical change in availability of one or more internal requirements, thereby altering cambial growth. Fritts (1966) presented a schematic diagram (Fig. 3.12) of possible sequential changes set in motion by environmental stresses, such as low precipitation or high temperature, culminating in narrow xylem rings in gymnosperms on semi-arid sites. According to this model, low precipitation might act specifically through increased internal water stress, stomatal closure, reduced photosynthesis, and inadequate food reserves, which allow only a narrow xylem ring to form. Internal water stress also might sequentially impede cell enlargement and differentiation from meristematic tissue, decrease needle elongation, and concurrently reduce synthesis of both carbohydrates and hormones, thereby causing a narrow xylem ring to be formed. High temperature might operate by increasing evaporation and internal water stress or, alternatively, increasing respiration and depleting food reserves sufficiently to inhibit cambial

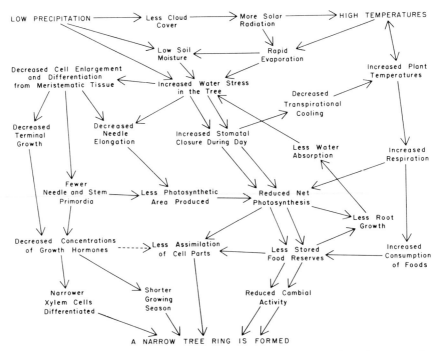

FIG. 3.12. Model of possible sequential events involved in production of narrow xylem rings as a result of hot, dry weather. [From Fritts (1966).]

activity. Although this model may place too much emphasis on food supply alone as specifically controlling cambial activity, it provides a good summary of complexities and interactions among various external and internal factors in control of cambial growth.

CARBOHYDRATES

Carbohydrates are translocated in the phloem along the entire cambial sheath and used in production of xylem and phloem cells as well as in expansion of the cambium. Both stored and currently produced carbohydrates are used in cambial growth, with the latter probably the most important (Kozlowski, 1962a; Kozlowski and Keller, 1966).

Considerable evidence shows that cambial growth usually is limited more by the rate of carbohydrate conversion to new tissues rather than solely by the amount of available food. For example, xylem production can be rapidly checked by late summer droughts when trees have substantial carbohydrate reserves (Kozlowski, 1962a). Cambial activity below a stem girdle is checked very rapidly even though carbohydrate supplies appear to be plentiful in the area of growth inhibition (Loomis, 1938; Evert and Kozlowski, 1967). Priestley (1962a,b) showed that only about one-third of the extractable carbohydrate of apple trees was consumed during growth. Hence, various data show that food supplies often are adequate but that growth is inhibited by internal blocks to food conversion into new tissues (Kozlowski and Keller, 1966).

Sources of Carbohydrates

Inasmuch as cambial activity below the buds is underway in many species before buds elongate, early season cambial growth of deciduous trees must depend on carbohydrate reserves. Correlated with early season cambial growth of deciduous trees of the Temperate Zone is depletion of reserve carbohydrates from storage parenchyma tissues such as pith, cortex, and ray cells (Cameron, 1923; Ishibe, 1935). Considerable evidence also shows that currently produced carbohydrates are rapidly translocated downward in the branches and stem and used in cambial growth. Several investigators have shown that large amounts of ^{14}C can be isolated from the alcohol-insoluble fraction of stem internodes within a few days after old needles of young pine trees are offered $^{14}CO_2$ (Gordon and Larson, 1968; Rangenakar and Forward, 1969; Dickmann and Kozlowski, 1970a). Such data indicate that current photosynthate is being incorporated into stem tissues. Larson (1969a), found that the bulk of the ^{14}C translocation to the stems of 5-year-old *Pinus resinosa* trees occurred within 3 days after the trees were given $^{14}CO_2$ and that practically all the ^{14}C incorporated into wall substance occurred during this period. However, Dickmann and Kozlowski (1970a) found that, after 1 week, the 1-year-old needles of 20-year-old, closely grown *Pinus resinosa* trees still retained almost 30 % of the recovered ^{14}C. Hence the rate of ulilization of current photosynthate in cambial growth of pines shows considerable variation.

Several investigators have studied the sources of carbohydrates used in cambial growth at various times during the growing season. A few examples will be given. Gordon and Larson (1968) noted that production of thick-walled xylem tracheids normally associated with latewood was correlated with maturation of current season's needles of *Pinus resinosa*. When shoots completed seasonal growth and no longer were a strong carbohydrate sink, there was an increased supply of current photosynthate for developing xylem tracheids. The increased downward export of carbohydrates after current needles matured coincided with an increase in secondary wall thickening in older stem internodes.

In *Pinus resinosa* cambial activity below the buds is underway by the time the buds open. In young trees most of the earlywood in older stem internodes is produced while shoots are elongating and during the early stages of needle expansion. The new needles do not contribute appreciable amounts of photosynthesis for cambial growth at this time. Rather, carbohydrates exported from the old needles are used in earlywood production. When the new needles are almost fully expanded they then begin to export large quantities of carbohydrates and these are used in xylem production. At the same time a change occurs in the direction of carbohydrate transport from the old needles, with transport primarily to the roots and very little upward to the new shoots. The increased carbohydrate supply following maturation of new needles is correlated with increased secondary wall thickening of tracheids indicative of latewood development. Toward the end of the growing season the new needles provide carbohydrates to the new buds and to cambial growth in upper stem internodes. At the same time the old needles provide carbohydrates for cambial growth of lower stem internodes. Late in the season all age classes of needles also translocate quantities of carbohydrates to the roots and reserve carbohydrates accumulate in parenchyma tissues throughout the tree (Gordon and Larson, 1968; Larson and Gordon, 1969).

In the heterophyllous species, *Populus deltoides*, new leaves are produced more or less continually during much of the summer (see Chapter 5, Volume I). A new leaf developing from the apex at first depends on carbohydrates from exporting leaves below. Although photosynthesis in the new leaf begins early, most of the carbohydrates are retained and used in growth and metabolism of the new leaf. Such leaves do not translocate large amounts of photosynthesis until they are almost fully expanded. At first a newly exporting leaf translocates carbohydrates upward until the newly formed leaf above approaches maturity. Translocation from that leaf then becomes bidirectional and, finally, basipetal. Thus the uppermost leaves supply the stem and roots, and intermediate leaves transport carbohydrates both upward and downward.

Only little structural tissue is formed in shoot regions when leaves are expanding. When a leaf is almost fully expanded the cambium of the stem internode to which the leaf is attached becomes active. A mature leaf preferentially provides carbohydrates to the internode to which it is attached, but also transports carbohydrates to a number of lower internodes. Thus many leaves contribute photosynthate for cambial growth of an internode. The proportion of current photosynthate used in cambial growth increases with tree size (Larson and Gordon, 1969).

As mentioned in Chapter 2, the xylem sheath laid down by the cambium varies at different stem heights of mature trees. Hence, utilization of the total carbohydrate pool is extremely variable over the stem axis. For example, in suppressed trees very little carbohydrate may be used in cambial growth at the stem base. By comparison, in vigorous, open-grown trees more carbohydrates are used in cambial growth in the lower than in the upper stem. These patterns reflect variations in amounts and physiological efficiency of leaves on branches located at different stem heights. In " average " pines the branches in the upper third of the crown contribute most to diameter growth of the stem. They are the most vigorous branches and they have the shortest translocation path to the main stem (Larson, 1969b).

Stiell (1969) studied the contributions of variously located branch whorls to xylem increment in 13-year-old *Pinus resinosa* trees. Cambial growth at various stem heights was studied following removal of single whorls of branches located at different levels in the crown. Cambial growth of an internode within the crown was influenced primarily by contributions of the branch whorl immediately above it. Cambial growth in the stem section just below the crown depended largely on contributions from all whorls. Cambial growth of no part of the main stem was wholly dependent on any one whorl of branches.

Respiratory Consumption of Carbohydrates

A substantial portion of the carbohydrates along the stem and branches is used in respiration near the cambium. Such consumption is restricted to the relatively few living cells of the sapwood and bark (Goodwin and Goddard, 1940). On the average, respiration is confined to cambial cells, and newly formed living xylem and phloem derivatives and to the small percentage of the sapwood cells which comprise the living axial and ray parenchyma cells. Goodwin and Goddard (1940) found higher rates of oxygen consumption in the phloem than in all but the most recent sapwood of *Acer rubrum* and *Fraxinus nigra*. In the inner sapwood the individual ray and axial parenchyma cells have high respiration rates, but these living cells comprise only a small portion of the xylem, which is made up mostly of dead cells. The rate of respiration in tree stems decreases rapidly from the outer to the inner sapwood, with the rate of decrease influenced by rates of xylem differentiation and differences in distribution of living cells among species. In *Fagus*, respiration decreased much more gradually than in *Quercus* from the cambium inward, reflecting differences in distribution of living cells (Möller, 1946).

HORMONAL GROWTH REGULATORS

Various hormonal growth regulators, including growth promoters and inhibitors, play a major role in such phases of cambial growth as cell division, increase in size of cambial derivatives, secondary wall thickening, transition from earlywood to latewood production, formation of reaction xylem and phloem, and cessation of cambial growth. Among the growth promoters auxins, gibberellins, and cytokinins appear to be variously involved.

It has long been known that shoots of woody plants exert an influence on cambial activity. Evidence for the regulatory role of shoot products on cambial activity exists in correlations between bud growth in the spring and basipetal migration of the xylem growth wave, initiation of xylem production, and arrested cambial activity in defoliated or disbudded trees, or below stem girdles.

Loomis (1935, 1938) and Wardrop (1957) found that normal cambial activity depended on uninterrupted phloem connections from the shoots to the cambium. Cambial growth was stopped rapidly by stem girdling at various times in the growing season to interrupt downward movement of shoot products in the phloem. If leaf-bearing branches were present below the ring, cambial growth continued below the branches. If the ring was made below the lowest branch, cambial growth below the ring ceased quickly.

Evert and Kozlowski (1967) showed in girdling experiments that normal development of xylem and phloem in *Populus tremuloides* depended upon a continuous supply of currently translocated regulatory substances, presumably hormones, from the leaves. Blocking the phloem during the dormant season or at various times during the growing season had marked effects on subsequent production and differentiation of xylem and phloem. When the phloem was interrupted during the dormant season, no xylem differentiation occurred below the block during the next growing season. However, when the phloem was blocked shortly after seasonal cambial activity began, the relatively few xylem elements produced were short and did not have normally thickened walls. The most conspicuous effect of isolating the lower stem from the shoot system by blocking the phloem was curtailment of

secondary wall formation in both xylem and phloem. When phloem blocks
were applied in mid-season, the first part of the annual xylem increment was
normal with respect to wall thickness and cell length. The cell walls of the
other cell types in the xylem varied from normal thickness in the first-formed
part of the increment to absence of thickening in the last part. The xylem
increment ended with several rows of parenchyma strands and scattered,
atypically short vessel members. The parenchyma cell walls were primary
in nature and unlignified; the vessel member walls were thickened and
lignified.

Phloem blocks applied during the dormant season did not prevent limited
phloem differentiation in the spring but prevented normal phloem development in *Populus tremuloides*. The ultimate effect of isolating the lower stem
from shoot products, either during the dormant or growing season, was
subdivision of all fusiform cambial cells into parenchymatous elements. The
ultimate effect on the newly-formed phloem was early death of sieve elements.
It was unlikely that cambial activity was affected directly by availability of
foods as axial and ray parenchyma cells of the phloem contained abundant
starch below the level of the severed phloem. Although food supplies apparently were adequate, cambial activity appeared to be checked by regulatory influences on food utilization. Loomis (1935) also found that girdling
of twigs at a time when the cortex, wood rays, and pith in the twigs were
filled with starch, stopped cambial growth abruptly. This indicated that
availability of food was not controlling growth directly and placed considerable emphasis on hormonal control of cambial growth.

Hormonal Control of Cambial Division

It is widely believed that auxin from active buds moves down tree stems
to initiate seasonal xylem production. Auxin in *Pinus radiata* increased in
the upper stem in late winter and in the mid and lower stem in mid-spring,
a pattern consistent with auxin moving down the stem at that time (Shepherd
and Rowan, 1967). In *Pinus sylvestris* the formation of new xylem below
buds in the spring is preceded by bud growth. In decapitated pine stems the
formation of new xylem does not occur until outgrowth of interfascicular
buds. Application of IAA or NAA to the cut surfaces of decapitated stems
induces xylem formation (Hejnowicz and Tomaszewski, 1969).

There apparently are wide differences among ring-porous and diffuse-
porous angiosperms in the pattern of basipetal spread of initiation of cambial
activity in the spring, with the process occurring much faster in ring-porous
trees. This suggests a fundamental difference between ring-porous and diffuse-
porous angiosperms with respect to degree of dependency on hormonal
supplies from the buds to the lower stem. Wareing (1951) found limited
cambial activity subsequent to disbudding of *Fraxinus excelsior* trees, and
none in *Acer pseudoplatanus*. In *Fraxinus excelsior* the stimulus to initiation

of cambial activity moved basipetally and was stopped by phloem interruption. Renewed cambial activity occurred some distance below the stem
girdle. However, the stimulus for such activity originated at positions of
adventitious buds, even though they had been removed earlier. In contrast,
in diffuse porous *Acer pseudoplatanus* and *Tilia europaea* trees, no cambial
activity was observed below nodes when there was no bud growth. Only
very weak activity occurred in the form of a few isolated vessels produced
where large buds had grown out. In both ring porous and diffuse porous
trees, vessels could originate from adventitious buds but their stimulation
was much stronger in ring porous species. Wareing (1951) postulated that
in ring porous species a reserve of auxin precursor that was present throughout the trees was available at the time of emergence from dormancy and
that, in contrast, diffuse porous species as a group accumulated little or no
such hormonal reserve.

Digby and Wareing (1966b) showed that in diffuse-porous trees the expanding buds appeared to be the primary source of auxins. There was a
gradient of auxin below the buds which was correlated with downward
spread of cambial activity. In contrast in ring porous species, an auxin precursor was present before buds opened and it was postulated that it was
converted to auxin at the time of bud opening generally throughout the tree
axis, accounting for rapid resumption of growth throughout the cambial sheath.

Digby and Wareing (1966b) confirmed the hypothesis of Wareing and
Roberts (1956) that continued cambial activity in ring porous species after
the cessation of shoot growth was due to auxin production by the mature
leaves. Both ring porous *Robinia pseudoacacia* and diffuse porous *Betula
pubescens* were given each of the following treatments: (1) long days for 5
weeks; (2) short days for 3 weeks (by which time extension growth ceased)
followed by short days for 2 weeks; and (3) short days for 3 weeks (by which
time extension growth ceased) followed by long days for 2 weeks. With both
Robinia and *Betula*, short-day treatment resulted in cessation of shoot
elongation or bud growth when plants were returned from short-day conditions. In *Robinia pseudoacacia*, high auxin levels were present in mature
leaves both after long-day and short-day treatment followed by long-day
treatment. Auxin was not detected in mature leaves in the short-day treatment.
These observations were interpreted as showing that continued cambial
activity under long-day conditions was regulated by auxin produced by
mature leaves. In *Betula pubescens* auxin was produced by mature leaves
under long days. No auxin was produced after change from short-day to
long-day conditions and, in this respect, *Betula* differed from *Robinia*. There
was an indication that in *Betula* a change occurred in the leaves under short-
day conditions so they subsequently could not produce auxin on transfer
to long-day conditions.

Evidence is also available that growth promoters other than auxin are important in control of cell division in the cambium. Tissue culture experiments with material derived from *Acer pseudoplatanus* cambium showed that GA, at concentrations of 15–50 ppm promoted cell division (Digby, Thomas, and Wareing, 1964). Stimulation of cell division was slightly enhanced by adding IAA. With increase in cell number as a result of adding GA, there was a corresponding decrease in mean cell size, indicating that GA was not promoting cell expansion to the same extent as it was stimulating cell division. Bradley and Crane (1957) found that application of GA stimulated xylem production in apricot spur shoots. Waisel, Noah, and Fahn (1966b) found similar results for *Eucalyptus camaldulensis*. The effects of GA, however, are not identical to those of auxin for Wareing, Hanney, and Digby (1964), DeMaggio (1966), and Digby and Wareing (1966a) reported that exogenous GA stimulated phloem production over xylem production. Cytokinins also promote cell division (Miller *et al.*, 1955). Bottomley *et al.* (1963) isolated kinin-like growth factors from woody plants and it is probable that cytokinins, as well as auxins, and gibberellins, play a role in control of cell division in the cambium.

Hormonal Control of Differentiation of Cambial Derivatives

Considerable evidence is available of hormonal control of various aspects of differentiation of cambial derivatives. Several growth regulators are involved, but with evidence at present available assigning a predominating role to auxin.

Several early investigators showed that exogenous auxin stimulated both cambial division and subsequent differentiation of xylem derivatives (Gouwentak, 1941). Voluminous evidence is available showing that auxin stimulates cell expansion (Leopold, 1964). IAA also increases incorporation of ^{14}C into cell walls (Ordin, 1958, 1960), emphasizing that auxin generally is important in regulation of cell differentiation.

Wareing, Hanney, and Digby (1964) applied IAA and GA alone and in combination to disbudded winter shoots of woody plants. Whereas both IAA and GA could promote cambial division only, IAA stimulated further differentiation of the xylem cells including increase in size, development of secondary walls, and lignification (Fig. 3.13).

Digby and Wareing (1966a) applied various concentrations of IAA and GA in lanolin paste to nondormant disbudded shoots of *Populus robusta*, *Vitis vinifera*, and *Robinia pseudoacacia*. Some tissue formed on the xylem side of the cambium when GA alone was applied but no differentiated xylem was produced in the absence of IAA. Cambial derivatives of *Populus robusta* did not elongate without IAA. There was a marked increase in fiber length between 0 and 100 ppm IAA, but no further increase between 100 and 500

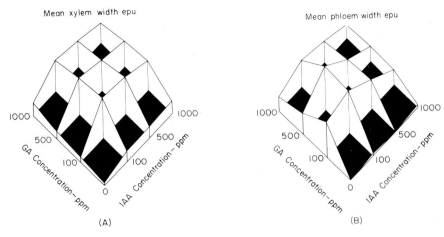

FIG. 3.13. Synergistic effects of gibberrellin (GA) and indoleacetic acid (IAA) on development of xylem (A) and phloem (B) in *Populus*. The growth regulator concentrations shown were those in lanolin and do not indicate concentration in the tissues. Xylem width and phloem width are given in eye-piece units (epu). [From Wareing, Hanney, and Digby (1964).]

ppm. Applied GA affected elongation of fibers, but only in the presence of IAA (Fig. 3.14). IAA application at 100 ppm also resulted in production of elongated vessel elements (Fig. 3.15). No further stimulation of elongation occurred when GA was applied.

Diameters of cambial derivatives also are controlled by auxin. Larson (1960, 1962a,b) showed that exogenously applied auxin increased tracheid diameter in *Pinus resinosa*. Digby and Wareing (1966a) applied a range of concentrations of IAA from 0 to 1000 ppm, with 100 ppm of GA in each case, to cut stumps of young *Robinia pseudoacacia* plants which had been subjected to short days and were not showing cambial activity. Vessel diameter was greater as IAA concentration was increased. When no IAA was included in a treatment, no differentiated xylem was produced.

Interactions among Growth Regulators in Control of Cambial Growth

Specific effects on cambial growth have been linked to individual growth regulators, with an important role assigned to auxin. Considerable evidence for the presence of auxin in cambial tissue is available. For example, Shepherd and Rowan (1967) confirmed this for *Pinus radiata* and Wodzicki (1968) for *Pinus sylvestris*. Balatinecz and Kennedy (1967) established an important role of auxin in earlywood–latewood relations. By applying auxin extracted from phloem of mature *Larix* trees they were able to induce earlywood cells in stems of young trees that had been producing latewood. Despite the existence of such evidence for a major role of auxin in regulation of cambial growth, other evidence indicates that normal cambial growth is the end result of balances of several growth regulators (including promoters and inhibitors) and synergistic effects among them. (Fig. 3.13).

Digby and Wareing (1966a) applied IAA and GA in various proportions to disbudded shoots of *Populus robusta* and studied subsequent cambial growth. When GA alone was applied, some xylem subsequently formed. However, no differentiated xylem was produced in the absence of IAA and fully differentiated xylem was produced with IAA alone. Maximum production of fully differentiated xylem occurred at low GA and high IAA concentrations. In contrast, phloem production was promoted by high GA and low IAA concentrations. No new phloem was produced with IAA alone, but a considerable amount formed with GA alone. IAA also promoted elongation of fibers and vessels. GA affected elongation of fibers, but only in the presence of IAA. In *Robinia pseudoacacia* vessel diameter increased with increasing IAA concentration. This suggested that in ring porous species there was a reduction in the endogenous auxin at the time of the earlywood to latewood transition.

The importance of synergisms among various growth regulators was further illustrated by Roberts and Fosket (1966) who found an interaction of GA and IAA in differentiation of wound vessel members. Wodzicki (1965) concluded that interactions between growth promoters and inhibitors were involved in regulation of differentiation of xylem in *Larix*. He studied

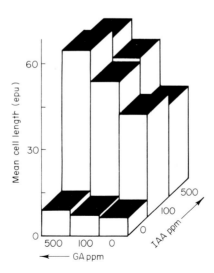

Fig. 3.14. Effect of IAA and GA on length of xylem fibers in *Populus robusta*. Vertical axis is length in eye-piece units (epu). [From Digby and Wareing (1966a).]

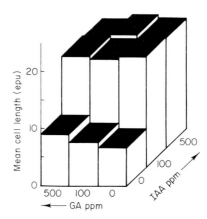

FIG. 3.15. Effect of IAA and GA on length of xylem vessels in *Populus robusta*. Vertical axis is cell length in eye-piece units (epu). [From Digby and Wareing (1966a).]

interactions of IAA with inhibitory substances extracted from *Larix* tissues. High concentrations of inhibitors reduced the effect of auxin on xylem differentiation. A slight synergistic action was shown between IAA and the inhibitors, at low concentrations of both substances. Adding to the complexity of studying internal control of cambial growth is the difficulty of interpreting experiments with exogenous growth regulators because they may stimulate metabolic activity to produce other internal growth regulators. Hejnowicz and Tomaszewski (1969) found that GA and cytokinins applied together with auxins to detopped *Pinus sylvestris* stems accelerated the cambial activity which had been induced by the auxins.

Robards, Davidson, and Kidwai (1969) applied aqueous solutions of IAA, NAA, 2,4-D, GA, FAP (6-furfurylaminopurine), myo-inositol, and sucrose singly and in mixtures to the apical ends of disbudded stem segments of *Salix*. After 4 weeks each of these substances had some effect on xylem differentiation. Production and differentiation of xylem cells were increased most when IAA, GA, and FAP were applied together but the response was greater when these were augmented by inositol or sucrose. When the chemicals were applied as mixtures their action was strongly synergistic. Such experiments further emphasize that only limited information can be obtained by exogenous applications of single substances and observing the plant response.

Evidence is also available of interactions of growth regulators and other internal factors, such as water deficits, in control of cambial growth (Doley and Leyton, 1968). This is discussed further in another section of this chapter.

Hormonal Control of Reaction Wood Formation

The formation of reaction wood is widely recognized as a geotropic phenomenon which involves internal redistribution of hormonal growth regulators and this is supported by strong evidence. For example, compression wood forms toward the focus of gravitational attraction under conditions of a reversed gravitational field. This has been demonstrated by growing trees upside down and having compression wood form on the morphologically upper sides of branches, which physically are the lower sides (Wershing and Bailey, 1942). When trees are grown on a revolving table the compression wood forms on the outer side of the stem (Jaccard, 1939).

The formation of reaction wood in both angiosperms and gymnosperms appears to be internally controlled by redistribution of hormonal growth regulators in inclined stems with auxin playing a primary role. Compression wood usually is associated with high auxin levels and tension wood with low auxin levels.

Necesany (1958) found that more auxin accumulated on the lower side of leaning angiosperm stems than on the upper side. This was confirmed by Leach and Wareing (1967) who noted a ratio of auxin of upper and lower sides of horizontal *Populus* stems to be about 40–60. However, they also found a greater concentration of inhibitors on the lower side.

Evidence for hormonal control of reaction wood formation comes from

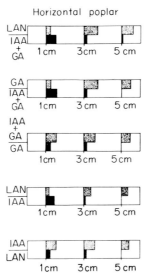

FIG. 3.16. Effect of indoleacetic acid (IAA) and/or gibberellin (GA) to apical ends of horizontal *Populus* shoots. The stippled and black areas indicate width of new xylem tissue on upper and lower sides at different distances from the apex. [From Wareing *et al.* (1964).]

tree responses to applications of hormonal growth regulators to tree stems. A few examples will be given. Necesany (1958) inhibited formation of tension wood on the upper side of inclined *Populus* shoots by high applications of auxin to that side. Hormonal regulation of reaction wood was further investigated by Wareing, Hanney, and Digby (1964). To test gravitational effects on hormonal distribution they applied IAA and GA, alone and together, to upper and lower halves of disbudded, horizontal *Populus* shoots and studied subsequent xylem development. At 1 cm from the point of treatment there was more cambial activity on either side depending on whether IAA was applied to the upper or lower half. At 3 and 5 cm, more xylem consistently formed on the upper side. GA in combination with IAA produced greater response than IAA alone. However, the same general pattern occurred with IAA as with both IAA and GA, indicating that only IAA was redistributed as a gravitational response (Fig. 3.16).

Because the lack of cambial activity on the lower side at 5 cm from the apical end might be due to too low or too high auxin concentrations, further tests were conducted. IAA was applied to the lower halves of apices of horizontal *Populus* shoots. GA plus IAA were applied to lower halves of other shoots, and in both sets IAA was applied to the lower side at 5 cm from the apex. As may be seen in Fig. 3.17 no new xylem formed subsequently on the lower side at 4 cm with IAA alone, and very little with both IAA and GA. However, at 1 cm beyond the second IAA application, abundant xylem formed. This emphasized that absence of xylem development at 5 cm was caused by auxin deficiency rather than supraoptimal concentrations.

The fact that gelatinous fibers sometimes are produced on the side opposite to that of maximum xylem production in angiosperm stems or branches suggests that there may be more than a single pathway to the gravitational stimulus. As suggested by Robards (1965), a growth hormone could be the

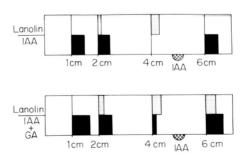

Fig. 3.17. Effect of second application of IAA to the lower side of horizontal *Populus* shoots at a point 5 cm from the apical end. See text for explanation. [From Wareing *et al.* (1964).]

starting point of two pathways, one leading to the development of gelatinous fibers and the other to variations in radial cambial division.

Although it has not been possible to induce formation of reaction xylem in angiosperms with auxin applications (Wardrop, 1965b), the responses of trees to applied antiauxins have been interpreted as evidence that formation of tension wood is associated with auxin deficiency. Kennedy and Farrar (1965a) applied 2,3,5-triiodobenzoic acid (TIBA) in lanolin paste to stems of 4-month-old *Ulmus americana* seedlings; TIBA is known to act as an IAA antagonist either through direct competition with auxin or by blocking its movement within the plant. The rapidly formed xylem which was produced in response to TIBA resembled tension wood. It had smaller vessels than normal xylem, and contained gelatinous fibers. Tension wood formation also was induced in stems of *Acer rubrum* seedlings by applications of TIBA to stems. IAA, NAA or 2,4-D suppressed the capacity of TIBA to induce formation of tension wood (Cronshaw and Morey, 1965; Morey and Cronshaw, 1968a). 2-4-dinitrophenol (DNP), which like TIBA interferes with polar auxin transport, also induced formation of tension wood in *Acer rubrum* seedlings (Morey and Cronshaw, 1968c). Also when *Acer rubrum* or *Ulmus americana* seedlings were placed horizontally, the normal differentiation of tension wood fibers was suppressed by IAA, NAA or 2,4-D (Morey and Cronshaw, 1968b). These observations further emphasized the importance of auxins in regulation of normal cambial growth.

Compression wood, which forms on the lower side of leaning gymnosperm stems and branches is believed to form because of a high auxin gradient, causing mobilization of foods. Wershing and Bailey (1942) caused compression wood to form by applying high concentrations of auxin to gymnosperm stems. The compression wood formed by the interaction of auxin and sucrose has large-diameter tracheids with very thick walls. Apparently the cambial zone of a vertically oriented tree stem appears to be a weaker sink for assimilates than is the cambium along the lower side of an inclined tree. It often is possible to induce compression wood to form with high applications of IAA. Such wood cannot be separated physically or chemically from a naturally occurring compression wood (Larson, 1969b).

Abnormal wood resembling compression wood often is produced as a result of infestation by the aphid, *Adelges piceae*. This insect feeds in cortical parenchyma cells of *Abies* species. It inserts its stylets intercellularly and injects saliva. The saliva appears to promote an abnormal concentration of growth hormones which cause the abnormal wood to form (Balch, 1952; Balch, Clark, and Bonga, 1954). The wood produced following *Adelges* infestation resembles compression wood in having wider xylem rings, dark red color, higher percentage of latewood, shorter and more rounded tracheids with intercellular spaces, thicker cell walls with helical checks, higher lignin content, and poorer physical properties than normal wood. However, there also are some important differences between compression wood and aphid-affected wood. For example, the number of rays in compression wood varies little or not at all from that in normal wood. Aphid-affected wood has about twice as many rays and larger rays, and many more xylem parenchyma strands than does normal wood (Smith, 1967).

Internal Water Deficits

Internal water deficits inhibit cambial growth through their effects on cell division, enlargement, and differentiation of cambial derivatives. The exact mechanism by which internal water deficit affects cambial growth is complicated and probably is partially indirect by inhibiting synthesis and downward translocation of carbohydrates and hormonal growth regulators. Water stress effects also appear to be partly direct through a water deficit in the cambial cells (Kramer, 1964).

Water deficits, which often develop rapidly in leaves, inhibit photosynthesis largely because of increased resistance to CO_2 diffusion resulting from stomatal closure and decreased permeability of mesophyll cells (Kozlowski, 1964). Even mild internal water deficits in leaves may decrease photosynthesis. Brix (1962) found that CO_2 uptake by *Pinus taeda* seedlings declined as diffusion pressure deficit (DPD) of leaves rose above 4 atm. When DPD reached 11 atm photosynthesis was negligible.

Water stresses in shoots also reduce production of growth promoters such as auxin. Furthermore, under water deficits the basipetal translocation of photosynthetic products from the leaves declines. Roberts (1964) observed that increasing internal water deficits in *Liriodendron tulipifera* leaves decreased both the uptake of radiocarbon by leaves and the amount translocated out of them. Decreased uptake of ^{14}C by leaves appeared to result from stomatal closure. The amount of radiocarbon translocated out of leaves, the rate of translocation, and the distance to which it was transported, were greatly reduced as internal water deficits increased.

Evidence is available that internal water deficits also have a direct inhibitory effect on cambial activity. The rate of cell division declines greatly during increasing internal stress. For example a total of only two xylem derivatives in a radial file were produced by *Pinus radiata* trees during a month of drought. Following a substantial rainfall and rehydration of trees, cambial activity accelerated until a maximum of 12 new cambial derivatives per file were produced per week (Shepherd, 1964). Within a few weeks, however, the trees were again exposed to drought and a rapid decline in cell size occurred along the whole length of the stem. The change in cell size was attributed to a rapid decrease in cell turgor which tended to override the effects of auxin in determining cell size. Considerable evidence is available that high turgor is required for cell enlargement and cell wall deposition. Reduction in turgor reduces enlargement of cells, even when auxin is present. Even mild internal water deficits reduced incorporation of ^{14}C into cell walls (Ordin, 1958; 1960). Whitmore and Zahner (1967) concluded that water deficits had a direct effect on cell wall metabolism of cambial derivatives, independent of control of cambial growth by crown tissues. Incceasing water deficit with polyethylene glycol influenced incorporation of glucose into cell walls of differentiating secondary xylem of *Pinus sylvestris* Tissues of

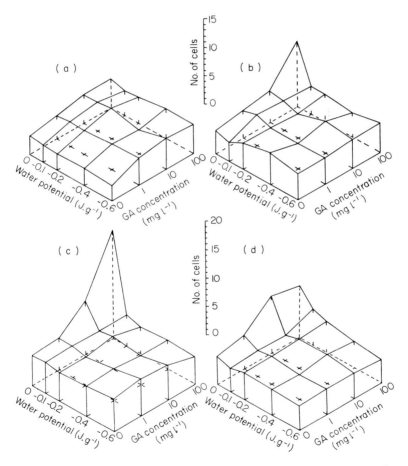

FIG. 3.18. Interactions between water potential and IAA and GA in their effects on production of cambial derivatives in *Fraxinus excelsior*. (a) Zero IAA; (b) 1 mgl^{-1} IAA; (c) 10 mg l^{-1} IAA; (d) 100 mg l^{-1} IAA. From Doley and Leyton (1968).]

TABLE 3.6

<small>EFFECTS OF WATER STRESS INDUCED BY POLYETHYLENE GLYCOL ON
ACTIVITY OF INCORPORATED GLUCOSE-^{14}C IN *Pinus sylvestris* CAMBIAL
DERIVATIVES[a]</small>

Treatment percent PEG (w/v)	Water potential (atm)			Counts/minute in total cell walls (mean ± SE)
	Initial	Final	Mean	
1	− 2.2	− 4.0	− 3.1	3971 ± 183
10	− 5.0	− 6.6	− 5.8	2680 ± 306
20	−14.1	−12.8	−13.5	2544 ± 298
30	−38.8	−19.4	−28.1	1858 ± 231

[a] From Whitmore and Zahner (1967).

developing xylem were excised and incubated in solutions containing labelled
glucose and varying concentrations of polyethylene glycol. Decreasing water
potential from −3.1 atm to −5.8 atm reduced incorporation of glucose into
cell walls by a third. A further decrease in water potential to −28.1 atm
reduced glucose formation by more than half (Table 3.6).

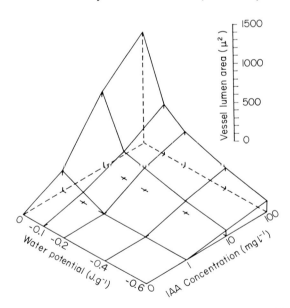

FIG. 3.19. Interaction between IAA concentration and water potential in their effects on
cross-sectional areas of lumens in vessels of *Fraxinus excelsior*. [From Doley and Leyton
(1968).]

Doley and Leyton (1968) studied the effects of water potential and hormonal growth promoters (IAA and GA) on cambial growth of *Fraxinus excelsior* stems. Water potential as well as IAA, GA, and their interactions had very marked effects on cambial growth (Figs. 3.18, 3.19). The effect of decreasing the water potential was to depress the effect of growth regulators. However, the greatest influence on cambial growth was exerted by water potential, with even small increases in water deficits inhibiting cell division and expansion.

Mineral Nutrients

Where a mineral deficiency exists the addition of fertilizers may be expected to accelerate cambial growth by increasing the physiological efficiency of existing foliage and sometime later by increasing the number and size of leaves by stimulating formation of shoot primordia and their subsequent expansion (Chapter 8, Volume I). The end result of these changes is an increased flow of growth regulating metabolites from the crown downward in the stem.

Data of Viro (1965) showed both an increase in chlorophyll content of needles and an increase in needle volume following addition of N fertilizers to *Picea abies* trees. In the second year after N fertilizers were added, the weight of new needles was greater by 48% than in unfertilized control trees. Maki (1960) noted that needles of *Pinus taeda* trees turned dark green within 2 weeks after N fertilizers were applied, emphasizing a rapid influence of fertilizers on chlorophyll synthesis in existing foliage.

The inhibitory effects of mineral deficiency on photosynthesis are well known (Kozlowski and Keller, 1966). Among the macronutrients nitrogen deficiency appears to inhibit photosynthesis more than lack of other elements. In apple trees, for example, photosynthesis of nitrogen-deficient leaves was only 37% of controls whereas leaves low in phosphorus and potassium had rates of about 91% of controls (Childers and Cowart, 1935). Keller and Koch (1962a) noted that at 40,000 lux net photosynthesis of nitrogen-deficient *Populus* x *euramericana* leaves was only 60% of that of high-nitrogen leaves. Keller and Wehrmann (1963) found also that nitrogen, chlorophyll content, and photosynthesis were well correlated in *Pinus* and *Picea* seedlings.

Phosphorus deficiency may block photosynthesis by interfering with phosphate-bound energy transfer of the ADP–ATP system. However, the inhibitory effect of phosphorus deficiency is rather weak. The rate of net photosynthesis may be decreased by potassium deficiency through inhibition of photosynthetic energy transfer and increased respiration (Pirson, 1958). Although magnesium is a part of the chlorophyll molecule, a deficiency of this element did not appreciably influence photosynthesis of *Populus* x *euramericana* (Neuwirth and Fritszche, 1964).

Deficiencies of various micronutrients have marked inhibitory effects on photosynthesis. A shortage of iron checks photosynthesis by causing chlorosis and influencing activity of enzymes. In *Populus americana* chlorophyll and iron contents of leaves were closely correlated. The rate of photosynthesis increased with iron content and light intensity up to 40,000 lux. At that light intensity absorption of CO_2 was decreased as much as half by iron deficiency. Leaves were small and palisade cells shorter than normal in iron-deficient trees (Keller and Koch, 1962b, 1964). Manganese deficiency reduced absorption of CO_2 by *Aleurites* largely by decreasing leaf areas (Reuther and Burrows, 1942). Copper and zinc deficiencies may reduce photosynthesis markedly even before symptoms are very obvious. For example, photosynthesis was reduced by 30% by zinc deficiency and 55% by copper deficiency before chlorosis or necrosis occurred. And when deficiency was severe, CO_2 uptake was reduced by 80% by copper deficiency and 62% by zinc deficiency (Loustalot *et al.*, 1945).

Control of Earlywood–Latewood Relations

Considerable interest has been shown in environmental and internal control of earlywood and latewood formation. Both density and specific gravity of wood are a function of the proportion of earlywood to latewood in the annual ring. Much of the interest in earlywood–latewood relations reflects the importance of specific gravity of wood to its utilization. For example, the most desirable *Pseudotsuga menziesii* wood for structural timber has been considered to be that of high specific gravity (Kennedy, 1961). Latewood, having a larger proportion of cell wall substance per unit of volume than the carlywood in the same ring, has a high specific gravity. In gymnosperms the average specific gravity of latewood often is about two to three times as high as that of earlywood. Specific gravity variations in four species of young pines of the southern United States were the following (Paul and Smith, 1950).

Species	Specific gravity	
	Earlywood	Latewood
Pinus palustris	0.280	0.690
Pinus taeda	0.310	0.625
Pinus echinata	0.265	0.600
Pinus elliottii	0.275	0.570

Within an annual xylem increment the width of the earlywood band generally decreases and width of the latewood band increases toward the stem base. This basic pattern can be modified to various degrees by a variety of influences, such as tree age, competition, crown size, site, moisture availability, cultural practices, and inheritance (Paul, 1950; Harris, 1955; Erickson and Lambert, 1958; Rendle and Phillips, 1958; Zahner and Whitmore, 1960; Larson, 1957; Smith and Wilsie, 1961; Kraus and Spurr, 1961; Zobel, 1961). These effects often are confounded but their influence appears to be mediated to a large extent through internal food, hormone, and water relations in the tree.

Earlywood tracheids form when internal control mechanisms favor their radial expansion over secondary wall thickening. In *Pinus resinosa*, radial expansion of tracheids usually occurs during the period of shoot growth as long as the needles are elongating. Later in the season, marked reduction in tracheid diameter to produce latewood occurs at the base of the stem and subsequently occurs upward in the stem and outward in the growth ring. Such a pattern continues until tracheids with narrow diameters (latewood) are laid down late in the season and before the cambium becomes dormant (Fig. 3.20).

In gymnosperm trees the earlywood tracheids are wider toward the base of the stem than at the top within the same xylem increment The transition between the last earlywood and first formed latewood tracheids of the annual ring also is sharper in the lower stem than in the upper stem. This is partly due to larger diameter earlywood cells and normal diameter latewood cells

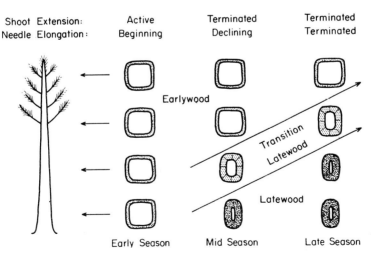

FIG. 3.20. Seasonal variation in formation of earlywood, transition latewood, and latewood at different stem heights in *Pinus resinosa*. [From Larson (1969b).]

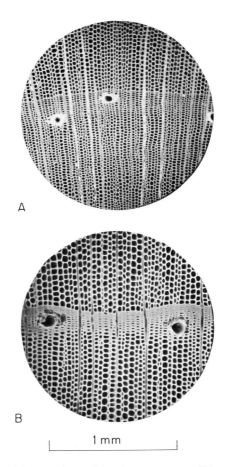

A

B

| 1 mm |

Fig. 3.21. Earlywood–latewood transition in upper stem (A) and lower stem (B) of 10-year-old *Pinus taeda* tree. The transition is sharper in the lower stem because of larger diameter earlywood cells and thicker walled latewood cells in the lower stem than in the upper stem. Photo courtesy U.S. Forest Service, Forest Products Laboratory.

in the lower stem. The very thick walls of latewood cells in the lower stem also contribute to the sharp transition. The narrow diameter earlywood cells in the upper stem contribute to making the earlywood–latewood transition less distinct than it is in the lower stem (Fig. 3.21).

Some tracheids fit the usual definition of latewood because of a decrease in radial diameter, without appreciable change in wall thickness. Other tracheids, however, become latewood because of an increase in wall thickness without change in radial diameter. Both dimensions show continuous change from the top of the stem toward the base until true latewood forms. In upper parts of the stem "transition latewood" often forms which cannot be conveniently classified as either true earlywood or latewood (Fig. 3.22) (Larson, 1969b).

In *Pinus resinosa* the beginning of cell wall thickening in latewood tracheids occurs after shoot elongation ceases, sometimes before and sometimes after the decrease in tracheid diameter (Larson, 1964). Changes in cell wall thickness are not as readily manipulated by environment as are changes in cell diameter. Such observations suggest that cell diameter and wall thickness of xylem cells may be regulated by different mechanisms. Hence, it appears likely that the internal control system which accounts for latewood formation may be rather complex and involve several processes and regulatory components.

HORMONAL CONTROL OF EARLYWOOD–LATEWOOD RELATIONS

As Larson (1962a, b, 1963a, c, 1964) emphasized, crown-produced hormones play a very important role in regulating tracheid diameter. He suggested that environmental factors such as photoperiod or drought affected shoot growth which in turn altered auxin synthesis and its basipetal translocation to directly regulate tracheid diameter in the stem. Larson (1960) stated that large diameter, earlywood cells were produced during the period of shoot growth and high auxin synthesis. Narrow diameter latewood cells were produced following cessation of terminal growth and consequent reduction in auxin synthesis. A growth inhibiting system could also become increasingly active at this time. Larson stated that any factor that caused terminal elongation to begin prematurely or to cease brought about a respective increase or decrease in cell diameter. The extent to which a change in terminal activity registered a concomitant change in tracheid development depended on the intensity of the apical stimulus. Thus a false ring originating

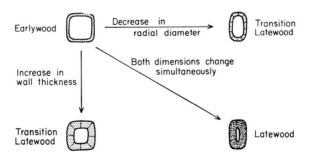

FIG. 3.22. Development of transition latewood in *Pinus resinosa* either by decrease in radial diameter or by increase in wall thickness. [From Larson (1969b).]

from a second flush of shoot growth might be evident only in the uppermost parts of the stem.

Larson's emphasis on the decisive influence of auxin in control of latewood formation was based on experiments with *Pinus resinosa* (Larson, 1964). In young plants of this species he found the transition from earlywood to latewood to coincide approximately with cessation of shoot elongation. As soon as internode extension ceased, needles began to elongate rapidly. At approximately the same time the formation of narrow diameter tracheids occurred, first at the base of the stem and then at successively higher levels. When Larson (1962a) subjected *Pinus resinosa* trees to short days the growth of needles was first reduced and later ceased, and this change was followed by a decrease in tracheid diameter. Finally all xylem production ceased. In trees subjected to long days, the needles continued to elongate and often became much longer than normal. Under long days the production of large diameter, earlywood type cells continued as needles elongated but eventually both needle growth and production of large diameter cells stopped.

Larson (1963c) found in irrigation experiments that under drought conditions *Pinus resinosa* trees responded rapidly by producing small diameter tracheids. He interpreted the effect of drought to be an indirect one. The direct effect of drought was considered to be on leaf development and the decrease in tracheid diameter to reflect the response of needles. In trees in which shoot growth, and especially needle elongation, was suppressed by short days, irrigation did not cause large diameter cells to form. Removal of current-year needles at the time of irrigation prevented production of large diameter cells in trees exposed to long or short days. Larson interpreted the influence of internal water deficits and photoperiod on tracheid diameter as indirect, involving first a direct effect on apical growth followed by changes in auxin synthesis. Auxin from the leaves was considered to be the specific, direct regulator of tracheid diameter and the influence of other factors, especially water deficits, to be indirect.

Some investigators have found certain aspects of the earlywood–latewood transition difficult to reconcile in terms of a mechanism involving auxin control alone. Zelawski (1957) and Wodzicki (1961) did not find a direct relation between shoot elongation and thickening of tracheid walls in *Larix polonica*. Zelawski (1957) reported that thick-walled tracheids could form during continued shoot extension under long photoperiods. Wodzicki (1961) further demonstrated that thin-walled tracheids could form even after shoot growth ceased. Some decrease of the radial diameter of tracheids occurred when the top of the main shoot only was subjected to short-day conditions while the lateral shoots remained intact, but such treatment did not change cell wall thickness. This might indicate that radial diameter of tracheids, unlike cell wall thickness, depended on extension growth of shoots. Wodzicki (1964) concluded that change in growth inhibitor content, rather than in growth promoter content, was the primary factor controlling cell wall thickening in *Larix decidua* tracheids under various photoperiodic conditions. Nevertheless, he also recognized an influence of growth promoters. His conclusions were based on (1) correlation between accumulation of inhibitors in the cortex and thickening of cell walls, (2) lack of correlation of cell wall thickening with growth promoters, (3) formation of thick-walled tracheids independent of shoot elongation, and (4) indirect evidence that differences in photosynthetic rates probably were not directly connected with different types of xylem formed under similar photoperiodic conditions.

In some species the correlation of seasonal changes of auxin and certain aspects of cambial activity is difficult. After a high accumulation in the spring the amount of auxin in shoots of many species declines rapidly and, relatively early in the growing season, it may be much less than shortly after cambial growth began. Wodzicki (1965), for example, could not detect auxin-like substances in the cortex of *Larix* as much as 60 days before latewood formation began. Hence, seasonal changes in cambial activity and full differentiation of the annual ring could not be explained solely by control of auxin-like substances. At the end of the season, however, inhibitors were present in the cortical tissues of *Larix*. These presumably were similar to those which accumulated under short-day conditions. The increase in inhibitors in cortical tissues was preceded by their accumulation in fully grown needles and shoot apices. Decapitation of shoots in plants under short-day conditions caused growth inhibitors to accumulate. Wodzicki concluded that the inhibitors were formed in the fully grown needles in late summer and transported to growth apices and cortical tissues. Accumulation of inhibitors in cortical tissues in late summer was followed closely by increase of cell number in the differentiated layer and, in turn, by formation of thick-walled tracheids. There was a time lag of about 30 days between increased accumulation of inhibitors in the cortex and production of thick-walled tracheids. Wodzicki (1965) emphasized the importance of interactions between growth promoters and inhibitors in control of xylem formation, with high concentrations of inhibitors reducing the promoting effect of auxin. At low concentrations of both substances a slight synergistic action was noted.

The evidence available at present is interpreted as showing that auxin undoubtedly plays a very important role in control of earlywood–latewood relations but its influence appears to be modified by the presence of other hormonal growth regulators. Wodzicki's (1965) observation of synergism between IAA and inhibitors in xylem differentiation of *Larix* would tend to support this view. Data presented by Balatinecz and Kennedy (1968) indicated that several endogenous growth regulators were involved to varying degrees in the mechanism of earlywood–latewood differentiation. They studied both the seasonal course of cambial activity and changes in endogenous growth substances in the cambial region of 40-year-old *Larix decidua* trees. They isolated 2 indole compounds from the cambium and tentatively identified them as 5-hydroxy IAA and IAA. They used a bioassay which involved the response of young *Larix* cambium and differentiating tracheids to isolated and synthetic growth regulators as a measure of biological activity. The bioassay showed that rapid cell division in the cambial zone and differentiation of earlywood tracheids in *Larix decidua* occurred with high concentrations of indolic growth promoting substances in the cambial zone and inner phloem. Reduction of cell division and production of latewood cells were associated with reduced concentrations of indolic growth promoting substances and increased concentrations of a phenolic growth inhibitor. These studies indicate that cambial growth appears to be regulated by the relative concentrations of different growth regulators rather than by auxin alone. This conclusion is supported by Kefford and Goldacre (1961) who emphasized that auxin was a predisposing agent rather than a determining one in plant growth.

WATER DEFICITS IN CONTROL OF EARLYWOOD–LATEWOOD RELATIONS

Water supply affects the time of latewood initiation, the length of time during which latewood is produced, and the transition between earlywood and latewood. Low water availability prompts early formation of latewood, and continued drought thereafter shortens the time during which latewood is produced. Krauss and Spurr (1961) found that in 1954 soil moisture

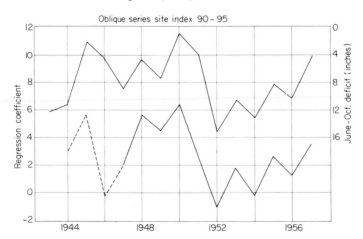

FIG. 3.23. Relation between latewood formation and summer water deficit. Upper curve represents soil water deficits, and the lower curve represents regression coefficients for latewood percentage on internodes from apex. [From Smith and Wilsie (1961).]

supplies in Michigan began to decline sharply on June 21, and drying continued until July 17 while the earlywood–latewood transition in *Pinus resinosa* lasted from June 28 to July 16. In 1955 soil moisture decline occurred earlier than in 1954, between May 23 and June 9, and the earlywood–latewood transition also occurred early, between May 27 and June 9. Kennedy (1961) reported that variation in latewood percentage between years was related significantly to precipitation. Highest latewood percentages were found in individual trees having the longest periods available for latewood formation. According to Smith and Wilsie (1961), large amounts of latewood were formed in *Pinus taeda* during years of low moisture stress, further emphasizing the influence of ample water supply in prolonging latewood growth (Fig. 3.23). Similarly, Foil (1961) found width of latewood in *Pinus caribaea* to be closely related to autumn moisture supply. Barrow's (1951) observation that *Pseudotsuga* trees growing nearest a river had higher latewood content than trees growing some distance away from the river further indicates the importance of available moisture in prolonging latewood production. The sharpness of transition between earlywood and latewood is influenced by level of available water near the latter part of the period of production. Harris (1955) noted that a severe drought at that time was reflected in a clear and sharp delineation of the earlywood–latewood boundary.

Zahner and Oliver (1962) emphasized the importance of internal water stress in earlywood–latewood relations. They showed that wood quality could be controlled by thinning and pruning. In *Pinus resinosa* trees released by thinning the changeover from earlywood to latewood occurred consistently about 2 weeks later than in the unthinned controls. The delay in changeover was associated with delay in soil moisture depletion and in periods of decreased diameter growth.

As Larson stated (1964), much evidence is available which indicates that internal water deficits may affect cambial growth indirectly by affecting metabolism of leaves. In addition, evidence is available of direct effects of water deficits on cambial growth. If cambial cells and their derivatives are severely dehydrated water deficits may play a more direct role in cell division and maturation because loss of turgor will then prevent auxin and food supplies from acting. That low cell turgor is one of the most common limitations on cell expansion is shown by experiments in which reduction of turgor decreased cell enlargement even in the presence of auxin (Ordin, 1950, 1960). Kramer (1964) pointed out that one or two days of high transpiration might produce sufficient internal water deficit in trees to stop growth immediately and directly because of low turgor, before a deficiency of auxin or carbohydrates could develop. However, water deficits which develop slowly over a period of days are accompanied by progressively reduced supplies of auxin and carbohydrates to the cambium.

In summary, it appears that both hormonal control and water deficits are involved in earlywood–latewood relations. In at least some species, interactions among growth regulators are involved, with auxin playing an important role. The available evidence also indicates that water deficits, operating both directly by controlling cell turgor and indirectly through crown metabolism, also appear to play an important role in control of earlywood and latewood formation.

Suggested Collateral Reading

Bormann, F. H. (1965). Changes in the growth pattern of white pine trees undergoing suppression. *Ecology* **46**, 269–277.

Church, T. W. (1949). Effects of defoliation on growth of certain conifers. *U.S. Forest Serv. Northeastern Forest Exp. Sta.* Paper 22.

Doley, D., and Leyton, L. (1968). Effects of growth regulating substances and water potential on the development of secondary xylem in *Fraxinus*. *New Phytol.* **67**, 579–594.

Duff, G. H., and Nolan, N. J. (1953). Growth and morphogenesis in the Canadian forest species. I. The controls of cambial and apical activity in *Pinus resinosa* Ait. *Can. J. Bot.* **31**, 471–513.

Evert, R. F., and Kozlowski, T. T. (1967). Effect of isolation of bark on cambial activity and development of xylem and phloem in trembling aspen. *Amer. J. Bot.* **54**, 1045–1055.

Forward, D. F., and Nolan, N. J. (1961). Growth and morphogenesis in the Canadian forest species. IV. Further studies of wood growth in branches and main axis of *Pinus resinosa* Ait. under conditions of open growth, suppression, and release. *Can. J. Bot.* **39**, 411–436.

Kozlowski, T. T. (1968). Soil water and tree growth. *In* "The Ecology of Southern Forests" (N. E. Linnartz, ed.), pp. 30–57. Louisiana State Univ. Press, Baton Rouge, Louisiana.

Kozlowski, T. T. (1969). Tree physiology and forest pests. *J. Forest.* **69**, 118–122.

Kozlowski, T. T., and Keller, T. (1966). Food relations of woody plants. *Bot. Rev.* **32**, 293–382.

Kramer, P. J. (1964). The role of water in wood formation. *In* "The Formation of Wood in Forest Trees" (M. H. Zimmermann, ed.) pp. 519–532. Academic Press, N.Y.

Kraus, J. F., and Spurr, S. H. (1961). Relationship of soil moisture to the springwood-summerwood transition in southern Michigan red pine. *J. Forest.* **50**, 510–511.

Larson, P. R. (1962). A biological approach to wood quality. TAPPI **45**, 443–448.

Larson, P. R. (1963). Stem form development in forest trees. *Forest Sci. Monogr.* **5**.

Larson, P. R. (1969). Wood formation and the concept of wood quality. *Yale Univ. School of Forest. Bull.* **74**.

Smith, D. M., and Wilsie, M. C. (1969). Some anatomical responses of loblolly pine to soil water deficiencies. TAPPI **44**, 179–185.

Wareing, P. F., Hanney, C. E. A., and Digby, J. (1964). The role of endogenous hormones in cambial activity and xylem differentiation. *In* "The Formation of Wood in Forest Trees" (M. H. Zimmermann, ed.), pp. 323–344. Academic Press, New York.

Westing, A. H. (1965). Formation and function of compression wood in gymnosperms *Bot. Rev.* **31**, 381–480.

Zahner, R. (1968). Water deficits and growth of trees. *In* "Water Deficits and Plant Growth" (T. T. Kozlowski, ed.), Vol. II, Chapter 5. Academic Press, New York.

Zahner, R., and Donnelly, J. R. (1967). Refining correlations of water deficits and radial growth in red pine. *Ecology* **48**, 525–530.

Zahner, R., and Oliver, W. W. (1962). The influence of thinning and pruning on the date of summerwood initiation in red and jack pines. *Forest Sci.* **8**, 51–63.

Zahner, R., and Stage, A. R. (1966). A procedure for calculating daily moisture stress and its utility in regressions of the tree growth on weather. *Ecology* **47**, 64–74.

.

Chapter 4

MEASUREMENT OF CAMBIAL GROWTH

Introduction

The objectives of different investigators in measuring and characterizing cambial growth are many and varied. For example, selection of measurement techniques often is influenced by biological, economic, or archeological considerations. Whereas some investigators are interested in estimates of gross cambial growth over a several-year period to determine increment in volume of wood in standing trees on large areas of land, others are interested in cambial growth over short-time periods and often in different parts of the same tree. Some biologists are concerned with minute details of cambial growth such as fine structure of the smallest elements of the cambium and its derivatives. Obviously the wide spectrum of interests among different investigators requires a variety of methods, with great variations in precision, to adequately characterize cambial growth increment in terms of individual objectives.

Measurement of Increase in Stem Radius, Diameter, or Girth

Many investigators have estimated certain aspects of cambial growth indirectly by measuring periodic changes in radius or diameter of growing tree stems or branches. For measurement of large increases in stem radius, diameter, or girth such instruments as dendrometers, calipers, and tapes, have been used. These measuring devices most commonly have been used to obtain readings on stems at breast height (4.5 ft above ground level). For measurements of out-of-reach diameters of trees, many different kinds of optical dendrometers (forks, calipers, and rangefinders) have been designed. Their accuracy and precision vary greatly. For a good discussion of the theory and usefulness of optical dendrometers the reader is referred to Grosenbaugh (1963).

Dendrometers have been very popular for measuring changes in stem diameters and supplying information on some aspects of tree growth. There are two basic types of dendrometers; those that measure changes in circumference by means of a band (Hall, 1944, Liming, 1957; Mesavage and Smith, 1960; Bormann and Kozlowski, 1962), and those that measure changes of a single radius through changing the distance between a fixed plane anchored in the wood and a point on the surface of the bark (Reineke, 1948; Daubenmire, 1945; Daubenmire and Deters, 1947; Tryon and Finn, 1949, Warrack and Jorgensen, 1950; Byram and Doolittle, 1950; Belyea, Fraser, and Rose, 1951; Gooding, 1952a; Fraser, 1952; Verner, 1962). A recording dendrometer or dendrograph, which provides a continuous and permanent record of diameter change on a chart driven by a clock mechanism, was described as early as 1921 by MacDougal. Since that time many modifications of recording dendrometers have been made (Fritts and Fritts, 1955; Impens and Schalck, 1965; Kuroiwa, Yoshino, and Takahashi, 1958).

Most dendrometers have been designed for use with large trees. However, some observations are available on periodic changes in stem diameters of small trees. For example, McCully (1952) and Farrar and Zichmanis (1960) measured diameter changes of seedlings with caliper micrometers. Their observations were widely spaced in time and did not give a continuous record of diameter changes. Kozlowski (1967a,b, 1968a) adapted the Fritts dendrograph for continuous measurement of diameter changes in tree seedlings. The instrument was mounted on a 30-inch-high frame constructed of galvanized band steel. The crossbar of the dendrograph was suspended on steel balls resting in small holes cut into a small projecting shelf of the frame (Fig. 4.1). The lower loading spring, which held the dendrograph tightly on the steel balls, was looped around a screw attached to a crossbar of the frame. A seedling stem was backed up against a removable steel plate held in place by tightened wing nuts. The dendrograph rod that was bearing on the opposite side of the stem registered changes in stem diameter which were transcribed to weekly charts on a rotating drum actuated by a clock mechanism. In general, the movement of the instrument was similar to that when mounted on a large tree, but the instrument recorded diameter change rather than radial fluctuations.

SOURCES OF ERROR

Diameter tapes, calipers, and dendrometers have provided much useful information on certain aspects of cambial growth, especially changes in volume growth of forest stands. However, these instruments have not always provided precise and accurate information on some aspects of cambial growth over short-time periods which are of particular interest to biologists.

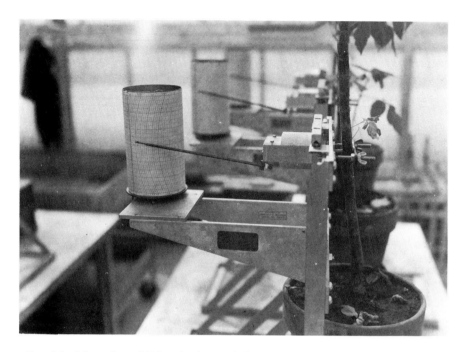

Fig. 4.1. Adaptation of Fritts dendrograph for continuous determination of diameter changes of small trees. For description see text.

This was emphasized by Bormann and Kozlowski (1962) who compared data on seasonal changes in girth of trees obtained with dial gauge dendrometers and vernier tree ring bands. The dial gauge dendrometer recorded radial changes of less than 40 μ that were not recorded or were recorded inaccurately by tree bands. Dial gauge dendrometers recorded stem shrinkage readily whereas tree ring bands did not. The bands also were inefficient in recording the first small increments of growth following cambial reactivation in the spring.

Measurements taken at only a single stem height or single radial position often do not provide reliable estimates of cambial growth of the tree as a whole. In suppressed trees, for example, xylem production often is negligible in the lower stem but appreciable in the upper stem (see Chapter 2). Hence, measurements taken at lower stem positions only will not provide data on cambial growth in the upper stem. Also, cambial growth of individual trees varies greatly around the stem circumference, often rendering of doubtful value an observation of radial increase at a single radial position only.

Many investigators have used measurements of initial increase in stem diameter at breast height to determine when seasonal cambial growth begins in a tree or species. Such measurements may be questioned because in some species appreciable xylem production and diameter increase occur in the upper stem first, and diameter increase in the lower stem may not be measurable until a considerably later date (see Chapter 2).

Changes in diameter of trees involve two major components: (1) addition and enlargement of cambial derivatives and (2) reversible changes in size resulting from hydration and thermal effects. Hence, the girth of a tree changes partly because shrinking and swelling are superimposed on cambial growth. Sometimes such reversible changes are negligible and can be disregarded. At other times, however, these hydration and thermal effects in trees are appreciable and may greatly exceed those resulting from cambial growth increment over short time periods. Consequently estimates of cambial growth from measurements of changes in stem girth sometimes can be very misleading. In the Temperate Zone, hydration changes in stem diameter generally are greater than thermal changes during the growing season.

Hydration Effects

Seasonal shrinkage of tree stems may constitute a sizable amount in comparison to expansion as a result of cambial growth (Figs. 4.2–4.4). For example, Bormann and Kozlowski (1962) recorded net weekly radial

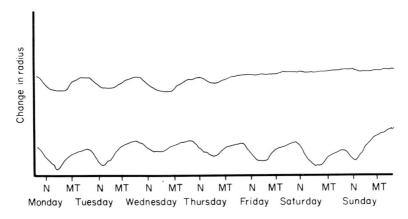

Fig. 4.2. Dendrograph traces showing shrinkage of *Pinus resinosa* stems in the afternoon followed by expansion during the night. N, noon; MT, midnight. The upper curve is for the week of July 10–17 and the lower curve for August 21–28. When cloudy and rainy weather prevailed (upper curve, latter part of the week) diurnal expansion and contraction of stems did not occur. [From Kozlowski (1968e).]

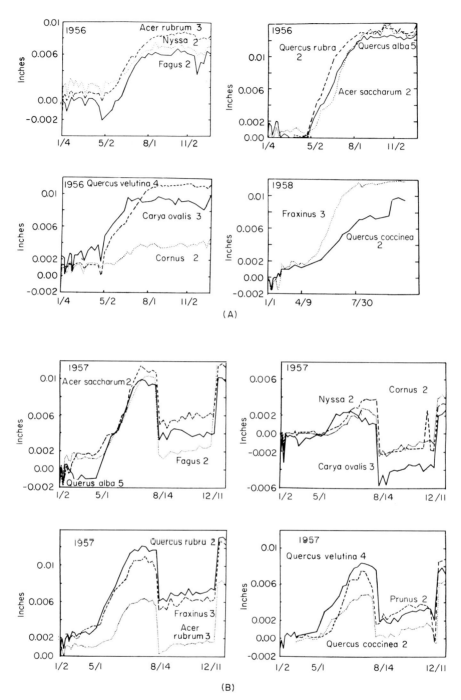

Fig. 4.3. Seasonal variations in radial change of several species of tree stems during (A) a normal year and (B) drought year. Note very large amount of stem shrinkage in August of the drought year. [From Buell *et al.* (1961).]

decreases in *Pinus strobus* stems. The amount of weekly decrease in stem radius was greater than the amount of weekly increase for many trees during the growing season. Dimock (1964) presented data showing that *Pseudotsuga menziesii* stems shrank constantly over the 6-week period of July 18 to August 29. Data of Buell *et al.* (1961) showed that during very severe droughts in New Jersey, external measurements of radial change of trees gave no useful indication of actual cambial increment (Fig. 4.3). For example, in 1957, a year of severe drought, a total of only 4.46 inches of rain was recorded for May, June, and July, as against a 9-year average of 9.97 inches. Radial increment of several species of deciduous trees, as determined with dendrometers, followed the usual positive course early in the season but radii began to decrease by mid-July. On August 7, a very large radial decrease was recorded, and by August 14, stems shrank so much that diameters of some trees were less than they were before the growing season started. Hence, in terms of radial change, all the irreversible cambial increment up to mid-August was masked by stem shrinkage. The trees remained in a severely shrunken condition and did not show any subsequent radial increase until soil moisture was replenished in December. At that time the stems expanded rapidly because of elimination of internal water stress.

Shortly following a rainfall a significant portion of radial increase of tree stems is accounted for by rehydration. Using dendrographs, Kozlowski, Winget, and Torrie (1962) recorded a pattern of significant radial increase of tree stems in Wisconsin each day that rain occurred during the growing season, only to be followed on the next day (if no rain occurred) by less radial increase, no increase, or shrinkage. For example, following a period of drought from July 4 to 12 there was a sudden and marked radial increase in *Quercus ellipsoidalis* stems associated with small amounts of precipitation on July 13, 17, and 20. Much less radial increase was recorded on days following these dates. After tree stems rehydrated and expanded as a result of 0.89 inches of rain on August 28, net shrinkage occurred during each of the several succeeding rainless days thereafter.

The amount of stem shrinkage has been correlated with rates of transpiration. For example, *Fraxinus americana* seedlings had higher transpiration rates and depleted soil moisture reserves more rapidly than did *Pinus strobus* seedlings. Stems of *Fraxinus* seedlings shrank more rapidly and to a greater extent in drying soil than did stems of *Pinus*. As soil dried, photosynthesis of both species was decreased; but it declined much faster in *Fraxinus* than in *Pinus* seedlings (Ogigirigi, Kozlowski, and Sasaki, 1970).

Radial increases or decreases in tree stems due to internal hydration changes often occur rapidly. However, expansion of stems following abundant rainfall often occurs faster than shrinkage caused by dehydration (Kozlowski and Peterson, 1962). MacDougal (1938) noted an increase in diameter of

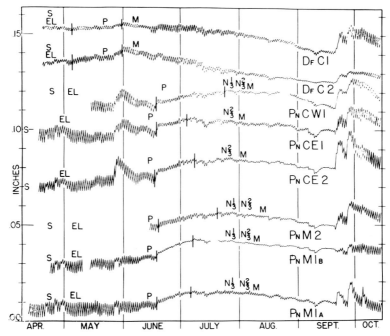

Fig. 4.4. Diurnal and seasonal changes of stem diameters of trees in southwestern Colorado. DfCl and DfC2 are *Pseudotsuga menziesii* trees from Navajo Canyon. PnCW1 is a *Pinus edulis* tree on a west-facing slope; PnCE1 and PnCE2 are *Pinus edulis* trees on an east-facing slope. PnM2 is a *Pinus edulis* tree on the mesa top. PnM1a and PnM1b represent a twin *Pinus edulis* tree on the mesa top with a dendrograph on each stem. Other symbols are: S, buds swelling; EL, bud elongation; P, pollen shedding; N 1/3, needles one-third full size; M, needles full size. Two vertical bars indicate interval of 90% radial increase. [From Fritts *et al.* (1965). Reproduced by permission of the Society for American Archaeology from American Antiquity, Vol. 31.]

oak trees within 2 hours after irrigation, following a 3-week period during which no significant changes occurred in stem girth.

Tree stems usually shrink slightly during the day because of net water loss by transpiration, and they rehydrate and expand at night. Shrinkage of trees during the day occurs even when they are growing in well-watered soils (Kozlowski, 1955, 1958, 1963b, 1965, 1967b,c). Ninokata and Miyazato (1959) found that maximum stem radii due to swelling were observed between 6 and 7 a.m. but shrinkage was greatest between 1 and 5 p.m. Using a very sensitive mirror dendrometer, Kuroiwa, Yoshino, and Takahashi (1958) observed daily radial variation in stems of *Paulownia* trees during the growing season. The rate of stem thickening was high at night and decreased to a negligible value shortly after sunrise. Thereafter, stem contraction occurred abruptly with minimal stem radii recorded before 3 p.m. Then the stem radius slowly increased and radial change accelerated rather suddenly beginning at about 3 p.m. Small daily fluctuations in stem radius were correlated with the amount of sunlight. Stems contracted when the sun shone and expanded when the sun went behind clouds. The response could be observed in 10 min. During the dormant season, however, the diurnal fluctuations essentially disappeared.

Radial changes in tree stems resulting from periodic seasonal and diurnal dehydration and rehydration often are of such magnitude that they cannot be disregarded in design of growth studies over short periods. Measurements of radial change of stems often show much more linear variation due to dehydration and hydration than to cambial growth increment (Kozlowski, 1968f). Fritts, Smith, and Stokes (1965) and Holmes and Shim (1968) showed that diurnal decrease in diameter of trees greatly exceeded the amount of cambial growth increment over a several-day period (Fig. 4.4, 4.5). Kern (1961) noted that on clear, dry days that were conducive to transpiration, diameters of *Picea* stems decreased from sunrise to early afternoon by up to 0.5 mm, amounts approximating a week's increment. However, on cloudy humid days there sometimes was a slight decrease in diameter. According to Holmes and Shim (1968) the amount of shrinkage of *Pinus canariensis* stems during daylight hours approximated eventual net cambial growth increment of 5 days.

In rapidly growing trees useful short-period estimates of cambial growth can often be obtained by connecting peaks or valleys of dendrograph traces

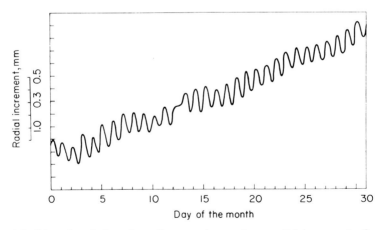

FIG. 4.5. Diurnal variations in radius superimposed on radial increment of a *Pinus canariensis* tree during March, 1965, in Australia. Note the effect of rain on March 13. [From Holmes and Shim (1968).]

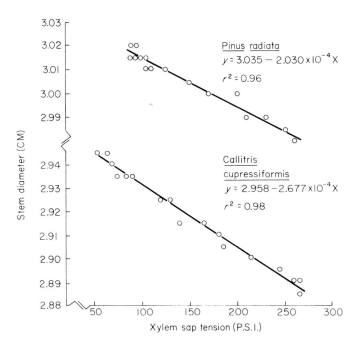

FIG. 4.6. Relation between stem diameter and xylem sap tension in two species of trees. [From Worrall (1966).]

obtained during successive days of clear weather. However, during periods of variable weather the separation of estimates of irreversible cambial growth increment from reversible shrinkage and expansion becomes difficult. The relationship between diurnal shrinkage and expansion and cambial growth increment often changes seasonally. For example, Kozlowski and Winget (1964) observed that the amount of diurnal stem shrinkage of *Populus tremuloides* and *Pinus resinosa* trees in northern Wisconsin varied greatly during the dormant season. Only small amounts of diurnal stem shrinkage occurred early in the growing season, followed by increased shrinkage in mid-season, and greatly decreased shrinkage in late summer after moisture reserves in the soil and in the trees were depleted by transpiration. To estimate cambial growth, measurements of radial changes with instruments such as dendrometers should obviously be taken at the same time on successive days to decrease the significant errors caused by hydration and dehydration of tree stems.

Correlation exists between short-time changes in stem diameter and internal water stress (Impens and Schalck, 1965; Worrall, 1966). The relationship between stem diameter and xylem sap tension of *Pinus radiata* and *Callitris cupressiformis* seedlings is shown in Fig. 4.6. Worrall (1966) used this correlation in a method for correcting diameter growth data for superimposed shrinkage and expansion. This involved measuring xylem sap tension on detached branches with a pressure bomb (Scholander *et al.*, 1965) at the time diameter measurements were made. A curve relating diameter and sap tension could then be used for estimating diameter at a standard tension. The good linear correlations between diameter and sap tension shown in Fig. 4.6 indicate that diameter changes due to internal water stress can be estimated by this technique. Inasmuch as there sometimes is a lag in diameter response to abrupt environmental changes (Kozlowski and Winget, 1964), sap tension and diameter should be measured after a period of equilibrium rather than immediately after a change in environmental conditions which influence stem hydration or dehydration.

    These few examples emphasize that because shrinking and swelling of tree stems and branches are superimposed on growth of tissues, radial or diameter changes over short periods of time should be interpreted with caution as estimates of cambial growth. Experiments by Kozlowski (1967a,b) showed that tree seedlings often shrank so rapidly during a soil drying cycle that diameter changes caused by cambial growth were completely masked (Fig. 4.7). Seedlings sometimes rehydrated and expanded appreciably in a matter of minutes after dry soil was irrigated. The use of dendrometers for precise determination of when cambial activity begins and ends is of doubtful value. Fielding and Millett (1941), for example, concluded that because of the constant and appreciable shrinking and swelling of *Pinus radiata* trees it was

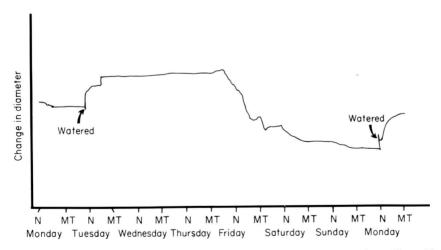

FIG. 4.7. Effect of soil drying on stem diameter of potted *Acer negundo* seedlings. N, noon; MT, midnight. The arrows indicate time of irrigation.

extremely difficult to determine with dendrometers exactly when cambial activity began or ended.

Shrinkage of Tapped Laticifers

The tapping of latex-producing trees, such as chicle (*Achras zapota*) and rubber (*Hevea brasiliensis*), results in rapid stem contraction (Karling, 1934; Gooding, 1952b). Using a sensitive dendrometer, Pyke (1941) showed that stem contraction of *Hevea brasiliensis* occurred below the tapping cut within a few seconds. The shrinkage, which averaged about 0.03 mm, often was completed within 3 min from the time of tapping. The magnitude of shrinkage was influenced by the time since last tapping and the time of day of tapping. Lustinec *et al.* (1969) observed that stem contraction of *Hevea brasiliensis* just below the cut occurred at once; whereas at increasing distances below the cut, the shrinkage began progressively later and recovery was slow.

The rapid shrinkage of laticifer stems associated with tapping apparently is the result of turgor changes and partial collapse of latex vessels because of the pressure of surrounding bark tissues. Gooding (1952b) outlined the following sequence of events after tapping in *Hevea*. When first tapped, the latex is highly concentrated and viscous. Tapping results in an internal pressure decrease at the cut ends of latex vessels. Resistance to latex movement is so great, however, that only a small amount is exuded. The pressure drops over a short length of the vessels. There is dilution in the affected areas but, even when diluted, the latex moves slowly because of its high viscosity. Resistance to latex movement, like turgor pressure, prevents water uptake at a high rate such as would occur if latex flowed more rapidly. After the incision has closed, the drop in pressure is transmitted slowly in the area below the cut. When the tree is tapped again the pressure drop is transmitted

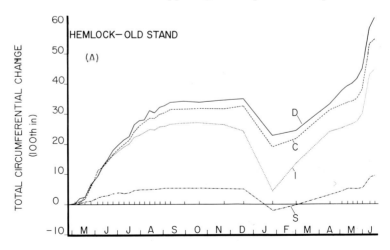

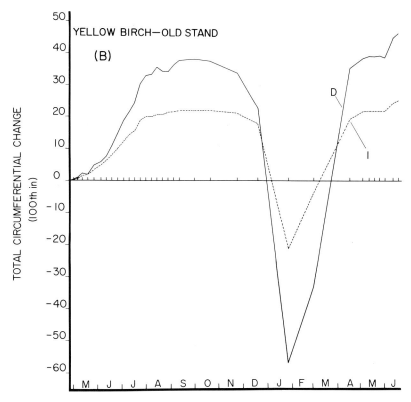

Fig. 4.8. Seasonal circumferential changes in various crown classes of yellow birch (*Betula alleghaniensis*) and eastern hemlock (*Tsuga canadensis*) in northern Wisconsin in 1962–1963. Crown classes included dominant (D), co-dominant (C), intermediate (I), and suppressed (S) trees. Winter contraction of stems of yellow birch (B) was much greater than that of eastern hemlock (A). [From Winget and Kozlowski (1965).]

farther than before because of the now somewhat lower viscosity of latex. Hence, there is more extensive dilution, giving a latex of even lower viscosity.

Thermal Effects

Direct thermal expansion and contraction of tree stems and branches often complicate indirect measurements of cambial growth (Kozlowski, 1965; McCracken and Kozlowski, 1965). As shown by Daubenmire and Deters (1947), an unseasonal drop in temperature not only decreases cambial activity but causes considerable stem shrinkage. The potential magnitude of thermal effects on radial change in stems is most easily demonstrated during the dormant season (Fritts and Fritts, 1955; Small and Monk, 1959). Using vernier bands, Winget and Kozlowski (1964) studied radial changes of tree

TABLE 4.1

TOTAL AND UNIT STEM EXPANSION DURING THE GROWING SEASON AND CONTRACTION DURING THE WINTER OF VARIOUS SPECIES AND CROWN CLASSES OF TREES GROWING ON DIFFERENT SITES IN NORTHERN WISCONSIN[a]

Species and stand	Crown class	D.b.h. range (in)	Total summer increase in circumference (.01 in/tree)	Total winter decrease in circumference (.01 in/tree)	Unit summer increase in circumference (0.0001 in/in)	Unit winter decrease in circumference (0.0001 in/in)	Winter decrease as percent of summer increase
Tilia americana Old 2	Dominant	13–19	26	107	28	127	453
	Sprouts	4–7	26	62	146	339	232
	Suppressed	4–7	29	53	80	332	184
Betula alleghaniensis Young	Dominant	8–12	31	37	122	148	121
	Intermediate	6–8	17	36	86	185	215
	Suppressed	3–5	4	20	26	147	565
Old 1	Dominant	15–23	38	95	62	162	261
	Intermediate	8–11	22	43	76	149	196
Acer saccharum Young	Dominant	7–17	41	38	111	105	94
	Suppressed	3–6	4	9	27	64	237
Old 1	Dominant	13–21	46	24	95	56	53
	Intermediate	6–10	36	11	173	55	32
	Suppressed	4–6	17	9	114	55	48
Old 2	Dominant	9–13	27	20	79	57	73
	Intermediate	6–9	16	12	69	50	73
	Suppressed	4–6	7	9	40	53	132
Tsuga canadensis Old 1	Dominant	16–25	35	12	69	33	48
	Co-Dominant	10–13	33	14	92	38	41
	Intermediate	9–12	27	23	81	68	84
	Suppressed	4–8	5	7	20	26	130
Old 2	Dominant	11–13	30	12	81	33	40
	Suppressed	4–7	11	8	84	48	75

[a] Data are for the 1962 Growing Season and 1962–1963 Winter. [From Winget and Kozlowski (1964).]

stems of several species throughout the year in northern Wisconsin. As may be seen in Fig. 4.8 all experimental trees showed a typical sigmoid growth curve during the growing season. The transition period from rapid to slow growth often showed temporary decreases in growth rates and small amounts of shrinkage due to summer drought. Generally this was followed by a period of little change or slow decrease in radial change through the late summer and autumn. Beginning in mid-December, all trees showed a marked decrease in radius as temperatures dropped rapidly. Stem shrinkage reached a maximum on January 26 and recovery was completed in April. The time of maximum shrinkage occurred in the coldest part of the winter when temperatures dropped to $-25°F$.

Surprisingly the amount of winter shrinkage was considerably more than the amount caused by summer hydration changes and, in more than half the cases studied, winter stem contraction exceeded the amount of total radial increase during the growing season. Some trees shrank over five times as much in winter as they had increased in diameter during the previous summer (Table 4.1). There were wide differences in shrinkage among species, with the order of shrinkage as follows: *Tilia americana* > *Betula alleghaniensis* > *Acer saccharum* > *Tsuga canadensis*, with little difference between *Acer* and *Tsuga*. Site differences also were apparent.

There is considerable evidence that much of the winter shrinkage of tree stems is localized in the bark. Wiegand (1906) collected twigs of *Salix cordata* at $-18°C$ and measured expansion on thawing of twigs with and without bark. More than half the total expansion was located in the bark. The bark expanded 13.5% whereas the wood expanded 2.5%. In Vermont, Marvin (1949) found that between 5:45 a.m. and 12:15 p.m. on April 4, the bark of *Acer saccharum* increased 82 μ in diameter and the xylem cylinder 55 μ. However, the bark changes were measured for a thickness of 1 cm. Since the xylem cylinder was 46 cm in diameter, 1 cm of the xylem diameter increased only 1.20 μ, emphasizing much greater unit change in the bark.

Winter contraction and expansion of tree stems with temperature change apparently occur very rapidly. Shortly after a cold spell beginning January 19 in North Carolina the outer layer of living tissue in *Pinus echinata* stems underwent a surprising contraction of 0.30 mm. This was equivalent to 10 times the mean daily shrinkage occurring during rapid spring growth. Recovery occurred immediately after the freezing weather ended, and stem expansion of 0.27 mm occurred within a day (Byram and Doolittle, 1950). Small and Monk (1959) made winter dendrometer measurements at 3 hr intervals for 6 days on *Fraxinus americana* stems together with air temperature measurements. The highest temperatures usually occurred around noon, and major radial increases were recorded then also. Lowest temperatures occurred at 6:30 a.m., which was the time of greatest stem contraction (Fig. 4.9).

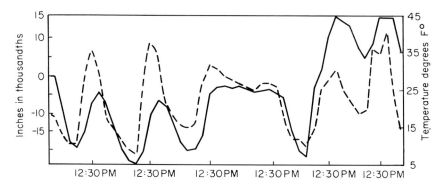

FIG. 4.9. Diurnal changes in stem radius of *Fraxinus americana* (solid line) and air temperature (dashed line). [From Small and Monk (1959).]

Among the various hypotheses advanced for stem contraction during low temperatures below freezing are (1) translocation of water to other parts of the tree, (2) reversible changes of free to bound water, and (3) continued transpiration while water absorption ceases (Byram and Doolittle, 1950). It seems unlikely that in deciduous trees winter transpiration from twigs and buds is of sufficient magnitude to account for the observed rapid changes in stem contraction. The view of Small and Monk (1959) that exosmosis from cells to intercellular spaces accounts for the marked and rapid contraction of tree stems as temperature decreases appears to be the most widely accepted explanation for the phenomenon.

Dendrochronology

The observation that ring width varies from year to year with climate has provided the basis for dendrochronology. Much repetition of ring width pattern among widely spaced trees and back through time has been identified. Actual dating techniques involve recognition of ring width patterns (especially narrow rings) associated with certain years and the cross matching of these patterns from living trees to successively older wood and charcoal fragments from historic or archeological sites (Stokes and Smiley, 1968). Dendrochronological techniques have been applied successfully to a correlation with climate, tracing of sea currents, and archeology (Giddings, 1962). Exact dates have been assigned to tree rings, archeological beams, and charcoal remnants when ring structures were identified. An archeological chronology was established in Mesa Verde National Park to AD 420 and living *Pinus aristata* trees yielded chronologies going back 4500 years (McGinnies, 1963).

The response of ring width to climate is more uniform in unfavorable years than in favorable ones, and narrow rings, therefore, are preferable to wide ones for dendrochronology. False and missing rings are a serious problem in dating, but the trained dendrochronologist can identify false rings microscopically by the fuzzy transitional demarcation line between small latewood-type cells and larger earlywood-type cells or by cross dating between known control plants (McGinnies, 1963). Since only trees with similar genetic background that are subjected to severe environmental stresses will cross date, often only a few trees in a locality are useful for study. According to McGinnies (1963), the best dendrochronological material in the United States has come from the western gymnosperms, including *Pinus ponderosa, Pseudotsuga menziesii, Pinus edulis, Juniperus scopulorum, Sequoia gigantea, Pinus aristata,* and *Pinus flexilis.* For further discussion of some of the problems involved in dendrochronology the reader is referred to Bannister (1963) and Stokes and Smiley (1968).

Microscopy

Magnification of cambium-produced tissues has been indispensable in studies of cambial growth. Practically all of the available definitive information on time of seasonal beginning and cessation of cambial growth, as well as the types and structure of cambial derivatives produced, has been derived by magnification and examination of transverse sections across the cambial zone, radial sections, or tangential sections along or on either side of the cambial zone. Microscopy has been invaluable in elucidating the structure of cambium-produced tissues and, when combined with measuring devices, to quantify cambial increments or determine sizes of various cambial-produced cells or their parts.

LINEAR MICROSCOPIC MEASUREMENT

As Isenberg (1958) emphasized, the accuracy of linear microscopic measurement is influenced by a variety of factors including sharpness and fineness of the micrometer scale, points of the object between which measurements are made, coarseness of the image of the markings on the micrometer scale, and the extent of their magnification. Outlines and details of the object depend on the focus, illumination, refractive index of the preparation, and resolving power of the microscope. Among popular methods of growth ring assessment are linear microscopic measurements of growth ring width (Eklund, 1949; Jazewitsch, Bettag, and Siebenlist, 1957) and accumulation of measurements. Linear cross sectional demensions of cambial derivatives usually are measured by one of three methods (Smith, 1967): (1) direct comparison with a graduated scale by use of traversing microscopes; (2) micrometer eyepieces; and (3) measurement with a graduated rule on projected images.

Because of variations in cross sectional shape of adjacent cells, Smith (1967) recommended measuring diameters of a number of cells and dividing the measurement by the cell count. To obtain average lumen diameter a useful procedure is to subtract the average double cell wall thickness, calculated from the sum of the double walls between adjacent lumens, from the average cell diameter. Cell wall thickness usually is measured as half the width of the double cell wall between adjacent lumens at its narrowest point.

Smith (1967) preferred to use traversing micrometers rather than micrometer eyepieces for measuring cell dimensions. The advantages cited for traversing micrometers were the following: (1) The size of the field over which measurements can be made is independent of magnification; (2) scale readings are direct readings of actual measurements and also are independent of magnification; (3) inaccuracies due to aberrations in the optical system are minimized by making measurements in the center of the field of view; and (4) cross hairs of the instrument serve as a marker for counting cells when measuring cell diameters of adjoining cells.

Traversing micrometers for measuring cell dimensions often are provided with dual or multiple linear movement. This makes it possible to accumulate two sets of measurements on separate scales. Smith (1965) described such an instrument which was used to measure cross sectional tracheid diameter and wall thickness. The microscope and stage traveled in opposite directions, making it possible to accumulate combined widths of double cell walls between the lumens on one scale and the combined widths of the lumens on the other (Smith and Miller, 1964). By counting the cells traversed, average wall thickness and tracheid diameter could be calculated. With such an instrument it also is possible to accumulate measurements of both radial and tangential diameters of various cambial derivatives (Liese and Meyer-Uhlenried, 1957).

Several investigators have used micrometer eyepieces to measure sizes of xylem increments or individual cambial derivatives (Jones, 1958; Saucier, 1963). Although micrometer eyepieces have been very useful they usually cause more eyestrain than do traversing micrometers. The use of micrometer eyepieces also requires calibration for each combination of ocular and objective as well as tube length (Smith, 1967).

Many quantitative measurements of cambial growth have been made directly with a graduated scale on projected images of tissue sections or photomicrographs. Hiller (1964), for example, used such a technique for estimating the size of fibril angles in tracheids. Measurements on projected images have also been used to determine fiber diameters and cell wall thickness of macerated fibers (Williams and Hamilton, 1961) and to measure cross sectional diameters of xylem elements (Haywood, 1950). A major advantage of this method over others is the marked increase in magnification that can be obtained. For proper use of the method excellent slide preparations of tissue sections are required.

Increment Cores

The increment borers which obtain cores representing the last rings of annual xylem increments of Temperate Zone trees have been useful in a variety of growth studies. They have been particularly useful in determinations of volume growth of forest stands (Meyer and Nelson, 1952) and in dendro-chronology (Stokes and Smiley, 1968). The auger of an increment borer conventionally is inserted into a standing tree at breast height (4.5 ft from the ground). Extracted cores usually are placed in protective holders, such as glass tubes or plastic straws, for transport to the laboratory (Hall, 1935; Fritz, 1939; Woods, 1951). The cores frequently require additional treatment in the laboratory. Several investigators have found that splitting cores to provide a flat clean surface facilitates measurement of annual xylem incre-ments (Krauss and Gärtner, 1938; Lumsden and Whyland, 1939). Examining cores of some species in transmitted light often is helpful (Reineke, 1941) as is the use of stains such as phloroglucin (Hornibrook, 1936). Measurements of annual growth increments in cores can be made either with or without magnification, depending on growth rate and the objectives of the investigator. A useful device for use with increment cores is the microscope and dial gauge described by Näslund (1942).

Scanning Methods

In recent years much attention has been given to "scanning" methods which variously characterize differences in physical characteristics of xylem cells in parts of an annual ring as well as in different rings. Some of the more important scanning methods will be reviewed briefly.

Determination of density of cells in various parts of xylem rings has been successfully accomplished by measurement of absorption by wood of a collimated beam of β particles. These high energy electrons lose energy as they pass through the wood as a result of interactions with electrons of the material in their pathway, and the number of such electrons depends on the amount of wood substance encountered. If the thickness of a sample is constant, the absorption varies only with density. Phillips (1960) determined variation in wood density by projecting a collimated beam of beta particles from a strontium 90 source through air-dry wood and measuring the number of particles absorbed. Phillips, Adams, and Hearmon (1962) improved the β-ray method and obtained a continuous chart record of density variations within annual rings (Fig. 4.10).

Marian and Stumbo (1960) described a technique of measuring growth rings based on graphical records obtained with a stylus tracer-type electronic instrument which transforms mechanical displacement of a stylus into

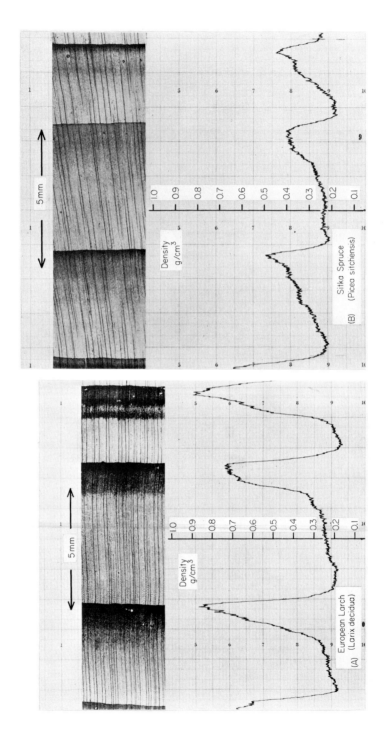

Density g/cm³

(B) Sitka Spruce (Picea sitchensis)

5mm

1.0 0.9 0.8 0.7 0.6 0.5 0.4 0.3 0.2 0.1

Density g/cm³

(A) European Larch (Larix decidua)

5mm

1.0 0.9 0.8 0.7 0.6 0.5 0.4 0.3 0.2 0.1

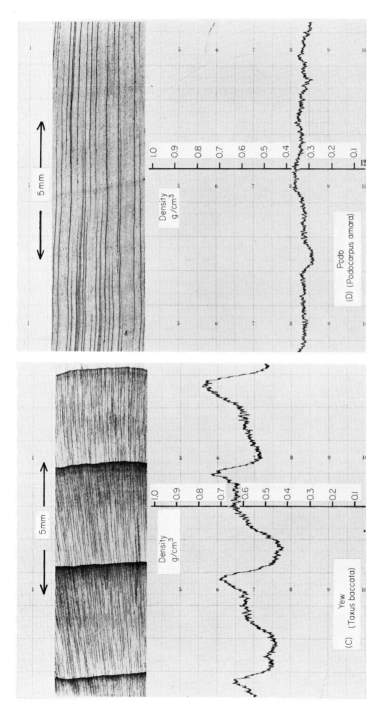

FIG. 4.10. Variations in cambial growth characteristics of four species as determined by the β-ray method. (A) *Larix decidua*, (B) *Picea sitchensis*, (C) *Taxus baccata* (D), *Podocarpus amara*. [From Phillips, Adams, and Hearmon (1962).]

electrical impulses. Cell-cavity and cell-wall dimensions, earlywood and latewood distribution within growth rings, porosity, cell-wall substance, and density can be determined with this technique.

Green and Worrall (1963) described a useful scanning microphotometer for characterizing certain aspects of xylem increments. By measuring light transmission by thin cross-sections of xylem they found the instrument useful in determining ring width, percent solids and percent voids, percent earlywood and percent latewood, total solids in earlywood and latewood, cell wall thickness, and lumen diameter, as well as information on occurrence of frost rings and compression wood. Some typical data obtained with this instrument are shown in Fig. 4.11.

Polge (1966) used a method for characterizing wood density which involved scanning with a densitometer of X-ray photographs of wood. The method involves variable absorption of X rays because of differences in wood density along increment cores. Radiographs of wood are scanned with a microdensitometer which provides a continuous record of variations in wood density along the increment core (Figs. 4.12, 4.13). The method is one of the best of the scanning techniques. It is nondestructive and very fast. The total time required does not exceed 2 min for determining density variations along a 10-cm long increment core. Reproducibility is satisfactory and the method has a high resolution power.

Harris and Polge (1967) and Polge (1969) compared the X-ray and β-ray techniques for measuring wood density. They concluded that the X-ray apparatus had superior resolving power and could be used to measure wood density of narrower growth layers than could the β-ray apparatus. The X-ray apparatus also was much faster. The time required to produce the photographic negative was approximately the same as the time for machining a specimen for the β-ray apparatus, but the rate of scanning was much faster. The β-ray apparatus was useful for examining xylem of fast grown gymnosperms but was less suitable than the X-ray technique for detailed studies of slow grown gymnosperms. In general, the X ray apparatus, although relatively expensive, had more refined capabilities than the β-ray technique.

Bark Slipping

When the cambium becomes active the bark "slips" over the wood. Following cambial dormancy in Temperate Zone trees, the slippage of bark occurs first below buds and moves down the branches and stem. Priestley, Scott, and Malins (1933) used the ease of peelability of bark strips to determine the time of year when the cambium was active in more than 30 species of angiosperms and 6 species of gymnosperms. With this method they also determined that the downward spread of cambial activity from the bases of buds was rapid in ring porous species and slow in diffuse porous species. Huber (1948) found that bark peelability of oaks moved down the stem so rapidly that the rate of such spread could not be determined. In *Picea*, however, he determined that peelability moved downward at a rate of approximately 1 meter per day.

Whereas the bark peelability method provides some rough estimates of when the cambium is active, it usually does not permit accurate dating of inception of cambial activity. This is borne out by data of several investigators who showed that, following cambial dormancy, bark slipping often preceded cambial division to produce xylem by several weeks. For example, Wilcox *et al.* (1956) reported that bark peeling in several species of angiosperms preceded cambial divisions by as much as a month.

Marking Partial Growth Increments

Investigators of cambial growth often find it necessary to identify the portion of an annual xylem increment which was produced up to a certain date. In this way tissue sections across the cambial zone can be made at the end of a growing season to include an entire growth increment in which the cells produced before and after critical dates can be readily identified. A few methods which have been used to label partial growth increments will be described briefly.

TILTING METHOD

Kennedy and Farrar (1965b) described a method of producing an internal mark in the xylem by tilting seedlings for short periods to produce an arc of reaction wood. The induced reaction wood cells could readily be identified microscopically in stem transections. A clear mark could be placed on the xylem of gymnosperm seedlings by tilting them for 2 days and then returning them to the vertical. The mark consisted of an arc of greatly lignified tracheids approximately 3 cells wide and extending for about half the stem circumference. Two arcs of reaction wood could be induced to identify a time interval during which specific cells were produced. Thus, the method could be used to determine the length of time necessary to initiate a new cambial derivative. This value multiplied by the number of immature cells between the cambium and wood permitted calculations of time required for complete differentiation of tracheids.

The specific response to tilting varied with the stage of maturation of xylem cells. During early stages of maturation, tilting stimulated cell division. In

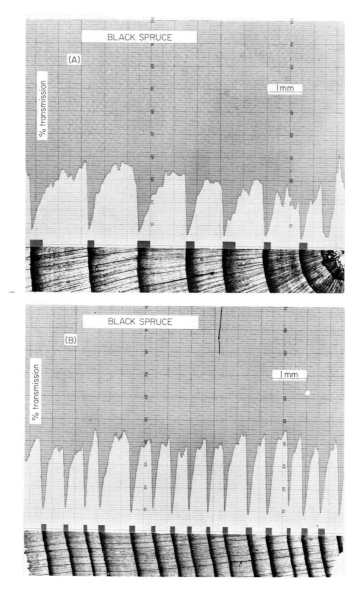

Fig. 4.11. Variations in xylem growth characteristics of *Picea mariana* as recorded by a scanning microphotometer. The shaded areas above the curves represent the solids in the section. The unshaded areas below represent the voids. Micrographs of the section scanned are shown below. [From Green and Worrall (1963).]

(A) Chart of wide, inner xylem rings (near the pith). The solid grey blocks at the bottom represent the amount of latewood. (B) Chart of narrow xylem rings in the mid-radius position. The solid grey blocks represent the amount of latewood. (C) Chart of section showing two xylem rings with compression wood. The thick-walled compression wood tracheids correspond to low transmission values. However, the earlywood band is narrower and has thicker-walled cells than do adjacent rings. (D) Chart showing frost rings which are indicated by the arrows.

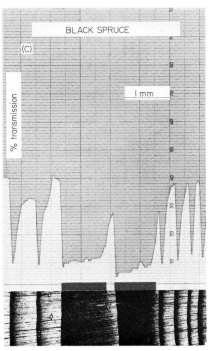

BLACK SPRUCE

(C)

% transmission

1 mm

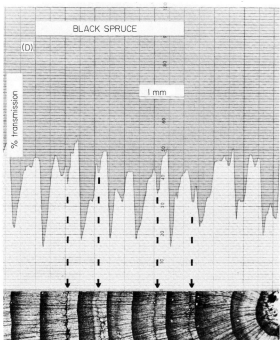

BLACK SPRUCE

(D)

% transmission

1 mm

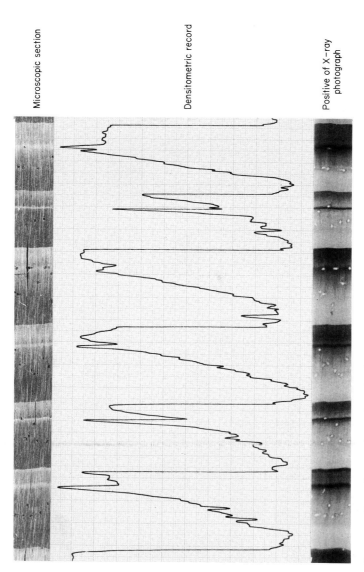

FIG. 4.12. Corresponding microscopic section, densitometric record, and X-ray photograph of xylem of *Pinus pinaster*. The X-ray photograph was obtained directly from an increment core. Note that small details on the wood section are also apparent in the X-ray photograph and densitometric record (×3). Photo courtesy of H. Polge.

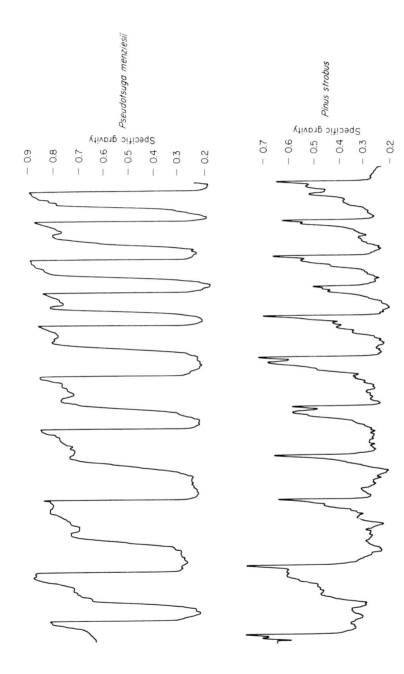

Fig. 4.13. Comparison of densitometric records of xylem of *Pseudotsuga menziesii* and *Pinus strobus* with corresponding specific gravity scales. Courtesy of H. Polge.

later stages, tilting caused altered shape, wall thickening, or degree of lignification of cells. Typical compression wood tracheids were formed only when the differentiating cells were on the underside of the tipped stem for the whole period of cell enlargement, thickening, and lignification.

RADIOLOGICAL METHOD

Waisel and Fahn (1965b) developed a method of studying cambial growth which involved exposing leaves of photosynthesizing trees to $^{14}CO_2$ and subsequently identifying, by radioactive techniques, the incorporated radio-carbon in the new cambial derivatives. As only the most recently deposited cell-wall materials were labeled with radioactive carbon, the newly divided and differentiated cells could be readily identified. When used together with histological techniques, the radiological method was quite useful in making precise distinctions between active and dormant cambium. It also was very useful in labeling the amount of seasonal cambial growth which occurred up to and after the time the test plant was offered $^{14}CO_2$. Thus the method is an especially useful, nondestructive technique for studies of environmental influences at various times during the growing season on cambial growth. The method has been used advantageously in studying effects of photoperiod and temperature on cambial growth of *Eucalyptus camaldulensis* (Waisel, Noah, and Fahn, 1966b) and for comparing seasonal activity of the phellogen with that of the cambium of *Robinia pseudoacacia* (Waisel, Liphschitz, and Arzee, 1967).

INJURING THE CAMBIAL ZONE

Late spring frost injury to the cambial zone (Chapter 2) has been useful in dating xylem increments because the time of occurrence of the frost is known. Both natural and artificial frost injuries have provided useful information (Studhalter, Glock, and Agerter, 1963).

Wolter (1968) inserted an insect mounting needle horizontally through the bark and into the cambial zone of a growing tree. The needle could either be left in the tree for future identification or the point of insertion marked and the needle removed immediately. The injury caused by the mechanical stimu-lation to the dividing and differentiating cells resulted in formation of ab-normal parenchymatous cells that could be identified microscopically in stem or branch transections made just above or below the point of needle insertion. Injury in the direction of the stem axis usually was confined to the length of the cambial initial pierced. Xylem cells formed subsequent to the time of needle insertion were normal.

Suggested Collateral Reading

Bormann, F. H. and Kozlowski, T. T. 1962. Measurements of tree ring growth with dial gage dendrometers and vernier tree ring bands. *Ecology* **43**: 289–294.

Evert, R. F. and Kozlowski, T. T. 1967. Effect of isolation of bark on cambial activity and development of xylem and phloem in trembling aspen. *Am. Jour. Bot.* **54**: 1045–1055.

Green, H. V. and Worrall, J. 1963. Wood quality studies. Part I. Scanning microphotometer for automatically measuring and recording certain wood characteristics. *Pulp and Paper Res. Inst. Canada. Tech. Rept.* 331.

Grosenbaugh, L. R. 1963. Optical dendrometers for out-of-reach diameters: a conspectus and some new theory. *Forest Sci. Monogr.* 4.

Hall, R. C. 1944. A vernier tree growth band. *Jour. Forestry* **42**: 742–743.

Harris, J. and Polge, H. 1967. A comparison of X-ray and beta ray techniques for measuring wood density. *Jour. Inst. Wood Sci.* **19**: 34–37.

Kennedy, R. W. and Farrar, J. L. 1965. Tracheid development in titled seedlings. *In* "Cellular Ultrastructure of Woody Plants" (W. A. Coté, ed.), pp. 419–453. Syracuse Univ. Press, Syracuse, New York.

Kozlowski, T. T. 1965. Expansion and contraction of plants. *Adv. Frontiers of Plant Sci.* **10**: 63–74.

Kozlowski, T. T. 1967. Diurnal variations in stem diameters of small trees. *Bot. Gaz.* **128**, 60–68.

Kozlowski, T. T. 1968. Soil water and tree growth. *In* "The Ecology of Southern Forests" (N. E. Linnartz, ed.), pp. 30–57. Louisiana State Univ. Press, Baton Rouge, Louisiana.

Kozlowski, T. T. and Winget, C. H. 1964. Diurnal and seasonal variation in radii of tree stems. *Ecology* **45**: 149–155.

McGinnies, W. G. 1963. Dendrochronology. *Jour. Forestry* **61**: 5–11.

Phillips, E. W. J., Adams, E. H. and Hearmon, R. F. S. 1962. The measurement of density variation within the growth rings in thin sections of wood using beta particles. *Jour. Inst. Wood Sci.* **10**: 11–28.

Polge, H. 1969. Further considerations about the X-ray and beta ray methods for determining wood density. *Jour. Inst. Wood Sci.* **23**: 39–44.

Small, J. A. and Monk, C. D. 1959. Winter changes in tree radii and temperature. *Forest Sci.* **5**: 229–233.

Smith, D. M. 1965. Rapid measurement of tracheid cross sectional dimensions of conifers: its application to specific gravity determinations. *Forest Prod. Jour.* **15**: 325–334.

Smith, D. M. 1967. Microscopic methods for determining cross-sectional cell dimensions. *U.S. Forest Service Research Paper FPL* 79.

Stokes, M. A. and Smiley, T. L. 1968. *In* "An Introduction to Tree-Ring Dating." Univ. Chicago Press, Chicago, Illinois.

Waisel, Y. and Fahn, A. 1965. A radiological method for the determination of cambial activity. *Physiologia Plant.* **18**: 44–46.

Winget, C. H. and Kozlowski, T. T. 1964. Winter shrinkage in stems of forest trees. *Jour. Forestry* **62**: 335–337.

Wolter, K. E. 1968. A new method for marking cambial growth. *Forest Sci.* **14**: 102–104.

Worrall, J. 1966. A method of correcting dendrometer measures of tree diameters for variations induced by moisture stress change. *Forest Sci.* **12**: 427–429.

Chapter 5

ROOT GROWTH

This chapter will discuss distribution and growth characteristics of roots of woody plants. Various specialized and modified root systems such as aerial roots, grafted roots, root buttresses, knee roots and pneumatophores, nodulated roots, and mycorrhizae will be discussed in Chapter 6.

Depth and Spread of Root Systems

Root growth characteristics of trees are greatly influenced by species, competition, rooting medium, and cultural practices (Kozlowski and Scholtes, 1948; Kozlowski, 1949). Several studies show that a number of angiosperm species have more ramified root systems than pines as shown in Table 5.1. Often the depth of rooting shows little relation to the size of the plant above ground. The effective rooting depth of tea (*Camellia thea*), for example, may be greater than that of tall shade trees. Studies in Nyasaland and Kenya showed that during droughts shade trees were affected earlier than tea bushes by water stress (Kerfoot, 1962). Although tea had most of its feeding roots distributed in the upper 3 feet of soil, it also had deep roots which ramified throughout a much greater volume of soil than did the roots of shade trees.

Roots of trees often spread laterally as far as or well beyond the width of the crown. (Fig. 5.1). However, the extent of lateral spread of roots varies greatly with site and especially soil types (Fig. 5.2). For example, Rogers and Booth (1959, 1960) found that roots of fruit trees growing on loam extended laterally about twice as far as the crown; on clay, about one and a half times; and on sand, three times. Roots of 20-year-old *Pinus sylvestris* trees on sandy soil in Wisconsin extended laterally about 7 times the average height of trees. Lateral roots of *Populus deltoides* in the same area extended laterally for more than 200 feet (S. A. Wilde and P. Mikola, personal communication).

196

TABLE 5.1

ORDERS, NUMBERS, AND LENGTHS OF GREENHOUSE-GROWN *Robinia pseudoacacia* AND *Pinus taeda* SEEDLINGS AND FOREST-GROWN *Quercus alba Pinus taeda* SEEDLINGS[a]

	Greenhouse-grown seedlings						Forest-grown seedlings					
	One primary root of *Robinia pseudoacacia* (4 months old)			*Pinus taeda* (4 months old)			*Pinus taeda* (one year old)			*Quercus alba* (one year old)		
Order	Roots (no)	Ave. length (cm)	Total length (cm)	Roots (no)	Ave. length (cm)	Total length (cm)	Roots (no)	Ave. length (cm)	Total length (cm)	Roots (no)	Ave. length (cm)	Total length (cm)
First	1	41.00	41.0	2	12.70	63.50	4	8.75	35.00	1	25.00	25.00
Second	104	7.30	759.8	251	0.33	82.62	66	0.81	53.70	84	1.33	112.00
Third	2340	1.08	2522.0	163	0.09	14.85	78	0.18	14.20	108	0.90	97.00
Fourth	3308	0.62	2051.7	0	—	—	0	—	—	0	—	—
Fifth	1276	0.52	653.7	0	—	—	0	—	—	0	—	—
Sixth	365	0.41	151.0	0	—	—	0	—	—	0	—	—
Seventh	20	0.38	7.5	0	—	—	0	—	—			
	7124		6186.7	419		160.97	148		96.90	196		234.00
						5.3 ft			3.2 ft			7.7 ft

Total length for *Robinia* seedling = 32,553.6 cm = 1068 feet

[a] From Kozlowski and Scholtes (1948).

Fig. 5.1. Root system of 16-year-old Cox's Orange Pippin apple tree on Malling II rootstock. [From Rogers and Head (1969).]

Species and Root Development

Kozlowski and Scholtes (1948) demonstrated very large differences among species in capacity for root development. A 4-month-old seedling of *Pinus taeda* grown without competition had only 419 roots and a total root length of 5.3 feet, whereas a *Robinia pseudoacacia* seedling of the same age had over 7000 roots and a total root length of 1068 feet (Table 5.1). A 6-month-old *Cornus florida* seedling had 2657 roots (total root length of 169 feet), while a *Pinus taeda* seedling of the same age developed only 767 roots (total root length of 12.7 feet) (Table 5.2). The severe effect of competition on root development is stressed by the observation that a 4-month-old *Pinus taeda* seedling developed several times as many roots as a one-year-old seedling growing in a forest (Table 5.2).

Differences in rooting habits of oak and pine were demonstrated by De Byle and Place (1959). They observed that northern pin oak (*Quercus ellipsoidalis*) and bur oak (*Q. macrocarpa*) rooted much more deeply than

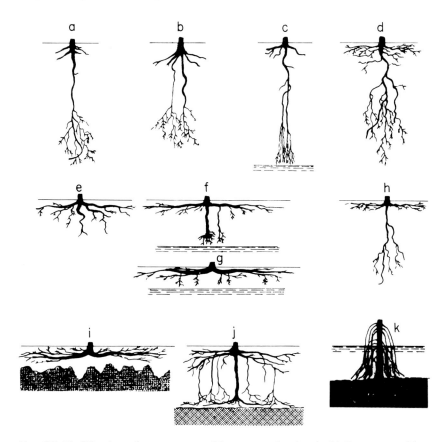

FIG. 5.2 Modification of root systems of forest trees by site. (a, b) Taproots and heart-roots with reduced upper laterals: patterns found in coarse sandy soils underlain by fine-textured substrata. (c) Taproot with long tassels, a structure induced by extended capillary fringe. (d) Superficial laterals and deep network of fibrous roots outlining an interlayer of porous materials. (e) Flattened heartroot formed in lacustrine clay over a sand bed. (f) Plate-shaped root developed in a soil with a reasonably deep ground water table. (g) Plate-shaped root formed in organic soils with shallow ground water table. (h) Bimorphic system of plate-like crown and heartroot or taproot, found in leached soils with a surface rich in organic matter. (i) Flatroot of angiosperms in strongly leached soil with raw humus. (j) Two parallel plate-roots connected by vertical joiners in a hardpan podzol. (k) Pneumato-phores of mangrove trees on tidal lands. [From Wilde (1958). Forest Soils, The Ronald Press Company, New York.]

jack pine (*Pinus banksiana*) (Table 5.3). Oak tap roots were traced to depths of more than 10 feet, but few pine roots were found below 3 feet. A much higher proportion of pine than oak roots occurred in the top few inches of soil, especially the horizontal roots up to 1 inch in diameter.

There often are hereditary differences in root growth in various species

TABLE 5.2.

VARIATION IN DEVELOPMENT OF ROOTS OF *Cornus florida*
AND *Pinus taeda* PINE SEEDLINGS[a]

Order	Cornus florida		Pinus taeda	
	No. of roots	Total length (cm)	No. of roots	Total length (cm)
First	1	44.1	1	32.2
Second	93	859.7	71	187.5
Third	1035	2714.4	496	146.1
Fourth	1336	1357.0	199	21.2
Fifth	191	168.1	0	0.0
Sixth	1	0.6	0	0.0
	2657	5143.9	767	0.0
Length (feet)		168.76		12.70

[a] Seedlings were 6 months old and grown in the absence
of competition. [From Kozlowski and Scholtes (1948)].

TABLE 5.3

ROOT DEVELOPMENT OF PURE OAK, MIXED OAK-PINE, AND PURE PINE STANDS GROWING
ON PLAINFIELD SAND IN CENTRAL WISCONSIN[a]

Forest type	Basal area (sq ft/acre)	Dry weight of roots to 5 ft depth		
		Total roots		Roots 2 mm diameter (g/sq ft)
		(g/sq ft)	(lb/acre)	
Pure oak	86.1	461	44,200	134
Mixed oak–pine	131.2	201	19,300	93
Pine	95.1	128	12,300	61

[a] From De Byle and Place (1959)

within the same genus. According to Krasilnikov (1960b), the descending
order of root penetration was *Euonymus europaea*, *E. maackii*, *E. hamilto-
niana*, *E. yedoensis*, and *E. verrucosa*. Maurer (1958) demonstrated the effect
of rootstock on the extent of root systems. He reported on a variety of walnut
that had been grafted both on *Juglans regia* and *J. nigra*. Both were shallow-
rooted but trees on the former rootstock were more vigorous and required
a wider spacing. Unusually widespreading root systems of sour orange
tree in Sardinia were noted by Baldini and Canu (1959). The roots grew

horizontally at a depth of 10–90 cm and extended to 3–4 times the radius of the crown.

There are many examples in the literature of woody plants that show an inherent capacity for unusually deep root penetration. Because the water in soil areas, which is not penetrated by roots generally, is unavailable to plants, the extent of root penetration and branching is a major factor in drought resistance of many species (Kozlowski, 1964). Albertson and Weaver (1945) linked the survival of *Quercus, Gleditsia, Juglans*, and *Maclura* during droughts to their capacity to produce deeply penetrating roots which utilized available water very efficiently.

Phillips (1963) reported an apparently authentic case of *Prosopis* roots that grew 175 feet below the soil surface near Tucson, Arizona. A good example of a tree with a deep and ramifying root system was the oak (*Quercus macrocarpa*) described by Weaver and Kramer (1932). This 65-year-old tree had a taproot which extended down to 14 feet and gave rise to 30 or more large branch roots. These main branches, which varied in diameter from 1 to 7 inches, extended outward for 20–60 feet. Many branches of the main laterals grew downward for 8–15 feet. According to Herre (1954), the desert shrub *Welwitschia mirabilis* may root to depths of 18 meters. In savanna type vegetation in Brazil several woody species, including *Jacaranda decurrens, Attalea exigua*, and *Andira* spp. have roots that penetrate the soil to 10 meters or more (Rawitscher *et al.*, 1943). Hayes and Stoeckeler (1935) classified hackberry, honey locust, bur oak, mulberry, and osage orange as deep rooters (10–20 feet). Green ash, American elm, red cedar, and box elder were in an intermediate group that formed roots down to 10 feet. Willow, cottonwood, and catalpa were more shallowly rooted. The success or failure of windbreak trees of the Southern High Plains in the United States was related to inherent capacity of various species to root deeply (Bunger and Thomson, 1938). Deep rooting species included Asiatic elm, osage orange, red cedar, and black locust with roots down to 27 feet. Roots of Russian mulberry and thornless honey locust grew down to 12 feet, whereas those of apricot, black walnut, and ash penetrated only to 5.5–7.5 feet. Studies of root growth of component species of hedges by Steubing (1960) showed that *Fraxinus excelsior, Sambucus nigra*, and *Populus alba* had extensive and deeply penetrating roots. In contrast, *Corylus avellana, Euonymus europaeus*, and *Ligustrum vulgare* had much more restricted roots that were generally confined to the surface soil layers.

Ordinarily in deep soils the trees with a tendency to develop a tap root are more resistant to windthrow than are those with a shallow and fibrous root system. This is not always true, however, and depends to some extent on soil depth. For example, *Picea* in a Vosges forest was more resistant than *Abies* to windthrow. This apparently was due to the presence at a shallow depth of rock substratum which prevented *Abies* from developing a taproot. Growth of the spreading, superficial root system of *Picea* was not impeded (Polge, 1960).

Many of the small absorbing roots of forest trees are confined to the soil surface layers (Kramer and Kozlowski, 1960). Numerous data support this and only a few examples will be given. According to Coile (1937) 90 % of the roots less than 0.1 inch in diameter were located in the upper 5 inches of soil in a North Carolina oak forest. In a Wisconsin oak–maple forest the greatest concentration of roots of 0.1–1.0 mm in diameter was in the A_1 horizon. The 0–8 inch depth had more than 80 % of the total root volume (Scully, 1942). Bilan (1960a) found in Texas that more than half the growth of 2-year-old loblolly pine (*Pinus taeda*) roots was in the top 3-inch soil layer and more than 70 % of the total root weight in the uppermost 6 inches.

Extreme shallow rooting has been shown for yellow birch (Redmond, 1957). In the Maritime provinces of Canada most of the organic matter under stands containing yellow birch (*Betula alleghaniensis*) was in the humus layer which rarely exceeded a depth of 6 cm. In pure stands of hardwoods in which *Betula* was a major component over three-fourths of the rootlets of *Betula alleghaniensis* were in the humus layer. In stands in which *Betula* was a minor component or which had a high proportion of gymnosperms more than 90 % of the *Betula* rootlets were in the humus layer (Table 5.4) (Redmond, 1957).

Longevity of Roots

Root systems of trees consist of the relatively large perennial roots and many short-lived small roots. There has been considerable controversy about the reasons for death of small roots, with some investigators considering root necrosis as normal physiological abscission. Others contend that unfavorable environmental conditions and various pests are mainly responsible. It appears likely that loss of small roots can be traceable to all of these causes, with some factors much more important than others on different sites. The development and decay of " feeder " roots or rootlets are influenced by such factors as species, age, soil fertility, and cultural practices (Kolesnikov, 1959). As root growth depends on carbohydrates and hormonal substances supplied by a healthy shoot system, the loss of leaves by abscission or defoliation by insects and fungi inevitably decreases formation of new roots and growth of existing ones. Furthermore, defoliation increases mortality of rootlets.

In healthy trees the loss of small roots sometimes occurs shortly after their formation. In apple trees, for example, small branches on roots lived

TABLE 5.4

<small>DISTRIBUTION OF ROOTLETS OF *Betula alleghaniensis* AT VARIOUS SOIL DEPTHS
IN STANDS OF VARYING COMPOSITION[a]</small>

Soil depth (cm)	Cumulative concentration of rootlets (%)		
	Hardwood 80% *Betula alleghaniensis*	Hardwood–softwood mixture	80% Hardwood–20% *Picea and Abies*
0–1	35.3	39.2	42.1
1–2	60.0	68.2	74.2
2–3	69.9	84.9	82.4
3–4	75.5	88.1	89.4
4–5	79.8	90.7	91.3
5–6	81.2	93.5	93.9
6–7	82.4	94.8	94.2
7–8	83.9	95.0	94.4
8–9	85.3	95.0	95.1
9–10	87.0	96.0	95.9
10–11	87.8	97.3	96.0
11–12	88.9	97.3	96.3

[a] From Redmond (1957).

only about a week even though the environment appeared to be suitable for growth (Childers and White, 1942). During any year, the greatest mortality of small roots appears to take place during the winter, possibly reflecting a starvation effect, at least in part. This was shown by Bode (1959) who found that more than 90% of the absorbing roots of *Juglans regia* were lost during the winter. According to Voronkov (1956), the dry weight of active roots of tea (*Camellia thea*) plants was 12–13% lower in February than in the previous December. By early April, however, new root growth had more than made up for the winter losses, and thereafter root growth was accelerated. In mature tea plants dead roots, as a proportion of the total at a soil depth of 30–50 cm, amounted to 4.3% in August, 4.2% in October, 5.3% in December, and 9.3% in February, emphasizing the relatively large winter losses.

There appears to be wide variability among species in the longevity of their small rootlets. Bosse (1960) showed that in apple seedlings the small absorbing roots began to decay in 80–100 days after their formation. In contrast, most absorbing rootlets of *Picea excelsa* usually lived from 3 to 4 years, but approximately 10% died during the first year while 20% remained alive for more than 4 years (Orlov, 1960). There is evidence of increasing root mortality with advanced tree age. For example, Copeland (1952) found that dead roots of 14- to 18-year-old shortleaf pine (*Pinus echinata*) and loblolly pine (*P. taeda*) trees averaged 2.0 and 3.7%, respectively, whereas in 34- to 42-year-old trees root mortality averaged 18.0 and 6.3% for these species.

EFFECT OF INSECTS AND DISEASES ON ROOT LONGEVITY

Mortality of rootlets is strongly influenced by fungal disease and insect attacks. Redmond (1959) examined some 60,000 rootlets from healthy *Abies balsamea* trees and found that less than 15% of the rootlets were dead. However, in trees fully or partially defoliated by spruce budworm, the amount of rootlet mortality was much greater. When defoliation destroyed more than 70% of the new leaves, rootlet mortality exceeded 30%. When 100% of the foliage was removed by budworm more than 75% of the rootlets died quickly (Table 5.5). When defoliation ceased or decreased in amount, new rootlets were produced rapidly, but this response varied considerably with tree age. Mature trees were less capable than young ones of producing new rootlets. Overmature trees did not produce new rootlets after new shoots had been totally defoliated for 4–5 years in succession, although they produced some new foliage before they died.

There appears to be a close relationship between dieback disease of birch and root deterioration following adverse climatic conditions. Hawboldt and Greenidge (1952) considered rootlet mortality as the initial symptom of the dieback disease. Pomerleau and Lortie (1962) demonstrated that deterioration of *Betula papyrifera* trees was related to depth of rooting. They reported a pattern of shallow rooting of trees following crown damage. In plots with trees having more than 90% of their foliage in a healthy, green condition, the average penetration of soil by roots was 8 inches and the average effective soil depth was 13 inches. Where the soil was less than 6 inches deep, the dieback was advanced, and less than 20% of the foliage was living. Table 5.6 and Fig. 5.3 show variations in vertical root distribution of 4 trees ranging from a healthy condition (tree No. 1) to an advanced stage of dieback (tree No. 4). Tree No. 1 had 98% of its crown showing normal foliage and a well developed root system that penetrated the soil to a depth greater than 50 inches. In contrast, tree No. 4 was almost dead. Only 2% of its foliage was alive and its root system was unusually shallow and sparsely developed. Trees 2 and 3 represented intermediate stages of birch dieback (Fig 5.3).

Pinus echinata trees affected by "littleleaf" disease had higher root mortality than did healthy trees (Table 5.7). Further, in healthy trees mortality was highest in roots less than 0.5 inches in diameter. On diseased trees, however, root mortality occurred to a considerable extent in all size classes of roots up to 1 inch in diameter (Copeland, 1952). Investigations by Jackson (1945) showed greater defects in root systems of pines of the southern United States with littleleaf disease than in healthy ones. Among important

TABLE 5.5.

MORTALITY OF ROOTLETS OF FIVE STANDS OF *Abies balsamea* IN 1956 AS RELATED TO HISTORY OF DEFOLIATION OF TREES BY SPRUCE BUDWORM[a]

Current foliage removal (%)							Tree size d.b.h.[b] (in)	Rootlet mortality (%)			
1950	1951	1952	1953	1954	1955	1956		0–15	31–50	76–99	100
									(number of trees)		
40	25	15	15	30	15	20	7–12	9	1		
5	5	5	5	30	65	90	3– 6	4	4	2	
10	60	100	100	95	10	0	4– 6		3	6	
5	5	5	50	70	100	80	4– 6		1	18	
65	100	100	100	100	80	40	8-12			3	10

[a] From Redmond (1959)
[b] Diameter at breast height

TABLE 5.6

DEPTH OF ROOTING AND AMOUNT OF ROOTLET MORTALITY
IN FOUR *Betula papyrifera* TREES IN VARYING STAGES OF
BIRCH DIEBACK[a]

Tree no.	Amount of living foliage (%)	Mean rooting depth (inches)	Average root mortality (%)
1	98	20	14
2	80	13	18
3	15	9	69
4	2	7	97

[a] The trees varied in age from 83 to 86 years and in diameter from 7.5 to 8 inches. [From Pomerleau and Lortie, (1962).]

defects were dieback of feeding roots, mortality of primary and lateral roots, cankers on the large roots, and excessive sloughing of bark from small roots. Diseased trees had 71% of the feeding roots with dieback as opposed to 17% for roots of healthy trees. Most of the feeding roots on diseased trees were stubby, and sometimes roots were reduced to spurlike structures with one or more replacement roots.

Progressive decay and loss of root systems of *Picea glauca* trees infested with *Polyporus tomentosus* was described by Whitney (1962). In early stages of the infection the trees had dead lateral roots one-fourth to three-fourths inches in diameter. In the early middle stages up to 40% of the root wood was decayed. In late stages, only 20% or less of the roots were alive and all of the main lateral roots were decayed. Although *Polyporus tomentosus* infected all root regions, heartwood usually was severely attacked. Table 5.8 demonstrates that there was at least a 50% increase, on the average, in rootlet mortality of infected trees over healthy ones.

Root Regeneration

The seed contains a radicle or root meristem in the embryo from which the first tap root develops. This first root branches and elongates to produce a ramified root system, or it may die back. Whereas lateral shoots on the stem originate from peripheral tissues, lateral roots arise from the deep-seated outer layer of the stele known as the pericycle (Fig. 5.4). During initiation of lateral roots, a group of pericyclic cells becomes meristematic and forms a protruding lateral root primordium which grows through the

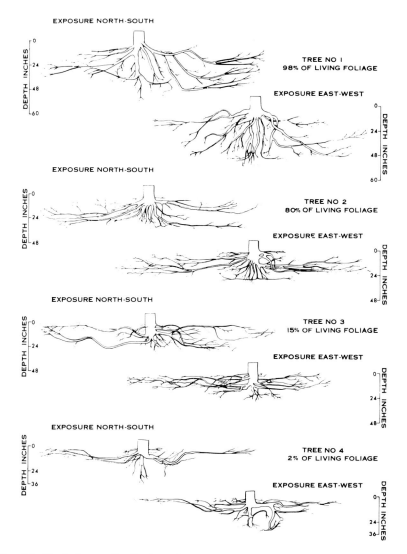

FIG. 5.3. Vertical root distribution of paper birch (*Betula papyrifera*) trees with varying amounts of living foliage. [From Pomerleau and Lortie (1962).]

endodermis, cortex, and epidermis. Before a lateral root breaks through the surface tissue of the main root, it develops a well-defined apical meristem and root cap. Both digestion of the surrounding tissue and mechanical pressure appear to be involved in outgrowth of lateral roots through the cortex.

TABLE 5.7

Root Mortality in Healthy and Littleleaf *Pinus echinata* Trees[a]

Soil	$\frac{1}{4}''$ Diameter		$\frac{1}{4}-\frac{1}{2}''$ Diameter		$\frac{1}{2}-1''$ Diameter		$1''$ and larger	
	Healthy	Littleleaf	Healthy	Littleleaf	Healthy	Littleleaf	Healthy	Littleleaf
Cecil	17	36	4	29	0	17	0	0
Davidson	14	34	12	24	0	9	0	0
Cataula	24	37	11	23	13	25	0	14
Vance	19	34	20	14	19	20	20	0
Mecklenburg	21	38	5	24	0	25	20	3

Dead roots (%) in various size classes

[a] From Copeland (1952).

TABLE 5.8

ROOTLET MORTALITY IN THREE HEALTHY *Picea glauca* TREES
AND SIX TREES INFECTED WITH *Polyporus tomentosus*[a]

	Tree no.	No. rootlets examined	% Dead
Healthy trees	1	2325	32.8
	2	1229	25.2
	3	130	26.2
Mean			30.1
Diseased trees	1	227	45.4
	2	123	80.4
	3	58	38.9
	4	65	31.8
	5	74	42.9
	6	259	39.6
Mean			47.8

[a] From Whitney (1962).

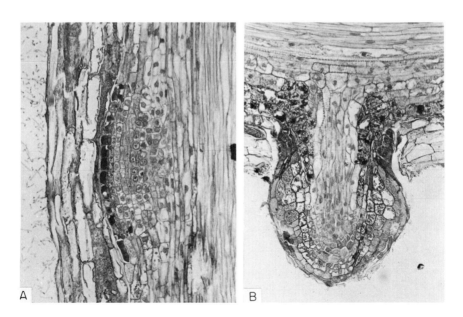

FIG. 5.4. Early stage (A) and late stage (B) of formation of lateral roots in *Pinus resinosa*. Photo courtesy of H. E. Wilcox.

ORIGIN OF ADVENTITIOUS ROOTS

Many woody plants form adventitious roots which may be defined as roots and their branches which do not originate at the root pole of the embryo. Adventitious roots commonly form on aerial plant parts, underground stems, and old roots of intact trees. The formation of adventitious roots on cuttings has accounted for successful propagation of many species.

Like normal lateral roots, adventitious roots may arise endogenously near vascular tissues. Subsequently they grow radially through various tissues and, preceding emergence from the stem or root, develop a promeristem, root cap, vascular cylinder, and cortex (Esau, 1965b). Adventitious roots may also develop from latent root primordia already present in "morphological roots," or they may develop from new primordia which originate from divisions of parenchyma cells in various tissues as in "wound induced roots." Wilcox (1955) emphasized differences in origin of normal lateral roots and those induced by root pruning. In each, the site of origin was related to proximity of vascular connections between the mother root and lateral. In unpruned roots, and those pruned before much secondary growth took place, the laterals originated in the pericycle which was near functioning xylem and phloem. However, in roots pruned after formation of a cambial cylinder, lateral replacement roots originated in the cambium.

Latent Root Primordia in Stems

According to Carlson (1938, 1950), latent root primordia are initiated during the first year and differentiate slowly. Additional primordia may form after the first year. As a stem increases in diameter, the root primordia increase in length, perpendicularly to the stem axis, in an amount equal to that of cambial growth. The root primordia can be stimulated to grow under proper conditions of darkness and moisture (Shapiro, 1958). Some of them probably remain dormant as long as the stem remains alive. Not all root primordia develop and the number which fails to grow usually increases with the age of the stem. Carlson (1950) reported latent root primordia in stems of several genera including *Pyrus, Acer, Thuja, Cupressus, Salix, Populus,* and *Ribes*. Carpenter (1961) found preformed root primordia in stems of *Citrus medica* seedlings. Most of the primordia appeared to have formed shortly after differentiation of the primary stem as indicated by their origin near the pith. Under suitable conditions the root primordia became active and in 1-year-old stems roots emerged within a week. Roots of cuttings usually emerged before basal callus was visible and appeared before the new adventitious roots which originated in the bark. Emergence of preformed roots was delayed for several weeks in old leafless stems with thick bark.

New Root Primordia

Bannan (1942) found that the origin of adventitious roots on wounded plants varied with species. For example, in *Taxus canadensis* adventitious roots originated from sectors of the cambium comprising fusiform initials and ray initials. In *Thuja occidentalis* and several species of *Juniperus* the root meristems originated in the phloem or cambial portions of unusually large xylem rays. In contrast, adventitious roots of *Abies balsamea*, *Picea glauca*, and *P. mariana* arose from dormant buds, and in *Larix laricina* they originated in the vicinity of dead or injured dwarf branches.

Callus formation at the base of cuttings appears to be required before rooting for some species but not for others. The origin of callus, a parenchymatous tissue formed by cell proliferation near wounds, varies with species. Although callus develops principally from newly formed derivatives of the cambium or from xylem rays, it may also originate in the pith and cortex (Barker, 1954; Rake, 1957). Snyder (1954) found callus originating primarily from the cambium and phloem parenchyma, but according to Buck (1954) callus tissues may form from any living cell that has not developed secondary walls.

The time of formation and origin of adventitious roots may be different in the juvenile and mature stage of the same species (Figs. 5.5, 5.6). Adventitious roots in the internodes of cuttings of juvenile phase plants of *Hedera helix* originated in phloem ray parenchyma above the basal cuts usually in 6–10 days. The roots emerged in one and a half to two weeks after the cuttings were made (Girouard, 1967a). As *Hedera helix* plants aged, the time needed for adventitious roots to form increased, and callus played an increasingly important role in the rooting of cuttings. In the mature growth phase, adventitious roots were initiating at the end of 2–4 weeks in phloem ray parenchyma of internodes and in callus near the basal end of cuttings. The adventitious roots emerged at the end of 3–5 weeks (Girouard, 1967b).

Knight (1926) reported that roots of cuttings of fruit trees usually appeared through basal callus. Cuttings of varieties which did not form callus died. In contrast, Swingle (1929) found callusing and rooting in *Malus* and *Salix* to occur independently of each other. Root production on hardwood cuttings of the gooseberry variety Keepsake did not depend on production of basal callus, but when callus formed on cuttings, root development was greater (Rake, 1957). Preformed root initials were not found in unplanted stems. Basal roots on cuttings originated from parenchyma cells near the cambium opposite a wood ray. Nodal roots originated from parenchyma cells near the cambium in the bud gap in a region of starch-filled ray cells. Satoo (1953) found that in cuttings of *Thujopsis*, the adventitious roots emanated primarily from callus tissue but also from stem tissues near the cut. Most of the roots from stem tissues originated in cells of the phloem region of primary ray

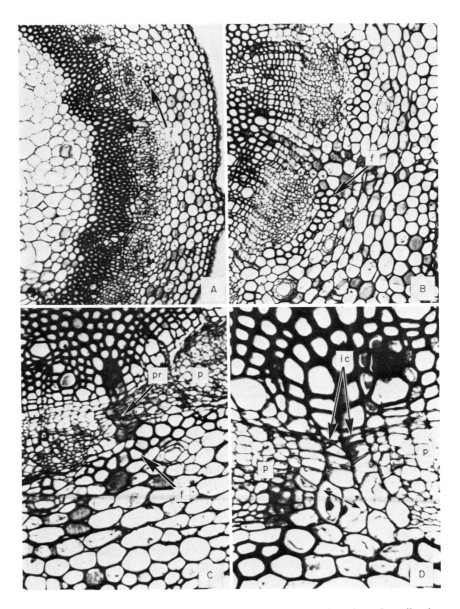

FIG. 5.5. Adventitious root formation in internodes of cuttings from juvenile phase plants of *Hedera helix*. (A) Transection of part of seedling stem showing few fibers external to phloem. (B) Transection of part of stem from a juvenile plant several years old. Fibers appear to form a mechanical barrier. (C) Transection of part of juvenile stem showing fibers which have differentiated external and tangential to a phloem ray. (D) Transection of part of stem showing derivatives of an anticlinal division in a phloem ray. Sample collected 6 days after the cutting was made. (E) Transection of part of juvenile stem showing root

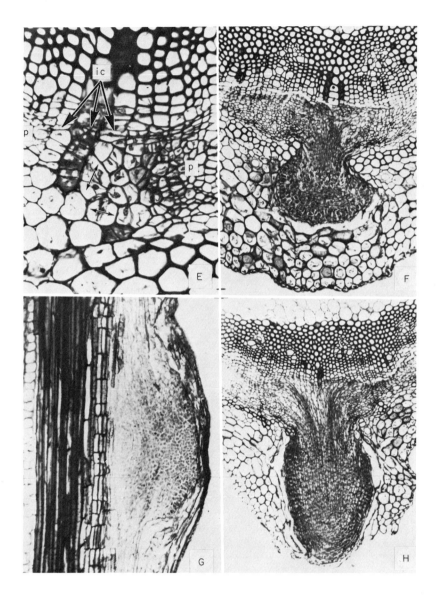

initial at a stage later than shown in D. Sample collected from base of 8-day-old cutting. (F) Transection of an adventitious root primordium in median view. Sample collected from base of 10-day-old cutting. (G) Longisection of an adventitious root primordium. Sample collected from base of 10-day old cutting. (H) Transection of young adventitious root which has penetrated the cortical and epidermal cells. A rootcap is well developed. Sample collected from base of 12-day-old cutting. f, Fibers; p, phloem; pr. phloem ray; ic, interfascicular cambium. [From Girouard (1967a). Reproduced by permission of the National Research Council of Canada.]

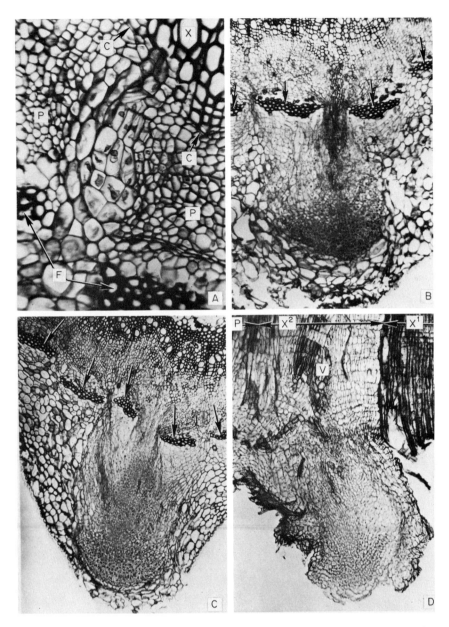

Fig. 5.6. Adventitious root formation in internodes of cuttings from adult phase plants of *Hedera helix*. (A) Median longitudinal section of young root initial. (B, C) Transections of stems with adventitious roots developing through cortical and epidermal tissues. Groups of fibers (arrows) do not impede root development. (D) Longisection of part of mature stem showing adventitious root which had formed in callus tissue derived from woundwood. C, Cambium; F, groups of fibers; P, phloem; V, vessels; X^1, primary xylem; X^2, secondary xylem. [From Girouard (1967b).]

tissue, either just below the leaf trace or from the leaf trace itself. According to Satoo (1955) most adventitious roots on cuttings of *Taxus cuspidata* and *Torreya nucifera* originated from callus tissues, as in *Cryptomeria*, *Thujopsis*, and *Thuja*, but some arose from phloem parenchyma near the cut as in *Abies* and *Picea*. Cameron and Thomson (1969) noted that adventitious roots on *Pinus radiata* cuttings did not arise directly by formation of new root meristems but were preceded either by lateral extension of callus xylem or by formation and extension of tracheid nests. At about the time that primordia emerged from the callus, true root meristems formed and developed rapidly, giving rise to protrusions which formed the first roots. Further appreciation of the variability of origin of adventitious roots may be gained from the work of Satoo (1956) who found roots of conifer cuttings to develop from cambial and phloem regions of ray tissues, leaf and branch traces, bud meristems and bud traces, irregular patches of parenchyma, and callus. In species difficult to root, however, the roots developed almost exclusively from callus tissue.

Root Hairs

The absorbing surface of roots of many species of woody plants is increased by development of root hairs These tubular outgrowths usually arise from the epidermis but in a few species they originate from cortical cells below the epidermis. Root hairs usually form in the area just behind the zone of most active meristematic tissue and they diminish in length toward the apex. They generally form after epidermal cell elongation slows (Cormack, 1949). The highly vacuolated and thin-walled root hairs vary in life-span. The majority live only a few hours, days, or weeks and are eliminated by changes of secondary thickening, including suberization and lignification (Kramer and Kozlowski, 1960). The zone of root hairs migrates because as old root hairs die new ones form regularly behind the growing point of an elongating root. Some trees, including *Gleditsia*, *Gymnocladus*, and Valencia orange, retain suberized or lignified root hairs for periods varying from months to years (MacDougal, 1921; Hayward and Long, 1942). Such persistent root hairs appear to be relatively inefficient in absorption.

Both hereditary differences among species and environmental factors influence the abundance of root hairs on trees (Kramer and Kozlowski, 1960) At times, many trees, such as avocado (*Persea*) and pecan (*Carya*), lack root hairs (Woodroof and Woodroof, 1934; Smith and Wallace, 1954). They also are absent on roots of some species of gymnosperms and on roots bearing mycorrhizae. Dittmer (1949) found root hairs growing on many species and found their presence to be consistent within a species. There was considerable variation in size of root hairs and the range of distribution among tree

species, but differences in size within any species were slight. The diameter
of root hairs was not correlated with length (Table 5.9). Root hairs often
were quite persistent and withstood considerable washing of roots. In one
Gleditsia plant the epidermis was being pushed off in strips by handling, but
the hairs were undamaged (Dittmer, 1949).

In *Pseudotsuga menziesii* root hairs occurred adjacent to root tips and at
considerable distance from growing points (McMinn, 1963). Kozlowski and
Scholtes (1948) found that roots of the average 7-week-old *Robinia pseudoacacia* seedling, grown in the greenhouse, developed over 11,000 root hairs
while *Pinus taeda* of the same age had less than 600 root hairs (Table 5.10).
The total root surface area of *Robinia pseudoacacia* was about 8 times that
of *Pinus taeda* per unit of root surface. Richardson (1953c) emphasized
differences in root hair production in *Acer pseudoplatanus* and *Quercus rubra*.
Acer had a normal pattern of root hair development, with the root hair
zone located just behind the growing tip and extending for 2–3 millimeters.
In contrast, *Quercus* had root hairs only on roots of the lowest order of
branching and these were produced only after growth ceased, in many
cases back from the root tip for the entire length of the roots. Variations
in size and distribution of root hairs among species are shown in Table
5.10.

TABLE 5.9

LENGTHS AND DIAMETERS OF ROOT HAIRS[a]

Species	Average diameter (μ) of root hairs on roots of:			Average length (μ) of root hairs on root of:		
	Main	Secondary	Tertiary	Main	Secondary	Tertiary
Celtis occidentalis	—	8	8	—	170	170
Ulmus pumila	—	—	10	—	—	200
Gleditsia triacanthos	—	13	13	—	200	180
Fraxinus lanceolata	—	5	5	—	370	370
Catalpa catalpa	—	10	10	—	250	250

[a] From Dittmer (1949).

TABLE 5.10

VARIATION IN DEVELOPMENT OF ROOTS AND ROOT HAIRS OF GREENHOUSE-GROWN, 7-WEEK-OLD *Robinia pseudoacacia* AND *Pinus taeda* SEEDLINGS[a]

	Root length (cm)	Root surface area (sq cm)	Root hairs (no)	Root hair surface area (sq cm)
Robinia pseudoacacia				
Primary	16.20	3.4466	1,166	3.6346
Secondary	115.62	15.7167	8,321	25.2172
Tertiary	30.60	3.1151	2,081	5.1759
Total	162.42	22.2784	11,568	34.0277
			520 root hairs per sq cm	
Pinus taeda				
Primary	6.45	2.7341	215	2.7973
Secondary	5.93	0.9683	371	2.0770
Total	12.38	2.7021	586	2.8743
			217 root hairs per sq cm	

[a] From Kozlowski and Scholtes (1948).

Primary Growth of Roots

A longitudinal section of the end of a young root typically has four cell regions of different character. At the tip is the protective cellular mass comprising the root cap. Behind it is the growing point, a meristematic region of small, thin-walled, cubical cells with dense cytoplasm. Mitotic figures often can be seen in this growing point, which usually is about a millimeter long. As the number of cells increases some are added to the root cap and others to the region of elongation located above the meristematic zone. It is in this region that the cells produced in the growing point rapidly increase their size, primarily in a longitudinal direction. Above the region of elongation is a zone of differentiation and maturation. Eventually the newly formed cells at the base of the region of elongation lose their capacity for further expansion and become differentiated into the epidermis, cortex, and stele.

As Kramer (1949) noted, considerable variation may be found among species and different roots in the delineation of root zones. The root cap, for example, does not occur in mycorrhizal roots of pines. The zone of differentiation often is difficult to measure because certain types of cells are differentiated at different distances from the root tip. Furthermore, the distance from the apex at which cells differentiate is a function of the rate of root growth (Riedhart and Guard, 1957). Wilcox (1954) found that various elements of slow growing roots of *Abies procera* matured closer to the apical initials than was the case in fast growing roots. For example, protoxylem elements were fully matured at 7 mm from the apex in actively growing roots, at 0.5 mm in a root sampled 4 days after elongation ceased, and at less than 0.05 mm in a root which had been dormant for a long time.

METACUTIZATION

Associated with cessation of root elongation is the process of metacutization which accounts for the presence of the dark brown cap which forms at the tip (Wilcox, 1954). The brown color then spreads until the whole root is colored. This process, the "Metakutisierung" of Müller (1906), involves lignification and suberization of cell walls of the cortex and dormant root cap. Many roots retain a white root tip even though a metacutization layer is present. Presence or absence of a white tip depends on how many layers of dead cells are cut off outside the metacutization layer.

In *Abies procera*, metacutization proceeded regularly in an acropetal direction. Initially the secondary endodermis developed downward to a region near the tip. From this level a zone of suberized cells curved outward near the boundary between the cortex and root cap. Although at this stage the initials were surrounded by the suberized layer they were not completely dormant but redivided briefly and the new tissue penetrated the enclosing layers. Such temporary growth activity was soon followed by dormancy and reforming of the metacutization layers (Wilcox, 1954). The orientation of the metacutization layer in relation to other root tissues is shown in Fig. 5.7.

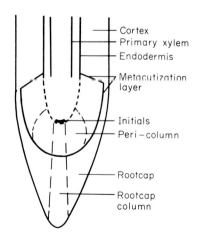

FIG. 5.7. Diagrammatic representation of tissue arrangement during metacutization in the root apex of *Abies procera*. [From Wilcox (1954).]

RATES OF ROOT ELONGATION

The growing root tip is pushed through the soil by the elongating cells and follows an irregular course around obstacles. Wilson (1964) found that roots commonly twisted as they grew. One root was twisted more than 4 times in a length of 22 meters. Time-lapse cinematography has revealed spiral movements of growing apple root tips (Head, 1965). As shown in Fig. 5.8, the direction of root tip growth was constantly changing with one

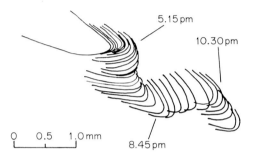

FIG. 5.8. Variations in direction of growth of elongating root tips of apple trees. The outline drawings were made at 15-min intervals from time-lapse photographs. [From Head (1965).]

complete cycle occurring in 6–7 hr. Only the apical 1.5–2.0 mm of the root showed displacement and the amplitude of the movements usually did not exceed the thickness of the root.

Seasonal Variations in Root Elongation

In analyzing seasonal growth of roots it is important to recognize two separate components: (1) elongation of existing roots and (2) initiation of laterals and their subsequent elongation. Therefore, growth periodicity of the total root system often is very different from that of individual roots within it. In the following discussion the root growth of the entire root system will be considered.

Root elongation in the Temperate Zone usually begins earlier in the spring than does shoot elongation in the same tree. Roots also grow for a longer time (Fig. 5.9) than above-ground parts of plants. The time interval between cessation of shoot expansion and of root elongation varies greatly among species. Root elongation may continue for many weeks after shoots stop expanding in species whose shoots are preformed in the bud and later expand rapidly. However, in heterophyllous and recurrently flushing species (Chapter 5, Volume I) root elongation often continues for only a slightly longer time than does shoot elongation. According to Lyr and Hoffmann (1967), the roots of angiosperm seedlings often showed maximum growth in early summer

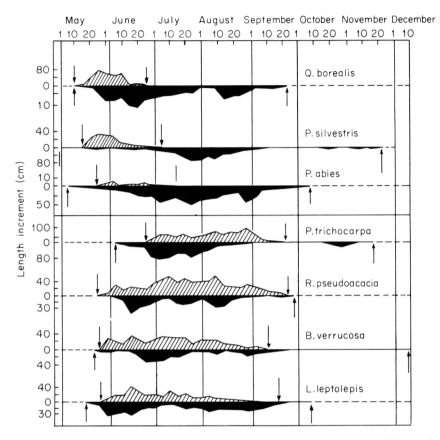

FIG. 5.9. Variations in seasonal shoot and root growth characteristics of eight species of forest trees. Shading indicates shoot growth and solid black represents root growth. Seasonal initiation and termination of growth are indicated by arrows. [From Lyr and Hoffmann (1967).]

whereas roots of gymnosperms grew somewhat more uniformly throughout the season.

Root growth of a number of genera, including citrus, occurs in cycles and these often appear to be responses to environmental changes. Whereas Reed and MacDougal (1937) reported two main surges of root growth for citrus in California, Schneider (1952), also in California, observed abundant root growth throughout December to April. Cooper (1957) found root growth of citrus in the Rio Grande Valley taking place in October, November, December, and January. He emphasized that citrus roots in California were dormant during the winter months when soil temperatures generally were lower than 55°F. Winter root growth of citrus usually takes place in Palestine,

South Africa, and the Rio Grande Valley where soil temperatures generally exceed 55°F.

During a cycle of root elongation, both the rate and duration of growth often vary with root order. For example, Wilcox (1968a) showed that during a growth cycle the primary roots of *Pinus resinosa* grew faster and for a longer time than first-order lateral roots which, in turn, grew faster and for a longer time than second-order laterals (Fig. 5.10).

Some idea of variability in root growth characteristics of apple trees in England may be gained from Fig. 5.11. Seasonal duration of root growth, as determined by number of white root tips at various times, was greater in Worcester Pearmain than in James Grieve or Crowley Beauty trees. Worcester Pearmain trees had a surge of root growth in April and May and one or two additional ones late in the season but the late-season pattern varied greatly among trees. James Grieve and Crowley Beauty trees had only one major surge of root growth. Rapid early-season root growth in James Grieve preceded that in Crowley Beauty and was correlated with earlier bud burst in the former.

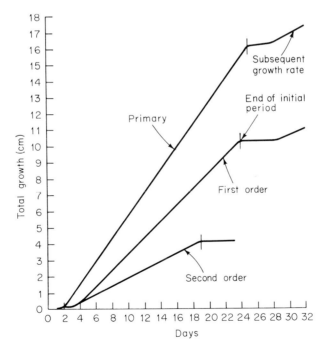

Fig. 5.10. Variations in rates of elongation of various orders of roots of *Pinus resinosa* seedlings. [From Wilcox (1968a).]

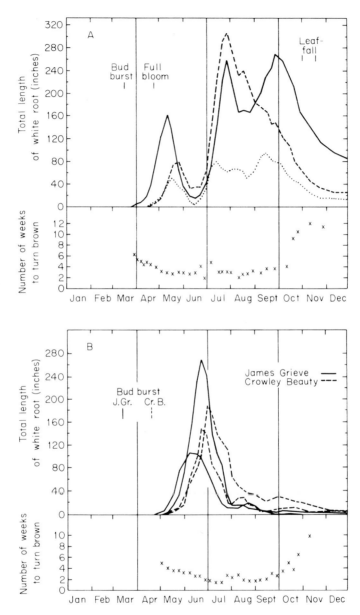

Fig. 5.11. Variations in seasonal patterns of root growth in England of three Worcester Pearmain apple trees (A) and 2 trees of James Grieve and Crowley Beauty (B). [From Head (1966).]

In Russia, the roots of fruit trees generally grew in two cycles of 2.5–3 months each, whereas shoots usually had only one growth flush lasting 2.5–3 months in May to July (Kolesnikov, 1955). However, the duration of root growth varied greatly in different areas. In the south, roots ceased growing during summer droughts and resumed growing later. Hence, growth occurred over a period of 5–6 months in May to July and October through November. Near Moscow in unusually wet years root growth occurred for 7–8 months. Kolesnikov (1960) noted that roots of cherry and plum grew more in autumn than roots of apple and pear. In the winter, however, apple and pear roots grew faster than those of cherry and plum.

The length of the growing season for roots varies at different soil depths. Growth in length of *Quercus robur* roots in the cis-Caspian lowland lasted for 10 months or more (April to January) but the duration of growth varied in different soil horizons. Root growth in the humus horizon lasted 3 months (late April–July) but in the leached horizon it lasted 5 months (May–October). At depths of 0–160 cm, root growth started when soil temperatures reached 15°C during the day, whereas in deeper horizons it began with temperatures of 10°. In the upper soil horizon root growth ceased in the middle of the growing season because of drought, but it often resumed in the autumn following rainfall (Karandina, 1961).

In the deep sands of the southeastern coastal plain of the United States development of very superficial root systems of scrub oaks (*Quercus laevis* and *Q. incana*) and longleaf pine (*Pinus palustris*) appears to be the result of an exceedingly unfavorable environment below the top few inches of soil (Woods, 1957). In that area plants of all species form a thick mat of fibrous roots in the upper 4–5 inches of soil. Below this there are very few roots. Rainfall distribution usually is restricted to the surface soil and nutrient-enriched organic matter is concentrated in the top 3 inches. In the winter, root growth often occurs in the surface soil which may be 10°F warmer than the soil at a depth of 9–12 inches.

In Israel, the main surge of root growth of *Pinus halepensis* occurred in winter when soil moisture content was high and temperatures were not low enough to restrict growth (Leshem, 1965). As may be seen in Table 5.11 the ratio of growing to dormant root tips was high from December to March. It decreased toward April and remained low during the dry summer season. There was an increase in growing roots toward autumn. Dormant roots resumed growth and new laterals appeared on long roots. There was neither complete cessation of root growth nor general growth activity at any time of the year. The percentage of growing roots varied from 70 to 80% during the most active period to as much as 10–15% during the dry season. Some root growth occurred during the dry season even when soil moisture was below wilting percentage but roots grew very slowly and briefly.

TABLE 5.11

SEASONAL VARIATIONS IN DORMANT AND GROWING ROOT TIPS OF *Pinus halepensis* AT
PANORAMA AND AT NEVE ILAN IN ISRAEL[a]

Month	Panorama			Neve Ilan		
	Number growing tips	Number dormant tips	Ratio of growing to dormant tips	Number growing tips	Number dormant tips	Ratio of growing to dormant tips
December	97	26	3.7	43	12	3.6
January	58	47	1.2	31	13	2.4
February	131	71	1.8	8	6	1.3
March	82	22	3.7	23	23	1.0
April	74	240	0.3	15	13	1.1
May	19	150	0.1	2	13	0.2
June	19	77	0.2	10	33	0.3
July	14	165	0.08	4	25	0.4
August	37	240	0.2	31	69	0.5
September	62	69	0.9	13	39	0.3
October	36	182	0.2	43	60	0.7
November	64	45	1.4	68	81	0.8

[a] From Leshem (1965)

Seasonal Root Growth of Nursery Stock

Stone and his colleagues in California have made valuable studies of seasonal variations in capacity of forest tree seedlings to regenerate roots. The root regenerating potential of tree seedlings depends on growth of intact short roots as well as capacity to initiate new roots on the few remaining long roots (Fig. 5.12). Whereas renewed growth activity in some species reflects elongation of short roots, in other species it involves both elongation of short roots as well as initiation of new ones (Stone, Jenkinson, and Krugman, 1962).

Much variation was shown among species and seasons in root regenerating potential. In general, in species which set dormant buds, such as *Pinus ponderosa*, *Pseudotsuga menziesii*, and *Abies concolor*, the capacity for root regeneration was low or absent during the summer. It increased during the autumn, continued to increase during the winter, and was highest prior to the time of bud break in the spring (Fig. 5.13). Root elongation of *Pinus ponderosa* seedlings transplanted to the greenhouse in July and August generally did not take place, but roots elongated during all other months. The pattern of root initiation was quite different, however, with roots forming

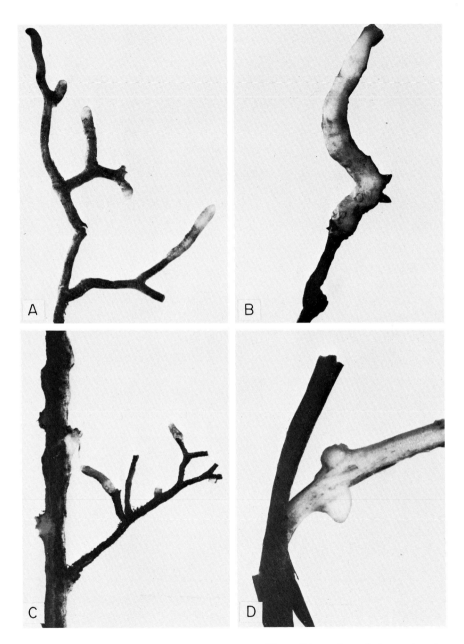

Fig. 5.12. Root growth of *Pinus ponderosa* seedlings. (A) portion of the root system showing lateral branching. Light colored tips show elongation. (B) An elongating lateral root with new growth shown by the light colored portion; (C) portion of the root system showing elongation of laterals and initiation of new laterals. Branched tips to the right are elongating and light spots at the left are recently initiated laterals. (D) Root with bark peeled away to show recently initiated lateral root. [From Stone and Schubert (1959).]

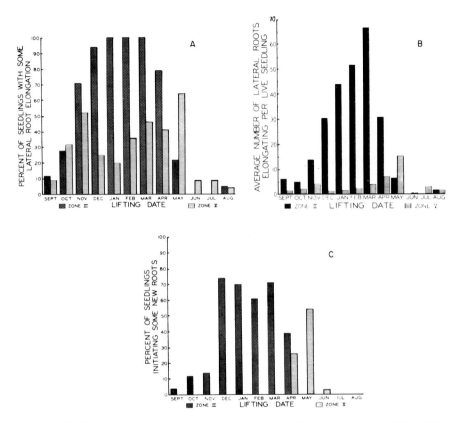

FIG. 5.13. Seasonal variations in root regeneration of *Pinus ponderosa* seedlings lifted from two California nurseries at various times during the year. Zone III data are for seed grown at the Placerville nursery and Zone V data for seed grown at the Mt. Shasta nursery. (A) Percent of seedlings showing some lateral root elongation within a month after being transplanted to the greenhouse; (B) average number of lateral roots per live seedling that showed some elongation within a month; (C) percent of seedlings showing root initiation within a month. [From Stone and Schubert (1959).]

only on seedlings transplanted from December to June 7 (Stone and Schubert, 1959). *Pseudotsuga menziesii* seedlings also exhibited marked seasonal periodicity in root growth, with a maximum in early spring. Root regenerating potential was primarily an expression of elongation of lateral roots rather than initiation and elongation of new ones. This emphasized the importance of preventing breakage and desiccation of existing roots during lifting and outplanting of nursery stock (Stone, Jenkinson, and Krugman, 1962). The seasonal variation in root growth of seedlings often varied somewhat among forest nurseries. As may be seen in Table 5.12 at the Mt. Shasta nursery in

TABLE 5.12

SEASONAL VARIATION IN ROOT REGENERATING POTENTIAL OF *Pinus ponderosa*
SEEDLINGS OBTAINED FROM FOUR CALIFORNIA NURSERIES[a]

Lifting date	Nursery				Total
	Mt. Shasta	Magalio	Placerville	Ben Lomard	
October 12	173	26	33	80	312
October 27	129	50	150	137	466
November 9	160	19	187	165	531
November 22	128	71	104	120	423
December 8	65	57	118	138	378
March 8	*105*	*187*	*265*	*289*	*846*
March 28	*220*	*76*	*189*	*156*	*641*
April 9	205	30	44	35	314
April 26	168	17	15	46	246
Total	1353	533	1105	1166	

[a] Data are numbers of roots showing new growth of 0.5 inch or more during one month in the greenhouse. The period of high root regenerating potential (March) is indicated by italics. [From Stone *et al.* (1963).]

California the autumn increase in potential for regeneration of roots began earlier, and the spring maximum and subsequent decline developed later than at other nurseries. Seedling size did not appear to influence root regeneration significantly. For example, root regeneration of large seedlings from the Placerville nursery did not differ significantly from that of small seedlings from the Mt. Shasta nursery.

Species which do not set a winter bud generally showed much less seasonal amplitude in capacity for root regeneration than did species which set a winter bud. Figure 5.14, for example, shows that *Pinus radiata*, which exhibits recurrent shoot flushing, had several peaks of root growth during the year (Krugman, Stone, and Bega, 1965).

Seasonal and species variations in capacity for root growth have important practical implications. This was emphasized by Stone, Jenkinson, and Krugman (1962) who observed that mortality of transplants and root regenerating potential were inversely related. On adverse sites, especially dry ones, successful planting often depends on rapid regeneration of roots. Hence, the planting of species showing marked seasonal periodicity in root regeneration potential must be confined to the time of year when high capacity for root growth occurs. On sites with high availability of soil moisture throughout the year, adjustment of planting schedules is less important. Species such as *Pinus radiata* with high potential for root growth throughout the year can be

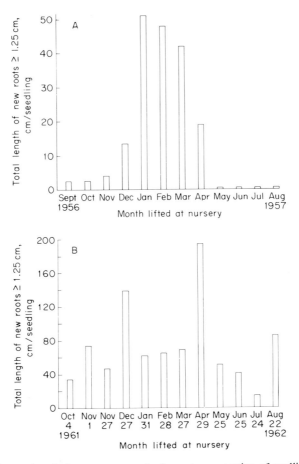

Fig. 5.14. Seasonal variations among species in root regeneration of seedlings. (A) *Pinus ponderosa,* which sets a dormant bud and, (B) *Pinus radiata* which does not set a dormant bud. [From Stone and Schubert (1959) and Krugman, Stone, and Bega (1965).]

planted on various sites without special consideration to peak periods of root regeneration. Stone and Jenkinson (1971) described a useful physiological grading system for ponderosa pine seedlings based on their expected root growth following planting. The system can be used for predicting root growth for specific planting dates. After seedlings are graded for root growth capacity the user can determine the capacities he will accept for various sites. The system shows promise for predicting seedling root growth for specific planting dates and thereby eliminate planting failures resulting from use of seedlings with inadequate capacity for root growth for a given environment.

The importance of root growth to survival of planted trees was shown by Bushey (1957). He related variation in survival among species to differences in loss of fibrous roots during transplanting and in regeneration of new roots. For example, *Ulmus americana*, which was easy to transplant, lost fewer roots during transplanting than *Quercus palustris*, which showed low survival. Furthermore, *Ulmus* planted in the autumn regenerated 4 times as many roots as *Quercus*. When *Quercus* was transplanted in the spring it showed higher survival than when planted in the autumn. Spring-transplanted trees also regenerated more new rootlets than those transplanted in the autumn, further emphasizing the importance of rapid root growth to survival.

Diurnal Variations in Root Elongation

The rate of root elongation of most individual roots of woody plants may vary from a fraction of a millimeter to well over 25 mm a day during the period of most active growth. According to Hoffmann (1966), a few roots of *Robinia pseudoacacia* and *Populus euramericana* showed exceptionally high elongation rates of about 5 cm per day. Some typical diurnal rates of root elongation are summarized in Table 5.13.

Elongation of *Prunus avium* roots at various times during the day differed by as much as 100% (Head, 1965). As may be seen in Table 5.14 roots made consistently more growth during the night than during the day. When growth was measured at 4-hr intervals for several days, the maximum growth of a root did not always occur during the same 4-hr period. However, maximum average elongation rates always occurred during one of the three 4-hr night periods and minimum rates during one of the day periods. Lyr and Hoffmann (1967) found root elongation of *Populus trichocarpa*, *Quercus borealis maxima*, *Pinus sylvestris*, and *Picea abies* to be from 30–60% greater at night than during the day.

Secondary Growth of Roots

Like stems, many roots increase in diameter through cambial production of xylem and phloem. Cambial growth of roots is similar in some respects and different in others to cambial growth of stems. This section will discuss some important aspects of cambial growth in roots.

SEASONAL INITIATION AND CESSATION OF CAMBIAL GROWTH IN ROOTS

As pointed out earlier, seasonal diameter growth in roots of Temperate Zone trees is initiated later and generally continues for a longer time than it does in the stem. The date of inception of cambial growth in the roots

TABLE 5.13

VARIATIONS IN RATES OF ROOT ELONGATION OF VARIOUS SPECIES OF TREES

Species	Root elongation (mm/day)	Remarks	Sources
Angiosperms			
Acer saccharum	0.6–1	March to June	Morrow (1950)
Betula pendula	15		Hoffmann (1966)
Malus spp.	25		Rogers (1939)
Populus trichocarpa	up to 28		Hoffmann (1966)
Populus euramericana	up to 50		Hoffmann (1966)
Quercus calliprinos	3	Arid region	Oppenheimer (1960)
Quercus robur	12		Hoffmann (1966)
Quercus borealis maxima	18		Hoffmann (1966)
Robinia pseudoacacia	up to 56		Hoffmann (1966)
Gymnosperms			
Larix leptolepis	10		Hoffmann (1966)
Picea abies	8		Hoffmann (1966a)
Pinus sylvestris	12		Hoffmann (1966)
Pinus echinata	up to 25		Reed (1939)
Pinus taeda	up to 25		Reed (1939)
Pinus taeda	0.17	Greenhouse, 5°C, normal light	Barney (1951)
Pinus taeda	5.2	Greenhouse, 25°C, normal light	Barney (1951)
Pinus taeda	0.23	Greenhouse, 35°C, normal light	Barney (1951)
Pinus mugho	5.4–6.5	Summer	Mason *et al.* (1970)
Pinus mugho	2.9–3.7	Autumn	Mason *et al.* (1970)
Pseudotsuga menziesii	up to 16		Hoffmann (1966)

varies greatly among species, among individual trees of the same species, and in different parts of the root system. The root cambium produces xylem first in roots located near the soil surface and later in those in deeper soil layers. Once xylem production is initiated in a root, the growth wave travels from the proximal to the distal end. Some evidence is available which shows that the migration of the cambial growth wave throughout the root system usually is slower than its progression along aerial tissues. In mature *Fagus sylvatica* and *Quercus robur* trees growing in fine-textured soil, 4–6 weeks elapsed between the time of initiation of cambial growth in roots near the soil surface and in those growing in deep soil layers (Ladefoged, 1952). In orange trees, cambial activity occurred in the stem and branches in April and spread to the main root within 2 weeks. Thereafter, the spread of cambial growth into the root system was slow; xylem production did not begin in

TABLE 5.14

AVERAGE ELONGATION RATES DURING THE DAY
AND NIGHT OF SIX *Prunus avium roots*[a]

Root number	Day growth (mm) 0400–1600 hr	Night growth (mm) 1600–0400 hr
1	3.9	6.25
2	2.3	2.7
3	3.4	5.0
4	3.3	3.9
5	4.0	5.75
6	3.6	4.15
Mean	3.8	4.9

[a]Data are based on measurements for 6-10 days
on each root. [From Head (1965).]

lateral roots until late July, and in some small roots not until the end of
September (Cameron and Schroeder, 1945). Sometimes xylem production
in the roots may begin before the descending wave of cambial growth reaches
the base of the stem. In old apple trees, for example, parts of the lower stem
had no new xylem while the stem above and the roots below were increasing
in diameter. Eventually the basipetal progression of the xylem growth wave
closed the gap which lacked new xylem in the lower stem (Knight, 1961).
The beginning of diameter growth in the roots did not appear to be related
to the depth of roots nor to their position relative to the branches.

It is difficult to generalize about the order of seasonal cessation of cambial
growth in roots because available data are few and contradictory. Whereas
some investigators believed that cessation of annual cambial growth proceeded from the root base to the root tip (Brown, 1935), others concluded
that cambial growth ceased first near root tips (MacDougal, 1938). In *Malus*,
cambial growth ceased first in small roots around November 1, but in the
main root some growth occurred until the end of November (Knight, 1961).
However, Fayle (1968) concluded that cessation of seasonal cambial activity
generally proceeded from the root tips toward the base and associated this
pattern with auxin deficiency occurring initially at the root tip. Studies on
variations in the time of cessation of cambial growth in roots are complicated
by differences in root environments, and presence or absence of buds,
sprouts, or branches near the base. Much more research is needed, under
controlled conditions, on timing and control of inception and cessation of
seasonal cambial growth in roots.

VARIATIONS IN CAMBIAL GROWTH IN ROOTS

Wide variations have been reported in cambial growth among roots of various species, roots of different trees of the same species, and various roots of the same tree. Cambial growth in roots is very much more irregular than in stems or branches. It varies markedly along the length of a given root and around its circumference, both with respect to the rate of xylem deposition and anatomy of cambial derivatives.

Variations Along Roots

Gradients occur along roots in size (length and diameter) and wall thickness of xylem cells and in the proportion of various xylem elements. Maximum xylem production consistently occurs at the root base. Many investigators have shown that annual xylem layers taper rapidly in the basal regions of roots and gradually beyond to the root tip (Fig. 5.15). Although local increases in xylem production sometimes occur beyond the zone of rapid taper, roots lack a consistent pattern of maximum xylem deposition at some point in the distal region which might be compared to the characteristic point of maximum thickening in the stem (Fayle, 1968). As may be seen in Fig. 5.16 the distribution and taper of the xylem sheath laid down along a given root vary appreciably from year to year. Drought caused a change in taper and a decrease in xylem production at the basal portion of the root during the drought year (1959 in Fig. 5.16) and subsequent years as well. Fayle (1968) found that a drought sometimes affected xylem production in *Pinus resinosa* roots for up to 3 years.

The rate of diameter growth in roots sometimes is very slow compared to

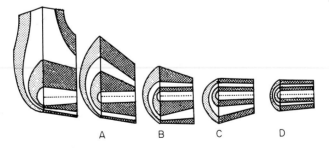

FIG. 5.15. Shifts in xylem production along a main lateral root of *Pinus resinosa*. In the young root xylem distribution was more or less even along the root (no shading in center). Subsequently (inner shading) xylem production was greatest on top near the base (A) and on the bottom further along the root (B), and even for the rest of the root length. As the tree enlarged, a shift in xylem production was evident (outer shading) with growth at (B) greatest on top, at (C) on the bottom, and more or less even beyond (D). [From Fayle (1968).]

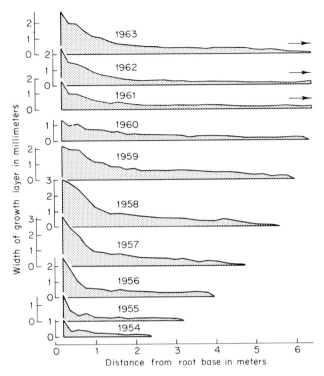

FIG. 5.16. Annual xylem production along a main lateral root of *Pinus resinosa*. [From Fayle (1968).]

their growth in length, causing rope-like forms of woody roots. For example, beyond the zone of rapid taper, the roots of *Acer rubrum* produced such narrow xylem rings that the roots seldom exceeded 2.5 inches in diameter (Wilson, 1964). Stout (1956) described a lack of tapering toward the distal ends in woody roots. In fact, he sometimes found greater root diameters at 20 feet from the root collar than at 10 feet.

Several investigators have reported consistent changes in the size of cambial derivatives along the length of individual roots. In roots which extend laterally for appreciable distances, the diameter and length of longitudinal xylem elements of roots of both gymnosperms and angiosperms increase with distance from the root collar. There may be a slight decrease in distal parts. In *Acer rubrum* surface lateral roots, for example, the diameter of earlywood vessels was slightly greater than in the same growth layer in the stem in the zone of rapid taper at the root base, and 2 to 3 times greater in the root at 2 meters from the base (Wilson, 1964). Fayle (1968) found that the relative size of vessels of a lateral root of a young *Tilia americana* tree at 10 cm from the base was 1.6 times greater than 15 cm up in the stem. Vessel diameters in the root at 60 and 120 cm from the root base were 2.4 and 2.6 times greater, respectively, than in the stem.

The consistent changes in cell size of cambial derivatives which occur along lateral roots apparently are not repeated, at least to the same degree, in main taproots, oblique roots, or vertical roots in the central rooting zone. For example, Fayle (1968) reported no marked changes in the relative size of vessels at 20- and 60-cm depths in the main vertical root of a *Tilia americana* sapling.

Wall thickness of xylem elements decreases from the root base toward the tip. The proportion of various xylem elements also changes along the root. For example, the proportion of wood volume occupied by vessels in lateral roots of *Tilia americana* increased with increasing distance from the root collar (Fayle, 1968). The changes along roots in sizes of cells, wall thickness, and proportion of cells of various types result in gradients of specific gravity. Often the most conspicuous change is a rapid decrease in specific gravity in the basal part of a root with increasing distance from the stem base (Fig. 5.17).

Variations Around the Root

Variations in rates of cambial growth around the root circumference, especially in horizontal roots, are marked and commonly produce roots which are very eccentric in cross section (Fig. 5.18). False and double xylem rings in roots are very common. The cambium may be active on one side of a root and dormant on the other for many years in otherwise normal roots. Uniform xylem deposition around a root circumference is very much an exception.

In the zone of rapid taper, large roots generally show greater xylem increment on the upper than on the lower surface. Young roots generally are circular in transection but later show a change toward greater xylem

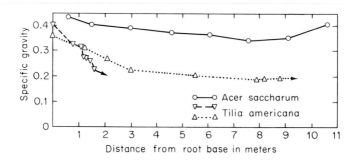

FIG. 5.17. Change in specific gravity along lateral roots of *Acer saccharum* and *Tilia americana*. [From Fayle (1968).]

Fig. 5.18. Transection of horizonal root of *Thuja occidentalis* showing marked eccentricity of cambial growth. U.S. Forest Service photo.

production on the upper side near the root base. Eccentric cambial growth of roots is particularly well known in tropical trees. The horizontal roots of many tropical species show much greater xylem production along the upper side than the lower one, leading to formation of buttresses (see Chapter 6).

At some distance from the root collar there may be a change in orientation of the growth eccentricity. For example, in young *Acer rubrum* roots the cambium produced about 2–10 relatively wide concentric xylem rings. Thereafter, cambial activity decreased and discontinuous rings were common among the narrow outer rings. Beyond the zone of rapid taper, the eccentricity of woody roots was reflected in oval, flattened, or grooved shapes. The orientation of the eccentricity was continually altered because the roots twisted as they grew through the soil (Wilson, 1964). Some discontinuous xylem rings disappeared entirely close to the stem, indicating that xylem production in roots was longitudinally discontinuous. Although xylem production is commonly greater on the upper than on the lower side in the basal portions of roots, exceptions have been noted. For example, in *Pinus strobus* roots the xylem rings usually were thickest on the lower side of roots close to the main stem, but the regularity of growth pattern disappeared a short distance from the stem (Brown, 1915).

Dimensional changes in size of tracheids and vessels in roots also vary from one annual ring to another and they differ within the same annual ring. In both gymnosperms and angiosperms, the smallest cells usually are found in the center of a root. In *Thuja occidentalis* lateral roots, tracheid diameters increased slightly from the inner to the outer wood (Bannan, 1941a). Fayle (1968) noted that at 30 cm from the base the vessels of roots of *Tilia americana*, *Betula allegheniensis*, and *Acer saccharum* were smaller in the interior rings than in outer ones.

Variations Among Roots

Great variability exists in patterns of xylem deposition in different roots of the same tree. Fayle (1968) noted that the occurrence of many eccentric and discontinuous xylem rings obscured any common patterns of cambial growth which may have existed among roots. Cambial growth in different roots of the same tree is influenced by location in the root system. There is much more change in structure of xylem along lateral roots than along vertical or oblique roots located in the central portion of a root system. The diameter and length of cambial derivatives are smaller in vertical and oblique roots, and walls are thicker, than in lateral roots at similar distances from the root crown (Fayle, 1968).

Control of Root Growth

The rate and duration of root growth vary seasonally and diurnally and with species, age of tree, and root environment. As root growth is regulated to a large degree by products produced by shoots it also varies with the environment of the crown.

Because of sensitivity of root growth to soil and site variations, existing species characteristics sometimes are subdued. Within and between years, tree roots adjust to a complex of constantly varying factors. The soil environment changes rapidly with depth and in each soil layer it varies from day to day, especially with respect to moisture, temperature, and aeration. Inherent growth periodicity of tree roots is subject to modification by these changes in environment. Hence, root growth may be expected to speed up and slow down during different seasons, and in different soil horizons. In warm climates some root growth may occur during every month of the year, but the rate varies greatly at different times during the year. For example, *Pinus taeda* and *Pinus echinata* roots in North Carolina grew throughout the year, but by far the most root growth occurred in April and May (Reed, 1939).

In New York State 80% of the root elongation of sugar maple (*Acer sacch-arum*) roots took place from mid-March to the end of June. However, the sensitivity of root growth to environment was illustrated when sugar maple roots grew during each month of a year which had an unusually mild winter (Morrow, 1950).

There has been considerable debate about whether or not roots undergo a state of deep-seated dormancy. Orlov (1957) observed growth of *Picea excelsa* roots in the field for a 2-year period and concluded that there was no inherent periodicity in root growth of this species. He considered that moisture and temperature mainly controlled growth. On the other hand, evidence of inherent growth periodicity of roots has accumulated. For example, Wilcox (1954) emphasized the cyclic growth of individual roots of *Abies procera* and suggested that the observed autonomous growth rhythm was determined largely within individual roots. Since food reserves were present before and after a growth flush, Wilcox concluded that food supply was not limiting to growth but that hormonal balance or accumulated toxic materials might have caused growth cessation. The root system of *Abies procera* as a whole grew in the greenhouse for 10 months of the year but certain individual roots did not elongate at all, whereas others reinitiated growth several times during the year. When an individual root stopped growing, a dark brown suberized tip resulted and resumption of growth was characterized by production of lighter-colored tissues. Up to 4 dark "collars" were detected in a single season's growth until suberization occurred at the end of the season. Individual roots had relatively short growth cycles varying from 2 to 6 weeks in length in the different roots. In incense cedar (*Libocedrus decurrens*) seedlings grown in the greenhouse there was both seasonal periodicity of growth and considerable variation in the growth pattern of different roots on the same tree (Wilcox, 1962b). No single root was active during the entire period of spring and early summer growth. The longest period of growth for an individual root was 63 days, from April 18 to June 17. Growth cycles of individual roots generally varied from 3 to 9 weeks. Roots of large diameter and the main laterals grew for longer periods than roots of small diameter of higher order. There also was a relationship between growth rate and root branching. In fast growing roots the laterals were more widely spaced than in slow growing roots, and the distance from the root apex to the first lateral root primordium also was greater in roots with a fast growth rate. Wilcox (1968a) found that under controlled environmental conditions, the growth cycles of individual *Pinus resinosa* roots varied in duration, intensity, and periodicity depending on stage of development, branching order, and position. The cyclic responses of roots under uniform environmental conditions indicated that root dormancy occurred in indi-vidual roots and arrested growth was not merely the result of adverse environmental conditions. Merritt (1959, 1968) also concluded that the pattern of growth in pine roots was endogenously controlled but environmental changes altered quantitative aspects of growth. Merritt (1959) found evidence of short-term cycles of root growth in *Pinus resinosa*, usually varying from 4 to 12 days, in initiation of new roots and elongation. Individual roots within a root system varied greatly in time of growth initiation and rate of elongation. The termination of growth also was variable and dormant roots were found at various times during the study.

CULTURAL PRACTICES AND ROOT DEVELOPMENT

That depth of rooting can be modified considerably by cultural practices was shown by Morita and Oguro (1951). Three months after mulching peach seedlings, most of the fine roots were concentrated in the surface 0–10 cm of soil. In cultivated trees, however, most of the fine roots were found at a depth of 20–60 cm, but below 60 cm the mulched trees had more roots than the cultivated trees. Slightly different effects of cultivation were noted by Cockroft and Wallbrink (1966) on root distribution of peach and pear trees. For both species cultivation prevented root growth in the surface 3 inches of soil, but it did not cause the entire root system to grow more deeply. With or without cultivation root distribution was greatest at about an 18-inch depth, and roots extended downward to about 36 inches (Table 5.15).

Bilan (1960a) grew *Pinus taeda* seedlings in an open field in eastern Texas

TABLE 5.15

EFFECT OF CULTIVATION ON ROOT DISTRIBUTION OF PEACH ROOTS[a]

Depth (in)	Root distribution				
	Cultivation			No cultivation—white clover sod	
	Root length (in)	Root weight (g)		Root length (in)	Root weight (g)
0–3	0	0		117	2.2
3–7	838	16.4		761	3.2
7–12	341	23.7		483	60.7
12–18	393	116.1		558	98.1
18–24	129	58.3		288	21.0
24–30	90	9.7		149	3.5
30–36	21	4.2		70	2.1
Total	1812	228.4		2426	190.8

[a] From Cockroft and Wallbrink (1966)

on variously prepared plots. When plots were protected by mulch, shade, or sod more than half the growth of 2-year-old roots occurred in the upper 3-inch soil layers. Scalping the site before planting increased dry weight development of the roots more than 4 times and resulted in less development of surface roots. When scalped soils were mulched, root development close to the soil surface was favored, probably because of improved water relations. Mulching also increased the length of lateral roots, and it decreased root branching and lignification. It also inhibited mycorrhizal formation. Combined mulching and shading affected root growth similarly to mulching alone and shading of bare scalped soil had no apparent effects on growth.

Soil and Root Development

Root form as well as depth and rate of root growth are markedly influenced by the rooting medium. For example, yearly root elongation of 6-year-old *Pinus strobus* trees on sandy soil averaged 18–20 inches whereas on clay soil it averaged only 5–10 inches (Stevens, 1931). In *Pinus ponderosa* seedlings, root branching was greatest in cindery soils and least in clayey soils near Flagstaff, Arizona. Laterals were numerous in loamy-rocky soils and moderately so in stoney-clayey and gravelly soils. Both clayey and cindery soils were limiting to seedling growth. Seedlings in clay soils had the longest roots and fewest laterals and fans. The fans were an extreme form of branchiness. Cindery soils had limited water holding capacity and roots growing in them were characterized by much branching and most abundant fans—both extremes of root development (Haasis, 1921). The effects of different textural grades of soil on root growth often are mediated in large part through differences in water holding capacity of soils. Large root systems of *Pinus taeda* and *Pinus echinata* developed when grown in soil with moisture content maintained close to field capacity (Kozlowski, 1949). However, when soil was allowed to dry down almost to the wilting point before rewatering, very sparse root systems resulted. In the deep sands of the southeastern Coastal Plain, roots of trees such as *Quercus laevis*, *Quercus incana* and *Pinus palustris* characteristically are very shallow (Woods, 1957). Generally all these species form a thick mat of fibrous roots within 4–5 inches from the surface and practically no roots occur below this level. These superficial root systems apparently result largely from the fact that available water and suitable temperature are localized in the upper few inches of soil.

Effect of Shoots on Root Growth

Root growth depends to a large degree on a supply of photosynthetic products and growth regulating hormones from the crown. Evidence for the important role of shoot products on root development comes from various sources and only a few examples will be given.

Complete defoliation of 9- and 10-year-old apple trees 4–6 weeks before natural leaf fall greatly reduced root growth for the remainder of the year (Fig. 5.19). As mentioned earlier, insect or fungus injury to leaf tissues impedes root growth and causes mortality of many roots. Interruption of basipetal translocation of shoot products to the roots by girdling the stem below the crown usually inhibits root growth rapidly and eventually leads to death of a tree. Soil moisture deficits may influence root growth driectly by affecting turgor in root cells, but they also do so indirectly by causing water deficits in shoots which inhibit photosynthesis and translocation of carbohydrates and growth regulators to the roots. Similarly the influence of other soil factors on root growth such as supply of nutrients and temperature is mediated to a large degree by way of metabolites produced by the shoot system. One-year-old tung (*Aleurites fordii*) seedlings with intact shoots produced 20 times more roots than trees with top growth curtailed by removal of developing buds along the stem (Neff and O'Rourke, 1951) (Table 5.16). On the other hand, severe pruning of tops of apple and plum trees stimulated shoot growth greatly. The more intense the shoot growth as a result of pruning the greater and more prolonged was the reduction in new white root production in midsummer, suggesting competition between roots and shoots for elaborated nutrients when reserves were not adequate at times of rapid utilization (Head, 1967).

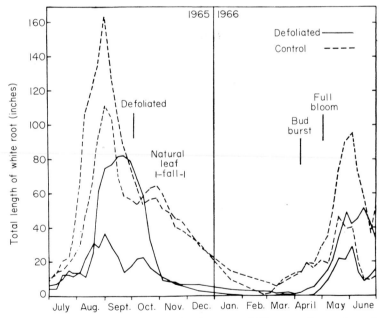

FIG. 5.19. Effects of defoliation on root development of Worcester Pearmain apple trees from July 1965 to June 1966. [From Head (1969).]

TABLE 5.16

EFFECTS OF SHOOTS ON ROOT GROWTH OF YOUNG
Aleurites fordii PLANTS[a]

Treatment	Average production of fibrous roots per tree(g)		
	April 20	May 20	June 15
Shoots intact	0.050	0.594	1.279
Shoot growth curtailed by bud removal	0.031	0.039	0.101

[a] Trees were planted on March 7. [From Neff and O'Rourke (1951).]

The extent, depth, configuration, and density of rooting often vary with crown size and vigor of trees. Root systems of 10-year-old *Pseudotsuga menziesii* trees consisted of a tap root and a few main laterals (Table 5.17). As the trees aged, the root system increased in length proportionally with increase in crown size. Much of the increase in total root length was traceable to secondary, tertiary, and quaternary branching. Within each age class the complexity of the root system varied greatly in different crown classes, with total length and branching in the following order: dominants > intermediates > suppressed trees. Often total root length of dominant trees was greater than in much older intermediate trees.

The influence of the shoot system on root growth varies with species and with age of the plant. In *Acer saccharinum* the growth of roots immediately after seed germination depended on food reserves in the cotyledons and, after these were exhausted, on current photosynthate (Richardson, 1956a). In first year seedlings of *Quercus rubra* grown under very low light intensities, removal of cotyledons did not affect the rate of root elongation, but the duration of root growth was reduced (Richardson, 1956c). The rate of growth was more closely related to dry weight of roots than to dry weight of shoots. Duration of root growth, however, was most closely related to the dry weight of the shoot system. This indicated a priority of food sources, with close dependence of root growth on the amount of reserves in the roots. Storage carbohydrates in roots were used before those in the shoots, and only when shoot reserves could no longer sustain root growth were the reserves in the acorn utilized.

According to Wassink and Richardson (1951), root growth of first year seedlings of *Acer pseudoplatanus* was much more sensitive to conditions affecting photosynthesis than was root growth of *Quercus rubra*. Reducing

TABLE 5.17

ROOT DEVELOPMENT IN THREE AGE CLASSES AND CROWN CLASSES OF *Pseudotsuga menziesii*[a]

Stand age and crown class	Average height (m)	Average diameter at 1.5 m (cm)	Average length of roots 1 cm diameter (cm)				Total and range
			Primary	Secondary	Tertiary	Quaternary	
10-Year-old-stand							
Dominant	2.5	2.5	99	38	—	—	137 (65–137)
Intermediate	1.8	1.0	31	—	—	—	31 (20–44)
Suppressed	0.9	—	7	—	—	—	7 (2–17)
25-Year-old-stand							
Dominant	20.0	15.7	1129	887	156	—	2172 (1747–2561)
Intermediate	10.0	8.1	484	257	10	—	751 (530–971)
Suppressed	5.0	5.1	55	51	—	—	106
55-Year-old-stand							
Dominant	39.0	45.7	2015	6400	3945	1555	13,915
Intermediate	26.0	26.0	1270	2205	1245	350	5070

[a] From McMinn (1963)

the light intensity from 4000 to 250 lux did not have a significant effect on root growth during the first day, but during the following night root growth was reduced by about half. On resuming the higher light intensity, the rate of root growth again changed during the night following the first day after the change. In contrast, the rate of root growth of *Quercus* remained constant at various light intensities, suggesting greater dependence of root growth of oak on stored carbohydrates. This conclusion was supported by the fact that abundant starch reserves were found in pith and parenchyma cells of the stem and roots of *Quercus*; whereas in *Acer*, starch was present only in isolated cells of the pith.

Kozlowski (1949) also demonstrated wide variations among species in root growth response to different light regimes. Although heavy shading reduced root growth of both oaks and pines, the growth of pine roots was reduced much more (Table 5.18). In trees grown in either light or shade, reserve carbohydrates were much higher in oak than in pine. Also, total food reserves were greater in light-grown pine than in shade-grown pine, but in oak there were no significant differences among plants grown in the light and shade. This was in accord with the observation of Kramer and Decker (1944) that oaks were very efficient in carrying on photosynthesis at low light intensities whereas pines were not.

Over short periods, the rate of root growth of first year seedlings of *Acer saccharinum* was closely correlated with rates of photosynthesis (Richardson, 1953a). A change in shoot environment which altered the rate of photosynthesis was followed within 12–24 hr by a response in root growth. For example, when shoot temperature was reduced from 20°–5°C, there was no significant change in root growth during the first day, but during the following

TABLE 5.18

Effect of Shading on Growth of *Pinus taeda* and *Quercus lyrata*[a]

Treatment	Height (cm)	Dry weight (g)		Root–shoot Ratio
		Roots	Shoots	
Pinus taeda				
Full light	42	25.2	20.1	1.25
Shade	35	6.1	7.2	0.84
Quercus lyrata				
Full light	59	44.1	21.1	2.01
Shade	66	38.7	20.1	1.92

[a] The plants were 3 years old when harvested and had been grown for 2 growing seasons in full light or shade. [From Kozlowski (1949).]

night the rate of root elongation was reduced about 65%. Twelve hours later root growth leveled off at approximately 16% of the rate when shoot temperature was maintained at 20°. Increasing shoot temperature from 5° back to 20° also increased the rate of root growth in 12 hr. Reducing the light intensity over the shoots or maintaining the shoots in an atmosphere devoid of detectable quantities of carbon dioxide also brought about reductions in root growth.

By the end of the first year and during the second year, the relation between current photosynthesis and root growth of *Acer saccharinum* changed to the extent that root growth appeared to be partly determined by carbohydrate reserves. Whereas in very young seedlings a decrease in light intensity from 5000 to 200 lux caused root elongation to decrease rapidly to a very low level, root growth was not reduced in second year seedlings for at least 7 days after light intensity was similarly reduced (Richardson, 1956a). Richardson (1956b) showed that if photosynthesis of first year seedlings of *Acer saccharinum* was limited by low light intensity for very long periods, root growth eventually stopped. Both the rate and duration of root growth were related to plant size. The speed of recovery from a limitation imposed on photosynthesis by low light intensity and rate and duration of root growth were directly related to dry weight of the plants, indicating that the amount of stored carbohydrate greatly influenced root growth. The rate and duration of root growth increased more per unit increase in dry weight of roots than per unit increase in weight of shoots or whole plants. These observations indicated that at low light intensities carbohydrate reserves in the roots were utilized in root growth before those in the stem influenced growth.

As emphasized earlier, it should not be inferred that growth depends only on available carbohydrates because, as Richardson (1953b) demonstrated, a hormonal stimulus also is required for the production of a healthy root system. Richardson (1957) concluded that at least two accessory growth factors were needed for root development in *Acer saccharinum*, one for root formation and the other for root elongation. Root formation required the presence of an active shoot, while root elongation depended on a stimulus provided by the leaves. Removing the terminal meristem by disbudding completely suppressed root formation but did not influence root elongation. The effect of the terminal meristem on root formation was replaceable with indoleacetic acid. Defoliation caused root elongation to cease but did not inhibit formation of new lateral roots. At the end of the season both stimuli (those controlling both root formation and root elongation) were transferred to the buds from the terminal meristem and leaves. Root growth at the end of the growing season occurred only when at least one physiologically nondormant bud was present (Richardson, 1958). Root growth required exposure of the shoots to low temperatures.

CONTROL OF ROOTING OF CUTTINGS

Rooting of stem cuttings is one of the best known methods of asexually propagating woody plants. This involves placing of stem pieces with one or more buds under conditions which favor root regeneration.

Many factors have been shown to affect rooting of cuttings. These include age of the tree from which cuttings are taken, the position of the cutting on the tree (see Chapter 3, Volume I), the type of cutting (e.g., "softwood" or "hardwood", the time of year when cuttings are taken, sex of the parent tree, nutrient status of the cutting, and environmental conditions under which cuttings are rooted (Doran, 1957; Cameron, 1968).

Often there is considerable seasonal variation in rootability of a given species. Cuttings of many trees (e.g., *Ilex glabra*) can be successfully rooted when taken over a period of weeks or months, but in other trees (e.g., *Fagus* and *Syringa*) the time limits are shorter. *Syringa vulgaris* is propagated better by softwood than by hardwood cuttings. Cuttings usually are taken while new shoots are growing, before or during flowering, or immediately thereafter. If cuttings are taken later, they root poorly and do not make appreciable top growth during the same season. The marked seasonal variability of rooting capacity of cuttings of *Salix atrocinerea* was emphasized by Vieitez and Pena (1968). They identified three different waves of rootability. One very active phase of root regeneration occurred during January, February, March, and April. A second lesser phase lasted from May to August. Both phases were separated by a marked decline of rootability in June. A third very minor phase of root initiation occurred from September to December. For further detailed information on seasonal rootability of a large number of species of woody plants the reader is referred to Doran (1957).

Anatomical Barriers to Rooting of Cuttings

Several investigators have reported correlation between the degree of stem sclerification and rooting capacity, with shoots of plants that root poorly showing considerable sclerification. For example, Beakbane (1961) found that in Conference pear, which roots poorly, the secondary phloem was encircled by a cylinder of mature thick-walled fibers which lacked living protoplasts. In contrast, in plants that rooted readily, most of the primary phloem parenchyma cells retained living protoplasts. Hence, in plants with high rooting capacity many phloem rays contacted living tissues at their distal ends, whereas phloem rays of plants which rooted poorly were often blocked by lignified tissues. The capacity for forming adventitious roots decreased as the continuity of a sclerenchymatous ring increased (Table 5.19). Beakbane (1961) reported similar anatomical relationships for a wide variety of stone fruits, flowering shrubs from temperate regions, and tropical plants.

TABLE 5.19

RELATION BETWEEN CAPACITY TO FORM ADVENTITIOUS ROOTS AND PHLOEM
STRUCTURE IN STEMS[a]

Variety	Rooting capacity	Continuity of fiber ring[b]	
		Percent	Mean
Apple rootstocks			
M. XIII		28	
M. V	Excellent	43	41
M. XI		52	
M. IV		59	
M. XVI	Good	64	64
M. II		69	
M. XII		69	
M. XXV	Fair	71	75
M. VIII		85	
Scion varieties			
Pear			
Conference	Poor	99	98
Williams Bon Chretien		96	

[a] From Beakbane (1961).
[b] Proportion of radii through the primary phloem blocked by sclerenchyma.

Ciampi and Gellini (1963) found poor rooting of *Olea europaea* stem cuttings having discontinuous sclerenchyma tissues. The thick-walled cells appeared to block emergence of primordia of adventitious roots. Gellini (1964) related poor rooting in cuttings to lignification of cell walls and formation of sclereids, regardless of discontinuity of sclerenchyma tissues.

In some species at least, the presence of sclerenchyma tissues does not appear to be a very serious mechanical barrier to rooting. Whereas phloem fibers are very rare in juvenile stems of *Hedera helix*, the mature phase of this species has a ring of fibers which encircle the phloem. However, these fibers are discontinuous and do not form a lignified cylinder (Goodin, 1965). As may be seen in Fig. 5.5 adventitious roots in the mature phase of *Hedera*, which originated in primary phloem ray parenchyma, developed through cortical and epidermal tissues and were not impeded by intense fiber formation (Girouard, 1967b). Sachs, Loreti, and DeBie (1964) concluded that differences in ease of rooting of olive, cherry, and pear cultivars were the result of restricted initiation of root primordia rather than to blocking of development of root primordia by sclerenchyma tissues.

Variations in capacity for growth of juvenile and adult tissues have been demonstrated in tissue cultures. For example, Stoutemyer and Britt (1965) showed that tissue cultures from the juvenile stage of *Hedera helix* had higher proliferation rates and larger cells than those from the adult phase (Table 5.20). Such differences were maintained over a 2-year period. This study showed that differences in cellular activity accompany the external morphological changes indicative of the growth phases. For such reasons, much attention has been given to the importance of endogenous substances which play an important regulatory role in development of adventitious roots.

Internal Control of Rooting of Cuttings

The initiation of adventitious roots appears to be regulated by a balance of several internal, basipetally translocated substances including carbohydrates, nitrogenous substances, hormonal growth regulators, and cofactors capable of acting synergistically with auxin. In a given system, any one of these internal requirements may play a controlling role in root initiation.

Root initiation by cuttings can be blocked by removal of leaves or buds or by phloem blockage, indicating the necessity of a phloem-translocated component. Stoltz and Hess (1966) found that the primary constituents which accumulated above stem girdles were carbohydrates, amino acids, and an unknown root promoting substance. The evidence for essentiality of carbohydrates for rooting comes from several sources. For example, increased rooting response is associated with high carbohydrate availability. Hess and Snyder (1955) found rooting capacity to be positively correlated with carbohydrate availability as regulated by light intensity and temperature control. Stoutemyer and Britt (1962) noted that wounding the bases of cuttings by splitting and prolonged soaking in a sucrose solution improved rooting responses to indolebutyric acid treatment, further emphasizing the importance of carbohydrates for rooting.

TABLE 5.20

GROWTH OF TISSUE CULTURES OF *Hedera helix*[a]

Type of tissue	Number of cultures	Mean initial weight (mg)	Mean final weight (mg)	Growth increment[b]
Adult	320	14.94	82.23	4.50
Reversion	320	15.23	100.38	5.59
Seedling	310	16.26	221.46	13.62

[a] From Stoutemyer and Britt (1965).

[b] Growth increment $= \dfrac{\text{Final weight} - \text{Initial weight}}{\text{Initial weight}}$

Some exogenous growth regulators such as auxin stimulate rooting and others, such as exogenous gibberellins or cytokinins applied at the base of cuttings, suppress rooting. However, in many species synthetic auxins do not overcome such limitations to rooting as the age of the parent plant and the time of year when cuttings are taken. Also auxins generally do not stimulate rooting on cuttings which are not known to root without them (Avery and Johnson, 1947).

Kinetin applied to leaves of *Acer rubrum* stimulated rooting of cuttings (Bachelard and Stowe, 1963). There was no evidence that kinetin stimulated rooting by altering the auxin–kinetin balance in the cuttings and it was postulated that leaf-applied kinetin may have stimulated rooting through some effect on nitrogen metabolism or anthocyanin formation. Bachelard and Stowe (1963) emphasized that, in addition to auxin, leaves were essential for optimal rooting of cuttings of *Acer rubrum* and *Eucalyptus camaldulensis*. Nitrogen compounds alone or together with sucrose appeared to play some role in this "leaf effect," but they did not replace the requirement for leaves completely or directly.

In at least some plants there is evidence that inhibitors play a contributory role in rooting of cuttings. For example, Paton *et al* (1970) showed that ontogenetic aging of *Eucalyptus grandis* seedlings involved a direct and quantitative relation between decrease in rooting capacity of stem cuttings and increase in rooting inhibitors in the tissue formed at the base of the cutting.

There is considerable evidence that high rooting capacity is associated with high levels of endogenous cofactors. Tissues of plants which are easy to root have been shown to have a higher content of rooting cofactors than tissues of plants which are difficult to root (Hess, 1962, 1965). Much interest has been shown in rooting cofactors of a variety of angiosperms, such as, *Hedera helix* (Girouard, 1969), *Prunus* (Challenger, Lacey, and Howard, 1965), *Pyrus* (Fadl and Hartmann, 1967), and *Salix* (Kawase, 1964). Rooting cofactors have also been studied in such gymnosperms as *Juniperus* (Lanphear and Meahl, 1966), *Pinus* (Zimmerman, 1963), and *Taxus* (Lanphear and Meahl, 1966).

Working with juvenile and mature forms of *Hedera helix*, Hess (1962) found at least four root promoting substances in a methanolic extract of juvenile tissues. As these substances were most active in promoting rooting when supplied to cuttings together with IAA, they appeared to be cofactors of IAA. One of the cofactors isolated from easy to root juvenile *Hedera helix* is isochlorogenic acid. Girouard (1969) extracted four rooting cofactors from juvenile and mature cuttings of *Hedera helix*. Cofactor 4, consisting of oxygenated terpenoids, had the highest root-inducing activity followed in order by cofactors 1, 3, and 2.

Domanski, Kozlowski, and Sasaki (1969) demonstrated highly significant influences of temperature, exogenous growth regulators, and temperature-growth regulator interactions on root initiation in *Salix viminalis* cuttings. Naphthaleneacetic acid (NAA) stimulated root formation and its effects were further enhanced by increasing the temperature from 22 to 25°C. In contrast to NAA, both gibberellic acid (GA) and benzyladenine inhibited root initiation. These experiments suggested regulation of rooting of cuttings by interactions of growth regulators and possible cofactors. As temperature increased toward an optimum for root initiation, the balance of endogenous growth regulators and possible cofactors may have changed to bring out the stimulatory effects of auxins over the inhibitory influence of cytokinins and gibberellins.

Based on the isolation of four rooting cofactors and available information on essentiality of carbohydrates, nitrogenous substances, and auxins for rooting, Hess (1969) presented an attractive model for internal control of adventitious root formation (Fig 5.20). According to this model, cuttings

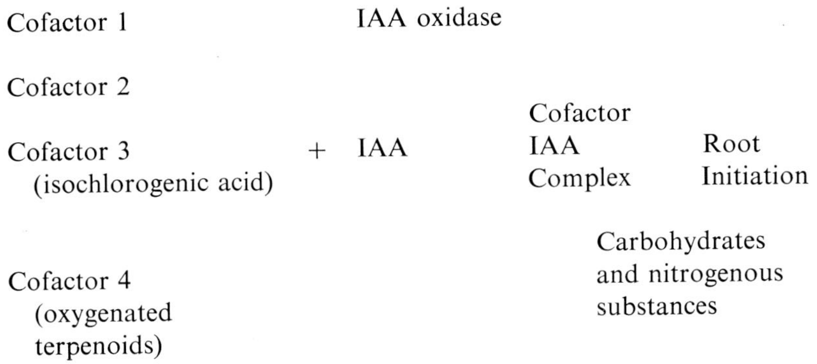

Cofactor 1   IAA oxidase

Cofactor 2
                                              Cofactor
Cofactor 3   +   IAA   IAA   Root
(isochlorogenic acid)   Complex   Initiation

                                              Carbohydrates
Cofactor 4   and nitrogenous
(oxygenated   substances
terpenoids)

FIG. 5.20. Internal factors controlling initiation of adventitious roots. [From Hess (1969).]

which are easy to root have all four rooting cofactors and sufficient IAA for cell division. Adventitious roots will form in such cuttings in the presence of adequate carbohydrates and nitrogenous substances. Deficiency of carbohydrates as a result of defoliation or low light intensity may inhibit root initiation. If supplies of carbohydrates and nitrogen compounds are adequate, the supply of IAA can be limiting to root formation.

Cuttings which are difficult to root may have ample supplies of nutritive substances, but may lack some of the rooting cofactors. Such cuttings do not initiate roots following applications of synthetic auxins. Variations in rooting ability among species may be traceable to differences in cofactors or balances among nutritive substances, auxins, and cofactors. In addition to the basipetally translocated components, there appear to be nonmobile or fixed cell components which are involved in the complex system which controls root initiation (Hess, 1969).

Suggested Collateral Reading

Esau, K. (1965). "Plant Anatomy." Chapter 17. Wiley, New York.

Fayle, D. C. F. (1968). Radial growth in tree roots. Faculty of Forestry, Univ. Toronto Tech. Rep. 9.

Girouard, R. M. (1967). Initiation and development of adventitious roots in stem cuttings of *Hedera helix. Can. J. Bot.* **45**, 1877–1881; 1883–1886.

Head, G. C. (1967). Effects of seasonal changes in shoot growth on the amount of un-suberized root on apple and plum trees. *J. Hort. Sci.*, **42**, 169–180.

Hess, C. E. (1969). Internal and external factors regulating root initiation. *In* "Root Growth," (W. J. Whittington, ed.), pp. 42–53, Butterworth, London.

Kozlowski, T. T. and Scholtes, W. H. (1948). Growth of roots and root hairs of pine and hardwood seedlings in the Piedmont. *J. Forest.* **46**, 750–754.

Lyr, H. and Hoffmann, G. (1967). Growth rates and growth periodicity of tree roots. *Int. Rev. Forestry Res.* **2**, 181–206.

Merritt, C. (1968). Effect of environment and heredity on the root growth pattern of red pine. *Ecology*, **49**, 34–40.

Rogers, W. S. and Booth, G. A. (1960). The roots of fruit trees. *Sci. Hort.* **14**, 27–34.

Whittington, W. J. (Ed.) (1969). "Root Growth," Butterworth, London.

Wilcox, H. (1954). Primary organization of active and dormant roots of noble fir, *Abies procera. Amer. J. Bot.* **41**, 818–821.

Wilcox, H. (1955). Regeneration of injured root systems in noble fir. *Bot. Gaz.* **116**, 224–234.

Wilcox, H. (1964). Xylem in roots of *Pinus resinosa* in relation to heterorhizy and growth activity. *In* "The Formation of Wood in Forest Trees," (M. H. Zimmerman, ed.), pp. 459–478, Academic Press, New York.

Chapter 6

SPECIALIZED AND MODIFIED ROOTS

Many woody plants have specialized or morphologically modified root systems which often have important implications in growth. This chapter will discuss several important types of such specialized root systems including aerial roots, grafted roots, root buttresses, knee roots and pneumatophores, nodulated roots, and mycorrhizae.

Aerial Roots

Although most roots are subterranean they are not exclusively so and many examples of root development above ground can be cited. Aerial roots may result from seed germination in a suitable above-ground medium which later is eroded away or decays to expose the roots. For example, seeds may germinate on stumps or in moss or litter patches in concavities of rocks above ground. Kozlowski and Cooley (1961) observed many exposed aerial roots of *Betula alleghaniensis*. These resulted when seeds germinated on old stumps and sent roots downward. After the stump decayed, the tree was supported by aerial "stilt" roots which often were completely fused. Such aerial roots were found up to 12 feet above ground level. Many horizontal aerial roots were found in trees which had become established after seeds germinated on a felled log. Subsequently the roots of such trees ran laterally along the log. After the log eventually decayed, the trees were supported by a fused mass of horizontal, almost parallel roots which extended outward at a height of approximately 2.5 feet off the ground for as far as 20 feet before turning downward into the soil (Fig. 6.1).

Normal subterranean roots of old trees may become aerial roots through exposure by soil erosion, road cuts, or other construction which disturbs the soil mass. Aerial roots may also develop adventitiously on parts of tree stems. Some tropical trees such as *Ficus elastica* send down aerial roots from their branches (Fig. 6.2). Aerial roots can also be induced on branches of many

Fig. 6.1. Fused mass of horizontal aerial roots of *Betula alleghaniensis* in northern Wisconsin. [From Kozlowski and Cooley (1961).]

trees by wrapping them in moist sphagnum. Such air layering is common practice with plant propagators who wish to reproduce plants that cannot be readily propagated by seed or other vegetative methods. A useful modification of this method involves wounding of a tree branch, applying a growth-regulating compound to the wound, and covering the wound with moist sphagnum followed by wrapping with waterproof paper or plastic. After roots form around the wound the rooted portion of the plant is severed and replanted (Kramer and Kozlowski, 1960). Various types of aerial roots are shown in Fig. 6.3.

Grafted Roots

Natural root grafting among trees is very widespread. The most usual type of root fusion appears to involve self grafts among roots of the same tree, but intraspecific grafts also occur commonly whereas interspecific grafts occur only rarely (Kozlowski, 1963a). True root grafts are characterized by

FIG. 6.2. India rubber tree (*Ficus elastica*) producing aerial roots from branches. U.S. Forest Service photo.

vascular connections which are brought about by union of cambium, phloem, and xylem of previously unconnected roots. According to Bormann (1966), growth patterns in developing grafts are controlled by tissue alignment of roots involved, with best development occurring between tissues having similar anatomical and physiological alignment. Conversely, tissues of

FIG. 6.3. Aerial roots. (A) Aerial roots of a small *Tsuga* tree growing over a *Pseudotsuga menziesii* burl. (B) Aerial roots of a *Tsuga* tree growing on a rock. The root collar of the tree is 8 feet off the ground. (C) Aerial roots of a *Betula alleghaniensis* tree which began growing as a seedling atop a stump. The tree was left on aerial "stilt" roots when the stump later decayed. U.S. Forest Service photo.

opposite polarity either do not graft or they grow abnormally. Many false grafts, which do not involve vascular connections, occur among unrelated species and these often are erroneously assumed to be true grafts.

Rao (1966) described the developmental anatomy of natural grafts of aerial roots of different thicknesses and presumably of different age. Initial contact between aerial roots was established by formation and fusion of epidermal hairs. As secondary growth increased the girth of roots, the cortices of adjacent roots approached each other and became compressed. Cortical tissues thinned in the compressed zone and fused marginally. Ray cells near the contact area became highly meristematic and produced many parenchyma cells to form a continuous parenchyma zone between the steles of the two roots. Cortical tissues, secondary phloem, and vascular cambia of both roots were interrupted by the new tissue. Subsequently, parenchyma cells below the fused regions of the cortex redifferentiated into vascular cambium which joined the original cambia of both roots. Hence, a continuous ring of vascular cambium was reorganized. The cork cambium differentiated to form a thick periderm with a smooth surface. Hence, the fused roots appeared externally as a single root.

Surveying the world's literature, Graham and Bormann (1966) found root grafting to occur in 150 species of woody plants, and it doubtless occurs in other species also. Kozlowski and Cooley (1961) found intraspecific root grafting to occur commonly in both angiosperms and gymnosperms in Wisconsin (Figs. 6.4, 6.5). Roots were fused in both saplings and old trees but the grafts were more plentiful among the older trees. Often trees were organically united by a complicated system of many intraspecific grafts. The main requirement for grafting appeared to be growth pressure. Feeder roots did not graft readily. The angle of approach did not seem important as roots were found to graft at various acute as well as right angles. Grafting was common over or adjacent to stones, indicating that growth pressure of one root on another one lodged against a stone promoted grafting. The presence of stones was not necessary, however, for where there were no stones, many grafts occurred, at various acute as well as right angles. In addition to established grafts, many cases of abrasion and callus development were observed where roots crossed, suggesting that fusions eventually would occur as a result of growth pressure at these points of contact. Bormann and Graham (1959) concluded that root grafting of *Pinus strobus* probably occurs under the whole range of soil conditions tolerated by the species population.

Rigg and Harrar (1931) noted considerable root grafting of bog species. They reasoned that wind sway caused the bark of roots to be worn off where they came in contact in the complicated ramifying growth of roots in sphagnum. A study by Kozlowski and Cooley (1961), however, showed that

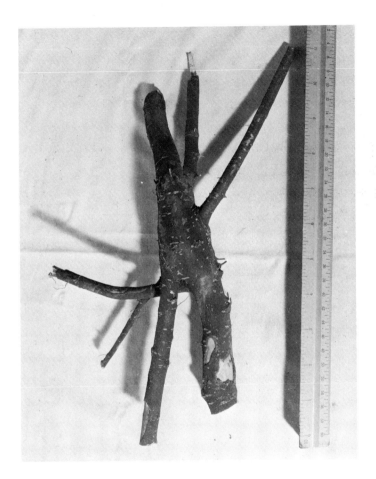

FIG. 6.4. Fused roots of *Acer saccharum* in northern Wisconsin. This compound graft formed on top of a large stone where the several roots crossed. [From Kozlowski and Cooley (1961).]

balsam fir (*Abies balsamea*) roots grafted readily even when trees were firmly rooted in soil. Their compatibility for grafting and growth pressure of contiguous roots apparently fulfilled the requirements for graft unions. LaRue (1934) also stressed that swaying of trees was not critical for root fusions in compatible species. He found root grafting of *Pinus strobus* trees growing in stiff clay where they could not have swayed sufficiently to wear away root bark by friction.

Plantations generally do not show root grafting until some critical age is reached, because the wide spacing among trees in early years precludes root

FIG. 6.5. Root grafts in closely-grown *Abies balsamea* trees. The stems were approximately 1.5 feet apart and the trees were bound together in units by numerous grafts of the larger roots. [From Kozlowski and Cooley (1961) Chicago Univ. Press].

contact. The proportion of root-grafted *Picea abies* trees in a Danish plantation increased from 3–5% at the time of the first thinnings to at least 25–35% by the time the trees were 40–60 years old (Holmsgaard and Scharff, 1963). In nurseries, root grafting often occurs among the closely grown plants at a relatively early age. Kuntz and Riker (1955), for example, noted that root grafting was common among 4-year-old red pines (*Pinus resinosa*) in nursery transplant beds. In red pine trees planted at a spacing of 6 × 6 feet, the youngest plantation in which root grafts among different trees were found was 15 years old (Armson and Van Den Driessche, 1959). Root grafting in white pine (*Pinus strobus*) was found in stands varying in age from 15 to 71 years. Numbers of grafts ranged from 1 to 35 between two trees (Bormann and Graham, 1959). Mature stands consisted of grafted communities of two to many trees with interspersed individual trees that were not grafted to others. According to Beskaravainyi (1956), half the trees in a 35- to 48-year-old pine plantation were joined together in an interconnected maze of root fusions. Jaroslavcev (1962) considered groups of root grafted *Cedrus atlantica* and *Cedrus deodara* trees as one " organism " having a single main stem, with the other stems acting as branches.

PHYSIOLOGICAL AND ECOLOGICAL IMPLICATIONS OF ROOT GRAFTING

There undoubtedly is considerable transfer of various materials, such as food, hormones, water, minerals, biocides, and spores, between trees through root grafts. Therefore, from a physiological viewpoint, many individual trees cannot really be regarded as completely self sufficient organic entities. Bormann (1966) presented evidence that relations between *Pinus strobus* trees connected by root grafts were influenced largely by translocation of organic substances, whereas transport of water and minerals was not very important. Water and minerals which moved in the xylem had a marked tendency to follow the grain of the wood to the crown. As xylem transport involves cross-grain movement, trees connected by functional root grafts could not divert large amounts of water and minerals from their partners. However, organic substances translocated in the phloem moved readily through grafts and both upward and downward in grafted partner trees. Kadambi (1954) described some interesting cases of root grafting involving aromatic trees. Following root fusion of sandalwood (*Santalum album*) and *Eugenia jambolana*, the fruit of the latter had the flavor and scent of the former. The wood of *Ficus*, which was root-grafted to the aromatic *Vateria indica*, had the aromatic odor of *Vateria*, which in turn exuded a latex like that of *Ficus*.

The importance of intertree food translocation through root grafts apparently varies with dominance of grafted partners. In studies of relationships between *Pinus strobus* trees whose roots were grafted together Bormann (1966) found that, when both trees were dominant, balanced exchanges of food occurred through root grafts. When a dominant tree was grafted to an intermediate or suppressed tree, net movement of food occurred to the smaller tree. When roots of a dominant tree were grafted to a living stump, the latter received small amounts of food from the dominant tree which, in turn, received small amounts of water and minerals. Both competition and intertree food translocation played roles in the development of naturally occurring *Pinus strobus* stands. Competition was far more important, however, because food translocation from a dominant tree could not prevent another tree from becoming suppressed as a result of competition.

Living Snags and Stumps

Adjacent trees whose roots are grafted together often develop very differently. One of these trees may maintain itself as a dominant whereas the other is progressively suppressed. Eventually its crown dies and a living snag or

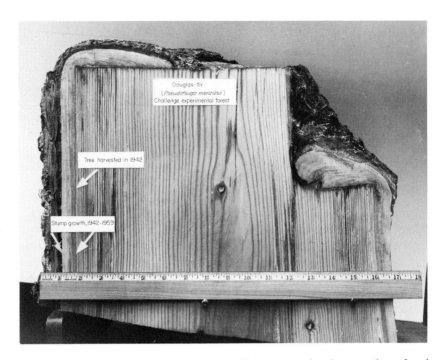

FIG. 6.6. Radial section through *Pseudotsuga* living stump showing new tissue forming across the cut surface. U.S. Forest Service Photo.

stump may persist (Fig. 6.6). Bormann (1966) found living tissue to a height of 3.3 meters on one side of a snag of *Pinus strobus* that was root-grafted to a vigorous dominant of the same species. The living tissue was localized over two roots grafted to the dominant tree. Roots on the opposite side of the snag were dead and apparently not grafted.

Most stumps die within a year or two after a tree is cut. However, a community of trees may be connected so effectively through root grafts that if all but one tree are cut, the remaining root systems can survive on carbohydrates and growth regulators supplied by the crown of the remaining tree (Garner, 1967). After the first thinnings in *Picea abies* stands in Denmark, the number of living stumps increased rapidly to an average of 200–300 per hectare by the time the stands were 40–60 years old. The number of grafts between a tree and a living stump varied from 1 to 8, but the average was 2.2 in one plot and 8 in another (Holmsgaard and Scharff, 1963). In Japan, Satoo (1964) found an average of 7 living stumps per 100 square meters in a 51-year-old *Chamaecyparis obtusa* plantation. The stumps continued to grow and formed xylem rings.

An interesting case involving transport of foods into a living stump through root grafts was described by Wold and Lanner (1965). In 1942 a stand of *Eucalyptus robusta* trees was selectively cut in Hawaii. A stump, 8 feet from a living tree remained alive for at least 20 years. In 1963 a windstorm removed the top of the tree, which responded by producing many epicormic branches from the bole. At the same time the adjacent living stump produced vigorous stool shoots from the callus rim at its upper edge (Fig. 6.7). These observations emphasized that the living stump was receiving carbohydrates and other growth requirements from the adjacent tree.

A living stump which is grafted to an intact tree may continue to produce a shell of xylem at a rate that may be greater or lesser than its normal growth (Lanner, 1961). In *Chamaecyparis obtusa*, the xylem rings formed in living stumps generally narrowed progressively. However, in some cases the xylem increments formed in the stumps were wider than those formed before the tops were severed (Satoo, 1964). The wood produced in living stumps gradually differentiates into sapwood and heartwood. Lanner (1961)

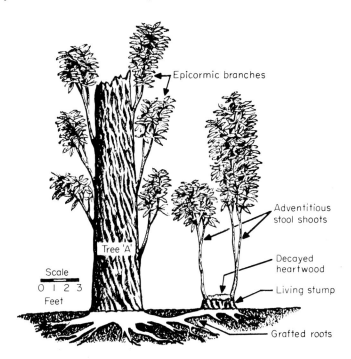

Fig. 6.7. Shoot development on stem of *Eucalyptus robusta* tree (left) in 1963 following wind breakage of main stem. At the same time the adjacent old stump (right) produced shoots. The stump was connected to the adjacent tree by root grafts. [From Wold and Lanner (1965).]

observed that in *Abies* and *Pseudotsuga* from the pith outward there was a sequence of original heartwood, original sapwood, new heartwood, and new sapwood.

Data of Bormann (1961) showed that stumps of *Pinus strobus* trees that were not grafted to intact trees stayed alive for only one growing season following cutting. When the trees were cut in early spring their stumps remained alive for practically the entire growing season; if cutting was done in the autumn and winter, however, the stumps usually died by the middle of the next growing season. The cambial region of stumps not grafted to intact trees did not show any mitotic activity during the season following cutting. In contrast, stumps grafted to intact trees remained alive for several years and produced new xylem and phloem increments annually. In one stand that had been cut 10 years previously one fourth of the stumps were alive.

Stumps grafted to intact trees often did not produce xylem and phloem around the entire stem circumference because only portions of the stump were alive. Also, the orientation of new wood elements in the stump changed after the tree was cut. Bormann (1961) cited a case in which xylem elements produced during the first season of stump growth were first vertically and later horizontally oriented. Bormann's data provided strong evidence for: (1) initiation of cambial activity in the stump by growth regulators provided by the donor tree; (2) dependence of growth of the stump on food from the donor tree; (3) possible exchanges of food and growth regulators between trees united by root grafts; and, (4) changes in direction of transport of such materials after cutting the stem of one of the grafted partners.

Lanner (1961) found that on some stumps only a single root comprised a translocation channel from a donor tree. In such cases only the part of the stump directly over the root remained alive. In living stumps a ring of callus tissue often formed around the top and sometimes grew across the entire cut surface (Fig. 6.6). Such callused stumps were protected from fungus and insect attack and showed remarkable longevity. Further evidence that living stumps often produce xylem over only part of their circumference is given by Holmsgaard and Scharff (1963).

Translocation of Herbicides

Various herbicides are readily transported from one tree to another through root grafts (Kozlowski, 1961). For example, Bormann and Graham (1960) noted that in a 30-year-old *Pinus strobus* plantation 43% of untreated trees were killed as a result of "backflash" or translocation of ammonium sulfamate from treated to untreated trees. Stout (1961) reported that half the residual *Pinus resinosa* trees were killed by backflash, and Fenton (1965) reported appreciable backflash of 2,4,5-T in *Liquidambar styraciflua* stands.

Some evidence is also available of transfer of material among plants whose roots are not actually fused. Bormann (1957) demonstrated with herbaceous plants that true vascular unions were not a prerequisite to interplant transfer. Graham and Bormann (1966) cited data on herbicide transfer among trees whose roots were not grafted together. Woods and Brock (1964) also noted that radioactive isotopes injected into stumps of one species were later localized in many other species to which they were not grafted. These data provide strong evidence of the importance of root exudation and subsequent uptake of materials by other trees as well as transfers of such substances by mycorrhiza-forming fungi and rhizospheric organisms.

Root Grafting and Disease Transmission

Incitants of some of the most destructive diseases of trees are translocated through root grafts. For example, *Fomes pini*, possibly the most destructive of wood decay fungi attacking the heartwood of living gymnosperms, is transmitted through root grafts in *Pseudotsuga menziesii* (Clark, 1949). Among other disease incitants transmitted through root grafts are *Armillaria mellea* in *Picea* (Wichmann, 1925), *Endothia gyrosa* in *Quercus velutina* (Weir, 1925), *Poria weirii* in *Pseudotsuga menziesii* (Wallis and Buckland, 1955), *Cerato-stomella ulmi* in *Ulmus americana* (Verrall and Graham, 1935), and *Cerato-cystis fagacearum* in *Quercus* (Kuntz and Riker, 1955). Local spread of oak wilt caused by *Ceratocystis fagacearum* occurs throughout grafts from tree to tree in a somewhat concentric pattern. According to Kuntz and Riker (1955), such radial spread involves only one or two "tree depths" in a season. Over a period of a few years a wilt pocket of up to a few acres may develop with dead trees in the center bordered by dying trees.

Excavation of roots by Verrall and Graham (1935) showed that almost all *Ulmus americana* trees more than 8 inches in diameter were connected by root fusions if the stems were 7 feet apart or less. Vessels discolored by *Ceratostomella ulmi*, the fungus causing Dutch elm disease, were traced through root grafts. The discoloration usually was confined to the roots, root collar, and lower stem, but it was absent from the crown, indicating that the disease incitant had entered through the grafted roots. In Illinois a definite relationship existed between the number of adjacent tree infections and the spacing distance between elms (Neely and Himelick, 1963). According to Himelick and Neely (1962), the spread of Dutch elm disease from affected to nearby healthy trees occurred when transmission by bark beetles was im-probable. Their results indicated that 43% of the elms closer than 16 feet and 29% of those closer than 26 feet were root-grafted (Table 6.1). Because of the high incidence of root grafting of trees for distances up to 25 feet they recommended spacing of elms at distances greater than 30 feet.

FIG. 6.8. Stages in development of buttresses caused initially by excessive cambial growth on the upper surfaces of horizontal roots. Photo courtesy Kepong Forest Research Institute, Malaysia.

FIG. 6.9. Spreading plank buttress of *Pterospermum javanicum*. Photo courtesy Kepong Forest Research Institute, Malaysia.

TABLE 6.1

Distance (ft) between treated and untreated trees	Number of untreated trees observed	Untreated trees grafted to treated trees	
		Number	%
5–10	9	3	33
11–15	14	7	50
16–20	29	6	21
21–25	20	5	25
26–30	13	—	—
31–35	2	—	—
36–40	1	—	—
	88	21	

[a] From Himelick and Neely (1962).

Root Buttresses

Many tropical species develop buttresses or somewhat flattened plates which are perpendicularly arranged to the lower portion of the stem. Buttresses vary widely in size and shape from thin plates to wide flutings. (Figs. 6.8–6.11). Their size increases with tree age, and in some mature trees they may extend upward along the stem and outward from the base for as much as 9–10 meters. Individual trees may form up to 10 buttresses but most buttressed trees usually have only 3 or 4.

Buttresses generally form only in trees with superficial root systems and well-developed, horizontal lateral roots. They begin to form from excessive cambial growth on the upper side of lateral roots. In young trees cambial growth is normal and lateral roots are concentric in cross section. After a few years, however, cambial growth along the upper sides of lateral roots accelerates greatly to produce excessive thickening until conspicuous buttresses form. Some trees begin to form buttresses rather early. For example, buttress formation in *Delonix regia* in Ceylon and *Terminalia superba* in Nigeria was confirmed for trees less than 5 years old (Petch, 1930; MacGregor, 1934).

Buttress formation is an inherited trait. It occurs commonly in tropical rain forest trees in the Dipterocarpaceae, Leguminosae, and Sterculiaceae. The expression of buttressing in species having inherent potential for it is

Fig. 6.10. Buttressing in *Pterygota horsfieldii* in Sarawak. Photo courtesy of Dr. P. Ashton.

regulated by environment. In the tropics buttressing is most prevalent at low altitudes and in areas of high rainfall. Soil depth appears to be most important in regulating buttress development (Richards, 1964).

The lower stems of buttressed trees are very eccentric and stem transections often are stellate. The stems of buttressed trees taper downward from the level to which buttresses ascend, and they also taper upward from this point. The downward tapering of stems is absent in young stems but develops progressively during buttress formation. Thus, formation of buttresses appears to involve a mechanism regulating preferential mobilization of cambial growth requirements by the buttressing sites.

FIG. 6.11. Buttresses of *Shorea mugongensis* in central Sarawak. Photo courtesy Dr. P. Ashton.

Knee Roots and Pneumatophores

A number of species of trees which usually grow in habitats subjected to periodic flooding characteristically develop various forms of "knee" roots or pneumatophores (Fig. 6.12). Such roots have been reported in such genera as *Taxodium, Avicennia, Sonneratia, Mitragyna, Phoenix, Pterocarpus, Amoora, Carapa, Heritiera, Ploiorium, Cratoxylon, Tristania, Symphonia,* and *Terminalia* (Groom and Wilson, 1925; Richards, 1964; Kramer and Kozlowski, 1960). Richards (1964) stated that knee roots produced by *Symphonia globulifera* in swamp forests of British Guiana sometimes were so abundant

F<small>IG</small>. 6.12. Abundant development of cypress "knees" in a dense stand of *Taxodium distichum* growing in South Carolina. U.S. Forest Service Photo.

that they impeded walking. The pneumatophores of swamp species vary somewhat in structure, origin, and function although many of them contain lenticels and assist in gas exchange by trees.

Knee roots of *Mitragyna stipulosa* in swamps developed by rapid local cambial activity as vertical protuberances of horizontal roots or by arching of a horizontal root above the surface (McCarthy, 1962). These pneumatophores grew above the swamp surface for a few centimeters before curving downward. As water levels increased, the roots kept pace by growing vertically and producing young pneumatophores from the top of the knee roots. The pneumatophores were covered with functioning lenticels at the water surface.

Mitragyna ciliata and *Symphonia globulifera* on waterlogged sites in West Africa form simple or compound knees. In *Mitragyna* a simple knee is always created by a root branch arising from a deep layer and then turning back into the soil. Gradually the looplike structure becomes buried in deposited mud and is subsequently stimulated to grow a new kneeroot out of the convex side of the primary loop. The branching occurs in an area of large lenticels. Hence, compound knees involving several layers of loops are formed and the root system thereby has access to the free atmosphere (Jenik, 1967).

Erect, lenticel-containing pneumatophores in *Amoora, Carapa*, and *Heritiera* are protuberances of roots that run horizontally beneath the mud (Groom and Wilson, 1925). They are produced by localized cambial activity and some are forked. In *Carapa* the forking is often the result of fusion of two pneumatophores, whereas in *Heritiera* forking results from bifurcation of pneumatophore tips. In *Avicennia*, which inhabits sites subject to tidal flooding, many vertical air roots emerge from the mud around the tree. Such roots apparently are involved in gas exchange and suck in air through lenticels when the tide falls.

A number of species produce "stilt" roots which emanate from the main stem of the tree, bend downward, and enter the soil. Stilt roots often branch and anastomose above ground and give rise to secondary and tertiary roots below ground.

The mangroves (*Rhizophora*) are perhaps the best known examples of trees which produce stilt roots, but such roots also form on a number of species found in freshwater swamps and rain forests. According to Richards (1964), stilt roots form on species of *Clusia* and *Tovomita* in South America, *Macaranga barteri* and *Uapaca* spp. in West Africa, and *Elaeocarpus littoralis, Xylopia ferruginea, Dillenia* (Fig. 6.13), *Eugenia,* and *Casuarina sumatrana* in Malaysia. Stilt roots also occur in some palms. Flattened stilt roots are found on *Virola surinamensis* in South America and on *Bridelia micrantha, Musanga cecropioides,* and *Santiriopsis trimera* in Africa.

Rhizophora has numerous and very thickly intermingled, arched stilt roots with surface lenticels connected to mud roots (Fig. 6.14). Scholander, Van Dam, and Scholander (1955) demonstrated the importance of such stilt roots as aerating channels for submerged roots. In *Rhizophora mucronata* in Malaysia, stilt roots develop very rapidly from the part of the root remaining above ground after the seed implants itself in the mud. Subsequently additional stilt roots develop from the stem, roots, and even branches as the tree increases in size. The height of root production and the spread of roots are influenced by site, with trees growing in shallow soils or subject to very deep inundation producing the greatest mass and spread of stilt roots. The stilt roots are light brown, smooth and soft when young, but after entering the ground they become very woody and tough. Eventually the stem of the tree may stand clear of the ground mounted on a group of stilt roots. The original tap root or lower portion of the stem, which gradually died, is visible in the center and often clear of the ground (Watson, 1928).

Although many pneumatophores are aerating organs which supply oxygen

Fig. 6.13. Stilt roots of *Dillenia reticulata*. Photo courtesy Kepong Forest Research Institute, Malaysia.

to submerged roots, this does not always seem to be the case with some kinds of " knees." When *Taxodium distichum* is grown in periodically flooded soil, it responds by producing vertical knees as a result of localized cambial activity on the upper surfaces of roots which are better aerated than the lower surfaces (Whitford, 1956). Data of Kramer, Riley, and Bannister (1952) indicated that oxygen was used locally by *Taxodium* knees and these did not serve as aerating organs for other parts of the tree. The pneumatophores of *Xylopia staudtii* of West African freshwater swamp forests have very thin cortex without air spaces and their compact secondary phloem does not appear to be a passage for gaseous exchange (Jenik, 1967).

FIG. 6.14. Stilt roots of *Rhizophora*. Photo courtesy Kepong Forest Research Institute, Malaysia.

Nodulated Roots

Nitrogen fixing root tubercles, or nodules, are characteristic of many species of Leguminosae (Fig. 6.15), but they also form on roots of many nonleguminous woody plants. As may be seen in Table 6.2 the root nodules of legumes and nonlegumes differ in several respects. Nodule formation in legumes results from penetration of roots by *Rhizobium* bacteria through root hairs or injuries along the roots. Uemura (1964) concluded that the weight of evidence favored actinomycetes as the causal agents of nodules in nonlegumes.

Two forms of nodules have been described on legumes, with the most common type occurring from infection of cortical parenchyma cells (Allen and Allen, 1958). Rarely nodules may also form from division of the pericycle. Whereas nodules of nonlegumes begin to form as simple structures resembling those of legumes, they soon begin to branch. Because of their branching (Fig. 6.16) and perennial habit, the nodules of nonlerumes develop in conspicuous clusters which, in some genera such as *Alnus* and *Ceanothus*, may

TABLE 6.2

Comparison of Leguminous and Nonleguminous Nodule Hypertrophies in the Angiospermae[a]

Criterion	Leguminous root nodules	Nonleguminous root nodules
Causal Organism		
Identity	*Rhizobium* spp.	Controversial
Invasive power	Well-defined	Not known
Mode of entry	Root hairs primarily	Uncertain; root hair invasion claimed
Localization	Intracellular	Intracellular
Mode of spread	Infection threads; host cell division	Mechanism described poorly or not at all
"In host" morphology	Bacteroid forms	"Bläschen" and sporangia stages
Strain differences	Common	Not known
Reinoculation	Established with pure cultures	Questionable; primarily with crushed nodule inocula
The nodule		
Morphology	Spherical, cylindrical, lobed	Coralloid
Size	1–10 mm; effective and ineffective types	2–6 mm clusters; ±60 mm after 10–15 years; efficiency differences not known
Anatomy	Organized tissues; four major zones	Modified roots; no tissue differentiation
Infection zone	Intrafasicular	Extrafasicular
Tissue culture	On excised roots	Not reported
Longevity	Short-lived on annuals; many years on perennials	Perennial
Rootlet production	From nodules of *Sesbania* and *Caragana* spp.	From nodules of *Myrica* and *Casuarina* spp.
The host		
Host range	1 plant family; ±1500 species	8 plant families; ±100 species
Infection site	Root cortex	Root cortex
Tissue differentiation	Pronounced; specialized	None
Nuclear changes in host cells	Polyploidy; distortion and disintegration of nuclei	Enlargement; amoeboid shapes; rupture of nuclear membrane
Plant growth response	Nonbeneficial to beneficial; growth enhanced, nitrogen fixed	Growth enhanced; nitrogen fixed; not proved in all associations
Importance	Major significance in agriculture	Ecology, reforestation, soil/plant conservation
Biochemistry		
Auxins	In large amounts	Reportedly present
Amino acids	±24 identified	±10 identified
Starch granules	Usually in noninvaded cells	In noninvaded cells (*A. glutinosa*)

TABLE 6.2 (*Continued*)

COMPARISON OF LEGUMINOUS AND NONLEGUMINOUS NODULE HYPERTROPHIES IN THE ANGIOSPERMAE[a]

Criterion	Leguminous root nodules	Nonleguminous root nodules
pH of tissue	Infected more acid than noninfected tissue, incl. plant root	Infected more acid than noninfected tissue, less acid than normal root
Vitamins	B_{12} synthesized	B_{12} present in *A. oregona*
Pigments	Leghemoglobin, choleglobin, methemoglobin; coproporphyrin	Anthocyanin, hemin, and hemoglobin
Phage	Present	Claimed, not proved

[a] From Allen and Allen (1965).

be as large as an orange (Fig. 6.17). In gymnosperms, the nodules have hairs resembling root hairs and they lack apical meristems. Nodule regeneration is accomplished by growth of an internal nodule formed by a secondary endodermis. As the inner nodule increases in size it crushes the old cortical tissues of the parent nodule.

Important nodulated nonlegumes include such gymnosperm genera as *Agathis, Araucaria, Libocedrus, Phyllocladus, Dacrydium,* and *Sciadopitys.* Root nodules have also been confirmed in some 100 species of angiosperms comprising 8 families (Allen and Allen 1965). The important nodulated woody genera of angiosperms include *Alnus, Casuarina, Coriaria, Elaeagnus, Hippophaë, Shepherdia, Comptonia (Myrica), Ceanothus,* and *Purshia.*

PHYSIOLOGICAL AND ECOLOGICAL SIGNIFICANCE OF ROOT NODULES

Bacteria in the nodules of legumes synthesize organic nitrogen compounds from carbohydrates of the host plant and nitrogen from the air. Root nodule fixation is especially important to trees in the southeastern United States, where forest trees grow together with herbaceous legumes (Kramer and Kozlowski, 1960).

As with early experiments on nodulated legumes, subsequent research demonstrated the capacity of nodules of nonleguminous woody plants to fix nitrogen. This was done by comparing growth of plants with and without nodules in a rooting medium lacking available nitrogen. One such experiment is summarized in Table 6.3. Many similar experiments showed that only nodulated plants grew vigorously and accumulated nitrogen in the absence of combined nitrogen (Fig. 6.18). They also showed that nodule tissues had a

Fig. 6.15. Root nodules of *Enterolobium cyclocarpum*. [From Allen and Allen (1936).]

higher nitrogen concentration than other root and shoot tissues. Removal of nodules often caused symptoms of nitrogen deficiency until new nodules formed (Bond, 1963). Confirmation of the nodules as the site of nitrogen fixation was provided by a variety of ^{15}N tests. For example, when Bond (1958) exposed roots of nodulated plants to ^{15}N, the nodules later showed the greatest accumulation of nitrogen. Furthermore, when a nodule was removed from a host, and it and the host later exposed separately to ^{15}N, fixation occurred only in the nodules. According to Stewart (1962), about 90% of the nitrogen fixed in *Alnus* nodules was rapidly translocated from the nodules to other tissues in the plant. Quick (1944) found that growth of *Ribes* plants approximately doubled when they were grown in vessels which previously contained *Ceanothus* roots, over plants grown in fresh soil. Similarly Hellmers

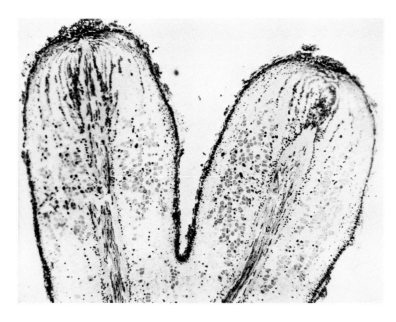

Fig. 6.16. Radial longitudinal section of branched nodule of *Alnus glutinosa*. [From Bond (1963).]

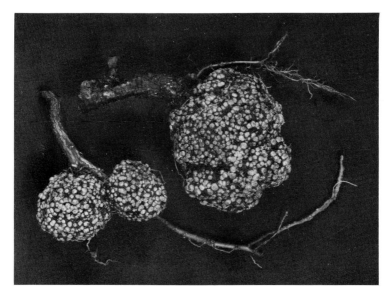

Fig. 6.17. Large clusters of root nodules on *Alnus glutinosa* ($\times$ 2/3). [From Bond (1958).]

TABLE 6.3

ACCUMULATION OF NITROGEN BY NODULATED PLANTS IN ROOTING MEDIA FREE OF COMBINED NITROGEN[a]

Species	Nitrogen accumulated per plant during first season (mg)	Subsequent accumulation (mg)
Alnus glutinosa	300	2500 by end of 2nd season
Myrica gale	146	5020 by end of 3rd season
Hippophaë rhamnoides	26	200 by end of 2nd season
Casuarina cunninghamiana	70	1400 after 2.5 seasons
Elaeagnus angustifolia	—	186 after 1.5 seasons
Coriaria myrtifolia	36	—

[a] From Bond (1963).

and Kelleher (1959) observed that growing *Ceanothus* plants first caused greatly increased nitrogen content in tomato plants grown in the same soil.

As Allen and Allen (1965) emphasized, the nodulated nonlegumes usually are shrubby pioneer perennial plants. For example, the capacity of nodulated roots of *Podocarpus lawrencei* to fix nitrogen contributed to the stabilizing capacity of this pioneer species in exposed rocky situations (Bergerson and Costin, 1964). The literature is rich with reports of *Alnus* fixing nitrogen and improving the site for adjacent plants or those succeeding *Alnus*; only a few examples will be given.

In Europe, *Alnus* has been used to prepare poor sites for subsequent forest plantings. According to Ovington (1956), soil in which *Alnus* was growing had a 30–50% higher nitrogen content than soil under *Pinus*, *Salix*, or *Fagus*. Tarrant (1961) reported even greater enrichment of soil by *Alnus*, with soil nitrogen 65% higher under *Pseudotsuga–Alnus* stands than under pure stands of *Pseudotsuga*. Virtanen (1957) interplanted *Alnus* trees among other forest trees and found those adjacent to *Alnus* to show growth stimulation through increased nitrogen availability. Nodulated seedlings of *Ceanothus velutinus* and *Alnus rubra* grown in low nitrogen soils had very beneficial effects on development of pine seedlings grown in the same soil. Two *Ceanothus* seedlings fixed at least 35 ppm of nitrogen, which became available for plant growth after the roots decomposed. *Alnus* fixed about half as much nitrogen as *Ceanothus* (Wollum and Youngberg, 1964). A variety of stunted, nitrogen-deficient plants covered the infertile stony substrate left by a retreating glacier in Alaska. *Alnus*, however, grew vigorously and deposited an average of 53 lbs of nitrogen per acre. This site was then suitable for invasion by *Picea sitchensis*, which eventually outgrew and succeeded *Alnus* (Crocker and Major, 1955).

FIG. 6.18. *Myrica gale* plants after one season's growth in solution free of combined nitrogen. Plants on left with nodules; those on right without nodules. [From Bond (1963).]

Alnus has also been shown to increase productivity of lakes by augmenting the nitrogen content of the soil and waters draining into the lake. For example, abundance of *Alnus tenuifolia* along the east shore only of a California lake provided opportunity for evalution of nitrogen fixation by this species. A very high accumulation of nitrogen on the *Alnus* side of the lake was demonstrated. After spring waters passed through *Alnus* humus they had about twice the stimulatory effect on growth of photoplankton as before (Goldman, 1961. For a good review of literature on amounts of nitrogen fixed by *Alnus* the reader is referred to Holmsgaard (1960).

Mycorrhizae

A number of soil fungi form symbiotic associations with the delicate un-suberized root tips of trees (Figs. 6.19–6.22) and play an important role in tree growth. Although these root–fungus associations are very widespread in nature they were not described until 1840 when Unger gave a superficial description of the fungus roots of *Monotropa* and *Pinus excelsa*. Such struc-tures were a subject of sporadic interest until 1885 when Frank published his first detailed studies and proposed the name, mycorrhiza (literally fungus-root) for them.

Inasmuch as mycorrhizae are formed by most forest trees they are a significant component of the forest ecosystem. Marks, Ditchburne, and Foster (1968) estimated that the top 6 inches of soil under a *Pinus radiata* stand contained about half a ton of mycorrhizae, about half of which consisted of viable associations. The fungal partners of these associations belong predominantly to the basidiomycetous fungi. The full range and extent of fungi which form mycorrhizae is still not completely known because the only way in which proof of an association can be established is in artificial culture—a technique subject to many criticisms. However, lists of mycorrhizal fungi have been compiled. Melin (1963) synthesized mycorrhizae with the following fungi: *Amanita, Boletinus, Boletus, Cantherellus, Clitophilus, Clitocybe, Cortinarius, Entoloma, Lactarius, Lepiota, Paxillus, Russulus,* and *Tricholoma.* Among the fungi suspected of forming mycorrhizae are *Gomphidius, Hebeloma, Hydnum, Hygrophorus,* and *Inocybe.* Two well-known fungi used frequently in experiments are *Rhizopogon* and *Scleroderma.*

STRUCTURE OF MYCORRHIZAE

Noelle (1910) published a detailed study on the unsuberized components of the root system of pine and made some of the most relevant discoveries on mycorrhizal structure. Most early investigations were conducted on mycorrhizae of gymnosperms and beech (*Fagus*). However, in the 1950's and 1960's studies of mycorrhizal structure were extended to numerous other plants.

Most mycorrhizal fungi fall into two very broad groups: the ectotrophic (or ectocellular) forms, and their variants, which exist both inside and outside the root; and the endotrophic (or endocellular) forms which exist entirely within the root cells. These associations always form in the cortical cells of the host roots and do not extend into the endodermis or stele. Usually the infection induces modifications in root morphology, with the character and physiology of the small absorbing rootlets dramatically altered.

Mycorrhizae do not form with all parts of the unsuberized root system of forest trees. The actual process of mycorrhizal formation is not well understood. However, the available evidence shows that the smaller, slower growing root surfaces are infected preferentially (Hatch, 1937; Wilson, 1951; Wilcox, 1968b). The rapidly growing large roots, especially those that eventually show secondary growth, do not form mycorrhizae. After a root is infected, its rate of growth slows down dramatically, possibly as a result of rapid loss of cell-wall-forming residues to the fungus. In gymnosperms the tips of infected roots branch many times, and the small root is converted into a cluster of short, dichotomous branches.

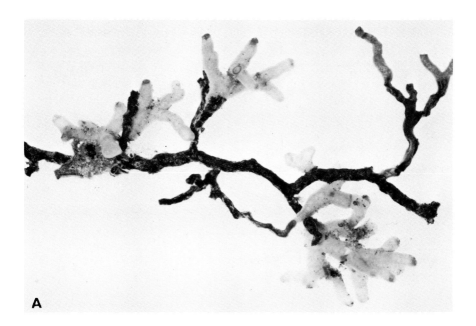

FIG. 6.19. Variation in mycorrhizal forms found on roots of *Pinus elliottii*. (A) and (B) White corraloid forms; (C) light brown coralloid form with bands on elements; (D) bifurcate form, with sheath, mycelium and shizomorphs pink-lavender in color. (E) Two forms on same rootlet. One is black and the other a white form growing from the former; (F) light brown bifurcate form (about × 6). U.S. Forest Service photo.

C

D

FIG. 6.20. Variations in mycorrhizae on *Pseudotsuga menziesii* roots. (A) Mycorrhizal cluster. (B) Grey, pinnate mycorrhiza. (C) Orange mycorrhiza. (D) Yellow mycorrhiza showing rhizomorphs of fungus symbiont. U.S. Forest Service photo.

Ectotrophic Mycorrhizae

This group contains forms in which the fungus produces a weft of hyphae on the root surface and the mycelia may form either thin, loosely woven tissue, tightly woven masses, or even compacted pseudoparenchymatous structures. A variety of other hyphal strands may radiate into the soil from this mantle. The fungus penetrates the cortex, forcing its way between the cortical cells without actually entering individual cells of the host. Marked cytological changes occur in the host (Foster and Marks, 1966, 1967) and these may be associated with modifications in root physiology. The fungi in the intercellular spaces are closely packed together and filled with glycogen whereas the adjacent host cells are depleted of their starch reserves. In root transections the cortical cells appear to be separated by a fungal net, frequently referred to as a Hartig net (Fig. 6.22C).

Some idea of similarities as well as quantitative and qualitative differences in ectotrophic mycorrhizae and uninfected roots of *Eucalyptus* in Australia may be gained from the work of Chilvers and Pryor (1965). Both mycorrhizal and uninfected roots had diarch steles, a single layer of cells in the pericycle and endodermis, two layers of cortical cells, and an epidermis (Fig. 6.22). Quantitative differences in structure include: (1) lack of production of root hairs by mycorrhizae and some root hairs in uninfected fine roots; (2) limited root cap tissue in mycorrhizae (rarely more than two cell layers between the apex and fungal sheath) and extensive root cap tissue in uninfected roots; and (3) occurrence of differentiation much closer to the apex in mycorrhizae than in uninfected roots. The morphology of mycorrhizal rootlets was similar to that which might occur from slow growth as a result of unfavorable environmental conditions and did not appear to be caused by any unique effect of the fungus. In contrast, some specific qualitative differences were ascribed to fungal infection. These included pronounced thickening of inner tangential and radial walls of the inner cortex in mycorrhizae and conspicuous radial elongation of epidermal cells of mycorrhizae. The structure of mycorrhizae of *Eucalyptus* was similar to those of European *Fagus sylvatica* as described by Harley (1968).

Ectotrophic mycorrhizae occur in a large number of economically important woody plants. They are found in the Pinaceae, Salicaceae, Betulaceae, Fagaceae, Juglandaceae, Caesalpinoideae, and Tiliaceae. Important genera of forest trees having ectotrophic mycorrhizae include *Pinus, Picea, Abies, Pseudotsuga, Cedrus,* and *Larix* among the gymnosperms, and *Quercus, Castanea, Fagus, Nothofagus, Betula, Alnus, Salix, Carya,* and *Populus* among the angiosperms (Meyer, 1966).

Ectendotrophic Mycorrhizae

Forms of this group are basically similar to ectotrophic forms with the exception that the fungus is both *intra-* and *inter*cellular. There is some doubt

Fɪɢ. 6.21. Fungal symbionts growing from individual mycorrhizae of *Pinus elliottii*. (A) Two different fungi emerging from plated mycorrhiza (about × 15). (B) Sketch of black mycorrhiza showing outgrowth of three different fungi: (a) is *Cenococcum graniforme*; (b) and (c) are different Basidiomycetes (about × 20). U.S. Forest Service photo.

whether this group represents a discrete mycorrhizal type or an advanced stage in the decline of the mycorrhizal association (Marks, Ditchburne, and Foster, 1968). Until additional evidence is available on details of host–fungus physiology, the significance of present systems of classification of mycorrhizae remains obscure.

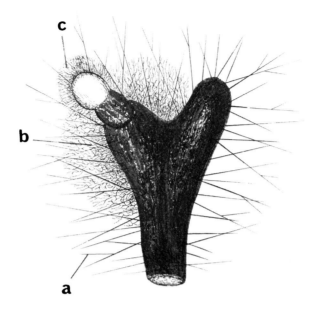

B

Pseudomycorrhizae

This is a rather common yet little understood form of "mycorrhizae" in which the fungus assumes a predominantly parasitic role (Levisohn, 1954). The fungus is predominantly intracellular, the mantles are thin and tenuous, and the Hartig net is coarse and beadlike. Seedlings grow very slowly when their roots are infected by pseudomycorrhizal fungi. The existence of such host–fungal associations highlights the difficulty in separating mycorrhizal associations into distinct groups and makes it obvious that all associations are not beneficial to the host tree.

Endotrophic Mycorrhizae

In these associations the fungus lives intracellularly and does not have any communication with the surface of the soil. These associations are usually formed with phycomycetous fungi and cause a lesser degree of change in the morphology of the host than in the ectotrophic forms (Hackaylo, 1957). Although endotrophic mycorrhizae are widely distributed in the plant kingdom, they are found only in tree species in the genera *Liriodendron, Acer, Liquidambar,* and various members of the Ericaceae.

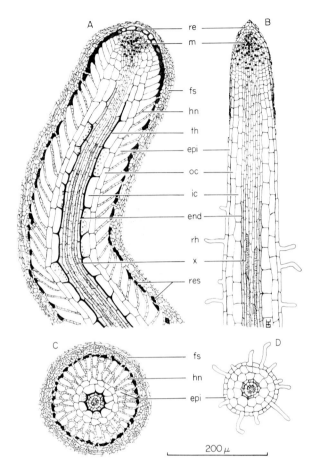

FIG. 6.22. Anatomy of mycorrhizal and uninfected roots of *Eucalyptus*. (A, B) Median longitudinal sections of mycorrhiza and uninfected root, respectively; (C, D) transverse sections through fully differentiated region of mycorrhiza and uninfected root, respectively. rc, Root cap; m, meristematic region; fs, fungal sheath or mantle; hn, Hartig net; th, thickened walls of inner cortex; epi, epidermis; oc, outer cortex; ic, inner cortex; end, endodermis (shaded to indicate extent of tannin impregnation); rh, root hair; x, lignified protoxylem (with reticulate to pitted thickening in both infected and uninfected roots); res, collapsed residues of cap cells. [From Chilvers and Pryor (1965).]

CLASSIFICATION AND NOMENCLATURE OF MYCORRHIZAE

Melin (1927) provided a simple description of a mycorrhiza based on the color of the mantle and the branching habit of the roots resulting from infection. Björkman (1941) made slight modifications of this sytem. Dominik (1955) made an extensive revision of the classification of ectrotrophic mycorrhizae based primarily on the color and structure of the mantle hyphae.

Trappe (1962) extended the classification further with a plea for more attention to changes in internal tissue structure. He drew attention to the significance of the tannin layer, its form and structure, to changes in the host cells, and the form and structure of the Hartig net. Wilde and Lafond (1967) questioned the validity of the terms ectotrophic, endotrophic, and ectendotrophic and proposed their replacement with terms which are more appropriate to the actual disposition of the fungus in and among the host tissues.

The problems of classifying mycorrhizae are numerous and until further facts on host–fungus physiology are obtained, most of the systems of classification will remain arbitrary. It must be emphasized that the types are only "form species" and may be subject to considerable variation. However, these classification systems can be used in ecological studies. Marks (1965) showed that seven mycorrhizal types could be identified on *Pinus radiata* in one locality. They had an overlapping mosaic distribution pattern which remained stable over a 3-year period of observation. Variation in mycorrhizal types is found not only in soils but also on the same root surface. It is possible to see one mycorrhizal form replaced by another on the same short root. However, such succession occurs only infrequently and an established association must be regarded as a stable entity (Marks and Foster, 1967).

ORGANISMS IN THE RHIZOSPHERE OF MYCORRHIZAE (OR MYCORHIZOSPHERE)

Frequently fungi form intimate associations with the surface of the root, actually penetrating between or into the superficial layers of the outer cortex. More than one fungus may be involved in forming the loosely knit mantles seen on the root surface and they can often be mistaken for a true mycorrhizal association. Wilde and Lafond (1967) pointed out that the superficial, extramatrical mycelia did not really form a "root fungus organ" and proposed that they be called "rhizoclenae" (literally root mantle). They further subdivided the rhizoclenae into "mycochlamydes," or loose fungal mantles covering roots wholly or partially, and "mycoplasts," or grumose fungal mantles, clusters of soil particles, and root sloughings (Fig. 6.23). These superficial associations appear to play an important role in nutrition of woody plants (Wilde, 1968a,b). Numerous bacteria are found in the mycorhizosphere and they differ qualitatively not only with different fungal associates but also with those found in uninfected roots. In electron microscope studies, Foster and Marks (1967), showed that the list of organisms found in the mycorhizosphere must be expanded to include algae, actinomycetes, and numerous other fungal forms. These are not identified in conventional plating techniques used to study mycorhizosphere organisms. All of these observations show that the flora (and possibly microfauna) on roots is more complex than often reported and is in need of further investigation.

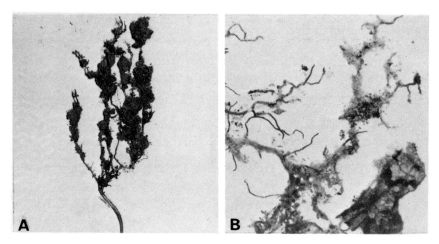

FIG. 6.23. Different forms of extra-matrical mycelia: A. *Mycochlamydes,* fungal mantles on roots of *Gilbertiodendron dewevrei* De Wild in equatorial forest of Congo; (B). *Mycoplasts,* grumose, mycelia-agglomerated organo-mineral clusters on roots of *Pinus strobus* in northern Wisconsin. These fimbrial root auxiliaries play an important part in the production of chelating agents and conversion of raw sources of nutrients into available form. (From Wilde, 1968b).

DISTRIBUTION OF MYCORRHIZAE

Research on distribution of mycorrhizae in soils has been complicated by lack of suitable techniques for making quantitative estimates. Usually these fungus–root associations are restricted primarily to the moderately acidic, well-aerated layers of the soil. Thus in dense compacted soils mycorrhizae may be found only in the very topmost zone, whereas in loose forest soils they occur to a considerably greater depth.

It appears that if the physical environment is conducive to mycorrhizal formation and the fungal inoculum is present in the soil, forest trees have little difficulty in forming these associations. However, situations are encountered where these associations are not formed when tree seedlings are introduced into a treeless environment. Curtis and Cottam (1950) showed that toxic substances given off by roots of prairie plants prevented the development of mycorrhiza-forming fungi which, in turn, inhibited tree growth (White, 1941).

In established forests there is a rich reservoir of potential mycorrhiza-forming fungi (Zak and Bryan, 1963) and often various environmental factors limit the formation of these structures.

Patterns of distribution of mycorrhizae in established forests have been the subject of many studies. Mikola and Laiho (1962) showed that in *Picea* stands the density of short root tips and mycorrhizae was greatest in the middle humus layer. It was low in mineral soil and decreased rapidly with

TABLE 6.4

DENSITY OF LIVING SHORT ROOT TIPS AT VARIOUS SOIL DEPTHS IN *Picea* STANDS AND THEIR
DISTRIBUTION INTO VARIOUS MYCORRHIZAL TYPES[a]

Root tips and mycorrhizal types	Humus layer			Mineral soil	
	0–1 cm	1–2 cm	2 + cm	0–2 cm	2–7 cm
Number of short root tips per cm^3	21	31	24	12	4
Young A mycorrhizae (%)	38.8	34.0	32.3	30.8	25.5
Old A mycorrhizae (%)	28.2	35.2	37.1	34.0	30.6
D_A mycorrhizae (%)	4.6	10.9	10.8	19.0	26.4
D_N mycorrhizae (%)	22.7	9.3	7.4	3.5	3.6
K mycorrhizae (%)	1.5	1.6	1.7	0.9	0.2
Pseudomycorrhizae (%)	4.2	9.0	10.7	11.8	13.6
Total	100	100	100	100	100

[a] From Mikola and Laiho (1962).

soil depth (Table 6.4). The rate at which the associations deteriorated increased rapidly. In deeper soil layers the proportion of pseudomycorrhizae
increased. Meyer (1967) in a highly informative investigation showed that
production of mycorrhizae in a gymnosperm forest was inversely related to
the productivity of the site and the texture of the soil. The more productive
sites had few mycorrhizae but a significantly greater proportion of these
were viable. In contrast, about 10 times more mycorrhizae were formed in
the less productive sites, yet the rate of deterioration in the associations was
very high. Marks, Ditchburne, and Foster (1968) made similar observations
in Australian plantations of *Pinus radiata*.

Mycorrhizal fungi often show marked survival potential. For example,
Mikola *et al.* (1964) noted that inoculation of pine seedlings with mycorrhizae was not delayed by heavy burning of slash and raw humus. However,
the mycorrhizal flora of soils rich in fungal symbionts can be destroyed by
prolonged flooding (Wilde, 1954).

RECIPROCAL RELATIONS BETWEEN MYCORRHIZAL FUNGI AND TREES

Much available evidence shows that trees and mycorrhizal fungi exist
symbiotically. The relationship appears to be one in which the tree supplies
carbohydrates and other metabolites which are beneficial to the fungus (Lewis
and Harley, 1965a,b,c). In turn, the fungus benefits the tree chiefly by increasing solubility of nitrogen, phosphorus, and other nutrients and thereby
making them more available from difficultly soluble sources (Bowen and
Theodorou, 1967). Zak (1964) postulated that mycorrhizal fungi may also
protect the higher symbiont from disease by utilizing excess carbohydrates

and thereby decreasing attractiveness of roots to pathogens, acting as a physical barrier, secreting fungistatic substances which were subsequently found by Marx (1969b), and favoring various protective organisms of the rhizosphere. For a more detailed discussion of the role of mycorrhizae in root disease the reader is referred to Zak (1964); Marx (1969a,b) and Marx and Davey (1969).

INFLUENCE OF MYCORRHIZAE ON TREE GROWTH AND ESTABLISHMENT

Although trees can be grown successfully without mycorrhizae under certain conditions, such as very high soil fertility, they usually grow much better with mycorrhizae. In fact, on most sites mycorrhizal fungi appear to be required for tree survival. A rich literature has accumulated on the improved growth of forest trees after mycorrhiza-free soils were inoculated with mycorrhizal fungi. A few examples will be given.

In Puerto Rico where pines are not native, attempts to introduce pine trees met with recurrent failure (Briscoe, 1959) until seedlings were inoculated with leaf mold imported from a pine forest in the United States. Thereafter, mycorrhizae developed and the trees grew satisfactorily. When such trees were 6 feet tall, those in an uninoculated area were only 10–12 inches high (Hacskaylo, 1961a).

Forest nursery failures in Australia, Philippines, South Africa, England, Hawaii, and Sweden occurred until soils were inoculated with appropriate mycorrhizal fungi (Hatch, 1936).

Wisconsin prairie soils did not provide suitable conditions for normal growth of trees whose root systems lacked mycorrhizae. Infestation of prairie soils with mycorrhizal fungi was confined mainly to the limits of root extension of adjacent forest stands. When seeds of conifers were planted on prairie soils, suitable germination was obtained, but subsequent development of tree seedlings was inhibited in the first whorl of leaves. However, the productive capacity of prairie soils was greatly improved by its inoculation with small amounts of forest humus or by planting of nursery stock that was known to have mycorrhizae (Figs. 6.24, 6.25). In a forest tree nursery in Iowa pine seedlings failed to grow unless they developed mycorrhizae. Seedling growth and mycorrhizal development were satisfactory only after the nursery soil was inoculated with duff and humus from a pine plantation (McComb, 1943). Mycorrhizal *Pinus virginiana* seedlings showed greatly increased height growth and produced twice as many short roots as did nonmycorrhizal plants. Field trial studies by Wright (1957) indicated that 2 + 0 nonmycorrhizal *Pinus ponderosa* nursery stock showed poorer survival than stock with mycorrhizae. Losses during the second year after planting were lower than after the first year, mostly because seedlings that originally lacked mycorrhizae acquired them after outplanting. In Iowa McComb and Griffith (1946) selected two

FIG. 6.24. Nine-month-old *Pinus strobus* seedlings raised for 2 months in sterile nutrient solution and then transplanted: (A) directly from nutrient solution to prairie soil; (B) from nutrient solution to forest soil for 2 weeks to inoculate seedlings with mycorrhizal fungi, then to prairie soil. [From Wilde (1968a).]

adjacent nursery beds which had never grown conifers before and which lacked mycorrhizal fungi. One bed was inoculated with duff and humus containing active mycorrhizal fungi. Part of each bed was then seeded to *Pinus strobus* and part to *Pseudotsuga menziesii*. Various fertilizer subtreatments were applied. After 2 years seedlings of both species made satisfactory growth in inoculated soils. On uninoculated soil fertilized with phosphorus, seedlings of *Pinus strobus* formed mycorrhizae and grew satisfactorily. In contrast, *Pseudotsuga menziesii* seedlings responded moderately to phosphorus addition but did not form mycorrhizae or grow normally. Inasmuch as *Pseudotsuga* seedlings made poorer growth in uninoculated, fertilized plots than in inoculated plots, even under conditions of high phosphorus, and no improvement in growth resulted from adding nitrogen and potassium, it appeared that there was a stimulus from the mycorrhizae in addition to the direct effect of phosphorus. McComb and Griffith (1946) suggested that the mycorrhizae increased growth by increasing metabolism and accelerating transfer of phosphorus and growth stimulators from the fungus to the seedlings.

The production of mycorrhizae in forest soils can be stimulated by application of fertilizers. This result is directly opposite to that obtained in many pot experiments conducted with impoverished soils where mycorrhizal production

Fig. 6.25. Influence of inoculation of prairie soil with mycorrhiza-forming fungi on growth of 6-month-old *Pinus radiata* seedlings. (A) Carrington prairie silt loam. (B) The same soil plus 0.2% of a forest soil (Plainfield sand) harboring mycorrhiza-forming fungi. (C) Plainfield sand. [From Wilde (1968b).]

is inhibited by balanced fertilizer regimes. Mycorrhizal formation has been promoted in some Australian plantations (G. Marks, personal communication) by mechanical disturbance of deep soil layers where the very high soil bulk density limits root development. Thus the interactions between formation of mycorrhizae, tree growth, and edaphic factors are complicated and require further study.

Mycorrhizae and Mineral Uptake

Much evidence is available which shows that mycorrhizal fungi play a very important role in increasing mineral uptake of the host tree. This has been confirmed, for example, by the research of Melin and his co-workers. Their experiments with radioactive elements demonstrated that mycorrhizal fungi transferred phosphorus, nitrogen, calcium, and sodium from the substrate to tree roots. Kramer and Wilbur (1949), who were among the first to use tracer techniques in mycorrhizal research, showed that mycorrhizal parts of pine roots accumulated larger quantities of ^{32}P than nonmycorrhizal ones. It was not clearly demonstrated, however, that the phosphorus of mycorrhizae had been absorbed by mycorrhizal hyphae. Melin and Nilsson (1950a) first exposed only mycorrhizal hyphae to ^{32}P and then introduced these to aseptic *Pinus sylvestris* seedlings. Subsequent measurements of radioactivity in the pine seedlings showed that nonmycorrhizal root tips contained only small amounts of ^{32}P whereas mycorrhizal tips contained much larger amounts. The isotope was readily translocated to the main roots, stem, and needles within a few hours.

Melin and Nilsson (1950b) showed that *Boletus variegatus* in mycorrhizal connection with *Pinus sylvestris* transferred nitrogen from a solution of ammonium salt to the roots of the higher symbiont. In other experiments ^{45}Ca was transferred by *Boletus mycelia* to mycorrhizal roots of tree seedlings and then was distributed throughout the seedlings (Melin and Nilsson, 1955). Melin, Nilsson, and Hacskaylo (1958) exposed mycorrhizal and nonmycorrhizal *Pinus virginiana* seedlings to $^{22}NaCl$ and 48 hr later analyzed the mycorrhizae and roots for distribution of the radioactive isotope. The mycorrhizal fungi contained the largest amount of the isotope (Table 6.5). The long root segments bearing only mycorrhizae also had considerable isotope, although they had about 40 % less than the mycorrhizae. Very little uptake of sodium was observed in nonmycorrhizal short roots and their corresponding long root segments. More sodium was accumulated by stems and needles than by nonmycorrhizal root segments, but less than by long root segments with mycorrhizae. These experiments confirmed the view that cations as well as phosphate ions and nitrogen were translocated to mycorrhizal trees through the mycorrhizae.

Stone (1950) failed to demonstrate beneficial mycorrhizal influences on phosphorus uptake by *Pinus radiata* seedlings grown in a synthetic soil containing ground phosphatic minerals. However, similar cultures of pine seedlings in Carrington silt loam demonstrated that infection of mycorrhizae resulted in increased phosphorus uptake and improved growth (Table 6.6). Nonmycorrhizal plants did not take up much phosphorus from untreated soils but they showed satisfactory growth after phosphate fertilizers were added. On the basis of these experiments, Stone (1950) placed great emphasis on improved phosphorus nutrition of the trees as an important role of mycorrhizal fungi in their symbiotic relationship.

Some investigators have questioned the importance of mycorrhizae in mineral uptake. Harley and McCready (1952), for example, worked with excised roots and suggested that the fungal sheath might actually be a barrier to absorption of minerals by tree roots. They showed that as much as 90 % of the phosphorus absorbed by excised roots in a few hours accumulated in the mycorrhizal mantle. Subsequent work by Harley and Brierley (1955) showed gradual movement of phosphorus from the mantle of the mycorrhizae to the root. In short-time experiments, nonmycorrhizal roots actually absorbed more phosphorus than did roots with mycorrhizae. As Morrison (1957, 1962a)

TABLE 6.5

RADIOACTIVITIES AND ESTIMATED AMOUNTS OF SODIUM TRANSLOCATION INTO ROOTS OF
Pinus virginiana SEEDLINGS[a]

Sample[b]	Dry weight of sample (mg)	cpm/sample (no)	cpm/ml dry weight (no)	Net sodium translocation (mμg/mg dry weight)
Mycorrhizal segments of root				
1 M	0.63	93.4	148.3	246
LR	0.48	29.0	60.4	100
2 M	0.51	66.6	130.6	216
LR	0.61	44.7	73.3	122
3 M	0.98	82.9	84.6	140
LR	0.84	34.4	41.0	68
Nonmycorrhizal segments of root				
1 W	0.84	8.5	10.1	17
LR	0.69	3.8	5.5	9
2 W	0.82	5.9	7.2	12
LR	1.01	8.1	8.0	13

[a] From Melin, Nilsson, and Hacskaylo (1958).
[b] M, mycorrhizae; W, nonmycorrhizal short roots; LR, long root bearing M or W.

TABLE 6.6

EFFECTS OF MYCORRHIZAE OF *Pinus radiata* SEEDLINGS ON PHOSPHORUS
UPTAKE AND DRY WEIGHT INCREMENT[a]

Treatment	Phosphorus content of needles (%)	Increase in total dry weight (g)	Increase in phosphorus content (mg)
Nonmycorrhizal	0.040 ± 0.001	1.99 ± 0.25	0.06 ± 0.11
Mycorrhizal	0.080 ± 0.008	3.71 ± 0.10	2.33 ± 0.07

[a] From Stone (1950).

demonstrated, this situation was reversed in longer time experiments. He found that shoots of intact nonmycorrhizal *Pinus radiata* plants received phosphorus rapidly at first, but the rate was not maintained very long. In contrast, shoots of mycorrhizal plants received phosphorus at a relatively constant rate, which was less than that of the initial phase, but greater than that of the second, slower phase in nonmycorrhizal plants. Hence, during the early period mycorrhizae actually impeded phosphorus uptake by the host, but thereafter enhanced its uptake. The fungus mantle apparently absorbed and accumulated phosphorus rapidly and then slowly transferred it to the host. Melin and Nilsson (1958) compared the transfer of radioactive phosphorus from the lower symbiont to both excised and intact pine roots. In intact plants phosphorus was readily transferred from the fungus to the host tissue and, when transpiration was high, phosphorus accumulation was several times higher than in decapitated plants. These experiments confirmed that mycorrhizae increase mineral uptake in intact plants.

In informative studies on the root environment and its relation to mineral absorption Bowen and Theodorou (1967) postulated that the volume of soil exploited by a mycorrhizal root was about 10 times greater than that of a nonmycorrhizal root with root hairs. The rationale behind this supposition was that the zone of efficient nutrient absorption in an uninfected root continuously moved along the soil as the root elongated. Consequently the volumes of soil that supplied nutrients by the process of diffusion were small. A mycorrhizal root, in contrast, was a longer-lived structure that did not "move" in the soil. Under conditions of restricted root development this made a mycorrhizal tree an effective competitor. Bowen and Theodorou (1967) also showed that the efficiency with which different mycorrhizal species of the same genus could assimilate and translocate phosphorus to the root differed considerably. Thus all mycorrhizal fungi did not have the same capacity to absorb mineral nutrients.

Unlike phosphorus, sulphur apparently moves quite rapidly through the mycelium of mycorrhizal fungi. Studies with ^{35}S by Morrison (1962b) showed lack of significant mycorrhizal influence on sulphur uptake by *Pinus radiata* shoots. This was true even when acute sulphur deficiency had been created in plants before they were used in the experiments. Mycorrhizae did not accumulate larger quantities of sulphur than nonmycorrhizal plants. Hence, in contrast to phosphorus, most of the sulphur was not metabolized by the fungus.

Rhizospheric Symbiosis

Most investigators have assigned a major role in tree nutrition to the short roots of ectotrophic mycorrhizae. However, Wilde (1968a,b) presented evidence that a significant part of the rhizosphere is made up of mantles of epirhizal mycelia which perform functions of symbiosis at least as efficiently as the mycelia which are imbedded in cortical tissues. Wilde suggested also that the peripheral mycelia played the most important role in nutrition of woody plants. He emphasized that, over the years, preoccupation with the nutritional importance of short roots of ectocellular mycorrhizae was partly the result of observations made on young seedlings grown in the greenhouse or nursery beds (e.g., plants grown under high light intensities, having high rates of photosynthesis, and producing short roots). Wilde noted that root systems of trees in dense stands in Wisconsin often had few or no mycorrhizal short roots. In seedlings reproduced under a forest canopy, the absorbing surface of short roots was negligible in comparison with active nonmycorrhizal roots and extramatrical mycelia (Fig. 6.26). Wilde also noted that additions of fertilizers to greenhouse cultures and nursery stock did not demonstrate any effect of density of short roots on mineral uptake. These observations suggested an important role in tree nutrition of rhizospheric fungi other than those which modify root structure.

In forest soils the usually abundant peripheral mycelia, which have a very extensive surface area, are in close contact with tree roots and derive energy from decomposition of root sloughings. Spyridakis, Chesters, and Wilde (1967) showed that chelating compounds formed in decomposition of tree roots were largely involved in transformation of biotite to kaolinate and sub-sequent availability of nutrients. For example, Iyer (1964) demonstrated much greater nutrient availability in soil samples in the immediate proximity of

FIG. 6.26. Roots of 3-year-old *Pinus strobus* seedlings grown in different environments. (A) Lack of mycorrhizal short roots on seedlings which grew under a dense forest canopy. (B) Extensive development of ectocellular mycorrhizae on seedlings grown in a forest nursery. [From Wilde (1968a).]

Pinus strobus and *P. resinosa* roots than in interrhizal spaces (Table 6.7). Experiments with isotopes have also shown that peripheral mycorrhizae are important components of the nutritional mechanism of trees (Wilde, 1968a,b). In addition, rhizospheric organisms other than fungi undoubtedly play a role in tree nutrition. Much more research is needed in identifying and quantifying the specific symbiotic roles of the various organisms of the rhizosphere.

FACTORS INFLUENCING MYCORRHIZAL DEVELOPMENT

Both the number and types of mycorrhizal fungi are influenced by various environmental factors especially light intensity, soil fertility, soil moisture, root exudates and biocides, aeration, and soil pH. Some of these controlling factors will be discussed briefly.

Light Intensity

Several investigators have reported that mycorrhizae developed best when the host tree was subjected to high light intensities. When Björkman (1949) grew *Pinus* and *Picea* seedlings under various degrees of shading he found mycorrhizal formation to be correlated with low light intensities. Harley and Waid (1955) studied growth of *Fagus* mycorrhizae under artificially produced light intensities. Various kinds of mycorrhizal fungi developed on the lateral

TABLE 6.7

VARIATIONS IN EXCHANGE CAPACITY AND NUTRIENT AVAILABILITY IN INTERRHIZAL SPACES AND IN THE PROXIMITY OF ROOTS OF *Pinus resinosa* AND *P. strobus* TREES[a]

	Reaction pH	Exchange capacity (meq/100 mg)	Available				
			N	P	K	Exch. Ca (meq/ 100 g)	Exch. Mg (meq/ 100 g)
Interrhizal spaces of coarse outwash sand	4.6	2.1	Trace	12	29	0.55	0.22
The same soil adhering to roots of *Pinus resinosa*	4.5	3.7	24	64	78	1.65	0.61
Interrhizal spaces of podzolic sandy loam	4.7	2.8	16	42	31	1.00	0.32
Aggregates of the same soil around roots of *Pinus strobus*	5.0	4.1	92	80	115	2.41	0.72

[a] From Iyer (1964).

roots between mid-July and the end of August, but only after the first true leaves developed. The types of mycorrhizae which are most abundant on *Fagus* trees in the forest appeared most commonly at very high light intensities, and they were absent on plants grown at low light intensities. Shading eventually led to a loss of seedling resistance to infection by parasites, whereas increases in light intensity caused mycorrhizal formation (see Zak, 1964). Hacskaylo and Snow (1959) reported that at a given nutrient level mycorrhizae developed best on 3 species of gymnosperms in full sunlight under natural daylength (Table 6.8). Either increasing daylength or interrupting the dark period changed the abundance of mycorrhizae. The alteration varied with species and depended on the intensity of the supplementary light.

Mineral Nutrition

At a given light intensity mycorrhizal formation usually varies inversely with soil fertility, especially in relation to available phosphorus, nitrogen, potassium, and calcium. As light intensity is increased the higher is the fertility level that permits a given mycorrhizal development. This general relationship applies over a rather wide range of nutrient availability, but it breaks down at extremes of deficiency or excess of minerals, as well as at unusually high light intensities.

Soil Moisture

It should be emphasized early in this section that there is some uncertainty as to how soil moisture supply affects formation of mycorrhizae. Griffin (1969)

TABLE 6.8

DEVELOPMENT OF MYCORRHIZAE ON ROOTS OF PINE SEEDLINGS GROWN IN FULL SUNLIGHT OR IN SHADE WITH VARIATIONS IN NUTRIENT LEVELS[a]

Light condition and nutrient level[b]	Prevalence of short roots with mycorrhizae (%)		
	Pinus virginiana	*Pinus taeda*	*Pinus strobus*
Full sunlight N_1	10–20	40–50	80–90
N_2	30–40	70–80	80–90
N_3	1–10	1–10	0
N_4	0	1–10	0
Shade N_1	0	0	0
N_2	0	1–10	0
N_3	1–10	1–10	0
N_4	0	0	0

[a] From Hacskaylo and Snow (1959).
[b] Shaded seedlings received about 10% of full sunlight. Nutrient levels increased progressively from N_1 to N_4.

showed that many species of fungi could grow in soils below pH 4.2. Although he did not work with basidiomycetous species, the mycelia of these fungi are readily observed in very dry soils. It appears likely that water deficits severely restrict the formation of new root surfaces available for colonization by mycorrhizal fungi and do not primarily affect the fungus directly.

Both the quantity and type of mycorrhizae formed are responsive to soil moisture availability. When several species of fungi invade a single host they often show variable sensitivity to soil moisture stress. Hence, mycorrhizal associations can be controlled by irrigation. Worley and Hacskaylo (1959) studied the effects of four soil moisture levels on mycorrhizal associations of *Pinus virginiana*. A white fungus, the major mycorrhiza-former when soil moisture was high, was absent under drought conditions. A black fungus, *Conococcum graniforme*, comprising only about a tenth of the mycorrhizae, formed under a low moisture content (Table 6.9). The mycorrhizae of a black fungus increased from 10 to 100% as moisture deficits increased. Apparently the black fungus was more vigorous at high moisture deficits, while the white fungus was less vigorous. Mikola and Laiho (1962) noted that the drought-resistant *Cenococcum graniforme* predominated in soil levels that were subjected to periodic drought. Excess moisture can destroy the mycorrhizal flora of soils rich in fungal symbionts. For example, submerged layers of peats and of abandoned beaver flowages had no mycorrhiza-forming fungi (Wilde, 1954).

Root Exudates and Biocides

A number of naturally occurring root exudates as well as applied chemicals profoundly affect mycorrhizal development. Natural root secretions include a wide variety of compounds including carbohydrates, amino acids, vitamins, organic acids, nucleotides, flavonones, enzymes, and other compounds (Rovira, 1965). Some compounds released from roots, such as hydrocyanic acid, glycosides, and saponins, are toxic to microorganisms.

TABLE 6.9

AVERAGE NUMBER OF BLACK AND WHITE MYCORRHIZAE PER SEEDLING ON *Pinus virginiana* GROWN UNDER FOUR SOIL MOISTURE LEVELS[a]

Watering period	White	Black	% Black
Every day	72.4	10.5	11.9
Every second day	18.4	8.3	59.9
Every third day	0.08	8.6	98.6
Every fourth day	0	2.4	100

[a] From Worley and Hacskaylo (1959).

Fungistatic root metabolites vary in different species. For example, inhibiting substances produced by tomato roots prevented entrance of tree mycorrhizal fungi into roots. In pine they prevented the mycorrhizal fungi from infecting certain parts of rootlets (Melin, 1962).

Handley (1963) found that under *Calluna* heathlands substances in extracts of healthy *Calluna* plants greatly inhibited growth of mycorrhizal Hymenomycetes on which the formation of mycorrhizal associations depended. The factor which inhibited growth of mycorrhizal fungi disappeared when growth of *Calluna* was suppressed, suggesting that it had to be continuously produced to remain at the inhibitory level.

Litter under forest trees contains water soluble substances which, when highly diluted, stimulate growth of mycorrhizal fungi and, when slightly diluted, inhibit their growth (Melin, 1946).

Applied Biocides

Some fungicides, insecticides, and herbicides check mycorrhizal growth variously but the degree of growth inhibition varies greatly with the chemical and dosage. Dosages as low as 0.25 lb/A of γ-isomer of benzene hexachloride inhibited mycorrhizal growth on *Pinus resinosa* seedlings. At dosages above 2 lbs/acre pine roots were severely malformed (Simkover and Shenefelt, 1951). Wilde and Persidsky (1956) evaluated effects of chlordane, benzene hexachloride, thiosan, calomel, formaldehyde, aluminum sulfate, allyl alcohol, and Stoddard solvent on mycorrhizal development. Although the specific effect varied with different biocides, all of them at high dosages produced symptoms of deterioration of mycotrophic organs. Benzene hexachloride and calomel were especially deleterious, causing destruction of the lower symbiont or partial disintegration of cortical cells of short roots and nonmycorrhizal root tissues. Sometimes the chemicals caused morphological modification of entire root systems. At low dosages of biocides, short roots showed irregular shapes of the fungal mantle as well as arrested penetration of mycelia and of development of the Hartig net. Persidsky and Wilde (1960) treated forest soil harboring mycorrhizal fungi with a combination of chlordane, thiosan, and allyl alcohol and then used this soil for inoculating mycorrhiza-free prairie soils seeded to *Pinus radiata*. Subsequent growth of tree seedlings indicated that the biocides virtually eliminated the mycorrhiza-forming organisms. Under a light application of chemical some of the fungi survived but their growth promoting efficiency was decreased by about half. According to Hacskaylo and Palmer (1957), methyl bromide at high concentrations prevented mycorrhizal formation on *Pinus virginiana* and *Pinus caribaea* seedlings. Vapam and Bedrench only partially prevented mycorrhizal development, whereas ethylene dibromide and nemagon had no obvious effects. Hacskaylo (1961b) found that mycorrhizal fungi of several genera including *Boletus, Amanita,* and *Russula* were completely inhibited at 8, 10, or 100 ppm of cycloheximide. *Cenococcum graniforme* showed high tolerance to the antibiotic as a concentration of 1000 ppm was required for its complete growth inhibition.

Repeated applications of mylone herbicide and Vapam decreased the productive capacity of soil by annihilating mycorrhiza-forming fungi (Iyer, 1964; Iyer and Wilde, 1965). The elimination of the fungi caused a greatly decreased absorption of certain nutrients by tree seedlings even from soils having large quantities of these nutrients in readily available form. These findings were reinforced by the observation of Henderson and Stone (1967) that fumigation with methyl bromide, Trizone, or Vapam resulted in reduced phosphorus uptake by coniferous seedlings in the nursery. Fortunately, all herbicides do not have deleterious effects on mycorrhizal fungi. For example, the herbicide DCPA(dimethyl 2,3,5,6-tetrachloroterephthalamate) promoted seedling growth without elimination of mycorrhiza-forming fungi (Iyer, 1965).

The quality of nursery stock which has been lowered by certain biocide treatments can be improved with applications of fermented sawdust compost and aluminum sulfate in solution (Iyer, Lipas, and Chesters, 1969). Such treatment decreased the succulence of tree crowns, increased the absorbing surface area of the roots, and preserved or reintroduced mycorrhiza-forming and extramatrical mycelia required for mycotrophic nutrient uptake.

INTERNAL REQUIREMENTS FOR MYCORRHIZAL ESTABLISHMENT AND DEVELOPMENT

Environmental factors affect mycorrhizal development primarily through their influence on the higher symbiont rather than directly on mycorrhizal fungi. Detailed studies on nutritional requirements of mycorrhizal fungi have established the indispensability of carbohydrates, nitrogen, vitamins, hormonal growth regulators, and other factors for development of the lower symbiont. Evidence also is available of the importance of additional unidentified metabolites. The various internal requirements for mycorrhizal growth will be discussed briefly.

Carbohydrates

Considerable evidence shows that mycorrhizal fungi depend on photosynthetically produced carbohydrates from the host. Experiments by Melin and Nilsson (1957) demonstrated, for example, that mycorrhizal Basidiomycetes obtained carbohydrates from tree roots. Pine seedlings that had been inoculated with mycorrhizal fungi were exposed to $^{14}CO_2$. After sufficient time had elapsed for translocation of tagged photosynthate to the roots, comparisons were made of hyphal sheaths of mycorrhizal and uninfected root tips. Considerable labeled photosynthate was rapidly transported from pine seedlings to the mycorrhizal mycelium. In fact, radioactivity values of fungal mantles were higher than those of uninfected roots, indicating higher concentrations of photosynthate in the former. Such transfer of materials appears to be necessary as an energy source for growth of mycorrhizal fungi. This was substantiated by Melin and his co-workers who demonstrated that mycorrhizal fungi associated with trees used glucose, maltose, and sucrose as energy sources (see Melin, 1962). Mycorrhizal fungi apparently differ greatly in their capacity for utilizing various kinds of carbohydrates, but most tree mycorrhizal Basidiomycetes use simple carbohydrates preferentially as energy sources.

Lewis and Harley (1965a,b,c) showed that transfer of carbohydrates from the host to the fungus depends on the latter functioning as a metabolic sink which receives and stores carbohydrates in forms that are not used by the host. Consequently there is no reciprocal flow. This is a characteristic common to some obligate parasites.

Mycorrhizal fungi do not appear to be able to satisfy their carbon requirements from the humus of forest soils which contain small amounts of soluble carbohydrates. This conclusion is based on experiments in which mycorrhizal fungi grew well in autoclaved raw humus from coniferous forests when sugar was added. Without the additional sugar, however, the fungi grew only negligibly. In contrast, the cellulose decomposing Basidiomycetes may fulfill necessary carbon requirements from the soil in addition to the roots. But even these fungi do not break down cellulose as long as carbohydrates are available from roots. When the supply from roots is cut off they utilize cellulose both from the roots and soil (Norkrans, 1950; Melin, 1962).

Although it seems clear that mycorrhizal fungi utilize carbohydrates provided by the host, there has not been agreement on whether or not correlations exist between the amount of soluble carbohydrates in the root system and the extent of mycorrhizal infection. Björkman (1942) presented data showing that such a causative correlation exists. Close correlation has also been shown between mycorrhizal frequency and factors controlling photosynthesis, especially light intensity and availability of nitrogen and phosphorus.

Some investigators have questioned whether a strong relation exists between carbohydrate supply in the roots and the degree of mycorrhizal infection. For example, Handley and Sanders (1962) and Meyer (1966) did not find an increase in mycorrhizal development with increasing light intensity. Handley and Sanders (1962) stated that in Björkman's experiments the root systems had different amounts of mycorrhizal development. Handley and Sanders (1962) concluded that mycorrhizal infection caused, rather than resulted from, the different carbohydrate concentrations found by Björkman. Meyer (1966) supported the conclusions of Handley and Sanders (1962). Harley and Lewis (1969) also raised questions about the validity of data because of questionable analytical procedures used by various investigators. Thus, although it is widely recognized that mycorrhizal fungi derive carbohydrates from the host, valid questions have been raised about quantitative correlations between carbohydrates in roots and the degree of development of mycorrhizal infection.

Vitamins

When grown in synthetic nutrient solutions in pure culture many species of mycorrhizal fungi have shown vitamin deficiencies. Most species tested have shown partial or total deficiency of thiamine (Melin, 1953, 1962). According to Melin (1953), partial deficiencies for thiamine may be affected by such environmental conditions as deficiency of oxygen and composition of the medium. In addition to a requirement for thiamine, various species of fungi have shown need for other vitamins. For example, Melin (1953) cited several investigators who found deficiencies of pantothenic acid in *Tricholoma imbricatum*, nicotinic acid in *T. fumosum*, biotin in *Cenococcum*, and inositol in *Rhizopogon roseolus*. Some species of mycorrhizal fungi have complex vitamin deficiencies and do not grow well in pure culture (Melin, 1953). As various fungal associates of the same tree species have different vitamin requirements, the main source of these may be the soil rather than the roots (Melin, 1962).

Nitrogen

Mycorrhizae differ in their capacity to utilize various nitrogen sources. For example, inorganic and organic ammonium salts were readily utilized by *Tricholoma* whereas nitrates were not (Norkrans, 1950). Although *Cenococcum graniforme* could use both nitrate and ammonium nitrogen it used the latter form preferentially when both were supplied (Mikola, 1948).

Considerable attention has been given to amino acids as nitrogen sources for the lower symbiont. Many tree mycorrhizal fungi are stimulated by one or several amino acids when grown *in vitro* in the presence of ammonium nitrogen (Melin, 1953). Nevertheless, various species of fungi differ markedly in their requirements for specific amino acids. Melin and Mikola (1948) found that at least 3 of 14 amino acids had a stimulating effect on growth of *Cenococcum*, with histidine accelerating growth more than any other amino acid tested. According to Melin (1963), most tree mycorrhizal Basidiomycetes were stimulated by glutamic acid but in different ways because of variable sensitivities to glutamic acid toxicity. Some species of the lower symbiont showed growth inhibition above rather low concentrations of glutamic acid. When added to nutrient media in certain concentrations, some amino acids apparently inhibit growth of mycorrhizal fungi. Such inhibition can be modified by other amino acids (Norkrans, 1950).

Other Metabolites

The roots of the higher symbiont produce unidentified essential metabolites for mycorrhizal fungi which were classed under the term " M-factor " by Melin (1962). Melin (1954) studied growth of mycorrhizal fungi in " maximum media " containing sugar, salts, vitamins, and amino acids. When mycorrhizal fungi were placed in such media with and without excised pine roots, their growth was greatly stimulated by the presence of roots. However, the magnitude of the growth promoting effect of the roots varied for different fungi, indicating various degrees of M-factor deficiency. *Boletus variegatus* and *Rhizopogon roseolus* were only partially deficient for the M-factor, whereas *Russula xerampelina* was wholly deficient or nearly so (Melin and Das, 1954). Experiments on growth of tree mycorrhizal fungi on agar plates in the presence of maximum media and tree roots showed that the M-factor exuded from the root to the rhizosphere. The M-factor also influenced spore germination of mycorrhizal Basidiomycetes (Melin, 1962). Apparently at least two substances comprise the M-factor. One is diffusible through plasma membranes and the other is retained in cells. The latter substance becomes available to fungi through their enzymic activity (Melin, 1963). Production of the M-factor is partly controlled by nutrient supplies in the root zone.

Hormonal Growth Regulators

Many mycorrhizal fungi produce auxinlike substances in pure culture. Culture filtrates of mycorrhizal fungi can induce dichotomous branching in the short roots of pine (Slankis, 1948, 1949, 1950, 1951). In low concentrations they stimulated root development and in high dosages they inhibited it. Under aseptic conditions Slankis was able to induce production of short roots in pine that closely resembled true mycorrhizae not only in general appearance but also in internal anatomy (Slankis, 1955, 1958a,b, 1963).

The action of these fungal hormones is closely related to physiology of the root and conditions in the external environment. For example, at low light intensities which will inhibit formation of mycorrhizae, auxins have little effect on the root, even at relatively high concentrations. Conversely, either in high light intensities or high carbohydrate availability, auxins stimulate production of mycorrhiza-like branches (Slankis, 1961, 1963). Slankis (1967) was able to convert mycorrhiza-like short roots formed in culture solutions with low nitrogen contents into fast-growing, long rootlike structures by greatly increasing the amount of ammonium nitrogen. Slankis' investigation is interesting in the light of Moser's (1959) observation that auxin production by mycorrhizal fungi in culture is diminished by high nitrogen concentrations.

In the light of an accumulating body of evidence which shows that growth of plants is controlled by hormonal interactions, the importance of growth regulators of fungal origin other than auxins in the mycorrhizal state must be considered. Harley and Lewis (1969) review available evidence which indicates that cytokinins are involved in establishment of the mycorrhizal condition. However, investigations on the role of growth regulators other than auxins on mycorrhizae have been few and much more research is needed along such lines.

Suggested Collateral Reading

Allen, E. K. and Allen, O. N. (1964). Non-leguminous plant symbiosis In "Microbiology and Soil Fertility." (C. M. Gilmour, and O. N. Allen, eds.), pp. 77–106. Oregon State Univ. Press, Corvallis, Oregon.

Bond, G. (1963). The root nodules of non-leguminous angiosperms. *Symp. Soc. Gen. Microbiol.* **13**, 72–91.

Bond, G. (1967). Fixation of nitrogen by higher plants other than legumes. *Ann. Rev. Plant Physiol.* **18**, 107–126.

Bormann, F. H. (1966). The structure, function, and ecological significance of root grafts in *Pinus strobus* L. *Ecol. Monogr.* **36**, 1–26.

Graham, B. F. Jr. and Bormann, F. H. (1966). Natural root grafts. *Bot. Rev.* **32**, 255–292.

Harley, J. L. (1969). "The Biology of Mycorrhiza." Leonard Hill, Ltd. London.

Harley, J. L. and Lewis, D. H. (1969). The physiology of ectotrophic mycorrhizas. In "Advances in Microbial Physiology." Vol. III. (Rose, A. H. and Wilkinson, J. F. eds.), pp. 53–81. Academic Press, London and New York.

Jenik, J. (1967). Root adaptations in West African trees. *J. Linn. Soc. (Bot.)* **60**, 25–29.

McCarthy, J. (1962). The form and development of knee roots in *Mitragyna stipulosa*. *Phytomorphology*, **12**, 20–30.

Melin, E. (1959). Mycorrhiza. *Encycl. Plant* Physiol II, 605–638.

Melin, E. (1962). Physiological aspects of mycorrhizae of forest trees. In "Tree Growth," (T. T. Kozlowski, ed.). Chapter 15. Ronald Press, New York.

Meyer, F. H. (1966). Mycorrhiza and other plant symbiosis. In "Symbiosis." Vol. I. (S. M. Henry, ed.), Chapter 4. Academic Press, New York.

Mikola, P. (1970). Mycorrhizal inoculation in afforestation. *Int. Rev. Forestry Res.* **3**, 123–196. Academic Press, New York.

Richards, P. W. (1964). "Tropical Rain Forest." Cambridge Univ. Press. Cambridge, England.

Scholander, P. F., van Dam, L. and Scholander, S. I. (1955). Gas exchange in the roots of mangroves. *Am. J. Bot.* **42**, 92–98.

Wilde, S. A. (1968). Mycorrhizae and tree nutrition. *Bioscience* **18**, 482–484.

Wilde, S. A. (1968). Mycorrhizae. Their role in tree nutrition and timber production. Univ. Wisconsin, *College of Agricultural and Life Sciences Res. Bull.* **272**.

Zak, B. (1964). Role of mycorrhizae in root disease. *Ann. Rev. Phytopath.* **2**, 377–392.

Chapter 7

FLOWERING

As outlined by Matthews (1963), the processes leading to development of mature seeds and fruits display several sequential stages including (1) enlargement of the inflorescence in the flower bud, (2) flowering, (3) pollination (transfer of pollen from anther to stigma), (4) fertilization (fusion of male and female gametes), (5) growth and differentiation of the embryo, (6) growth of the seed and fruit to maturity, and (7) ripening of fruits and cones. The first three of these phases will be discussed in the present chapter and the others in Chapter 8.

Floral Structure and Arrangement

As Kramer and Kozlowski (1960) emphasized, many botanists often restrict the term "flower" to angiosperms. However, this volume will use the term more broadly, in line with common usage of horticulturists and foresters, and treat the young cones or strobili of gymnosperms as flowers also.

ANGIOSPERMS

Typical complete flowers of angiosperms bear four types of organs in their receptacles (Fig. 7.1). The outermost of these are the sepals which together make up the calyx. Above the sepals are the petals, collectively called the corolla. The sepals and petals together comprise the perianth. Most flowers have a regular or actinomorphic corolla, with petals similar in shape and size and the flower showing radial symmetry. Some flowers, as in the Leguminosae, have an irregular or zygomorphic corolla and exhibit bilateral symmetry. Inside the perianth are two kinds of reproductive organs. These are the pollen-producing stamens, collectively called the androecium, and the carpels which comprise the gynoecium. Typically the mature carpel resembles a folded or rolled leaf blade with appressed or fused margins. A flower may have a single carpel or more than one. The carpel usually consists of a lower,

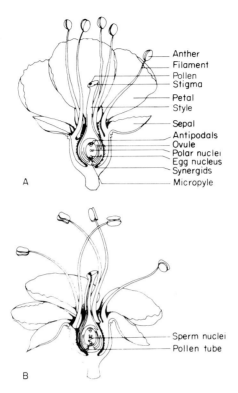

FIG. 7.1. Typical flower before and after fertilization. (A) Flower before fertilization; (B) flower shortly after union of sperm nucleus and egg nucleus. Some petals have fallen and stamens are withered. [After Biale (1954) Scientific American.]

fertile part, the ovary, and an upper sterile part, the style. At the top of the style is the stigma on which the pollen grains land prior to fertilization of immature seeds or ovules. The ovary interior may have a single cavity, called a locule, or more than one locule separated from each other by partitions. The ovules may be attached to the walls of the ovary or to partitions between locules. The ovule is important in reproduction as it is the site of megaspore formation and development of the female gametophyte called the embryo sac.

The typical mature ovule, which consists of the nucellus enclosed by one or more integuments, is attached to the ovule-bearing region, the placenta, by a stalk called the funiculus. At the top of the integument is a narrow opening, the micropyle. The region of the ovule in which the integuments merge with the funiculus is called the chalaza. Fusion among parts of the ovule is common. Usually the integuments are fused to each other and, for variable distances, to the nucellus.

The structure and form of ovules vary appreciably among species. Integuments may be lacking or there may be several and they may vary in thickness. In some species the nucellus is small; in others very large. Outgrowths other than integuments sometimes are present. The orientation of ovules is variable also. For example, at one extreme are atrapous (orthotropous) ovules with a nucellar apex so aligned that it points away from the funiculus. At the other extreme are anatropous ovules which are completely turned so the nucellar apex points toward the funiculus. Intermediate forms of ovule orientation also are well known (Maheshwari, 1950).

On the basis of ovary position flowers may be classified as hypogynous, perigynous, or epigynous. In an hypogynous flower the receptacle is convex or cone-shaped, and the whorls of floral parts are situated above each other with sepals the lowest and carpels the highest. In a perigynous flower the receptacle is more or less concave, the carpel(s) is attached to the center, and the sepals, petals, and stamens arise at the margin so they appear to be attached around rather than below the ovary. In an epigynous flower the receptacle is concave and not only surrounds the ovary but is fused to it, with other floral parts appearing to originate from the top of the ovary.

Woody plants show many examples of floral modifications and often lack some of the parts of the complete flower. For example, flowers of *Populus* and *Juglans* lack a corolla and those of *Salix* lack both calyx and corolla (Fig. 7.2). Another floral modification involves fusion of floral parts. In *Vitis* and

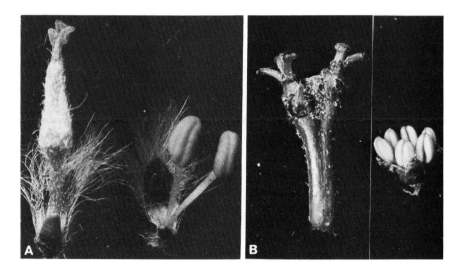

FIG. 7.2. (A) Pistillate and staminate flowers of *Salix*. (B) Pistillate and staminate flowers of *Quercus rubra*. Photo courtesy of W. M. Harlow.

Rhododendron, for example, carpels are fused, in *Catalpa* petals are fused, and in *Viburnum* sepals are fused. Fusion of parts of the perianth or carpels may date from the time of their origin or may have developed at a later stage of evolution.

Some flowers have nectaries. These are surface areas or organs which secrete a sweet liquid, called nectar, which attracts bees and other insects. Eames (1961) distinguished between two general types of nectaries: (1) localized areas which secrete nectar, and (2) nectar secreting organs which have been transformed from their original form and function. Nectaries may develop on both reproductive and vegetative tissues. Floral nectaries may occur close to the base of perianth parts (e.g., *Hibiscus*), as a shallow or concave ring between the stamens and base of the ovary (e.g., *Cercis siliquastrum*, *Robinia*, *Prunus*, and *Rubus*) or between the stamens and styles when an inferior ovary is present (e.g., *Eucalyptus*) or as a distinct ring around the base of the ovary (e.g., *Citrus*). Extrafloral nectaries often occur on the teeth of leaves (Fahn, 1967).

Nectaries may excrete nectar in several ways including: (1) diffusion through thin-walled epidermal cells; (2) diffusion from thin-walled epidermal papillae; (3) excretion from the tips of hairs; (4) excretion through stomata specially modified for this function; and (5) excretion as a result of rupture of the cuticle caused by swelling of the outer wall (Fahn, 1967). In *Magnolia* the entire flower has been termed a nectary because nectar diffuses through petal cuticles and is excreted through stomatal pores on petal bases and carpel surfaces (Eames, 1961).

Whereas flowers of many fruit trees are very showy those of most forest trees are very inconspicuous. Usually flowers of forest trees are so small and lacking in unusual coloration that they go unnoticed to the casual observer. There are some exceptions, however. *Magnolia*, for example, produces large and fragrant, terminal bell-shaped flowers that may measure 2–12 inches across depending on species. The white yellowish or greenish flowers of *Magnolia* have 6–12 petals and many stamens and pistils on a long axis. The large cup-shaped flowers of *Liriodendron*, which resemble tulips and lilies, also are showy. They have six greenish and orange petals, many long stamens, and many pistils on a narrow axis. The flowers of *Cornus florida* stand out because the flower clusters are surrounded by 4–6 large and attractive, white or pinkish petallike bracts. A marked contrast to the subdued flowers of most forest trees is presented by the showy flowers of many orchard trees and woody plants of ornamental value. Some examples of tree flowers are shown in Fig. 7.3.

Flowers of angiosperms are borne individually or, more commonly, in groups on various types of inflorescences. Flowers of apple trees are produced in clusters of three to seven (usually five). As in apple, the pear flower bud

FIG. 7.3. Flowering in Angiosperms. (A) Flowers of *Pyrus communis*; (B) flowers of *Robinia pseudoacacia*; (C) staminate and pistillate flowers of *Acer nigrum*; (D) flowers of *Tilia americana*; (E) pistillate flowers of *Populus deltoides*; (F) staminate flowers of *Populus deltoides*. U.S. Forest Service Photo.

opens into a terminal cluster of about five flowers. In olive (*Olea*), flowers are borne in paniculate inflorescences, each consisting of about 15 flowers. The inflorescences appear on shoots 1 or sometimes 2 years old. The flowers are either perfect, with functioning stamens and pistil, or staminate with the pistil aborted.

In *Magnolia* and *Liriodendron* the flowers occur singly in leaf axils. In *Prunus serotina* and *Acer pennsylvanicum* they are born in racemes; in *Populus*, *Betula*, and *Alnus* in catkins; in *Aesculus* in panicles and in *Sambucus* and *Viburnum* in cymes (Fig. 7.4).

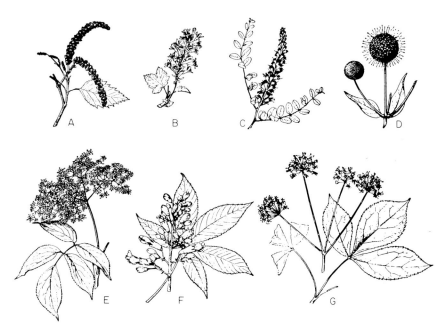

FIG. 7.4. Various types of inflorescences. (A) catkin of *Alnus*; (B) raceme of *Ribes*; (C) spike of *California*; (D) head of *Cephalanthus*; (E) cyme of *Sambucus*; (F) panicle of *Aesculus*; and (G) umbel of *Aralia*. From Woody Plant Seed Manual (1948).

Some forest trees are monecious, with staminate and pistillate flowers on the same plant as in *Betula* and *Alnus*. Others, such as *Diospyros*, *Populus*, and *Salix* are dioecious and bear staminate and pistillate flowers on separate plants. It should be obvious that a staminate tree will not produce seed. A few genera, such as *Aesculus*, have perfect flowers, bearing both stamens and pistils as well as staminate and pistillate flowers in addition. Still another combination occurs in *Rhamnus* and *Fraxinus* which have perfect flowers as well as either staminate or pistillate flowers.

GYMNOSPERMS

The calyx, corolla, stamens, and pistil are absent in gymnosperms. The flowers of gymnosperms consist of staminate and ovulate cones or strobili which, in most species, are produced on the same trees. The many small staminate strobili which produce pollen in pollen sacs are relatively short-lived. The more persistent and larger ovulate or pistillate strobili bear naked ovules on scales. Some examples of staminate and ovulate strobili of gymnosperms are shown in Fig. 7.5.

Floral Initiation and Development

As discussed in Chapter 3, Volume I, the capacity for flowering in woody plants is confined to the adult state. Even after the tree age or size denoting attainment of flowering capacity is reached, many trees fail to flower regularly. Hence, strong environmental and internal control of floral induction occur after attainment of adulthood. Such controls are discussed further in Chapter 9, this volume.

In many angiosperm trees of the Temperate Zone, flower primordia form rather early in the season preceding the spring in which the flowers open. Although the specific time of induction varies among species, for a large number of woody plants of the North Temperate Zone it takes place between early May and late July (Matthews, 1963). For example, after completion of vegetative growth in late June, nearly all of the buds of mature *Acer pseudoplatanus* trees were vegetative and later the apex of most of these buds entered into a transitional stage and finally a floral one. By cell division and enlargement the floral apex formed an inflorescence that remained undeveloped throughout the winter. Rapid development was resumed in the spring, and trees bloomed in late May and early June (Anderson and Guard, 1964).

The time of floral initiation is influenced by weather, site conditions, and management practices (Chapter 9). Therefore, the period of floral initiation changes somewhat from year to year and it varies in different parts of the natural range of a species. The degree of structural differentiation of flowers during the first season varies greatly among species.

Some variations in time of flower initiation have been observed for different shoot locations. In *Malus*, for example, flowers are initiated later in terminal buds of shoots than of spurs. They also are initiated later in terminal buds of spurs on 2-year-old shoots than on 3-year-old shoots. Within a flower cluster the central flower forms after the lateral flowers but it develops more rapidly (Zeller, 1955).

FIG. 7.5. Flowering in gymnosperms. (A) Staminate and ovulate strobili of *Pseudotsuga menziesii*; (B) staminate and ovulate strobili of *Tsuga caroliniana*; (C) staminate strobili of *Pinus elliottii* shortly before shedding pollen; (D) ovulate strobili of *Taxodium distichum*; (E) receptive ovulate strobilus of *Abies nobilis*; (F) staminate strobili of *Abies nobilis*, showing swollen pollen sacs about 1-day before shedding. U.S. Forest Service Photo.

FLORAL ONTOGENY IN ANGIOSPERMS

A flower develops from an apical meristem, with floral parts arising at the receptacle tip as rounded protuberances of meristematic activity. Usually development is acropetal with sepals appearing first, followed in order by petals, stamens, and carpels. Early stages of development of floral appendages resemble those of leaf formation at the stem tip. The floral parts arise by periclinal divisions in subsurface layers of apical meristems. These divisions are followed by others which include anticlinal divisions. Growth in length and width of floral parts follows as a result of apical and marginal growth (Esau, 1965b).

Perianth

After the leaf-like, sterile sepals and petals arise from periclinal divisions in subsurface layers they grow upward, at first by apical growth and then by intercalary growth. The perianth primordia increase in width by both marginal and intercalary growth. The sepals and petals consist of ground parenchyma and an abaxial and adaxial epidermis. The vascular system is poorly developed. The color of petals is traceable to carotenoid and anthocyanin pigments (Paech, 1955).

Stamens

A stamen primordium originates on the floral receptacle. Expansion of stamens involves apical growth at first and intercalary growth later. The stamen soon lengthens rapidly and assumes the form of the anther. The filament generally remains short until late stages of floral development.

The stamen typically consists of a sterile filament which supports the fertile anther. The anther generally has two pollen sacs in each of two lobes. The lobes are separated by a zone of sterile connective tissue. The ground tissue of the anther, filament, and connective is parenchymatous.

Next to the anther epidermis is a layer of wall cells called the endothecium which develops secondary thickenings as the anther matures. Adjacent to the endothecium are one to three layers of cells which become crushed when meiosis occurs in the microspore mother cells. The innermost wall layer of the anther, the tapetum, has an important physiological function in nutrition of pollen mother cells and young microspores.

Pollen Formation.   Early in anther ontogeny cells in the central zone of each of the four corners are distinguishable by their large, dense cytoplasm and large nuclei. These cells, called archesporial cells, divide periclinally to produce outer cells which form the tapetum. The inner cells, following this division, form the primary sporogenous cells. These may differentiate as microspore mother cells or give rise to mother cells by mitotic divisions. Each mother cell then undergoes two successive meiotic divisions to form a tetrad of haploid microspores (pollen grains). In most cases the pollen grains separate and lie freely in the pollen sac. In some species, however, the pollen grains remain in tetrads when mature; in still others the tetrads of pollen grains stick together.

Pollen grains differ markedly in size and morphological details, even within the same species. The size limits of pollen grains vary from about 5–200 μ. However, neither the size nor the shape of an individual pollen grain is fixed; they vary with hydration. The pollen grain is enclosed in a membrane or sporoderm consisting of an intine layer on the inside, which consists of pectin, and a thick outer exine layer made up of a high molecular weight terpene called sapropellin. Most pollen grains have one to many apertures or thin parts in the exine through which the pollen tube eventually emerges. Pollen apertures are morphologically classified as either pores or furrows. Pores tend to be isodiametric with rounded ends, whereas furrows are elongated and have acute ends. The apertures of angiosperm pollen are more distinct than those of gymnosperm pollen.

Male Gametophyte. The mature microspore has a large nucleus, dense cytoplasm, and a thin wall. After it grows considerably the microspore germinates. As a result of the first division two cells form: the larger vegetative (or tube) cell and the smaller, peripherally located generative cell. The generative cell is formed during late stages of anther development. The generative cell divides once to form two male gametes.

Carpels

The carpels grow as a result of activity in both apical and marginal meristems. The primordium of a primitive carpel is crescent-shaped at first but it soon widens. The more advanced carpel arises as a tubular structure from a ring-shaped primordium. Fusion of carpels occurs commonly and in a variety of forms in different species. Fusion may occur throughout the length of a carpel and involve stigmas, styles, and ovaries. It may occur at the base or apex only, or at both the base and apex, leaving the carpels free in the central region. Fusion rarely occurs by the middle only. Fusion may involve the entire lateral walls or only parts of them. Carpels of many plants are closed partly congenitally and partly ontogenetically (Eames, 1961).

Ovule. Stages in ovule development are shown in Fig. 7.6. The ovule develops from the placenta of the ovary. The ovule primordium is conical and has a rounded apex. The first sporogenous cell is located below the protoderm at the primordium apex. The inner (or single) integument forms below the nucellar apex by periclinal divisions in the protoderm. The integument grows more rapidly than the nucellus and encloses it. If an outer

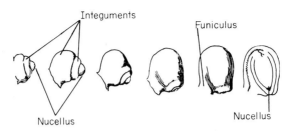

FIG. 7.6. Stages in development of an anatropous ovule. [From "Plant Morphology" by Haupt (1953). Used with permission of McGraw-Hill Book Company.]

integument forms it originates in the protoderm lower than and in a manner similar to that of the inner integument. Often the outer integument fails to grow sufficiently to reach the apex of the ovule. In curved (e.g., anatropous) ovules the integuments grow more on the convex than on the concave side of the ovule.

Female Gametophyte. Sporogenous cells mature as megaspore mother cells with large nuclei, dense cytoplasm, and thin walls. Megaspores form in tetrads as a result of meiosis in the spore mother cells. Typically one of the four cells enlarges to become the embryo sac mother cell and the other three cells degenerate rather rapidly.

Following enlargement and three successive mitotic divisions of the megaspore, an embryo sac with eight nuclei is formed (Fig. 7.1). The three nuclei at the micropylar end (the egg and two synergids) have walls as do the three antipodals at the chalazal end. The polar nuclei, located in the middle of the embryo sac, remain unwalled. As the embryo sac develops, the tissues surrounding it, such as the nucellus and parts of the integument, may be destroyed. Many deviations from the typical eight-nucleate embryo sac occur. For further details of embryo sac development the reader is referred to Maheshwari (1950) and Eames (1961).

FLORAL ONTOGENY IN GYMNOSPERMS

This section will briefly discuss the initiation and development of fertile parts of staminate and ovulate strobili of gymnosperms prior to fertilization. Fertilization and subsequent development of ovulate strobili and seeds to maturity will be discussed in Chapter 8.

Staminate and ovulate strobili of gymnosperms form on differently located shoots; they may be initiated at different times, indicating dissimilar internal requirements. In *Pinus* the numerous, staminate strobili form at the base of the current year's growth in the lower portion of the crown. On the same tree the ovulate strobili are concentrated in the upper crown and sometimes are clustered near the end of the current year's growth. In *Picea* staminate strobili occur along twig growth of the previous year whereas ovulate strobili are borne terminally. In *Tsuga* staminate strobili form at leaf bases and ovulate strobili are terminal. In *Pseudotsuga* staminate strobili are borne along twigs, and ovulate strobili are generally terminal on short twigs, in the upper crown. In *Sequoia* staminate and ovulate strobili usually are borne at the ends of twigs, but staminate strobili sometimes are lateral. In *Thuja* staminate and ovulate strobili are borne singly at the ends of different twigs on a tree. In *Larix laricina* staminate strobili occur mainly on 1- or 2-year-old branchlets. Ovulate strobili are most common on 2- to 4-year-old wood but they also occur on branchlets 5–10 or more years old. In *Abies* staminate and ovulate strobili develop in spring from buds formed along 1-year-old twigs. In *Abies balsamea* ovulate strobili occur primarily in the top 4–5 feet of the crown, and staminate strobili in the area about 10 feet below.

In adult trees staminate and ovulate strobili of gymnosperms often are differentiated at different times, with the former usually initiated first. For example, *Pinus elliottii* staminate strobili were initiated at the end of June and ovulate strobili in late August (Mergen and Koerting, 1957). Primordia of staminate strobili of *Pinus densiflora* formed early in September, about 2 weeks before those of ovulate strobili were initiated. Larson (1961) noted that in young *Pinus banksiana* trees staminate strobili occurred on basal portions of the new shoot of older lateral branches, whereas ovulate strobili occurred primarily at the end of the main shoot, indicating earlier initiation of the staminate strobili. Hashizume (1962) noted that staminate strobili of *Cryptomeria japonica* were initiated from late June to late September and ovulate strobili from mid-July to mid-September.

Staminate Strobilus

The staminate strobilus of *Pinus* is made up of a number of spirally arranged scales (microsporophylls) (Fig. 7.7). Each of the microsporophylls bears two microsporangia on the undersurface. When the strobilus, whose primordia were differentiated during the previous growing season, appears in the spring, sporogenous cells in the microsporangium produce many spore mother cells. Each spore mother cell undergoes meiosis to produce a tetrad of microspores. The nucleus of each microspore now has n chromosomes. Microspores develop thick walls before they separate and enlarge. Subsequently they germinate within the sporangium. Nuclear divisions follow to produce a mature pollen grain consisting of four cells. The nuclei of two of these cells, the prothallial cells, degenerate. The remaining two cells include a generative cell and a tube cell. The microsporangia (which are now called pollen sacs) split, and the pollen grains are released.

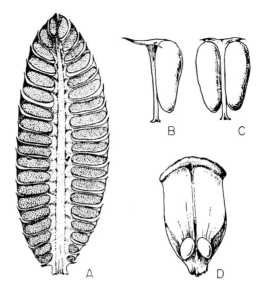

FIG. 7.7. (A) Staminate strobilus of *Pinus nigra*; (B,C) side and abaxial views of micro-sporophyll; (D) ovuliferous scale with two ovules. [From "Plant Morphology" by Haupt, 1953). Used with permission of McGraw-Hill Book Company.]

Ovulate Strobilus and Ovule

The ovulate strobilus consists of a central axis bearing ovulate scales, each of which is borne in the axis of a bract (Fig. 7.8A). Two ovules appear as protuberances on the upper side of an ovuliferous scale. An ovule is comprised of an integument surrounding a megasporangium. At the end of the ovule near the strobilus axis is an opening, the micropyle, through which pollen grains may enter. The megasporangium has one large megaspore mother cell which, by meiosis, produces a row of four megaspores. The nucleus of each of these cells has *n* chromosomes. Usually the megaspore farthest from the micropyle develops into a female gametophyte and the other three megaspores disintegrate (Fig. 7.8B, and C).

The functional megaspore enlarges and nuclear divisions continue until many free nuclei are formed. Eventually division stops and cell walls are laid down between the nuclei, forming a multicellular female gametophyte (megagametophyte) (Fig. 7.9). Division in the megaspore and enlargement of the megagametophyte occur over a period of several months in most gymnosperms. In *Pinus* 13 months elapse between the origin of the megaspore and formation of the mature megagametophyte. During late megagameto-phyte development two or more archegonia differentiate at the micropylar end. The ovule now consists of integuments, nucellus and megagametophyte with several archegonia, each with an egg enclosed.

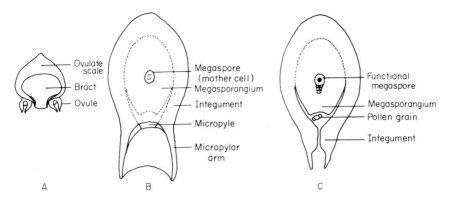

FIG. 7.8. Early development of ovule of *Pinus strobus*. (A) Ovule and ovulate scale at time of pollination as seen from below. (B) Single ovule at time of pollination. (C) Single ovule shortly after pollination showing swollen integument and nearly closed micropyle. [After Wilson and Loomis (1967).]

The megagametophyte of gymnosperms and the endosperm of angiosperms have similar nutritive functions but they differ in several ways. The megagametophyte is formed prior to fertilization, has nuclei with n chromosomes, and produces archegonia. By comparison, the endosperm of angiosperms forms after fertilization, has $3n$ chromosomes, and does not produce archegonia.

Periodicity of Flowering

In fruit trees the buds which produce flowers may or may not contain leaves. For example, in stone fruits such as peach, plum, apricot, and almond only flowers open from flower buds. These plump and rounded buds are easily distinguished from the smaller and more sharply pointed shoot buds. In apple, pear, and quince trees and in flower buds of pecan and walnut, initials of both flowers and shoots occur in the same bud. The terminal part of the shoot which develops from such a bud contains a single flower or flower cluster. The basal part has leaves and shoot buds develop in the leaf axils. In persimmon (*Diospyros*) the tip portion of the bud consists of shoot apical meristem and flowers develop laterally in leaf axils.

In forest trees there sometimes are problems in distinguishing between vegetative and flower buds and, in the latter group, between male and female flower buds. Whereas the globose flower buds of *Acer rubrum* and *A. saccharinum* are readily distinguished from the smaller, more elongated vegetative buds, the male and female flower buds cannot be identified without dissection. In the dioecious *Acer negundo* and *Fraxinus* spp. the flower buds

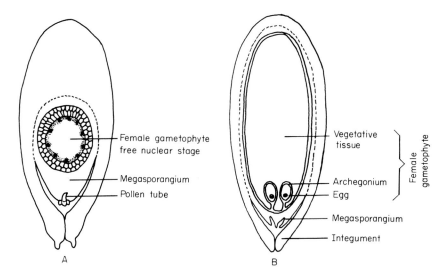

FIG. 7.9. Later stages in development of ovule of pine. (A) Female gametophyte at end of first season of growth. Note the closed micropyle. (B) Mature female gametophyte just before fertilization. [After Wilson and Loomis (1967).]

of female trees cannot be separated by macroscopic examination from the vegetative buds.

Stages in opening of flowers and expansion of leaves of apple are shown in Fig. 7.10. Flowers open largely as a result of expansion of cells formed in the bud. Anthesis usually occurs rapidly with full size of flowers sometimes attained in a day or two (Kramer and Kozlowski, 1960). The periodicity of flowering is exceedingly variable among Temperate Zone and tropical species as well as within each of these groups.

FLOWERING PERIODICITY OF TEMPERATE ZONE TREES

Woody plants of the Temperate Zone show variation between and within years in flowering periodicity. A few genera such as *Jasminum, Hamamelis,* and *Alnus* open flowers during the cold season but most other species do so during the warm season. Although the actual dates of flowering of a species vary from year to year at a given site, the flowering sequence among species is usually maintained. In the United States, trees with a wide geographic distribution, such as *Cornus florida,* may be expected to flower in northern states as much as a few months after they bloom in the South. For example, *Cornus florida* bloomed in Glen St. Mary, Florida in mid-February, in St. Louis, Missouri in early April, and in Columbus, Ohio in early May (Wyman, 1950). Some idea of the annual sequence of flowering of forest trees and ornamental woody plants in the vicinity of Boston, Massachusetts may be

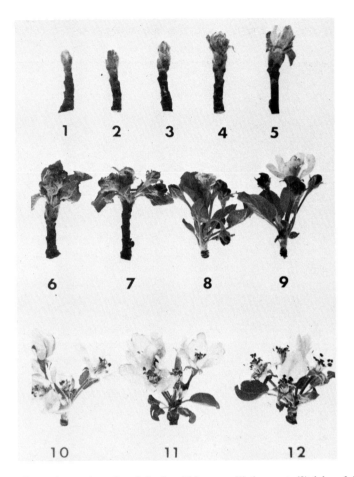

FIG. 7.10. Stages in opening of apple bud and blossom: (1) dormant, (2) delayed dormant, (3) and (4) early prepink, (5) and (6) prepink, (7) early pink, (8) full pink, (9) early bloom, (10) and (11) full bloom, (12) petal fall or calyx. [From Powell, Janson, and Sharvelle (1965).]

gained from Table 7.1. Variation in time of flowering in different years is emphasized by Tydeman's (1964) observation that over a 43-year period the date of full bloom of Cox's Orange Pippin apple trees in England varied from April 15th to May 23rd. The flowering season for apple trees lasts about a week or two, with considerable difference among varieties in time of blossom opening. Red Astrachan, Early Harvest, Faneuse, McIntosh, Oldenburg, and Wagner are considered early blossoming. The late flowering varieties include Beauty, Northern Spy, Greening, and Rome Beauty. Most other commercial varieties flower in midseason.

TABLE 7.1

Approximate Time of Flowering of Woody Plants in the
Arnold Arboretum, Boston, Massachusetts[a]

Forest trees	Ornamentals

March
  Acer saccharinum
  Salix spp.

Early April
  Acer rubrum   *Cornus mas*
  Ulmus americana   *Hamamelis japonica*

Mid-April
  Acer negundo   *Rhododendron dauricum*
  Betula spp.   *Rhododendron mucronulatum*
  Carcidiphyllum japonicum   *Forsythia europaea*

Late April
  Amelenchier canadensis   *Acer circinatum*
  Acer platanoides   *Magnolia kobus*
                                   Pieris floribunda
                                   Prunus canescens

Early May
  Acer saccharum   *Crataegus arnoldiana*
  Carpinus coroliniana   *Magnolia soulangeana*
  Prunus pensylvanica   *Malus floribunda*
                                   Malus robusta
                                   Prunus sieboldi
                                   Rhododendron mucronatum

Mid-May
  Aesculus hippocastanum   *Malus bracteata*
  Cercis canadensis   *Malus sargenti*
  Cornus florida   *Rhododendron albrechti*
  Quercus spp.   *Rhododendron vaseyi*
  Prunus virginiana   *Sambucus pubens*
                                   Syringa vulgaris
                                   Viburnum carlesi

Late May
  Rhamnus cathartica   *Acer ginnala*
  Cornus stolonifera   *Crataegus crus-galli*
  Magnolia virginiana   *Laburnum* spp.
  Prunus serotina   *Rhododendron nudiflorum*
                                   Viburnum lentago
                                   Viburnum tomentosum

TABLE 7.1 (*Continued*)

APPROXIMATE TIME OF FLOWERING OF WOODY PLANTS IN THE
ARNOLD ARBORETUM, BOSTON, MASSACHUSETTS[a]

Forest trees	Ornamentals
Early June	
Cladrastis lutea	*Cornus kousa*
Ilex opaca	*Rhododendron arbutifolium*
Robinia pseudoacacia	*Rhododendron catawbiense*
	Rhododendron calendulaceum
	Viburnum cassinoides
	Viburnum sargenti
Mid-June	
Diospyros virginiana	*Robinia viscosa*
Gymnocladus dioicus	*Rhododendron arborescens*
Ilex glabra	*Spiraea veitchii*
Liriodendron tulipifera	*Spiraea watsoniana*
Sambucus nigra	*Viburnum molle*
Catalpa speciosa	*Viburnum pubescens*
Late June	
Rhus typhina	*Cornus macrophylla*
	Rhododendron maximum
Early July	
Rhus glabra	*Rhododendron viscosum*
	Spiraea salicifolia
	Tilia tomentosa
	Tilia petiolaris
Mid-July	
	Kolreuteria paniculata
	Tamarix pentandra
Late July	
Oxydendrum arboreum	*Abelia schumanni*
August	
	Abelia grandiflora
	Rhus copallina
September	
	Baccharis halimifolia
	Franklinia alatamaha
October	
Hamamelis virginiana	

[a] From Wyman (1950).

Species with flowers appearing at the same time often differ greatly in the time of their floral initiation. *Prunus glandulosa, Spiraea thunbergi, Cornus mas, Forsythia ovata,* and *Hamamelis vernalis* flower in the early spring. Whereas the first two of these species initiated flowers in late summer or early autumn of the previous season, flowers of the other species were initiated in early summer (Carpenter and Watson, 1965).

Bingham and Squillace (1957) summarized the literature on flowering periodicity in pines. They found that duration of staminate and ovulate flowering in individual pine trees was uniform within and between species, averaging about a week, and usually not exceeding 2 weeks. In pine stands of a single species, staminate flowering averaged about 2.5 weeks, but could vary from a few days to 10 weeks. Ovulate flowering usually averaged about 3 weeks and often extended for 2–5 weeks. Elevation and latitude, through their effects on temperature, had a strong effect on flowering dates. Most pines showed a delay in flowering of about 5 days with each degree of latitude northward. The effects of elevation were shown by a 5-day delay in flowering on *Pinus monticola* per 1000 feet of added elevation.

Occasionally exceptions to these generalizations can be cited. For example, *Tectona grandis* has a long flowering period within an inflorescence. *Pinus radiata* also has an unusually long flowering period, a characteristic associated with its multinodal character. Unfolding of female flowers on one tree occurred over a period of 2 months or more (Fielding, 1960). As may be seen in Table 7.2 there is also considerable clonal variation in flowering characteristics of *Pinus radiata.*

TABLE 7.2

CLONAL VARIATION IN TIME OF OPENING OF OVULATE STROBILI IN RELATION TO TIME OF POLLINATION OF *Pinus radiata* IN AUSTRALIA[a]

Clone No.	Ovulate strobili		Staminate strobili	
	Date on which first ovulate strobili opened	Date on which last ovulate strobili opened	Date of first pollen spread	Date of last pollen spread
7	Aug. 29	Oct. 2	Sept. 12	Oct. 2
440	Sept. 19	Sept. 19	Sept. 19	Oct. 2
446	Aug. 7	Oct. 2	Sept. 12	Oct. 2
507	Sept. 12	Oct. 2	Sept. 19	Oct. 10
536	Aug. 29	Oct. 2	Sept. 12	Oct. 10
546	Sept. 19	Oct. 2	Sept. 19	Oct. 10
559	Sept. 25	Sept. 25	Sept. 19	Oct. 20

[a] From Fielding (1960).

Flowering in Relation to Leafing

The time of opening of flowers of deciduous trees is correlated with rather definite stages of leaf development in a manner which varies among species. Flowers appear before leaves in a number of species including *Populus grandidentata, P. tremuloides, P. deltoides, Fraxinus nigra, F. americana*, and *Ulmus americana*. In *Alnus rubra* the flowers expand before or with the leaves. In *Betula lenta, B. alleghaniensis*, and *Salix nigra* flowers open at about the time the leaves begin to expand. In contrast, the flowers of *Nyssa sylvatica* do not appear in the spring until the leaves are nearly grown. *Robinia pseudoacacia* flowers appear about a month after the leaves. The flower clusters of *Tilia americana* emerge in June or July, some 6–8 weeks after the leaves develop. In *Fagus sylvatica* female flowers appeared shortly after trees began to leaf out and male flowers were evident when leafing out was completed (Nielsen and Schaffalitzky de Muckadell, 1954).

That there is no strong control of the relationship of time of flowering and leafing within a genus is shown by wide variations in time of flowering of different species of *Quercus*. Flowers of *Quercus nigra* and *Q. phellos* appear shortly before the tree produces leaves; *Q. alba* flowers emerge at about the same time as the leaves; *Q. palustris* flowers appear with leafing or just after the new leaves appear; *Q. stellata* flowers when the leaves are about a third grown; and *Q. velutina* flowers when the leaves are half grown. Although domestic cherries flower before the leaves appear, *Prunus serotina* does not flower until the leaves are almost fully grown.

FLOWERING PERIODICITY OF TROPICAL TREES

As in Temperate Zone species the flowering of many tropical trees is correlated with rather definite stages of leafing. For example, flowering of *Erythrina indica* in Malaysia occurs on old wood before new leaf growth; in *Cratoxylon formosum* and *Cassia fistula* flowering takes place simultaneously with growth of new shoots, and in *Lagerstroemia* and *Peltophorum* at the time of ending of growth of leafy shoots (Holttum, 1940).

Some tropical trees are easily classified on the basis of their flowering periodicity. However, rigid classification is difficult for many other species because their flowering patterns vary greatly with environment, especially with seasonal distribution of rainfall and photoperiodic regimes. For example, Wright (1905) noted that certain species, which generally were considered to show nonseasonal flowering, tended to flower seasonally when grown some distance from the equator, as in Java and Ceylon. *Theobroma cacao* flowers throughout the year in Costa Rica where rainfall is nonseasonal and there is little seasonal temperature change. By comparison, in the states of Bahia and

Espirito Santo, Brazil, which have distinct rainy seasons, flowering of *Theobroma* is essentially restricted to the wet months of October to June.

Woody tropical plants are noteworthy for their variable patterns of flowering. This was emphasized by Corner (1940) in Malaysia where *Terminalia* and *Parkia* flower annually. Other trees including *Lagerstroemia* and *Cassia fistula* have variable patterns; still others, such as *Wormia suffruticosa* and *Adinandra dumosa*, produce flowers more or less continuously. *Homalium grandiflorum* changes foliage annually but flowers only at 20-year intervals. Leaves of *Knema Hookeriana* remain on the tree for 2 or 3 years, but its branches produce flowers twice a year.

Several investigators have classified tropical trees on the basis of flowering periodicity. The useful classification of Alvim (1964), which is similar to that of Koriba (1958), lists tropical woody plants in four broad groups:

(1) *Everflowering Species.* These species produce flowers continuously throughout the year. Examples include *Hibiscus* spp., *Ficus* spp., and *Carica papaya.*

(2) *Nonseasonal Flowering Species.* These species exhibit variation in flowering periodicity from plant to plant and from branch to branch. They become seasonal flowering species at some distance from the equator. Examples include *Spathodea campanulata*, *Michelia champaca*, *Cassia fistula*, *Cassia splendens*, and *Lagerstroemia flos-reginae.*

(3) *Gregarious Flowering Species.* These species flower at indefinite times of the year. Anthesis occurs more or less simultaneously in all plants of a species over a wide area. In gregarious species flower buds form regularly but they remain closed for long periods (weeks or months) and are stimulated to open by marked environmental changes. They flower almost invariably when rain follows a period of drought. For example, *Coffea* flowers a rather definite number of days after rain, close to 7 days for *Coffea arabica* and 3 days for *C. rupestris*. In Nigeria *Prevostea heudelotii* flowers during March and April, from 5–8 days after a rain (Rees, 1964a). As may be seen in Fig. 7.11 flowering of *Coffea rupestris* occurred anytime during early January to mid-April, but only after rain or irrigation. By mid-April the trees usually had no unopened flower buds remaining. The limiting of flower production to January to mid-April in Nigeria appeared to be related to daylength since short days appear to be necessary for initiation of flower buds in *Coffea* (Piringer and Borthwick, 1955). A dry period prior to an effective rain increases flower production in *Coffea*. Artificial watering during the dry season is followed by rather sporadic flowering. For example, when Alvim (1960) maintained a low level of moisture stress by weekly irrigation, the flower buds of *Coffea* failed to open. In contrast, when he allowed soil moisture to approach the wilting percentage before irrigating, abundant flowering followed each irrigation. He suggested that water stress, like chilling, removed an inhibitor responsible for dormancy.

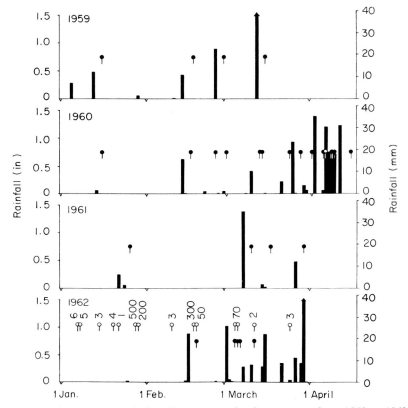

FIG. 7.11. Flowering record of *Coffea rupestris* for four seasons from 1959 to 1962 in southern Nigeria. The histograms represent rainfall and the symbols the dates on which flowering took place. For 1962 data are given for a watered plant (open circles) and for one growing under natural conditions (closed circles). The numbers by the open circles represent the numbers of flowers produced on the indicated date. [From Rees (1963a).]

In southern Nigeria the ornamental shrub, *Clerodendron incisum* produces large numbers of flowers at irregular intervals throughout the year (Rees, 1964b). Flowering is highly correlated with heavy rainfall during the wet season, with rainfall above a certain minimum during the dry season, and with temperature below a maximum in the absence of rain. There is a lag response of 25–33 days between the timing of the external stimulus and flowering response (Fig. 7.12). *Clerodendron* shows no indication of flower buds at the time of the external stimulations. Therefore, the lag response · encompasses both growth of flower buds and their subsequent opening. Buds grow slowly at first, 1.8 mm in 10 days and 5–8 mm in 3 weeks. During the 5 days before opening the buds grow rapidly to a final length of about 13 cm. Rees (1964b) stated that water stress did not directly cause flowering,

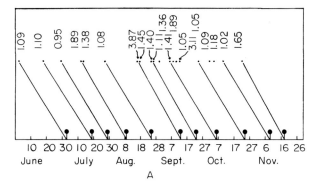

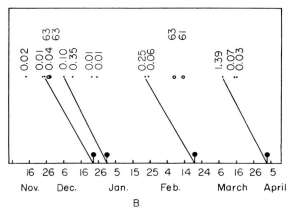

FIG. 7.12. Variations in flowering of (A) *Clerodendron incisum* during the wet season of 1960 and (B) the dry season of 1960–1961. In (A) and (B) each day is marked with a point above when more than 1.0 in rain fell; the amount of rainfall is given in inches. The symbols below show a flowering response. The diagonal lines link flowering responses with initiating rainfall. In (B) minimum temperatures below 65°F (18°C) are also shown. [From Rees (1964b).]

but that temperature decreases associated with each effective rainfall were more directly involved. This conclusion was based on the long lag response together with the lack of microscopic flower buds at the time of the temperature drop.

According to Alvim (1964), species of *Bambusa*, *Strobilanthes*, *Hopea*, and *Schornia* flower gregariously at very long intervals. *Bambusa*, for example, flowers in from 7 to 13 years in southern Brazil and up to 30 years elsewhere (Alvim, 1964; Walter, 1962). *Bambusa* plants die after their fruits ripen.

(4) *Seasonal Flowering Species.* These species flower seasonally in areas with alternating rainy and dry seasons or seasonal variations in daylength. They often become everflowering or nonseasonal in certain areas.

Flowering in Seasonal Tropical Climates

In the seasonal climates of Nigeria where the periods of November to January and February to April are dry, the opening of flowers of most trees occurs between November and April (Njoku, 1963). In most species the flowers appear with new leaves on the new shoot at the time of bud opening. In *Monodora tenuifolia* and *Bosquueia angolensis* the swelling of compound buds can already be seen in October, although the flowers do not open until February or March.

In the seasonal climate of Trinidad flowering appears to be equally divided between wet and dry seasons and between the "in-leaf" and "out-of-leaf" condition. Fruiting, however, occurs predominantly in the dry season. According to Beard (1946), about half of the deciduous trees of Trinidad flower during the rainy season when they are in leaf, and they fruit during the dry season after leaf fall. About one fourth of the trees flower during the dry season and fruit during the same or next dry period. An additional one fourth of the deciduous trees flower during the dry season and drop their fruit during the subsequent rains. Only a negligible number of species flower and fruit during the rainy season.

Flowering in Nonseasonal Tropical Climates

Richards (1964) has given a good account of flowering periodicity in tropical rain forests. In evergreen tropical forests flowering may be seen throughout the year. Some species produce blossoms almost continuously and others do so in periodic surges. However, even in very nonseasonal climates flowering maxima occur at certain times of the year. In most rain forest climates flower production reaches a maximum at the end of the dry season, but it often continues into the early part of the wet season. Sometimes another surge of flowering takes place at the beginning of the dry season just when rain stops. According to Koriba (1958), flower formation in Singapore is induced mainly in the dry spells of February and July. Flowering follows about 2 months later, and fruiting is at a maximum in July and January. Davis and Richards (1933) presented evidence that flowering was more seasonal in upper than in lower strata of the forest. In British Guiana, for example, trees of upper strata tended to show two major flowering seasons whereas those of lower ones appeared to flower throughout the year.

The great majority of rain forest trees appear to flower at more or less regular intervals, but the pattern varies considerably among species. Individual trees within species and branches within trees often flower at different times. Some idea of species variations in flowering periodicity in the tropical rain forest of the New Hebrides is given in Table 7.3. In that area there is no dry season, but the months of June to October are considerably less wet and slightly cooler than other months.

TABLE 7.3

SPECIES VARIATIONS IN TIMES OF FLOWERING (Fl) AND FRUITING (Fr) OF TROPICAL RAIN FOREST SPECIES IN THE NEW HEBRIDES[a]

Species	Sept.	Oct.	Nov.	Dec.	Jan.	Feb.	March	April	May	June	July	Aug.
Corymborchis veratrifolia		Fl Fr	Fr	—	Fl		—	—	—	Fl	—	—
Ficus copiosa	Fr	Fr	Fr	Fr	Fr	Fr	Fr	—	—	Fr	Fr	—
Piper methysticum	Fl	Fl Fr	Fl Fr	Fl Fr	Fl Fr	Fl	Fr	—	Fl Fr	Fr	Fr	Fr
Garuga floribunda	Fl		—	—	—	Fl	—	—	—	—	—	—
Castanospermum australe	Fl Fr	Fl	Fl	Fl Fr	Fl	—	—	—	—	—	—	—
Eugenia spp.	Fr	Fl	Fl	Fl	Fl		—	Fr	Fr	—	—	—
Barringtonia samoensis	Fl Fr	Fl Fr	Fl Fr	Fl Fr	Fl	Fl	—	—	Fr	Fl		Fl Fr
Psychotria spp.	Fr	Fl Fr	Fl Fr	Fl	Fl Fr	—	—	—	Fl:	—	—	Fr
Geophila herbacea	Fl Fr	Fl Fr	Fl Fr	Fl Fr	Fl Fr	Fl Fr	Fr	Fl	Fl	Fl Fr	Fl Fr	Fl

[a] Horizontal lines denote absence of both flowers and fruits [From Baker and Baker (1936). Published by permission of The Linnean Society of London.]

Pollination

It is well known that a good flowering year does not always produce a large fruit or seed crop. A major factor contributing to lack of correlation between flowering and seed production is deficient pollination. Other factors may be involved also (e.g., self-fertilization, adverse weather conditions, and insect and rodent pests). This is discussed further in Chapter 9.

PRODUCTION AND SHEDDING OF POLLEN

Voluminous quantities of pollen are produced by trees, with the amount varying with site, species, trees within species, and different locations on trees. The amount of pollen produced also varies greatly from year to year. Much more pollen is produced by wind-pollinated species than by insect-pollinated species. According to Faegri and Iverson (1964), a 10-year-old branch system of *Fagus* may produce more than 28 million pollen grains; in *Betula*, *Picea*, and *Quercus* more than 100 million; and in *Pinus* about 300 million grains.

Annual variations in pollen production are much greater for some species than for others. For example, from 1947 to 1959 maximum pollen production in *Pinus sylvestris* in Finland exceeded the average for these years by only 50%, but in *Picea abies* the average was exceeded by 353% (Table 7.4). Sarvas (1962) found large fluctuations in pollen dispersal among stands, individual trees, and various parts of trees. Often the south side of a tree produced more pollen than the north side. In *Pinus sylvestris* the male flowers were fewer in number at the very top of the crown, and pollen production was lower than in the middle and lower parts of the crown. Often the tops had no male flowers.

Although species vary widely in the time of pollen shedding, the process usually occurs rather rapidly, often in a period of a few days. Complete pollen dissemination from a tree required only a few hours in *Quercus prinoides* and about 3 days in *Quercus alba* (Sharp and Chisman, 1961). Dorman and Barber (1956) noted a consistent pattern over the southern United States in the sequence of pollen ripening among pines, with *Pinus elliottii* first followed by *P. palustris*, *P. taeda*, and *P. echinata*. Variations in pollen collection dates of different species of pines growing in Placerville, California are shown in Fig. 7.13. Some idea of the time of pollen ripening of southern pines at two different locations may be gained from Table 7.5. Shedding of *Pinus sylvestris* pollen of several stands in Finland occurred during a 5- to 10-day period. An individual stand shed its pollen in 2 or 3 days less than this and an individual tree within even a shorter period. The period of pollen shedding was longer for *Pinus sylvestris* than *Picea abies*, *Betula verrucosa*, or *B. pubescens* (Sarvas, 1955a,b, 1962). During a year of heavy pollen crop, the greatest

TABLE 7.4

Seasonal Variations in Pollen Production by *Pinus sylvestris* and *Picea abies* in Finland[a]

| | Flowering year | | | | | | | | | | | | | |
	1947	1948	1949	1950	1951	1952	1953	1954	1955	1956	1957	1958	1959	Average
Pinus sylvestris														
g/m²	2.77	2.28	2.98	5.13	5.92	7.39	3.61	4.93	4.97	2.29	2.85	7.31	4.10	4.35
%	64	52	69	118	136	170	83	113	114·	53	66	168	94	100
Picea abies														
g/m²	0.06	0.25	0.12	0.03	1.44	0.34	0.20	0.90	0.04	3.44	0.32	0.53	2.28	0.76
%	8	33	16	4	190	45	26	118	5	453	42	70	300	100

[a] From Sarvas (1962).

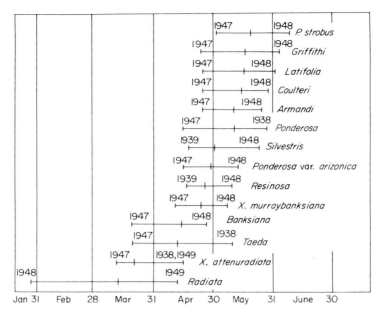

FIG. 7.13. Pollen collection dates for pines at Placerville, California. [From Duffield (1953).]

TABLE 7.5

TIME OF POLLEN RIPENING OF SOUTHERN PINES AT TWO LOCATIONS[a]

Species	California[b]		Mississippi	
	Start	End	Start	End
Pinus elliottii	Feb. 1	Feb. 9	March 31[c]	—
Pinus palustris	Feb. 16	March 11	—	—
Pinus taeda	Feb. 22	March 11	March 23	May 10
Pinus echinata	Feb. 26	April 7	April 3	April 23
Pinus virginiana	—	—	April 11	April 23
Pinus rigida	—	—	April 8	April 29

[a] From Dorman and Barber (1956).
[b] At elevation of 2700 feet.
[c] Average pollen collection date.

dispersal occurred during a day near the middle of the flowering period. During years of low male flowering, however, a peak day of maximum pollen could not be readily identified. Under certain weather conditions some parts of trees lose pollen more readily than other parts. For example, dehiscence of anthers in catkins of *Quercus* progressed downward in the tree so that those on the low branches were the last to lose pollen. This pattern followed that of anther emergence, but trees in open fields did not conform to this pattern (Sharp and Chisman, 1961).

POLLEN DISPERSION

The transfer of tree pollen from the anther to the stigma is accomplished chiefly by wind and insects, but birds and other animals may also be involved in some species. There are various gymnosperms which rely on wind pollination and, among the angiosperms, *Populus, Quercus, Fraxinus, Ulmus, Carya,* and *Platanus.* Insect pollination occurs in such fruit trees as apple (*Malus*), pear (*Pyrus*), fig (*Ficus*), and avocado (*Persea*) and in such genera of forest trees of the Temperate Zone as *Tilia, Acer,* and *Salix.* Many fruit trees are pollinated by bees. As the bees extract nectar from the interior of flowers they pick up pollen in their leg hairs. Such pollen is transported by the bees and later scraped off onto stigmas of flowers which are visited by the bees. A very interesting example of zoogamous pollination occurs in all species of fig (*Ficus*). Pollination in this genus involves activity of chalcid wasps which cannot develop anywhere except in the receptacles of figs. As there is a period of several weeks to months between maturation of pistillate and staminate flowers in an individual fig, pollination cannot be accomplished with pollen from the staminate flowers of the same fig. When wasps enter a fig cavity they bring pollen and it subsequently is deposited on a stigma. Some species of wasps have pollen-holding concavities (corbiculae) on the front legs and mesosternum for carrying pollen. Other wasps, which lack such pollen-carrying structures, may transport pollen in their digestive tracts or adhering to various parts of their bodies (Ramirez, 1969).

In general, the greater and more effective the zoogamous pollination the more restricted is the amount of pollen produced and liberated. Nevertheless, a few zoogamous trees (e.g., *Tilia*) produce as much pollen as do wind-pollinated species (Hyde and Williams, 1945). Only a negligible fraction of the voluminous pollen rain produced by wind pollinated species settles on stigmata and the rest is lost. In most wind pollinated species, including *Picea, Fagus, Corylus, Alnus,* and *Betula* the pollen is dry and the grains fall apart to provide a maximum number of pollen grains. However, in *Ulmus, Tilia, Acer, Larix, Castanea,* and *Pinus* at least one fourth of the grains adhere in small clumps. In insect-pollinated genera, such as *Salix, Malus,* and *Pyrus,* the pollen grains occur in more frequent and larger clumps.

Effect of Climate on Pollen Dispersal

Climatic conditions, especially temperature, humidity, and wind, have profound effects on male flowering and shedding of pollen. Temperature exerts an effect directly by altering metabolism of trees and indirectly by influencing humidity. According to Sarvas (1962), humidity influences pollen dispersal by controlling evaporation of water from the exothecium cells surrounding the anthers and thereby influencing their opening. During rainy periods the opening of anthers often stops. The important effect of temperature is emphasized by Sarvas' (1962) observation that most pollen in Finland was shed on the warmest day in most of the years under study. Flowering during late spring was delayed until the air warmed appreciably. Often only a single warm day after a cold spring was required for pollen shedding and distribution. The effect of temperature also is emphasized by latitudinal and altitudinal variations in the time of ripening of pollen (Fig. 7.14).

Climatic fluctuations also appear to be responsible for large diurnal variations in pollen dispersal. In Finland the daily cycle showed a maximum dispersal around mid-day and almost complete cessation of pollen spread at night. These fluctuations reflected temperature and humidity changes. In Finland the days are warm and nights very cool during the flowering period. Also the relative humidity often drops below 50% during the day but approaches 100% at night. On the few days when relative humidity was unusually low at night the dispersal of pollen was abundant during the night (Sarvas, 1962).

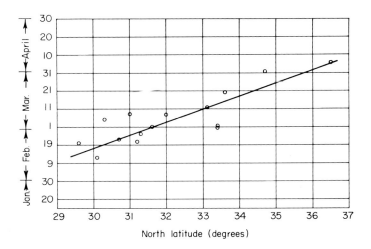

Fig. 7.14. Pollen ripening of *Pinus taeda* in relation to latitude. [From Dorman and Barber (1956).]

Pollen Dispersion Distance

The pollen of most species of trees migrates to greater distances than does the seed. Hence, pollen migration rates are extremely important in determining natural regeneration. Forest geneticists are especially interested in implications of pollen dispersion distances of trees in seed orchards, seed collection, controlled pollinations, and development of local races (Wright, 1953).

Two conflicting views on pollen dispersion have appeared in the literature: (1) that the amount of pollen dispersed from individual trees decreases rapidly with distance from the tree (Wright, 1952, 1953); and (2) that large amounts of pollen are transported for long distances (Strand, 1957). There is, of course, considerable variation among species in the distance of their pollen dispersal. Pollens of *Picea, Pseudotsuga, Pinus,* and *Fraxinus* have among the shortest dispersion distances and rapid rates of fall. By comparison, the pollens of *Populus, Ulmus, Juglans,* and *Corylus* exhibit much longer dispersion distances (Table 7.6). However, there does not appear to be a marked

TABLE 7.6

RELATIVE DISPERSION DISTANCE OF POLLEN
GRAINS OF FOREST TREES[a,b]

Pinus cembroides var. *edulis*
Pseudotsuga menziesii
Cedrus spp.
Picea excelsa
Fraxinus spp.
Corylus avellana
Juglans regia
Ulmus americana
Populus deltoides
Populus nigra var. *italica*

[a] Species are listed in order of increasing dispersion distance.
[b] From Wright (1952).

difference in dispersion distance between insect- and wind-borne pollen and no obvious correlation between pollen size and dispersion distance. For example, large pollen grains of *Pseudotsuga* traveled as far as small *Fraxinus* grains (Wright, 1953).

Wright (1953, 1962) provided persuasive evidence that most airborne pollen is shed rather close to the tree that produced it. Therefore, most pollination usually occurs in trees close to a seed tree. Wright (1952, 1953) showed, for example, that pollen of some forest trees traveled only a few hundred feet (Table 7.7). Very little pollen was distributed beyond 100 feet from an isolated

TABLE 7.7

VARIATIONS AMONG SPECIES IN POLLEN DISPERSION[a]

Species	Pollen dispersion distance (feet)
Fraxinus americana	55–150
Pseudotsuga menziesii	60
Populus deltoides	1000 or more
Ulmus americana	1000 or more
Picea abies	130
Cedrus atlantica	240
Cedrus libani	140
Pinus cembroides var. *edulis*	55

[a] From Wright (1953).

TABLE 7.8

POLLEN COLLECTED AT VARYING DISTANCES FROM AN ISOLATED *Pinus elliottii* TREE[a]

Distance from source (feet)	Grains per 2.71 cm²		
	Jan. 28	Jan. 29	Jan. 31, Feb. 2, Feb. 3[b]
0	78	204	45
25	28	79	23
50	30	53	7
75	17	38	20
100	7	28	0
150	9	16	0
200	1	13	2
300	0	8	0
400	4	4	0
500	0	6	0
1000	0	6	0
1500	3	1	0
2000	0	2	0
2500	0	2	0
2850	0	0	0
Total	177	460	97

[a] From Wang, Perry, and Johnson (1960).
[b] Totalled grain counts of 3 days pollen samples.

Pinus elliottii tree (Table 7.8). Silen (1962) confirmed that pollen counts from a *Pseudotsuga menziesii* tree showed a maximum in distribution near the tree, a sharp decline with distance up to 300 feet, and then a leveling off at greater distances. The large amount of pollen far from the tree was explained as originating from distant sources.

In addition to direct observation of pollen dispersal, Wright (1962) outlined three other lines of evidence showing that most pollen is distributed for limited distances only: (1) only little gymnosperm pollen remains in the air overnight; (2) uncommon exotic trees which are not completely isolated set very little sound seed to open pollination (Wright, 1955); and (3) most natural hybrids are reported to occur with their parents.

Some long distance migration of pollen occurs. For example, Sarvas (1955b) found a greater rain of pollen on a ship 12 miles from the coast of Finland than in the forest along the shore. In Sweden, Andersson (1963) found that during a year of heavy pollen production some rocky islands located 2.5–5 miles from the nearest forest had a layer of *Picea* pollen about a centimeter deep. Lanner (1966b) suggested that pollen can be lifted upward and carried for great distances by independently moving air masses. Masses of pollen may subsequently be washed out of the air and deposited by raindrops.

Wright (1953) emphasized the paramount importance of pollen dispersion distance in regeneration of forest trees and especially in forest genetics work. For example, in cutting a mixed hardwood stand leaving one seed tree of *Fraxinus americana* per acre will result in spacing male and female trees about 300 feet apart. This will result in about 1 % pollination, whereas increasing the number of seed trees to provide spacing of 200 feet between male and female trees will increase by 15 times the percentage of ovules pollinated. In seed orchards expected contamination can be determined by isolation strips of different widths on the basis of pollen dispersion distances. For example, with isolation strips of only 1 σ (Table 7.9) considerable contamination may be expected and little contamination with strips of 5 σ. Pollen dispersion distances also provide information for estimating seed production at varying distances from pollen sources. Pollen dispersion data also are useful in estimating probabilities of formation of races. The number of breeding individuals in the neighborhood, N, (largest populations within which breeding takes place at random) is determined by population density and distance of pollen dispersion. From the size of N the effect on race formation can be determined. With small pollen dispersion distance and small N, frequent uncrossed gaps in the range of a species and distinct local races may be expected. By comparison, with large pollen dispersion distance and large N rapid interchange of genes occurs, and there is little formation of races. For a more detailed analysis of important practical aspects of pollen dispersion distance the reader is referred to Wright (1962).

RECEPTIVITY OF FEMALE FLOWERS TO POLLEN

An essential requisite for pollination is receptivity of the stigma when viable pollen reaches it. In most species the period of stigma receptivity

TABLE 7.9

Expected Contamination in Seed Orchards Surrounded by Isolation Strips of Different Widths[a]

Width of isolation strip[b]	Percentage of contaminating pollen at distances inside seed orchard				
	0	0.5 σ	1 σ	3 σ	5 σ
Assuming equal pollen production of all trees					
1 σ	61.6	15.4	6.1	0.31	0.020
2 σ	28.0	4.2	1.6	0.076	0.0049
3 σ	8.7	1.0	0.38	0.020	0.0012
5 σ	0.57	0.065	0.020	0.0012	0.00007
10 σ	0.0005	0.00006	0.00002	0.000001	0.00000007
Assuming pollen production per tree 1000 times as great for outside as for inside trees					
5 σ	85.1	39.4	20.0	1.2	0.07
10 σ	0.5	0.06	0.02	0.001	0.00007

[a] From Wright (1953).

[b] Distances are given in terms of σ, which is, for *Fraxinus americana*, 50 to 150 feet; *Cedrus atlantica*, 240 feet; *Cedrus libani*, 140 feet; *Pinus cembroides* var. *edulis*, 55 feet; *Pseudotsuga menziesii*, 60 feet; *Picea abies*, 130 feet; *Ulmus americana*, *Populus deltoides*; and *P. nigra* var. *italica*, 1000 feet or more.

usually lasts for a few days, but it may vary from a few hours as in mango (*Mangifera*) to as much as 2 weeks in *Fagus*. In *Acer saccharum* the receptive period lasted about 3 days. Germination of pollen grains on *Acer* stigmas occurred first about 23 hr after buds opened. Maximum receptivity of the stigma, as estimated by germination of pollen and growth of pollen tubes, occurred 38 hr after bud opening. Germination of pollen grains was last recorded at 102 hr after bud burst and, by that time, pollen tube growth was greatly reduced. Penetration of the stigma by pollen tubes did not occur later than 95 hr after bud burst (Gabriel, 1966). In *Castanea* the female flowers did not become fully receptive to pollen until 5–13 days after anthesis of male catkins. Most trees remained receptive for a week or more (Nienstaedt, 1956). Unpollinated *Fagus sylvatica* flowers were receptive to pollen for 10–14 days. This long period included the entire time of pollen release and even extended beyond it (Nielsen and Schaffalitzky de Muckadell, 1954).

In gymnosperms the period of pollen receptivity of female flowers usually is short and may not exceed a few days. For example, strobili of *Picea glauca* were receptive to pollen for 3–5 days with some variation evident among individual trees. Pollen shedding coincided rather closely with female receptivity (Nienstaedt, 1948). One study of *Pinus* showed the period of maximum receptivity of an individual strobilus to vary from 3 to 7 days (Cumming and Righter, 1948). Whereas in *Pinus* there appeared to be considerable variation in timing of pollen receptivity among strobili on the same tree, in *Pseudotsuga* only little variation occurred within trees (Duffield, 1950). There often is considerable variation from year to year in the time of female receptivity of a given species.

Suggested Collateral Readings

Childers, N. F. (1961). "Modern Fruit Science." Horticultural Publications. Rutgers University, New Brunswick, N.J.

Eames, A. J. (1961). "Morphology of Angiosperms." Chapters 2 to 7. McGraw-Hill, N.Y.

Esau, K. (1965). "Plant Anatomy." Chapter 18. Wiley, New York.

Faegri, K. and Iversen, J. (1964). "Textbook of Pollen Analysis." Hafner Publishing Co., New York.

Fahn, A. (1967). "Plant Anatomy." Chapter 19. Pergamon Press, Oxford.

Fowells, H. A. (1965). Silvics of forest trees of the United States. *U.S. Forest Service, Agriculture Handbook* **271**.

Haupt, A. W. (1953). "Plant Morphology." Chapters 8 and 9. McGraw-Hill, New York.

Kramer, P. J. and Kozlowski, T. T. (1960). "Physiology of Trees." Chapter 13. McGraw-Hill, New York.

Leopold, A. C. (1964). "Plant Growth and Development." Chapters 13 and 14. McGraw-Hill, New York.

Maheshwari, P. and Singh, H. (1967). The female gametophyte of gymnosperms. *Biol. Rev.* **42**, 88–130.

Matthews, J. D. (1963). Factors affecting the production of seed by forest trees. *Forestr. Abstracts* **24**, i xiii.

Richards, P. W. (1964). "Tropical Rain Forest." Cambridge Univ. Press, London and New York.

Sarvas, R. (1962). Investigations on the flowering and seed crop of *Pinus sylvestris*. *Commun Inst. Forest Fenniae* **53**, 1–198.

Wright, J. W. (1962). "Genetics of Forest Tree Improvement." FAO Forestry and Forest Products Study 16, Rome, Italy.

Wyman, D. (1950). Order of bloom. *Arnoldia*. **10**, 41–56.

Chapter 8

FRUIT, CONE, AND SEED DEVELOPMENT

Introduction

When a flower has been successfully pollinated, growth of the ovary is stimulated and floral parts such as stamens and pistils usually wilt and abscise. Such changes, which characterize the transformation of a flower into a young fruit, comprise fruit set (Leopold, 1964). After fertilization occurs, the ovary usually develops into a fruit and the ovule becomes a seed. The development of fruits of angiosperms and cones or strobili of gymnosperms differs in several respects; thus, they will be discussed separately.

Fruit Growth in Angiosperms

A fruit is generally considered to be a matured ovary together with such parts which adhered to it during its development (Kramer and Kozlowski, 1960). As fruits reflect the structure of the flower from which they are derived they vary greatly because of differences in structure of flowers and because of distinctive ontogenies of fruits derived from similar flowers. Nitsch (1965) considered the concept of a fruit in physiological rather than morphological terms. According to Nitsch, a fruit consists of tissues which support the ovules and whose development depends on physiological changes which take place in these ovules. He considered this concept applicable not only to fruits with seeds but also to seedless fruits as ovules originally were present in them also.

Botanists have long classified tree fruits as simple, aggregate, or multiple. Simple fruits, which may be fleshy or dry, consist of a single ripened ovary and sometimes adhering sepals, stamens, and other parts. The fruits of most woody angiosperms are classified as simple. Simple fleshy fruits include berries and drupes. In a berry the whole pericarp becomes fleshy (e.g., grape, banana). The fruit of citrus, called a hesperidium, is a berry with a leathery

rind. Drupes are fleshy fruits in which the exocarp is a thin skin, the mesocarp is thick and fleshy, and the endocarp is hard and stony. The endocarp
or pit encloses one (sometimes more) seeds. Examples are peach, plum, olive,
cherry, and apricot.

The pome fruit (e.g., apple, pear, quince) is characteristic of a subfamily
of Rosaceae. According to Robbins, Weier, and Stocking (1957) most of
the flesh of the pome fruit is derived from the floral tube which consists of
fused bases of sepals, petals, and stamens. The fleshy exocarp is united with
floral tube tissues. Both mesocarp and endocarp are fleshy and not easily
separated.

In dry simple fruits the entire pericarp becomes dry and often hard. An
example of a dry dehiscent fruit is the legume which consists of one carpel
that splits along two seams (e.g., fruits of *Gleditsia*, *Robinia*). The samara
(e.g., fruit of *Acer*, *Fraxinus*), is an example of a dry indehiscent fruit.
The nut (e.g., fruit of *Quercus*, *Corylus*) is a single-seeded fruit similar
to an achene but with a thick, hard pericarp. The capsule (e.g., fruit of
Populus) consists of two or more fused carpels and splits open in various
ways.

Aggregate fruits (e.g., raspberry, blackberry) consist of a cluster of ripened
ovaries produced by a single flower and borne on the same receptacle.
Multiple (compound) fruits [e.g., fruits of mulberry, fig, osage-orange
(*Maclura*)] are clusters of several to many ripened ovaries produced by
several flowers crowded on the same inflorescence.

The common names applied to many fruits often are misnomers in a strict
botanical sense. For example blackberries and raspberries are aggregates of
drupes rather than berries. The fruit of mulberry (*Morus*) is not a berry but
a multiple fruit made up of small nutlets surrounded by sepals. A coconut
is really a drupe rather than a nut (Fuller and Tippo, 1949). Some examples
of fruits of forest trees are shown in Fig. 8.1.

For comprehensive treatments of the details and complexities of anatomical
development of different fruits of angiosperm trees the reader is referred to
the following: apple, *Malus pumila* (MacArthur and Wetmore, 1941;
MacDaniels, 1940; Tukey and Young, 1952); Cherry, *Prunus cerasus* (Tukey,
1935); Pecan, *Hicoria pecan* (Woodroof and Woodroof, 1927); plum, *Prunus
domestica* (Sterling, 1953); pear, *Pyrus communis* (Bain, 1961); apricot,
Prunus armeniaca (Jackson and Coombe, 1966a); grape, *Vitis vinifera* (Harris,
Kriedemann, and Possingham, 1968); avocado, *Persea americana* (Valmayor,
1964); orange, *Citrus sinensis* (Bain, 1958); rubber, *Hevea brasiliensis* (Muzik,
1954); oak, *Quercus alba* and *Q. velutina* (Mogenson, 1966); walnut,
Juglans regia (Nast, 1935); and macadamia, *Macadamia ternifolia* (Jones,
1939).

FIG. 8.1. Fruits of forest trees: (A) *Alnus rugosa*; (B) *Liquidambar styraciflua*; (C) *Acer saccharum*; (D) *Magnolia grandiflora*; (E) *Fraxinus americana*; (F) *Ulmus thomasii*. U.S. Forest Service Photos.

PHASES OF FRUIT GROWTH

Nitsch (1965) considers the life history of a fruit to consist of the following major phases:

1. A preanthesis phase, during which growth occurs primarily by cell multiplication
2. A phase at anthesis, during which the critical processes of pollination and fertilization of the ovule occur
3. A postfertilization phase of growth, with cell enlargement predominating in the fruit and cell multiplication in the seed
4. A maturation phase, consisting of fruit ripening followed by senescence.

Fruits of most woody angiosperms of the United States ripen in the autumn of the year they are formed, usually from September to November. There are numerous exceptions, however, with fruits of some species reaching full size within a month after pollination, as in *Fraxinus pennsylvania*; others, such as some species of *Quercus*, require two growing seasons to mature.

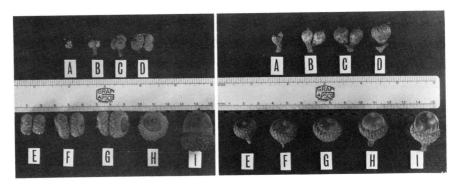

FIG. 8.2. Variations in duration of development of acorns of *Quercus alba* (left) and *Quercus velutina* (right).

Left	Right
A. May 29. 24 days after pollination	May 13. 1 year and 8 days after pollination
B. June 11. 37 days after pollination	May 29. 1 year and 24 days after pollination
C. June 23. 49 days after pollination	June 11. 1 year and 37 days after pollination
D. July 6. 62 days after pollination	June 23. 1 year and 37 days after pollination
E. July 12. 68 days after pollination	July 6. 1 year and 62 days after pollination
F. July 18. 74 days after pollination	July 12. 1 year and 68 days after pollination
G. July 25. 81 days after pollination	July 18. 1 year and 74 days after pollination
H. July 30. 86 days after pollination	July 30. 1 year and 86 days after pollination
I. Sept. 10. 128 days after pollination	Sept. 4. 1 year and 22 days after pollination

From Mogenson (1966).

Whereas acorns of red or black oaks mature the second year, those of white oaks ripen the first year (Fig. 8.2). Acorns of most species in both of these groups usually mature in September and October. Fruits of *Ulmus* mature very rapidly. For example, in *Ulmus americana* the flowers appear before the leaves unfold and fruits ripen as early as late February in the southern United States and June in northern states. The samaras of *Ulmus thomasii* and *U. rubra* are mature by the time the leaves are only half grown. *Populus* fruits also ripen early, often before the leaves are fully expanded. Fruits of *Populus tremuloides* usually ripen in May or June, about 6 weeks after flowering. Although *Tilia americana* fruits ripen in September or October, the period of fruit development is short as flowers in this species do not appear until June or July, about 6 to 8 weeks after leaves expand.

Acer species are rather variable with respect to time of maturing fruit. Whereas fruits of *Acer nigrum* mature in September or October those of *Acer rubrum* ripen from March to late June. *Acer saccharinum* fruits ripen from April to mid-June. In species having extensive ranges, the precise time of fruit ripening varies with climate and location.

FERTILIZATION

The essentials of the ovule inside the ovary are the outer integuments, the micropylar opening opposite the stalk end, and the embryo sac which occupies most of the ovule. In angiosperms the embryo sac generally contains eight nuclei before fertilization. The three located at the micropylar end consist of the egg nucleus and two synergids. Two polar nuclei are located in the central part of the embryo sac, and the three nuclei at the end opposite the micropyle are the antipodals (see Fig. 7.1).

When viable pollen grains are placed on a receptive stigma they imbibe water, germinate to produce pollen tubes, and activate their enzymes. After pollen penetrates the stigmatic surface it grows between cells of the style by secreting enzymes which soften the pectins of the middle lamella. A number of additional enzymes, which are secreted by pollen as it grows, promote changes in metabolism of tissues of the style and probably produce substrates for pollen growth (Stanley, 1964).

Growth of the pollen tube can be characterized by a sigmoid curve. Active elongation of the tube occurs only near the tip. Pollen tubes often grow very rapidly and some may expand several millimeters per hour.

Pollen tubes grow at various rates through the style and into the ovary which contains the ovules. Although many pollen tubes reach the ovars, only one enters the ovule. The tube nucleus and generative nucleus of the pollen grain enter the pollen tube when it is formed. The generative nucleus undergoes an early mitotic division to produce two sperms. When the ovule is reached, the pollen tube enters the embryo sac and discharges its two sperms. One of these fuses with the egg and the other with the two polar nuclei to form an endosperm nucleus. After fertilization is completed and the zygote formed, the remaining nuclei of the embryo sac, consisting of two synergids and three antipodals, usually degenerate. Conditions are then conducive to further development of the fruit and seed.

Because of rapid growth of pollen tubes, the time span between pollination and fertilization generally is rather brief. According to Maheshwari (1950), only 24–48 hr elapse between pollination and fertilization in the majority of angiosperms. However, there are marked variations among species; fertilization in *Coffea arabica* occurs in 12–14 hr after pollination (Mendes, 1941), in 24–120 hr in *Juglans regia* (Nast, 1935), 3–4 months in *Corylus avellana* (Hagerup, 1942), 5–7 months in *Hamamelis virginiana* (Shoemaker, 1905), and 12–14 months in some species of *Quercus* (Bagda, 1948, 1952). In *Hamamelis* and *Quercus* there is an overwintering of pollen tubes.

POSTFERTILIZATION DEVELOPMENT

After fertilization there is intense activity characterized by rapid growth of the endosperm and translocation of food into the enlarging ovule. Normal growth and differentiation of the embryo, the sporophyte of the new generation, depend on the endosperm. As the embryo increases in size it draws on the contents of endosperm cells and in some species may consume nearly the whole endosperm. The mature endosperm is rich in carbohydrates, fats, proteins, and growth hormones. In *Malus* the endosperm accumulated large amounts of growth regulators (Luckwill, 1948, 1954). Gibberellin-like substances occur in endosperm of *Aesculus californica, Persea americana, Prunus amygdalus, P. armeniaca, P. domestica* (Phinney *et al.*, 1957), and *Cocos nucifera* (Radley and Dear, 1958).

As summarized by Maheshwari and Rangaswamy (1965), several different lines of evidence attest to the importance of the endosperm as a nurse tissue for growth of the embryo. At the time of fertilization the embryo sac lacks an appreciable amount of food. As the endosperm grows, however, it accumulates enough food to supply the developing embryo. The zygote usually does not divide until after considerable endosperm growth takes place. Furthermore, the embryo develops normally only when the endosperm is organized. Should endosperm abortion occur, growth of the embryo is subsequently inhibited.

Polyembryony

Sometimes multiple embryos develop in seeds of some angiosperm trees. For example, polyembryony has been reported in such species as *Alnus rugosa* (Woodworth, 1930), *Casuarina equisetifolia* (Swamy, 1948), *Citrus*

(Leroy, 1947), *Juglans nigra* (Robyns, 1938), *Mangifera indica* (Sachar and Chopra, 1957), and *Quercus macrolepis* (Bagda, 1952).

Polyembryony has been classified as either false or true. False polyembryony involves fusion of two or more nucelli or development of two or more embryo sacs within the same nucellus. In true polyembryony the additional embryos arise in the embryo sac either by cleavage of the zygote or from the synergids and antipodal cells. Adventive embryos also are an example of true polyembryony. The adventive embryos arise from tissues outside the embryo sac (e.g., cells of the nucellus or integuments). Ultimately they enter the embryo sac where they grow to maturity. Adventive embryos differ from sexual embryos in having a lateral position, irregular shape, and lack of suspensor. Adventive embryos, which originate from nucellar tissue, are well known in *Citrus* and *Mangifera indica*. In several species polyembryony has been linked to genetic causes and appears to be caused by hybridization. (Maheshwari and Sachar, 1963).

Polyembryony has been of particular practical importance in propagating certain species of trees. For example, adventive embryos, which inherit characters of the maternal parent, have been used to provide genetically uniform seedlings of *Mangifera indica* and *Citrus*. In *Citrus* they have been used as orchard stock on which grafts from other types have been made. In addition, *Citrus* clones which have deteriorated after repeated vegetative reproduction have been restored to original seedling vigor with nucellar embryos (Maheshwari and Sachar, 1963). Such vegetative invigoration, or "neophysis," may be traceable to hormonal influences of the embryo sac. Hofmeyer and Oberholzer (1948) raised better *Citrus* seedlings from adventive embryos than from cuttings. The difference was attributed to infection of cuttings with virus diseases and absence of disease in nucellar embryos.

Parthenocarpy

Ordinarily the development of mature fruits requires fertilization of the egg. In a few species, however, fruits are set and mature without seed development and without fertilization of an egg. Such fruits, called parthenocarpic fruits, are well known in some figs, pears, apples, peach, cherry, plum, and citrus. Parthenocarpy also occurs in several genera of forest trees including some species of *Acer*, *Ulmus*, *Fraxinus*, *Betula*, *Diospyros*, and *Liriodendron*.

Some types of parthenocarpy require pollination and others do not. For example, fruit development in citrus and banana may occur without pollination. In other species of fruit trees such as cherry and peach, seedlessness may occur because the embryo aborts before the fruit matures. In some species pollination stimulates fruit development but fruits mature without the pollen tube reaching the ovule (Leopold, 1964).

The physiology of parthenocarpy is not well understood. Parthenocarpic fruits tend to form in fruits having many ovules, suggesting they are a source of chemicals which promote fruit set and development. The fact that ovules are sites of auxin synthesis and that spraying of plants or treating of pistils with synthetic auxin has caused fruit-set in some species suggests that auxins are important in fruit-set. However, as such treatments have not been effective in causing setting of parthenocarpic fruits in most deciduous orchard trees (except fig, pear, and some varieties of apple) an additional factor seems to be important for fruit set. Chemical induction of parthenocarpy is most successful with species which naturally produce parthenocarpic fruits. In olive, avocado, and mango auxin applications can cause initial fruit-set, but pollination is necessary for continued fruit development. Setting of fruits with auxins often causes developing embryos, which may have been fertilized, to abort (Leopold, 1964). The role of growth regulators in development of parthenocarpic fruits is discussed further in Chapter 9.

GROWTH CURVES OF DEVELOPING FRUITS

Two generalized growth patterns for angiosperm fruits are well known. In the first type, as for apple and pear, the growth curve is sigmoid, with the fruit enlarging more or less continuously during the season. The precise shape of the curve differs somewhat with variety as shown in Fig. 8.3. For example, the curve for gross development of Early Harvest apples resembled a straight line, whereas for each successively later-ripening variety the growth curve flattened as the season progressed. The rate of growth was also a varietal characteristic, with late-ripening varieties growing more slowly than early-ripening ones (Tukey and Young, 1942). The second type of growth curve, as for stone fruits such as peach, cherry, apricot, and plum, is a double growth curve which shows development occurring in three stages. During stage I the ovary, nucellus, and integuments of the seed grow rapidly, whereas the embryo and endosperm develop little. During stage II the endosperm and embryo grow rapidly, but the ovary does not increase much in size. Sclerification of the pit also begins. The amount of endosperm material decreases greatly by the end of stage II and the embryo increases to full size. Finally, in stage III a new surge of rapid growth or swelling begins again and continues until ripening. The duration of these growth stages is quite variable. As may be seen in Table 8.1 stage II may last about a month in late-ripening varieties, and only a few days in early-ripening ones. Neither of these two major types of growth patterns is distinctive for each morphological type of fruit. According to Leopold (1965), growth of some berries, pomes, simple fruits, and accessory fruits can be characterized by one or the other type of growth curve.

Fruit growth may reflect a variety of internal changes, such as cell division,

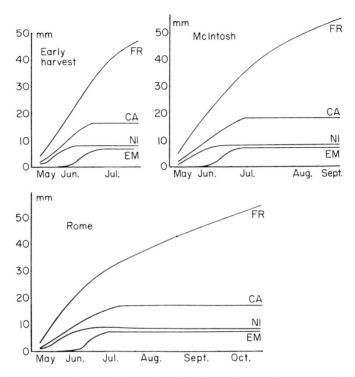

FIG. 8.3. Increase in length of the embryo (EM), nucellus and integuments (NI), carpel (CA), and whole fruit (FR) of Early Harvest, McIntosh, and Rome apples from full bloom to fruit ripening. [From Tukey and Young (1942). Chicago Univ. Press.]

cell enlargement, and development of intercellular spaces. The early growth of most fruits is traceable to cell division and late growth to cell enlargement. In the developing fruit of *Prunus cerasus* most of the size increase prior to bloom was the result of cell division. After bloom, however, virtually all growth was traceable to cell enlargement (Tukey and Young, 1939).

Following pollination and for some time thereafter, cell division generally continues but declines to a negligible amount when cell enlargement becomes prominent. The length of time during which cell division occurs following pollination varies with species and variety. For example, after pollination cell division lasted for about 20 days in Granny Smith apple (Bain and Robertson, 1951), 30 days in peach (Addoms, Nightingale, and Blake, 1930), and plum (Sterling, 1953), 25–30 days in early pear variety "Yakumo," and 45 days in late pear variety "Okusankichi" (Toyama and Hayaski, 1957). Thereafter, size of these fruits increased rapidly by cell enlargement only. Fruit growth in avocado (*Persea gratissima*) is an exception to the pattern

TABLE 8.1

DURATION OF STAGES OF FRUIT DEVELOPMENT IN *Prunus cerasus*[a]

Variety	Stage I (days)	Stage II (days)	Stage III (days)	Full bloom to ripening (days)
Early Richmond	22	5	14	41
Montmorency	22	12	23	57
English Morello	21	28	17	66

[a] From Tukey (1935).

of cell division followed by cell enlargement. In *Persea* cells of mature fruits are not much larger than those of young fruits, emphasizing that size increase results from continued cell multiplication throughout fruit development (Schroeder, 1953).

The size of mature fruits appears to be correlated with cell size in some species and with cell numbers in others. In apple, for example, variation in size of fruits at maturity was due primarily to differences in cell numbers and only to a small extent to mean cell size. Size increase also was related to large numbers of intercellular spaces which formed during the latter phases of fruit development (Bain and Robertson, 1951). In contrast, the ultimate size of cherry fruits was closely related to the size of cells in the fleshy parts of the fruit (Tukey and Young, 1939).

Growth of Various Parts of Fruits

The rates and timing of growth of different parts of fruits may or may not be in phase with growth of the fruit as a whole. A few examples will be given to emphasize variability among species in growth patterns of different parts of fruits.

In most angiosperms the embryo remains very small in size until appreciable fruit development occurs. Rapid growth of the embryo takes place only during late stages of development. In apple the carpel blade reaches full length early, as do the nucellus and integuments. The embryo remains microscopic in size for a long time and begins rapid growth only shortly before the nucellus and integuments are fully grown (Tukey and Young, 1942). Growth of the embryo in cherry and peach is very restricted during rapid growth of the pericarp, nucellus, and integuments. Embryos grow rapidly, however, during the mid-period (stage II) of arrested development of the fruit as a whole. In *Macadamia* embryo growth is delayed for 90 days after fertilization (Jones, 1939). The carpel of *Hevea brasiliensis* fruits grows first leaving a space which the seed later fills. After this time the embryo makes its most rapid growth. According to Muzik (1954), maximum size of *Hevea* seeds was not attained until 10–14 days after maximum fruit size.

Variations in growth of different fruit parts of three cherry varieties (cultivars), ripening at different seasons, are shown in Fig. 8.4. The fleshy pericarp developed in three stages, with the duration of stage I nearly identical for all three varieties. The duration of stage II varied greatly among varieties and was directly correlated with the date of ripening. The length of stage III varied among cultivars and was not correlated with the sequence of ripening. The nucellus and integuments grew rapidly, beginning at full bloom, and ceased growing early (stage I); the time was about the same in all three cultivars. Embryo growth was arrested until growth of the nucellus

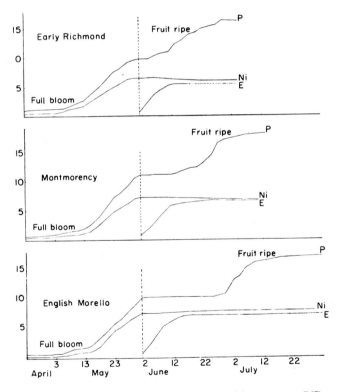

FIG. 8.4. Growth curves of the pericarp (P), nucellus and integuments (NI), and embryo (E) of three varieties of cherry ripening at different seasons. The time of rapid increase of embryo growth and related inhibition of growth of the nucellus and integuments and pericarp was similar for all varieties. Periods of rapid embryo increase also were similar but rates of pericarp development were not. [From Tukey (1935).]

and integuments essentially stopped, about 20–23 days after full bloom. Beginning about June 1, the embryo enlarged rapidly and completed its growth in 18–25 days, with very slight differences apparent in embryo growth of the three varieties.

The sigmoid growth curve of the whole orange differs greatly from the growth curve of the peel. Bain (1958) considered the development of orrnge fruits to occur in three stages. The first stage was characterized by cell divisions in all tissues and intensive synthesis of cellular components. Size increase at this early stage was traceable primarily to growth of peel tissues. During the second stage, cell divisions occurred only in the external layers of the peel and growth resulted largely from enlargement of cells of the endocarp. During the final period, growth slowed down and the endocarp filled with juice.

Shrinkage and Expansion of Fruits

During their development fruits increase in size because of cell division and expansion. Superimposed on such growth changes are reversible changes in size because of fruit hydration and dehydration. Over short time periods the reversible size changes resulting from variations in fruit hydration often are much greater than the growth changes. Fruits tend to shrink during the day and expand at night (Fig. 8.5). The loss of water by transpiration during the day sets up a gradient toward the leaves, and water is extracted from fruits while absorption from the soil is inadequate to supply the leaves.

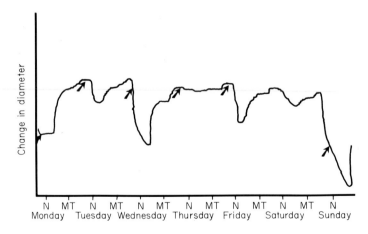

Fig. 8.5. Diurnal contraction and expansion of fruits of *Prunus cerasus* as a result of changes in internal water balance. Arrows indicate times of irrigation. [From Kozlowski (1968a).]

When transpiration declines late in the day and ceases during the night, the fruits tend to refill with water (Kozlowski, 1965, 1968a). For example, Bartholomew (1926) showed that during the afternoon of a hot, dry day lemons decreased in diameter and became soft but they recovered turgor at night. During a 48-hr period lemons attached to the tree lost up to 35% more water than detached ones, indicating that attached lemons served as a water reservoir for other tissues. The drier the soil became, the greater was the amount of water withdrawn from the lemon fruits and the longer the diurnal period of internal water deficit. Tukey (1959) noted that young developing apples shrank shortly after sunrise and reached their smallest size of the day around noon. Shortly thereafter they began to expand and regained their initial size in the late afternoon. Diurnal shrinkage and swelling have been reported for a variety of fruits of both orchard and forest trees (Magness, Degman, and Furr, 1935; Schroeder and Wieland, 1956; Kozlowski, 1965, 1968a; Chaney and Kozlowski, 1969a, 1970), and forest trees (Chaney and Kozlowski, 1969b).

The amount of diurnal shrinkage and swelling of fruits is controlled by factors affecting transpiration, the degree of water stress in fruits, and stage of fruit maturity. Tukey (1960) reported high statistical correlations between the amount of daily shrinkage of apples and factors influencing transpiration. Harley and Masure (1938) also found strong negative correlation between daily growth of apples and evaporating power of the air. The relation between transpiration rate and fruit shrinkage was further demonstrated by Schroeder and Wieland (1956). They followed diurnal contraction and expansion of avocado fruits on two separate trees. In mid-morning one of the trees was sprayed with water to wet the leaf surfaces. The fruits had been covered to avoid the spray. Within a few minutes after spraying, the fruit of the sprayed tree stopped shrinking, and within another 10 min its diameter actually increased. During the rest of the day the fruit of the sprayed tree shrank only slightly. By comparison, the fruit on the unsprayed tree shrank constantly until mid-afternoon.

Chaney and Kozlowski (1969a,b) measured diurnal changes in diameters of fruits of several species of forest trees. During a large part of the period of fruit development, diurnal shrinkage occurred in very hard fruits (e.g., *Quercus rubra*) as well as soft fruits (e.g., *Prunus serotina*). The major factor causing diurnal expansion and contraction of fruits appeared to be translocation of water into and out of fruits. Chaney and Kozlowski (1969b) found that during much of the growing season percent moisture of fruits of several species of forest trees usually was low during the day and high during the night. To a large degree the diurnal increases or decreases in percent moisture were the result of movement of water into or out of fruits. However, daily changes in dry weight of fruits sometimes also contributed to influencing diurnal changes in percent moisture of fruits. Chaney and Kozlowski (1971) observed a lag response of shrinkage of Calamondin orange fruits to increases in vapor pressure deficits of the air. Leaves began to shrink at sunrise when stomata opened and transpiration began, but fruits began to shrink about 1.5 hr later (Fig. 8.6). The changes in fruit diameter were attributed to internal redistribution of water set in motion

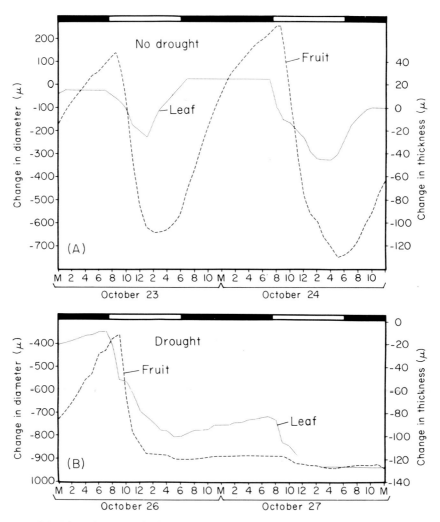

FIG. 8.6. Diurnal changes in diameters of fruits and thickness of leaves of Calamondin orange under conditions of no drought (A) and severe drought (B). Both contraction and expansion of leaves occurred earlier than in fruits. Black bars = night; open bars = day. [From Chaney and Kozlowski (1971).]

by high transpiration. Evidence that water moved from fruits to leaves was obtained in an experiment showing higher moisture contents in leaves or branches with attached fruits than in leaves on branches without fruits. These observations indicate that a water potential gradient from the fruits to the leaves develops during the day and water is translocated from the fruit along a free energy gradient (Fig. 8.7). Klepper (1968) found such a gradient between fruits and leaves of pear trees. During midday the leaves showed a minimum water potential of −15 to −20 bars whereas the fruits showed a slightly less negative minimum. According to Kaufmann (1970) the diurnal changes in water potential of the exocarp of orange fruits of about 5.6 bars were similar to those which occurred in leaves.

Young fruits often show less diurnal shrinkage than old ones. Rokach (1953), for example, found that fruits of the Shamouti orange were not an effective water reservoir for other plant tissues prior to June 1, by which date the fruit had not yet reached the size of a large olive. After June 1, however, water was readily withdrawn from the oranges in midday. Tukey (1959) found that diurnal contraction of Fairhaven peaches was rare during May and the first half of June, but during the last half of June shrinkage occurred commonly. Kozlowski (1968a) noted that diurnal shrinkage of Montmorency cherry fruits varied with their stage of growth and often was low or absent

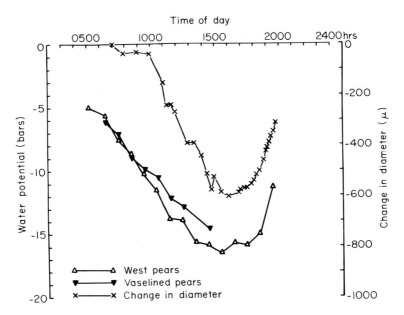

Fig. 8.7. Relation between water potential of pear fruits, with and without a vaseline coating, and fruit diameter. [From Klepper (1968).]

in immature fruits. In contrast, cherry fruits in a mid-stage of development showed marked diurnal shrinkage and expansion. On bright clear days shrinkage usually began in the early morning and continued until mid- or late afternoon when fruits began to expand. When soil moisture contents were maintained at high levels by frequent irrigation the amount and timing of fruit shrinkage were correlated with conditions affecting transpiration, and these varied greatly from day to day. As fruits approached maturity they showed a strong tendency for water uptake and afternoon expansion, and only very limited contraction. In nearly mature cherries afternoon expansion tended to predominate even when soil was dry. Mature fruits could be made to shrink appreciably, however, by very high internal water deficits.

RIPENING OF FRUITS

Ripening of fruits is correlated with a number of changes in metabolism which are driven by respiratory energy. Changes associated with fruit ripening include loss of chlorophyll to unmask other pigments, softening of the fruit flesh, development of odor and flavor, and decrease in dry weight. These changes are paralleled by precise chemical alterations such as production of ethylene, changes of insoluble to soluble pectins, conversion of starch to sugar in some fruits, and disappearance of tannins in others. Several of these changes are general and occur in many fruits. Although most fruits ripen on the tree a few, such as avocado, will not do so. Ripening of normally tree-ripened fruits can be accelerated by picking.

Respiration plays a dominant role throughout fruit development. The rate of respiration is high during the stage of cell division. It increases during cell enlargement and maturation, increases abruptly in a climacteric burst after maturation, and then declines.

Edible fruits have been classified into a group showing a marked climacteric, and a group lacking such a pronounced respiratory burst. Among the climacteric fruits are those of apple, apricot, avocado, banana, mango, papaya, papaw, peach, pear, and plum. Examples of nonclimacteric fruits are cherry, fig, grape, grapefruit, lemon, and orange.

Changes associated with fruit ripening are linked to the climacteric in many species. For example, the drop in respiration following the climacteric peak is rather sharp and terminates in physiological breakdown or fungal invasion. Biale (1960) considered the climacteric to be a critical stage identifying the end of fruit development and maturation and the beginning of senescence. A number of changes associated with ripeness occur at or shortly after the climacteric. For example, fruits change color (green to yellow in some varieties of apple, pear, banana, and papaya; green to red in plums and mangoes; green to dark brown in some varieties of avocado). Changes in color may result from disappearance of chlorophyll (e.g., banana) or formation of carotenoid pigments (e.g., orange). Also the flesh may soften. In pear, "eating ripeness" occurs at the climacteric peak. In apples, bananas, and avocados the highest state of edibility occurs shortly after the climacteric peak.

Role of Ethylene

Much interest has been shown in the role of ethylene, an unsaturated hydrocarbon, in fruit ripening as it is commonly produced by fruits. In concentrations as low as 1 ppm ethylene accelerates loss of chlorophyll from citrus fruits and transformation of starch to sugar in banana fruits. Production of ethylene varies among fruits. Biale, Young, and Olmstead (1954), for example, described the following three types of fruits with respect to a climacteric and ethylene production: (1) fruits with a pronounced climacteric and producing significant amounts of ethylene (e.g., avocado, banana, apple, pear and plum); (2) fruits with a pronounced climacteric but not producing ethylene (e.g., mango); and (3) fruits not exhibiting a climacteric and not producing ethylene under normal conditions (e.g., lemon, orange).

There has been some question as to whether ethylene is a product of ripening or a cause of it. Biale, Young, and Olmstead (1954) found that some fruits (e.g., mango) did not produce ethylene during the climacteric rise and other fruits (e.g., avocado) produced ethylene after the climacteric burst began. They concluded that ethylene was a product of fruit ripening which further stimulated ripening processes. Leopold (1964), however, reviewed the results of several investigations which indicated that even in mango enough preclimacteric ethylene was produced to cause the respiratory burst. These investigations showed that fruit ripening, in general, is accelerated by ethylene and, in fruits which produce appreciable ethylene, a respiratory climacteric follows.

Flavor

Development of fruit flavor is influenced by both physical changes during development and chemical constituents. As mentioned, transformation of insoluble to soluble pectins occurs in cell walls of ripening fruits. Rupture of some of the cells follows and juices are released into spaces between cells, and thereby the taste of fruits is enhanced.

Flavor of fruits is determined by a balance between sugars, acid, and astringent components. Sucrose, glucose, and fructose are the major sugars present in varying proportions in different fruits. In apples all three sugars are present; in peaches and apricots sucrose predominates; in cherry, glucose and fructose make up the bulk of sugars present.

Organic acids increase in amount and affect flavor of growing fruits. The organic acids probably are translocated into the fruits from the leaves as indicated by decreases in acid content of fruits following reduction of leaf area and higher acid contents in the center than in the periphery of grapes and apples. The concentration of organic acids in fruits is relatively high, often amounting to 1–2% of fresh weight in apples and pears and up to 4% in black currants. The most important organic acids of fruits are malic in pome fruits, citric in citrus, tartaric in grapes, and isocitric in blackberries. Many other fruits contain a mixture of these acids (Nitsch, 1953). Flavor is also associated with aroma provided by such constituents as amyl esters of formic, acetic, caproic, and caprylic acids (Chandler, 1957).

Softening of Fruits

Softening of fruits is related to changes in pectic compounds and hydrolysis of starch or fats. During fruit development, insoluble protopectin is laid down in primary cell walls and in some fruits (e.g., apple, pear, citrus) it accumulates to high concentrations. Changes from insoluble pectins (e.g., protopectin and calcium pectate) to soluble pectins such as pectin, pectic acid, and pectinic acid are closely related to ripening. Pectic changes during ripening probably are due to the activity of protopectinase. Between the green and ripe stages soluble pectins in peaches may increase by a factor of 2, in apple by 12, and in pear by 20 (Biale, 1958). In overripe fruits pectic substances tend to disappear and fruits soften greatly. In ripening citrus fruits changes in pectic compounds are similar to those of apples and pears but they are quantitatively smaller. In final stages of fruit senescence, protoplasts may disintegrate and cell walls collapse. The actual breakdown of fruits appears to be linked to disorganization of metabolic processes rather than to depletion of foods.

Abscission of Reproductive Structures

The process of abscission of flowers and fruits is basically similar to that in leaves. Floral structures abscise as parts of flowers, entire flowers, or inflorescences. Cell division usually does not precede shedding of petals and the abscission layer is not well differentiated. Separation of petals results from softening of the middle lamella (Esau, 1965b). The investigations of Lott and Simons (1964, 1966, 1968a,b) showed the same general patterns of development of floral cup and style abscission zones in a number of species of *Prunus*. However, important differences also were found among species in rates of development of abscission zones, with those of *P. cerasus* and *P. avium* developing more rapidly than those of *P. persica* and *P. armeniaca* (Table 8.2).

TABLE 8.2

VARIATION IN RATE OF DEVELOPMENT OF FLORAL TUBE AND STYLE ABSCISSION IN
Prunus SPECIES[a]

		Days from anthesis to		
Species	Cultivars	Petal fall	Floral tube abscission zone evident	Style abscission
P. avium	"Starking Hardy Giant"	3–4	5–6	3–4
P. avium	"Stark Gold"	3–4	5–6	5–6
P. cerasus	Montmorency	3–4	5–6	5–6
P. armeniaca	Wilson Delicious	3–5	6–8	18–20
P. persica	12 cultivars	3–6	7–10	20–24

[a] From Lott and Simons (1968b).

Abscission of fruits occurs not only when fruits are mature but also shortly after pollination and fruit set or during growth of the young embryo. Abscission of immature fruits is an especially serious problem with apples, pears, oranges, and grapefruits. In apple, three normal periods of fruit drop occur. These include "early drop" between the time of initial ovary enlargement and beginning of endosperm development, "June drop" of young fruits, and the preharvest drop.

Premature abscission of fruits of wind pollinated species of forest trees also is well known. For example, most of the potential acorn crop of *Quercus alba* often abscises prematurely (Table 8.3). Williamson (1966) found that from early May to mid-July (the period of pollination, ovule development, and fertilization) almost 90% of *Quercus alba* acorns were shed prematurely. Sweet and Thulin (1969) reported that in a seed orchard of *Pinus radiata* about half of all ovulate strobili initiated aborted during the first year after pollination. Conelet drop started at the time of receptivity, reached a peak 4–6 weeks later, and then decreased in intensity.

The location of the abscission layers of fruits varies with species. Pome fruits abscise at the base of the pedicel. The fruitlets of plum abscise with attached stems in the first two of the three seasonal waves of fruit drop, and without stems in the third drop. Two abscission zones occur in sweet cherry (*Prunus avium*), with fruits separating either between the pedicel and peduncle or between the peduncle and spur. In plum, mango, avocado, and orange, the separation of fruits at maturity occurs at the base of the fruit (Stösser, Rasmussen, and Bukovac, 1969a). After fruits of many tropical species form their stalks, they separate from them by a second abscission

TABLE 8.3

<small>Percentage of Abscission of Acorns at Various Development Stages[a]</small>

	1962		1963	
Development stage	Starting date	Percent abscissions	Starting date	Percent abscissions
Pollination	April 30	55.6	April 24	28.4
Ovule development	May 17	10.6	May 20	37.9
Fertilization	June 4	15.8	June 6	18.1
Embyro development	July 6	16.7	July 3	10.5
Maturation	Sept. 19	1.3	Sept. 20	5.1
		100.00		100.00

[a] From Williamson (1966)

layer. The shedding of fruits together with their stalks is also common in Temperate Zone forest trees such as *Salix, Populus, Tilia, Robinia,* and *Ulmus.*

Some idea of the extent and sequence of abscission of reproductive structures of Washington Navel orange may be gained from the study of Erickson and Brannaman (1960) in California. Abscission of buds, flowers, or fruits occurred from February to July. Almost half of the buds dropped before they opened. Abscission of open flowers amounted to 16.7% of all flower buds initiated. Abscission of small fruits continued throughout and following the flowering period. Small fruits abscised either at the base of the ovary or at the base of the pedicel. Abscission at the base of the pedicel occurred about 10 times as commonly as at the base of the ovary. Most abscission occurred when fruits were very small (Table 8.4).

ANATOMICAL AND CHEMICAL CHANGES DURING ABSCISSION OF FRUITS

Shedding of fruits may or may not involve the formation of a well differentiated abscission layer. For example, an abscission layer does not form at maturity of *Prunus avium* fruits. In contrast, in *Prunus cerasus* a distinct abscission layer forms between the fruit and pedicel (Fig. 8.8). Abscission of reproductive structures may also occur with or without prior cell division. For example, when flowers or immature fruits of apple are shed, cell enlargement and cell division precede abscission. However, cell division does not take place prior to shedding of mature apples (Esau, 1965b).

The important anatomical and chemical changes in the developing abscission layer have been studied for several economically important fruits including apples (MacDaniels, 1936; McCown, 1943), mangos and avocados

TABLE 8.4

NUMBER OF REPRODUCTIVE STRUCTURES (BUDS, FLOWERS, AND FRUITS)
ABSCISED PER TREE FROM WASHINGTON NAVEL ORANGE AT RIVERSIDE
CALIFORNIA[a]

Diameter of ovary (mm)	Buds	Flowers	Fruits		Total
			With pedicel	Without pedicel	
1 or less	59,635	674	1002	12	61,323
2	22,790	14,939	13,953	344	52,026
3	10,804	15,295	25,043	541	51,683
4	3114	2321	13,469	589	19,493
5		6	3853	460	4319
6			2399	634	3033
7			1250	643	1893
8			586	450	1036
9			417	663	1080
10			179	462	641
11			77	357	434
12			37	275	312
13			20	194	214
14			7	137	144
15			7	118	125
16			3	79	82
17			2	71	73
18			2	55	57
19			2	40	42
20				32	32
21 or more				232	232
Total	96,343	33,235	62,308	6388	198,274
Average no. of mature fruits per tree					419
Total flower buds per tree					198,693
Percent	48.5	16.7	31.4	3.2	Crop = 0.2

[a] From Erickson and Brannaman (1960).

(Barnell, 1939), oranges (Wilson and Hendershott, 1968), and cherries
(Stösser, Rasmussen, and Bukovac, 1969a, b).

In sour cherry (*Prunus cerasus*) fruits, the formation of the abscission
zone was first evident when the fruit had almost finished enlarging (12–15
days before maturity) and was complete within 8–10 days (Stösser, Rasmussen, and Bukovac, 1969a). The abscission layer, which was composed
of five to eight rows of cells, appeared as an arc which extended from the
point of juncture of the pedicel and fruit and almost to and across the base

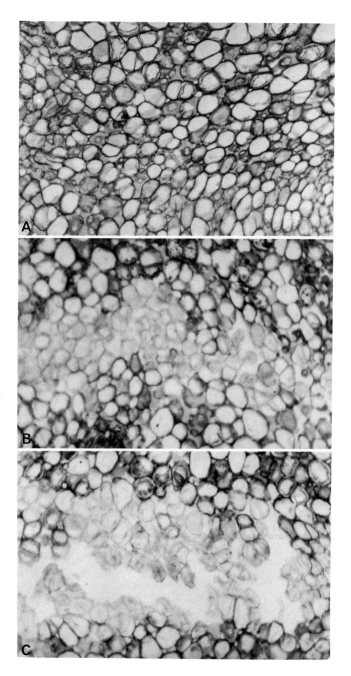

FIG. 8.8. Development of the abscission layer of the fruit of sour cherry (*Prunus cerasus*). (A) Longitudinal section through the potential abscission zone between the fruit and pedicel. (B) Early development of the abscission layer as shown by lower affinity of cells in the central part of the photo for haematoxylin. (C) Well developed abscission layer with separation occurring between cells. The layer at this stage is typical of layers present in fully mature fruits. Photo courtesy of M. J. Bukovac.

of the stony pericarp. An abscission layer did not form across the vascular bundle. Development of the abscission layer involved separation of cells without rupture of cell walls, followed by collapse of cells. Walls of cells in the abscission layer usually were thinner and less rigid than those of cells nearby.

Chemical changes associated with formation of the abscission layer involved a partial enzymic breakdown of cell wall constituents, including pectic materials, noncellulosic polysaccharides, and cellulose (Stösser, Rasmussen, and Bukovac, 1969b). In addition, Ca and Mg moved out of walls of cells in the abscission zone before or during its late development. The loss of Ca and Mg as well as degradation of pectins, which are known to act as cementing agents between cells, would account for separation of cells. The abscission layer usually was complete at the time of fruit maturity but the fruits remained attached until vascular bundles were physically broken.

In citrus fruits only few distinct histological differences exist between tissue of the abscission zone and the adjoining tissue. However, the cells of the separation layer tend to be slightly smaller and more compact than the adjoining cells. The clear protoplasm of cells in the abscission zone of immature fruits tends to darken and become noticeably granular as fruits approach maturity. Large quantities of starch also accumulate in the separation layer at maturity. As starch increases, and during abscission, methylated pectins and total pectins disappear from the separation layer. With advent of abscission, lignification occurs in cells on the fruit side of the separation layer. As lignification of cells continues after abscission, a protective layer is formed (Wilson and Hendershott, 1968).

Prevention of Fruit Abscission

Several naphthalene and phenoxy compounds applied as sprays are used in standard orchard practice to prevent preharvest drop of fruits. For example, naphthaleneacetic acid (NAA) has been successfully used to prevent drop of apples; 2,4-dichlorophenoxyacetic acid (2,4-D) for preventing dropping of apples, pears, oranges, and grapefruits; and 2,4,5-trichlorophenoxyacetic acid (2,4,5-T) for apples and apricots (Cooper et al., 1968). Often varieties of fruit trees may differ in their sensitivity to these compounds. For example, Grimes Golden apple was sensitive to 2,5-dichlorophenoxyacetic acid (2,5-D) but insensitive to 2,4-D and 2,4,5-T. By comparison, the response of York Imperial apple to these materials was just the reverse. The conventional naphthalene and phenoxy sprays accelerate fruit ripening and pose a hazard if the crop cannot be harvested on time. Abscission of some fruits such as apple can also be prevented by growth retardants such as B-995. This compound reduces elongation of shoots and also decreases preharvest drop of apples to a degree similar to that caused by NAA and 2,4-D sprays.

STIMULATION OF ABSCISSION OF BLOSSOMS AND FRUIT

Horticulturists often remove some of the blossoms at bloom or shortly thereafter in order to reduce alternate bearing and increase the size and quality of the potential fruit crop. Thinning of the excessive crop often is considered necessary for species which have excessively heavy bloom. The most obvious effect of thinning is an increase in fruit size resulting from an increase in the amount of leaf surface allotted per fruit.

Thinning of blossoms or young fruits with chemical sprays has been a growing horticultural practice. Some of the chemicals used include weak solutions of dinitrophenol, dinitrocresol compounds, or other dinitro compounds, or the growth regulator NAA, or its sodium salt or amide. For a good discussion of the problems involved in chemical thinning of blossoms of fruit trees the reader is referred to Chandler (1957) and Childers (1961).

It is often desirable to stimulate fruit abscission at harvest time and this can also be accomplished with chemicals. Cooper *et al.* (1968) presented a good discussion of several types of chemicals which cause fruit abscission. One important group includes ascorbic acid which at high levels induces fruits to produce ethylene and promote abscission. Leaves treated with ascorbic acid also produce some ethylene but not enough to cause much defoliation. Another group of chemicals which stimulate abscission of mature fruits includes inhibitors of protein synthesis, such as cycloheximide. Low concentration (about 30 μ moles/liter) sprayed on the fruit causes ethylene formation which moves freely and masks the effect of the slow-moving inhibitor.

Cone Development in Gymnosperms

In some genera of gymnosperms, such as *Taxus*, the single seed is surrounded by a fleshy aril whereas in most other genera including *Abies*, *Picea*, *Pinus*, *Pseudotsuga*, *Sequoia*, and *Tsuga* the reproductive structures consist of seed-bearing cones (strobili). Attached to the main axis of a mature strobilus are bracts and in the axil of each of these is a scale which bears exposed seeds (see Fig. 7.9). In mature strobili of most gymnosperm genera the bract is usually smaller than the scale. There are some exceptions, however, and in *Pseudotsuga* and species of *Abies* and *Larix* the bracts are large and conspicuous.

In most genera of gymnosperms (e.g., *Abies*, *Larix*, *Picea*, *Pseudotsuga*) the strobili ripen during the first season. However, the time elapsed between pollination and ripening of strobili of pines of the Temperate Zone usually involves 15 or 16 months over two summers and one winter. This timetable of events can be readily modified by climate. Mirov (1962) emphasized that as the equator was approached, the reproductive development of pines was modified. In Nicaragua, for example, ovulate strobili of tropical pines continued to develop during the winter and matured in a little over a year. In the mountains of Java, *Pinus merkusii* pollen was produced and shed intermittently throughout the year. Ovulate strobili and mature cones also were recorded throughout the year.

FERTILIZATION AND EMBRYO DEVELOPMENT

Because most detailed investigations of development of strobili and seeds of gymnosperms have been conducted on pines, this section will refer particularly to fertilization and embryo development of *Pinus*. Some differences in pollination and fertilization between *Pinus* and other genera of gymnosperms will also be summarized.

Fertilization

Gymnosperm pollen is disseminated by wind. Cross pollination commonly occurs because ovulate strobili of many species are concentrated in upper branches and staminate strobili in lower branches. The time span between pollination and fertilization varies among gymnosperm genera from a few days to several months. Pollen grains remain dormant on the nucellus for a few days in *Picea*, 3 weeks in *Pseudotsuga*, 3 months in *Keteleeria evelyniana*, and 9 months in *Cedrus*. In *Pinus* the tube nucleus enters the pollen tube shortly after pollination but the antheridial cells remain in place. The pollen tube rests in this condition for almost a year. The antheridial cell divides the following spring and forms a stalk and body cell. These then enter the pollen tube. In *Pinus* and *Pseudotsuga* the body cell divides a week before fertilization (Konar and Oberoi, 1969).

The exact time between pollination and fertilization differs somewhat with climatic variations. For example, in southern Finland fertilization in *Pinus sylvestris* usually takes place in July. In 1957 it occurred between July 13 and 15, some 13 months and 4 days after pollination. However, in 1959 when early summer temperatures were high, fertilization occurred on June 30, with the interval between pollination and fertilization only 12 months and 13 days. At northern limits of the range of *Pinus sylvestris*, seed development is so slow that fertilization may not take place before winter (Sarvas, 1962).

After the wind-borne pollen of *Pinus* arrives on the stigmatic surface of the micropyle within the ovulate strobilus, it is transported through the micropylar canal to the receptive surface of the nucellus. In *Pinus*, secretion of a micropylar fluid plays an important role in pollination. The fluid fills the micropylar canal during the receptive period. Pollen which is present on surfaces covered by the fluid becomes incorporated in it. The fluid is then withdrawn and absorbed by the nucellus (Doyle, 1935; McWilliam, 1958). Doyle (1935) noted that in *Pinus sylvestris* the pollen grains adhered to the essentially stigmatic micropylar extension. A fluid secretion gradually filled the micropylar canal to the level of the rim and ran up as a film between the arms. Secretion of the fluid occurred for several nights in succession but in unpollinated ovules the fluid seldom was found during the day. Pollen on the arms was caught in the fluid which was then rapidly (within 10 minutes or less) reabsorbed.

The pollination mechanism of *Pinus* differs considerably from that of other gymnosperm genera. Doyle and O'Leary (1935) studied ovular structure in relation to pollination in *Tsuga*, *Cedrus*, *Pseudotsuga*, and *Larix*. In contrast to *Pinus*, all of these genera failed to produce a micropylar fluid that was associated with securing of pollen. In *Tsuga* the pollen lodged on the bracts and scales, with the tubes germinating *in situ* and growing toward the micropyle of the ovule, as in *Araucaria*. In *Cedrus*, *Pseudotsuga*, and *Larix* the micropyle had a stigmatic function. In *Cedrus* the pollen was caught on a flaring micropyle, with the nucellus growing to contact the pollen grains.

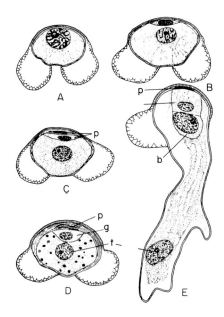

Fɪɢ. 8.9. Development of pollen tube of *Pinus nigra*: (A) pollen grain, (B,C,D,E,) sequential stages in development of pollen tube; p, Prothallial cells; t, tube nucleus; g, generative cell; s, stalk cell; b, body cell. From "Plant Morphology" by Haupt (1953). Used with Permission of McGraw-Hill Book Company.

In *Larix* and *Pseudotsuga* the pollen was trapped on a large and swollen stigmatic development on one side of the micropylar edge. According to Doyle and Kane (1943), pollination mechanisms in most species of *Picea* are similar to those of *Pinus*.

When the micropylar fluid of *Pinus* evaporates, the pollen grains germinate to form a pollen tube that grows downward into the nucellus (Fig. 8.9). As mentioned, the pollen tube grows slowly in the apex of the nucellus for about a year after pollination. Then it grows rapidly through the rest of the nucellus to the entrance of an archegonium and discharges its contents into the egg cell (Fig. 8.10). In *Pinus nigra* this final growth phase of the pollen tube takes about 10 days (McWilliam and Mergen, 1958). The larger of the two male nuclei fuses with the egg nucleus. The smaller male nucleus usually stays in the upper part of the egg together with the tube nucleus and remnants of the stalk cell. The male and female nuclei form a chromosome group arranged on a spindle. Two successive mitotic divisions in the fertilized egg form four free nuclei. These pass to the base of the egg and form the initial cells of the proembryo (Fig. 8.11).

Embryogeny

General features common to embryogeny of all gymnosperms include differentiation of a proembryo into tiers, extensive development of a suspensor, and frequent occurrence of polyembryony. Roy Chowdhury (1962) described similarities and differences in embryogeny of various groups of gymnosperms. In most genera the proembryo consists of three tiers but the proembryo of Pinaceae has four tiers. The Pinaceae also differ from other gymnosperms in having a suspensor which does not elongate but comprises a group of four quiescent rosette cells.

Some differences in embryogeny between Pinaceae and other gymnosperms are shown in Fig. 8.12. In Pinaceae both tiers of the two-tiered proembryo divide, resulting in four tiers at the base of the archegonium: the lowest embryonal tier (E), the primary suspensor tier (S), rosette tier (R), and upper tier (U) (Fig. 8.12A, B). The S cells, which elongate together, are the primary suspensors. After cells of the E tier divide transversely, the proximal cells elongate to form secondary suspensors or embryonal tubes (Fig. 8.12C, D). The derivation of the suspensor tier in Pinaceae is quite different from other groups of gymnosperms. In most members of the Taxodiaceae, Cupressaceae, Podocarpaceae, Cephalotaxaceae, and Taxaceae the mature proembryo is three-tiered with a variable number of cells in each tier (Fig. 8.12). This is the result of division of the upper or open tier of the two-tiered proembryo. The middle tier is designated as the prosuspensor. The prosuspensor elongates carrying embryonal cells at the apex (Fig. 8.12F). As prosuspensors degenerate, cells of the embryonal mass elongate as embryonal tubes and make up

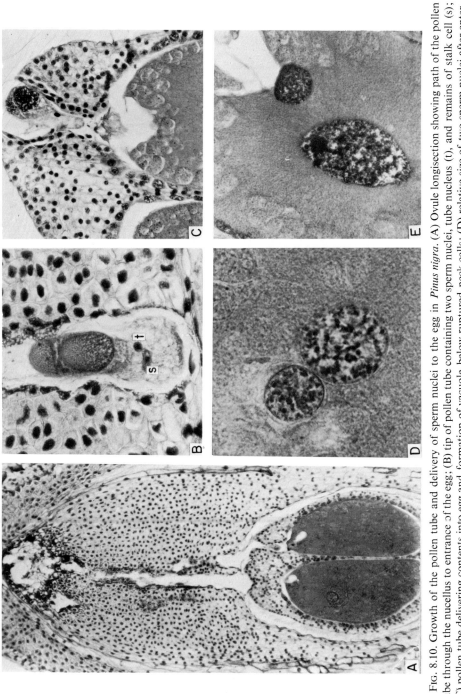

FIG. 8.10. Growth of the pollen tube and delivery of sperm nuclei to the egg in *Pinus nigra*. (A) Ovule longisection showing path of the pollen tube through the nucellus to entrance of the egg; (B) tip of pollen tube containing two sperm nuclei, tube nucleus (t), and remains of stalk cell (s); (C) pollen tube delivering contents into egg and formation of vacuole below ruptured neck cells; (D) relative size of two sperm nuclei after entering egg. The large one is the functional sperm nucleus; (E) functional sperm nucleus approaching the egg nucleus. [From McWilliam and Mergen (1958) Chicago Univ. Press.]

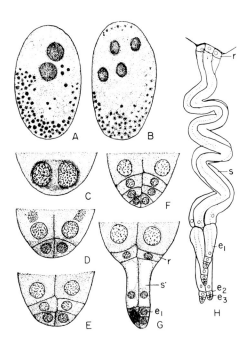

FIG. 8.11. Early embryogeny of *Pinus monophylla*. (A) proembryo with two nuclei; (B) proembryo with four nuclei; (C) two of four nuclei located at base of the egg; (D) eight-celled proembryo; (E) three tiers of four cells each; (F) four tiers of four cells each; (G) elongating cells of the suspensor tier; (H) later stage of *Pinus banksiana*. e, e_2, e_3, Secondary suspensor cells. [From "Plant Morphology" by Haupt (1953). Used with permission of McGraw-Hill Book Company.]

secondary suspensors which replace dying prosuspensor cells (Fig. 8.12 I) (*Taxus*). In some genera (e.g., *Sciadopitys*) the embryonal cells divide transversely after considerable elongation of the prosuspensor cells has occurred. Daughter cells toward the prosuspensor elongate and become primary suspensors (Fig. 8.12 G). When only one cell participates the suspensor is called primary (Fig. 8.12 G) but when more than one cell is involved, it is called a secondary suspensor (Fig. 8.12 H). An embryo may have all three types of suspensors (e.g., *Sciadopitys*) or a prosuspensor and secondary suspensor (e.g. *Taxodium* and *Cryptomeria*).

Elongation of suspensor cells forces the lower cells into gametophyte tissue. Suspensors elongate sufficiently to cause their twisting. In gymnosperms the gametophyte tissue in which the embryo is embedded has the same function as the endosperm of angiosperms. The embryo derives its nutrition from the gametophyte. Growth requirements for the embryo probably are initially formed by breakdown of reserve materials in the

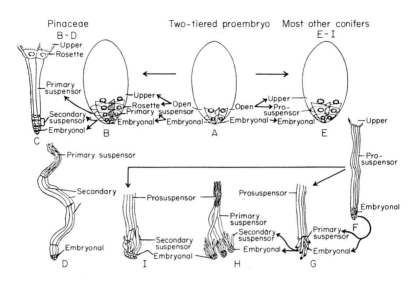

FIG. 8.12. Origin of various types of suspensors in conifers. (A) Two-tiered proembryo; (B–D) figures showing derivation of primary and secondary suspensors in Pinaceae; (E–I) figures showing derivation of prosuspensor, primary, and secondary suspensors in most other conifers. [From Roy Chowdhury (1962).]

gametophyte. These substances are absorbed by the embryo and resynthesized into complex molecules such as starch and proteins (Maheshwari and Singh, 1967).

In Pinaceae separate embryos form from each of the four terminal cells. Usually one of the largest of the four primary embryos survives and the others abort to give the mature seed a single embryo. The mature embryo has a hypocotyl with a radicle at the suspensor end and a plumule at the other end. The plumule is surrounded by cotyledons which vary in number in different genera. The stem tip is recognizable before cotyledon primordia appear.

Polyembryony

The presence of more than one embryo is a dominant feature of embryogeny of Pinaceae. Two types of polyembryony occur in gymnosperms: (1) simple polyembryony in which additional embryos result from fertilization of several archegonia in a gametophyte; and (2) cleavage polyembryony in which several embryos arise from splitting of embryonal cells of a single zygote. In cleavage polyembryony it sometimes can be determined at a very early stage of development which of the embryos will be successful (determinate cleavage polyembryony). At other times it is difficult to predict early which embryo will be successful (indeterminate cleavage polyembryony). All genera of Pinaceae exhibit simple polyembryony. Cleavage polyembryony occurs in *Pinus, Cedrus, Tsuga, Taxodium Cryptomeria, Cunninghamia, Sequoia,* and *Podocarpus.*

Even though multiple fertilization takes place in the female gametophyte of *Pinus,* most mature seeds of this genus have only a single embryo. For example, Buchholz (1946) stated that in more than 98% of pine seeds only one embryo matures. Occasionally, however, *Pinus* has more than one embryo per seed (Berlyn, 1962; Cayford and Waldron, 1965). The occurrence of multiple embryos appears to be higher in pines with large seeds than in those with small ones. Berlyn (1962) reported the occurrence of four embryos per mature seed in approximately one-third of the seeds of *Pinus lambertiana* and *P. cembra* examined and in a few seeds of *P. strobus.* There was a progressive reduction in size and development of embryos in a given seed, with the embryo furthest from the micropyle being the largest and most differentiated. In another study Berlyn (1967) found eight embryos present in one *Pinus lambertiana* seed.

PARTHENOCARPY

Development of unpollinated strobili with fully formed but usually empty seeds occurs in a number of genera of gymnosperms. Parthenocarpy is common in *Abies, Juniperus, Larix, Picea, Taxus,* and *Thuja* and has also been reported in *Chamaecyparis, Cryptomeria, Pseudotsuga,* and *Tsuga* (Orr-Ewing, 1957). Only rarely does parthenocarpy occur in *Pinus,* however. For example, only 0.4% of *Pinus sylvestris* cones had completely aborted ovules (Sarvas, 1962) and only one out of 76 developing cones of *Pinus resinosa* had no developing ovules (Dickmann and Kozlowski, 1971).

DURATION AND TIMING OF CONE DEVELOPMENT

Some idea of similarities and differences in strobilus development of different gymnosperm genera in the Temperate Zone may be gained by comparing the timing of significant events in reproductive growth of *Pinus resinosa, Pseudotsuga menziesii,* and *Abies balsamea.*

In central Wisconsin the strobilus or conelet of *Pinus resinosa* first becomes externally visible in late May or early June at the distal end of a growing shoot. However, primordia of strobili are differentiated during the previous growing season. Pollination occurs in early June while the ovuliferous scales are separated from one another. The strobilus begins to enlarge after pollination and the scales close. By late July the strobilus has lengthened to 10–12 mm and little additional increase in length occurs during the rest of the first year (Lyons, 1956). Meanwhile the pollen grains have germinated but the pollen tube stops growing and is quiescent during late summer and winter (Stanley, 1958). Megaspores do not form until approximately 3 weeks after emergence of the ovulate strobilus. Successive cell and nuclear division of one of the megaspores result in an enlarged megagametophyte. A period of winter dormancy follows.

The cones resume growing early in the spring of the second season and attain their final length by early July. Growth of the megagametophyte also resumes in early spring, but the pollen tube does not grow until just before fertilization occurs. Fertilization takes place around mid-June of the second year. Embryo development follows and seeds ripen by early September in Wisconsin (Dickmann and Kozlowski, 1969a).

Important events in growth of *Pseudotsuga menziesii* cones throughout their 17-month developmental cycle at Corvallis, Oregon, were studied by Owens and Smith (1964, 1965). Initiation of lateral vegetative, staminate and ovulate primordia occurred during the second week of April. These reproductive tissues were formed about a month before vegetative buds opened and at the same time as the current season's ovulate strobili opened. Cataphylls were initiated from early April to mid-July and bract initiation was continued from mid-July to early October. Scales were initiated early in September and continued until the strobilus became dormant early in November. Growth was resumed early the following March and the strobilus buds burst approximately a month later. The strobili achieved maximum size early in July. Maturation occurred in July and August and it generally was completed in September. The timing and duration of significant events are summarized in Table 8.5.

After the first year, the dormant strobili were only 2.7 mm long. They resumed growing in March and elongated to about 8 cm by July 1. During this early period the vascular tissues were initiated and partially differentiated, with subsequent differentiation occurring throughout the strobilus until September. Both cell division and cell elongation accounted for growth in length of the strobilus. Cell division predominated before pollination, whereas cell elongation accounted for most growth following pollination.

The bracts elongated rapidly and increased from 1.5 mm to 2 cm in 60 days. They expanded primarily as a result of intercalary growth and cell elongation. The outermost subepidermal cells differentiated into hypodermal tissue. Maturation of mesophyll began at the tip of the bract. Transfusion tissue was present in the exposed part of the bract. The bracts grew faster than the scales and were the first to reach maximum size.

Although there was considerable variation in the rate of growth of different scales they elongated on the average about 2.5 cm in 90 days. The scales became spoon-shaped as a result of marginal growth. During strobilus enlargement the exposed part of the scale was green and the covered

TABLE 8.5

Timing of Events in Bud and Strobilus Development of *Pseudotsuga menziesii* near Corvallis, Oregon[a]

Event	Date	Elapsed time from bud initiation (mo.)
All buds		
Lateral bud primordia initiated	Early April	Ovulate buds burst
Zonation become apparent	Mid-May	1.5
Cataphyll initiation complete, apical enlargement occurs, leaf, bract, or microsporophyll initiation begins	Mid-July	3.5
Ovulate Strobilus		
Beginning of scale initiation	Early Sept.	5
All bracts initiated	Early Oct.	6
All scales initiated and ovulate buds become dormant	Early Nov.	7
Ovulate buds resume growth	Early March	11
Ovulate buds burst and pollination occurs	Early April	12
Fertilization	Early June	14
Elongation of strobilus complete	Early July	15
Maturation complete, strobilus opens, seeds released	Early Sept.	17

[a] From Owens and Smith (1965)

part white. Before strobili opened, however, the scales turned brown. During ovule development the scale thickened by cell division especially in the vicinity of the growing ovule. Differentiation of seed wings began at about the time of pollination, and the wings were fully developed in early July, about 60 days before strobili opened. The seed wings usually separated from the scales in late August.

As mentioned, strobili of *Abies balsamea* mature in one growing season. However, buds differentiating into staminate and ovulate strobili can be identified microscopically in the spring, approximately a year before pollination. Some idea of early post-dormancy development of staminate and ovulate strobili from the time of dormancy to the end of the receptive stage of ovulate strobili, in New Brunswick, Canada, may be gained from Fig. 8.13.

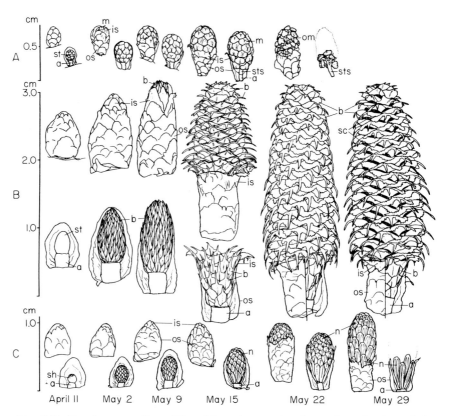

FIG. 8.13. Development of strobili and lateral vegetative shoots from the time of dormancy to end of the receptive stage in the ovulate strobilus of *Abies balsamea* in New Brunswick, Canada. (A) Staminate strobilus: by date, left = entire bud and strobilus, right = bud scales partially removed to show base of strobilus and part of axis. (a) Bearing bud scales, (is) inner bud scale, (os) outer bud scale, (m) microsporophyll, (om) open microsporangium, (st) strobilus, (sts) strobilus stalk. (B) ovulate strobilus; April 11 to May 15, upper = entire bud and strobilus; lower = bud scales partially removed to show base of strobilus and part of axis. (a) Bearing bud scales: May 22 and 29 strobilus with bud scales removed from right to show base of strobilus; (b) bract, (sc) ovuliferous scale. (C) Lateral vegetative shoot: by date, left = entire bud and shoot, right = bud scales partially removed to show base of shoot and part of axis. (a) Bearing bud scales; (n) needle, (sh) shoot. [From Powell (1970)].

In early April the proportional volume of buds occupied by strobilus or shoot was greatest in staminate and least in vegetative buds. The strobilus buds opened earlier than the vegetative buds. The latter opened about 10 days after the ovulate buds, by which time pollen was being shed and ovulate strobili were receptive. Staminate strobili elongated considerably just before shedding pollen (Fig. 8.13 A). Mature staminate strobili which varied from red-purple to yellow in color, turned brown after pollen was shed and they subsequently abscised over a period of months. Growth of ovulate strobili was rapid during early development (Fig. 8.13 B). As ovuliferous scales appeared between the bracts (Fig. 8.13 B, May 20) the receptive period ended. The bracts were at first lanceolate and incurved, but by mid-May the shape of the bract had changed as a result of elongation and widening in the basal half. The bracts became reflexed after bud bursting (Fig. 8.13 B, May 15 and 22).

After reaching the ovulate strobilus some of the pollen grains sift down between the ovuliferous scales and rest on the micropylar tip before being drawn into the nucellus. The pollen tubes begin to grow slowly and about a month elapses before fertilization occurs (in late June in southern Canada). Embryo development follows. The mature seed consists of the embryo, megagametophyte, a thin layer of nucellus, and a hard seed coat. In the autumn the ripening strobili become gray in color and the scales dehydrate and fall from the persistent central axis of the strobilus (Bakuzis and Hansen, 1965).

INCREASE IN SIZE AND DRY WEIGHT OF STROBILI AND SEEDS

In pines which ripen strobili over a 2-year period, most increase in size and dry weight of strobili occurs during the second year of their development (Fig. 8.14). For example, when growth of first-year strobili (conelets) of *Pinus resinosa* in Wisconsin ended they were only about one fortieth the weight, one thirtieth the volume, and one third the length of mature strobili at the

FIG. 8.14. Strobili of *Pinus elliottii* in three stages of development (from left to right): 2 years, 1 year, and 1 month. U.S. Forest Service Photo.

end of their second year of development (Dickmann and Kozlowski, 1969a).

Seasonal patterns of increase in dry weight and size of first- and second-year strobili of *Pinus resinosa* in Wisconsin are shown in Figs. 8.15 and 8.16. The dry weight of first-year strobili increased at a steady rate until late September, by which time the average cone weighed slightly less than 0.2 g. Patterns of dry weight increment were similar during each of three successive growing seasons. The length and width of first-year strobili increased until mid-July and changed little thereafter. At the end of the first season, an average strobilus was 8 mm wide and 14–15 mm long.

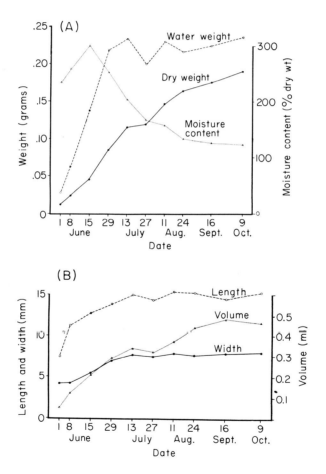

FIG. 8.15. Seasonal changes in dry weight, weight of water (per conelet), and percent moisture of first-year conelets of *Pinus resinosa* (A). Seasonal changes in length, width, and volume of first-year conelets (B). [From Dickmann and Kozlowski (1969b).]

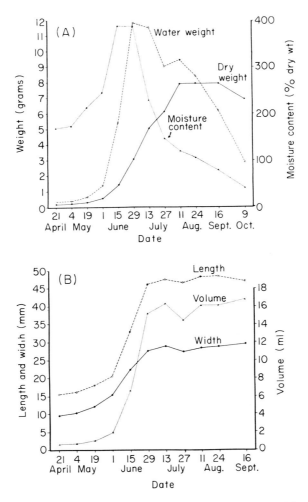

FIG. 8.16. Seasonal changes in dry weight, weight of water (per strobilus), and percent moisture of second-year strobili of *Pinus resinosa* (A). Seasonal changes in length, width, and volume of second-year strobili (B). [From Dickmann and Kozlowski (1969b).]

During the second year of development, *Pinus resinosa* strobili resumed growing in mid-April. Dry weight increase was slow during May but increased rapidly during early June and continued at a high rate until early August when maximum dry weight was recorded. Dry weight of the average second-year strobilus increased from less than 0.2 g in April to nearly 8 g in August. Seasonal patterns of dry weight increase of different second-year strobili were similar in 3 successive years, but strobili were small in 1966

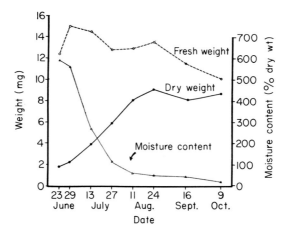

FIG. 8.17. Changes in fresh weight, dry weight, and percentage moisture of developing *Pinus resinosa* seeds from just after fertilization to maturity. [From Dickmann and Kozlowski (1969b).]

because of severe infestation of cone insects. Most increase in size of second-year strobili occurred in June when the volume of the individual strobilus increased from less than 2 ml to more than 15 ml and strobilus length increased from 20 mm to more than 45 mm. The second-year strobili reached maximum size about a month before maximum dry weight increase was recorded.

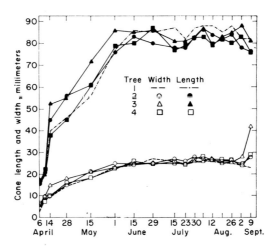

FIG. 8.18. Changes in length and width of ovulate strobili of four *Pseudotsuga menziesii* trees in Corvallis, Oregon. [From Ching and Ching (1962).]

Seasonal changes in dry and fresh weight and moisture content of fertilized ovules or seeds of *Pinus resinosa* are shown in Fig. 8.17. Dry weight increment of seeds was rapid from June until late August with no net gain in dry weight recorded thereafter. Moisture content (as percent of dry weight) decreased sharply from a late June average of near 600 to 50 % in late August. Subsequently, moisture content of seeds decreased gradually to 17% by early October.

Changes in width and length of ovulate strobili of *Pseudotsuga menziesii* (which require one year for maturation) are shown in Fig. 8.18. Length of strobili increased rapidly to a maximum by June 1. Width of strobili increased from 6 mm (excluding bracts) on April 24 to 24 mm on June 1, when maximum width was approached. Sudden increases of width of strobili in early September were traceable to expansion of scales. Overall dry weight changes of strobili followed a typical sigmoid pattern (Fig. 8.19) but the scales stopped gaining dry weight in July, whereas seeds increased in dry weight until September. From early June to August dry weight of strobili increased, moisture content rapidly decreased, and weight of fertilized seeds increased as the seed enlarged.

In *Abies balsamea* in Fredricton, New Brunswick, Canada, elongation of staminate strobili (which require one year for maturation) followed a normal sigmoid form (Fig. 8.20). However, increase in length of ovulate strobili

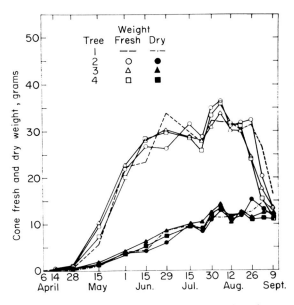

FIG. 8.19. Changes in fresh and dry weight of ovulate strobili of four *Pseudotsuga menziesii* trees in Corvallis, Oregon. [From Ching and Ching (1962).]

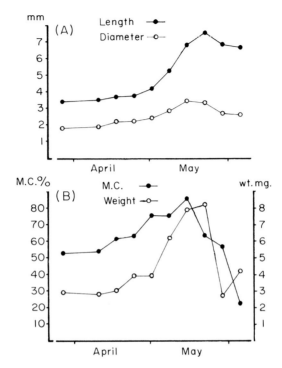

FIG. 8.20. Changes in length and diameter (A) and moisture content and dry weight (B) of staminate strobili of *Abies balsamea*. [From Powell (1970)].

occurred in two stages (Fig. 8.21). The first stage, which occurred before the strobili were receptive, accompanied the grand period of bract growth. The second stage was associated with the grand period of growth of ovuliferous scales. The two stages were not obvious if growth was expressed as dry weight increment. Elongation of strobili stopped in mid-July but dry weight increased until mid-August. The continued dry weight increase was largely the result of embryo growth in the seeds.

PHYSIOLOGY OF CONE DEVELOPMENT

This section will consider some aspects of carbohydrate, mineral, and water relations during growth and development of strobili. The role of hormonal growth regulators in control of reproductive growth will be discussed in Chapter 9.

Carbohydrates

The rapidly developing strobili of gymnosperms require large amounts of carbohydrates. The contribution of photosynthesis by green strobili to their

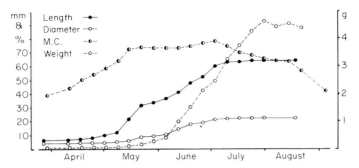

FIG. 8.21. Changes in length, diameter, dry weight, and moisture content of ovulate strobili of *Abies balsamea*. [From Powell (1970).]

own growth appears to be inadequate to provide carbohydrates in needed amounts (Dickmann and Kozlowski, 1970b). However, ample evidence is available of diversion of carbohydrates into growing strobili. Dickmann and Kozlowski (1968, 1970a) reported a preferential mobilization of currently produced carbohydrates by reproductive tissues of *Pinus resinosa*. A changing seasonal pattern in the source of current photosynthate for cone development was also shown. The 1-year-old needles were the major source of current photosynthate for cone development early in the season. In June the 2- and 3-year-old needles also contributed some current photosynthate for cone development, but after late June their contribution was slight. The supply of carbohydrates from old needles declined late in the season as cones mobilized increasingly more carbohydrates from needles produced during the current year.

Ching and Ching (1962) showed that in early April the few starch grains present were small and disoriented throughout *Pseudotsuga* strobili (Ching and Ching, 1962). By the end of April the grains increased progressively in size and number. By June 1, when the strobili achieved maximum size, starch grains filled all the parenchyma cells. This condition persisted until mid-July when starch was concentrated near the seed in the scale. Starch grains then gradually shifted to the embryo and surrounding tissues. As the seed matured the number of starch grains decreased. The scales apparently served as temporary storage sites for carbohydrates required for seed growth.

In *Pseudotsuga* more carbohydrates were utilized by seeds than by cone scales for respiration and synthesis of structural and reserve materials. As may be seen in Table 8.6, the seeds absorbed about 4 times as much glucose as the scales during early development and about twice as much during later stages. Respiration of both seeds and scales decreased with maturity, but seeds had a higher rate of oxygen uptake than the scales.

Dickmann and Kozlowski (1969b) studied changes in extractable reserves

TABLE 8.6

ABSORPTION OF GLUCOSE-6-^{14}C IN DEVELOPING CONE SCALES AND
SEEDS OF *Pseudotsuga menziesii*[a]

Days after pollination	Total absorption (μg/g dry wt per 6 hrs)	
	Scale	Seed
75	487 ± 15	1523 ± 39
85	274 ± 18	683 ± 39
95	227 ± 11	523 ± 7
105	109 ± 4	189 ± 57

[a] From Ching and Fang (1963).

and structural carbohydrates during development of first-year and second-year strobili of *Pinus resinosa* in Wisconsin. Major changes in composition occurred only during the last 3 months of development. The major components of strobili during the first year and the early part of the second year included both reserves and products of current synthesis. During this period, reserves increased at a rate which paralleled the overall weight increase of young strobili and comprised about half their dry weight. Carbohydrates accumulated at a rate commensurate with their incorporation into storage and structural materials or losses in respiration. For these reasons, reserves remained rather stable during the first season and during April and May of the second season of strobilus development (Figs. 8.22, 8.23).

During the latter part of the second season of strobilus development, marked compositional changes occurred (Fig. 8.23). There was a shift from high levels of reserves and low levels of structural materials, expecially cellulose, to a reversal in their relative proportions. The amount of extractable reserves increased rapidly from early May until the end of June. Subsequently, reserves increased gradually until early August, although their concentrations decreased sharply after mid-June. At the same time, a sharp increase in cellulose was recorded and continued until August. The data showed that large amounts of reserve carbohydrates were converted to cellulosic secondary cell wall components from mid-June to September. Whereas starch was abundant in scales and pith of strobili in late June, it had virtually disappeared from the strobili by early September, further indicating conversion of reserves to structural materials.

The decrease in reserve carbohydrates of maturing strobili also is associated with mobilization of reserves by seeds. For example, Ching and Ching (1962) noted that starch grains disappeared from scales of *Pseudotsuga menziesii*

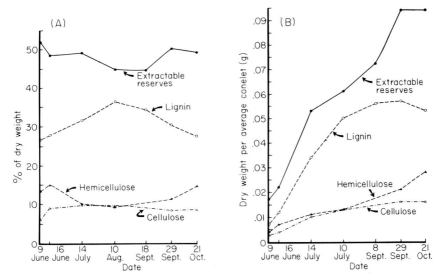

FIG. 8.22. Seasonal changes in extractable reserves, lignin, hemicellulose, and cellulose of first-year conelets of *Pinus resinosa*. Data are given in concentration (percent of dry weight) (A) and in weight per conelet (B). [From Dickmann and Kozlowski (1969b).]

strobili at the time they began to increase in the embryo. Krugman (1966) observed that gametophytes and embryos of *Pinus lambertiana* from strobili collected in mid-August increased in dry weight if seeds were stored in strobili, but not if they were removed from the strobili and stored in vermiculite, indicating translocation of reserve materials from cone scales to seeds.

Mineral Relations

Dickmann and Kozlowski (1969c) studied mineral relations of first- and second-year ovulate strobili and developing seeds of *Pinus resinosa*. Mineral nutrients moved rapidly into growing strobili, but as they matured, accumulation was reduced. Finally mobile nutrients were translocated out of senescing strobili.

During the first year the major macronutrients moved steadily into developing strobili. The rate and magnitude of accumulation were in the following order: $N > K > P > Ca > Mg$. However, the concentration of N decreased, whereas that of the other macronutrients was rather stable. Micronutrients also moved into strobili during the first year (Fig. 8.24).

The seasonal pattern of uptake and accumulation of nutrients during the second year of strobilus development differed from the first-year pattern. During the period of rapid growth of strobili following fertilization, uptake of macro- and micronutrients continued. However, translocation of Mn into

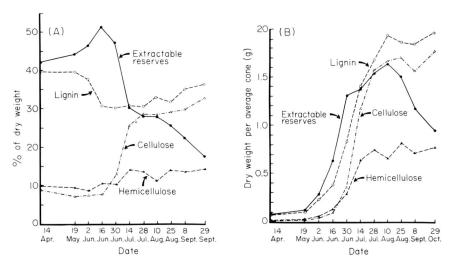

FIG. 8.23. Seasonal changes in extractable reserves, lignin, hemicellulose, and cellulose of second-year strobili of *Pinus resinosa*. Data are given in concentrations (percent of dry weight) (A) and in weight per strobilus (B). [From Dickmann and Kozlowski (1969b).]

strobili stopped abruptly in mid-June when strobili reached their maximum size. Beginning in mid-July, N, P, and K began moving out of maturing strobili. Other macro- and micronutrients continued to accumulate in strobili during the entire second year of growth (Fig. 8.25).

At the same time that mature strobili were beginning to senesce, N, P, K, Mg, Mn, Zn, and Fe were rapidly mobilized by developing seeds. Nitrogen accumulated in high concentrations. Senescing strobilus tissue apparently supplied much of the N, P, and K that was translocated into seeds. Calcium was present in low concentrations in seeds whereas Na accumulated in large amounts. Aluminum did not move into seeds after fertilization occurred (Fig. 8.26).

Water Relations

Seasonal patterns of hydration are different in first-year strobili than in second-year strobili. In first-year strobili of *Pinus resinosa* there was a rapid period of hydration which lasted until mid-June. Thereafter, the weight of water in strobili remained stable, but percent moisture content decreased primarily because of increasing dry weight (Dickmann and Kozlowski, 1969a).

Water moved into second-year strobili until late June, but percent moisture reached a maximum during mid-June. Maximum water content was recorded at about the time the strobili achieved maximum size but were still increasing

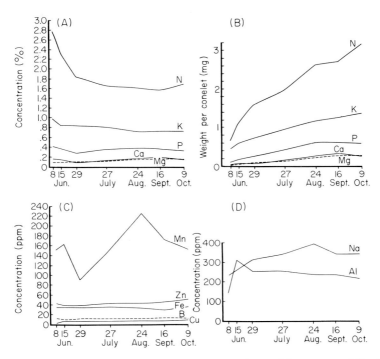

Fig. 8.24. Seasonal changes in macro- and micronutrients of first-year strobili of *Pinus resinosa*. (A) Changes in concentration of macronutrients. (B) Changes in weight of macronutrients per strobilus. (C) Changes in concentration of micronutrients. (D) Changes in concentration of Na and Al. [From Dickmann and Kozlowski (1969c).]

in dry weight. Thereafter, the strobili dehydrated and shrank rapidly until they matured (Figs. 8.16 and 8.27). Thus, stabilization in dry weight accompanied by continued dehydration characterized the stage immediately prior to strobilus maturity.

A similar pattern of rapid dehydration of maturing strobili has been reported for a number of other species of gymnosperms. Beaufait (1960), Cram and Worden (1957), and Pfister (1967) also reported rapid decreases in percent moisture of *Pinus banksiana*, *Picea glauca*, and *Abies grandis* strobili as they approached maturity. In *Pseudotsuga* strobili the average moisture content was high in early April (482%), decreased to 362% after pollination, then increased rapidly until the end of June. Thereafter, moisture content decreased throughout the season until it averaged only 16% in early September when strobili were opening. The scales dehydrated more slowly than the maturing seeds (Table 8.7).

The opening of strobili apparently is caused by drying rather than by

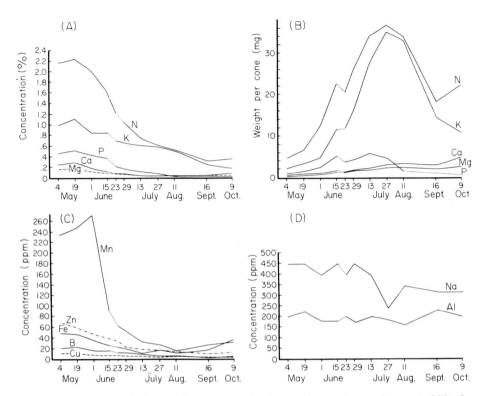

FIG. 8.25. Seasonal changes in macro- and micronutrients of second-year strobili of *Pinus resinosa*. (A) Changes in concentration of macronutrients. (B) Changes in weight of macronutrients per strobilus. (C) Changes in concentration of micronutrients. (D) Changes in concentration of Na and Al. [From Dickmann and Kozlowski (1969c).]

growth. Willis (1917) noted that *Pseudotsuga* cones did not begin to open until at least 20% of their water was lost. All strobili were fully opened by the time they lost about half of their water. Harlow, Coté, and Day (1964) demonstrated that opening of strobilus scales was related to greater shrinkage of ventral tissues than dorsal ones. They found that the dorsal zone of a scale of the strobilus of pine consisted principally of wood fibers and the ventral zone was made up of a band of short, rectangular thick-walled cells. The dorsal fibrous tissues showed little variation in lengthwise dimensions as they dried. In contrast, the ventral tissues shrank longitudinally by 10–13% depending on species.

During certain stages of strobilus development, the decrease in percent moisture and dry weight of strobili may be traced primarily to rapid increase in dry weight rather than to translocation of water from the strobilus. For

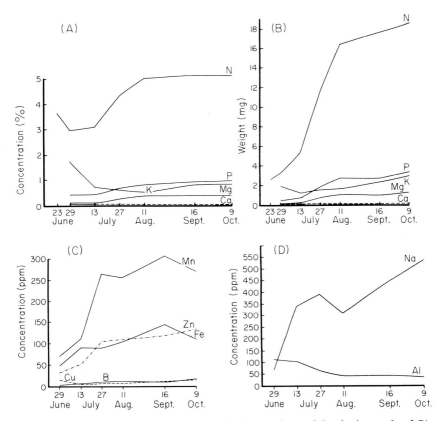

FIG. 8.26. Seasonal changes in macro- and micronutrients of developing seeds of *Pinus resinosa*. (A) Changes in concentration of macronutrients. (B) Changes in weight of macronutrients in seeds per strobilus. (C) Changes in concentration of micronutrients. (D) Changes in concentration of Na and Al. [From Dickmann and Kozlowski (1969c).]

example, whole strobili, scales, and seeds of *Picea glauca* and *Larix laricina* achieved their highest percentage moisture content, approximately 400% in late May or early June (Clausen and Kozlowski, 1965). They then showed an overall seasonal decrease in percent moisture until reaching their lowest values, less than 50%, in September. An initial increase in percent moisture between late May and early June was the result of an increase in actual moisture content which exceeded the dry weight increase. From early June to late July the percentage moisture decreased markedly even though actual water weight per strobilus remained the same or even increased. The decrease in percent moisture was traceable to a greater proportional increase in dry weight. After the beginning of August, by which time the increase in dry weight was completed, the decrease in percentage moisture resulted primarily

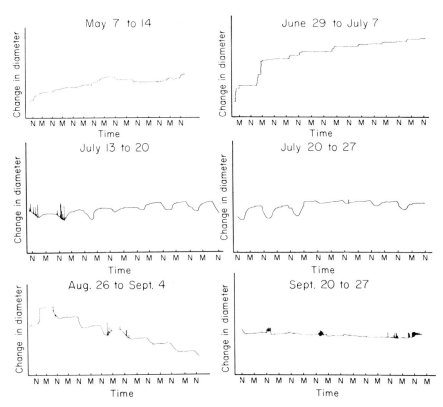

FIG. 8.27. Diameter changes in second-year *Pinus resinosa* strobili. N = noon; M = midnight. [From Dickmann and Kozlowski (1969a).]

TABLE 8.7

CHANGES IN FRESH WEIGHT, DRY WEIGHT, AND MOISTURE CONTENT OF DEVELOPING CONES, SCALES, AND SEEDS OF *Pseudotsuga menziesii*[a]

Days after pollination	Fresh weight (mg)		Dry weight (mg)		Moisture Content (% dry weight)	
	Scale	Seed	Scale	Seed	Scale	Seed
75	710.5	25.4	137.6	3.9	80.8	84.6
85	662.9	26.8	173.0	5.7	73.9	78.2
95	578.4	22.4	174.0	6.6	69.7	70.8
105	711.1	25.1	236.8	11.9	66.7	59.4

[a] From Ching and Fang (1963).

from dehydration. Hence, percent moisture of developing strobili and seeds may change because of water translocation into or out of tissues, changes in dry weight, or both.

Diurnal Shrinkage and Expansion of Cones

Superimposed on dimensional growth changes of strobili are reversible size changes which reflect changes in hydration. During a mid-period of development, strobili often shrink during the day and expand at night (Dickmann and Kozlowski, 1969a; Chaney and Kozlowski, 1969c). The amount of diurnal shrinkage and expansion of strobili varies with the stage of strobilus development. Chaney and Kozlowski (1969c) showed that *Picea glauca* and *Pinus banksiana* strobili made intermittent stepwise increases in diameter early in their development. Strobili expanded during the evening and night, while vapor pressure deficit of the air was decreasing or low and did not change in diameter during the daytime when vapor pressure deficit was high. In a mid-stage of strobilus development, reversible diurnal expansion and contraction of strobili occurred; these fluctuations were inversely correlated with vapor pressure deficits (Fig. 8.28). Maturing strobili decreased in diameter in a stepwise pattern. Diurnal shrinkage of maturing *Picea glauca* strobili was recorded when vapor pressure deficit was increasing or high and no appreciable diameter change occurred when vapor pressure deficit was low. Dickmann and Kozlowski (1969a) noted that although some expansion of maturing *Pinus resinosa* strobili occurred at night the dimensional change was consistently less than the amount of shrinkage during the day, resulting in net daily diameter decrease.

Periodicity of Reproductive Growth

There has been much concern about the failure of trees to produce large fruit or seed crops each year. A good example of regular seasonal periodicity in reproductive growth is the biennial or alternate bearing of fruit trees. Whereas the number of flowers and fruits varies only slightly from year to year in some varieties, in others a heavy flower and fruit crop is produced one year and little or none the following year. The tendency for alternate bearing is much greater in apple varieties York Imperial and Golden Delicious than in Rome Beauty or Jonathan. Alternate flowering and bearing of fruit is a physiological characteristic of individual trees as well as parts of trees. Some trees in an orchard bear heavily one year while neighboring trees have few flowers and fruits, only to produce an abundant crop the next year. Furthermore, within a tree, one branch may produce flowers and fruits while the remainder of the tree fails to do so. The next year the reverse occurs,

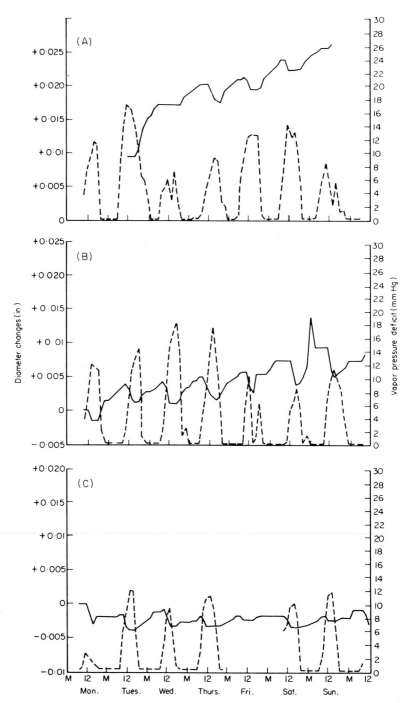

FIG. 8.28. Diurnal variations in diameters of *Pinus banksiana* strobili and changes in vapor pressure deficit at various times during the growing season. (A) July 10–17; (B) July 17–24; (C) July 24–31. [From Chaney and Kozlowski (1969c).]

with the previously fruiting branch remaining vegetative. The bearing sequence can be readily altered by early destruction of reproductive structures. For example, when early frost damage destroys a fruit crop, the normally bearing year becomes a vegetative one. The subsequent year becomes one of heavy fruiting and the biennial habit is continued (Davis, 1957).

Reproductive growth of many forest trees is irregular and unpredictable. However, fruit and seed production occurs much more regularly in plantation grown trees than in natural forest stands. The amount of seed produced by forest trees varies greatly among species and from year to year. Wide variations in annual seed production can be shown by comparing species which tend to produce good seed crops annually (e.g., *Nyssa aquatica*, *Magnolia grandiflora*, *Celtis laevigata*) with those that have good seed crops at intervals of several years (e.g., *Fagus grandifolia*). Some species tend to have good seed crops at fairly regular intervals (e.g., *Fraxinus* spp., *Acer saccharum*); others produce good seed crops irregularly (e.g., *Juglans nigra*, *Liriodendron tulipifera*). Between good seed years, seed crops are often light and sometimes may be total failures. Usually, seed production cycles tend to be more regular if the period between good crops is short than when it is long. Associated species of forest trees often vary greatly in seed and cone production. For example, *Tsuga heterophylla* is a very prolific seeder and *Abies grandis* and *Pinus monticola* are light seeders. *Tsuga heterophylla* trees are often densely covered with hundreds of cones. By comparison a good cone crop for *Abies grandis* is one of 40 cones or more, and a fair crop is 21 to 40 cones. A crop of 40 cones per tree is rated as good for *Pinus monticola*.

Wide variations often occur in seed production among different species of the same genus of forest trees. For example, *Acer rubrum* and *A. saccharinum* tend to have good seed crops annually, whereas *A. saccharum* has them at 2- to 5-year intervals. Among the oaks *Quercus phellos* produces good seed crops nearly every year; *Q. velutina* and *Q. macrocarpa* every 2 or 3 years; *Q. muehlenbergii* every 2–5 years; *Q. prinus* with periodicity which varies over the range of the tree, but with good seed crops occurring about once in 4–7 years; and *Q. alba*, which is considered a prolific seeder generally, having irregular heavy crops, often 4–10 years apart.

Among the poplars, *Populus trichocarpa*, *P. balsamifera*, and *P. deltoides* var. *deltoides* generally produce good seed crops annually; by comparison, *P. grandidentata* and *P. tremuloides* have good seed crops only once every 4–5 years, with light crops in most intervening years. The amount of seed produced is influenced by age, size, and vigor of individual trees. Dominant, widely spaced trees of a given species produce most seed if they are adequately pollinated.

Effects of Reproductive Growth on Vegetative Growth

The amount of fruit or seed crop usually is negatively correlated with vegetative growth (Davis, 1957). In addition to suppressing vegetative growth, heavy fruiting and seed production also alter the balance between roots and shoots. Proebsting (1958) demonstrated that in bearing Elberta peach trees vegetative growth was suppressed over a 3-year period. Tingley (1936) reported that heavy fruiting by apple trees caused the formation of intraannual rings of wood, presumably because of carbohydrate diversion into the fruit. Singh (1948) also found that heavy fruiting reduced stem and root growth. His work showed that the physiological condition of the tree at the beginning of an "off" or nonbearing year was different from that of an "on" or bearing year. Leaf area per spur of off-year trees was nearly twice as great as that of on-year trees during the critical period of fruit bud formation.

Under certain conditions the relationship between vegetative and reproductive growth is positive. This may occur when variations in tree vigor predominate over differences in reproductive growth. When both vegetative and reproductive growth are influenced by fertilizers, for example, a high positive correlation often results between vegetative and reproductive increment (Havis and Cullinan, 1946).

The relationship between vegetative and reproductive growth may be considered to be linear over a considerable range but often this does not hold when fruit crops are abnormally high or low. As shown in Fig. 8.29 the growth–fruit yield relationship is more likely to be represented by the curve A-A^1 rather than B-B^1 (Proebsting, 1958). In the range of very low fruit production the efficiency of the tree appears to be lowered by some internal factor, possibly accumulation of photosynthetic products. In the range of very high fruit production the physiological efficiency of the tree is increased. This might be the result of rapid removal of photosynthetic products.

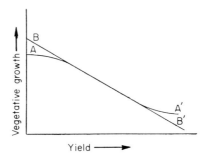

FIG. 8.29. Relations between vegetative growth and reproductive growth under extremes of cropping. For explanation see text. [From Proebsting (1958).]

SUPPRESSION OF VEGETATIVE GROWTH BY REPRODUCTIVE GROWTH

Considerable evidence shows that apical and cambial growth of fruit trees and forest trees is suppressed by reproductive growth. A few examples will be given for each group.

Fruit trees

In a comprehensive study covering a 25-year-period, Rogers and Booth (1964) showed strong negative correlation between fruit yield of apple trees and the amount of shoot growth during the year following fruiting. In trees on a variety of rootstocks, a heavy fruit crop was followed by reduced shoot growth the next year and a light crop was followed by increased shoot growth (Table 8.8). The increase in shoot growth in years following light fruit crops varied from 45% on a dwarfing rootstock to 6% on a very vigorous one. The decreases in growth following large fruit crops ranged from 53-9% on different rootstocks. No significant correlations were found between fruit yield and the current year's shoot growth, or with shoot growth of 1 or 2 years previously (Table 8.9). Barlow's (1964) regression analyses showed that shoot growth of apple trees was related to the size of the fruit crop, after it exceeded a certain threshold weight on the tree. For each 10 lb of fruit above a threshold of 10 lb for trees on Malling XVI rootstocks, there was a decrease in shoot length of 11.3 and 3.3 meters for trees lightly and heavily pruned, respectively. For trees on Malling IX rootstocks above a threshold of 3 lb of fruit per tree, 10 lb of fruit reduced shoot elongation by 9.4 and 12.5 meters for lightly and heavily pruned trees, respectively. According to Schumacher (1963), the main difference in shoot growth between biennially bearing trees in their bearing and nonbearing years was in

TABLE 8.8

EFFECT OF FRUITING ON SHOOT GROWTH IN APPLE TREES DURING THE
SUCCEEDING YEAR[a]

Amount of fruit crop[b]	Rootstocks					
	M.IX	M.VII	M.II	M.I	M.IV	M.XVI
Low	+ 10	+ 8	+ 18	+ 21	+ 22	+ 17
Medium	− 2	+ 7	− 2	− 7	+ 6	+ 39
High	− 11	− 13	− 36	− 25	− 20	− 21

[a] Data are means for 25 years, 1929–1954, for Lane's Prince Albert on different rootstocks. Data are given as meters per tree above or below previous year. From Rogers and Booth (1964).

[b] Low fruit crop = more than 20% below the 5-year running mean yield for each rootstock; high fruit crop = more than 20% above the 5-year running mean yield for each rootstock.

TABLE 8.9

Correlation Coefficients for Fruit Yield of Apple Trees
and Amount of Shoot Growth in the Same Year and in the
Following Year[a]

Rootstock	Fruit yield and shoot growth in same year	Fruit yield and shoot growth in following year
M.IX	0.05	− 0.53[b]
M.VII	− 0.22	− 0.47[c]
M.I	− 0.12	− 0.47[c]
M.II	− 0.17	− 0.62[d]
M.IV	− 0.20	− 0.45[c]
M.XVI	− 0.06	− 0.27

[a] Data for 25 years, 1929–1954. From Rogers and Booth (1964). [b] Significant at 1% level. [c] Significant at 5% level. [d] Significant at 0.1% level.

the amount of second flushing of shoots by each group. During a non-bearing year more than one fifth of the shoots produced a second growth flush, whereas in the bearing year only 3.5% of the shoots flushed twice. Trees that bore fruit annually produced second growth flushes on 8% of the shoots.

Maggs (1963) removed blossoms from 2-year-old apple trees at the time of flowering or removed fruits on May 30. After blossoms were removed, the trees increased more in dry weight and produced more and larger leaves and larger stems than did fruiting trees (Fig. 8.30). Removal of fruits also resulted in stimulation of cambial growth.

As may be seen in Table 8.10 diversion of metabolites to reproductive tissues greatly altered the growth balance of the rest of the tree. Fruiting trees had about 50% more foliage in proportion to total vegetative growth and 50% less root system than deblossomed trees. Although the fruiting trees were more leafy than nonfruiting trees, they produced more total dry matter per unit of leaf surface in vegetative and reproductive growth than did nonfruiting trees.

Barlow (1966) showed in deblossoming experiments that fruiting in apple trees decreased both the number of long shoots and their proportion of all shoots in a tree. The effect of fruiting was much less severe on initiation of shoot growth than on its continuation. Barlow's data indicated that severe competition between fruit and shoot meristems began only when the fruitlets began to develop actively (Tables 8.11, 8.12).

Avery (1969) reported an overall inhibitory effect of fruiting in apple trees

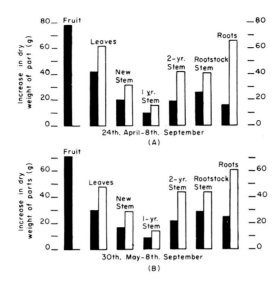

FIG. 8.30. Dry weight increment of parts of cropping apple trees (black bars) and noncropping trees (open bars). (A) From deblossoming on April 24 to September 12; (B) from defruiting on May 30 to September 12. [From Maggs (1963).]

on shoot growth of the tree as a whole. In addition he found that growth of individual shoots was influenced by the proximity of fruits, with decreased leaf size the first observed effect of fruiting.

Mochizuki (1962) investigated growth, carbohydrate distribution, and mineral relations of 9-year-old apple trees. In 1957 half of the experimental trees were deflorated at blossom time, and in 1958 the remaining trees were similarly treated. Root and cambial growth were reduced rapidly and markedly by fruiting, whereas the effects on shoot and leaf growth were delayed and less pronounced.

As may be seen in Table 8.13 root and cambial growth of apple trees were significantly decreased in 1957 by fruiting whereas shoot and leaf growth were not. In 1958, however, shoot growth of the trees which bore fruit in 1957 was reduced over that of trees not producing fruit in 1957. In 1957 the starch content of leaves and twigs did not vary significantly between bearing and nonbearing trees. In contrast, the roots of fruiting trees had a reduced starch content beginning in mid-June.

Mochizuki (1962) treated bearing and nonbearing apple trees with $^{14}CO_2$ on four dates (June 3, July 7, July 30, and August 25) corresponding to 26, 60, 83, and 109 days after normal flowering time. After the June 3 treatment, most of the photosynthate was distributed to the leaves and the remainder

TABLE 8.10

EFFECT OF REMOVAL OF BLOSSOMS OR FRUITS FROM 1-YEAR-OLD APPLE TREES ON
DISTRIBUTION OF VEGETATIVE INCREMENT[a]

	Percent distribution of vegetative growth					
	Leaves	New stem	1-Year-stem	2-Year stem	Rootstock	Roots
Deblossomed trees	24	12	6	16	16	26
Fruiting trees	32	15	7	14	20	12
Defruited trees	20	12	6	19	18	25
Fruiting trees (May 30–Sept. 8)	23	13	7	17	22	18

[a] From Maggs (1963).

to other plant parts. It was already evident in June that small roots of
flowering trees had slightly lower carbohydrate levels than deflorated trees.
These differences were accentuated after subsequent deflorating treatments.
After July 7, there was considerably more photosynthate in roots of bearing
trees than of nonbearing ones. These differences became even greater after
the July 30 and August 25 deflorating treatments. Following the last treatment to bearing trees, most of the carbohydrates were supplied to the fruits.
When the rapidly growing fruits were mobilizing large amounts of available
carbohydrates, the roots and main stem received proportionally much less
than the leaves of fruiting over nonfruiting trees, but this was not adequate
to supply the added requirements of the developing fruits. The growth
inhibition of small roots in fruiting trees already began in June of the bearing
year and was correlated with reduction in available carbohydrates at that

TABLE 8.11

PERCENTAGE OF LONG SHOOTS ON TWO VARIETIES OF DEBLOSSOMED AND BEARING APPLE
TREES[a]

		Deblossomed trees		Bearing trees	
Variety	Year	Heavy pruning	Light pruning	Heavy pruning	Light pruning
Worcester	1964	35	32	4	1
	1965	29	28	8	5
Cox	1964	15	11	12	6
	1965	27	17	11	5

[a] From Barlow (1966).

TABLE 8.12

EFFECT OF FRUIT BEARING IN APPLE TREES ON NUMBER OF LONG SHOOTS[a] PER TREE AND
AVERAGE SHOOT LENGTH DURING 1958–1963[b]

	Deblossomed trees		Bearing trees	
	Heavy pruning	Light pruning	Heavy pruning	Light pruning
On M.XVI rootstocks				
Number	1817	2901	1450	1664
Length (cm)	49	24	47	23
On M.IX rootstocks				
Number	924	992	213	197
Length (cm)	20	14	13	10

[a] Greater than 3 inches long.
[b] From Barlow (1966)

time. Nitrogen and potassium in small roots were available in excess at the time when root growth was first reduced.

Lenz (1967) demonstrated strong dominance of fruit growth over vegetative development of Washington Navel orange. Experiments with rooted plants carrying 0, 1, 2, or 3 orange fruits showed that increased number of orange fruits resulted in reduced vegetative development. Furthermore, reduction in leaf area by defoliation 4 weeks after fruit set depressed vegetative growth more than it inhibited fruit development. The balance between vegetative and reproductive growth also affected fruit quality.

Forest Trees

Blais (1952) measured several thousand shoots of flowering and non-flowering *Abies balsamea* trees. The shoots of flowering trees averaged 0.9 inches in length, and those of nonflowering trees averaged 2.0 inches. Branches of flowering trees had almost twice as many buds per unit length of branches as nonflowering trees. Because of heavy flower production in 1947 up to half of the vegetative buds on some flowering trees failed to develop and the shoots which grew were short and had poorly developed needles. In contrast, on nonflowering trees most vegetative buds developed normally.

Morris (1951) demonstrated that trees produced heavy seed crops in alternate years. During each seed year both shoot growth and radial growth were inhibited. There were deviations from the general pattern, however,

TABLE 8.13

Distribution of Dry Weight in Fruiting and Nonfruiting (Deflorated) Apple Trees during 1957, the Year of Fruiting, and 1958, the Year following Fruiting[a]

	1957											
	Nonfruiting trees							Fruiting trees				
	Apr. 10	May 28	June 18	July 28	Sept. 1	Oct. 15	Nov. 15	June 18	July 28	Sept. 1	Oct. 15	Nov. 15
Leaves	—	2.5	15.4	15.6	11.1	8.5	9.3	20.6	15.1	9.2	7.7	9.1
Shoots	—	0.6	4.3	7.1	6.8	7.6	7.7	4.0	7.7	5.5	9.2	6.7
Branches and trunk	64.7	59.5	55.8	52.1	56.4	57.6	57.7	50.1	47.7	54.3	47.5	53.5
Roots	35.3	37.4	24.5	25.3	25.9	26.4	25.4	23.1	23.2	16.0	19.9	18.8
Fruits	—	—	—	—	—	—	—	2.1	6.3	14.9	15.2	21.9

	1958							
	Nonfruiting trees in 1957				Trees fruiting in 1957			
	Apr. 15	May 25	June 25	July 26	Apr. 15	May 25	June 25	July 26
Leaves	—	8.2	14.8	14.2	—	9.0	9.2	9.4
Shoots	—	—	1.9	3.9	—	—	1.0	3.2
Branches and trunk	69.0	64.1	57.8	56.6	77.0	68.8	67.7	65.0
Roots	20.9	27.7	25.5	24.9	23.0	22.2	22.1	22.5

[a] Dry weight in various plant parts is given in percent of total. From Mochizuki (1962).

during the drought years of 1921, 1923, 1926, and 1946 when very little radial growth occurred.

Within individual trees foliage production was low in the parts of the crown that flowered profusely (Morris, 1951). More foliage was produced in 1946 than 1945. As may be seen in Table 8.14 the increase was much greater on flowering than nonflowering trees. Production of foliage also was reduced in 1947 over 1946. However, flowering trees in 1947 produced only 27% as much foliage as in 1946, while foliage production in nonflowering trees was reduced to only 84% of the 1946 values.

Years of abundant cone production in *Pseudotsuga menziesii, Abies grandis,* and *Pinus monticola* were correlated with low xylem production. No relation was found between ring width and size of cone crop in prior to later years. This suggested that the carbohydrates mobilized in

TABLE 8.14

Foliage Production of *Abies balsamea* in Two Successive Years[a,b]

	(1) 1946/1945		(2) 1947/1946	
	Flowering	Nonflowering	Flowering	Nonflowering
Number of shoots	144	120	91	118
Length of shoots	110	104	46	78
No. needles per shoot	114	102	67	88
Length of needles	112	107	66	93
Weight per needle	110	101	45	81
Weight of needles per shoot	125	103	30	71
Total weight of needles	180	124	27	84

[a] In (1) flower production was negligible in the later year and light in the earlier (1946/1945) whereas in (2) flower production was heavy in the later year and negligible in the earlier (1947/1946). Amounts of foliage for the later year are given in percent of those for the earlier year.

[b] From Morris (1951).

reproductive growth largely represented currently produced photosynthate (Eis, Garman, and Ebell, 1965).

Tappeiner (1969) studied the effect of cone production on vegetative growth of 35- to 50-year-old *Pseudotsuga menziesii* trees. In 1962, which was an excellent seed year, the cone-bearing trees produced from 450 to 2500 cones per tree. By comparison, in 1965 which was a light seed year, the same trees produced only 50 to 460 cones per tree. In cone producing trees, shoot and needle elongation was less in 1962 and 1965 than in 1961, 1963, or 1964 (Fig. 8.31). Cone crops, as evidenced by peduncle remains, always were associated with restricted shoot and needle growth (Fig. 8.32). Cambial growth also was greatly reduced by the heavy 1962 cone crop. However, the light cone crop of 1965 did not cause a conspicuous reduction in xylem increment. The reduction of shoot and needle growth in 1962 and 1965 apparently was caused largely by cone production and not by other factors, such as weather. This conclusion was supported by the observation that growth of trees which did not produce cones in 1962 and 1965 did not differ from their growth in 1961, 1963, or 1964.

Data are also available on suppression of vegetative growth by reproductive growth in angiosperm forest trees. During good seed years, for example, the width of annual rings in *Fagus sylvatica* was reduced to about half of that in years of low seed production. Heavy seed production also reduced xylem increment for 2 years thereafter (Holmsgaard, 1962).

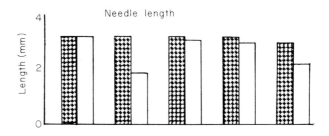

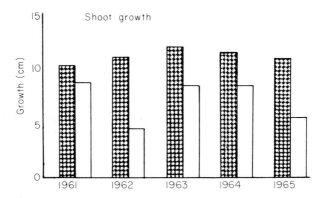

FIG. 8.31. Needle length and shoot elongation on cone-bearing (open bars) and non-bearing (shaded bars) of *Pseudotsuga menziesii* trees from 1961–1965. [From Tappeiner (1969).]

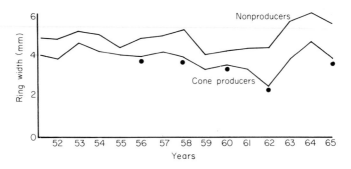

FIG. 8.32. Xylem ring width at breast height on cone-producing and nonproducing *Pseudotsuga menziesii* trees from 1961 to 1965. The black dots indicate cone years. [From Tappeiner (1969).]

Suggested Collateral Reading

Biale, J. B. (1958). Postharvest physiology and biochemistry of fruits. *Annu. Rev. Plant Physiol.* **1**, 183–206.

Biale, J. B. (1960). The postharvest biochemistry of tropical and subtropical fruits. *Adv. Food Res.* **10**, 293–354.

Cooper, W. C., Rasmussen, G. K., Rogers, B. J., Reece, P. C. and Henry, W. H. (1968). Control of abscission in agricultural crops and its physiological basis. *Plant Physiol* **43**. Part B, 1560–1576.

Dickmann, D. I. and Kozlowski, T. T. (1969). Seasonal growth patterns of *Pinus resinosa* Ait. pistillate strobili in central Wisconsin. *Can. J. Bot.* **47**, 839–848.

Esau, K. (1965). "Plant Anatomy." Chapters 19 and 20. Wiley, New York.

Fowells, H. A. (1965). Silvics of forest trees of the United States. *U.S. Forest Service, Agriculture Handbook No.* **271**.

Hansen, E. (1966). Postharvest physiology of fruits. *Annu. Rev. Plant Physiol.* **17**, 459–480.

Kozlowski, T. T. and Keller, T. (1966). Food relations of woody plants. *Bot. Rev.* **32**, 293–382.

Kramer, P. J. and Kozlowski, T. T. (1960). "Physiology of Trees." Chapter 13. McGraw-Hill, New York.

Leopold, A. C. (1964). "Plant Growth and Development." Chapters 15–17. McGraw-Hill, New York.

Maheshwari, P. (1950). "An Introduction to the Embryology of Angiosperms." McGraw-Hill, New York.

Maheshwari, P. (Ed.) (1963). "Recent Advances in the Embryology of Angiosperms." Catholic Press, Ranchi, India.

Nitsch, J. P. (1965). Physiology of flower and fruit development. *Encycl. Plant Physiol.* **15**. Part 1: 1537–1647.

Owens, J. N. and Smith, F. H. (1964). The initiation and early development of the seed cone on Douglas-fir. *Can. J. Bot.* **42**, 1031–1047.

Owens, J. N. and Smith, F. H. (1965). Development of the seed cone of Douglas-fir following dormancy. *Can. J. Bot.* **43**, 317–332.

Powell, G. R. (1970). Postdormancy development and growth of microsporangiate and megasporangiate strobili of *Abies balsamea*. *Can. J. Bot.* **48**, 419–428.

Roy Chowdhury, C. (1962). The embryogeny of conifers: a review. *Phytomorphology*, **12**, 313–338.

Chapter 9

CONTROL OF REPRODUCTIVE GROWTH

Introduction

As mentioned in Chapter 3, Volume I, once the juvenile stage of growth is passed and the capacity for reproductive growth is achieved by a tree, it is usually retained thereafter. Nevertheless, fruit and seed production of many adult trees is disturbingly irregular. Failure of a fruit or seed crop in adult trees often results from internal blocks at one of the sequential phases of reproductive growth, such as floral induction, flowering, pollination fertilization, embryo growth, or fruit and seed ripening.

Although much is known about combinations of environmental factors which favor various stages of reproductive growth, the specific nature of the internal controls through which environmental effects are mediated is not understood as well. It is well known, however, that development of flowers and fruits involves a series of physiological signals which sequentially regulate the differentiation of tissues and organs, growth of each of these, and cessation of growth as each reaches maturity. The complexity of these interrelated events may be illustrated by growth of an ovary into a fruit. First, the ovary receives a signal to grow as the flower develops until bloom. Then a signal causes slowing or stopping of growth until pollination occurs. At that time a signal stimulates another surge of growth which continues until the time of embryo growth (e.g., in stone fruits), at which time growth may again slow down or cease. Following embryo enlargement, fruit growth is again stimulated until maturity when yet another signal terminates growth (Leopold, 1962). The ultimate success of the reproductive phase depends on maintaining source-sink relations which favor mobilization of metabolites to various reproductive tissues at decisive stages of their development.

This chapter will discuss some aspects of internal and external control of reproductive growth at critical stages of development. It will also review some practical methods for stimulating fruit and seed production by trees.

Floral Induction

The shoot tip carries out the sequential morphogenic steps which produce stem and leaves. At a given internal signal the genes which control the production of leaves and stem are turned off and those for controlling flower induction turned on.

Induction of flower buds in deciduous fruit trees begins shortly after the leaves form and development of the buds continues throughout the growing season and during the winter. Flower formation in fruit trees depends on an adequate leaf surface. In apples, for example, strong positive correlations exist between the presence of subtending leaves and floral differentiation even though leaves are present at adjacent nodes, indicating a highly localized effect. That currently produced leaf products are required for floral initiation is shown by experiments in which flowers form in girdled branches only when a critical minimum number of leaves is present. An increase in the number of leaves is reflected in differentiation of more flowers (Davis, 1957).

Floral induction is influenced by light intensity and is associated with high rates of photosynthesis, long days, and high levels of nutrition. The tendency for floral induction is high when adequate nitrogen and high carbohydrate levels occur in branches (Shoemaker and Teskey, 1959). It appears doubtful, however, that leaves and fruits influence floral induction solely by regulating carbohydrate supply. Rather it is more likely that complex hormonal controls, involving balances of growth promoters and growth inhibitors, are involved in such regulation. There is considerable evidence that initiation of flower buds depends on a supply of metabolites in excess of requirements of shoots, fruits, and roots and this is mediated by an hormonal system (Jackson, 1969).

Although carbohydrate and nitrogen levels of trees are greatly influenced by alternate bearing, the data of Lewis, Coggins, and Hield (1964) for mandarin leaves suggested that they are not directly responsible for the repetitive cycle of bearing followed by no bearing. As may be seen in Table 9.1 carbohydrate levels of leaves were correlated with the bearing cycle and fruit production. In the spring of 1962, after the 1961–1962 crop had been harvested, starch levels in leaves of trees that had produced a small number of fruits were approximately twice as high as those of trees with large crops. Trees that produced large crops in 1961 did not flower or set crops in 1962; the reverse was true of trees that failed to produce fruit in 1961. By the autumn of 1962 the leaves of trees that had low starch content and failed to set a 1962 crop had approximately double the starch concentration of trees with a large fruit crop in 1962. The effects of fruiting on nitrogen generally were similar to those on carbohydrates. A heavy bearing year depleted nitrogen reserves so they were not adequate for a crop the following

TABLE 9.1

RELATIONS BETWEEN BIENNIAL FRUIT PRODUCTION IN *Citrus reticulata* AND CARBOHYDRATE AND NITROGEN CONTENTS OF LEAVES[a,b]

Sampled in Spring, 1962

Orchard	Starch			Total sugar			Nitrogen		
	On 1961	Off 1961	On 1961 + NAA	On 1961	Off 1961	On 1961 + NAA	On 1961	Off 1961	On 1961 + NAA
Stonehill	18.3	26.9	—	22.8	28.8	—	1.59	1.95	—
Seaview	27.7	54.5	37.4	31.9	34.3	31.8	1.69	1.97	1.91
Pettis	38.6	87.2	—	35.5	42.4	—	1.83	2.17	—

Sampled in Fall, 1962

Orchard	Starch			Total sugar			Nitrogen		
	On 1961	Off 1961	On 1962 + NAA	On 1962	Off 1962	On 1962 + NAA	On[c] 1962	Off[c] 1962	On 1962[c] + NAA
Stonehill	60.2	30.2	29.4	38.7	30.1	29.6	—	—	—
Seaview	15.9	6.5	6.8	28.5	24.3	30.4	1.72	1.88	1.88
Pettis	40.2	23.0	—	34.5	27.5	—	—	—	—

[a] Carbohydrates are expressed as milligrams of glucose per gram of fresh weight and N values as percent of dry weight.

[b] From Lewis, Coggins, and Hield (1964).

[c] Sampled in spring, 1963.

year. When there was no significant fruit competition, the reserves in the leaves increased and a heavy crop of fruit followed.

When naphthalepeacetic acid (NAA) was applied to mandarin trees in the spring of the bearing year it thinned the crops and stimulated fruit production during the subsequent off-year. Yet NAA treatment did not significantly affect carbohydrate levels. These observations emphasized that although carbohydrate and nitrogen levels were greatly influenced by alternate bearing, the control of such alternation appeared to be linked to a hormone-sensitive regulatory mechanism in the tree (Lewis, Coggins, and Hield, 1964).

Fulford (1962, 1965, 1966a,b,c) studied various aspects of floral induction in apple trees. He reported that the activity of the apical meristem and subsequent development of primordia into bud scales were controlled by self-regulating mechanisms. The rate of production of primordia was controlled by the younger leaf primordia in the bud which themselves were controlled by the foliage. The apical meristem itself was controlled by inhibitory influences of adjacent primordia. The foliage did not control the apical meristems for that would have caused its maximum inhibition and limit the production of primordia during the time when leaves were rapidly expanding —the reverse of what actually happened. The inhibitory effect of the adjacent primordia was related to their metabolism and therefore was affected by environmental influences, as was the apical meristem. An increased activity of the apical meristem was balanced through increased inhibition by the adjacent primordia. The inhibitory effect of the youngest primordia depended on how much they were inhibited by older primordia. The expanding foliage influenced the youngest primordia directly during early phases of bud development, but at later stages the foliage influenced only the older primordia in the bud (compare a, b, and c, Fig. 9.1). The influence of foliage leaves varied with seasonal influences and with interaction of other parts of the tree.

Fulford (1962) showed that in biennially bearing apple trees the fruits produced a factor which prevented buds from becoming fruit buds. Flower induction in the biennially fruiting variety Miller's Seedling apple occurred after the spur leaves had stopped expanding. The developing fruits slowed down the rate of development of spur buds after early June. Removal of fruits after mid-June caused rapid acceleration in rate of production of primordia in the buds. Fulford (1966c) also noted that failure to form flowers on fruiting trees was associated with occurrence of a long plastochron (time interval between initiation of two successive leaf primordia) in buds. He concluded that absence of flower formation on fruiting trees involved hormonal controls rather than a competitive effect of the fruit for nutrients. He suggested that the long plastochron was due to the inhibitory effect of

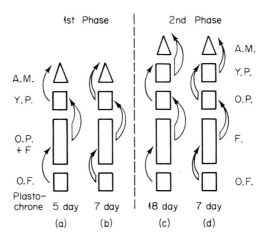

FIG. 9.1. Model of control of production of primordia in apple buds. The arrows indicate the inhibitory effect of organs on each other. The thickness of the arrow represents degrees of inhibition. A.M. = apical meristem; Y.P. = adjacent primordia; O.P. = older primordia; F. = expanding foliage; O.F. = other parts of the tree. [From Fulford (1965).]

the fruit on older primordia of the bud, an effect which did not occur until after the resting buds had begun to form.

Pollination

Voluminous evidence is available which illustrates the importance of pollination to the development of viable seeds. For example, the large proportion of empty seeds in *Betula verrucosa*, *B. pubescens*, and *Picea abies* resulted largely from lack of fertilization because of incomplete pollination. Similarly, low viability of *Liriodendron tulipifera* seeds appears to result from lack of fertilization caused by ineffective pollination during the brief receptive period of the stigma. Boyce and Kaeiser (1961) found normal development of ovules, embryo sacs, and egg cells in this species. Pollen formed normally, and the tube nucleus and two sperm cells were structurally normal. When pollination was ineffective, the embryo sac disintegrated and left a cavity in the nucellus. Finally, in late summer, disintegration of the nucellus resulted in an empty seed consisting of a seedcoat plus nucellar remains. The importance of pollination is also emphasized by the observation that if ovules of gymnosperms are left unpollinated they gradually collapse, mostly during the first growing season. Furthermore, the female strobilus as a whole often deteriorates from insufficient pollination and usually abscises during the first growing season or at the beginning of the second (Sarvas, 1962).

The majority of economically important trees must be cross pollinated. Some deciduous orchard varieties, such as sweet cherries and many varieties of plum, are self-sterile and many varieties of apples and pears are partially so. Self-sterility may result from a number of causes including (1) bearing of staminate and pistillate flowers on separate plants, (2) sterility of pollen, (3) giving off of pollen too late to fertilize eggs of the same variety or before the pistils become receptive, and (4) inability of pollen of self-incompatible clonal varieties to fertilize eggs of the same varieties (e.g., many varieties of plum, cherry, and almond).

Self-incompatibility varies in degree. Most varieties of peach are completely self-compatible and set as much fruit from self-pollination as from cross pollination. As most varieties of apple, pear, plum, and sweet cherry are self-unfruitful and require cross pollination, it is customary to interplant pollinizer varieties among them. Bees must first visit such a pollinizer before they can pollinate the flowers of the main variety with compatible pollen. Many varieties of fruit trees which will set fruit from self-pollination will set more fruit from cross pollination with compatible varieties.

Fertilization

Transport of the male cell to the egg cell represents a very critical process in reproduction. Ultimate success in seed and fruit production depends on growth of the pollen tube to the ovary and occurrence of syngamy followed by embryo development. Barriers to crossability are well known and include (1) failure of pollen grains to germinate on the stigma, (2) bursting of pollen tubes in the style, (3) failure of tubes to grow through the style, and (4) slow growth of pollen tubes so they do not reach the ovules before flowers abscise. Sometimes pollen tubes enter the embryo sac but sterility may result from lack of fusion of male gamete and egg nucleus, or inhibition of subsequent embryo development (Johri and Vasil, 1961). Information on the nature of pollen incompatibility is not extensive but some evidence shows that expression of incompatibility reactions is linked to protein metabolism. Incompatibility can often be reduced or eliminated by changing the temperature regime of the pistil before or after pollination, removal of floral parts, irradiation of the pistil, or by use of various chemicals (Rosen, 1968).

It is common practice to determine pollen viability *in vitro* to estimate probability of success when pollen is applied to the stigma. Such tests have limitations, however, as maximum growth of pollen tubes *in vitro* is generally less than the amount that would be required for the pollen tubes to reach the ovule and for fertilization to occur. A number of external and internal factors influence the rate of growth of the pollen tube, with the response varying with species of pollen and its pretreatment. Factors which influence pollen germination are those which control amount and activity of pollen enzymes. Stanley (1967) divided the factors influencing *in vitro* growth of pollen tubes into primary factors (those which must be present in the medium and within a narrow optimum range) and secondary ones (those whose concentration can vary over a wide range or when added to the medium will increase pollen tube growth only slightly). Stanley included temperature, moisture, pH, oxygen, osmotic pressure, cations, anions, and carbohydrates as primary factors. He considered secondary factors to be growth hormones, CO_2, micronutrients, and irradiation. The most important factors influencing *in vivo* growth of pollen are chemicals in the pollen, chemistry and structure of the tissue through which the pollen tube grows, and numbers and types of pollen present. Moisture and temperature are major environmental factors influencing pollen tube growth. Boron affects pollen germination and tube elongation more than any known hormone, vitamin, or chemical. According to Johri and Vasil (1961), the effect of boron may involve promotion of absorption and metabolism of sugars by forming sugar–borate complexes, increasing oxygen uptake, and participating in synthesis of pectic materials for walls of elongating pollen tubes.

Internal Requirements for Reproductive Growth

Internal requirements for growth of flowers and fruits include carbohydrates, minerals, hormonal growth regulators, and water. These will be discussed separately.

CARBOHYDRATES

Growing reproductive tissues mobilize large amounts of carbohydrates. Although flowers usually do not synthesize foods, they may represent a significant drain on those produced elsewhere. For example, expansion of flowers in *Aleurites*, which was initiated before vegetative growth, consumed carbohydrate reserves (Sell and Johnston, 1949). Some idea of the drain of flowering on available food may be gained from Ovington's (1963) observation that spring production of catkins in *Populus tremuloides* was equal in dry weight to approximately one fourth of the dry weight of annual foliage production. The massive drain on carbohydrates by fruits was emphasized by Shaw (1934). Individual Rhode Island greening apple trees produced 364 pounds of fruit during a 32-year period, or an average of 11.4 pounds annually. Heinicke (1937) estimated that over a third of the total photosynthate of apple trees was diverted into fruit growth.

When a fruit is set, it becomes a powerful sink which can mobilize large amounts of carbohydrates from vegetative tissues. Some green fruits carry on limited photosynthesis but usually they do not appear to supply more than a very small amount of the food required for their own development. For example, photosynthesis by green fruits of lemons, orange, avocado, apple, grape, and plum was too low to contribute appreciably to their own growth (Bean and Todd, 1960; Todd, Bean, and Propst, 1961; Kidd and West, 1947; Van der Meer and Wassink, 1962; Kriedemann, 1968b). Photosynthesis by rapidly expanding green strobili of *Pinus resinosa* was not adequate to balance their high respiratory evolution of CO_2. Thus, most of the carbohydrates incorporated into strobili which were growing rapidly were mobilized from other sources (Dickmann and Kozlowski, 1970b).

Both reserve and currently produced carbohydrates are used by developing fruits. In *Fagus*, *Persea*, and *Citrus*, large amounts of carbohydrate reserves were mobilized from twigs and branches by developing fruits (Gäumann, 1935; Cameron and Borst, 1938; Cameron and Schroeder, 1945). By comparison, the high carbohydrate demands of apple fruits were reported to be supplied directly by current photosynthesis (Murneek, 1933). Almost 90% of the ^{14}C taken up by apple leaves was translocated to adjacent fruits (Hansen, 1967).

Reproductive growth of some forest trees has been shown to utilize large amounts of carbohydrate reserves, Gäumann (1935) estimated that during a year of heavy seed production the reproductive tissues of *Fagus* trees required 40–50 times as much reserve food as did the leafy branches.

Stone fruits are particularly strong sinks for photosynthetic assimilates. For example, in the early growth stages of both peach (*Prunus persica*) and apricot (*Prunus armeniaca*) the developing fruits competed successfully with nearby expanding foliage for current photosynthate. Even when stone fruits were completely ripe they acted as the major carbohydrate sink (Kriedemann, 1968a). The strong carbohydrate-mobilizing capacity of fruits was also emphasized by the observation of Cannell and Huxley (1969) that during the dry season in Kenya, practically all the ^{14}C-assimilates were translocated into fruits of *Coffea arabica* trees.

As may be seen in Fig. 9.2 the primary difference in the starch cycle of fruiting branches of three cultivars of peach trees which matured fruits at different times was variation in starch level as fruits approached harvest. The decrease in starch content in Coronado and Elberta trees, the slowing down of starch accumulation in Corona trees prior to harvest, and large starch increase subsequent to harvest were interpreted as demonstrating preferential use of photosynthate by the ripening fruits. The cultivar which matured its fruit earliest showed the greatest preharvest starch decrease, whereas the latest maturing cultivars showed the lowest decrease.

There sometimes is considerable competition for carbohydrates among

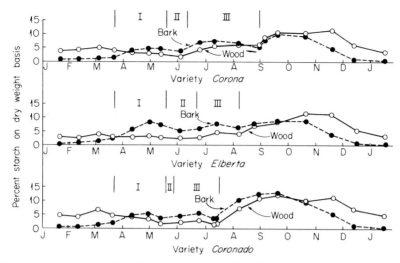

Fig. 9.2. Seasonal variations in starch content of fruiting branches of three varieties of peach trees which matured fruits at different times. Three stages in fruit growth are shown by numerals I, II, and III. Date of harvest is indicated by short vertical arrows. [From Ryugo and Davis (1959).]

young and old fruits on the same tree. For example, in Southern California Valencia orange trees flower and set fruit while the previous fruit crop is still on the tree. The mature fruit crop often remains on the tree for as long as 5 months before it is harvested. Such "on-tree" storage tends to accentuate alternate bearing and to decrease yield of the crop following the late harvest (Jones and Cree, 1954). As may be seen in Table 9.2 late harvesting of oranges resulted in lower fruit production than did consistent early or mid-season removal of the fruit crop. The time of harvesting also affected fruit

TABLE 9.2

INFLUENCE OF TIME OF HARVESTING OF VALENCIA ORANGES ON YIELD PER TREE[a]

Time of harvest[b]	Fruits per Tree		Packed boxes per tree	Percent "fancy" fruit by volume
	Number	Pounds		
Early	1,017	294	3.63	70.8
Midseason	815	244	3.03	67.2
Late	707	204	2.47	56.4

[a] Data are averages for 12 years [From Jones and Cree (1954).]

[b] Picking dates varied slightly from year to year. Main picking dates were: early, June 4; midseason, July 24; and late, September 21.

quality. No significant decrease in fruit quality was shown from early to midseason harvest, but a late harvest caused a significant decrease in the quality of subsequent crops. Jones *et al.* (1964) showed that when both old and young fruits were on the tree at the same time, there was considerable competition among them for available carbohydrates. The old fruits used up carbohydrates in respiration and growth. Late harvesting of fruits reduced available carbohydrates in the leaves, and this effect was apparent several months after the fruits were removed (Table 9.3). Hence, the earlier the fruit crop was removed, the greater was the amount of carbohydrates available for the next crop.

MINERALS

Much evidence shows that minerals are involved in all major phases of reproductive growth, including initiation of floral primordia, setting of a fruit crop, controlling the growth rate of fruit and its size at harvest, and influencing mature fruits by affecting quality and preharvest drop. A balanced supply of minerals ensures normal development of reproductive tissues primarily by maintaining a large, physiologically active leaf surface which in turn produces the metabolites and growth regulators required for development of flowers, fruits, and seeds.

The important key nutrient for reproductive growth of orchard trees is nitrogen. In most regions, and especially on sandy areas, enough nitrogen

TABLE 9.3

FRESH WEIGHT AND CARBOHYDRATE CONTENT OF VALENCIA ORANGE TREES AS INFLUENCED BY THE TIME OF FRUIT REMOVAL[a]

Leaf weight and carbohydrate components	Date of fruit removal in 1961			Significance
	May 25	July 25	October 4	
Fresh wt./20 leaves (g)	0.844	0.734	0.758	[b]
Reducing sugar (% DW)	3.95	3.64	3.56	[b]
Sucrose (% DW)	3.96	3.79	3.79	NS
Total sugar (% DW)	7.91	7.43	7.35	[b]
Starch (% DW)	2.64	2.78	2.82	[c]
Starch (mg/leaf)	8.78	8.24	8.76	NS
Total carbohydrate (mg/leaf)	35.74	31.29	31.96	[b]

[a] Trees were sampled January 25, 1962 [From Jones *et al.* (1964),]
[b] Significant at 1% level.
[c] Significant at 5% level.
NS Not significant

TABLE 9.4

Distribution of Total Nitrogen in Grams in Organs of the Apple Spur System of Two Apple Varieties at Various Times During the Growing Season[a]

| | May 1 | May 15 | | June 15 | July 15 | | |
	Control	Control	Deblossomed (April 15)	Control	Control	Deblossomed (April 15)	Defruited (May 15)
Jonathan							
New Growth	0.144	0.112	0.116	0.109	0.127	0.097	0.116
Old growth	0.133	0.142	0.169	0.094	0.133	0.207	0.122
Fruits	0.183	0.828	—	2.670	6.701	—	—
Leaves	0.711	1.121	1.290	0.815	0.814	1.231	0.940
Totals	1.171	2.203	1.575	3.688	7.775	1.535	1.178
Paynes Late Keeper							
New growth	0.128	0.118	0.099	0.148	0.114	0.128	0.123
Old growth	—	0.143	0.123	0.109	0.093	0.142	0.117
Fruits	0.071	0.586	—	2.010	4.385	—	—
Leaves	0.535	0.859	0.971	0.907	0.796	1.283	1.058
Totals	0.734	1.706	1.193	3.174	1.553	1.553	1.298

[a] From Murneek (1925).

is lost by leaching to reduce it to a critical level of deficiency. Hence, it must be replaced annually. Potash, magnesium, and boron probably are next in importance for reproductive growth, but other nutrient elements also may be deficient in some areas.

During early development of apple spurs, nitrogen reserves of the tree are used in large quantities by leaves and in lesser amounts by flowers and fruits. Later in the season the leaves become the main source of nitrogen for the rapidly developing fruits. According to Murneek (1925), of some 50 lb of nitrogen taken up per acre by bearing apple trees, almost half eventually found its way into the fruit crop. This approximated two thirds of the amount of nitrogen that was returned to the soil through leaf fall.

Murneek (1925) found that after flowering there was no significant change in the amount of nitrogen in new or old parts of apple spurs. Leaves took up sufficient nitrogen very early in the season for their development. At the time of flowering over 60% of the total nitrogen was found in the leaves. Removal of blossoms or fruits increased total nitrogen in the older part of the spur, but mostly in the leaves. By July 15, when apple fruits were only half grown, 86 and 82% of the nitrogen in the spur system was localized in the fruits (Table 9.4).

Deficiency of some of the minor elements greatly decreases fruit quality (Fig. 9.3). For example, boron deficiency is associated with internal or external cork formation in apple fruits. Fruits of boron-deficient trees often have lesions and are dwarfed, misshapen, and cracked. The fruits of boron-deficient olive trees become deformed because the mesocarp and exocarp at the end of the fruit do not develop and the endocarp, which is unaffected, protrudes through the apex of the olive. Boron deficiency in pear causes shallow depressions in the fruit surface and corky tissues in the flesh. Severely affected fruits may be misshapen and cracked. The blossoms of boron-deficient trees may not develop fruit (Kienholz, 1942). In apricot, boron deficiency caused internal browning and formation of corky tissues in the pericarp, external cracking, and browning and shriveling of the fruit (Bullock and Bensen, 1948). The importance of minerals for reproductive growth is discussed further in the section on stimulation of reproductive growth.

HORMONAL GROWTH REGULATORS

Leopold (1962) cited evidence indicating that hormonal growth promoters are involved in regulating each step of reproductive growth. For example, auxin which stimulates growth of the flower and floral stalk may come from the ovary of the flower, the base of the inflorescence, and from the flower stalk itself. Pollination of the ovary brings additional auxin to the reproductive structure. Pollen contains auxin and growth of the pollen tube

FIG. 9.3. Advanced copper deficiency symptoms in Comice pear shoots and fruits. Photo courtesy East Malling Research Station.

promotes synthesis of even more auxin. Fruit growth may also require auxin which is synthesized in the seed region of the fruit.

Several hormonal growth regulators play a dominant role in controlling fruit development. For many years auxin alone was considered to regulate growth of fruits. However, more recent data on the natural occurrence of gibberellins, cytokinins, and various growth inhibitors in reproductive tissues, in addition to auxins, emphasize that theories assigning control of fruit growth to auxin alone are no longer adequate. The prevailing view is that fruit growth is controlled by complex interactive influences of several growth regulators including at least auxins, gibberellins, cytokinins, and possibly inhibitors.

As may be seen in Fig. 9.4 peak levels of different hormones are not attained at the same time but occur one after another during fruit growth. Hence, high levels of hormone activity are present, enabling fruits to compete successfully with developing vegetative tissues (Crane, 1969).

Luckwill, Weaver, and MacMillan (1969) reported that apple seeds produced a sequence of different hormones during their development in the

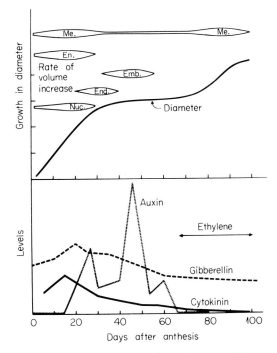

FIG. 9.4. Fruit growth as related to rate of volume increase of its parts and to levels of hormones. The levels of hormones bear no relation to one another but only to time after anthesis. ME = mesocarp; EN = endocarp; NUC = nucellus; END = endosperm; EMB = embryo. [From Crane (1969).]

fruit. The appearance and disappearance of various hormones was related to successive stages of development of the endosperm and embryo. The first stage of seed development, characterized by development of a free nuclear endosperm and negligible embryo growth was associated with presence of cytokinins (Zwar, Bottomley, and Kefford, 1963). This stage was followed by development of the cellular primary endosperm and appearance of two indole auxins (Luckwill, 1957). The second stage of development was associated with rapid growth, digestion of the nucellus and primary endosperm, and formation of a secondary endosperm which formed a sheath around the fully grown embryo. During this stage two gibberellins were present. During the final maturation period of the seed the gibberellin content decreased rapidly (Luckwill, Weaver, and MacMillan, 1969).

Crane and van Overbeek (1965) placed considerable emphasis on the presence of seeds in control of fruit growth. As early as 1936 Tukey showed that the presence of embryos or seeds was critical for normal fruit development in orchard trees. Destruction of peach and cherry embryos affected both the size of fruits and time of fruit ripening. The influence of seeds varied from growth inhibition to stimulation depending on the stage of fruit growth. Whereas early embryo destruction inhibited growth of fruits and sometimes caused their abscission, late destruction (in the third stage of pericarp development) stimulated growth (Tukey, 1936).

Young ovules often influence ovary growth in flower buds but their effect becomes much more apparent after fertilization. Apples with few seeds often fail to achieve normal size, and they tend to abscise early. When seeds are unevenly distributed, the fruit grows irregularly and becomes misshapen. Other evidence for the importance of seeds in fruit growth is provided by correlations between seed number and fruit length or weight of the flesh (Nitsch, 1953). The influence of seeds on fruit development is modified somewhat by leaf area. With an extensive leaf area and high photosynthetic efficiency, comparatively large fruits are often produced in the presence of few seeds (Murneek, 1954).

Crane and van Overbeek (1965) suggested that a major function of the fertilized ovule or seed in fruit growth was to synthesize hormones which initiated and maintained a metabolic gradient along which foods and hormones were translocated from other parts of the plant. Mobilization of metabolites appears to be a general feature of hormonal effects as shown in studies of apical dominance, senescence, and abscission in addition to investigations of fruit growth.

Auxins

It has been shown that auxin occurs in pollen, and during growth of the pollen tube it is produced in the style and ovary. Its importance in fruit growth is also demonstrated by its stimulating influence on growth of the ovary and following its application to some unpollinated plants such as fig and grape. Nevertheless, most species of woody plants do not set fruits following auxin application. Furthermore, fruits set by exogenous auxin applications often grow abnormally. This has been shown for avocado, apple, apricot, and pear fruits.

Because the stimulating effects of auxin on cell enlargement are well known and because increase in size of fruits results primarily from cell expansion, much early emphasis was placed on auxin alone in regulation of fruit growth. The importance of auxin was supported by evidence of high correlations between fruit size and seed development as well as increase in volume growth of some fruits in response to exogenous auxins. For example, application of auxins to species such as apricot, blackberry, grape, orange, and prune stimulated fruit growth (Crane and Brooks, 1952; Marth and Meader, 1944; Weaver and Williams, 1950; Stewart and Hield, 1950; Harris and Hansen, 1955). The size and shape of some fruits, including grape, pear, apple, and blueberry are highly correlated with seed number. In strawberry the growth of fruits is closely related to the number of achenes present (Nitsch, 1950).

As mentioned, a substantial body of evidence indicates that auxin alone does not control fruit growth. For example, in apple, grape, and peach the variations in total seed auxins were not well correlated with sigmoid growth curves of fruits (Luckwill, 1948; Coombe, 1960; Nitsch *et al.*, 1960; Stahly and Thomson, 1959). In *Vitis*, correlations between auxin levels, moristematic activity in seeds, and growth of fruits existed in stage I only. Coombe (1960) related the enlargement of fruits in subsequent stages to their mobilization of carbohydrates, which in turn caused osmotic water uptake. Fruit growth appeared to be controlled more by levels of gibberellins than by auxins, or by synergistic effects of both. Crane (1964) summarized the state of knowledge of auxin effects on fruit growth. He pointed out that the physiologically important "bound" auxins were largely ignored in early studies. Furthermore, the auxin assays used in early studies of fruit growth obscured the possible role of inhibitors in reproductive growth. Even the methods of auxin extraction had limitations. It now appears that the early overemphasis on auxin as the sole hormonal controller of fruit growth tended to obscure the role of other important hormonal substances in fruit development.

Gibberellins

In recent years the importance of gibberellins on fruit growth has been emphasized. Fruits of some species such as fig, pear, apple, and currant can be set with auxin, but they can be set as well or better with gibberellins. Furthermore, gibberellins increase fruit set in plants, such as *Citrus*, whereas auxin is generally ineffective (Soost and Burnett, 1961; Hield, Coggins, and Garber, 1965).

Gibberellins have been useful in producing parthenocarpic stone fruits whereas auxins generally are ineffective (Primer and Crane, 1957; Crane, Primer, and Campbell, 1960; Crane, Rebeiz, and Campbell, 1961). Whereas applied gibberellin induced parthenocarphy in *Rosa arvensis*, auxin did not. Synergistic effects between gibberellin and naphthaleneacetamide in producing parthenocarpic *Rosa spinosissima* fruits have been shown (Jackson and Prosser, 1959). Gibberellin-like growth regulators have been demonstrated in peach fruits where they influence endocarp development and regulate cell division and enlargement of the mesocarp (Bradley and Crane, 1962; Crane, Primer, and Campbell, 1960; Crane, Rebeiz, and Campbell, 1961; Crane, 1964). Apparently normal parthenocarpic peaches are produced following gibberellin application. Crane (1964) suggested this indicated that gibberellin or gibberellin-like substances were the only growth regulators produced in seeds of pollinated fruits that were absent in unfertilized ovaries. In contrast, in cherry both auxins and GA appear to be required for development of parthenocarpic fruits (Rebeiz and Crane, 1961). Hence, the hormonal requirements for fruit set and growth appear to be quite variable among species.

Extracts of young seeds of almond, apricot, and plum show gibberellin-like activity (Phinney *et al.*, 1957). Coombe (1960) found that extracts of mature stems of seeded and seedless varieties of grape (*Vitis*) had gibberellin-like activity, while berries of only seedless varieties showed it. Growth of only seedless varieties was accelerated by GA. Coombe (1960) therefore concluded that gibberellins were important in growth of seedless grapes.

Gibberellin activity in the seed, endocarp, and mesocarp of apricot fruits correlated well with growth rates in these tissues for the first 60 days after anthesis (Fig. 9.5). Gibberellin activity increased following anthesis and reached a maximum 20 days after anthesis. The seed had the greatest gibberellin activity and the endocarp the least. Thereafter, the concentration of gibberellin-like substances declined in all three tissues, the decrease being most rapid in the endocarp and slowest in the mesocarp (Jackson and Coombe, 1966b).

Cytokinins

The importance of cytokinins in fruit growth has been postulated. The presence of cytokinins has been shown indirectly by stimulation of cell division in tissue explants by extracts of seeds and fruits of apple, plum, peach, pear, and quince (Letham and Bollard, 1961; Crane, 1964). Steward and Simmonds (1954) observed that in most species the stimulation of fruit set involved promotion of cell division. They noted the presence of a cytokinin in young fruits of parthenocarpic bananas and little or none of the cytokinin in nonparthenocarpic banana ovaries. Goldacre and Bottomley

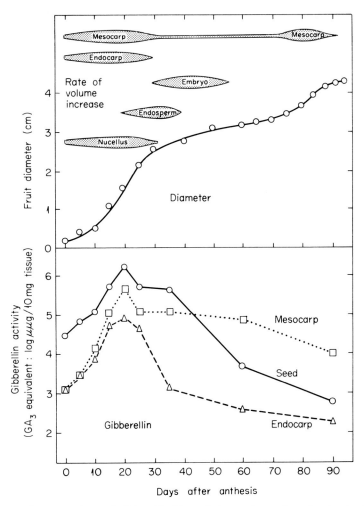

Fig. 9.5. Concentrations of gibberellin-like substances in methanol extracts of seed, endocarp, and mesocarp of apricots compared with their rate of growth during development. [From Jackson and Coombe (1966b).]

(1959) found cytokinins in the flesh of apple fruits until they were 3 weeks old at which time cell division ceased. Following addition of the extracted cytokinin, cell division in apple fruits resumed after the third week of development.

Black Corinth grape clusters dipped in a cytokinin solution 4 days after anthesis produced berries about 3 times the size of untreated berries. At 100 and 500 ppm cytokinin was very effective in promoting parthenocarpy in the Calimyrna fig (*Ficus carica*) (Crane and van Overbeek, 1965). The figs so produced were morphologically similar to those produced with auxin or gibberellin. Hence, it was demonstrated that any of these three endogenous hormones needed for fig growth could be supplied by tissues other than seeds.

INHIBITORS

Although a number of growth inhibiting substances occur in fruits and seeds, progress in their extraction and identification has been slow (Crane, 1964). The application of abscisic acid promotes abscission of young fruits, causes parthenocarpy, accelerates sensescence, and inhibits or promotes flower induction in different species. Although it is not established that these responses are controlled by endogenous abscisic acid, it is tempting to conclude that in some of them, abscisic acid is having a functional role. As abscisic acid is known to inhibit gibberellin-controlled responses and to interact with cytokinins (Crane, 1969), it may have an important regulatory function in fruit development. Some evidence is available which indicates that floral induction in *Olea* involves a change in balance between endogenous growth promoters and inhibitors (Badr, Hartmann, and Martin, 1970) and that increased activity of an endogenous inhibitor may cause reduction of fruit growth in *Persea* (Gazit and Blumenfeld, 1970). Much more research is needed on the role of abscisic acid and other inhibitors in growth of reproductive tissues of woody plants.

WATER

As Zahner (1968) emphasized, it is more difficult to generalize about the effects of water deficits on reproductive growth than on vegetative growth. One important reason for this is that the timing of the reproductive growth cycle varies greatly among species, with some requiring only a few months to initiate and mature fruits and other species requiring as much as several years. Thus, a severe drought may occur while one species is in bloom and another, on the same site, is already maturing fruits. Furthermore, many different stages of reproductive growth often occur on a tree at the same time. The effects of water deficits on fruit growth vary with the timing, duration, and degree of water stress. The influence of water deficit may be direct at certain stages of reproductive growth and indirect, through effects on vegetative growth, at other stages.

Severe internal water deficits are inhibitory to each of the phases of reproductive growth. Flower formation often is suppressed by severe water deficits and the effect of a drought may not be obvious until the subsequent year when flower buds open. For example, low soil moisture availability during July, August, and September resulted in reduction in the number of flower buds differentiated in apricot trees, a delay in the time of differentiation of flower buds, and slow development of buds which differentiated at the normal time. Early, uniform, and rapid development of flower buds was assured by irrigation once before and 3 times after harvest (Brown, 1953). Internal water deficits in olive (*Olea europaea*) trees at any stage between the appearance of floral primordia and full bloom were correlated with a low number of flowers per inflorescence (Hartmann and Panetsos, 1961). Water deficits early in the period of floral development were especially critical to the number of inflorescenses produced. Short periods of water stress at various stages of reproductive growth were almost as inhibitory to fruit set as those which extended throughout the entire reproductive period. Modlibowska (1961) noted great sensitivity of reproductive growth of apple trees to water stress 2–4 weeks before the blossoms were due to open. A drought during that critical period caused abnormal flowers to form.

Both the size and quality of fruits are regulated by availability of water during the period of fruit enlargement and preceding it. Smith (1966), for example, derived a regression equation relating coconut yields in a particular year in Trinidad with integrated soil moisture deficit over the 29 months preceding the beginning of a crop year. The correlation between crop yield and the integrated deficit was high, -0.81, with yield more closely related to the integrated deficit than to rainfall. Nevertheless, growing fruits are able to compete rather successfully with vegetative tissues for available water. This is shown by much more rapid inhibition of vegetative growth than fruit growth during severe droughts. Veihmeyer and Hendrickson (1952) emphasized that growth of pears, peaches, apples, and grapes in California was not appreciably reduced as soil moisture declined over the range from field capacity to the wilting percentage. Ordinarily if fruit trees reduced soil moisture to the permanent wilting percentage for only a few days and irrigation followed, the growth of fruits was not greatly affected. However, if the soil remained at the wilting percentage for a long time, the growth of fruits was inhibited. Following prolonged and severe droughts the fruits did not again attain the size they would have achieved, even if the trees were irrigated.

Butijn (1962) observed that fruit growth of apple was affected much less than shoot growth as soils dried. He recorded a decrease in apple yields of only about 10% if the soil moisture content was maintained near the wilting percentage for several weeks during the most susceptible period—about 4–6 weeks before harvesting. When soil moisture content dropped below the wilting percentage, growth of both shoots and apple fruits ceased and did not resume even if the soil was rewetted. Furthermore, after a severe drought, the lost growth of fruit was not restored.

As mentioned, water deficits also alter fruit quality. The highest quality of fruits was obtained when trees had available water throughout the growing season, but there were no obvious differences in quality when the soil moisture content was high or low, provided a large portion of the root system was not in soil which had reached the wilting percentage (Veihmeyer and Hendrickson, 1952). Severe droughts for several weeks prior to harvest produced peaches of tough, leathery texture. Under similar conditions pears matured later than when provided with a continuous supply of readily available water. Prolonged severe drought not only reduced the size of grapes but also resulted in a darker wine than was produced without drought.

Beneficial Effects of Water Deficits

Several investigators have reported that a mild water stress at a critical time in the reproductive cycle often increases initiation of flower buds by inhibiting vegetative growth. For example, Swarbrick and Luckwill (1953) concluded that restricted flower-bud formation in apple trees during some years was correlated with high summer rainfall which caused shoot growth to continue late into summer. Ito *et al.* (1953, 1954) noted that high availability of water and nitrogen to peach trees stimulated lush vegetative growth which in turn impeded formation and development of flower buds. Similarly, drought conditions preceding and during the floral initiation period hastened the appearance of flower buds of *Litchi chinensis*. The stimulatory effect on floral initiation was exerted through inhibition of vegetative growth (Nakata and Suehisa, 1969).

Internal water deficits of short duration have also been beneficial in overcoming dormancy of flower buds in some species. For example, when *Coffea* trees were irrigated weekly, the flower buds failed to open (Alvim, 1960). By comparison, when soil was allowed to dry until it approached the wilting percentage and was then irrigated, flower buds subsequently opened readily. Alvim (1960) suggested that a water stress requirement for breaking dormancy in *Coffea* flower buds accomplished what chilling did in many other species.

There is some evidence that mild water deficits sometimes are beneficial to certain stages of fruit growth. Tukey (1960), for example, suggested that some diurnal shrinkage of apple fruits was conducive to their enlargement. He noted that small apples near the base of the crown showed less diurnal shrinkage than did large apples near the top. He suggested that substances conducive to fruit enlargement were produced by temporary and mild diurnal water stress.

Stimulation of Reproductive Growth

Horticulturists and foresters have long practiced methods which increase the size and quality of fruit and seed crops of trees by stimulating floral initiation and subsequent growth of flowers and fruits. As mentioned in Chapter 3, Volume I, flowering often can be induced in young trees by manipulating the environment to make them grow as rapidly as possible until they reach the critical size necessary for flowering. To promote flowering thereafter, rapid tree growth should be stimulated because there is a close correlation between vigor of adult trees and their flowering capacity. Among the most successful treatments for stimulating flowering and fruiting in trees are use of dwarfing rootstocks, adding fertilizers, irrigating, releasing trees from competition, and applying chemical growth retardants. Combinations of added fertilizers and irrigation have often produced greatly accelerated reproductive growth. Matthews (1963) urged that such treatments should be performed regularly when possible to ensure regularity of large flower and seed crops in high-value trees, as in seed orchards. Flowering can also be induced in individual trees by various emergency treatments, such as girdling, bark inversion, root pruning, grafting, or bending and knotting of stems and branches. However, some of these emergency measures may be harmful over a period of years and may not be advisable in many situations. Some of the methods for promoting flowering and fruiting in trees will be discussed briefly.

DWARFING ROOTSTOCKS

One of the most widely used methods of producing fruit trees which bear fruit early and heavily involves propagating a desired variety on a dwarfing rootstock. In such trees seasonal shoot extension often ceases early and translocation of metabolites is directed toward the reproductive phase. For example, some varieties of apple worked on Malling IX rootstocks may grow to only about a third of normal size and they often produce fruit at a very early age. Some rootstocks may even cause certain varieties of fruit trees to bear heavily at an early age without materially impeding vegetative growth. Weak rootstocks also tend to increase the size of fruit, probably by decreasing vegetative growth, and they may hasten fruit ripening. Vegetative growth of some fruit trees can also be reduced and flowering stimulated by inserting a stem piece of a dwarfing stock between a vigorous rootstock and a vigorous scion variety. For further discussion of types of rootstocks used with various fruit trees the reader is referred to Shoemaker and Teskey (1959) and Hartmann and Kester (1968).

FERTILIZERS

Mineral requirements of reproductive tissues are high. For example, almost a third of the 1.3 to 1.5 lb of nitrogen absorbed per apple tree per year is used in fruit growth. In years of heavy fruiting very little nitrogen is stored in trees and reserves may become depleted. This section will discuss the effects of fertilizers on various aspects of reproductive growth of both fruit trees and forest trees.

Fruit Trees

Extensive data are available which emphasize the important role of fertilizers in initiation of floral primordia, fruit set, and growth of fruits. A few examples will be given.

Initiation of Floral Primordia. Fertilizer experiments with several species of orchard trees show that mineral supply influences initiation of floral primordia. The most dramatic effects have been achieved by adding nitrogen. For example, floral initiation in *Malus* was stimulated by nitrogen fertilizers. The added nitrogen also reduced the tendency toward alternation of flowering. It appeared that a deficiency of nitrogen in unfertilized trees was limiting growth of leaf tissues sufficiently to prevent maximum initiation of flowers (Bradford, 1924). During bloom of citrus, nitrogen is mobilized by flowers from leaves and the number of flowers is related to nitrogen levels (Cameron and Appleman, 1934; Cameron *et al.*, 1952; Smith and Reuther, 1950). According to Shear (1966), nitrogen fertilizers increased differentiation of pistillate blossom buds in tung (*Aleurites fordii*) during the first year of application. These buds develop into the crop during the subsequent year.

Fruit Set. When a deficiency of a given mineral element occurs, fruit set after bloom may be inhibited. Evidence for this is available from experiments in which fruit set was increased by additions of the deficient element to various orchard trees at the appropriate time. For example, fruit set in apple was appreciably increased by application of sodium nitrate at the time of bloom (Knowlton and Hoffman, 1932). On unfertile soils in California, the addition of 4 lb of nitrogen around each olive tree increased fruit set and yields. Whereas unfertilized trees set only 6.3 fruits per 100 inflorescences, those receiving nitrogen fertilizers set 48 fruits per 100 inflorescences. Trees grown on more fertile soils responded much less to added nitrogen (Hartmann, 1958). Another example of the importance of minerals to fruit set was provided by Proebsting (1934) who noted that adding 5–10 lb of sodium nitrate in the spring to Bartlett pear trees increased fruit set and yield by approximately 25%. Although fruit set is inhibited most commonly by deficiencies of macronutrients, especially nitrogen, deficiency of minor elements sometimes may also be involved. For example, Batjer and Thompson

(1949) were able to increase fruit set of pear with sprays of 25 and 125 ppm of boron applied during bloom.

Although fertilizer nitrogen has been traditionally applied to fruit trees in the spring, both flowering and fruiting of some varieties can be improved by supplementary nitrogen applied later in the season. For example, summer applications of nitrogen fertilizers to some varieties of fruit trees resulted in flowers that were more vigorous and more likely to set fruit than those which received fertilizer only in the spring (Williams, 1963, 1965). The ovules of the vigorous flowers remained capable of fertilization for twice as long as those of normal flowers. Hill-Cottingham (1963) showed that the highest yield of fruit came from trees initially well supplied with nitrogen and given a supplementary application before flowering. Hill-Cottingham and Williams (1967) noted that the time of application of nitrogen fertilizers influenced several aspects of flowering and fruit set of Lord Lambourne apple trees. In trees which received no fertilizer and those receiving fertilizer in the spring (early April) or autumn (late October), flower initiation took place in late July or early August. However, in trees which received fertilizer only in the summer (early August) after shoot extension ceased, flower primordia were not initiated until September. Development of flower buds was accelerated during September on trees given nitrogen in the summer. From the end of November until March no additional differentiation occurred on control trees or those given fertilizer in the spring, but it continued in trees given fertilizer either in the summer or autumn. Trees which had been given nitrogen either in the previous summer or autumn produced flowers 4 to 5 days sooner than other trees. Those given nitrogen in the summer had large flowers and large green leaves. Flowers on trees given nitrogen in the autumn were smaller. When blossoms were self-pollinated, virtually no fruit set occurred in control trees or those given nitrogen fertilizer in the spring. In contrast, trees given nitrogen in the summer showed appreciable fruit set and those given nitrogen in the autumn a heavy fruit set. Some effects of nitrogen applied at various times on flowering and abscission of fruitlets in apple are shown in Fig. 9.6.

Delap (1967) studied effects of timing of nitrogen applications on flowering and fruit setting of young apple trees. Control trees received a continuous low supply of nitrogen during 2 years. Treated trees received additional nitrogen supplies in the spring, summer, or autumn. Each of the supplementary nitrogen applications increased flower production. In addition, summer and autumn applications produced more fertile blooms than did spring applications (Table 9.5). Flowering was affected both directly by increasing the intensity of blossom production and indirectly by increasing shoot growth and hence the number of buds. The increase in fruit set by summer and autumn applications of nitrogen over spring applications was associated with greater longevity of ovules and a longer receptive period in

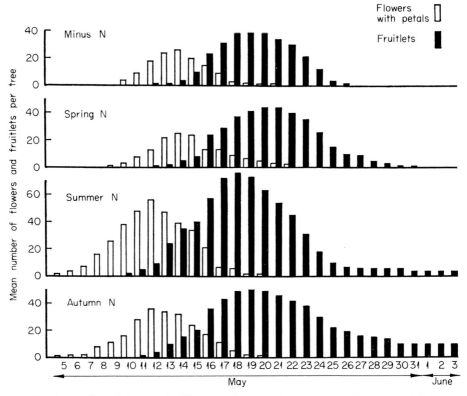

FIG. 9.6. Effect of nitrogen fertilizers applied at various times on flowering and fruitlet abscission of Lord Lambourne apple trees. [From Hill-Cottingham and Williams (1967).]

the stigmas. Williams (1965) showed that in trees receiving nitrogen fertilizers only in the spring of the previous year, the flowers continued viable ovules for about 7–9 days. However, flowers from trees given additional nitrogen in the previous summer contained ovules capable of remaining viable for 12–13 days.

Growth Rate of Fruits and Size at Harvest.   An extensive literature is available on the stimulation of fruit yield by added minerals, especially nitrogen: e.g., apple (Boynton *et al.*, 1950), cherry (Philp, 1947), citrus (Koo, Reitz, and Sites, 1958), olive (Hartmann, 1958, 1962), peach (Proebsting, 1937), and pear (Proebsting, 1961). For a review of the important literature pertaining to orchard trees the reader is referred to Childers (1966a,b).

Both the rate of fruit growth and its ultimate size at harvest are controlled by relations between numbers of fruit and leaf surface. Adding nitrogen fertilizers may decrease the average size of the harvested fruit if floral initiation and fruit set are increased proportionally more than leaf growth (Tukey

TABLE 9.5

Effect of Amount and Timing of Adding Nitrogen on Flowering and Fruit Set of Young Apple Trees[a]

	Date	Low N[b] (control)	Spring N[c]	Summer N[c]	Autumn N[c]	Moderate N[d]
Percent of clusters at pink bud stage	May, 1962	40.2	36.8	36.1	59.7[e]	47.6
No. of blossom clusters	May, 1962	46.9	48.4	47.1	56.9[e]	59.6[f]
No. of axillary clusters	May, 1963	5.9	27.8[e]	49.6	26.4[e]	51.5
No. of spur clusters	May, 1963	46.7	41.1	41.1	53.9	47.7
No. of spur clusters	April, 1964	84.3	93.0	129.4[g]	118.0[f]	139.4[g]
Total number of fruitlets	11 June 1964	24.8	20.0	101.0[g]	103.8[e]	146.5[g]
Percent set	11 June 1964	5	4	14[g]	19[g]	19[g]

[a] From Delap (1967).
[b] Continuously supplied with complete nutrient solution containing 1 meq NO$_3$/liter.
[c] Same solution as b but nitrate level increased to 16 meq/liter.
[d] Continuously supplied with complete nutrient solution containing 4 meq NO$_3$/liter.
[e,f,g] Differs significantly from control at $P = 0.05$, 0.01, and 0.001, respectively.

and Anderson, 1929). However, if added nitrogen does not greatly increase floral initiation and fruit set, it often subsequently greatly increases the size of the mature fruit (Fisher, Boynton, and Skodvin, 1948).

Forest Trees

It is well known that forest trees growing on infertile sites often produce few seeds and these often are of poor quality. Sarvas (1962) observed, for example, that flowering and seed production of *Pinus sylvestris* were stimulated as soil fertility increased. A number of investigators have shown that addition of fertilizers stimulated both flowering and seed production of forest trees. When fertilizers are used with a combination of crown release or irrigation, the results are usually better than when fertilizers are used alone. A few examples of stimulation of flowering and seed production in forest trees will be given.

Wenger (1953) applied 25 or 50 lbs of 7-7-7 fertilizer per tree to 25- and 40-year-old *Pinus taeda* seed trees. In the 25-year-old stand the lightly fertilized trees produced 98 cones per tree; heavily fertilized trees produced 123 cones per tree in the first effective year (third growing season after treatment), compared to 36 cones per control tree. The 40-year-old trees did not respond significantly to the addition of fertilizer.

Hoekstra and Mergen (1957) applied 20 or 40 lbs per tree of 7-7-7 or 3-18-6 fertilizers to 21-year-old *Pinus elliottii* trees in the spring of 1954. Fertilizer application resulted in an average increase of flower production of 59% over controls (Table 9.6). Nitrogen apparently was most important in stimulation of flowering. The 7-7-7 fertilizer was more than twice as effective as the 3-18-6 fertilizer even though the latter had more phosphorus and almost as much potassium as the former. The effect of fertilizers on flowering persisted for 2 years.

TABLE 9.6

Effect of Adding Fertilizer on Female Flowers per Bud on 21-Year-Old *Pinus elliottii* Trees During Two Successive Years[a]

| Year | Type and amount of fertilizer per tree[b] | | | | Control |
| | 7–7–7 | | 3–18–6 | | |
	20 lbs	40 lbs	20 lbs	40 lbs	
1955	0.66	0.65	0.30	0.53	0.30
1956	0.41	0.42	0.26	0.46	0.15

[a] From Hoekstra and Mergen (1957).
[b] Fertilizers were applied during the third week of April 1954.

Steinbrenner, Duffield, and Campbell (1960) applied 100 or 200 lbs/acre of nitrogen and P_2O_5 in four combinations to 20-year-old *Pseudotsuga menziesii* trees. First-year seed production was 1.2 lbs/acre on control plots; 4.5 lbs/acre on plants receiving 100 lbs/acre of each nutrient; and 10.3 lbs/acre on plots receiving 200 lbs of each nutrient. The treatments were repeated. In the second spring following the first fertilizer application, 37% of the control trees produced flowers; 56% of those receiving 100 lbs/acre of each nutrient produced flowers; and 75% of those treated with 200 lbs/acre of nitrogen and phosphate produced flowers. Most of the beneficial response was attributed to the effect of nitrogen.

Beginning in 1958 Shoulders (1967) applied annually 250, 500, or 1000 lbs/acre of 15-25-10 fertilizer to 45-year-old *Pinus palustris* trees in heavily thinned stands. The number of flowers produced was counted on individual trees during the years 1959–1965. The applied fertilizer stimulated flower production in a complex manner, with rainfall and individual tree variables modifying the fertilizer effect. Trees were classified first as having either high or low inherent flowering capacity. Those with both high and low flowering capacity responded to fertilizers, but unfertilized high-flowering trees produced more flowers than the fertilized low producers in most years (Fig. 9.7). The flowering response to fertilizers was influenced by rainfall prior to flower bud differentiation, which occurred in July and August. When available soil moisture was low, the applied fertilizer reduced flower production.

Annual additions of 100 lbs/acre of 15-25-10 fertilizer to heavily thinned cultivated stands of *Pinus palustris* or *Pinus elliottii* in March greatly stimulated flower and cone production in Louisiana (Shoulders, 1968). Fertilized *Pinus palustris* trees had twice as many flowers and 1.5 times as many cones as trees which had not received fertilizer (Fig. 9.8). Over a 4-year period the addition of fertilizer to *Pinus palustris* trees accounted for an increase of 8460 female flowers and 1340 mature cones per acre. By comparison, the addition of fertilizer at the same rate to *Pinus elliottii* stands increased production by 4330 cones per acre.

In the spring and early summer of 1964, Barnes and Bengston (1968) applied a total of 150 lbs/acre of nitrogen fertilizer as ammonium nitrate to 7-year-old *Pinus elliottii* trees in Florida. Irrigation treatments also were added to provide at least an inch of water (rainfall plus irrigation) per week during December and February, and at least 2 inches of water per week during the rest of the year. Irrigated plots received 14 inches of water more than the unirrigated plots. Both the addition of fertilizers and irrigation stimulated flowering but the former treatment had the much greater effect. The number of female flowers was twice as high in trees receiving fertilizer (31 flowers per tree) as in trees without fertilizer (15 flowers per tree). Male

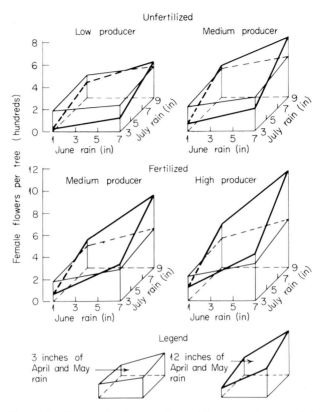

Fig. 9.7. Effect of fertilizers and rain on estimated flower production of *Pinus palustris*. Data are for low, medium, and high producing trees with different rates of fertilization and rainfall in the spring and summer preceding flower-bud formation. Average flower yields were assumed to be 150 per tree for low, 235 for medium, and 320 for high producers. Flower production 2 years earlier was 60, 90, and 120, respectively. [From Shoulders (1967).]

flowering was not affected by addition of fertilizers. Irrigation did not affect female flowering but increased the number of male flowers.

For stimulating flower bud formation in forest trees of the Temperate Zone, fertilizers usually are applied in the early spring before new flower buds are differentiated (Matthews, 1963). The time when added fertilizers affect seed production differs among species because of variations in the time required to ripen seed. For example, the influence of fertilizer applications in the spring of a given year to pines will be shown in flowering in the spring of the next year and in the ripened seeds during the autumn of the second year. As some gymnosperms and angiosperms ripen seeds in one growing season, fertilizers applied in the spring of one year will affect both the flowers and

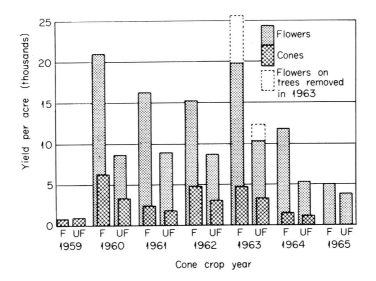

FIG. 9.8. Stimulation of reproductive growth with fertilizers. Flowers and cones of *Pinus palustris* on cultivated and heavily thinned plots that were unfertilized (UF) or given annually 1000 lbs/acre of 15–25–10 fertilizer in one application (F). [From Shoulders (1968)].

seed crop during the next year. The greatest effect of fertilizers appears to be exerted on a single seed crop of forest trees. Hence, continuous high production of seeds usually requires repeated fertilizer applications (Matthews, 1963).

IRRIGATION

Irrigation may be useful and practical in stimulating flowering and fruiting in areas which are dry during the period of floral induction. However, the effects of irrigation are complex and vary with such factors as rainfall regime, soil type, species, and timing and amount of irrigation.

Induction of ovulate strobili in some pines of the southern United States was increased by high availability of soil moisture during spring growth and lower availability of moisture just before differentiation of strobili. For example, increases in February and March rainfall increased the flowering response of *Pinus elliottii* to fertilization, whereas high rainfall in April or May through July decreased it (Shoulders, personal communication). These results differed somewhat from those obtained with *Pinus palustris*. High rainfall in April, May, June, and July of the year before flowering greatly stimulated flowering in *Pinus palustris* (Shoulders, 1967). Trees receiving fertilizers as well as unfertilized trees required high rainfall for maximum flowering (Fig. 9.6). They produced fewest flowers when high rainfall in April and May was followed by low rainfall in June and July. Flowering also was improved with increasing June and July rainfall, but the amount of increase varied with inherent flowering capacity, rate of fertilizer application, and rainfall during April and May.

Some investigators have found that irrigation, especially on deep sandy soils, did not effectively stimulate reproductive growth of pines of the southern United States. For example, Bengston (1969) concluded that irrigation during the first 5 years after establishment of pine seed orchards in north central Florida was of doubtful value for increasing vegetative growth and cone production. Irrigation had a depressing effect on production of ovulate strobili, but it stimulated pollen production. The annual rainfall in the area of Bengston's study averages 50 inches, and half that amount falls from June to September.

The variable flowering responses to irrigation of pines growing on soils of different moisture-holding capacity and increases of variable rainfall indicate that additional research is needed on internal water deficits in tissues and reproductive responses under various irrigation regimes.

Hendrickson and Veihmeyer (1942) studied growth of fleshy fruits in several California orchards. In the coast region in years of normal rainfall, pear and apple trees on medium or fine-textured soils did not reduce soil moisture content to the permanent wilting percentage until late in the season. A significant reduction in fruit growth as a result of water deficit occurred only when the available soil moisture was depleted. By comparison, pear orchards in the interior valley of California reduced soil moisture to the permanent wilting percentage in the top 4–6 feet of soil in late June or early July, at which time growth of pears decreased. Fruit growth was not appreciably retarded, however, during the period when soil was drying from field capacity to wilting percentage. On the basis of these experiments it was recommended that irrigation did not materially improve fruit growth until the wilting percentage of soil was approached or reached.

Although the work of Veihmeyer and Hendrickson emphasized that fruit growth can compete successfully with vegetative growth as soil dries, it should not be assumed that growth of all fruits will be unaffected in drying soil until the permanent wilting percentage is reached. For example, Lewis, Work, and Aldrich (1939) reported that growth of pears on trees in drying soil began to slow down before the permanent wilting percentage was reached, and while 60–80% of the water in the available range was present. Their experiment was conducted with trees growing in a heavy clay soil. They suggested that maintaining normal growth of pears would require frequent irrigation to maintain moisture content at a value above 60% of the available range (between field capacity and wilting percentage).

Veihmeyer and Hendrickson (1960) found irrigation to increase yields in fruit and nut orchards in California where the winter storage of water usually is depleted before the end of the growing season. Response to irrigation appeared slowly and often was not evident for several years. This emphasized the importance of irrigating high-value plantations early in arid regions to increase survival and, many years later, to stimulate reproductive growth. Uriu and Magness (1967) summarized several studies which showed beneficial effects of irrigation or both yield and quality of fruits of deciduous trees, including apples, pears, peaches, plums, cherries and almonds.

Evergreen fruit trees are grown in subtropical areas which may be humid, semi arid, or arid. Whereas irrigation usually is not required in humid zones except during dry periods, it is essential in arid regions. Hilgeman and Reuther (1967) described irrigation needs and practices for tropical fruit trees, including citrus, avocado, date palm, and olive. They emphasized that irrigation increased yields primarily by maintaining available water in the entire root zone during the period of fruit set. Irrigation following fruit set was much less important.

THINNING OF FOREST STANDS

Foresters have long been concerned about the failure of many forest trees to produce a seed crop under the severe competition which trees undergo in natural forest stands. In dense forest stands close correlations exist between tree vigor and capacity for flowering and fruiting. This was demonstrated by Fowells and Schubert (1956) who noted that in many coniferous forests almost all cones were produced by dominant trees and only very few by intermediate and suppressed trees combined. For example, in *Pinus lambertiana* stands in California, about 98 % of the cones were borne by dominant trees. Codominant trees produced about 1.5 % of the cones in the stands and intermediate and suppressed trees collectively had only a negligible number.

Within a tree crown the vigor of branches also influences fruit and cone development. This is well illustrated in gymnosperms. For example, in *Pinus resinosa* the more vigorous branches in the upper and middle thirds of the crown produced larger cones than did less vigorous branches of the lower third. The largest cones generally were located within the middle third of the crown. In general, larger cones were produced on secondary lateral branches than on tertiary branches (Dickmann and Kozlowski, 1971). The quality of seeds was related to cone size. Cone volume was positively corelated with number of full seeds per cone, total dry weight of seeds per cone, and number of scales per cone. The number of scales per cone was correlated with number of seeds per cone. The differences in cone and seed production within trees can be related to variations in vigor of shoots on different axes (Kozlowski and Ward, 1961). Hard (1964) also reported good correlations between cone production and branch size in *Pinus resinosa*, further emphasizing the importance of vigorous shoot growth to cone development.

Further support for the importance of tree vigor to flowering and fruiting comes from observations of increased flower and seed crops in residual trees following thinning of stands. Wenger (1954) thinned *Pinus taeda* trees during the winter of 1946–1947. Flowering of the residual trees was soon affected as an increased number of flower buds was formed during the first growing season after cutting. In 1949, the first year that release could affect mature cone production, and a very poor seed year, each released tree produced an average of 51 cones, whereas unreleased control trees produced only 5 cones each. The very significant effect of stand thinning carried over into 1950 and 1951, with released trees producing 107 and 132 cones per tree and control trees bearing only 16 and 48 cones during the same 2 years. Crown release of pine trees often is followed by increase in pollen production which, in turn, is reflected in an increase in the number of viable seeds per cone (Matthews, 1963).

CHEMICAL GROWTH RETARDANTS

A number of investigators have demonstrated rather dramatically that certain chemicals which retard vegetative growth of ornamental woody plants and some fruit trees also stimulate reproductive growth. Among the most effective of these chemicals are N-dimethylaminosuccinamic acid (B9 or Alar) and 2-chloroethyl trimethyl ammonium chloride (Cycocel or Chlormequat). Trees treated with these chemicals exhibit short internodes, early cessation of shoot growth, and early and prolific formation of fruit buds. Responses to these chemicals vary among species and also between cultivars of a given species (Cathey, 1964; McGuire, Kitchin, and Davidson, 1965; Edgerton and Hoffman, 1965; Luckwill, 1968, 1970).

Some evidence indicates that the effects of growth retardants on vegetative growth and reproductive growth are independent. In Eureka lemon, for example, chemicals which increased flower bud induction and fruit set as well also stimulated shoot growth (Monselise, Goren and Halevy, 1966). Batjer, Williams and Martin (1964) increased production of fruit buds over an entire apple tree by spraying only the lower part of the tree with B9. Reduced vegetative growth was restricted to the sprayed branches. Luckwill (1970) suggested that this response may have been caused by translocation of the growth retarding chemical from the treated branches to the roots where it influenced production of a xylem-translocated hormone which subsequently stimulated floral initiation throughout the tree.

GIRDLING

Cutting through the bark and into the xylem has been shown to suppress vegetative growth beneath the girdle and to stimulate fruit and seed production in a variety of orchard and forest trees. This method impedes basipetal translocation of carbohydrates and growth regulators in the phloem. When downward movement of organic solutes is blocked they tend to diffuse into the xylem and are translocated upward in the transpiration stream. Hence, they concentrate in the leaves and other tissues near those involved in reproduction and thereby stimulate fruit and seed production. For example, Furr and Armstrong (1956) demonstrated that girdling the trunks of grapefruit trees greatly stimulated the rate of floral induction in early autumn and winter. Stephens (1964) was able to stimulate production of ovulate strobili by stem girdling in 22-year-old *Pinus strobus* trees but not in 3- to 14-year-old trees. Girdling also increased production of strobili on individually treated branches. Treatment in the summer of the year before flowering increased the yield of strobili, which otherwise would have been low. However, no stimulation of reproductive growth by girdling was apparent when production of strobili generally was high. Bilan (1960b) found stem girdling to stimulate cone production in *Pinus taeda*, and Pond (1936) reported that about 50% of girdled black ash (*Fraxinus nigra*) trees produced seeds whereas only 10% of the control trees did so.

BARK INVERSION

Removal of a ring of bark from a tree and replacing it in an inverted position has been shown to promote flowering. Sax (1957, 1958) found that if he imposed such treatments before July to 2- or 3-year-old apple trees their vegetative growth was inhibited but they produced fruits and flowers the following year (Table 9.7). Bark inversions on individual branches caused flowering on those branches in trees that normally would not flower for several years. As may be seen in Table 9.8 bark inversion generally was ineffective if imposed after July 1, e.g., after flower primordia normally were differentiated.

Sax (1958) stated that impeding of phloem transport by bark inversion probably operated primarily by blocking polar auxin transport. Although the effect of bark inversion is temporary it usually persists for more than one year. Even double inversion with vertical seams on opposite sides of the stem results in only temporary effects. Apparently, the phloem-translocated materials move downward first through the regenerated bark of the upper vertical seam and then move through the new bark of the seam of the lower inversion. Eventually normal transport is established through regenerated bark tissues (Sax, 1957, 1958).

TABLE 9.7

EFFECT OF BARK INVERSION IN 1954 ON FRUITING, FLOWERING AND DIAMETER GROWTH OF 5-YEAR-OLD APPLE TREES. DATA ARE FOR 12 TREATED AND 12 CONTROL TREES.[a]

Treatment	No. of fruit per tree 1955	No. of flower clusters per tree 1956	Average stem diameter 1956 (cm)
Bark inverted	3	2	5.2
Control	43	70	5.1
Difference	40	68	0.1
LSD 5%	19	20	0.3

[a] From Sax (1957).

TABLE 9.8

EFFECT OF TIME OF YEAR OF BARK INVERSION ON FLOWERING OF INDIVIDUAL BRANCHES OF APPLE TREES.[a]

Time of bark inversion in 1954	Number of trees	Flower clusters per branch		
		1955	1956	Total
June 22	13	51	16	67
July 4	13	24	19	33
July 14	13	8	17	25
July 27	13	5	30	35
Control	13	2	2	3

[a] From Sax (1957).

ROOT PRUNING

Flowering of woody plants has been stimulated by root pruning alone or in combination with other treatments (Bergmann, 1955; Stephens, 1964). For example, removal of part of the root system increased production of ovulate strobili of 7-year-old *Pinus elliottii* trees (Hoekstra and Mergen, 1957). Root pruning also stimulated initiation of ovulate strobili in 14- and 22-year-old *Pinus strobus* trees (Stephens, 1964). Pruning initially reduced the functional root system but it also eliminated root competition and stimulated formation of new roots to form an effective, multibranched root system. A combination of girdling of branches and root pruning was more effective in stimulating flowering than was root pruning alone (Table 9.9).

TABLE 9.9

Effect of Root Pruning and Branch Girdling on Production of Ovulate Strobili in 22-Year-Old *Pinus strobus* Trees[a]

Flower year		Branches per treatment	Not girdled		Girdled	
			Control	Pruned	Control	Pruned
1960[b]	No fertilizer added	10	0	0	0	0
	Fertilizer added	30	0	5	4	28
1961[c]	No fertilizer added	30	0	7[d]	10	30[d]
	Fertilizer added	90	0	0	1	11

[a] From Stephens (1964).

[b] Trees treated July 1959 with five trees receiving each treatment.

[c] Fifteen trees received each treatment.

[d] A single unfertilized root-pruned tree had seven strobili on control branches and 29 on girdled branches.

Grafting

Flowering has sometimes been accelerated by such techniques as grafting on related species, grafting on dwarfing rootstocks, grafting mature scions into seedlings, or grafting or budding in crowns of mature fruiting trees. When scions are taken from adult trees and grafted to seedling rootstocks in the juvenile, nonflowering state, they soon flower. This technique is used in seed production in clonal seed orchards (Matthews, 1963). Visser (1964) stimulated flowering by shortening the juvenile phase of apple seedlings by budding them on Malling IX rootstocks. Tydeman (1961) reported that seedling apples on Malling IX rootstocks showed 43% flowering in 6 years in contrast to 3% in controls. Campbell (1961) also stimulated flowering through shortening the juvenile phase of apple seedlings by budding them on apomictic rootstocks from *Malus sikkimensis*. Sorensen (1943) induced very early flowering by budding of *Hevea* in crowns of mature trees at an age of 4–10 years. Grafting techniques, in general, have been more successful in stimulating flowering of orchard trees than of forest trees. As Matthews (1963) emphasized, the difficulty of rooting cuttings or layering of several forest tree genera, including *Larix*, *Pinus*, *Pseudotsuga*, *Fraxinus*, and *Fagus*, poses special problems in selecting clonal rootstocks for seed orchards.

Bending or Knotting of Stems and Branches

Arching or maintaining shoots horizontally often inhibits vegetative growth and promotes flower initiation (Champagnat, 1954). Longman and Wareing

(1958) found flowering in young *Larix leptolepsis* trees to be influenced by the position of the branches in relation to the gravitational field. As branch angle measured from the vertical upward was increased, the amount of flowering increased. Wareing and Nasr (1961) studied the effects of shoot orientation on vegetative growth of apple, cherry, plum, and black currant. Trees were maintained horizontally throughout the growing season and their growth was compared with vertical controls. As may be seen in Table 9.10 shoot elongation of horizontal trees was greatly checked. Extension of shoots was inhibited the most in cherry and plum and was due to reduced internode length as well as to a decreased number of internodes. In apples and currants, however, growth inhibition was brought about primarily through a decrease in internode length. As may be seen in Table 9.11 looping or knotting of stems of young trees checks subsequent vegetative development but it stimulates flowering and fruiting. Three to five seasons after stems of young apple seedlings were knotted, the trees were only one third to a half as large as control trees. McIntosh trees or knotted *Malus sikkimensis* averaged 53 flower clusters per tree as against none for the controls (Sax, 1957).

TABLE 9.10

EFFECT OF SHOOT POSITION ON AVERAGE SHOOT ELONGATION OF APPLE, CHERRY, PLUM, AND BLACKCURRANT[a]

Species and Treatment	Mean shoot elongation (cm)	Mean internode length (cm)	Mean number of internodes
Cherry			
Horizontal	21.4	1.6	13.6
Vertical	51.8	2.5	20.7
Apple			
Horizontal	52.9	1.7	31.3
Vertical	69.3	2.1	32.7
Plum			
Horizontal	84.8	1.0	82.0
Vertical	116.9	1.1	102.0
Blackcurrant			
Horizontal	42.7	1.2	35.5
Vertical	59.0	1.7	35.1

[a] From Wareing and Nasr (1961).

TABLE 9.11

EFFECT OF STEM KNOTTING IN 1951 ON DIAMETER GROWTH AND FLOWERING OF BUDDED
VARIETIES OF APPLE IN 1955[a]

Variety and stock	Treatment	Number of trees	Cross sectional area of stem $(cm)^2$	No. of trees flowering
McIntosh/Sik	Control	9	22	2
	Knotted in 1951	9	18	5
Difference			4	+ 3
LSD 5%			2.1	+ 3
McIntosh/Sarg/Sik	Control	5	14	0
	Knotted in 1951	5	8	5
Difference			6	+ 5
LSD 5%			2.2	

[a] From Sax (1957).

Suggested Collateral Reading

Chandler, W. H. (1957). "Deciduous Orchards." Lea and Febiger. Philadelphia.

Childers, N. F. (1961). "Modern Fruit Science." Horticultural Publications. Rutgers University. New Brunswick, New Jersey.

Childers, N. F. (1966a). "Fruit Nutrition." Horticultural Publications. Rutgers University. New Brunswick, New Jersey.

Childers, N. F. (1966b). "Nutrition of Fruit Crops." Horticultural Publications. Rutgers University. New Brunswick, New Jersey.

Crane, J. C. (1964). Growth substances in fruit setting and development. *Annu. Rev. Plant Physiol.* **15**, 303–326.

Crane, J. C. (1969). The role of hormones in fruit set and development. *HortScience*, **4**, 108–111.

Jackson, D. I. (1969). Effect of water, light, and nutrition on flowerbud initiation in apricots. *Aust. J. Biol. Sci.* **22**, 69–75.

Johri, B. M. and Vasil, I. K. (1961). Physiology of pollen. *Bot. Rev.* **27**, 325–381.

Luckwill, L. C. and Cutting, C. V. (eds.) (1970). "Physiology of Tree Crops." Academic Press, London and New York.

Matthews, J. D. (1963). Factors affecting the production of seed by forest trees. *Forestry Abstracts* **24**, i–xiii.

Nitsch, J. P. (1965). Physiology of flower and fruit development. *Encycl. Plant Physiol.* **15**. Part 1, 1537–1647.

Pratt, H. K. and Goeschl, J. D. (1968). The role of ethylene in fruit ripening. *In* "Biochemistry and Physiology of Plant Growth Substances." pp. 1295–1302, (F. Wightman and G. Setterfield eds.), Runge Press, Ottawa.

Schneider, G. W. and Scarborough, C. C. (1960). "Fruit Growing." Prentice Hall. Englewood Cliffs, New Jersey.

Shoemaker, J. S. (1955). "Small-Fruit Culture." McGraw-Hill, New York.

Shoemaker, J. S. and Teskey, B. J. E. (1959). "Tree Fruit Production." Wiley, New York.

Stanley, R. G. (1964). Physiology of pollen and pistil. *Sci. Progress* **52**, 122–132.

BIBLIOGRAPHY

Addicott F. T., and Lyon, J. L. (1969). Physiology of abscisic acid and related substances. *Ann,. Rev. Plant Physiol.* **20**, 139–164.

Addoms, G. T., Nightingale, G. T., and Blake, M. A., (1930). Development and ripening of peaches as correlated with physical characteristics, chemical composition and histological structure of the fruit flesh. II. Histology and microchemistry. *N. J. Agr. Exp. Station Bull.* **507**.

Ahlgren, C. E. (1958). Adventitious roots and shoots of wilding white pine at the Quetico-Superior Wilderness Research Area. *Univ. Minnesota Forest. Note* **70**.

Albertson, F. W., and Weaver, J. E. (1945). Injury and death or recovery of trees in prairie climate. *Ecol. Monogr.* **15**, 395–433.

Alfieri, F. J., and Evert, R. F. (1965). Seasonal phloem development in *Pinus strobus. Amer. J. Bot.* **52**, 626–627.

Alfieri, F. J., and Evert, R. F. (1968). Seasonal development of the secondary phloem in *Pinus. Amer. J. Bot.* **55**, 518–528.

Allen, E. K., and Allen, O. N. (1958). Biological aspects of symbiotic nitrogen fixation. *Encycl. Plant Physiol.* **8**, 48–118.

Allen, E. K., and Allen, O. N. (1965). Nonleguminous plant symbiosis. In "Microbiology and Soil Fertility" (C. M. Gilmour and O. N. Allen, eds.), pp. 77–106. Oregon State Univ. Press, Corvallis, Oregon.

Allen, O. N., and Allen, E. K. (1936). Root nodule bacteria of some tropical leguminous plants. I. Cross inoculation studies with *Vigna sinensis* L. *Soil Sci.* **42**, 61–76.

Alvim, P. de T. (1960). Moisture stress as a requirement for flowering of coffee. *Science* **132**, 354.

Alvim, P. de T. (1964). Tree growth periodicity in tropical climates. *In* "The Formation of Wood in Forest Trees" (M. H. Zimmermann, ed.) pp. 479–496. Academic Press, New York.

Anderson, N. F., and Guard, A. T. (1964). A comparative study of the vegetative, transitional and floral apex of *Acer pseudoplatanus* L. *Phytomorphology* **14**, 500–508.

Anderson, B. J., and Evert, R. F. (1965). Some aspects of phloem development in *Quercus alba. Amer. J. Bot.* **52**, (Part 2), 627.

Anderssen, F. G. (1932). Chlorosis of deciduous fruit trees due to a copper deficiency. *J. Pomol.* **10**, 130–146.

Andersson, E. (1963). Seed stands and seed orchards in the breeding of conifers. *Proc. World Consult. Forest. Genetics and Forest Tree Improvement. II FAO/FORGEN* **63** (8/1), 1–18.

Andrews, S. R., and Gill, L. S. (1939). Determining the time branches on living trees have been dead. *J. Forest.* **37**, 930–935.

Armson, K. A., and Van Den Driessche, R. (1959). Natural root grafts in red pine (*Pinus resinosa* Ait.). *Forest. Chron.* **35**, 232–241.

Artschwager, E. (1945). Growth studies on guayule (*Parthenium argentatum*) *US Dep. Agr. Tech. Bull.* **885**, 1–19.

Artschwager, E. (1950). The time factor in the differntiation of secondary xylem and phloem in pecan. *Amer. J. Bot.* **37**, 15–24.

Arzee, T., Liphschitz, N., and Waisel, Y. (1968). The origin and development of the phellogen in *Robinia pseudacacia. New Phytol.* **67**, 87–93.

Avery, D. J. (1969). Comparisons of fruiting and deblossomed maiden apple trees, and of non-fruiting trees on a dwarfing and an invigorating rootstock. *New Phytol.* **68**, 323–336.

Avery, G. S., and Johnson, E. B. (1947). "Hormones and Horticulture." McGraw-Hill, New York.

Bachelard, E. P., and Stowe, B. B. (1963). Rooting of cuttings of *Acer rubrum* L. and *Eucalyptus camaldulensis* Dehn. *Aust. J. Biol. Sci.* **16**, 751–767.

Badr, S. A., Hartmann, H. T. and Martin, G. C. (1970). Endogenous gibberellins and inhibitors in relation to flower induction and inflorescence development in the olive. *Plant Physiol.* **46**, 674–679.

Bagda, H. (1948). Morphologische und physiologische Untersuchungen über Valonia Eichen (*Quercus macrolepis* Ky.) im Haci-Kadin-Tal bei Ankara, *Ankara Univ. Tip. Fak. Mecm.* **1**, 89–125.

Bagda, H. (1952). Untersuchungen über den weiblichen Gametophyten der Valonia Eichen (*Quercus macrolepis* Ky.) *Rev. Fac. Sci. Univ. Istanbul* **17**, 77–94.

Bailey, I. W. (1920). The cambium and its derivative tissues. II. Size variations of cambium initials in gymnosperms and angiosperms. *Amer. J. Bot.* **7**, 355–367.

Bailey, I. W., and Faull, A. F. (1934). The cambium and its derivative tissues. IX. Structural variations in the redwood, *Sequoia sempervirens*, and its significance in the identification of fossil woods. *J. Arnold Arboretum* **15**, 233–254.

Bain, J. M. (1958). Morphological, anatomical, and physiological changes in the developing fruit of the Valencia orange, *Citrus sinensis* (L.) Osbeck. *Aust. J. Bot.* **6**, 1–25.

Bain, J. M. (1961). Some morphological, anatomical, and physiological changes in the pear fruit (*Pyrus communis* var. Williams Bon Chrétienne) during development and following harvest. *Aust. J. Bot.* **9**, 99–123.

Bain, J. M., and Robertson, R. N. (1951). Physiology and growth of apple fruits. I. Cell size, number and fruit development. *Aust. J. Sci. Res. Ser.* **B. 4**, 75–91

Baker, J. R., and Baker, I. (1936). The seasons in a tropical rain forest. *J. Linn. Soc. London Zool.* **39**, 507–519.

Bakuzis, E. V., and Hansen, H. L. (1965). "Balsam Fir." Univ. Minnesota Press, Minneapolis, Minnesota.

Balatinecz, J. J., and Kennedy, R. W. (1967). Mechanism of earlywood-latewood differentiation in *Larix decidua*. TAPPI *4th Forest Biol. Conf.*: 36–55.

Balatinecz, J. J., and Kennedy, R. W. (1968). Mechanism of earlywood-latewood differentiation in *Larix decidua*. TAPPI **51**, 414–422.

Balch, R. E. (1952). Studies of the balsam wooly aphid, *Adelges Piceae* (Ratz.) and its effects on balsam fir, *Abies balsamea* (L). *Mill. Can. Dep. Agr. Publ.* **867**.

Balch, R. E., Clark, J., and Bonga, J. M. (1964). Hormonal action in production of tumours and compression wood by an aphid. *Nature* (*London*) **202**, 721–722.

Baldini, E., and Canu, S. (1959). Ulteriori indagini sul sistema radicale degli agrumi. *Riv. Ortoflorofruitticolt. Ital.* **43**, 233–254.

Bamberg, S., Schwarz, W., and Tranquillini, W. (1967). Influence of daylength on the photosynthetic capacity of stone pine (*Pinus cembra* L.) *Ecology* **48**, 264–269.

Bannan, M. W. (1941a). Wood structure of *Thuja occidentalis*. *Bot. Gaz.* (*Chicago*) **103**, 295–309.

Bannan, M. W. (1941b). Variation in wood structure in roots of native Ontario conifers. *Bull. Torrey Bot. Club* **68**, 173–194.

Bannan, M. W. (1942). Notes on the origin of adventitious roots in the native Ontario conifers. *Amer. J. Bot.* **29**, 593–598.

Bannan, M. W. (1950). The frequency of anticlinal divisions in fusiform cambial cells of *Chamaecyparis*. *Amer. J. Bot.* **37**, 511–519.

Bannan, M. W. (1951a). The reduction of fusiform cambial cells in *Chamaecyparis* and *Thuja*. *Can. J. Bot.* **29**, 57–67.

Bannan, M. W. (1951b). The annual cycle of size change in the fusiform cambial cells of *Chameacyparis* and *Thuja*. *Can. J. Bot.* **29**, 421–437.

Bannan, M. W. (1953). Further observations on the reduction of fusiform cambial cells in *Thuja occidentalis*. *Can. J. Bot.* **31**, 63–74.

Bannan, M. W. (1955). The vascular cambium and radial growth in *Thuja occidentalis* L. *Can. J. Bot.* **33**, 113–138.

Bannan, M. W. (1956). Some aspects of the elongation of fusiform cambial cells in *Thuja occidentalis*. *Can. J. Bot.* **34**, 175–196.

Bannan, M. W. (1957a). Girth increase in white cedar stems of irregular form. *Can. J. Bot.* **35**, 425–434.

Bannan, M. W. (1957b). The relative frequency of the different types of anticlinal divisions in conifer cambium. *Can. J. Bot.* **35**, 875–884.

Bannan, M. W. (1957c). The structure and growth of the cambium. *TAPPI* **40**, 220–225.

Bannan, M. W. (1960a). Ontogenetic trends in conifer cambium with respect to frequency of anticlinal division and cell length. *Can. J. Bot.* **40**, 795–802.

Bannan, M. W. (1960b). Cambial behavior with reference to cell length and ring width in *Thuja occidentalis* L. *Can. J. Bot.* **38**, 177–183.

Bannan, M. W. (1962). The vascular cambium and tree-ring development. *In* "Tree Growth" (T. T. Kozlowski, ed.), Chapter 1. Ronald Press, New York.

Bannan, M. W. (1964). Tracheid size and anticlinal divisions in the cambium of *Pseudotsuga*. *Can. J. Bot.* **42**, 603–631.

Bannan, M. W. (1965a). The length, tangential diameter, and length/width ratio of conifer tracheids. *Can. J. Bot.* **43**, 967–984.

Bannan, M. W. (1965b). Ray contacts and rate of anticlinal division in fusiform cambial cells of some Pinaceae. *Can. J. Bot.* **43**, 487–507.

Bannan, M. W. (1966). Spiral grain and anticlinal divisions in the cambium of conifers. *Can. J. Bot.* **44**, 1515–1538.

Bannan, M. W. (1967). Anticlinal divisions and cell length in conifer cambium. *Forest Prod. J.* **17**, 63–69.

Bannan, M. W. (1968). Polarity in the survival and elongation of fusiform initials in conifer cambium. *Can. J. Bot.* **46**, 1005–1008.

Bannan, M. W., and Bayly, I. L. (1956). Cell size and survival in conifer cambium. *Can. J. Bot.* **34**, 769–776.

Bannister, B. (1963). Dendrochronology. *In* "Science in Archaeology," (D. Brotherwell and E. Higgs, eds.), pp. 161–176. Basic Books, Inc., New York.

Barghoorn, E. S., Jr. (1940a). Origin and development of the uniseriate ray in the Coniferae. *Bull. Torrey Bot. Club* **67**, 303–328.

Barghoorn, E. S., Jr. (1940b). The ontogenetic development and phylogenetic specialization of rays in the xylem of dicotyledons. I. The primitive ray structure. *Amer J. Bot.* **27**, 918–928.

Barghoorn, E. S., Jr. (1941a). The ontogenetic and phylogenetic specialization of rays in the xylem of dicotyledons. II. Modification of the multiseriate and uniseriate rays. *Amer. J. Bot.* **28**, 273–282.

Barghoorn, E. S., Jr. (1941b). The ontogenetic development and phylogenetic specialization of rays in the xylem of dicotyledons. III. The elimination of rays. *Bull. Torrey Bot. Club* **68**, 317–490.

Barker, W. G. (1954). A contribution to the concept of wound repair in woody stems. *Can. J. Bot.* **32**, 486–490.

Barlow, H. W. B. (1964). An interim report on a long-term experiment to assess the effect of cropping on apple tree growth. *Annu. Rep. East Malling Res. Sta.* 1963 (1964).

Barlow, H. W. B. (1966). The effect of cropping on the number and kinds of shoots on four apple varieties. *Annu. Rep. East Malling Res. Sta.* 1965, 120–124.

Barnell, E. (1939). Studies in tropical fruits. V. Some anatomical aspects of fruit fall in two tropical arboreal plants, *Ann. Bot.* **3**, 77–89.

Barnes, R. L., and Bengston, G. W. (1968). Effects of fertilization, irrigation, and cover cropping on flowering and on nitrogen and soluble sugar composition of slash pine. *Forest Sci.* **14**, 172–180.

Barney, C. W. (1951). Effects of soil temperature and light intensity on root growth of loblolly pine seedlings. *Plant Physiol.* **26**, 146–163.

Barrow, G. P. (1951). Loss of weight of three Douglas-fir poles. *Quart. J. Forest.* **45**, 235–236.

Bartholomew, E. T. (1926). Internal decline of lemons. III. Water deficit in lemon fruits caused by excessive leaf evaporation. *Amer. J. Bot.* **13**, 102–117.

Bartholomew, E. T., and Reed, H. S. (1943). General morphology, histology and physiology *In* "The Citrus Industry" (H. J. Webber and L. D. Batchelor, eds.), pp. 669–717. Univ. California, Berkeley.

Bassett, J. R. (1964a). Diameter growth of loblolly pine trees as affected by soil moisture availability. *USDA Forest Serv. Res. Pap.* **50–59**.

Bassett, J. R. (1964b). Tree growth as affected by soil moisture availability. *Soil Sci. Soc. Amer. Proc.* **28**, 436–438.

Bassett, J. R. (1966). Seasonal diameter growth of loblolly pines. *J. Forest.* **64**, 674–676.

Batjer, L. P., and Thompson, A. H. (1949). Effect of boric acid sprays applied during bloom upon the set of pear fruits. *Proc. Amer. Soc. Hort. Sci.* **53**, 141–142.

Batjer, L. P., Williams, M. W. and Martin, G. C. (1964). Effects of N-dimethylamino-succinamic acid (B.9) on vegetative and fruit characteristics of apples, pears, and sweet cherries. *Proc. Amer. Soc. Hort. Sci.* **85**, 11–19.

Beakbane, A. B. (1961). Structure of the plant in relation to adventitious rooting. *Nature (London)* **192**, 954–955.

Beakbane, A. B. (1965). Anatomical changes associated with juvenile to mature growth phase transition in *Hedera. Nature (London)* **208**, 504–505.

Bean, R. C., and Todd, G. W. (1960). Photosynthesis and respiration in developing fruits. I. $C^{14}O_2$ uptake by young oranges in light and dark. *Plant Physiol.* **35**, 425–429.

Beard, J. S., (1946). The natural vegetation of Trinidad. *Oxford Forest. Mem. No.* **20**.

Beaufait, W. R. (1960). Some effects of high temperatures in the cones and seeds of jack pine. *Forest Sci.* **6**, 194–199.

Belyea, R. M., Fraser, D. A., and Rose, A. H. (1951). Seasonal growth of some trees in Ontario. *Forest. Chron.* **27**, 1–6.

Benjamin, D. M. (1955). The biology and ecology of the red-headed pine sawfly. *USDA Tech. Bull.* **1118**.

Bengston, G. W. (1969). Growth and flowering of clones of slash pine under intensive culture: early results. *Southeastern Forest Exp. Sta. Pap.* **SE–46**.

Benic, R. (1955). Growth-ring width as a factor in the quality of *Fraxinus augustifolia* wood. *Sumarstvo* (*Beograd*) **8**, 534–545. *Forest. Abstr.* **17**, 3229 (1956.)

Bergerson, F. J., and Costin, A. B. (1964). Root nodules on *Podocarpus lawrencei* and their ecological significance. *Aust. J. Biol. Sci.* **17**, 44–48.

Bergmann, F. (1955). Försök med tvangsfruktiticering av tall gran och björk. *Svensk. Skogsvardsföreningens Tidskr.* **53**, 275–304.

Berlyn, G. P. (1961). Factors affecting the incidence of reaction tissue in *Populus deltoides* Bartr. *Iowa J. Sci.* **35**, 367–424.

Berlyn, G. P. (1962). Developmental patterns in pine polyembryony. *Amer. J. Bot.* **49**, 327–333.

Berlyn, G. P. (1964). Recent advances in wood anatomy. The cell wall in secondary xylem. *Forest Prod. J.* **14**, 467–476.

Berlyn, G. P. (1967). The structure of germination in *Pinus lambertiana*. *Yale Univ. School Forest. Bull.* **71**.

Berlyn, G. P., and Mark, R. E. (1965). Lignin distribution in wood cell walls. *Forest Prod. J.* **15**, 140–141.

Bernstein, A., and Fahn, A. (1960). The effect of annual and bi-annual pruning on the seasonal changes in xylem formation in the grape vine. *Ann. Bot.* **24**, 159–171.

Beskaravainyi, M. M. (1956). The formation of groups in pine plantings of the Kamyshinsk Forest Improvement Support Point (in Russian). *Agrobiologiya* **1956** (1), 143–146 [*Biol. Abstr.* **32** (11), 38517 (1958)].

Bethel, J. S. (1941). The effect of position within the bole upon fiber length of loblolly pine (*Pinus taeda* L.) *J. Forest.* **39**, 30–33.

Biale, J. B. (1954). The ripening of fruit. *Sci. Amer.* **190**, 40–44.

Biale, J. B. (1958). Postharvest physiology and biochemistry of fruits. *Annu. Rev. Plant Physiol.* **1**, 183–206.

Biale, J. B. (1960). The postharvest biochemistry of tropical and subtropical fruits. *Advan. Food Res.* **10**, 293–354.

Biale, J. B., Young, R. E., and Olmstead, A. (1954). Fruit respiration and ethylene production. *Plant Physiol.* **29**, 168–174.

Bilan, M. V. (1960a). Root development of loblolly pine seedlings in modified environments. *Austin State Coll. Dep. Forest. Bull.* **4**.

Bilan, M. V. (1960b). The stimulation of cone and seed production in pulpwood size loblolly pine. *Forest Sci.* **6**, 207–220.

Bingham, R. T., and Squillace, A. E. (1957). Phenology and other features of the flowering of pines, with special reference to *Pinus monticola*, Dougl. *Res. Paper* 53 N. *Region and Intermountain Forest and Range Exp. Sta.*

Bisset, I. J. W., and Dadswell, H. E. (1949). The variation of fibre length within one tree of *Eucalyptus regnans*. F. V. M. *Aust. Forest.* **13**, 86–96.

Bisset, I. J. W., and Dadswell, H. E. (1950). The variation in cell length within one growth ring of certain angiosperms and gymnosperms. *Aust. Forest.* **14**, 15–29.

Björkman, E. (1941). Die Ausbildung und Frequenz der Mycorrhiza in mit Asche gedüngten und ungedungten Teilen von entwassertem Moor. *Medd. Skogsforsoksanst.* **32**, 255–296.

Björkman, E. (1942). Über die Bedingungen der Mykorrhizabildung bei Kiefer und Fichte. *Symb. Bot. Uppsal.* **6**, 1–190.

Björkman, E. (1944). The effect of strangulation on the formation of mycorrhiza in pine. *Sv. Bot. Tidskr.* **38**, 1–14.

Björkman, E. (1949). The ecological significance of the ectotrophic mycorrhizal association in forest trees. *Sv. Bot. Tidskr.* **43**, 224–262.

Blais, J. R. (1952). The relationship of the spruce budworm (*Choristoneura fumiferana*, Clem.) to the flowering condition of balsam fir (*Abies balsamea* (L.) Mill.) *Can. J. Zool.* **30**, 1–29.

Bode, H. R. (1959). Über den Zusammenhang zwischen Blattenfaltung und Neubildung der Saugwurzeln bei *Juglans. Ber. Deut. Bot. Ges.* **72**, 93–98.

Bond, G. (1958). Symbiotic nitrogen fixation by non-legumes. *In* "Nutrition of the Legumes." (E. G. Hallsworth, ed.) pp. 216–231. Proc. 5th. Easter School Agr. Sci. Univ. Nottingham. Butterworth, London.

Bond, G. (1963). The root nodules of non-leguminous angiosperms. *Symp. Soc. Gen. Microbiol.* **13**, 72–91.

Bormann, F. H. (1957). Moisture transfer between plants through intertwined root systems. *Plant Physiol.* **32**, 48–55.

Bormann, F. H. (1961). Intraspecific root grafting and the survival of eastern white pine stumps. *Forest Sci.* **7**, 247–256.

Bormann, F. H. (1965). Changes in the growth pattern of white pine trees undergoing suppression. *Ecology* **46**, 269–277.

Bormann, F. H. (1966). The structure, function, and ecological significance of root grafts in *Pinus strobus* L. *Ecol. Monogr.* **36**, 1–26.

Bormann, F. H., and Graham, Jr., B. F. (1959). The occurrence of natural root grafting in eastern white pine, *Pinus strobus* L. and its ecological implications. *Ecology* **40**, 677–691.

Bormann, F. H., and Graham, Jr., B. F. (1960). Translocation of silvicides through root grafts. *J. Forest.* **58**, 402–403.

Bormann, F. H., and Kozlowski, T. T. (1962). Measurements of tree ring growth with dial gage dendrometers and vernier tree ring bands. *Ecology* **43**, 289–294.

Bosse, G. (1960). Die Wurzelentwicklung von Apfelkonen und Apfelsämlingen während der ersten drei Standjahre. *ErwObstbl.* **2**, 26–30.

Bosshard, H. H. (1951). Variabilität der Elemente des Eschenholzes in Funktion von der Kambiumtätigkeit. *Schweiz Z. Forstw.* **102**, 648–665.

Bottomley, W., Kefford, N. P., Zwar, J. A., and Goldacre, P. L. (1963). Kinin activity from plant extracts. I. Biological assay and sources of activity. *Aust. J. Biol. Sci.* **16**, 395–406.

Bowen, G. D., and Theodorou, C. (1967). Studies on phosphate uptake by mycorrhizas. *Rep. Sec. 24. 14th IUFRO Congr. Munich.*

Boyce, S. G., and Kaeiser, M. (1961). Why yellow-poplar seeds have low viability. *Central States Forest Exp. Sta. Tech. Pap.* **186**.

Boynton, D., Burrell, A. B., Smock, R. M., Compton, O. C., Cain, J. C., and Beattie, J. M. (1950). Responses of McIntosh apple orchards to varying nitrogen fertilization and weather. *Cornell Univ. Agr. Sta. Mem.* **290**.

Bradford, F. C. (1924). Nitrogen-carrying fertilizers and the bearing habits of mature apple trees. *Mich. Agr. Exp. Sta. Spec. Bull.* **127**

Bradley, M. V., and Crane, J. C. (1957). Gibberellin-stimulated cambial activity in stems of apricot spur shoots. *Science* **126**, 972–973.

Bradley, M. V., and Crane, J. C. (1962). Cell division and enlargement in mesocarp parenchyma of gibberellin-induced parthenocarpic peaches. *Bot. Gaz.* (*Chicago*) **123**, 243–246.

Braun, H. J. (1955). Beiträge zur Entwicklungsgeschichte der Markstrahlen. *Bot. Studien (Jena)* **4**, 73–131.

Bray, J. R. (1966). Similarity of tree growth in northern Scandinavia, polar Urals, and the Canadian Rockies. *J. Glaciol.* **6**, 321.

Brier, G. W. (1948). Northern hemisphere surface pressure and climatic fluctuations and vegetation growth in northern Finland. *Nature (London)* **161**, 730–731.

Briscoe, C. B. (1959). Early results of mycorrhizal inoculation of pine in Puerto Rico. *Carib. Forest.* **20**, 73–77.

Brix, H. (1962). The effect of water stress on the rates of photosynthesis and respiration in tomato plants and loblolly pine seedlings. *Physiol. Plant.* **15**, 10–20.

Brix. H. (1967). An analysis of dry matter production of Douglas-fir seedlings in relation to temperature and light intensity. *Can. J. Bot.* **45**, 2063–2072.

Brown, A. B. (1935). Cambial activity, root habit and sucker development in two species of poplar. *New Phytol.* **34**, 163–179.

Brown, D. S. (1953). Effects of irrigation on flower bud development and fruiting in the apricot. *Proc. Amer. Soc. Hort. Sci.* **61**, 119–124.

Brown, H. P. (1915). Growth studies in forest trees. 2. *Pinus strobus* L. *Bot. Gaz. (Chicago)* **59**, 197–241.

Buchholz, J. T. (1946). Volumetric studies of seeds, endosperms, and embryos in *Pinus ponderosa* during embryonic differentiation. *Bot. Gaz. (Chicago)* **108**, 232–244.

Buck, G. J. (1954). The histology of the bud graft union in roses. *Iowa State Coll. J. Sci.* **28**, 587–602.

Buell, M. F., Buell, H. F., Small, J. A. and Monk, C. D. (1961). Drought effect on radial growth of trees in the William L. Hutcheson Memorial *Forest Bull. Torrey Bot. Club* **88**, 176–180.

Bullock, R. M., and Benson, N. R. (1948). Boron deficiency in apricots. *Proc. Amer. Soc. Hort. Sci.* **51**, 199–204.

Bunger, M. T., and Thomson, H. J. (1938). Root development as a factor in the success or failure of windbreak trees in the Southern High Plains. *J. Forest.* **36**, 790–803.

Bushey, D. J. (1957). Regeneration of the root systems of pin oak (*Quercus palustris*) and American elm (*Ulmus americana*) following transplanting in the fall and spring. *Abst. Doctoral Dissertations No.* **52**. Ohio State Univ. Press, Columbus, Ohio.

Butijn, J. (1962). Water requirements of pome fruits. *Inst. for Land and Water Management Res., Wageningen. Tech. Bull.* **27**.

Byram, G. M., and Doolittle, W. T. (1950). A year of growth for a shortleaf pine. *Ecology* **31**, 27–35.

Cameron, R. J. (1968). The propagation of *Pinus radiata* by cuttings. Influences affecting the rooting of cuttings. *N.Z. J. Forest.* **13**, 78–89.

Cameron, R. J. and Thomson, G. V. (1969). The vegetative propagation of *Pinus radiata*: root initiation in cuttings. *Bot. Gaz.* **130**, 242–251.

Cameron, S. H. 1923. Storage of starch in the pear and apricot. *Proc. Amer. Soc. Hort. Sci.* **20**, 1–3.

Cameron, S. H., and Appleman, D. (1934). Total N in developing flowers and young fruits of the Valencia orange. *Proc. Amer. Soc. Hort. Sci.* **32**, 204–207.

Cameron, S. H., and Borst, G. (1938). Starch in the avocado tree. *Proc. Amer. Soc. Hort. Sci.* **36**, 255–258.

Cameron, S. H., Mueller, R. T., Wallace, A., and Sartori, E. (1952). Influence of age of leaf, season of growth, and fruit production on the size and inorganic composition of Valencia orange leaves. *Proc. Amer. Soc. Hort. Sci.* **60**, 42–50.

Cameron, S. H., and Schroeder, C. A. (1945). Cambial activity and starch cycle in bearing orange trees. *Proc. Amer. Soc. Hort. Sci.* **46**, 55–59.

Campbell, A. I. (1961). Shortening the juvenile phase of apple seedlings. *Nature* (*London*) **191**, 517.

Cannell, M. G. R. and Huxley, P. A. (1969). Seasonal differences in the pattern of assimilate movement in branches of *Coffea arabica* L. *Ann. Appl. Biol.* **64**, 345–357.

Carlson, M. C. (1938). The formation of nodal adventitious roots in *Salix cordata*. *Amer. J. Bot.* **25**, 721–725.

Carlson, M. C. (1950). Nodal adventitious roots in willow stems of different ages. *Amer. J. Bot.* **37**, 555–556.

Carpenter, E. D., and Watson, D. P. (1965). The initiation and differentiation of flower buds of four rosaceous ornamental shrubs. *Proc. Amer. Soc. Hort. Sci.* **86**, 806–808.

Carpenter, J. B. (1961). Occurrence and inheritance of preformed root primordia in stems of citron (*Citrus medica* L.) *Proc. Amer. Soc. Hort. Sci.* **77**, 211–218.

Casperson, G. (1960). Über die Bildung von Zellwänden bei Laubhölzern. I. Mitteilung Feststellung der Kambiumactivität durch Erzeugen von Reaktionsholz. *Ber. Deut. Bot. Ges.* **73**, 349–357.

Cathey, H. M. (1964). Physiology of growth retarding chemicals. *Annu. Rev. Plant Physiol.* **15**, 271–302.

Cayford, J. H., and Waldron, R. M. (1965). Multiple jack pine seedlings. *Can. J. Bot.* **43**. 481–482.

Chalk, L. (1930). The formation of spring and summerwood in ash and Douglas-fir. *Oxford Forest. Mem. No.* **10**.

Chalk, L. (1937). A note on the meaning of the terms earlywood and latewood. *Leeds Phil. Soc. Proc.* **3**, 324–325.

Challenger, S., Lacey, H. J., and Howard, B. H. (1965). The demonstration of root promoting substances in apple and plum rootstocks. *Ann. Rep. E. Malling Res. Sta.* 1964, 124–128.

Champagnat, P. (1954). "The Pruning of Fruit Trees." Crosby, Lockwood and Sun, London.

Chandler, W. H. (1957). "Deciduous Orchards." Lea and Febiger, Philadelphia, Pennsylvania.

Chaney, W. R., and Kozlowski, T. T. (1968). Relation of vapor pressure deficits to diurnal expansion and contraction of fruits of forest trees. *Bull. Ecol. Soc. Amer.* **49**, 69.

Chaney, W. R., and Kozlowski, T. T. (1969a). Seasonal and diurnal expansion and contraction of fruits of forest trees. *Can. J. Bot.* **47**, 1033–1038.

Chaney, W. R., and Kozlowski, T. T. (1969b). Seasonal and diurnal changes in water balance of fruits, cones, and leaves of forest trees. *Can. J. Bot.* **47**, 1407–1417.

Chaney, W. R., and Kozlowski, T. T. (1969c). Seasonal and diurnal expansion and contraction of *Pinus banksiana* and *Picea glauca* cones. *New Phytol.* **68**, 873–882.

Chaney, W. R., and Kozlowski, T. T. (1969d). Diurnal expansion and contraction of leaves and fruits of English Morello cherry. *Ann. Bot.* **33**, 691–699.

Chaney, W. R., and Kozlowski, T. T. (1971). Water transport in relation to expansion and contraction of leaves and fruits of Calamondin orange. *J. Hort. Sci.* **46**, 71–81.

Chang, Y. (1954a). Bark structure of North American conifers. *US Dep. Agr. Tech. Bull.* **1095**.

Chang, Y. (1954b). Anatomy of common North American pulpwood barks. *Tappi Monogr. No.* **14**.

Chattaway, M. M. (1933). Ray development in the Sterculiaceae. *Forestry* **7**, 93–108.

Chattaway, M. M. (1938). The wood anatomy of the family Sterculiaceae. *Phil. Trans. Roy. Soc. London Ser.* **B228**, 313–365.

Chattaway, M. M. (1953). The anatomy of bark. I. The genus *Eucalyptus*. *Aust. J. Bot.* **1**, 402–433.

Chattaway, M. M. (1955). The anatomy of bark. V. *Eucalyptus* species with stringy bark. *Aust. J. Bot.* **3**, 165–169.

Cheadle, V. I., and Esau, K. (1964). Secondary phloem of *Liriodendron tulipifera. Univ. Calif. Publ. Bot.* **36**, 143–252.

Childers, N. F. (1961). "Modern Fruit Science." Horticultural Publ. Rutgers Univ., New Brunswick, New Jersey.

Childers, N. F. (Ed.). (1966a). "Fruit Nutrition." Horticultural Publ. Rutgers Univ., New Brunswick, New Jersey.

Childers, N. F. (1966b). "Nutrition of Fruit Crops." *Horticultural* Publ. Rutgers Univ., New Brunswick, New Jersey.

Childers, N. F., and Cowart, F. F. (1935). The photosynthesis, transpiration, and stomata of apple leaves as affected by certain nutrient deficiencies. *Proc. Amer. Soc. Hort. Sci.* **33**, 160–163.

Childers, N. F., and White, D. G. (1942). Influence of submersion of the roots on transpiration, apparent photosynthesis, and respiration of young apple trees. *Plant Physiol.* **17**, 603–618.

Chilvers, G. A., and Pryor, L. D. (1965). The structure of Eucalypt mycorrhizas. *Aust. J. Bot.* **13**, 245–259.

Ching, T. M., and Ching, K. K. (1962). Physical and physiological changes in maturing Douglas-fir cones and seed. *Forest Sci.* **8**, 21–31.

Ching, T. M., and Fang, S. C. (1963). Utilization of labeled glucose in developing Douglas-fir seed cones. *Plant Physiol.* **38**, 551–554.

Chowdhury, K. (1939). The formation of growth rings in Indian trees. I. *Indian Forest Rec. Util.* **2**, 1–39.

Church, T. W. (1949). Effects of defoliation on growth of certain conifers. U.S. Forest Service. *Northeastern Forest Exp. Sta. Pap.* **22**.

Ciampi, C., and Gellini, R. (1963). The origin and development of adventitious roots in *Olea europaea.* The importance of anatomical structure in root development. *Nuovo G. Bot. Ital.* **70**, 62–74 [*Hort. Abstr.* **35**, (4422) (1965)].

Clark, J. W. (1949). Infections of *Fomes pini* through root grafts of Douglas-fir. M.S. thesis. Univ. of Washington, Seattle.

Clausen, J. J., and Kozlowski, T. T. (1965). Seasonal changes in moisture contents of gymnosperm cones. *Nature (London)* **206**, 112–113.

Cockerham, G. (1930). Some observations on cambial activity and seasonal starch content in sycamore (*Acer Pseudo-Platanus*) *Proc. Leeds Phil. Lit. Soc. Sci. Sect.* **2**, 64–80.

Cockrell, R. A. (1941). A comparative study of the wood structure of several South American species of *Strychnos. Amer. J. Bot.* **28**, 32–41.

Cockroft, B., and Wallbrink, J. C. (1966). Root distribution of orchard trees. *Aust. J. Agr. Res.* **17**, 49–54.

Coile, T. S. (1937). Distribution of forest tree roots in North Carolina Piedmont soils. *J. Forest* **35**, 247–257.

Coombe, B. G. (1960). Relationships of growth and development to changes in sugars, auxins, and gibberellins, in fruits of seeded and seedless varieties of *Vitis vinifera. Plant Physiol.* **35**, 241–250.

Coombe, D. E. (1960). An analysis of the growth of *Trema guineensis. J. Ecology* **48**, 219–231.

Coombe, D. E., and Hatfield, W. (1962). An analysis of the growth of *Musanga cecropioides. J. Ecol.* **50**, 221–234.

Cooper, W. C. (1957). Periodicity of growth and dormancy in citrus—a review with some observations of conditions in the lower Rio Grande Valley of Texas. *J. Rio. Grande Hort. Soc.* **11**, 3–10.

Cooper, W. C., Rasmussen, G. K., Rogers, B. J., Reece, P. C., and Henry, W. H. (1968). Control of abscission in agricultural crops and its physiological basis. *Plant Physiol.* **43** (Part B), 1560–1576.

Copeland, O. L., Jr. (1952). Root mortality of shortleaf and loblolly pine in relation to soils and littleleaf disease. *J. Forest.* **50**, 21–25.

Copes, D. (1967). Grafting incompatability in Douglas fir. *Proc. Int. Plant Propagators Soc. Annu. Mtg.* 130–138.

Copes, D. (1969). Graft union formation in Douglas-fir. *Amer. J. Bot.* **56**, 285–289.

Cormack, R. G. H. (1949). The development of root hairs in angiosperms. *Bot. Rev.* **15**, 583–612.

Corner, E. J. H. (1940). "Wayside Trees of Malaya," Vol. 1. Gov. Printing Office, Singapore.

Coté, W. A. Jr. (Ed.). (1965). "Cellular Ultrastructure of Woody Plants." Syracuse Univ. Press, Syracuse, New York.

Coté, W. A. Jr. (1967). *In* "Wood Ultrastructure". Washington Univ. Press, Seattle.

Cowling, E. B., and Merrill, W. (1966). Nitrogen in wood and its role in wood deterioration. *Can. J. Bot.* **44**, 1539–1554.

Cram, W. H., and Worden, H. H. (1957). Maturity of white spruce cones and seed. *Forest Sci.* **3**, 263–269.

Crane, J. C. (1964). Growth substances in fruit setting and development. *Annu. Rev. Plant Physiol.* **15**, 303–326.

Crane, J. C. (1969). The role of hormones in fruit set and development. *Hort. Sci.* **4**, 108–111.

Crane, J. C., and Brooks, R. M. (1952). Growth of apricot fruits as influenced by 2,4-5-trichlorophenoxyacetic acid application. *Proc. Amer. Soc. Hort. Sci.* **59**, 218–224.

Crane, J. C., Primer, P. E., and Campbell, R. C. (1960). Gibberellin induced parthenocarpy in *Prunus. Proc. Amer. Soc. Hort. Sci.* **75**, 129–137.

Crane, J. C., Rebeiz, C. A., and Campbell, R. C. (1961). Gibberellin induced parthenocarpy in the J. H. Hale peach and the probable cause of "button" production. *Proc. Amer. Soc. Hort. Sci.* **78**, 11–118.

Crane, J. C., and Overbeek, J. van. (1965). Kinin-induced parthenocarpy in the fig, *Ficus carica* L. *Science* **147**, 1468–1469.

Crocker, R. L., and Major, J. (1955). Soil development in relation to vegetation and surface age at Glacier Bay, Alaska. *J. Ecol.* **43**, 427–448.

Cronshaw, J. (1965a). The organization of cytoplasmic components during the phase of cell wall thickening in differentiating cambial derivatives of *Acer rubrum. Can. J. Bot.* **43**, 1401–1407.

Cronshaw, J. (1965b). Cytoplasmic fine structure and cell wall development in differentiating xylem elements. *In* "Cellular Ultrastructure of Woody Cells" (W. A. Coté, Jr., ed.), pp. 99–124. Syracuse Univ. Press, Syracuse, New York.

Cronshaw, J., and Morey, P. R. (1965). Induction of tension wood by 2,3,5-tri-iodobenzoic acid. *Nature (London)* **205**, 816–818.

Cronshaw, J., and Wardrop, A. B. (1964). Organization of cytoplasm in differentiating xylem of *Pinus radiata. Aust. J. Bot.* **12**, 15–23.

Cumming, W. C., and Righter, F. I. (1948). Methods used to control pollination of pines in the Sierra Nevada of California. *USDA Circ.* **792**.

Curtis, J. T., and Cottam, G. (1950). Antibiotic and autotoxic effects in prairie sunflower. *Bull. Torrey Bot. Club* **77**, 187–191.

Dadswell, H. E. (1958). Wood structure variations occurring during tree growth and their influence on properties. *J. Inst. Wood Sci.* **1**, 11–33.

Dadswell, H. E., and Wardrop, A. B. (1956). Structure, properties, and formation of tension wood. *Proc. 8th Int. Bot. Congr.* Part 4, Sec. 13, 85–10.

Daubenmire, R. F. (1945). An improved type of precision dendrometer. *Ecology* **26**, 97–98.

Daubenmire, R. F., and Deters, M. E. (1947). Comparative studies of growth in deciduous and evergreen trees. *Bot. Gaz. (Chicago)* **109**, 1–12.

Davis, J. D., and Evert, R. F. (1965). Phloem development in *Populus tremuloides. Amer. J. Bot.* **52**, 627.

Davis, L. D. (1957). Flowering and alternate bearing. *Proc. Amer. Soc. Hort. Sci.* **70**, 545–556.

Davis, T. A. W., and Richards, P. W. (1933). The vegetation of Moraballi Creek, British Guiana; an ecological study of a limited area of Tropical Rain Forest. Parts I and II. *J. Ecol.* **21**, 350–384; **22**, 106–155.

De Byle, N. V., and Place, I. C. M. (1959). Rooting habits of oak and pine on Plainfield sand in central Wisconsin. *Univ. Wisc. Forest. Res. Note* **44**.

Decker, J. P. (1944). Effect of temperature on photosynthesis and respiration in red and loblolly pines. *Plant Physiol.* **19**, 679–688.

Delap, A. V. (1967). The effect of supplying nitrate at different seasons on the growth, blossoming and nitrogen content of young apple trees in sand culture. *J. Hort. Sci.* **42**, 149–167.

Delisle, A. L. (1954). The relationship between the age of the tree and rooting of cuttings of white pine. *Proc. Indiana Acad. Sci.* **64**, 60–61.

DeMaggio, A. E. (1966). Phloem differentiation: Induced stimulation by gibberellic acid. *Science* **152**, 370–372.

DeMaggio, A. E. (1969). Dormancy regulation: hormonal interaction in maple (*Acer platanoides*). *Can. J. Bot.* **47**, 1165–1169.

Denisov, A. K. (1960). Razvitie pridatocnyh kornej v pescanom aljuvii drevesnymi i Kustarnikovymi porodami juznoj tajgi. *Bot. Z.* **45**, 1516–1522.

Derr, W. F., and Evert, R. F. (1967). The cambium and seasonal development of the phloem in *Robinia pseudoacacia. Amer. J. Bot.* **54**, 147–153.

Deshpande, B. P. (1967). Initiation of cambial activity and its relation to primary growth in *Tilia americana* L. Ph.D. dissertation. Univ. Wisconsin, Madison, Wisconsin.

Dickmann, D. I., and Kozlowski, T. T. (1968). Mobilization by *Pinus resinosa* cones and shoots of C^{14}-photosynthate from needles of different ages. *Amer. J. Bot.* **55**, 900–906.

Dickmann, D. I., and Kozlowski, T. T. (1969a). Seasonal growth patterns of *Pinus resinosa* Ait. pistillate strobili in central Wisconsin. *Can. J. Bot.* **47**, 839–848.

Dickmann, D. I., and Kozlowski, T. T. (1969b). Seasonal variations in reserve and structural components of *Pinus resinosa* Ait. cones. *Amer. J. Bot.* **56**, 515–521.

Dickmann, D. I., and Kozlowski, T. T. (1969c). Seasonal changes in the macro and micro-nutrient composition of ovulate strobili and seeds of *Pinus resinosa* Ait. *Can. J. Bot.* **47**, 1547–1554.

Dickmann, D. I., and Kozlowski, T. T. (1970a). Mobilization and incorporation of photo-assimilated ^{14}C by growing vegetative and reproductive tissues of adult *Pinus resinosa* Ait. trees. *Plant Physiol.* **45**, 284–288.

Dickmann, D. I., and Kozlowski, T. T. (1970b). Photosynthesis by rapidly expanding green strobili of *Pinus resinosa. Life Sci.* **9**, 2(10), 549–552.

Dickmann, D. I., and Kozlowski, T. T. (1971). Cone size and seed yield in red pine. *Amer. Midl. Naturalist* **85**, 431–436.

Digby, J., Thomas, T. H., and Wareing, P. F. (1964). Promotion of cell division in tissue cultures by gibberellic acid. *Nature (London)* **203**, 547–548.

Digby, J., and Wareing, P. F. (1966a). The effect of applied growth hormones on cambial division and the differentiation of the cambial derivatives. *Ann. Bot.* **30**, 539–548.

Digby, J., and Wareing, P. F. (1966b). The relationship between endogenous hormone levels in the plant and seasonal aspects of cambial activity. *Ann. Bot.* **30**, 607–622.

Dimock, E. J. (1964). Simultaneous variations in seasonal height and radial growth of young Douglas-fir. *J. Forest.* **62**, 252–255.

Dinwoodie, J. M. (1961). Tracheid and fibre length in timber. A review of literature. *Forestry* **34**, 125–144.

Dinwoodie, J. M. (1963). Variation in tracheid length in *Picea sitchensis* (Carr.) *Dep. Sci. Ind. Res. Forest Prod. Res. Spec. Rep. (London)* **16**.

Dittmer, H. J. (1949). Root hair variations in plant species. *Amer. J. Bot.* **36**, 152–155.

Doley, D., and Leyton, L. (1968). Effects of growth regulating substances and water potential on the development of secondary xylem in *Fraxinus*. *New Phytol.* **67**, 579–594.

Domanski, R., Kozlowski, T. T., and Sasaki, S. (1969). Interactions of applied growth regulators and temperature on root initiation in *Salix* cuttings. *J. Amer. Soc. Hort. Sci.* **94**, 39–41.

Dominik, T. (1955). Vorschlag einer neuer Klassifikation der ektotrophen Mykorrhizen auf morphologisch-anatomischen Merkmalen begrundet. *Rocz. Nauk. Pol.* **14**, 223–245.

Doran, W. L. (1957). Propagation of woody plants by cuttings. Univ. Massachusetts. *Exp. Sta. Bull.* **491**.

Dorman, K. W., and Barber, J. C. (1956). Time of flowering and seed ripening in southern pines. *Southeast. Forest Exp. Sta. Pap.* **72**.

Dormling, I. (1963). Anatomical and histological examinations of the union of scion and stock in grafts of Scots pine (*Pinus silvestris* L.) and Norway spruce (*Picea abies* (L.) Karst.). *Stud. Forest. Suec.* **13**.

Douglass, A. E. (1946). Precision of ring dating in tree-ring chronologies. *Univ. Arizona Bull.* **16**.

Doyle, J. (1935). Pollination in *Pinus*. *Sci. Proc. Roy. Dublin. Soc.* **21**, 181–190.

Doyle, J. (1945). Developmental lines in pollination mechanisms in the Coniferales. *Sci. Proc. Roy. Dublin Soc.* **24**, 43–62.

Doyle, J., and Kane, A. (1943). Pollination in *Tsuga pattoniana* and in species of *Abies* and *Picea*. *Sci. Proc. Roy. Dublin Soc.* **23**, 57–70.

Doyle, J., and O'Leary, M. (1935). Pollination in *Tsuga, Cedrus, Pseudotsuga* and *Larix*. *Sci. Proc. Roy. Dublin Soc.* **21**, 191–204.

Duff, G. H., and Nolan, N. J. (1953). Growth and morphogenesis in the Canadian forest species. I. The controls of cambial and apical activity in *Pinus resinosa* Ait. *Can. J. Bot.* **31**, 471–513.

Duffield, J. W. (1950). Techniques and possibilities for Douglas-fir breeding. *J. Forest.* **28**, 41–45.

Duffield, J. W. 1953. Pine collection dates—annual and geographic variation. *Calif. Forest and Range Exp. Sta. Res. Note* **85**.

Eames, A. J. (1961). "Morphology of the Angiosperms." McGraw-Hill, New York.

Eames, A. J., and MacDaniels, L. H. (1947). "An Introduction to Plant Anatomy." McGraw-Hill Book Co., New York.

Echols, R. M. (1958). Variation in tracheid length and wood density in geographic races of scotch pine. *Yale Univ. School Forestry Bull.* **64**.

Edgerton, L. J. and Hoffman, M. B. (1965). Some physiological responses of apple to *N*-dimethyl amino succinamic acid and other growth regulators. *Proc. Amer. Soc. Hort. Sci.* **86**, 28–36.

Eggler, W. A. (1955). Radial growth in nine species of trees in southern Louisiana. *Ecology* **36**, 130–136.

Eis, S., Garman, E. H., and Ebell, L. F. (1965). Relation between cone production and diameter increment of Douglas fir (*Pseudotsuga menziesii* (Mirb.) Franco, Grand fir

(*Abies grandis* (Dougl.). Lindl.), and western white pine (*Pinus monticola* Dougl.). *Can. J. Bot.* **43**, 1553–1559.

Ekdahl, I. (1941). Die Entwicklung von Embryosack und Embryo bei *Ulmus glabra* Huds. *Sv. Bot. Tidskr.* **35**, 143–156.

Eklund, B. (1949). Skogsforkingsinst. Arsringsmätningmaskiner. *Medd. Fran Skogsforskn Inst. Stockholm* **38**, 1–77.

Elliott, G. K. (1960). The distribution of tracheid length in a single stem of Sitka spruce. *J. Inst. Wood Sci.* **5**, 38–47.

Erickson, H. D., and Lambert, G. M. G. (1958). Effect of fertilization and thinning on chemical composition, growth, and specific gravity of young Douglas-fir. *Forest Sci.* **4**, 307–315.

Erickson, L. C., and Brannaman, B. L. (1960). Abscission of reproductive structure and leaves of orange trees. *Proc. Amer. Soc. Hort. Sci.* **75**, 222–229.

Esau, K. (1948). Phloem structure in the grapevine and its seasonal changes. *Hilgardia* **18**, 217–275.

Esau, K. (1964). Structure and development of the bark in dicotyledons. *In* "The Formation of Wood in Forest Trees" (M. H. Zimmermann, ed.), pp. 37–50. Academic Press, New York.

Esau, K. (1960). "Anatomy of Seed Plants." Wiley, New York.

Esau, K. (1965a). "Vascular Differentiation in Plants." Holt, Rinehart, and Winston, N.Y.

Esau, K. (1965b). "Plant Anatomy." Wiley, New York.

Esau, K. (1965c). Anatomy and cytology of *Vitis* phloem. *Hilgardia* **37**, 17–72.

Esau, K. (1965d). On the anatomy of the woody plant. *In* "Cellular Ultrastructure of Woody Plants" (W. A. Coté, ed.), pp. 35–50. Syracuse Univ. Press, Syracuse, New York.

Esau, K. (1966). Exploration of the food conducting system in plants. *Amer. Sci.* **54**, 141–157.

Esau, K., and Cheadle, V. I. (1969). Secondary growth in *Bougainvillea*. *Ann. Bot.* **33**, 807–818.

Evert, R. F. (1960). Phloem structure in *Pyrus communis* L. and its seasonal changes. *Univ. Calif. Publ. Bot.* **32**, 127–194.

Evert, R. F. (1961). Some aspects of cambial development in *Pyrus communis*. *Amer. J. Bot.* **48**, 479–488.

Evert, R. F. (1963a). Ontogeny and structure of the secondary phloem in *Pyrus malus*. *Amer. J. Bot.* **50**, 8–37.

Evert, R. F. (1963b). The cambium and seasonal development of the phloem in *Pyrus malus*. *Amer. J. Bot.* **50**, 149–159.

Evert, R. F. (1963c). Sclerified companion cells in *Tilia americana*. *Bot. Gaz.* (*Chicago*) **124**, 262–264.

Evert, R. F., and Alfieri, F. J. (1965). Ontogeny and structure of coniferous sieve cells. *Amer. J. Bot.* **52**, 1058–1066.

Evert, R. F., and Kozlowski, T. T. (1967). Effect of isolation of bark on cambial activity and development of xylem and phloem in trembling aspen. *Amer. J. Bot.* **54**, 1045–1055.

Evert, R. F., Murmanis, L., and Sachs, I. B. (1966). Another view of the ultrastructure of *Cucurbita* phloem. *Ann. Bot.* **30**, 563–585.

Evert, R. F., Tucker, C. M., Davis, J. D., and Deshpande, B. P. (1969). Light microscope investigation of sieve element ontogeny and structure in *Ulmus americana*. *Amer. J. Bot.* **56**, 999–1017.

Ewart, A. J., and Mason-Jones, A. J. (1906). Formation of red wood in conifers. *Ann. Bot.* **20**, 201–204

Fadl, M. S., and Hartmann, H. T. (1967). Isolation, purification, and characterization of an endogenous root-promoting factor obtained from basal sections of pear hardwood cuttings. *Plant Physiol.* **42**, 541–549.

Faegri, K., and Iversen, J. (1964). "Textbook of Pollen Analysis." Hafner, New York.

Faegri, K., and Van der Pijl. L. (1966). "The Principles of Pollination Ecology." Macmillan (Pergamon), New York.

Fahn, A., and Arnon, N. (1963). The living wood fibers of *Tamarix aphylla* and the changes occurring from sapwood to heartwood. *New Phytol.* **62**, 99–104.

Fahn, A., Waisel, Y., and Binyamini, L. (1968). Cambial activity in *Acacia raddiana.* *Ann. Bot.* **32**, 677–686.

Fahn, A. (1967). "Plant Anatomy." Pergamon Press, Oxford.

Farrar, J. L. (1961). Longitudinal variations in the thickness of the annual ring. *Forest. Chron.* **37**, 323–331.

Farrar, J. L., and Zichmanis, H. (1960). The accurate measurement of diameter changes in small stems. *Annual Ring* (Fac. Forest., Univ. Toronto) pp. 16–17.

Fassi, B. (1960). Die Verteilung der ektotrophen Mykorrhizen in der Streu in Kongo. *In* "Mykorrhiza." Int. Mykorrhizasymposium. G. Fisher-Verlag, Jena.

Fayle, D. C. F. (1968). Radial growth in tree roots. *Fac. Forest., Univ. Toronto Tech. Rep.* **9.**

Fegel, A. C. (1941). Comparative anatomy and varying physical properties of trunk, branch and root wood in certain northeastern trees. *N.Y. State Coll. Forest., Syracuse, New York, Tech. Bull.* **55**.

Fenton, R. H. (1965). Root grafts and translocation of 2,4,5-T in young sweet-gum stands. *J. Forest.* **63**, 16–18.

Fielding, J. M. (1960). Branching and flowering characteristics of Monterey pine. *Austral. Forest. Timber Bur. Bull.* **37**.

Fielding, J. M., and Millett, M. R. O. (1941). Some studies of the growth of Monterey pine (*Pinus radiata*) I. Diameter growth. *Forest Bur. Bull. Aust.* **27**, 33 pp.

Finn, R. F., and White, D. P. (1966). Commercial fertilizers increase growth in a yellow-poplar plantation. *J. Forest.* **64**, 809–810.

Fisher, E., Boynton, D., and Skodvin, K. (1948). Nitrogen fertilization of the McIntosh apple with leaf sprays of urea. *Proc. Amer. Soc. Hort. Sci.* **51**, 23–32.

Foil, R. R. (1961). Late season soil moisture shows significant effect on width of slash pine summerwood. *La. Agr. Exp. Sta. Bull. Forest. Note* **44**.

Forward, D. F., and Nolan, N. J. (1961). Growth and morphogenesis in the Canadian forest species. IV. Further studies of wood growth in branches and main axis of *Pinus resinosa* Ait. under conditions of open growth, suppression, and release. *Can. J. Bot.* **39**, 411–436.

Foster, R. C., and Marks, G. C. (1966). The fine structure of the mycorrhizas of *Pinus radiata* D. Don. *Aust. J. Biol. Sci.* **19**, 1027–1038.

Foster, R. C., and Marks, G. C. (1967). Observations on the mycorrhizas of forest trees. II. The rhizosphere of *Pinus radiata*. D. Don. *Aust. J. Biol. Sci.* **20**, 915–926.

Fowells, H. A., and Schubert, G. H. (1956). Seed crops of forest trees in the pine region of California. *USDA Tech. Bull.* **1150**.

Frank, A. B. (1885). Ueber die auf Wurzelsymbiose beruhende Ernährung gewisser Bäume durch unterirdische Pilze. *Ber. Deut. Bot. Ges.* **3**, 128–145.

Fraser, D. A. (1952). Initiation of cambial activity in some forest trees in Ontario. *Ecology* **33**, 259–273.

Fraser, D. A. (1956). Ecological studies of forest trees at Chalk River, Ontario, Canada. II. Ecological conditions and radial increment. *Ecology* **37**, 777–789.

Fraser, D. A. (1962). Apical and radial growth of white spruce (*Picea glauca* (Moench) Voss) at Chalk River, Ontario, Canada. *Can. J. Bot.* **40**, 659–668.

Fritts, H. C. (1956). Radial growth of beech and soil moisture in a central Ohio forest during the growing season of 1952. *Ohio J. Sci.* **56**, 17–28.

Fritts, H. C. (1958). An analysis of radial growth of beech in a central Ohio forest during 1954—1955. *Ecology*, **39**, 705–720.

Fritts, H. C. (1959a). The relation of radial growth to maximum and minimum temperatures in three tree species. *Ecology* **40**, 261–265.

Fritts, H. C. (1959b). The growth-environmental relationships of mature forest trees. *Yearb. Amer. Phil. Soc.* **1959**, 269–270.

Fritts, H. C. (1960). Multiple regression analysis of radial growth in individual trees. *Forest Sci.* **6**, 334–349.

Fritts, H. C. (1962). The relation of growth ring widths in American beech and white oak to variations in climate. *Tree-Ring Bull.* **25**, 2–10.

Fritts, H. C. (1966). Growth rings of trees: their correlation with climate. *Science* **154**, 973–979.

Fritts, H. C. (1967). Tree-ring analysis (Dendroclimatology) *In* "Encyclopedia of Atmospheric Sciences and Astrogeology" (R. W. Fairbridge, ed.), pp. 1008–1027. Reinhold, New York.

Fritts, H. C., and Fritts, E. C. (1955). A new dendrograph for recording radial changes of a tree. *Forest Sci.* **1**, 271–276.

Fritts, H. C., Smith, D. G., Cardis, J. W., and Budelsky, C. A. (1965). Tree-ring characteristics along a vegetation gradient in northern Arizona. *Ecology* **46**, 393–401.

Fritts, H. C., Smith, D. G., and Stokes, M. A. (1965). The biological model for paleoclimatic interpretation of Mesa Verde tree-ring series. *Amer. Antiquity* **31**, 101–121.

Fritz, E. (1939). Increment core handling. *J. Forest.* **37**, 491–492.

Fulford, R. M. (1962). The development of apple spur buds in relation to leaves and fruits XVI *Int. Hort. Congr.* **3**, 343–346.

Fulford, R. M. (1965). The morphogenesis of apple buds. I. The activity of the apical meristem. *Ann. Bot.* **29**, 167–180.

Fulford, R. M. (1966a). The morphogenesis of apple buds. II. The development of the bud. *Ann. Bot.* **30**, 25–38.

Fulford, R. M. (1966b). The morphogenesis of apple buds. III. The inception of flowers. *Ann. Bot.* **30**, 207–219.

Fulford, R. M. (1966c). The morphogenesis of apple buds. IV. The effect of fruit. *Ann. Bot.* **30**, 597–606.

Fuller, H. J., and Tippo, O. (1949). "College Botany." Holt, New York.

Furr, J. R., and Armstrong, W. W. (1956). Flower induction in Marsh grapefruit in the Coachella Valley, California. *Proc. Amer. Soc. Hort. Sci.* **67**, 176–182.

Gabriel, W. J. (1966). The onset and duration of stigma receptivity in sugar maple flowers. *Forest Sci.* **12**, 14–18.

Gane, R. (1934). Production of ethylene by some ripening fruits. *Nature* (*London*) **134**, 1008.

Gane, R. (1936). A study of the respiration of bananas. *New Phytol.* **35**, 383–402.

Garner, R. J. (1967). "The Grafter's Handbook," 2nd Ed. Faber and Faber, London.

Gates, C. T., Bouma, D., and Groenewegen, H. (1961). The development of cuttings of the Washington Navel orange to the stage of fruit set. III. The fruiting cutting. *Aust. J. Agr. Res.* **12**, 1081–1088.

Gäumann, E. (1935). Der Stoffhaushalt der Buche. (*Fagus sylvatica* L.) im Laufe eines Jahres. *Ber. Deut. Bot. Ges.* **45**, 591–597.

Gazit, S. and Blumenfeld, A. (1970). Cytokinin and inhibitor activities in the avocado fruit mesocarp. *Plant Physiol.* **46**, 334–336.

Gellini, R. (1964). Studio sulla radicazione de talee di *Ficus carica* L. Osservazioni salla struttura e sullo suillupo di radici preformata. *In* "Atti delle Giornate di Studio su la Propagazione della Specie Legnose," pp. 198–219. Universita di Pisa, Institutio di Coltirazioni Arboree.

Giddings, J. L. (1962). Development of tree-ring dating as an archeological aid. *In* "Tree Growth" (T. T. Kozlowski, ed.), Chapter 6. Ronald Press, New York.

Ginzburg, C. (1963). Some anatomic features of splitting of desert shrubs. *Phytomorphology* **13**, 92–97.

Girouard, R. M. (1967a). Initiation and development of adventitious roots in stem cuttings of *Hedera helix*. Anatomical studies of the mature growth phase. *Can. J. Bot.* **45**, 1883–1886.

Girouard, R. M. (1967b). Initiation and development of adventitious roots in stem cuttings of *Hedera helix*. Anatomical studies of the juvenile growth phase. *Can. J. Bot.* **45**, 1877–1881.

Girouard, R. M. (1969). Physiological and biochemical studies of adventitious root formation. Extractible rooting cofactors from *Hedera helix*. *Can. J. Bot.* **47**, 687–699.

Glerum, C., and Farrar, J. L. (1966). Frost ring formation in the stems of some coniferous species. *Can. J. Bot.* **44**, 879–886.

Glock, W. S. (1937). Observations on the western juniper. *Madrono* **4**, 21–28.

Glock, W. S., and Agerter, S. R. (1962). Rainfall and tree growth. *In* "Tree Growth" (T. T. Kozlowski, ed.), Chapter 2. Ronald Press, New York.

Glock, W. S., and Agerter, S. R. (1963). Anomalous patterns in tree rings. *Endeavour* **22**, 9–13.

Glock, W. S., Agerter, S. R., and Studhalter, R. A. (1964). Tip growth in trees of west Texas and Maryland. *Advan. Frontiers Plant Sci.* **9**, 15–106.

Glock, W. S., Studhalter, R. A., and Agerter, S. R. (1960). Classification and multiplicity of growth layers in the branches of trees at the extreme lower border. *Smithson. Misc. Collect.* **4421**.

Godman, R. M. (1959). Winter sunscald of yellow birch. *J. Forest.* **57**, 368–369.

Goldacre, P. L., and Bottomley, W. (1959). A kinin in apple fruitlets. *Nature (London)* **184**, 555–556.

Goldman, C. R. (1961). The contribution of alder trees (*Alnus tenuifolia*) to the primary productivity of Castle Lake, Calif. *Ecology* **42**, 282–287.

Gomez, J. B., and Thai, C. K. (1967). Alignment of anatomical elements in the stem of *Hevea brasiliensis*. *J. Rubber Res. Inst. Malaya* **20**, 91–99.

Goo, M. (1961). Development of flower bud in *Pinus densiflora* and *P. thunbergii*. *J. Jap. Forest Soc.* **43**, 306–309.

Goodin, J. R. (1965). Anatomical changes associated with juvenile-to-mature growth phase transition in *Hedera*. *Nature (London)* **208**, 504–505.

Gooding, E. G. B. (1952a). Studies in the physiology of latex. III. Latex flow on tapping *Hevea brasiliensis*: associated changes in trunk diameter and latex concentration. *New Phytol.* **51**, 11–29.

Gooding, E. G. B. (1952b). A note on Pyke's dendrometer. *New Phytol.* **51**, 258–259.

Goodwin, R. H., and Goddard, D. R. (1940). The oxygen consumption of isolated woody tissues. *Amer. J. Bot.* **27**, 234–237.

Gordon, J. C., and Larson, P. R. (1968). Seasonal course of photosynthesis, respiration, and distribution of ^{14}C in young *Pinus resinosa* trees as related to wood formation. *Plant Physiol.* **43**, 1617–1624.

Gore, H. C. (1911). Studies in fruit respiration. *USDA Bur. Chem. Bull.* **142**.

Gouwentak, C. A. (1941). Cambial activity as dependent on the presence of growth hormone and the non-resting condition of stems. *Proc. Amsterdam Acad. Sci.* **44**, 654–663.

Graham, B. F., Jr., and Bormann, F. H. (1966). Natural root grafts. *Bot. Rev.* **32**, 255–292.

Graham, S. A., and Knight, F. B. (1965). "Principles of Forest Entomology." McGraw-Hill, New York.

Green, H. V., and Worrall, J. (1963). Wood quality studies. Part 1. Scanning microphotometer for automatically measuring and recording certain wood characteristics. *Pulp Pap. Res. Inst. Can. Tech. Rept.* **331**.

Griffin, D. M. (1969). Soil water in the ecology of fungi. *Annu. Rev. Phytopath.* **7**, 289–310.

Grigsby, H. C. (1967). Irrigation and fertilization of seed orchards. *Proc. Southeastern Area Forest Nurserymen's Conf.* pp. 121–130.

Grillos, S. J., and Smith, F. H. (1959). The secondary phloem of Douglas-fir. *Forest Sci.* **5**, 377–388.

Groom, P., and Wilson, S. E. (1925). On the pneumatophores of paludal species of *Amoora, Carapa,* and *Heritiera. Ann. Bot.* **39**, 9–24.

Grosenbaugh, L. R. (1963). Optical dendrometers for out-of-reach diameters: a conspectus and some new theory. *Forest Sci. Monogr.* **4**.

Guard, A. T., and Postlethwait, S. N. (1958). Relation of the formation of annual rings to multiple flushes of growth in several species of *Quercus. Indiana Acad. Sci.* **67**, 104–106.

Haasis, F. W. (1921). Relation between soil type and root form of western yellow pine seedlings. *Ecology* **2**, 292–303.

Haberland, F. P., and Wilde, S. A. (1961). Influence of thinning of red pine plantation on soil. *Ecology* **42**, 584–586.

Hacskaylo, E. (1957). Mycorrhizae of trees with special emphasis on physiology of ectrotrophic types. *Ohio J. Sci.* **57**, 350–357.

Hacskaylo, E. (1961a). Factors influencing mycorrhizal development in some cultural practices. *Rec. Advan. Bot.* II, 1744–1748.

Hacskaylo, E. (1961b). Influence of cycloheximide on growth of mycorrhizal fungi and on mycorrhizae of pine. *Forest Sci.* **7**, 376–379.

Hacskaylo, E., and Palmer, J. G. (1957). Effects of several biocides on growth of seedling pines and incidence of mycorrhizae in field plots. *Plant Disease Rep.* **41**, 354–358.

Hacskaylo, E., and Snow, Jr., A. G. (1959). Relation of soil nutrients and light to prevalence of mycorrhizae on pine seedlings. *U.S. Forest Serv. Northeast. Forest Exp. Sta. Pap.* **125**.

Hagem, O. (1962). Additional observations on the dry matter increase of coniferous seedlings in winter. *Medd. Vestlandets Forstl. Forsk. (Bergen)* **37**, 5.

Hagerup, O. (1942). The morphology and biology of the *Corylus* fruit. *Kl. Danske Vidensk Selskab.* **17**, 1–32.

Hall, R. C. (1935). Handling and filing increment cores. *J. Forest.* **33**, 821–822.

Hall, R. C. (1944). A vernier tree growth band. *J. Forest.* **42**, 742–743.

Haller, M. H., Rose, D. H., Lutz, J. M., and Harding, P. L. (1945). Respiration of citrus fruits after harvest. *J. Agr. Res.* **71**, 227–259.

Handley, W. R. C. (1963). Mycorrhizal associations and Calluna heathland afforestation. *Brit. Forest. Commun. Bull. (London)* **36**.

Handley, W. R. C., and Sanders, C. J. (1962). The concentration of easily soluble reducing substances in roots and the formation of ectotrophic mycorrhizal associations—a reexamination of Björkman's hypothesis. *Plant Soil* **16**, 42–61.

Hansen, E. (1966). Postharvest physiology of fruits. *Annu. Rev. Plant Physiol.* **17**, 459–480.

Hansen, P. (1967). ^{14}C-studies on apple trees. I. The effect of the fruit in the translocation and distribution of photosynthates. *Physiol. Plant.* **20**, 382–392.

Hard, J. S. (1964). Vertical distribution of cones in red pine. *U.S. Forest Serv. Res. Note* **LS-51.**

Harkin, J. M. (1969). Lignin and its uses. *U.S. Forest Serv. Res. Note* **FPL-0206.**

Harley, C. P., and Masure, M. P. (1938). Relation of atmospheric conditions to enlargement rate and periodicity of Winesap apples. *J. Agr. Res.* **57**, 109–124.

Harley, J. L. (1968). "The Biology of Mycorrhiza," 2nd ed. Leonard Hill Ltd., London.

Harley, J. L., and Brierley, J. K. (1955). The uptake of phosphate by excised mycorrhizal roots of the beech. VII. Active transport of P^{32} from fungus to host during uptake of phosphate from solution. *New Phytol.* **54**, 296–301.

Harley, J. L., and Lewis, D. H. (1969). The physiology of mycorrhizas. *In* "Advances in Microbial Physiology" (A. H. Rose and J. F. Wilkinson, eds.), pp. 53–78. Academic Press, New York.

Harley, J. L., and McCready, C. C. (1952). The uptake of phosphate by excised mycorrhizal roots of the beech. II. Distribution of phosphorous between host and fungus. *New Phytol.* **51**, 342–348.

Harley, J. L., and Waid, J. S. (1955). Effect of light upon the roots of beech and its surface population. *Plant Soil* **7**, 96–112.

Harlow, W. M., Coté, Jr., W. A., and Day, A. C. (1964). The opening mechanism of pine cone scales. *J. Forest.* **62**, 538–540.

Harris, E. H. (1955). The effect of rainfall on the latewood of Scots pine and other conifers in East Anglia. *Forestry* **28**, 136–140.

Harris, J. M. (1952). Discontinuous growth layers in *Pinus radiata. New Zealand Forest. Prod. Res. Notes* **1**, 1–10.

Harris, J. M., Kriedemann, P. E., and Possingham, J. V. (1968). Anatomical aspects of grape berry development. *Vitis* **7**, 106–119.

Harris, J. M., and Polge, H. (1967). A comparison of x-ray and beta ray techniques for measuring wood density. *J. Inst. Wood Sci.* **19**, 34–42.

Harris, R. W., and Hansen, C. J. (1955). The effects of 2,4-5-trichlorophenoxyacetic acid on the development and maturation of the French prune. *Proc. Amer. Soc. Hort. Sci.* **66**, 73–78.

Hartman, F. (1943). Frage der Gleichgewichtsreaktion von Stamm und Wurzel heimischer Waldbäume. *Biol. Generalis* **17**, 367–418.

Hartmann, H. T. (1958). Some responses of the olive to nitrogen fertilizers. *Proc. Amer. Soc. Hort. Sci.* **72**, 257–266.

Hartmann, H. T. (1962). Olive growing in Australia. *Econ. Bot.* **16**, 31–44.

Hartmann, H. T., and Panetsos, C. (1961). Effects of soil moisture deficiency during floral development on fruitfulness in the olive. *Proc. Amer. Soc. Hort. Sci.* **78**, 209–217.

Hartmann, H. T. and Kester, D. E. (1968). "Plant Propagation—Principles and Practices." Prentice-Hall, Englewood Cliffs, New Jersey.

Hashizume, H. (1962). Initiation and development of flower buds in *Cryptomeria japonica. J. Jap. Forest. Soc.* **44**, 312–319.

Hatch, A. B. (1936). The role of mycorrhizae in afforestation. *J. Forest.* **34**, 22–29.

Hatch, A. B. (1937). The physical basis of mycotrophy in the genus *Pinus. Black Rock Forest Bull.* **6**, 1–168.

Haugen, R. K. (1967). Tree ring indices. A circumpolar comparison. *Science* **158**, 773–775.

Haupt, A. W. (1953). "Plant Morphology." McGraw-Hill, New York.

Havis, L., and Cullinan, F. P. (1946). Second report on the effects of cover crops in a peach orchard. *Proc. Amer. Soc. Hort. Sci.* **48**, 27–36.

Hawboldt, L. S., and Greenidge, K. N. H. (1952). Dieback of yellow birch and rootlet mortality in Nova Scotia. *Can. Dep. Agr. Forest. Biol. Div. Bi-monthly Progr. Rep.* **8**(6), 1.

Hayes, F. A., and Stoeckeler, J. H. (1935). Soil and forest relationships of the shelterbelt zone. *In* Possibilities of shelterbelt planting in the Plains region. *US Forest Serv. Spec. Bull.* pp. 111–155.

Hayward, H. E., and Long, E. M. (1942). The anatomy of the seedling and roots of the Valencia orange. *USDA Tech. Bull.* **786**.

Haywood, G. (1950). Effect of variations in size and shape of fibers on papermaking properties. TAPPI **33**, 370–383.

Head, G. C. (1965). Studies of diurnal changes in cherry root growth and nutational movements of apple root tips by time-lapse cinematography. *Ann. Bot.* **29**, 219–224.

Head, G. C. (1966). Estimating seasonal changes in the quantity of white unsuberized root on fruit trees. *J. Hort. Sci.* **41**, 197–206.

Head, G. C. (1967). Effects of seasonal changes in shoot growth on the amount of unsuberized root on apple and plum trees. *J. Hort. Sci.* **42**, 169–180.

Head, G. C. (1969). The effects of fruiting and defoliation on seasonal trends in new root production on apple trees. *J. Hort. Sci.* **44**, 175–181.

Heinicke, A. J. (1937). Some cultural conditions influencing the manufacture of carbohydrates by apple leaves. *Proc. N.Y. Hort. Soc.* pp. 149–156.

Hejnowicz, A., and Tomaszewski, M. (1969). Growth regulators and wood formation in *Pinus silvestris. Physiol. Plant.* **22**, 984–992.

Hejnowicz, Z. (1961). Anticlinal division, intrusive growth, and loss of fusiform initials in nonstoried cambium. *Acta. Soc. Bot. Pol.* **30**, 729–748.

Hejnowicz, Z. (1968). The structural mechanism involved in the changes of grain in timber. *Acta Soc. Bot. Pol.* **37**, 347–365.

Helander, A .B. (1933). Variations in tracheid length of pine and spruce. *Found. Forest Prod. Res. Finland. Publ.* **14**.

Hellmers, H., and Kelleher, J. M. (1959). *Ceanothus leucodermis* and soil nitrogen in Southern California mountains. *Forest Sci.* **5**, 275–278.

Helms, J. A. (1964). Apparent photosynthesis of Douglas-fir in relation to silvicultural treatment. *Forest Sci.* **10**, 432–443.

Henderson, C. S., and Stone, E. L. (1967). Interactions of phosphorous availability, mycorrhizae, and soil fumigation of coniferous seedlings. *Agronomy Abstr. Washington, D.C.*, p. 134.

Hendrickson, A. H., and Veihmeyer, F. J. (1942). Readily available soil moisture and the sizes of fruit. *Proc. Amer. Soc. Hort. Sci.* **40**, 13–18.

Hepting, G. H. (1945). Reserve food storage in shortleaf pine in relation to little-leaf disease. *Phytopathology* **35**, 106–119.

Herre, M. (1954). *Welwitschia mirabilis* Hook. I. From seed to seed in the botanic garden of the University of Stellenbosch, C. P. *J. S. Afr. Bot.* **20**, 23–24.

Herrero, J. (1956). Incompatibilidad entre patron e injerto. III. Comparacion de sintomas producidas por incompatibilidad y por el anillado del tronco. *An. Aula Dei* **4**, 262–265.

Herrick, E. H. (1932). Further notes on twisted trees. *Science* **46**, 406–407.

Hess, C. E. (1957). A physiological analysis of rooting in cuttings of juvenile and mature *Hedera helix*. Ph.D. thesis. Cornell University, Ithaca, New York.

Hess, C. E. (1962). A physiological analysis of root initiation in easy and difficult-to-root cuttings. *Rep. 16th Int. Hort. Congr.* **1**, 375–381.

Hess, C. E. (1965). Rooting cofactors—identification and function. *Proc. Int. Plant. Prop. Soc.* **15**, 181–186.

Hess, C. E. (1969). Internal and external factors regulating root initiation. *In* "Root Growth" (W. J. Whittingham, ed.), pp. 42–53. Butterworth, London.

Hess, C. E., and Snyder, W. E. (1955). A physiological comparison of the use of mist with other propagation procedures used in rooting cuttings. *14th Int Hort. Congr.* II, 1133.

Hield, H. Z., Coggins, Jr., C. W., and Garber, M. J. (1965). Effect of gibberellin sprays on fruit set of Washington Navel orange trees. *Hilgardia* **36**, 297–311.

Hilgeman, R. H. and Reuther, W. (1967). Evergreen tree fruits. *In* "Irrigation of Agricultural Lands." (R. M. Hagan, H. R. Haise, and T. W. Edminster, eds.), Chapter 36. *Amer. Soc. Agron. Monograph* **11**. Madison, Wisconsin.

Hill-Cottingham, D. G. (1963). Effect of time of application of fertilizer nitrogen on the apple trees grown in sand culture. *J. Hort. Sci.* **38**, 242–251.

Hill-Cottingham, D. G., and Williams, R. R. (1967). Effect of time of application of fertilizer nitrogen on the growth, flower development and fruit set of maiden apple trees, var. Lord Lambourne, and on the distribution of total nitrogen within the trees. *J. Hort. Sci.* **42**, 319–338.

Hiller, C. H. (1964). Estimating the size of the fibril angle in latewood tracheids of slash pine. *J. Forest.* **62**, 249–252.

Himelick, E. B., and Neely, D. (1962). Root-grafting of city-planted American elms. *Plant Dis. Rep.* **46**, 86–87.

Himelick, E. B., Neely, D., and Crowley, Jr., W. R. (1965). Experimental field studies on shade tree fertilization. *Ill. Nat. Hist. Surv. Div. Biol. Notes* **53**.

Hoekstra, P. E., and Asher, W. C. (1962). Diameter growth of pole-size slash pine after fertilization. *J. Forest.* **60**, 341–342.

Hoekstra, P. E., and Mergen, F. (1957). Experimental induction of female flowers on young slash pine. *J. Forest.* **55**, 827–831.

Hoffmann, G. (1966). Verlauf der Tiefendurchwurzelung und Feinwurzelbildung bei einigen Baumarten. *Arch. Forstwiss.* **15**, 825–856.

Hofmeyer, J. O. J., and Oberholzer, P. C. V. (1948). Genetic aspects associated with the propagation of Citrus. *Farming S. Afr.* **23**, 201–208.

Holdheide, W. (1951). Anatomie mitteleuropaischer Gehölzrinden. *In* "Handbuch der Mikroskopie in der Technik." (H. Freund, ed.), **Bd. 5**, pp. 195–367. Umsachen-Verlag, Frankfurt.

Holmes, G. D., and Cousins, D. A. (1960). Applications of fertilizers to checked plantations. *Forestry* **33**, 54–73.

Holmes, J. W., and Shim, S. Y. (1968). Diurnal changes in stem diameter of Canary Island pine trees (*Pinus canariensis*, C. Smith) caused by soil water stress and varying microclimate. *J. Exp. Bot.* **19**, 219–232.

Holmsgaard, E. (1960). Kvaelstofbindingens strrelse hos el. *Det. Forstl. Forsøgsvaesen i Danmark* **26**, 253–270.

Holmsgaard, E. (1962). Influence of weather on growth and reproduction of beech. *Commun. Inst. Forst. Fenni.* **55**, 1–5.

Holmsgaard, E., and Olsen, H. C. (1966). Experimental induction of flowering in beech. *Det. Forstl. Forsøgsvaesen i Danmark* **30**, 1–17.

Holmsgaard,E., and Scharff, O. (1963). Levende stødi rødgransevoks-ninger. *Det. Forstl. Forsøgvaesen i Danmark* **28**, 99–150.

Holttum, R. E. (1940). On periodic leaf changes and flowering of trees at Singapore. II. *Gard. Bull. Singapore* **11**, 119–175.

Hornibrook, E. M. (1936). Further notes on measurement and staining of increment cores. *J. Forest.* **34**, 815–816.

Huber, B. (1939). Das Siebröhrensystem unserer Bäume und seine jahreszeitlichen Veränderungen. *Jahrb. Wiss. Bot.* **88**, 176–242.

Huber, B. (1948). Physiologie der Randenschälung bei Fichte und Eichen. *Forstwiss. Centralbl.* **67**, 129–164.

Hughes, J. F. (1965). Tension wood: a review of literature. *Forest. Abstr.* **26**, 1–16.

Hustich, I. (1948). The Scotch pine in northernmost Finland and its dependence on the climate in the last decades. *Acta Bot. Fenn.* **42**, 4–75.

Hyde, H. A., and Williams, D. A. (1945). Pollen of lime (*Tilia* sp.) *Nature (London)* **155**, 457.

Impens, I. I., and Schalck, J. M. (1965). A very sensitive electric dendrograph for recording radial changes of a tree. *Ecology* **46**, 183–184.

Isenberg, I. H. (1958). "Pulp and Paper Microscopy," 3rd ed. Inst. Paper Chemistry, Appleton, Wisconsin.

Ishibe, O. (1935). The seasonal changes in starch and fat reserves of some woody plants. *Kyoto Imp. Univ. Bot. Inst. Publ.* **42**.

Isonogle, I. T. (1944). Effects of controlled shading upon the development of leaf structure in two deciduous species. *Ecology* **25**, 404–413.

Ito, H., Ogaki, C., Tatsuno, Y., Kamata, H., and Inoue, I. (1953). Ecological investigation of peach trees on volcanic black soil. II. Effects of soil properties on top and root growth of peach trees in orchards with black soil of various profiles. (Japanese). *Bull. Bur. Hort. Sect. Kanagawa Agr. Exp. Sta.* **1**, 68–78.

Ito, H., Ogaki, C., Tatsuno, Y., Kumata, H., and Inoue, I. (1954). Ecological investigation of peach trees on volcanic black soil. III. Relation of soil chemical composition to shoot growth, fruit bud formation and fruit development (Japanese). *Bull. Hort. Sect. Kanagawa Agr. Exp. Sta.* **2**, 16–25.

Ito, M. (1957). The state of the seasonal variation of xylem elements in one growth ring of chestnut tree (*Castanea crenata* S. et Z.) Sci. Rept. Faculty of Liberal Arts and Education. *Gifu Univ. Gifu Japan (Nat. Sci.)* **2**, 75–79.

Iyer, J. G. (1964). Recent developments in mycotrophy of trees. *Progr. Rep. Soil Sci. Dept. Univ. Wisconsin (Processed)*.

Iyer, J. G. (1965). Effect of Dacthal 75 on the growth of nursery stock. *Tree Planters Notes* **71**, 13–16. Washington, D.C.

Iyer, J. G., Lipas, E., and Chesters, G. (1969). Correction of mycorrhizal deficiencies of tree nursery stock produced on biocide-treated soils. *North Amer. Mycorrhizal Conf. Urbana, Illinois*.

Iyer, J. G., and Wilde, S. A. (1965). Effect of Vapam biocide on the growth of red pine seedlings. *J. Forest.* **63**, 703–704.

Jaccard, P. (1939). Tropisme et bois de réaction provoqué par la force centrifuge. *Bull. Soc. Bot. Suisse* **49**, 135–147.

Jackson, D. I. (1969). Effects of water, light, and nutrition on flower-bud initiation in apricots. *Aust. J. Bot. Sci.* **22**, 69–75.

Jackson, D. I., and Coombe, B. G. (1966a). The growth of apricot fruit. I. Morphological changes during development and the effects of various tree factors. *Aust. J. Agr. Res.* **17**, 465–477.

Jackson, D. I., and Coombe, B. G. (1966b). Gibberellin-like substances in developing apricot fruit. *Science* **154**, 277–278.

Jackson, G. A. D., and Prosser, M. V. (1959). The induction of parthenocarpic development in *Rosa* by auxins and gibberellic acid. *Naturwiss.* **46**, 407–408.

Jackson, L. W. R. (1945). Root defects and fungi associated with the littleleaf disease of southern pines. *Phytopathology* **35**, 91–105.

Jackson, L. W. R. (1952). Radial growth of forest trees in the Georgia Piedmont. *Ecology* **33**, 336–341.

Jackson, L. W. R. (1959). Loblolly pine tracheid length in relation to position in tree. *J. Forest.* **57**, 366–367.

Jackson, L. W. R., and Morse, W. E. (1965). Tracheid length variation in single rings of loblolly, slash, and shortleaf pine. *J. Forest.* **63**, 110–112.

Jaroslavcev, G. D. (1962). Natural root grafting in the forests of the Yalta leskhoz (in Russian) *Lesn. Hoz.* **15**, 49–64. [*Forest. Abstr.* **24**, 278 (1963).]

Jazewitsch, W. von., Bettag, G., and Siebenlist, H. (1957). Eine neue Jahrringmess machino mit elecktrischer Messerwertregistrierung. *Holz Roh. Werkst.* **15**, 241–244.

Jeffrey, W. W. (1959). White spruce rooting modifications on the fluvial deposits of the lower Peace River. *Forest. Chron.* **35**, 304–311.

Jenik, J. (1967). Root adaptations in west African trees. *J. Linn. Soc. (Bot.)* **60**, 25–29.

Johri, B. M., and Vasil, I. K. (1961). Physiology of pollen. *Bot. Rev.* **27**, 325–381.

Jones, G. B. (1958). Variations in cell wall thickness in Norway spruce. *Picea abies* Karst. *J. Oxford Univ. Forest Soc. Ser.* **4**(6), 35–43.

Jones, W. W. (1939). A study of the developmental changes in composition of the *Macadamia. Plant Physiol.* **14**, 755–768.

Jones, W. W., and Cree, C. B. (1954). Effect of time of harvest on yield, size and grade of Valencia oranges. *Proc. Amer. Soc. Hort. Sci.* **64**, 139–145.

Jones, W. W., Embleton, T. W., Steinacker, M. L., and Cree, C. B. (1964). The effect of time of fruit harvest on fruiting and carbohydrate supply in the Valencia orange. *Proc. Amer. Soc. Hort. Sci.* **84**, 152–157.

Kadambi, K. (1954). Instances of the fusion of the tissues of different trees. *Indian Forest.* **80**, 726.

Kaeiser, M., and Boyce, S. G. (1965). The relationship of gelatinous fibers to wood structure in eastern cottonwood (*Populus deltoides*). *Amer. J. Bot.* **52**, 711–715.

Karandina, S. N. (1961). O prodolzitel'nosti rosta rostovyh kornej duba (*Quercus robur* L.) v tecenie goda. *Soobshch. lab. Lesoved. Nauk SSSR. Moskva No.* **4**, 54–69. [*Forest. Abstr.* **23**, 243 (1962).]

Karling, J. S. (1934). Dendrograph studies in *Achras zapota* in relation to optimum conditions for tapping. *Amer. J. Bot.* **21**, 161–193.

Kaufman, C. M. (1968). Growth of horizontal roots, height, and diameter of planted slash pine. *Forest Sci.* **14**, 265–274.

Kaufmann, M. R. (1970). Water potential components in growing citrus fruits. *Plant Physiol.* **46**, 145–149.

Kawana, A., and Kawaguchi, M. (1957). Several aspects of the overmoist forestry on the sea coast of Kujukuri. III. On the colored growth bands appearing in the well-grown planted Sugi seedlings. *J. Jap. Forest. Soc.* **39**, 323–327.

Kawase, M. (1964). Centrifugation, rhizocaline, and rooting in *Salix alba. Physiol. Plant.* **17**, 855–865.

Kefford, N. P., and Goldacre, P. L. (1961). The changing concept of auxin. *Amer. J. Bot.* **48**, 643–650.

Keller, T., and Koch, W. (1962a). Der Einfluss der Mineralstoffernährung auf CO_2-Gaswechsel und Blattpigmentgehalt der Pappel. I. Stickstoff. *Mitt. Schweiz. Anst. Forstl. Versuchs.* **38**, 253–282.

Keller, T., and Koch, W. (1962b). Der Einfluss der Mineralstoffernährung auf CO_2-Gaswechsel und Blattpigmentgehalt der Pappel. II. Eisen. *Mitt. Schweiz. Anst. Forstl. Versuchs.* **38**, 282–318.

Keller, T., and Koch, W. (1964). The effect of iron chelate fertilization of poplar upon CO_2 uptake, leaf size, and content of leaf pigments and iron. *Plant Soil* 20, 116–126.

Keller, T., and Wehrmann, J. (1963). CO_2-Assimilation, Wurzelatmung und Ertrag von Fichten-und Kiefernsämlingen bei unterschiedlicher *Mineralstoffernährung. Mitt. Schweiz. Anst. Forstl. Versuchs.* 39, 217–242.

Kennedy, R. W. (1961). Variation and periodicity of summerwood in some second-growth Douglas-fir. TAPPI 44, 161–166.

Kennedy, R. W., and Farrar, J. L. (1965a). Induction of tension wood with the anti-auxin 2,3,5-triiodobenzoic acid. *Nature (London)* 208, 406–407.

Kennedy, R. W., and Farrar, J. L. (1965b). Tracheid development in tilted seedlings. *In* "Cellular Ultrastructure of Woody Plants" (W. A. Coté, Jr., ed.), pp. 419–453. Syracuse Univ. Press, Syracuse, New York.

Kerfoot, O. (1962). Tea root systems. *World Crops* 14, 140–143.

Kern, K. G. (1961). Ein Beitrag zur Zuwachsmessung mit den Arnberg Mikrodendrometer. *Allg. Forst Jagdztg.* 132, 206–212.

Kidd, F., and West, C. (1947). A note on the assimilation of carbon dioxide by apple fruits after gathering. *New Phytol.* 46, 274–275.

Kienholz, J. R. (1942). Boron deficiency in pear trees. *Phytopathology* 32, 1082–1086.

Klepper, B. (1968). Diurnal patterns of water potential in woody plants. *Plant Physiol.* 43, 1931–1934.

Knight, R. C. (1926). The propagation of fruit tree stocks by stem cuttings. *J. Pomol.* 5, 248–266.

Knight, R. C. (1961). Taper and secondary thickening in stems and roots of the apple. *Annu. Rep. East Malling Res. Sta.* pp. 65–71 1960 (1961).

Knowlton, H. E., and Hoffman, M. B. (1932). The fertilization of apple orchards. III. A comparison of nitrate of soda and sulfate of ammonia. *W. Va. Agr. Exp. Sta. Bull.* 252.

Knudson, L. W. (1916). Cambial activity of certain horticultural plants. *Bull. Torrey Bot. Club* 40, 533–537.

Koehler, A. (1931). More about twisted grain in trees. *Science* 73, 477.

Kolesnikov, V. A. (1955). [Something new in the study of the root system of fruit trees] (Russ.) *Sady Ogorody* 5, 44–49 [*Hort. Abstr.* 25, 3552 (1955).]

Kolesnikov, V. A. (1959). (The growth of axial and absorbing roots of top and small fruit plants throughout their annual life cycle.) (Russ). *Izv. Timaryazev Selskokhoz. Akad.* 1, 127–128. [*Hort. Abstr.* 29, 3233 (1959).]

Kolesnikov, E. V. (1960). The study of the root system of fruit trees by the adsorption method. *Izv. Timaryazev. Selskokhoz. Akad.* 4, 34–42.

Konar, R. N., and Oberoi, Y. P. (1969). Recent work on reproductive structures of living conifers and taxads—a review. *Bot. Rev.* 35, 89–116.

Koo, R. C. J., Reitz, H. J., and Sites, J. W. (1958). A survey of the mineral status of Valencia orange in Florida. *Fla. Agr. Exp. Sta. Bull.* 604.

Koriba, K. (1958). On the periodicity of tree growth in the tropics, with reference to the mode of branching, the leaf fall, and the formation of the resting bud. *Gard. Bull.* 17, 11–81.

Kosceev, A. L. (1953). The silvicultural significance of adventitious roots on tree species in waterlogged clear-felled areas. *Dept. Forest. Ottawa.* (Transl. from *Tr. Inst. Lesa. No.* 13, 116–129).

Kozak, A., Sziklai, O., Griffith, B. G., and Smith, J. H. G. (1963). Variation in cone and seed yield from young, open-grown Douglas firs on the U.B.C. research forest. *Univ. British Columbia Fac. Forest. Res. Pap.* 57.

Kozlowski, T. T. (1949). Light and water in relation to growth and competition of Piedmont forest tree species. *Ecol. Monogr.* **19**, 207–231.

Kozlowski, T. T. (1955). Tree growth, action and interaction of soil and other factors. *J. Forest.* **53**, 508–512.

Kozlowski, T. T. (1957). Effects of continuous high light intensity on photosynthesis in forest trees. *Forest Sci.* **3**, 220–225.

Kozlowski, T. T. (1958). Water relations and growth of trees. *J. Forest.* **56**, 498–502.

Kozlowski, T. T. (1961). Challenges in forest production-physiological implications. *In* "Challenges of Forestry," pp. 91–124. State Univ. Coll. Forest., Syracuse, New York.

Kozlowski, T. T. (1962a). Photosynthesis, climate and growth of trees. *In* "Tree Growth" (T. T. Kozlowski, ed.), Chapter 8. Ronald Press, New York.

Kozlowski, T. T. (ed.), (1962b). "Tree Growth." Ronald Press, New York.

Kozlowski, T. T. (1963a). Characteristics and improvement of forest growth. *Adv. Frontiers Plant Sci.* **2**, 73–136.

Kozlowski, T. T. (1963b). Growth characteristics of forest trees. *J. Forest.* **61**, 655–662.

Kozlowski, T. T. (1964). "Water Metabolism in Plants." Harper, New York.

Kozlowski, T. T. (1965). Expansion and contraction of plants. *Advan. Frontiers Plant Sci.* **10**, 63–74.

Kozlowski, T. T. (1967a). Diurnal variation in stem diameters of small trees. *Bot. Gaz. (Chicago)* **128**, 60–68.

Kozlowski, T. T. (1967b). Continuous recording of diameter changes in seedlings. *Forest Sci.* **13**, 100–101.

Kozlowski, T. T. (1967c). Water relations of trees. *Proc. Midwest Chapt. Int. Shade Tree Conf.* **1–13**.

Kozlowski, T. T. (1968a). Diurnal changes in diameters of fruits and tree stems of Montmorency cherry. *J. Hort. Sci.* **43**, 1–15.

Kozlowski, T. T. (1968b). Growth and development of *Pinus resinosa* seedlings under controlled temperatures. *Advan. Frontiers Plant Sci.* **19**, 17–27.

Kozlowski, T. T. (ed.) (1968c). "Water Deficits and Plant Growth." Vol. I. Development, Control, and Measurement. Academic Press, New York.

Kozlowski, T. T. (ed.) (1968d). "Water Deficits and Plant Growth." Vol. II. Plant Water Consumption and Response. Academic Press, New York.

Kozlowski, T. T. (1968e). Water balance in shade trees. *Proc. 44th Int. Shade Tree Conf.* 29–42.

Kozlowski, T. T. (1968f). Soil water and tree growth. *In* "The Ecology of Southern Forests" (N. E. Linnartz, ed.), pp. 30–57. La. State Univ. Press, Baton Rouge, Louisiana.

Kozlowski, T. T. (1969). Tree physiology and forest pests. *J. Forest.* **69**, 118–122.

Kozlowski, T. T. and Cooley, J. C. (1961). Root grafting in northern Wisconsin. *J. Forest.* **59**, 105–107.

Kozlowski, T. T. Hughes, J. F., and Leyton, L. (1966). Patterns of water movement in dormant gymnosperm seedlings. *Biorheology* **3**, 77–85.

Kozlowski, T. T., Hughes, J. F., and Leyton, L. (1967). Dye movement in gymnosperms in relation to tracheid alignment. *Forestry* **40**, 209–227.

Kozlowski, T. T., and Keller, T. (1966). Food relations of woody plants. *Bot. Rev.* **32**, 293–382.

Kozlowski, T. T., Kuntz, J. E., and Winget, C. H. (1962). Effect of oak wilt on cambial activity. *J. Forest.* **60**, 558–561.

Kozlowski, T. T., and Peterson, T. A. (1962). Seasonal growth of dominant, intermediate, and suppressed red pine trees. *Bot. Gaz. (Chicago)* **124**, 146–154.

Kozlowski, T. T., and Scholtes, W. H. (1948). Growth of roots and root hairs of pine and hardwood seedlings in the Piedmont. *J. Forest.* **46**, 750–754.

Kozlowski, T. T. and Ward, R. C. (1961). Shoot elongation characteristics of forest trees. *Forest Sci.* **7**, 357–368.

Kozlowski, T. T., and Winget, C. H. (1963). Patterns of water movement in forest trees. *Bot. Gaz. (Chicago)* **124**, 301–311.

Kozlowski, T. T., and Winget, C. H. (1964). Diurnal and seasonal variation in radii of tree stems. *Ecology* **45**, 149–155.

Kozlowski, T. T., Winget, C. H., and Torrie, J. H. (1962). Daily radial growth of oak in relation to maximum temperature. *Bot. Gaz. (Chicago)* **124**, 9–17.

Kramer, P. J. (1949). "Plant and Soil Water Relationships." McGraw-Hill, New York.

Kramer, P. J. (1962). The role of water in tree growth. *In* "Tree Growth." (T. T. Kozlowski, ed.), pp. 171–182. Ronald Press, New York.

Kramer, P. J. (1964). The role of water in wood formation. *In* "The Formation of Wood in Forest Trees" (M. H. Zimmermann, ed.), pp. 519–532. Academic Press, New York.

Kramer, P. J. (1969). "Plant and Soil Water Relations: A Modern Synthesis." McGraw-Hill, New York.

Kramer, P. J., and Decker, J. P. (1944). Relation between light intensity and rate of photosynthesis of loblolly pine and certain hardwoods. *Plant Physiol.* **19**, 350–358.

Kramer, P. J., and Kozlowski, T. T. (1960). "Physiology of Trees." McGraw-Hill, New York.

Kramer, P. J., Riley, W. S., and Bannister, T. T. (1952). Gas exchange of cypress (*Taxodium distichum*) trees. *Ecology* **33**, 117–121.

Kramer, P. J., and Wilbur, K. M. (1949). Absorption of radioactive phosphorus by mycorrhizal roots of pine. *Science* **110**, 8–9.

Krasilnikov, P. K. (1960a). Adventitious roots and the root system of *Pinus sibirica* in the central Sayan Mountains. [(Transl. *Forest. Prod. Lab. Can. No.* 12, by H. Bernard from *Bot. Z.* **41**, 1194–1206, (1956)].

Krasilnikov, P. K. (1960b). Some characteristics of the root systems of five species of *Euonymus* at the age of two years in the Leningrad region (Russian) *Bot. Zh.* **45**, 394–397.

Kraus, J. F., and Spurr, S. H. (1961). Relationship of soil moisture to the springwood-summerwood transition in southern Michigan red pine. *J. Forest.* **50**, 510–511.

Krauss, G., and Gärtner, G. (1938). Ein Schneideapparat für die Zurichtung von Bohrspänen. *Tharandter Forstl. Jahrb.* **89**, 436–441.

Kremers, R. E. (1957). The occurrence of lignin precursors. TAPPI **40**, 262–268.

Kremers, R. E. (1963). The chemistry of developing wood. *In* "The Chemistry of Wood" (B. L. Browning, ed.), Chapter 8. Interscience, New York.

Kremers, R. E. (1964). Cambial chemistry, a way of looking at a stick of pulpwood. TAPPI **47**, 292–296.

Kriedemann, P. E. (1968a). ^{14}C translocation patterns in peach and apricot shoots. *Aust. J. Agr. Res.* **19**, 775–780.

Kriedemann, P. E. (1968b). Observations on gas exchange in the developing Sultana berry. *Aust. J. Biol. Sci.* **21**, 907–916.

Krugman, S. (1966). Artificial ripening of sugar pine seed. *US Forest Serv. Res. Pap.* **PSW-32**.

Krugman, S., Stone, E. C., and Bega, R. V. (1965). The effects of soil fumigation and lifting date on the root-regenerating potential of Monterey pine planting stock. *J. Forest.* **63**, 114–119.

Kuntz, J. E., and Riker, A. J. (1955). The use of radioactive isotopes to ascertain the role of root grafting in the translocation of water, nutrients, and disease-inducing organisms. *Int. Conf. Peaceful Uses Atomic Energy (Geneva, Switzerland) Proc.* **12**, 144–148.

Kuroiwa, K., Yoshino, R., and Takahashi, G. (1958). Daily growth curve of Paulownia. II. Variation in the growing season. *J. Jap. Forest. Soc.* **40**, 139–145.

Labyak, L. F., and Schumacher, F. X. (1954). The contribution of its branches to the main stem growth of loblolly pine. *J. Forest.* **52**, 333–337.

Ladefoged, K. (1952). The periodicity of wood formation. *Dan. Biol. Skr.* **7**, 1–98.

Langdon, O. G. (1963). Growth patterns of *Pinus elliottii* var. *densa. Ecology* **44**, 825–827.

Lanner, R. M. (1961). Living stumps in the Sierra Nevada. *Ecology* **42**, 170–173.

Lanner, R. M. 1966a. Adventitious roots of *Eucalyptus robusta* in Hawaii. *Pac. Sci.* **20**, 379–381.

Lanner, R. M. (1966b). Needed: a new approach to the study of pollen dispersion. *Silvae Genet.* **15**, 50–52.

Lanphear, F. O., and Meahl, R. P. (1963). Influences of endogenous rooting cofactors and environment on seasonal fluctuation in root initiation of selected evergreen cuttings. *Proc. Amer. Soc. Hort. Sci.* **83**, 811–818.

Lanphear, F. O., and Meahl, R. P. (1966). Influence of the stock plant environment on the rooting of *Juniperus horizontalis* "Plumosa." *Proc. Amer. Soc. Hort. Sci.* **89**, 666–671.

Larson, P. R. (1956). Discontinuous growth rings in suppressed slash pine. *Tropical Woods* **104**, 80–99.

Larson, P. R. (1957). Effect of the environment on the percentage of summerwood and specific gravity of slash pine. *Yale Univ. School Forest. Bull.* **63**.

Larson, P. R. (1960). A physiological consideration of the springwood–summerwood transition in red pine. *Forest Sci.* **6**, 110–122.

Larson, P. R. (1961). Influence of date of flushing on flowering in *Pinus banksiana. Nature (London)* **192**, 82–83.

Larson, P. R. (1962a). The indirect effect of photoperiod on tracheid diameter in red pine. *Amer. J. Bot.* **49**, 132–137.

Larson, P. R. (1962b). Auxin gradients and the regulation of cambial activity. *In* "Tree Growth" (T. T. Kozlowski, ed.), Chapter 5. Ronald Press, New York.

Larson, P. R. (1962c). A biological approach to wood quality. TAPPI **45**, 443–448.

Larson, P. R. (1963a). Stem form and silviculture. *Proc. Soc. Amer. Forest.* pp. 103–107.

Larson, P. R. (1963b). Stem form development in forest trees. *Forest Sci. Monogr.* 5.

Larson, P. R. (1963c). The indirect effect of drought on tracheid diameter in red pine. *Forest Sci.* **9**, 52–62.

Larson, P. R. (1964). Some indirect effects of environment on wood formation. *In* "The Formation of Wood in Forest Trees" (M. H. Zimmermann, ed.), pp. 345–365. Academic Press, New York.

Larson, P. R. (1965). Stem form of young *Larix* as influenced by wind and pruning. *Forest Sci.* **11**, 412–424.

Larson, P. R. (1966). Changes in chemical composition of wood cells associated with age in *Pinus resinosa. Forest Prod. J.* **16**, (3), 37–45.

Larson, P. R. (1967). Effects of temperature on the growth and wood formation of ten *Pinus resinosa* sources. *Silvae Genet.* **16**, 58–65.

Larson, P. R. (1968). Assessing wood quality of fertilized coniferous trees. *In* "Forest Fertilization," pp. 275–280. T.V.A., Muscle Shoals, Alabama.

Larson, P. R. (1969a). Incorporation of ^{14}C in the developing walls of *Pinus resinosa* tracheids (earlywood and latewood). *Holzforschung* **23**, 17–26.

Larson, P. R. (1969b). Wood formation and the concept of wood quality. *Yale School Forest. Bull.* **74.**

Larson, P. R., and Gordon, J. C. (1969). Photosynthesis and wood yield. *Agr. Sci. Rev.* **7,** 7–14.

LaRue, C. D. (1934). Root grafting in trees. *Amer. J. Bot.* **21,** 121–126.

Leach, R. W. A., and Wareing, P. F. (1967). Distribution of auxin in horizontal woody stems in relation to gravimorphism. *Nature (London)* **214,** 1025–1027.

LeBarron, R. K. (1945). Adjustment of black spruce root systems to increasing depth of peat. *Ecology* **26,** 309–311.

Lenz, F. (1967). Relationships between the vegetative and reproductive growth of Washington Navel orange cuttings (*Citrus sinensis* L. Osbeck). *J. Hort. Sci.* **42,** 31–39.

Leopold, A. C. (1962). The roles of growth substances in flowers and fruits. *Can. J. Bot.* **40,** 745–755.

Leopold, A. C. (1964). "Plant Growth and Development." McGraw-Hill, New York.

Leroy, J. F. (1947). La polyembryonie chez les *Citrus* son interet dans la culture et amelioration. *Rev. Int. Bot. Appl. Paris* **27,** 483–495.

Leshem, B. (1965). The annual activity of intermediary roots of the Aleppo pine. *Forest Sci.* **11,** 291–298.

Letham, D. S., and Bollard, E. G. (1961). Stimulants of cell division in developing fruits. *Nature (London)* **191,** 1119–1120.

Levisohn, I. (1954). Aberrant root infections of pine and spruce seedlings. *New Phytol.* **53,** 284–290.

Lewis, D. H., and Harley, J. L. (1965a). Carbohydrate physiology of mycorrhizal roots of beech. I. Identity of endogenous sugars and utilization of exogenous sugars. *New Phytol.* **64,** 224–235.

Lewis, D. H., and Harley, J. L. (1965b). II. Utilization of exogenous sugars by uninfected and mycorrhizal roots. *New Phytol.* **64,** 238–255.

Lewis, D. H., and Harley, J. L. (1965c). Movement of sugars between host and fungus. *New Phytol.* **64,** 256–269.

Lewis, L. N., Coggins, Jr., C. W., and Hield, H. Z. (1964). The effect of biennial bearing and NAA on the carbohydrate and nitrogen composition of Wilking Mandarin leaves. *Proc. Amer. Soc. Hort. Sci.* **84,** 147–151.

Lewis, M. R., Work, R. A., and Aldrich, W. W. (1939). Influence of different quantities of moisture in a heavy soil on rate of growth of pears. *Plant Physiol.* **10,** 309–323.

Liese, W., and Meyer-Uhlenried, K. H. (1957). Zur quantitativen Bestimmung der verschiedenen Zellarten im Holz. *Z. Wiss. Mikrosk. m. Tech.* **63,** 269–275.

Liese, W., and Ammer, V. (1962). Anatomische Untersuchungen un extrem drehwüchsigem Kieternholz. *Holz Roh. Werks.* **20,** 339–346.

Liming, F. G. (1957). Homemade dendrometers. *J. Forest.* **55,** 575–577.

Lodewick, E. (1928). Seasonal activity of the cambium in some northeastern trees. *N.Y. State Coll. Forest., Syracuse, N. Y. Tech. Publ.* **23.**

Longman, K. A., and Wareing, P. F. (1958). Effect of gravity on flowering and shoot growth in Japanese larch (*Larix leptolepis* Murray). *Nature (London)* **182,** 379–381.

Loomis, W. E. (1935). Translocation and growth balance in woody plants. *Ann. Bot.* **49,** 247–272.

Loomis, W. E. (1938). Relation of condensation reactions to meristematic development. *Bot. Gaz. (Chicago)* **99,** 814–824.

Lott, R. V., and Simons, R. K. (1964). Floral tube and style abscission in the peach and their use as physiological reference points. *Proc. Amer. Soc. Hort. Sci.* **85,** 141–153.

Lott, R. V., and Simons, R. K. (1966). Sequential development of floral-tube and style abscission in the Montmorency cherry (*Prunus cerasus* L.) *Proc. Amer. Soc. Hort. Sci.* **88**, 208–218.

Lott, R. V., and Simons, R. K. (1968a). The developmental morphology and anatomy of floral-tube and style abscission in the 'Wilson Delicious' apricot (*Prunus armeniaca* L.). *Hort. Res.* **8**, 67–73.

Lott, R. V., and Simons, R. K. (1968b). The morphology and anatomy of floral tube and style abscission and of associated floral organs in the 'Starking Hardy Giant' cherry (*Prunus avium* L.). *Hort. Res.* **8**, 74–82.

Loustalot, A. J., Burrows, F. W., Gilbert, S. G., and Nason, A. (1945). Effect of copper and zinc deficiencies on the photosynthetic activity of the foliage of young tung trees. *Plant Physiol.* **20**, 283–288.

Luckwill, L. C. (1948). The hormone content of the seed in relation to endosperm development and fruit drop in the apple. *J. Hort. Sci.* **24**, 32–44.

Luckwill, L. C. (1954). The auxins of the apple seed and their role in fruit development. *Proc. 8th Int. Bot. Congr. Sec.* **11/12**, 377.

Luckwill, L. C. (1957). Studies of fruit development in relation to plant hormones. IV. Acidic auxins and growth inhibitors in leaves and fruits of the apple. *J. Hort. Sci.* **32**, 18–33.

Luckwill, L. C. (1968). The effect of certain growth regulators on growth and apical dominance of young apple trees. *J. Hort. Sci.* **43**, 91–101.

Luckwill, L. C. (1970). The control of growth and fruitfulness of apple trees. *In* "Physiology of Tree Crops" (L. C. Luckwill and C. V. Cutting, eds.), pp. 237–254. Academic Press, London and New York.

Luckwill, L. C. and Cutting, C. V. (eds.) (1970). "Physiology of Tree Crops." Academic Press, London and New York.

Luckwill, L. C., Weaver, P., and MacMillan, J. (1969). Gibberellins and other growth hormones in apple seeds. *J. Hort. Sci.* **44**, 413–424.

Lumsden, G. Q., and Whyland, W. P. (1939). A pocket increment core slicer. *J. Forest.* **37**, 900–901.

Lustinec, J., Simmer, J., and Resing, W. L. (1969). Trunk contraction of *Hevea brasiliensis* due to tapping. *Biol. Plant.* **11**, 236–244.

Lyford, W. H., and Wilson, B. F. (1964). Development of the root system of *Acer rubrum* L. *Harvard Forest Pap.* **10**.

Lyons, A. (1956). The seed production capacity and efficiency of red pine cones (*Pinus resinosa* Ait.). *Can. J. Bot.* **34**, 27–36.

Lyr, H., and Hoffmann, G. (1967). Growth rates and growth periodicity of tree roots. *Int. Rev. Forest. Res.* **2**, 181–206.

MacArthur, M., and Wetmore, R. H. (1941). Developmental studies in the apple fruit in the varieties McIntosh and Red Wagener. II. An analysis of development. *Can. J. Res.* **C19**, 371–382.

MacDaniels, L. H. (1936). Some anatomical aspects of apple flower and fruit abscission. *Proc. Amer. Soc. Hort. Sci.* **34**, 122–129.

MacDaniels, L. H. (1940). The morphology of the apple and other pome fruits. *Cornell Exp. Sta. Mem.* **230**.

MacDougal, D. T. (1921). Growth in trees. *Carnegie Inst. Wash. Publ.* **307**.

MacDougal, D. T. (1938). "Tree Growth." Chronica Botanica, Waltham, Massachusetts.

MacDougal, D. T., and Dufrenoy, J. (1944). Mycorrhizal symbiosis in *Asplectrum, Corallorhiza*, and *Pinus*. *Plant Physiol.* **19**, 440–465.

MacGregor, W. D. (1934). Silviculture of the mixed decidous forest of Nigeria. *Oxford Forest. Mem.* **18**.

Maggs, D. H. (1963). The reduction in growth of apple trees brought about by fruiting. *J. Hort. Sci.* **38**, 119–128.

Magness, J. R., Degman, E. S., and Furr, J. R. (1935). Soil moisture and irrigation investigations in eastern apple orchards. *US Dept. Agr. Tech. Bull.* **491**.

Maheshwari, P. (1950). "An Introduction to the Embryology of Angiosperms." McGraw-Hill, New York.

Maheshwari, P., and Rangaswamy, N. S. (1965). Embryology in relation to physiology and genetics. *In* "Advances in Botanical Research," Vol. 2. (R. D. Preston, ed.), pp. 219–321. Academic Press, New York.

Maheshwari, P., and Sachar, R. C. (1963). Polyembryony. *In* "Recent Advances in the Embryology of Angiosperms" (P. Maheshwari, ed.). Chapter 9 Catholic Press, Ranchi, India.

Maheshwari, P., and Singh, H. (1967). The female gametophyte of gymnosperms. *Biol. Rev.* **42**, 88–130.

Maki, T. E. (1960). Some effects of fertilizers on loblolly pine. *7th Int. Congr. Soil Sci.* **III**, 363–375.

Marian, J. E., and Stumbo, D. A. (1960). A new method of growth ring analysis and the determination of density by surface texture measurements. *Forest Sci.* **6**, 276–291.

Marks, G. C. (1965). The classification and distribution of the mycorrhizas of *Pinus radiata*. *Aust. Forest.* **29**, 238–251.

Marks, G. C., Ditchburne, N., and Foster, R. C. (1968). Quantitative estimates of mycorrhiza population in radiata pine forests. *Aust. Forest.* **32**, 26–38.

Marks, G. C., and Foster, R. C. (1967). Succession of mycorrhizal associations on individual roots of radiata pine. *Aust. Forest.* **31**, 193–201.

Marr, J. W. (1948). Ecology of the forest-tundra ecotone on the east coast of Hudson Bay. *Ecol. Monogr.* **18**, 117–144.

Marth, P. C., and Meader, E. M. (1944). Influence of growth-regulating chemicals on blackberry fruit development. *Proc. Amer. Soc. Hort. Sci.* **45**, 293–299.

Marvin, J. W., (1949). Changes in bark thickness during sap flow in sugar maple. *Science* **109**, 231–232.

Marx, D. H. (1969a). The influence of ectotrophic mycorrhizal fungi on the resistance of pine roots to pathogenic infections. I. Antagonism of mycorrhizal fungi to root pathogenic fungi and soil bacteria. *Phytopathology* **59**, 153–163.

Marx, D. H. (1969b). The influence of ectotrophic mycorrhizal fungi on the resistance of pine roots to pathogenic infection. II. Production, identification, and biological activity of antibiotics produced by *Leucopaxillus cerealis* var. *piceina. Phytopathology* **59**, 411–417.

Marx, D. H., and Davey, C. B. (1969). The influence of ectotrophic mycorrhizal fungi on the resistance of pine roots to pathogenic infection. IV. Resistance of naturally occurring mycorrhizae to infection by *Phytophthora cinnamomi. Phytopathology* **59**, 559–565.

Mason, G. F., Bhar, D. S., and Hilton, R. J. (1970). Root growth studies on Mugho pine. *Can. J. Bot.* **48**, 43–47.

Matthews, J. D. (1963). Factors affecting the production of seed by forest trees. *Forest. Abstr.* **24**, i–xiii.

Maurer, K. J. (1958). Unterlageneinfluss und Wurzelverlauf bei der Walnuss. *Neue Deut. Obstb.* **4**, 82.

McCarthy, J. (1962). The form and development of knee roots in *Mitragyna stipulosa. Phytomorphology* **12**, 20–30.

McComb, A. L. (1943). Mycorrhizae and phosphorus nutrition of pine seedlings in a prairie soil nursery. *Iowa Agr. Exp. Sta. Res. Bull.* **314**.

McComb, A. L., and Griffith, J. E. (1946). Growth stimulation and phosphorus absorption of mycorrhizal and non-mycorrhizal white pine and Douglas-fir seedlings in relation to fertilizer treatment. *Plant Physiol.* **21**, 11–17.

McCown, M. (1943). Anatomical and chemical aspects of abscission of fruits of the apple. *Bot. Gaz. (Chicago)* **105**, 212–220.

McCracken, I. J., and Kozlowski, T. T. (1965). Thermal contraction in twigs. *Nature (London)* **208**, 910–912.

McCully, W. G. (1952). Measuring diameter changes in small stems. *Ecology* **33**, 300–301.

McGinnies, W. G. 1963. Dendrochronology. *J. Forest.* **61**, 5–11.

McGuire, J. J., Kitchin, J. T. and Davidson, R. (1965). The effect of different growth retardants on the growth and flowering of *Rhododendron obtusum* 'Hinodegiri'. *Proc. Amer. Soc. Hort. Sci.* **86**, 761–763.

McMinn, R. G. (1963). Characteristics of Douglas-fir root systems. *Can. J. Bot.* **41**, 105–122.

McWilliam, J. R. (1958). The role of the micropyle in the pollination of *Pinus. Bot. Gaz. (Chicago)* **120**, 109–117.

McWilliam, J. R., and Mergen, F. (1958). Cytology of fertilization in *Pinus. Bot. Gaz. (Chicago)* **119**, 246–249.

Melin, E. (1927). Studier över Barrträdsplantans utveckling i råhumus. *Medd. Skogs-försöksanst. Stockholm.* **23**, 433–484.

Melin, E. (1946). Die Einfluss von Waldstreuextracten auf das Wachstum von Bodenpilzen mit besonderer Berückssichtigung der Wurzelpilze von Bäumen. *Symb. Bot. Upsal.* **8**(3), 1–116.

Melin, E. (1953). Physiology of mycorrhizal relations in plants. *Annu. Rev. Plant Physiol.* **4**, 325–346.

Melin, E. (1954). Growth factor requirements of mycorrhizal fungi of trees. *Sv. Bot. Tidskr.* **48**, 86–94.

Melin, E. (1962). Physiological aspects of mycorrhizae of forest trees. *In* "Tree Growth" (T. T. Kozlowski, ed.), Chapter 15. Ronald Press, New York.

Melin, E. (1963). Some effect of forest tree roots on mycorrhizal *Basidiomycetes. Symp. Soc. Gen. Microbiol.* **13**, 125–145.

Melin, E., and Das, V. S. R. (1954). Influence of root metabolites on the growth of tree mycorrhizal fungi. *Physiol. Plant.* **7**, 851–858.

Melin, E., and Mikola, P. (1948). Effects of some amino acids on the growth of *Cenococcum grandiforme. Physiol. Plant.* **1**, 109–112.

Melin, E., and Nilsson, H. (1950a). Transfer of radioactive phosphorus to pine seedlings by means of mycorrhizal fungi. *Physiol. Plant.* **3**, 88–92.

Melin, E., and Nilsson, H. (1950b). Transport of labelled nitrogen from an ammonium source to pine seedlings through mycorrhizal mycelium. *Sv. Bot. Tidskr.* **46**, 281–285.

Melin, E., and Nilsson, H. (1955). Ca^{45} used as indicator of transport of cations to pine seedlings by means of mycorrhizal mycelium. *Sv. Bot. Tidskr.* **49**, 119–122.

Melin, E., and Nilsson, H. (1957). Transport of C^{14}-labelled photosynthate to the fungal associate of pine mycorrhizae. *Svensk. Bot. Tidskr.* **51**, 166–186.

Melin, E., and Nilsson, H. (1958). Translocation of nutritive elements through mycorrhizal mycelia to pine seedlings. *Bot. Notiser* **111**, 251–256.

Melin, E., Nilsson, H., and Hacskaylo, E. (1958). Translocation of cations to seedlings of *Pinus virginiana* through mycorrhizal mycelium. *Bot. Gaz. (Chicago)* **119**, 243–245.

Mendes, A. J. T. (1941). Cytological observations in *Coffea*. VI. Embryo and endosperm development in *Coffea arabica* L. *Amer. J. Bot.* **28**, 784–789.

Mergen, F. (1954). Anatomical study of slash pine graft unions. *Fla. Acad. Sci. Quart. J.* **17**, 237–245.

Mergen, F. (1955). Grafting slash pine in the field and in the greenhouse. *J. Forest.* **53**, 836–842.

Mergen, F. (1958). Distribution of reaction wood in eastern hemlock as a function of its terminal growth. *Forest Sci.* **4**, 98–109.

Mergen, F., and Koerting, L. E. (1957). Initiation and development of flower primordia in slash pine. *Forest Sci.* **3**, 145–155.

Merritt, C. (1959). Studies in the root growth of red pine (*Pinus resinosa* Ait.). Ph.D. Thesis Univ. Michigan, Ann Arbor, Michigan.

Merritt, C. (1968). Effect of environment and heredity on the root-growth pattern of red pine. *Ecology* **49**, 34–40.

Mesavage, C., and Smith, W. S. (1960). Timesavers for installing dendrometer bands. *J. Forest.* **58**, 396.

Metcalfe, C. R., and Chalk, L. (1950). "Anatomy of the Dicotyledons." Clarendon Press, Oxford.

Meyer, F. H. (1966). Mycorrhiza and other plant symbioses. *In* "Symbiosis," (S. M. Henry, ed.), Vol. I, Chapter 4. Academic Press, New York.

Meyer, F. H. (1967). Feinwurzelverteilung bei Waldbäumen in Abhängigkeit vom Substrat. *Forstarchiv.* **38**, 286–290.

Meyer, H. A., and Nelson, F. B. (1952). Accuracy of forest growth determination based on the measurement of increment cores. *Penn. State Univ. Agr. Exp. Sta. Bull.* **547**.

Mikola, P. (1948). On the physiology and ecology of *Cenococcum graniforme*, especially as a mycorrhizal fungus of birch. *Commun. Inst. For. Fenn.* **36**, 1–104.

Mikola, P., 1950. Puiden kasvun vaihteluista ja niden merkityksestä Kasvututkimuksissa. *Commun. Inst. For. Fenn.* **38.5**, 1–131.

Mikola, P. (1951). Kasvun luonnollinen kehitys. *Eripainos Metsät. Aikakauslehdestä.* **2**, 1–4.

Mikola, P. (1962). Temperature and tree growth near the northern timber line. *In* "Tree Growth" (T. T. Kozlowski, ed.), Chapter 16. Ronald Press, New York.

Mikola, P. and Laiho, O. (1962). Mycorrhizal relations in the raw humus layer of northern spruce forests. *Commun. Inst. For. Fenn.* **55**, 1–13.

Mikola, P., Laiho, O., Erikäinen, J., and Kuvaja, K. (1964). The effect of slash burning on the commencement of mycorrhizal association. *Acta Forest. Fenn.* **77**, 1–12.

Miller, C. O., Skoog, F., Okumura, F. S., von Saltza, M. H., and Strong, F. M. (1955). Structure and synthesis of kinetin. *J. Amer. Chem. Soc.* **77**, 2662–2663.

Mironov, V. V. (1959). Pridatocnye korni derev'ev Priroda Moskva **48**, 118 (Russ.) (*Forest. Abstr.* **21**, (250), (1960)).

Mirov, N. T. (1962). Phenology of tropical pines. *J. Arnold Arboretum Harvard. Univ.* **43**, 218–219.

Mochizuki, T. (1962). Studies on the elucidation of factors affecting the decline in tree vigor in apples as induced by fruit load. *Bull. Fac. Agr. Hirosaki Univ.* **8**, 40–124.

Modilbowska, I. (1961). Effect of soil moisture on frost resistance of apple blossom including some observations on "ghost" and "parachute" blossoms. *J. Hort. Sci.* **36**, 186–196.

Moehring, D. M, and Ralston, C. W. (1967). Diameter growth of loblolly pine related to available soil moisture and rate of soil moisture loss. *Soil Sci. Soc. Amer. Proc.* **31**, 560–562.

Mogenson, H. L. (1966). A contribution to the anatomical development of the acorn in *Quercus* L. *Iowa State J. Sci.* **40**, 221–255.

Möller, C. M. (1946). Untersuchungen über Laubmenge, Stoffverlust und Stoffproduktion des Waldes. *Det Forstl. Forsgsøvaesen i Danmark.* **17**, 1–287.

Monselise, S. P., and Goren, R. (1969). Flowering and fruiting—interactions of exogenous and internal factors. *Proc. 1st Int. Citrus Symp.* **3**, 1105–1112.

Monselise, S. P., Goren, R., and Halevy, A. H. (1966). Effects of B.9, Cycocel and benzo-thiazole oxyacetate on flower bud induction of lemon trees. *Proc. Amer. Soc. Hort. Sci.* **89**, 195–200.

Morey, P. R., and Cronshaw, J. (1966). Induced structural changes in cambial derivatives of *Ulmus americana. Protoplasma* **62**, 76–85.

Morey, P. R., and Cronshaw, J. (1968a), Developmental changes in the secondary xylem of *Acer rubrum* induced by various auxins and 2,3,5-tri-iodobenzoic acid. *Protoplasma* **65**, 287–313.

Morey, P. R., and Cronshaw, J. (1968b). The effect of plant growth substances on the development of tension wood in horizontally inclined stems of *Acer rubrum* seedlings. *Protoplasma* **65**, 379–391.

Morey, P. R., and Cronshaw, J. (1968c). Induction of tension wood by 2,4-dinitrophenol and auxins. *Protoplasma* **65**, 393–405.

Morita, Y., and Oguro, E. (1951). Studies on the physical properties of soil in relation to fruit tree growth. III. Soil moisture and tree growth (3) the influence of mulching upon the soil moisture and root distribution of peach seedlings. *J. Hort. Assoc. Japan*, **20**, 11–18.

Mork, E. (1928). Die Qualität des Fichtenholzes unter besonderer Rücksichtnahme auf Schleif-und Papierholz. *Pap.-Fabrik.* **26**, 741–747.

Mork, E. (1960). Om sambandet mellom temperatur, toppskuddtilvekst og arringens vokst og tervedning hos gran (*Picea abies* (L.) Karst.) *Medd. Norske Skogforsokoy.* 16. **56**, 227–261.

Morris, R. F. (1951). The effects of flowering on the foliage production and growth of balsam fir. *Forest. Chron.* **27**, 40–57.

Morrison, T. M. (1957). Mycorrhiza and phosphorus uptake. *Nature (London)* **179**, 907–908.

Morrison, T. M. (1962a). Absorption of phosphorus from soils by mycorrhizal plants. *New Phytol.* **61**, 10–20.

Morrison, T. M. (1962b). Uptake of sulphur by mycorrhizal plants. *New Phytol.* **61**, 21–27.

Morrow, R. R. (1950). Periodicity and growth of sugar maple surface layer roots. *J. Forest* **48**, 875–881

Moser, M. (1959). Beitrage zur Kenntnis der Wuchsstoff-beziehungen im Bereich ektotro-phen Mykorrhizen. *Areh. Mikrobiol.* **34**, 251–269.

Mosse, B. (1962). Graft-incompatability in fruit trees with particular reference to its underlying causes. *Tech. Commun. Bur. Hort. Plantation Crops, E Malling*, **28**.

Moyle, R. C., and Zahner, R. (1954. Soil moisture as affected by stand conditions. *Southern Forest Exp. Sta. Occasional Pap.* **137**.

Müller, H. (1906). Über die Metakutisierung der Wurzelslpitze und über di verkorkten Scheiden in den Achsen der Monocotyledone. *Bot. Z.* **64**, 53–84.

Murmanis, L. and I. B. Sachs. 1969. Seasonal development of secondary xylem in *Pinus strobus* L. *Wood Sci. Tech.* **3**, 177–193.

Murneek, A. E. (1925). Is fruiting of the apple an exhaustive process? *Proc. Amer. Soc. Hort. Sci.* **22**, 196–200.

Murneek, A. E. (1930). Quantitative distribution and seasonal fluctuation of nitrogen in apple trees. *Proc. Amer. Soc. Hort. Sci.* **27**, 228–231.

Murneek, A. E. (1933). Carbohydrate storage in apple trees. *Proc. Amer. Soc. Hort. Sci.* **30**, 319–321.

Murneek, A. E. (1954). The embryo and endosperm in relation to fruit development with special reference to the apple, *Malus sylvestris*. *Proc. Amer. Soc. Hort. Sci.* **64**, 573–582.

Mustanja, K. J., and Leaf, A. L. (1965). Forest fertilization research, 1957–1964. *Bot. Rev.* **31**, 151–246.

Muzik, T. J. (1954). Development of fruit, seed, embryo, and seedling of *Hevea brasiliensis*. *Amer. J. Bot.* **41**, 39–43.

Myers, C. A. (1963). Vertical distribution of annual increment in thinned ponderosa pine. *Forest Sci.* **9**, 394–404.

Nakata, S., and Suehisa, R. (1969). Growth and development of *Litchi chinensis* as affected by soil moisture stress. *Amer. J. Bot.* **56**, 1121–1126.

Nanson, A. (1965). Stimulation de la production de strobiles femelles don un verger à graines de *Pinus sylvestris* L. par application d'engrais. *Silvae Genet.* **14**, 94–97.

Narayanaswami, S., and Norstog, K. (1964). Plant embryo culture. *Bot. Rev.* **30**, 587–628.

Näslund, M. (1942). Den gamla norrländska granskogens reaktionsförmäga efter genomhuggning. *Medd. Statens Skogsför.* **33**, 1–212.

Nast, C. G. (1935). Morphological development of the fruit of *Juglans nigra*. *Hilgardia* **9**, 345–381.

Necesany, V. (1958). Effect of β-indoleacetic acid on the formation of reaction wood. *Phyton (Buenos Aires)* **11**, 117–127.

Neely, D., and Himelick, E. B. (1963). Root graft transmission of Dutch elm disease in municipalities. *Plant Dis. Rep.* **47**, 83–85.

Neff, M. S., and O'Rourke, E. (1951). Factors affecting the initiation of new roots in newly transplanted tung trees. *Proc. Amer. Soc. Hort. Sci.* **57**, 186–190.

Nesbitt, W. A. (1942). Aerial roots from old tree wound. *Plant Physiol.* **17**, 689–690.

Neuwirth, G., and Fritzsche, K. H. (1964). Untersuchungen über den Einfluss verschiedener Düngergaben auf das gasstoffwechselökologische Verhalten einjähriger Pappel-Steckholzantwuchse. *Arch. Forstw.* **13**, 233–246.

Nielsen, P. C., and Schaffalitzky de Muckadell, M. (1954). Flower observations and controlled pollination in *Fagus*. *Z. Forstgenet Forstpflanzenzüchtung* **3**, 1–16.

Nienstaedt, H. (1956). Receptivity of the pistillate flowers and pollen germination tests in genus *Castanea*. *Z. Forstgenetik Forstpflanzenzuchtung* **5**, 40–45.

Nienstaedt, H. (1958). Receptivity of female strobili of white spruce. *Forest Sci.* **4**, 110–115.

Nicholls, J. W. P. (1967). Assessment of wood qualities for tree breeding. IV. *Pinus pinaster* grown in western Australia. *Sylvae Genet.* **16**, 21–28.

Ninokata, K., and Miyazato, M. (1959). Measurement of daily variation of the diameter of trunks by the electrical strain gauge. *Bull. Fac. Agr. Kagoshima Univ.* **8**, 76–88.

Nitsch, J. P. (1950). Growth and morphogenesis of the strawberry as related to auxin. *Amer. J. Bot.* **37**, 211–215.

Nitsch, J. P. (1953). The physiology of fruit growth. *Annu. Rev. Plant Physiol.* **4**, 199–236.

Nitsch, J. P. (1965). Physiology of flower and fruit development. *Encycl. Plant Physiol.* **15**, (1), 1537–1647.

Nitsch, J. P., Pratt, C., Nitsch, C., and Shaulis, N. J. (1960). Natural growth substances in Concord and Concord Seedless grapes in relation to berry development. *Amer. J. Bot.* **47**, 566–576.

Njoku, E. (1963). Seasonal periodicity in the growth and development of some forest trees in Nigeria. *J. Ecol.* **59**, 617–624.

Noel, A. R. A. (1968). Callus formation and differentiation at an exposed cambial surface. *Ann. Bot.* **32**, 347–359.

Noelle, W. (1910). Studien zur vergleichenden Anatomie und Morphologie der Koniferwurzeln mit Rücksicht auf die Systematik. *Bot. Z.* **68**, 169–266.

Nomoto, N., Kasanaga, H., and Monsi, M. (1959). Dry matter production by *Chamaecyparis pisifera* in winter. *Bot. Mag. Tokyo* **72**, 450–455.

Norkrans, B. (1950). Studies in growth and cellulolytic enzymes of *Tricholoma*: with special reference to mycorrhiza formation. *Symb. Bot. Upsal.* **11**, 1–126.

Northcote, D. H. (1963). Changes in the cell walls of plants during differentiation. *Symp. Soc. Exp. Biol.* **17**, 157–174.

Northcott, D. L. (1957). Is spiral grain the normal pattern. *Forest. Chron.* **33**, 335–352.

Noskowiak, A. S. (1963). Spiral grain in trees. A review. *Forest Prod. J.* **13**, 266–275.

Obaton, M. (1960). Les lianes ligneuses a structure anormale des fôrets denses d'Afrique occidentale. *Ann. Sci. Nat. Bot. Biol. Veg. Ser.* **12**, (1), 1–220.

Ogigirigi, M. A., Kozlowski, T. T., and Sasaki, S. (1970). Effect of soil drying on stem shrinkage and photosynthesis of tree seedlings. *Plant Soil* **32**, 33–49.

Onaka, F. (1950). The longitudinal distribution of radial increments in trees. *Kyota Univ. Forest.* **18**, 1–53.

O'Neil, L. C. (1963). The suppression of growth rings in jack pine in relation to defoliation by the Swaine jack-pine sawfly. *Can. J. Bot.* **41**, 227–235.

Oppenheimer, H. R. (1960). Adaptation to drought: xerophytism. In plant–water relationships in arid and semi-arid conditions. *Rev. Res.* UNESCO, 105–138.

Ordin, L. (1958). The effect of water stress on the cell wall metabolism of plant tissue. *In* "Radioisotopes in Scientific Research," Vol. IV, pp. 553–564. MacMillan (Pergamon), New York.

Ordin, L. (1960). Effect of water stress on cell wall metabolism of Avena coleoptile tissue. *Plant Physiol.* **35**, 443–450.

Orlov, A. J. (1957). Nabljudenija nad sosuscimi kornajami eli (*Picea excelsa* Link.) v estestvennyh uslovijan. *Bot. Zh.* **42**, 1172–1181.

Orlov, A. J. (1960). Rost i vozrastnye izmenenija sosuscih kornej eli *Picea excelsa Link.* *Bot. Z.* **45**, 888–896.

Overbeek, J. van. (1962). Endogenous regulators of fruit growth. *Proc. Plant Sci. Symp. Campbell Soup Co. Camden, New Jersey.* 37–58.

Orr-Ewing, A. L. (1957). Possible occurrence of viable unfertilized seeds in Douglas-fir. *Forest Sci.* **3**, 243–248.

Overbeek, J. van, and Gregory, J. L. (1945). A physiological separation of two factors necessary for the formation of roots on cuttings. *Amer. J. Bot.* **32**, 336–341.

Ovington, J. D. (1956). Studies of the development of woodland conditions under different trees. IV. The ignition loss, water, carbon and nitrogen content of the mineral soil. *J. Ecol.* **44**, 171–179.

Ovington, J. D. (1963). Flower and seed production. A source of error in estimating woodland production, energy flow and mineral cycling. *Oikos* **14**, 148–153.

Owens, J. N. (1969). The relative importance of initiation and early development of cone production in Douglas-fir. *Can. J. Bot.* **47**, 1039–1049.

Owens, J. N., and Smith, F. H. (1964). The initiation and early development of the seed cone on Douglas-fir. *Can. J. Bot.* **42**, 1031–1047.

Owens, J. N., and Smith, F. H. (1965). Development of the seed cone of Douglas-fir following dormancy. *Can. J. Bot.* **43**, 317–332.

Packer, W. J., Chalmers, D. J., and Baxter, P. (1963). Supplementary irrigation of Jonathan apple trees. *J. Agr. Victoria Aust.* **61**, 453–460.

Paech, K. (1955). Colour development in flowers. *Annu. Rev. Plant Physiol.* **6**, 273–298.

Panshin, A. J., De Zeeuw, C., and Brown, H. P. (1964). "Textbook of Wood Technology," Vol. I. McGraw-Hill, New York.

Parmeter, J. R., Kuntz, J. E., and Riker, A. J. (1956). Oak wilt development in bur oaks. *Phytopathology* 46, 423–436.

Patel, R. N. (1963). Spiral thickening in normal and compression wood. *Nature (London)* 198, 1225–1226.

Patel, R. N. (1965). A comparison of the anatomy of the secondary xylem in roots and stems. *Holzforschung* 19, 72–79.

Paton, D. M., Willing, R. R., Nicholls, W., and Pryor, L. D. (1970). Rooting of stem cuttings of *Eucalyptus*: A rooting inhibitor in adult tissue. *Aust. J. Bot.* 18, 175–183.

Paul, B. H. (1950). Wood quality in relation to site quality of second-growth Douglas-fir. *J. Forest.* 48, 175–179.

Paul, B. H., and Smith, D. M. (1950). Summary on growth in relation to quality of southern yellow pine. *US Forest Prod. Lab. Rep. Madison, Wisconsin.* D1751.

Peace, T. R. (1962). "Pathology of Trees and Shrubs." Clarendon Press, Oxford.

Persidsky, D. J., and Wilde, S. A. (1960). The effect of biocides on the survival of mycorrhizal fungi. *J. Forest.* 58, 522–524.

Pessin, L. J. (1934). Annual ring formation in *Pinus palustris* seedlings. *Amer. J. Bot.* 21, 599–604.

Petch, T. (1930). Buttress roots. *Annu. Rep. Bot. Gard. Peradeniya* 11, 277–285.

Pfeiffer, H. (1926). Das abnorme Dichenwachstum. *Linsbauer Handb. Pfl. Anat. (Berlin).* 9.

Philipson, W. R., and Ward, J. M. (1965). The ontogeny of the vascular cambium in the stem of seed plants. *Biol. Rev.* 40, 534–579.

Pfister, R. D. (1967). Maturity indices for grand fir cones. *US Forest Serv. Res. Note* INT-58.

Phillips, E. W. J. (1960). The beta ray method of determining the density of wood and the proportion of summerwood. *J. Inst. Wood Sci.* 5, 16–28.

Phillips, E. W. J., Adams, E. H., and Hearmon, R. F. S. (1962). The measurement of density variation within the growth rings in thin sections of wood using beta particles. *J. Inst. Wood Sci.* 10, 11–28.

Phillips, W. S. (1963). Depth of roots in soil. *Ecology* 44, 424.

Philp, G. L. (1947). Cherry culture in California. *Calif. Agr. Ext. Circ.* 46, 1–51.

Phipps, R. L. (1961). Analysis of five years dendrometer data obtained with three deciduous forest communities of Neotoma, *Ohio Agr. Exp. Sta. Res. Circ.* 105.

Phinney, B. O., West, C. A., Ritzel, M., and Neely, P. M. (1957). Evidence for "gibberellinlike" substances from flowering plants. *Proc. Nat. Acad. Sci.* 43, 398–404.

Piringer, A. A., and Borthwick, H. A. (1955). Photoperiodic responses of coffee. *Turrialba* 5, 72–77.

Pirson, A. (1958). Mineralstoffe und Photosynthese. *Encyl. Plant Physiol.* 4, 355–381.

Pisek, A., and Tranquillini, W. (1954). Assimilation und Kohlenstoffhaushalt in der Krone von Fichten (*Picea excelsa* Link) und Rotbuchenbäumen (*Fagus silvatica* L.) *Flora* 141, 237–270.

Pisek, A., and Winkler, E. (1958). Assimilationsvermögen und Respiration der Fichte (*Picea excelsa*) in verschiedener Höhenlage und der Zirbe (*Pinus cembra* L.) an der alpinen Waldgrenze. *Planta* 51, 518–543.

Pisek, A., and Winkler, E. (1959). Licht-und Temperaturabhängigkeit der CO_2-Assimilation von Fichte (*Picea excelsa* Link.), Zirbe (*Pinus cembra* L.) and Sonnenblume (*Helianthus annuus.* L.) *Planta* 53, 532–550.

Polge, H. (1960). Sensibilité relative du sapin pactine et de l'epicea commun aux crups de vent. *Rev. Forest. Fr.* 12, 637–642.

Polge, H. (1966). Etablissement des courbes de variation de la densite du bois par exploration densitometrique de radiographies d'echantillons préléves a la tariere sur des arbres vivants. *Ann. Sci. Forest.* **23**, 1–206.

Polge, H. (1969). Further considerations about the x-ray and beta ray methods for determining wood density. *J. Inst. Wood Sci.* **23**, 39–44.

Pollard, D. F. W., and Wareing, P. F. (1968). Rates of dry matter production in forest tree seedlings. *Ann. Bot.* **32**, 573–591.

Pomerleau, R., and Lortie, M. (1962). Relationships of dieback to the rooting depth of white birch. *Forest Sci.* **8**, 219–224.

Pond, J. D. (1936). Girdling for seed production. *J. Forest.* **34**, 78–79.

Powell, D., Janson, B., and Sharvelle, E. G. (1965). Diseases of apples and pears in the midwest. *Univ. Illinois Ext. Circ.* **909**

Powell, G. R. (1970). Postdormancy development and growth of microsporangiate and megasporangiate strobili of *Abies balsamea. Can. J. Bot.* 48, 419–428.

Pratt, H. K., and Goeschl, J. D. (1968). The role of ethylene in fruit ripening. *In* "Biochemistry and Physiology of Plant Growth Substances," (F. Wightman and G. Setterfield, eds.), pp. 1295–1302. Runge Press, Ottawa.

Priestley, C. A. (1962a). Carbohydrate resources within the perennial plant. *Commun. Bur. Hort. Plantation Crops. Tech. Commun.* **27.**

Priestley, C. A. (1962b). The location of carbohydrate resources within the apple tree. *Proc. XVI. Int. Hort. Congr.* **1**, 319–327.

Priestley, J. H. (1935). Radial growth and extension growth in the tree. *Forestry* **9**, 84–95.

Priestley, J. H., Scott, L. I., and Malins, M. E. (1933). A new method of studying cambial activity. *Proc. Leeds. Phil. Lit. Soc. Sci. Sect.* **2**, 365–374.

Primer, P. E., and Crane, J. C. (1957). Growth regulator induced parthenocarpy in apricots. *Proc. Amer. Soc. Hort. Sci.* **70**, 121–124.

Proebsting, E. L. (1934). A fertilizer trial with Bartlett pears. *Proc. Amer. Soc. Hort. Sci.* **30**, 55–57.

Proebsting, E. L. (1937). Fertilizing deciduous fruit trees in California. *Calif. Agr. Exp. Sta. Bull.* **610.**

Proebsting, E. L. (1958). A quantitative evaluation of the effect of fruiting on growth of Elberta peach trees. *Proc. Amer. Soc. Hort. Sci.* **71**, 103–109.

Proebsting, E. L. (1961). Response of Bartlett pear to nitrogen in California. *Calif. Ag.* 15(6), 14–15.

Pyke, E. E. (1941). Trunk diameter of trees of *Hevea brasiliensis:* experiments with a new dendrometer. *Nature (London)* **148**, 51–52.

Quamme, H. A., and Nelson, S. H. (1965). Root promoting substances in the juvenile phase of *Malus robusta. Can. J. Plant Sci.* **45**, 509–511.

Quick, C. R. (1944). Effects of snowbrush on the growth of Sierra gooseberry. *J. Forest* **42**, 827–832.

Radley, M., and Dear, E. (1958). Occurrence of gibberellin-like substances in the coconut. *Nature (London)* **182**, 1098.

Rake, B. A. (1957). The development of adventitious roots on hardwooa cuttings of gooseberries. *J. Hort. Sci.* **32**, 195–198.

Ramirez, W. B. (1969). Fig wasps: mechanism of pollen transfer. *Science,* **163**, 580–581.

Rangnekar, P. V., and Forward, D. F. (1969). Foliar nutrition and growth in red pine: the fate of photoassimilated carbon in a seedling tree. *Can. J. Bot.* **47**, 897–906.

Rao, A. N. (1966). Developmental anatomy of natural root grafts in *Ficus globosa. Aust. J. Bot.* **14**, 269–276.

Rawitscher, F., Ferri, M. G., and Rochid, M. (1943). Profundidade dos solos e vegetacao em campos cerrados do Brasil meridional. *Ann. Acad. Bras. Sci.* **15**, 267–294.

Rebeiz, C. A., and Crane, J. C. (1961), Growth regulator induced parthenocarpy in the Bing cherry. *Proc. Amer. Soc. Hort. Sci.* **78**, 69–75.

Redmond, D. R. (1957). Observations on rootlet development in yellow birch. *Forest. Chron.* **33**, 208–212.

Redmond, D. R. (1959). Mortality of rootlets in balsam fir defoliated by the spruce budworm. *Forest Sci.* **5**, 64–69.

Reed, H. S., and MacDougal, D. T. (1937). Periodicity in the growth of the young orange tree. *Growth* **1**, 371–373.

Reed, J. F. (1939). Root and shoot growth of shortleaf and loblolly pines in relation to certain environmental conditions. *Duke Univ. School Forest. Bull.* **4**.

Rees, A. R. (1964a). Some observations on the flowering behavior of *Coffea rupestris* in southern Nigeria. *J. Ecol.* **52**, 1–7.

Rees, A. R. (1964b). The flowering behavior of *Clerodendron incisum* in southern Nigeria. *J. Ecol.* **52**, 9–17.

Reineke, L. H. (1941). A new increment core instrument and coring wrinkles. *J. Forest.* **39**, 304–309.

Reineke, L. H. (1948). Dial gage dendrometers. *Ecology* **29**, 208.

Reinken, G. (1963). Wachstum, Assimilation und Transpiration von Apfelbäumen und ihre Beeinflussung durch Phosphor. *Phosphorsäure* **23**, 91–108.

Rendle, B. J., and Phillips, E. W. J. (1958). The effect of rate of growth (ring width) on the density of softwoods. *Forestry* **31**, 113–120.

Reukema, D. L. (1959). Missing annual rings in branches of young Douglas-fir. *Ecology* **40**, 480–482.

Reukema, D. L. (1961). Crown development and its effect on stem growth of six Douglas-firs. *J. Forest.* **59**, 370–371.

Reuther, W., and Burrows, F. W. (1942). Effect of manganese sulfate on the photosynthetic activity of frenched tung foliage. *Proc. Amer. Soc. Hort. Sci.* **40**, 73–76.

Richards, P. W. (1964). "Tropical Rain Forest." Cambridge Univ. Press, Cambridge, England.

Richardson, S. D. (1953a). Studies of root growth in *Acer saccharinum* L. I. The relation between root growth and photosynthesis. *Proc. Kon. Akad. Wetensch. Amsterdam* **C56**, 185–193.

Richardson, S. D. (1953b). Studies of root growth in *Acer saccharinum* L. II. Factors affecting root growth when photosynthesis is curtailed. *Proc. Kon. Ned. Akad. Wetensch. Amsterdam* **C56**, 346–353.

Richardson, S. D. (1953c). A note on some differences in root-hair formation between seedlings of sycamore and American oak. *New Phytol.* **52**, 80–82.

Richardson, S. D. (1956a). Studies of root growth in *Acer saccharinum* L. III. The influence of seedling age on the short term relation between photosynthesis and root growth. *Proc. Kon. Ned. Akad. Wetensch. Amsterdam* **C59**, 416–427.

Richardson, S. D. (1956b). Studies of root growth in *Acer saccharinum*. V. The effect of a long-term limitation of photosynthesis on root growth rate in first-year seedlings. *Proc. Kon. Ned. Akad. Wetensch. Amsterdam* **C59**, 694–701.

Richardson, S. D. (1956c). On the role of the acorn in root growth of American oak seedlings. *Med. van de Landbouwhogeschool, Wageningen.* **56**, 1–18.

Richardson, S. D. (1957). Studies of root growth in *Acer saccharinum* L. VI. Further effects of the shoot system on root growth. *Proc. Kon. Akad. Wetensch. Amsterdam* **C60**, 624–629.

Richardson, S. D. (1958). Bud dormancy and root development in *Acer saccharinum*. *In* "The Physiology of Forest Trees" (K. V. Thimann, ed.), Chapter 20. Ronald Press, New York.

Richardson, S. D., and Dinwoodie, J. M. (1960). Studies on the physiology of xylem development. I. The effect of night temperature on tracheid size and wood density in conifers. *J. Inst. Wood Sci.* **6**, 3–13.

Riedhart, J. M., and Guard, A. T. (1957). On the anatomy of the roots of apple seedlings. *Bot. Gaz. (Chicago)* **118**, 191–194.

Riedl, H. (1937). Bau und Leistungen des Wurzelholzes. *Jahrb. Wiss. Bot.* **85**, 1–95.

Rigg, G. B., and Harrar, E. S. (1931). The root systems of trees growing in sphagnum. *Amer. J. Bot.* **18**, 391–397.

Robards, A. W. (1965). Tension wood and eccentric growth in crack willow (*Salix fragilis* L.) *Ann. Bot.* **29**, 419–431.

Robards, A. W., Davidson, E., and Kidwai, P. (1969). Short-term effects of some chemicals on cambial activity. *J. Exp. Bot.* **20**, 912–920.

Robbins, W. W., Weier, T. E., and Stocking, C. R. (1957). "An Introduction to Plant Science." Wiley, New York.

Roberts, B. R. (1964). Effects of water stress on the translocation of photosynthetically assimilated carbon-14 in yellow poplar. *In* "The Formation of Wood in Forest Trees" (M. H. Zimmermann, ed.), pp. 273–288. Academic Press, New York.

Roberts, L. W., and Fosket, D. E. (1966). Interactions of gibberellic acid and indoleacetic acid in the differentiation of wound vessel members. *New Phytol.* **65**, 5–8.

Robyns, W. (1938). Sur un cas de polyembryonie dans le *Juglans nigra* L. *Ann. Soc. Sci. Bruxelles Ser.* 2 **58**, 120–129.

Rogers, W. S. (1939). Root studies. VIII. Apple root growth in relation to rootstock, soil, seasonal, and climatic factors. *J. Pomol. Hort. Sci.* **17**, 99–130.

Rogers, W. S., and Booth, G. A. (1959, 1960). The roots of fruit trees. *Sci. Hort.* **14**, 27–34.

Rogers, W. S., and Booth, G. A. (1964). Relationship of crop and shoot growth in apple. *J. Hort. Sci.* **39**, 61–65.

Rogers, W. S., and Head, G. C. (1969). Factors affecting the distribution and growth of roots in perennial woody species. *In* "Root Growth" (W. J. Whittington, ed.), pp. 280–295. Butterworth, London.

Rokach, A. (1953). Water transfer from fruits to leaves in the Shamouti orange tree and related topics. *Palestine J. Bot.* **8**, 146–151.

Rommell, L. (1937). Kvistrensning och övervallning hos okvistad och torrkvistad tall. *S. Skogsvärdsföreningens Tidskr.* **35**, 299–328.

Rommell, L. (1940–41). Kvistningsstudier å tall och gran. *Medd. Från Statens Skogsförsöksan Stalt* **32**, 143–194.

Rose, A. H. (1958). The effect of defoliation on foliage production and radial growth of quaking aspen. *Forest Sci.* **4**, 335–342.

Rosen, W. G. (1968). Ultrastructure and physiology of pollen. *Annu. Rev. Plant Physiol.* **19**, 435–462.

Rovira, A. D. (1965). Plant root exudates. *Bot. Rev.* **35**, 17–34.

Roy Chowdhury, C. (1962). The embryogeny of conifers: A review. *Phytomorphology* **12**, 313–338.

Ryugo, K., and Davis, L. D. (1959). The effect of the time of ripening on the starch content of bearing peach branches. *Proc. Amer. Soc. Hort. Sci.* **74**, 130–133.

Rudinsky, J. A., and Vité, J. P. (1959). Certain ecological and phylogenetic aspects of the pattern of water conduction in conifers. *Forest Sci.* **5**, 259–266.

Sachar, R. C., and Chopra, R. N. (1957). A study of the endosperm and embryo in *Mangifera* L. *Indian J. Agr. Sci.* **27**, 219–228.

Sachs, I. B., Clark, I. T., and Pew, J. C. (1963). Investigation of lignin distribution in the cell wall of certain woods. *J. Polymer Sci.* **C2**, 203–212.

Sachs, R. M., Loreti, F., and DeBie, J. (1964). Plant rooting studies indicate sclerenchyma tissue is not a restricting factor. *Calif. Agr.* **18**,(9), 4–5.

Saeki, T., and Nomoto, N. (1958). On the seasonal change of photosynthetic activity of some deciduous and evergreen broadleaf trees. *Bot. Mag. Tokyo* **71**, 235–241.

Sakai, A. (1962). Studies on the frost hardiness of woody plants. I. The causal relation between sugar content and frost hardiness. *Contr. Inst. Low Temp. Sci. Hokkaido Univ. Ser.* **B11**, 1–40.

Sakai, A. (1968). Mechanism of desiccation damage of forest trees in winter. *Contr. Inst. Low Temp. Res. Hokkaido Univ. Ser.* **B15**, 15–35.

Sanio, K. (1872). Ueber die Brösse der Holzzellen bei der gemeinen Kiefer (*Pinus silvestris*), *Jahrb. Wiss. Bot.* **8**, 410–420.

Sarvas, R. (1955a). Investigations into the flowering and seed quality of forest trees. *Commun. Inst. Forest Fenn.* **45**.

Sarvas, R. (1955b). Ein Beitrag zur Fernverbreitung des Blütenstaubes einiger Waldbäume. *Z. Forstgenet. Forstpflanzenz.* **4**, 137–142.

Sarvas, R. (1962). Investigations on the flowering and seed crop of *Pinus silvestris*. *Commun. Inst. Forst. Fenni.* **53**, 1–198.

Sasaki, S., and Kozlowski, T. T. (1967). Effects of herbicides on carbon dioxide uptake of pine seedlings. *Can. J. Bot.* **45**, 961–971.

Sass, J. E. (1932). Formation of callus knots on apple grafts as related to the histology of the graft union. *Bot. Gaz.* (*Chicago*) **94**, 364–380.

Satoo, S. (1953). Origin and development of adventitious roots in *Thujopsis dolabrata* cuttings. *J. Jap. Forest. Soc.* **35**, 220–225.

Satoo, S. (1955). Origin and development of adventitious roots in layered branches of 4 species of conifers. *J. Jap. Forest. Soc.* **37**, 314–316.

Satoo, S. (1956). Anatomical studies on the rooting of cuttings in conifer species. *Bull. Tokyo Univ. Forests* **51**, 111–157.

Satoo, T. (1964). Natural root grafting and growth of living stumps of *Chamaecyparis obtusa*. *Tokyo Univ. Forests. Misc. Inf. No.* **15**.

Satoo, T., Kunagi, R., and Kumekawa Z. (1956). Materials for the studies of growth in stands. 3. Amount of leaves and production of wood in an aspen (*Populus davidiana*) second growth in Hakkaido. *Bull. Tokyo Univ. Forest.* **52** 33–58.

Satoo, T., Negisi, K., and Senda, M. (1959). Materials for the studies of growth in stands. 5. Amount of leaves and growth in plantations of *Zelkowa serrata* applied with crown thinning. *Bull. Tokyo Univ. Forest* **55**, 101–123.

Satoo, T., and Senda, M. (1958). Materials for the studies of growth in stands. 4. Amount of leaves and production of wood in a young plantation of *Chamaecyparis obtusa*. *Bull. Tokyo Univ. Forest* **54**, 71–100.

Saucier, J. R. (1963). Within tree variations of fiber characteristics of green ash. M. S. Thesis. Univ. of Georgia, Athens, Ga.

Sax, K. (1957). The control of vegetative growth and the induction of early fruiting of apple trees. *Proc. Amer. Soc. Hort. Sci.* **69**, 68–74.

Sax, K. (1958). Experimental control of tree growth and reproduction. *In* "The Physiology of Forest Trees" (K. V. Thimann, ed.), Chapter 32. Ronald Press, New York.

Schaad, N. W., and Wilson, E. E. (1970). Structure and seasonal development of phloem of *Juglans regia*. *Can. J. Bot.* **48**, 1049–1053.

Schneider, G. W., and Scarborough, C. C. (1960). "Fruit Growing." Prentice-Hall, Englewood Cliffs, New Jersey.

Schneider, H. (1952). The phloem of the sweet orange tree trunk and the seasonal production of xylem and phloem. *Hilgardia* **21**, 331–366.

Schneider, H. (1954). Condition of phloem of sour orange tree trunk in winter. *Hilgardia* **22**, 583–591.

Schneider, H. (1955). Ontogeny of lemon tree bark. *Amer. J. Bot.* **42**, 893–905.

Schoch-Bodmer, H., and Huber, B. (1952). Local apical growth and forking in secondary fibers. *Proc. Leeds Phil. Lit. Soc. (Sci. Sec.)* **6**(1), 25–32.

Scholander, P. F., Hammel, H. T., Bradsheet, E. D., and Hemmingsen, E. A. (1965). Sap pressure in vascular plants. *Science* **148**, 339–346.

Scholander, P. F., van Dam, L., and Scholander, S. I. (1955). Gas exchange in the roots of mangroves. *Amer. J. Bot.* **42**, 92–98.

Schroeder, C. A. (1953). Growth and development of the Fuerte avocado fruit. *Proc. Amer. Soc. Hort. Sci.* **61**, 103–109.

Schroeder, C. A., and Wieland, P. A. (1956). Diurnal fluctuations in size in various parts of the avocado tree and fruit. *Proc. Amer. Soc. Hort. Sci.* **68**, 253–258.

Schumacher, R. (1963). Triebwachstum und Blatt-Frucht-Verhältnis regelmässig und alternierend tragender Bäume. *Schweiz. Z. Obst-u. Weinb.* **72**, 229–233.

Scully, N. J. (1942). Root distribution and environment in a maple-oak forest. *Bot. Gaz. (Chicago)* **103**, 492–517.

Scurfield, G., and Wardrop, A. B. (1962). The nature of reaction wood. VI. The reaction anatomy of seedlings of woody perennials. *Aust. J. Bot.* **10**, 93–105.

Sell, H. M., and Johnston, F. A. (1949). Biochemical changes in terminal tung buds during their expansion prior to blossoming. *Plant Physiol.* **24**, 744–752.

Shapiro, S. (1958). The role of light in the growth of root primordia in the stem of the Lombardy poplar. *In* "The Physiology of Forest Trees" (K. V. Thimann, ed.), Chapter 22. Ronald Press, New York.

Sharp, W. M., and Chisman, H. H. (1961). Flowering and fruiting in the white oaks. I. Staminate flowering through pollen dispersal. *Ecology* **42**, 365–372.

Sharples, A., and Gunnery, H. (1933). Callus formation in *Hibiscus rosa-sinensis* L. and *Hevea brasiliensis* Müll. Arg. *Ann. Bot.* **47**, 827–840.

Shaw, J. K. (1934). The lifetime yield of an apple orchard. *Proc. Amer. Soc. Hort. Sci.* **31**, 35–38.

Shear, C. B. (1966). Tung nutrition. *In* "Fruit Nutrition" (N. F. Childers, ed.), pp. 549–568. Horticultural Publications, Rutgers University. New Brunswick, New Jersey.

Shepherd, K. R. (1964). Some observations on the effect of drought on the growth of *Pinus radiata* D. Don., *Aust. Forest.* **28**, 7–22.

Shepherd, K. R. (1967). Growth patterns and growth substances in radiata pine. *Aust. Forest.* **31**, 294–302.

Shepherd, K. R., and Rowan, K. S. (1967). Indoleacetic acid in cambial tissue of radiata pine. *Aust. J. Biol. Sci.* **20**, 637–646.

Shipman, R. D., and Rudolph, V. J. (1954). Factors influencing height growth of planted yellow-poplar in southwestern Michigan. *Mich. State Univ. Tech. Bull.* **242**.

Shiroya, T., Lister, G. R., Slankis, V., Krotkov, G., and Nelson, C. D. (1966). Seasonal changes in respiration, photosynthesis, and translocation of the ^{14}C labelled products of photosynthesis in young *Pinus strobus* L. plants. *Ann. Bot.* **30**, 81–91.

Shoemaker, D. N. (1905). On the development of *Hamamelis virginiana*. *Bot. Gaz. (Chicago)* **39**, 245–266.

Shoemaker, J. S. (1955). "Small-Fruit Culture." McGraw-Hill, New York.

Shoemaker, J. S., and Teskey, B. J. E. (1959). "Tree Fruit Production." Wiley, New York.

Shoulders, E. (1967). Fertilizer application, inherent fruitfulness, and rainfall affect flowering of longleaf pine. *Forest Sci.* **13**, 376–383.

Shoulders, E. (1968). Fertilization increases longleaf and slash pine flower and cone crops in Louisiana. *J. Forest.* **66**, 192–197.

Silen, R. R. (1962). Pollen dispersal considerations for Douglas-fir. *J. Forest.* **60**, 790–795.

Simkover, H. G., and Shenefelt, R. D. (1951). Effect of benzene hexachloride and chlordane on certain soil organisms. *J. Econ. Ent.* **44**, 426.

Singh, L. B. (1948). Studies in biennial bearing. III. Growth studies in the "on" and "off" year trees. *J. Hort. Sci.* **24**, 123–148.

Sinnott, E. W., and Bloch, R. (1939). Changes in intercellular relationships during the growth and differentiation of living plant tissues. *Amer. J. Bot.* **26**, 625–634.

Siren, G. (1963). Tree rings and climatic forecasts. *New Sci.* **346**, 18–20.

Skene, D. S. (1969). The period of time taken by cambial derivatives to grow and differentiate into tracheids in *Pinus radiata*. D. Don. *Ann. Bot.* **33**, 253–262.

Slankis, V. (1948). Einfluss von Exudaten von *Boletus variegatus* auf die dichotomische Verzweigung isolierter Kiefernwurzeln. *Physiol. Plant.* **1**, 390–400.

Slankis, V. (1949). Wirkung von β-Indolylessigsäure auf die dichotomische Verzweigung isolierter Wurzeln von *Pinus sylvestris* L. *Sv. Bot. Tidskr.* **43**, 603–607.

Slankis, V. (1950). Effect of α-naphthaleneacetic acid on dichotomous branching of isolated roots of *Pinus silvestris*. *Physiol. Plant.* **3**, 40–44.

Slankis, V. (1951). Über den Einfluss von β-Indolylessigsäure und andere Wirkstoffen auf das Wachstum von Kiefernwurzeln. *Symb. Bot. Upsal.* **11**, 1–63.

Slankis, V. (1955). Causality of morphogenesis of mycorrhizal pine roots. *Proc. Can. Phytopath Soc.* **22**, 20–21.

Slankis, V. (1958a). Mycorrhiza of forest trees. *First North American Forest Soils Conf. Mich. State Univ. East Lansing, Mich.*, pp. 130–137.

Slankis, V. (1958b). The role of auxin and other exudates in mycorrhizal symbiosis of forest trees. *In* "The Physiology of Forest Trees" (K. V. Thimann, ed.), Chapter 21. Ronald Press, New York.

Slankis, V. (1961). On the factors determining the establishment of ectotrophic mycorrhizae of forest trees. *Rec. Advan. Botany. IXth Int. Bot. Congr.* 1960, pp. 1738–1742.

Slankis, V. (1963). Der gegenwärtiger Stand unseres Wissens von der Bildung der ectotrophen Mycorrhizen bei Waldbäumen. *In* "International Mycorrhiza Symposium" (W. Rawald and H. Lyr, eds.), pp. 175–183. G. Fischer, Verlag Jena.

Slankis, V. (1967). Renewed growth of ectotrophic mycorrhizae as an indication of an unstable symbiotic relationship. IUFRO *Congr. Sec.* **24**, Munich, 84–99.

Small, J. A., and Monk, C. D. (1959). Winter changes in tree radii and temperature. *Forest Sci.* **5**, 229–233.

Smith, D. M. (1965). Rapid measurement of tracheid cross sectional dimensions of conifers: its application to specific gravity determinations. *Forest Prod. J.* **15**, 325–334.

Smith, D. M. (1967). Microscopic methods for determining cross-sectional cell dimensions. *US Forest Serv. Res. Pap.* **FPL 79**.

Smith, D. M., and Miller, R. B. (1964). Methods of measuring and estimating tracheid wall thickness of redwood (*Sequoia sempervirens* (D. Don) Endl.) TAPPI **47**, 599–604.

Smith, D. M., and Wilsie, M. C. (1961). Some anatomical responses of loblolly pine to soil-water deficiencies. TAPPI **44**, 179–185.

Smith, F. H. (1967). Effects of balsam wooly aphid (*Adelges piceae*) infestation on cambial activity in *Abies grandis*. *Amer. J. Bot.* **54**, 1215–1223.

Smith, G. W. (1966). The relation between rainfall, soil water and yield of copra on a coconut estate in Trinidad. *J. Appl. Ecol.* **3**, 117–125.

Smith, P. F., and Reuther, W. (1950). Seasonal changes in Valencia orange trees. I. Changes in leaf dry weight, ash, and macronutrient elements. *Proc. Amer. Soc. Hort. Sci.* **55**, 61–72.

Smith, R. L., and Wallace, A. (1954). Preliminary studies of some physiological root characteristics in citrus and avocado. *Proc. Amer. Soc. Hort. Sci.* **63**, 143–145.

Snyder, W. E. (1954). The rooting of leafy stem cuttings. *Nat. Hort. Mag.* **33**, 1–18.

Soe, K. (1959). Anatomical studies of bark regeneration following scoring. *J. Arnold Arboretum Harvard Univ.* **40**, 260–267.

Soost, R. K., and Burnett, R. H. (1961). Effects of gibberellin on yield and fruit characteristics of Clementine mandarin. *Proc. Amer. Soc. Hort. Sci.* **77**, 194–201.

Sorensen, H. G. (1943). Crown budding for healthy *Hevea. Agr. Americas* **2**, 191–193.

Sorensen, R. W., and Wilson, B. F. (1964). The position of eccentric stem growth and tension wood in leaning old oak trees. *Harvard Forest Pap.* **12**.

Spyridakis, D. E., Chesters, G., and Wilde, S. A. (1967). Kaolinization of biotite as a result of coniferous and deciduous seedling growth. *Soil Sci. Soc. Amer. Proc.* **31**, 203–210.

Spurr, S. H., and Hyvärinen, M. J. (1954). Compression wood in conifers as a morphogenetic phenomenon. *Bot. Rev.* **20**, 551–560.

Srivastava, L. M. (1963). Secondary phloem in the Pinaceae. *Univ. Calif. Publ. Bot.* **36**, 1–142.

Srivastava, L. M. (1964). Anatomy, chemistry, and physiology of bark. *Int. Rev. Forest. Res.* **1**, 204–274.

Stahly, E. A., and Thompson, A. H. (1959). Auxin levels of developing Halehaven peach ovules. *Maryland Agr. Exp. Sta. Bull.* **A-104**.

Stanley, R. G. (1958). Methods and concepts applied to a study of flowering in pine. *In* "The Physiology of Forest Trees" (K. V. Thimann, ed.), Chapter 31. Ronald Press, New York.

Stanley, R. G. (1964). Physiology of pollen and pistil. *Sci. Progr.* **52**, 122–132.

Stanley, R. G. (1967). Factors affecting germination of the pollen grain. *Proc. XIV IUFRO Congr.*, **24**, 38–59.

Stark, R. W., and Cook, J. A. (1957). The effects of defoliation by the lodgepole needle miner. *Forest Sci.* **3**, 376–395.

Steinbrenner, E. C., Duffield, J. W., and Campbell, R. K. (1960). Increased cone production of young Douglas-fir following nitrogen and phosphorus fertilization. *J. Forest.* **58**, 105–109.

Stephens, G. R., Jr. (1964). Stimulation of flowering in eastern white pine. *Forest Sci.* **10**, 28–34.

Sterling, C. (1953). Developmental anatomy of the fruit of *Prunus domestica* L. *Bull. Torrey Bot. Club* **80**, 457–477.

Steubing, L. (1960). Wurzeluntersuchungen an Feldschutzhecken. *Z. Acker- und Pflanzenbau (Berlin)* **110**, 332–341.

Stevens, C. L. (1931). Root growth of white pine. *Yale Univ. School of Forestry Bull.* **32**.

Steward, F. C., and Simmonds, N. W. (1954). Growth promoting substances in the ovary and immature fruit of the banana. *Nature (London)* **173**, 1083.

Stewart, C. M. (1966). The chemistry of secondary growth in trees. *Div. Forest Prod. Tech. Pap.* **43**. CSIRO, Melbourne, Australia.

Stewart, C. M. (1969). The formation and chemical composition of hardwoods. APPITA **22**, 32–60.

Stewart, W. D. P. (1962). A quantitative study of fixation and transfer of nitrogen in *Alnus. J. Exp. Bot.* **13**, 250–256.

Stewart, W. S. and Hield, H. Z. (1950). 2,4-D and citrus fruit sizes. *Calif. Agr.* **4**(4), 5–6.

Stiell, W. M. (1969). Stem growth reaction in young red pine to the removal of single branch whorls. *Can. J. Bot.* **47**, 1251–1256.

Stokes, M. A. and Smiley, T. L. (1968). "An Introduction to Tree-Ring Dating." Univ. Chicago Press, Chicago, Illinois.

Stoltz, L. P., and Hess, C. E. (1966). The effect of girdling upon root initiation: auxin and rooting cofactors. *Proc. Amer. Soc. Hort. Sci.* **89**, 744–751.

Stone, E. C., and Jenkinson, J. L. (1971). Physiological grading of ponderosa pine nursery stock. *J. Forest.* **69**, 31–33.

Stone, E. C., Jenkinson, J. L., and Krugman, S. L. (1962). Root-regenerating potential of Douglas-fir seedlings lifted at different times of the year. *Forest Sci.* **8**, 288–297.

Stone, E. C., and Schubert, G. H. (1959). Root regeneration by ponderosa pine seedlings lifted at different times of the year. *Forest Sci.* **5**, 322–332.

Stone, E. C., Schubert, G. H., Benseler, R. W., Baron, F. J., and Krugman, S. L. (1963). Variation in the root-regenerating potentials of ponderosa pine from four California nurseries. *Forest Sci.* **9**, 217–225.

Stone, E. L. (1950). Some effects of mycorrhizae on the phosphorus nutrition of Monterey pine seedlings. *Soil Sci. Soc. Amer. Proc.* **14**, 340–345.

Stösser, R., Rasmussen, H. P., and Bukovac, M. J. (1969a). A histological study of abscission layer formation in cherry fruits during maturation. *J. Amer. Soc. Hort. Sci.* **94**, 239–243.

Stösser, R., Rasmussen, H. P., and Bukovac, M. J. (1969b). Histochemical changes in the developing abscission layer in fruits of *Prunus cerasus* L. *Planta* **86**, 151–164.

Stout, B. B. (1956). Studies of the root systems of deciduous trees. *Black Rock Forest Bull.* **15**.

Stout, B. B. (1961). Season influences the amount of backflash in a red pine plantation. *J. Forest.* **59**, 897–898.

Stoutemyer, V. T., and Britt, O. K. (1962). Growth phases and the propagation of *Hedera*. *Proc. Amer. Soc. Hort. Sci.* **80**, 589–592.

Stoutemyer, V. T., and Britt, O. K. (1965). The behavior of tissue cultures from English and Algerian ivy in different growth phases. *Amer. J. Bot.* **52**, 805–810.

Strain, B. R., and Johnson, P. L. (1963). Corticular photosynthesis and growth in *Populus tremuloides. Ecology* **44**, 581–584.

Strand, L. (1957). Pollen dispersal. *A. Forstgenet.* **6**, 129–136.

Struckmeyer, B. E., and Roberts, R. H. (1942). Investigations on the time of blossom induction in Wealthy apple trees. *Proc. Amer. Soc. Hort. Sci.* **40**, 113–119.

Studhalter, R. A., Glock, W. S., and Agerter, S. R. (1963). Tree growth. *Bot. Rev.* **29**, 245–365.

Studholme, W. P., and Philipson, W. R. (1966). A comparison of the cambium in two woods with included phloem: *Heimerliodendron brunonianum* and *Avicennia resinifera. N.Z. J. Bot.* **4**, 355–365.

Swamy, B. G. L. (1948). A contribution to the life history of *Casuarina. Proc. Amer. Acad. Arts. Sci.* **77**, 1–32.

Swan, H. S. D. (1965). Reviewing the scientific use of fertilizers in forestry. *J. Forest.* **63**, 501–508.

Swan, H. S. D. (1966). Studies of the mineral nutrition of Canadian pulpwood species. *Pulp Paper Res. Inst. Canada Tech. Rep.* **464**.

Swarbrick, T., and Luckwill, L. C. (1953). The factors governing fruit bud formation. *In* "Science and Fruit" (T. Wallace and R. W. Marsh, eds.), pp. 99–109. Univ. Bristol, Bristol, England.

Sweet, G. B. and Thulin, I. J. (1969). The abortion of conelets in *Pinus radiata. N.Z. J. Forest.* **14**, 59–67.

Swingle, C. F. (1929). A physiological study of rooting and callusing in apple and willow. *J. Agr. Res.* **39**, 81–128.

Tappeiner, J. C. (1969). Effect of cone production on branch, needle, and xylem ring growth of Sierra Nevada Douglas-fir. *Forest Sci.* **15**, 171–194.

Tarrant, R. F. (1961). Stand development and soil fertility in a Douglas-fir-red alder plantation. *Forest Sci.* **7**, 238–246.

Tepper, H. B., and Hollis, C. A. (1967). Mitotic reactivation of the terminal bud and cambium of white ash. *Science* **156**, 1635–1636.

Thornber, J. P., and Northcote, D. H. (1961a). Changes in the chemical composition of a cambial cell during its differentiation into xylem and phloem tissues in trees. 1. Main components. *Biochem. J.* **81**, 449–455.

Thornber, J. P., and Northcote, D. H. (1961b). Changes in the chemical composition of a cambial cell during its differentiation into xylem and phloem tissues. 2. Carbohydrate constituents of each main component. *Biochem. J.* **81**, 455–464.

Thornber, J. P., and Northcote, D. H. (1962). Changes in the chemical composition of a cambial cell during its differentiation into xylem and phloem tissues in trees. 3. Xylan, glucomannan, and α-cellulose fractions. *Biochem. J.* **82**, 340–346.

Tingley, M. A. (1936). Double growth rings in Red Astrachan. *Proc. Amer. Soc. Hort. Sci.* **34**, 61.

Tison, A. (1903). Les traches foliares des coniferes dans leur rapport avec l'epaississement de la tige. *Mem. Linn. Soc. Normandy* **21**, 1902–1921.

Tizio, R., Pons, G. A., Trione, S. O., and Trippi, V. S. (1963). Estudios sobre enraizamiento en vid. VII. Auxinas, inhibidores y la capacidad rizogena de las estaces. *Phyton* **20**, 1–12.

Todd, G. W., Bean, R. C., and Propst, B. (1961). Photosynthesis and respiration in developing fruits. II. Comparative rates at various stages of development. *Plant Physiol.* **36**, 69–73.

Toyama, S., and Hayaski, S. (1957). Studies on the fruit development of Japanese pears. I. On the flesh cell division, cell enlargement and the relation between cell-size and fruit size of some varieties. *J. Hort. Assoc. Jap.* **25**, 274–278.

Trappe, J. M. (1962). Fungus associates of ectotrophic mycorrhizae. *Bot. Rev.* **28**, 538–606.

Tryon, H. H., and Finn, R. F. (1949). On obtaining precise diameter measurements on hardwoods using the dial gage. *J. Forest.* **47**, 396–397.

Tucker, C. M., and Evert, R. F. (1969). Seasonal development of the secondary phloem in *Acer negundo. Amer. J. Bot.* **56**, 275–284.

Tukey, H. B. (1935). Growth of the embryo, seed, and pericarp of the sour cherry (*Prunus cerasus*) in relation to season of fruit ripening. *Proc. Amer. Soc. Hort. Sci.* **31**, 125–144.

Tukey, H. B. (1936). Development of cherry and peach fruits as affected by destruction of the embryo. *Bot. Gaz. (Chicago)* **98**, 1–24.

Tukey, H. B., and Anderson, L. C. (1929). Five years results with fertilizers in three Hudson River Valley orchards. *NY State (Geneva) Agr. Exp. Sta. Bull.* **574**.

Tukey, H. B., and Young, J. O. (1939). Histological study of the developing fruit of the sour cherry. *Bot. Gaz. (Chicago)* **100**, 723–749.

Tukey, H. B., and Young, J. O. (1942). Gross morphology and histology of developing fruit of the apple. *Bot. Gaz. (Chicago)* **104**, 3–25.

Tukey, L. D. (1959). Periodicity in growth of fruits of apples, peaches, and sour cherries with some factors influencing this development. *Bull. Penn. Agr. Exp. Sta.* **661**.

Tukey, L. D. (1960). How apples grow—some recent findings. *Penn. Fruit News* **39**(2), 12, 14, 16, 18.

Tydeman, H. M. (1961). Rootstock influence on the flowering of seedling apples. *Nature (London)* **192**, 83.

Tydeman, H. M. (1964). The relation between time of leaf break and of flowering in seedling apples. *Annu. Rep. East Malling Res. Sta.* 1963–1964, 70–72.

Uemura, S. (1964). Isolation and properties of microorganisms from root nodules of non-leguminous plants. A review with extensive bibliography. *Bull. Gov. Forest Exp. Sta. Tokyo* 167.

Unger, F. (1840). Beiträge zur Kenntnis der parasitischen Pflanzen. Erster oder anatomisch-physiologischen Theil. *Ann. Wiener Mus. Natur.* 2, 13–60.

Uriu, K. and Magness, J. R. (1967). Deciduous tree fruits and nuts. *In* "Irrigation of Agricultural Lands." (R. M. Hagan, H. R. Haise, and T. W. Edminster, eds.). Chapter 35. *Amer. Soc. Agron. Monograph* 11, Madison, Wisconsin.

Valmayor, R. V. (1964). Cellular development of the avocado from blossom to maturity. Ph.D. thesis. Univ. Florida, Gainesville, Florida.

Van Buijtenen, J. P. (1958). Experimental control of environmental factors and their effect upon some aspects of wood anatomy in loblolly pine. *TAPPI* 41, 175–178.

Van der Meer, Q. P., and Wassink, E. C. (1962). Preliminary note on photosynthesis in green plum fruits. *Med. van de Landbouwhogeschool, Wageningen.* 62, 1–9.

Vasiljevic, S. (1955). Onekim karakteristikama grade dvostrukihlaznih-prstenova prirasta. *Glas. Summarskog Fac. (Beograd)* 9, 311–315.

Veihmeyer, F. J., and Hendrickson, A. H. (1952). The effects of soil moisture on deciduous fruit trees. *Proc. 13th Int. Hort. Congr.* I, 306–319.

Veihmeyer, F. J., and Hendrickson, A. H. (1960). Essentials of irrigation and cultivation of orchards. *Calif. Agr. Exp. Sta. Circ.* 486.

Veretenikov, A. V. (1959). Otmiranie i regeeneratsiya kornevvi sistemy *Pinus sylvestris* L. v. zavisimosti ot uslovii snabzheniya koreobitameogo sloya pochoy kislorodom vozdukka. *Bot. Z.* 44, 202–209.

Verner, L. (1962). A new kind of dendrometer. *Idaho Agr. Exp. Sta. Bull.* 389.

Verrall, A. F., and Graham, T. W. (1935). The transmission of *Ceratostomella ulmi* through root grafts. *Phytopathology* 25, 1039–1040.

Vieitez, E., and Pena, J. (1968). Seasonal rhythm of rooting of *Salix atrocinerea* cuttings. *Physiol. Plant.* 21, 544–555.

Viro, P. J. (1965). Estimation of the effect of forest fertilization. *Commun. Inst. Forest. Fenn.* 593, 5–42.

Virtanen, A. I. (1957). Investigations on nitrogen fixation by the alder. II. Associated culture of spruce and inoculated alder without combined nitrogen. *Physiol. Plant.* 10, 164–169.

Visser, T. (1964). Juvenile phase and growth of apple and pear seedlings. *Euphytica* 13, 119–129.

Vité, J. P. (1959). Observations on the movement of injected dyes in *Pinus ponderosa* and *Abies concolor*. *Contr. Boyce Thompson Inst.* 20, 7–26.

Vité, J. P., and Hendrickson, W. H. (1959). Die Orientierung der Holzfasern im Douglasienstamm. *Allgem. Forstz.* 14, 166–168.

Voronkov, V. V. (1956). The dying off of the feeder root system in the tea plant. (Russ.) *Doklady vsesojuz. Akad. Seljsk. Nauk.* 21, 22–24. [*Hort. Abstr.* 27, 2977, (1957)].

Waisel, Y., and Fahn, A. (1965a). The effect of environment on wood formation and cambial activity in *Robinia pseudoacacia* L. *New Phytol.* 64, 436–442.

Waisel, Y., and Fahn, A. (1965b). A radiological method for the determination of cambial activity. *Physiol. Plant.* 18, 44–46.

Waisel, Y., Noah, I., and Fahn, A. (1966a). Cambial activity in *Eucalyptus camaldulensis* Dehn. I. The relation to extension growth in young saplings. *La-Yaaran* 16, 103–108.

Waisel, Y., Noah, I., and Fahn, A. (1966b). Cambial activity in *Eucalyptus camaldulensis* Dehn. II. The production of phloem and xylem elements. *New Phytol.* 65, 319–324.

Waisel, Y., Liphschitz, N., and Arzee, T. (1967). Phellogen activity in *Robinia pseudacacia* L. *New Phytol.* **66**, 331–335.

Wallis, G. W., and Buckland, D. C. (1955). The effect of trenching on the spread of yellow laminated root rot of Douglas fir. *Forest. Chron.* **31**, 356–359.

Walter, H. (1962). "Die Vegetation der Erde in ökologischer Betrachtung." G. Fischer, Jena.

Wang, C. H., Perry, T. O., and Johnson, A. G. (1960). Pollen dispersion of slash pine (*Pinus elliottii* Engelm.) with special reference to seed orchard management. *Silvae Genet.* **9**, 65–92.

Wardlaw, C. W., and Leonard, E. R. (1936). Studies in tropical fruits. I. *Ann. Bot.* **50**, 622–653.

Wardrop, A. B. (1954). Observations on crossed lamellar structures in the cell walls of higher plants. *Aust. J. Bot.* **2**, 154–164.

Wardrop, A. B. (1957). The phase of lignification in the differentiation of wood fibers. TAPPI **40**, 225–243.

Wardrop, A. B. (1961). The structure and organization of thickened cell walls. *Rep. Forest. Prod. Aust.* 476.

Wardrop, A. B. (1964a). The reaction anatomy of arborescent angiosperms. *In* "The Formation of Wood in Forest Trees" (M. H. Zimmermann, ed.), pp. 405–456. Academic Press, New York.

Wardrop, A. B. (1964b). The structure and formation of the cell wall in xylem. *In* "The Formation of Wood in Forest Trees" (M. H. Zimmermann, ed.), pp. 87–134. Academic Press, New York.

Wardrop, A. B. (1964c). Changes in cell wall structure and cytoplasmic organization during differentiation of xylem. *Proc. 10th Int. Bot. Congr.* Abstr. p. 205.

Wardrop, A. B. (1965a). Cellular differentiation in xylem. *In* "Cellular Ultrastructure of Woody Plants." (W. A. Coté, Jr., ed.), pp. 61–97. Syracuse Univ. Press, Syracuse, New York.

Wardrop, A. B. (1965b). The formation and function of reaction wood. *In* "Cellular Ultrastructure of Woody Plants." (W. A. Coté, Jr., ed.), pp. 371–390. Syracuse Univ. Press, Syracuse, New York.

Wardrop, A. B., and Bland, D. E. (1958). The process of lignification in woody plants. *Proc. 4th Int. Congr. Biochem.* **2**, 92–116.

Wardrop, A. B., and Dadswell, H. E. (1952). The nature of raction wood. III. Cell division and cell wall formation in conifer stems. *Aust. J. Sci. Res.* **B5**, 385–398.

Wardrop, A. B., and Dadswell, H. E. (1953). The development of the conifer tracheid. *Holzforschung* **7**, 33–39.

Wardrop, A. B., and Dadswell, H. E. (1955). The nature of reaction wood. IV. Variations in cell wall organization of tension wood fibers. *Aust. J. Bot.* **3**, 177–189.

Wardrop, A. B., and Harada, H. (1965). The formation and structure of the cell wall in fibres and tracheids. *J. Exp. Bot.* **16**, 356–371.

Wareing, P. F. (1951a). Growth studies in woody species. III. Further photoperiodic effects in *Pinus silvestris*. *Physiol. Plant.* **4**, 41–56.

Wareing, P. F. (1951b). Growth studies in woody species. IV. The initiation of cambial activity in ring-porous species. *Physiol. Plant.* **4**, 546–562.

Wareing, P. F. (1958a). The physiology of cambial activity. *J. Inst. Wood Sci.* **1**, 34–42.

Wareing, P. F. (1958b). Reproductive development in *Pinus sylvestris In* "The Physiology of Forest Trees" (K. V. Thimann, ed.), Chapter 35. Ronald Press, New York.

Wareing, P. F. (1964). Tree physiology in relation to genetics and breeding. *Unasylva* **18**, 1–10.

Wareing, P. F., Hanney, C. E. A., and Digby, J. (1964). The role of endogenous hormones in cambial activity and xylem differentiation. *In* "The Formation of Wood in Forest Trees" (M. H. Zimmermann, ed.), pp. 323–344. Academic Press, New York.

Wareing, P. F., and Nasr, T. A. A. (1961). Gravimorphism in trees. I. Effects of gravity on growth and apical dominance in fruit trees. *Ann. Bot.* **25**, 321–340.

Wareing, P. F., and Roberts, D. L. (1956). Photoperiodic control of cambial activity in *Robinia pseudoacacia* L. *New Phytol.* **55**, 289–388.

Warrack, G., and Jorgensen, C. (1950). Precision measurements of radial growth and daily radial fluctuations in Douglas fir. *Forest. Chron.* **26**, 52–66.

Wassink, E. C., and Richardson, S. D. (1951). Observations on the connection between root growth and shoot illumination in first-year seedlings of *Acer pseudoplatanus* L. and *Quercus borealis maxima* (Marsh) Ashe. *Proc. Kon. Ned. Akad. Wetensch. Amsterdam.* **C54**, 503–510.

Watson, J. G. (1928). Mangrove forest on the Malay peninsula. *Malayan Forest Records* **6**, 1–240.

Weaver, J. E., and Kramer, J. (1932). Root system of *Quercus macrocarpa* in relation to the invasion of prairie. *Bot. Gaz. (Chicago)* **94**, 51–85.

Weaver, R. J., and Williams, W. O. (1950). Response of flowers of Black Corinth and fruit of Thompson Seedless grapes to application of plant growth regulators. *Bot. Gaz. (Chicago)* **11**, 477–485.

Weir, J. R. (1925). Notes on the parasitism of *Endothia gyrosa* (Schw.) Fr. *Phytopathology.* **15**, 489–491.

Wellner, C. A., and Lowery, D. P. (1967). Spiral grain—a cause of pole twisting. *US Forest Serv. Res. Pap.* **INT-38**.

Wenger, K. F. (1953). The effect of fertilization and injury on the cone and seed production of loblolly pine trees. *J. Forest.* **51**, 570–573.

Wenger, K. F. (1954). The stimulation of loblolly pine seed trees by preharvest release. *J. Forest.* **52**, 115–118.

Wershing, H. F., and Bailey, I. W. (1942). Seedlings as experimental material in the study of "redwood" in conifers. *J. Forest.* **40**, 411–414.

Westing, A. H. (1961). Changes in radial symmetry in the leaders of eastern white pine following inclination. *J. Forest.* **59**, 17–19.

Westing, A. H. (1965a). Formation and function of compression wood in gymnosperms. *Bot. Rev.* **31**, 381–480.

Westing, A. H. (1965b). Compression wood in the regulation of branch angle in gymnosperms. *Bull. Torrey Bot. Club* **92**, 62–66.

Westing, A. H., and Schulz, H. (1965). Erection of a leaning eastern hemlock tree. *Forest Sci.* **11**, 364–367.

Whalley, B. E. (1950). Increase in girth of the cambium in *Thuja occidentalis*. *Can. J. Res. Sect.* **C28**, 331–340.

White, D. P. (1941). Prairie Soil as a medium for tree growth. *Ecology* **22**, 398–407.

Whitford, L. A. (1956). A theory on the formation of cypress knees. *Elisha Mitchell Sci. Soc. J.* **72**, 80–83.

Whitmore, F. W., and Zahner, R. (1966). Development of the xylem ring in stems of young red pine trees. *Forest Sci.* **12**, 198–210.

Whitmore, F. W., and Zahner, R. (1967). Evidence for a direct effect of water stress in the metabolism of cell wall in *Pinus*. *Forest Sci.* **13**, 397–400.

Whitmore, T. C. (1962a). Studies in systematic bark morphology. I. Bark morphology in Dipterocarpaceae. *New Phytol.* **61**, 191–207.

Whitmore, T. C. (1962b). Studies in systematic bark morphology. II. General features of bark construction in Dipterocarpaceae. *New Phytol.* **61**, 208–220.

Whitmore, T. C. (1963). Why do trees have different sorts of bark? *New Sci.* **16**, 330–331.

Whitney, R. D. (1962). Studies in forest pathology. XXIV. *Polyporus tomentosa* Fr. as a major factor in stand-opening disease of white spruce. *Can. J. Bot.* **40**, 1631–1658.

Wichmann, H. E. (1925). Wurzelwachsungen und Stockuberwallung bei Abietineen. *Zentralbl. Ges. Forstw.* **51**, 250–258.

Wiegand, K. M. (1906). Some studies regarding the biology of buds and twigs in winter. *Bot. Gaz.* (*Chicago*) **41**, 373–424.

Wilcox, H. (1954). Primary organization of active and dormant roots of noble fir, *Abies procera. Amer. J. Bot.* **41**, 818–821.

Wilcox, H. (1955). Regeneration of injured root systems in noble fir. *Bot. Gaz.* (*Chicago*) **116**, 221–234.

Wilcox, H. (1962a). Cambial growth characteristics. *In* "Tree Growth" (T. T. Kozlowski, ed.), Chapter 3. Ronald Press, New York.

Wilcox, H. (1962b). Growth studies of the root of incense cedar, *Libocedrus decurrens*. II. Morphological features of the root system and growth behavior. *Amer. J. Bot.* **49**, 237–245.

Wilcox, H. (1968a). Morphological studies of the root of red pine, *Pinus resinosa*. I. Growth characteristics and patterns of branching. *Amer. J. Bot.* **55**, 247–254.

Wilcox, H. (1968b). Morphological studies of the roots of red pine, *Pinus resinosa*. II. Fungal colonization of roots and the development of mycorrhizae. *Amer. J. Bot.* **55**, 686–700.

Wilcox, H., Czabator, F. J., Girolami, G., Moreland, D. E., and Smith, R. F. (1956). Chemical debarking of some pulpwood species. *N.Y. State Coll. Forest. Tech. Publ.* **77**. Syracuse Univ., Syracuse, New York.

Wilde, S. A. (1954). Mycorrhizal fungi: their distribution and effect on tree growth. *Soil Sci.* **78**, 23–31.

Wilde, S. A. (1958). *In* "Forest Soils." Ronald Press, New York.

Wilde, S. A. (1968a). Mycorrhizae and tree nutrition. *Bioscience* **18**, 482–484.

Wilde, S. A. (1968b). Mycorrhizae: their role in tree nutrition and timber production. *Univ. Wisconsin, Coll. Agr. Life Sci. Res. Bull.* **272**.

Wilde, S. A., and Lafond, A. (1967). Symbiotrophy of lignophytes and fungi: its terminological and conceptual deficiencies. *Bot. Rev.* **33**, 99–104.

Wilde, S. A., and Persidsky, D. J. (1956). Effect of biocides on the development of ectotrophic mycorrhizae in Monterey pine seedlings. *Proc. Soil Sci. Soc. Amer.* **20**, 107–110.

Williams, Jr., C. B. (1967). Spruce budworm damage symptoms related to radial growth of grand fir, Douglas-fir, and Engelmann spruce. *Forest Sci.* **13**, 274–285.

Williams, R. F., and Hamilton, J. R. (1961). The effect of fertilization on four wood properties of slash pine. *J. Forest.* **59**, 662–665.

Williams, R. R. (1963). The effect of nitrogen on the self-fruitfulness of certain varieties of cider apples. *J. Hort. Sci.* **38**, 52–60.

Williams, R. R. (1965). The effect of summer nitrogen applications on the quality of apple blossom. *J. Hort. Sci.* **40**, 31–41.

Williamson, M. J. (1966). Premature abscissions and white oak acorn crops. *Forest Sci.* **12**, 19–21.

Willis, C. P. (1917). Incidental results of a study of Douglas-fir seed in the Pacific Northwest. *J. Forest.* **15**, 991–1002.

Wilson, B. F. (1963). Increase in cell wall surface area during enlargement of cambial derivatives in *Abies concolor. Amer. J. Bot.* **50**, 95–102.

Wilson, B. F. (1964). Structure and growth of woody roots of *Acer rubrum* L. *Harvard Forest Pap.* **11**.

Wilson, B. F. (1967). Root growth around barriers. *Bot. Gaz. (Chicago)* **128**, 79–82.

Wilson, B. F. (1968). Effect of girdling on cambial activity in white pine. *Can. J. Bot.* **46**, 141–146.

Wilson, B. F., Wodzicki, T., and Zahner, R. (1966). Differentiation of cambial derivatives: proposed terminology. *Forest Sci.* **12**, 438–440.

Wilson, C. L., and Loomis, W. E. (1967). "Botany." Holt, New York.

Wilson, J. (1951). Microorganisms in the rhizosphere of beech. Ph.D. Thesis. Oxford Univ.

Wilson, W. C., and Hendershott, C. H. (1968). Anatomical and histochemical studies of abscission of oranges. *Proc. Amer. Soc. Hort. Sci.* **92**, 203–210.

Winget, C. H., and Kozlowski, T. T. (1964). Winter shrinkage in stems of forest trees. *J. Forest.* **62**, 335–337.

Winget, C. H., and Kozlowski, T. T. (1965). Seasonal basal area growth as an expression of competition in northern hardwoods. *Ecology* **46**, 786–793.

Wodzicki, T. (1961). Investigations on the kind of *Larix polonica* Roc. wood formed under various photoperiodic conditions. II. Effect of different light conditions on wood formed by seedlings grown in greenhouse. *Acta Soc. Bot. Pol.* **30**, 111–131.

Wodzicki, T. (1964). Photoperiodic control of natural growth substances and wood formation in larch (*Larix decidua* D.C.). *J. Exp. Bot.* **15**, 584–599.

Wodzicki, T. (1965). Annual ring of wood formation and seasonal changes of natural growth inhibitors in larch. *Acta Soc. Bot. Pol.* **34**, 117–151.

Wodzicki, T. (1968). On the question of occurrence of indole-3-acetic acid in *Pinus silvestris*. *Amer. J. Bot.* **55**, 564–571.

Wold, M. L., and Lanner, R. M. (1965). New stool shoots from a 20-year-old swamp-mahogany *Eucalyptus* stump. *Ecology* **46**, 755–756.

Wollum, A. G., and Youngberg, C. T. (1964). The influence of nitrogen fixation by non-leguminous woody plants on the growth of pine seedlings. *J. Forest.* **62**, 316–321.

Wolter, K. E. (1968). A new method for marking cambial growth. *Forest Sci.* **14**, 102–104.

Woodroof, J. G., and Woodroof, N. C. (1934). Pecan root growth and development. *J. Agr. Res.* **49**, 511–530.

Woodroof, J. G., and Woodroof, N. C. (1927). The development of the pecan nut (*Hicoria pecan*) from flower to maturity. *J. Agr. Res.* **34**, 1049–1063.

Woods, F. W. (1951). A storage container for increment cores. *J. Forest.* **49**, 707.

Woods, F. W. (1957). Factors limiting root penetration in deep sands of the southeastern coastal plain. *Ecology* **38**, 357–359.

Woods, F. W., and Brock, K. (1964). Interspecific transfer of Ca^{45} and P^{32} by root systems. *Ecology* **45**, 886–889.

Woodworth, R. H. (1930). Cytological studies in the Betulaceae. III. Parthenogenesis and polyembryony in *Alnus rugosa*. *Bot. Gaz. (Chicago)* **89**, 402–409.

Worley, J. F., and Hacskaylo, E. (1959). The effect of available moisture on the mycorrhizal association of Virginia pine. *Forest Sci.* **5**, 267–278.

Worrall, J. (1966). A method of correcting dendrometer measures of tree diameters for variations induced by moisture stress change. *Forest Sci.* **12**, 427–429.

Wright, E. (1957). Importance of mycorrhizae to ponderosa pine seedlings. *Forest Sci.* **3**, 275–280.

Wright, H. (1905). Foliar periodicity of endemic and indigenous trees in Ceylon. *Annu. Bot. Gdns. Peradeniya* **2**, 415–417.

Wright, J. W. (1952). Pollen dispersion of some forest trees. *Northeastern Forest Exp. Sta. Pap.* **46**.

Wright, J. W. (1953). Pollen dispersion studies; some practical applications. *J. Forest.* **51**, 114–118.

Wright, J. W. (1955). Species crossability in spruce in relation to distribution and taxonomy. *Forest Sci.* **1**, 319–349.

Wright, J. W. (1962). Genetics of Forest Tree Improvement. *FAO Forestry Forest Prod. Study*, Rome **16**.

Wyman, D. (1950). Order of bloom. *Arnoldia* **10**, 41–56.

Yanagihara, T. (1958). On the time of flower bud differentiation of Japanese larch. I. *J. Jap. Forest. Soc.* **40**, 343–344.

Yanagihara, T. (1959). On the time of flower bud differentiation of Japanese larch. II. *J. Jap. Forest. Soc.* **41**, 164–166.

Yazawa, K., and Fukazawa, K. (1959). Studies on the relation between physical properties and growth conditions for planted Sugi (*Cryptomeria japonica* D. Don) in central District of Japan, V. On the specific gravity, fiber saturation point and volumetric shrinkage of the spring and summerwood. *Hokkaido Univ. Exp. Forest. Res. Bull.* **20**, 93–117.

Young, H. E., and Kramer, P. J. (1952). The effect of pruning on the height and diameter growth of loblolly pine. *J. Forest.* **50**, 474–479.

Zahner, R. (1955). Soil water depletion by pine and hardwood stands during a dry season. *Forest Sci.* **1**, 258–264.

Zahner, R. (1958). September rains bring growth gains. *US Forest Ser. Southern Forest Exp. Sta. Forest. Note* **113**.

Zahner, R. (1968). Water deficits and growth of trees. *In* "Water Deficits and Plant Growth" (T. T. Kozlowski, ed.), Vol. II, Chapter 5. Academic Press, New York.

Zahner, R., and Donnelly, J. R. (1967). Refining correlations of water deficits and radial growth in red pine. *Ecology* **48**, 525–530.

Zahner, R., and Oliver, W. W. (1962). The influence of thinning and pruning on the date of summerwood initiation in red and jack pines. *Forest Sci.* **8**, 51–63.

Zahner, R., and Stage, A. R. (1966). A procedure for calculating daily moisture stress and its utility in regressions of tree growth on weather. *Ecology* **47**, 64–74.

Zahner, R., and Whitmore, F. W. (1960). Early growth of radially thinned loblolly pine. *J. Forest.* **58**, 628–634.

Zak, B. (1964). Role of mycorrhizae in root disease. *Annu. Rev. Phytopathol.* **2**, 377–392.

Zak, B., and Bryan, W. C. (1963). Isolation of fungal symbionts from pine mycorrhizae. *Forest Sci.* **9**, 270–278.

Zasada, J. C., and Zahner, R. (1969). Vessel element development in the earlywood of red oak (*Quercus rubra*). *Can. J. Bot.* **47**, 1965–1971.

Zeevart, J. A. D. (1962). Physiology of flowering. *Science* **137**, 723–731.

Zelawski, W. (1957). Dalsze badania reakcji fotoperiodycznej siewek modrzewia (*Larix europaea* D.C.). *Acta. Soc. Bot. Pol.* **26**, 79–103.

Zeller, O. (1955). Entwicklungsverlauf auf der Infloreszenknospen einiger Kern und Steinobstsorten. *Angew. Bot.* **29**, 69–89.

Zimmerman, R. (1963). Rooting cofactors in some southern pines. *Proc. Int. Plant Prop. Soc.* **13**, 71–74.

Zimmermann, M. H. (1961). Movement of organic substances in trees. *Science* **133**, 73–79.

Zobel, B. (1961). Inheritance of wood properties in conifers. *Silvae Genet.* **10**, 65–70.

Zwar, J. A., Bottomley, W., and Kefford, N. P. (1963). Kinin activity from plant extracts. II. Partial purification and fractionation of kinins in apple extract. *Aust. J. Biol. Sci.* **16**, 407–415.

AUTHOR INDEX

Numbers in italics refer to the pages on which the complete references are listed

SUBJECT INDEX

A

Abscisic acid, 420
Abscission
    of floral parts, 341, 358–360, 364
    of fruits, 329, 358–364, 416, 425, 426
    of leaves, 20, 21, 138, 202
Absorption of water, 131
Actinomorphy, 306
Actinomycetes, 287
Additive division, 1
ADP–ATP system, 157
Adult stage, 211, 214, 247, 402
Adventitious buds, 146
Adventitious roots, 210–215, *see also*
    Rooting of cuttings
Adventive embryos, 347
Aerial roots, 196, 251, 252
Aggregate fruits, 341, 342
Aging, 65, 86, 107, 130, 203, 204, 242, 257,
    384, *see also* Fruit senescence
Air layering, 252
Albuminous cells, 22
Alternate bearing, *see* Biennial bearing
Amino acids, 40, 272, 299, 303
Androecium, 306
Annual ring, *see* Cambial growth
Anomalous cambial growth, 51, 59–62, *see
    also* Cambial growth
Anthocyanin, 248, 273
Apical meristems, 105, 126, 207, 244, 273
Auxins, 126, 144, 145–155, 157, 161–165,
    231, 248, 249, 272, 304, 348, 363,
    415–417
Axial parenchyma, 35, 41, 115, 144, 145
Axillary buds, 13

B

Backflash, 262, 265
Bark cracks, 38, 79
Bark flap, 57
Bark inversion, 435, 436
Bark patterns, 100–102
Bark shedding, 100–102, 206
Bark slipping, 188, 189
Bark stress, 38
Basal area increment, 120
Basidiomycetes, 278, 284, 299, 301, 302,
    304
Beta ray method, 185–188
Biennial bearing, 389, 391, 392, 397, 403,
    405
Birefringence, 30
Biseriate ray, 38, *see also* Rays
Bois rouge, 92
Bordered pit, 71
Bound water, 182
Branch trace, 215
Branching, 105
Bud dormancy, *see* Dormant buds
Bud opening, 12–14, 146, 221, 320, 321, 327,
    374
Bud scales, 14
Bud shield, 57
Bud trace, 13, 14, 215

C

Calipers, 168
Callose, 11, 36, 37
Callus, 54, 55, 136, 211–215, 256, 261